THE NATURE OF MANAGEMENT AND ORGANIZATIONS
Challenges in the Canadian Context

Len Karakowsky
York University

Captus Press

THE NATURE OF MANAGEMENT AND ORGANIZATIONS
Challenges in the Canadian Context

Cover artwork by Deborah Karakowsky.

National Library of Canada Cataloguing in Publication

Karakowsky, Len
    The nature of management & organizations: challenges in the Canadian context / Len Karakowsky. — 1st ed.

Includes bibliographical references and index.
ISBN 1–55322–035–8

    1. Management. I. Title. II. Title: Nature of management & organizations.

HD58.7.K37 2002   658   C2002–901694–0

Captus Press Inc.
Units 14 & 15, 1600 Steeles Avenue West, Concord, Ontario L4K 4M2
Telephone: (416) 736–5537
Fax: (416) 736–5793
Email: Info@captus.com
Internet: http://www.captus.com

Canada ▪ We acknowledge the financial support of the Government of Canada through the Book Publishing Industry Development Program (BPIDP) for our publishing activities.

0 9 8 7 6 5 4 3 2
Printed in Canada

Table of Contents

III.   THE LANDSCAPE OF ORGANIZATIONS

IV. LOOKING OUTSIDE: THE CONTEXT OF ORGANIZATIONS

Preface

What is the value of reading about management and organizations? Consider the context within which we all live and work. From schools, to hospitals, to multinational corporations, there is little in our lives that is not somehow connected to, or influenced by, organizations. An understanding of the nature of organizations, consequently, offers insight into the very nature of our society — a society of organizations.

In recent years, we have also witnessed dramatic change in our society of organizations. Clearly, we live in a rapidly changing environment. Business is influenced by a host of factors that exist outside the walls of the company, including: technological advances, the globalization of the workplace, the changing role of government, and the continued "re-engineering" of organizational structures, to name but a few. The aim of this text is to introduce the student to many of these critical concerns facing today's organizations. However, I hope that you find this book goes beyond a mere presentation of current issues affecting organizations.

A fundamental aim of any university education is to encourage critical thinking skills. I have tried to develop this book with that objective in mind. That is, this book is not so much a description of business practices or a "how to" of managing a business; rather, it is intended as a springboard for critically examining how organizations are designed, how they are managed, and what central challenges they face. It presents the reader with questions, concepts, theories and ideas. And it is aimed at encouraging students to think about these concepts and assess how they might add value to an understanding of the nature of organizations and management.

As with the completion of any book, much thanks must be given to the many individuals who contributed directly or indirectly to the writing process. First, I wish to thank Randy Hoffman, Pauline Lai and all the staff at Captus Press for their tremendous effort in preparing this book for publication. I am also grateful to Professor Diane Jurkowski, Rosenda Brown and the rest of my colleagues at York University for their input and suggestions. And certainly I owe much to my students for their feedback during the various stages of this book. Finally, I must express my gratitude to my dear wife, Debbie, whose support and encouragement made all this possible.

Prof. Len Karakowsky
York University
Toronto, Canada

Introduction

The central aim of this book is:

- To examine current issues affecting the management of organizations.
- To offer insight into the unique challenges present in the Canadian business context.
- To help generate conceptual frameworks for identifying and analyzing key issues within organizations and their environment.
- To encourage critical thinking regarding the nature of organizations and the challenges of managing in the workplace.

This book presents conceptual frameworks, ideas and theories drawn from the work of management scholars and organizational research. In order to enhance critical thinking skills, each chapter emphasizes concept application through the infusion of extensive "real-life" business illustrations, largely drawn from the Canadian popular press. Each chapter begins with an **Organizational Insider** that reports current real-life business issues and themes explored within the chapter. The chapters are also filled with real-life business illustrations, summarized within the **Let's Talk Business** exhibits. Each chapter also contains an end-of-chapter **Case Application** with questions. These cases are also largely drawn from the Canadian popular press, and are intended to give you an opportunity to apply chapter concepts to real business contexts.

In addition to encouraging critical thinking skills, this book is equally concerned with relating ideas and issues voiced by practitioners and communicated through such popular press sources as *BusinessWeek*, *Canadian Business*, *Fortune*, *Report on Business*, *The Globe and Mail*, and *The National Post*. For example, **Related Readings** (included at the end of each chapter) typically explore ideas that were initiated in the chapter, and expose you to a variety of management voices — both academic and practitioner. The questions following each Related Reading should make for lively class discussions.

STRUCTURE OF THE BOOK

Section I: Introduction

Chapter 1 presents the broader context within which managers manage — the environment of organizations. This chapter helps us appreciate the challenges of developing managerial strategies to cope with the environment. It describes the context within which much of our examination of organizations and management occurs. The framework employed is one that underscores both internal forces and external forces directed at the organization. The ability to adequately address both types of forces will, ultimately, determine the organization's fate.

Section II: Looking Inside: Managing Organizations

In Section II, you are introduced to the notion of "managing". Understanding the nature of managing is an important concern for any member of any organization. What, indeed, does it mean to manage people, and what roles are played by the manager? Chapter 2 presents a glimpse into the world of managers. Any organization must be managed — that is, in very simple terms, an organization must generate a set of goals, and these goals must be accomplished. What is the role of the manager in generating goals and ensuring that these goals are fulfilled? What is the best way to manage people? The aim of Chapter 2 is to provide a better sense of what managing is all about, to offer insight into the different styles of managing, and to identify the various approaches or philosophies that have been generated with regard to managing people. Chapter 3 explores, in more detail, one important aspect of the job of the manager — making decisions. In fact, regardless of your role in any organization, decision making is clearly a fundamental aspect of every job! All members of any organization are called upon to make decisions, whether the decisions are routine or non-routine. While decision making is a pervasive element of organizational life, ironically, we often fail to critically evaluate the process through which decisions are generated. This chapter encourages us to think critically about this managerial function as a means to maximize our decision-making effectiveness.

Section III: The Landscape of Organizations

In Section III, we explore the world of organizations. Chapter 4 outlines specific challenges to designing organizational features. How do elements of organizational structure resolve the challenges inherent in managing an organization? There are different ways of thinking about the anatomy of organizations. Chapter 4 offers insight into the nature of the "organizational landscape". It offers a road map for understanding why organizations look the way they do. Chapter 5 examines the future of organizational structure and design. Are the traditional methods of designing organizations still valid? What factors suggest whether certain structures will succeed or fail? Specifically, what is the relationship between strategy and structure? What new organizational forms are arising? These are among the issues addressed in this chapter. Chapter 6 examines a specific type of organization — the small business. Among the central questions addressed is, what are the challenges and opportunities faced by small business owners and entrepreneurs? Chapter 7 examines the organizations whose purpose is not based on profits. We consider the non-profit landscape and its role in the Canadian context. This chapter discusses the challenges that such organizations confront, and the responses they are making to address those challenges.

Section IV: Looking Outside: The Context of Organizations

This section presents several issues that encourage you to reconsider the current status of organizations and their ability to adapt to the challenges of the present and future. Chapter 8 discusses organizations in the global or international context. This chapter explores the notion of globalization, and outlines a number of central considerations in any organizational efforts to expand internationally. Chapter 9 considers the roles that government can play with regard to business, and how these roles have been changing. Issues such as privatization, deregulation and the facilitation of trade agreements are discussed. Chapter 10 considers challenges for practitioners with regard to managing organizations in a responsible and ethical manner. This relates to the underlying issue of business ethics and corporate social responsibility.

Section V: The Future

Chapter 11 explores the issue of change. What is change, and how do organizations experience change? We will consider factors that either create or reduce resistance to change in organizations. This chapter also discusses the notion of the learning organization, and addresses the question of whether organizations are capable of facilitating learning and development among their members. In addition, the role of technology is examined, as well as those factors that have influenced innovation in the Canadian business context.

I

Introduction

1

Organizational Context: Looking Inside and Outside

Is Canadian business headed for a dismal future, or one that is bright? How, indeed, does one make sense of the current state of Canadian business? Assessing the prospects of organizations requires a careful examination of the contexts within which organizations operate. Much of this chapter and, indeed, this book is intended to address the internal and external context of organizations and those factors that critically impact the functioning and fate of business.

LEARNING OBJECTIVES

By the end of the chapter, you should be able to:

1. Define three characteristics of organizations that play a central role in their success or failure.
2. Identify the forces that comprise the specific and general environments of organizations.
3. Discuss the nature of the external forces confronting organizations.
4. Explain the importance of each of the external forces within the Canadian business context.
5. Describe the framework that this text will employ to examine the nature of organizations and management.

Organizational Insider ─────────────────────────────────

The Best of Times . . .

[T]here is a remarkable story unfolding in Canada.... Our corporate sector has adopted, as its strategy, a degree of accommodation to the promising technology revolution that has advanced us to a competitiveness standing internationally that is well above our previous standing.... We have established ourselves as one of the lead countries in the continuing fight against renewed inflation.... The real story has been the improvement in Canada's export performance, not only to the United States but also to Europe, Latin America and the Far East. ... a super-competitive Canadian dollar [has been an important contributing factor] to the improvements in Canada's current account. But there has been one other development that promises sustained long run continuing improvement: the huge rise in Canadian productivity growth that has resulted from intense restructuring and strong business investment.... A more profound, confidence-boosting development has been the restructuring taking place in the corporate sector, the government and in our schools to accommodate to the realities of rapid technological advances that are redesigning competitiveness throughout the globe.... What is apparent is the fact that Canadian companies, following the lead set by those in the United States, are aggressively restructuring in ways that are the surprise, and the delight, of Canada watchers. Moreover, this restructuring is evident in all areas of the economy: manufacturing and non-manufacturing alike; and, to be even more positive, there is no evidence of an end in sight.[1]

... Canadian companies actually boosted productivity faster than their U.S. counterparts in 12 out of 19 industrial sectors between 1989 and 1997.... We see plenty of Canadian individuals and enterprises well positioned for global success.... Canada has come a long way since 1991, in the private and public sectors alike....[2]

. . . or the Worst of Times?

Canada simply isn't keeping up. Productivity levels here are hurting our competitiveness and our image in world markets. The Canadian Association of Management Consultants has warned the productivity gap between Canada and the US has widened 25% in the past two decades, resulting in a 20% drop in Canadians' standard of living relative to Americans' since 1961.[3]

We must face up to our weaknesses. Canada has a handful of companies that are large in domestic terms. But it is a different story when they are viewed in the world market, in which Canada has barely 3% of the wealth. In this global light, our largest companies are dwarfed by their foreign competitors, which are growing faster than our own companies, often through consolidation.[4]

[T]he mindset of corporate Canada — fixated on the U.S. and only intermittently interested in the rest of the world. It turned out to be a fiction that Canada-US free trade would allow Canadian companies first to conquer the US market and then make the leap to the rest of the world. Canada's trade pattern is more bilateral with the US now than a decade ago, despite Team Canada's missions.[5]

[Citing a 2001 report, "The Marginalization of Corporate Canada", by Isaiah Litvak for the Canadian Institute of International Affairs:]

If Canada is to be anything more than an economic appendage to the United States in the years ahead, then we need to do some pretty serious thinking about our future. Increasing continental integration is sharply reducing Canada's capacity to make decisions that affect its economic future. Yet unless we can strengthen our indigenous capacity for wealth creation through a strong base of Canadian companies, we will be unable to sustain our quality of life or continue as a distinct and sovereign country in North America.[6]

Sources:

1. Lloyd C. Atkinson, "Canada: A remarkable story is unfolding" *Business Credit* (January 2001) 103(1). Reproduced from Business Credit Magazine with permission from the National Association of Credit Management.
2. Thomas D'Aquino and David Stewart-Patterson, Comment: "Forget Porter: Canadian industries are better off than you think" *The Globe and Mail* (May 9, 2001), A15.
3. Jason Kirby, "It's getting loonie" *Canadian Business* (February 18, 2002) 75(3): 11.
4. Gordon Nixon, "We can't sit back and allow all of our industries to become globally insignificant" *The Globe and Mail* (July 5 2001): B11.
5. Jeffrey Simpson, "When corporate Canada is too big for Canada" *The Globe and Mail* (June 22, 2001): A13.
6. David Crane, "Canadian business is losing its voice" *The Toronto Star* (November 11, 2001): B1.

MAKING SENSE OF ORGANIZATIONS AND MANAGEMENT

Who do we believe — the doomsayers, or the optimists, regarding the future of business enterprise in Canada? We cannot help but be struck by the different voices we hear and the different stories we read regarding our future as working Canadians. **Are we living in the best of times, or the worst of times?** One thing is for sure — we live in **confusing times!** How do we make sense of our status in the business context? Where are we headed?

What factors influence the "health" of business in the Canadian economy? What determines the ultimate success or failure of an organization? How does one identify what possibly lies ahead? Perhaps the most productive way is to get a sense of how organizations are currently functioning, and identify some ongoing challenges they face. To do this, we can look inside and outside organizations. That is, we can consider key issues that can be defined as existing within the boundaries of the organization; and we can examine issues that are part of the organization's external environment. This chapter sets the stage for that examination.

INSIDE AND OUTSIDE ORGANIZATIONS

Inside the Organization: The Internal Context

What goes on within the walls of an organization — that is, what comprises the internal context of organizations? In Chapters 2, 3, 4 and 5 we will consider more closely the internal context of organizations. This book will focus, internally, on three fundamental concepts: people, structure and strategy, and goals. Looking inside organizations involves a consideration of how people within organizations are managed. Chapter 2 considers the notion of management, and discusses perspectives on managing people. Organizations' fates are intrinsically bound up with the quality of decisions that are generated inside the organization. Consequently, Chapter 3 considers how decisions are made, and how organizations might fall victim to decision disasters. Chapters 4 and 5 continue to look inside the organization to consider how organizations are designed, and why they have decided to undergo dramatic change. Below, we will expand this description of our examination of organizations from the inside.

People

Chapter 2 considers the nature of the members who comprise an organization and how they manage and are managed. It does not matter whether they are small businesses (Chapter 6), non-profit organizations (Chapter 7) or a giant multinational corporation (Chapter 8); any type of organization must be managed. Organizations are made up of people and, consequently, this factor is clearly one that must be carefully examined. How do we manage people within the organization? Regardless of your role in organizations, no doubt at some point in your career you will be required to apply some sort of management or leadership skills in the conduct of your job. Simply working in organizations is a reason to be familiar with how organizational life operates and understand what exactly is involved in the art or science of management. Given the importance of this issue, we will take a closer look at it in more detail in Chapter 2.

Structure

Chapters 4 and 5 consider the internal context of the organization with regard to how it is designed and the implications of organizational design and redesign. As we discuss in Chapter 4, organizational structure is a deliberately planned network or pattern of relationships that exists among individuals in various roles or positions. This includes the formal hierarchy of authority, the distribution or grouping of work (for example, into departments), and the rules or procedures that control and coordinate behaviour in the organization.

The structure of many organizations has been radically redesigned in recent years. Organizations in just about every industrialized nation have been undergoing change. While some companies have reduced their levels of hierarchy or laid off employees at all levels, others have undergone a concurrent change in their whole business process, while other have simply closed down. In order to understand what is happening — and, more important, why it is happening — we need to understand more about the design or structure of organizations. This is the aim of Chapters 4 and 5 — to offer an insight into the anatomy of organizations and, ultimately, to explain why organizations are being redesigned.

Strategy and Goals

Deciding what strategies the organization should pursue is a key task of managers. Managers are continually faced with the task of making decisions, both minor and major, on a daily basis. Whether it is when to schedule the next staff lunch or what approach to take to the new product advertising campaign, the decisional role of manager is a commonly played role. But how much do we know about how decisions are made? Is it possible to teach managers how to make good decisions? What can we gain from an examination of the process of decision making? Chapter 3 is intended to offer a framework for understanding the process of decision making and to draw attention to the biases that influence the wisdom of decision-makers and that can, consequently, set the stage for decision fiascos. We will begin our examination with a look at the classical model of decision making, and then move on to consider more recent efforts at understanding how decisions are made. We will look at the area of risky decision making — decisions made with risk or uncertainty — and consider what factors influence our decisions to take on risk or to avoid risk. Chapter 3 concludes with a consideration of how we might minimize decision biases and, consequently, help reduce the risk of engaging in a decision fiasco.

In Chapters 4 and 5, we will consider why organizations are designed the way they are and how they attempt to achieve their goals. It is useful, for now, to consider the

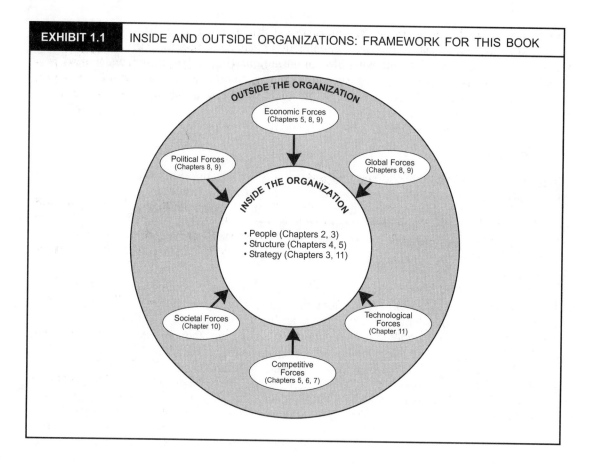

EXHIBIT 1.1   INSIDE AND OUTSIDE ORGANIZATIONS: FRAMEWORK FOR THIS BOOK

purpose of organizations, or their goals, in broad terms. Exhibit 1.1 illustrates the framework we adopt in this book, and also identifies the environment of business, which we discuss below.

Outside the Organization: The External Context

Specific and general environments. We can refer to the external context of organizations as the environment of organizations. Management scholars have typically defined the environment of an organization along two dimensions: the organization's specific or task environment, and the organization's general environment. Each factor in an organization's external environment can be considered as existing in two spheres: a general sphere or environment that would encompass the external environments of all organizations in a society; and a specific sphere or environment within which the organization directly operates. This specific sphere has been referred to as the environmental domain of the organization. For example, changes in the international environment may be a common factor for all organizations with, say, trade agreements affecting Canadian industry in general. However, some industries may have been differentially affected by changes in the international environment via trade agreements. Not all organizations within an industry or within different industries are equally affected by changes in the environment. There are changes that affect all or some industries, and there are changes or factors that influence the direct sphere or environment of the organizations.

Specific or Task Environment

Any organization is surrounded by external stakeholders. These are parties or groups that have direct influence on the organization's ability to obtain resources and generate outputs. Stakeholders have some kind of stake or interest in the organization, and could include such parties as: the organization's customers, suppliers, the labour pool from within which the organization obtains employees, competitors, unions, distributors, creditors, the local public, and the government. While not all of these stakeholders may exist or exert influence on every organization, they are the types of factors that potentially constitute the specific environment of an organization.

Any organization needs to consider the needs of consumers and the strategies taken by competitors, and organizations must respond to the behaviours of suppliers, distributors, unions, the government, etc. For example, Bell Canada is an organization that has operated within the telecommunications industry for many years. It relies on the Canadian labour pool for employees, and has attempted to offer services that it feels will be valuable to Canadian customers and profitable to the company. Its specific environment has changed in recent years. For example, the government has exerted much influence on the activities of this company, and has also changed the nature of Bell's competitors. (See Let's Talk Business 1.1.)

LET'S TALK BUSINESS 1.1   BELL CANADA

Regulations regarding who can enter this industry have changed over the years, and essentially have resulted in Bell facing many more competitors than it did initially. In 2001, the government's *Broadband Task Force* released a report recommending the Chrétien government change foreign ownership rules to permit greater foreign investment in Canadian telecommunications companies, and consequently, increase competition in this industry. Part of the aim for this initiative would be to encourage the supply of high-speed Internet service to all communities in Canada as soon as possible. Companies such as AT & T have been lobbying the Canadian government and the Canadian Radio-telephone and Telecommunications Commission (CRTC) to relax foreign ownership regulations in this industry and to force Bell to offer access to its wires to competing service providers at wholesale prices.[1]

Source: [1] James Baxter, "Majority against foreign-owned media: poll Decima research: But study finds foreign investment not opposed" *Southam News* (July 6, 2001).

Changes to any aspects of an organization's specific environment, whether these changes are government regulations, competitive changes, changes in consumer tastes, etc., can dramatically change the behaviour or strategy of the organization. It is not possible to ignore various stakeholder groups — an organization, to function effectively, must respond to, and engage in interaction with, the various stakeholder groups.

General Environment

The sphere surrounding the organization's specific environment is typically referred to as the general environment. The forces that make up the general environment ultimately shape the specific environment of the organization. Consequently, the general environment will also influence the organization's ability to obtain resources. General environmental factors typically include: economic, political, competitive, technological, societal, and global forces.

Economic Forces

Whether it is a recession or strong economic health in Canada, the economic environment acts as a strong influence on the present and future prospects of any organization. Moreover, given the strong global ties in Canada, we can also consider the international economic environment as exerting an influence on Canadian organizations. Certainly, we understand the strong influence that the United States and its economy exert on Canadian business.

Any organization, in considering how it will obtain resources from the environment, must ask the question: Is the economy healthy, or weak? Organizations are continuously forced to adapt to changing economic conditions. Downsizings are more likely to occur in lean times than in rich. The use of a temporary workforce was partly an outcome of the recession that occurred in the 1990s and the consequent introduction of massive downsizings and layoffs of permanent members of the workforce. Economic changes have also facilitated changes to the nature of the employer–employee relationship. Lifetime employment appears to be a thing of the past. Consider the 1950s or the 1970s — these were times when employment actually meant security. The dominant model was long-term employment stability. However, a change to these implicit employment promises occurred sometime in the 1980s, when the age of downsizing began, with large, secure organizations beginning to lay off employees. Part-time and temporary work arrangements have become much more common than in the past.

Political Forces

Political forces can exert influence at both the specific and general levels. The government's push toward deregulating many industries was not solely aimed at the telecommunications industry, but rather was designed to welcome more competitors into the Canadian business sector and facilitate freer trade between Canada and the United States. The reduction in trade barriers worldwide has also opened the doors for increasing presence of foreign competition in many industries. Deregulation and privatization, discussed in another chapter, are clear examples of the importance of considering the effect of governmental

EXHIBIT 1.2 THE EXTERNAL CONTEXT OF ORGANIZATIONS

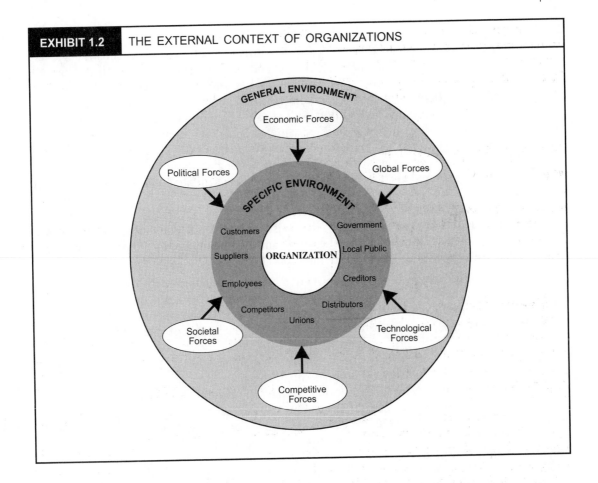

changes on business strategy. Are government regulations facilitating, or restricting, certain business strategies? The political environment of business can dictate changes in how business competes, or what services it offers and how they can be offered. As we will discuss in a later chapter, the deregulation of protected industries in the 1980s and 1990s created competition for companies where no real competition had previously existed. Industries such as telecommunications, banking, energy, and aerospace were dramatically affected by these governmental/regulatory changes. As the dominant companies in these industries were forced to compete in an open market, some responded by downsizing their workforce.

In a general sense, the traditional relationship of government with business is clearly undergoing change. The trend toward increased government involvement after World War II seems to have reversed by about 1980. In fact, some observers have suggested that this massive disposal of government-owned assets and the reduction of government controls in the business sector indicate a minor revolution of sorts. We will examine this issue in more detail in Chapter 9.

Competitive Forces

Competitive forces operate at two levels for any organization. As mentioned above, an organization will have its own set of competitors, and yet the force of competition can be viewed from a more general level. For example, globalization, as discussed elsewhere in this book, opens the floodgates for competitors in many industries. Clearly, the number of competitors and the nature of competition will dictate changes in organization design and strategy. Competition, both domestic and foreign, certainly has demanded an acceleration in innovation among firms in many industries. Organizations, to compete effectively, must continually create new and better methods of serving customers. While globalization has opened up larger markets for businesses, it has also facilitated much higher levels of competition.

Below, we will consider the competitive environment in the Canadian business context. For now, it is useful to note that when we consider players in the business context, we are really potentially looking at three broad forms of organizations. Three fundamental forms of business ownership can be defined as follows:

1. a sole proprietorship: a business owned directly and managed by one person. This happens to be the most common form of business ownership.
2. a partnership: two or more people who are legally co-owners of the business.
3. a corporation: a legal entity that exists separately from the people who own it.

In contrast to the first two forms above, a corporation is formed separate and distinct from its owners. While the owners hold shares in the corporation, the business is a separate legal entity. This is the notion of the corporation. So what does this mean? This means that a corporation can, for example, buy or sell property, or it can sue or be sued in its own name. The bulk of Canadian businesses are sole proprietorships. There are about 100,000 corporations in Canada, and they make up only about 17% of the total number of businesses. Ironically, however, they generate the largest volume of sales. Corporations account for about 87% of total sales volume, while sole proprietorships account for only about 9% of total sales volume. Of course, organizations may not simply be for-profit business. We will consider the nature and types of non-profit business in Chapter 7.

Technological Forces

Technological forces that surround organizations play a central role in how an organization functions, how it obtains resources and, ultimately, how effectively it competes. The technological environment exerts influence across industries. For example, in the case of Bell Canada, the increase in the number of competitors in the telecommunications industry was partly a consequence of the ability of smaller businesses to enter the industry with the increasingly sophisticated technology that formerly was the domain of big business, given its costly nature. However, with technological advances came reductions in operating costs and, hence, the ability to attract more competitors who could now afford to enter the industry.

Change in technology is a constant, and a force that permits and demands organizational change. Benefits from technology have included the ability to gain more flexibility in work arrangements. Telework, or telecommuting, essentially means that, given today's technology, an employee can work from home. Typically, with the aid of a modem or fax machine, business need not be conducted from a formal office. This has also contributed to increased flexibility with regard to the hours of work. It is clear that an organization will certainly continue to be affected by this environmental factor.

Societal Forces

Societal forces have an important impact on organizations. The nature of a society certainly is an entrenched part of any organization's general environment. For example, we have witnessed an increasing concern for individual welfare in the workplace as societies become more cognizant of human rights and how people could be treated. Consequently, we have witnessed in the workplace an increasing emphasis on organizational justice — how employees are treated. This has translated into greater laws governing fairness in the workplace. One such area that has been dramatically affected is compensation. Pay equity has been among numerous issues examined in redressing inconsistencies in pay treatment among men and women, for example. We have also witnessed an increasing emphasis on merit-based pay, and pay-for-performance — which all attempt to more closely link actual effort to performance instead of keeping things like seniority-based pay, which bases pay on the number of years you have been with the organization.

Business must respond to society. Consumer tastes change, for example, and business must adapt to such changes. Similarly, the types of organizations that serve societal demands can change. The aging population suggests that greater emphasis needs to be placed on such industries as the health care sector. In addition, society has a certain set of ethics or values, and these can influence the type of behaviour that organizations will manifest in that society. From a societal standpoint, it is not difficult to understand the importance of adequately addressing the issue of the ethical behaviour of business organizations and their constituents. All sectors of society, including organizations themselves, are drastically affected by a variety of forms of unethical behaviour. There is a growing belief that organizations are social actors responsible for the ethical and unethical behaviour of their employees. Critics of business argue that organizational leaders must examine more closely the "moral sense-making" within organizations, or the moral conflicts that arise in routine operations and decisions, in addition to responsibilities to external constituencies. The tolerance of unethical behaviour in a society would seem to be a precursor to the acceptance of corporate unethical behaviour. This is an issue that we will more fully explore in Chapter 10.

Global Forces

Global forces, in many ways, are forces that could be embedded in general economic, political, technological, or societal forces — but simply are international in nature.

The tragic and devastating events of September 11, 2001 following the terrorist attacks in the United States resulted in a chain reaction of international consequences, including changes in economic and political forces acting on organizations. Global events have an increasingly important impact on local organizations. While there is no universally agreed-upon definition of globalization, it is useful to consider this concept as a process: that is, a process involving the integration of world economies. The presence of trade blocs reflects the accelerating pace with which nations are integrating their economies. Globalization also includes the globalization of markets — the notion that consumer preferences are converging around the world. Whether it is for products made by McDonald's, Sony, The

Gap or Nike, organizations are increasingly marketing their goods and services worldwide. On the other side, production is increasingly becoming a global affair. Businesses will set up operations wherever it is least costly to do so.

Certainly, international trade agreements are global agreements among governments that are changing the nature and functions of many businesses. A Canadian organization may not simply consider consumers within the domestic borders, but may have a significant consumer market overseas; this demands a knowledge of global societies, global competitors, and other forces that exist on an international level.

The global forces of the general environment underscore the increasingly tangled web of players in the global business context — domestic and foreign competitors, domestic and foreign workers, domestic and foreign industry, government, national cultures and economies. How business is conducted in light of trade agreements and global arrangements is a key issue for our entire society. And this is a theme we will explore more fully in Chapter 8.

THE EXTERNAL ENVIRONMENT IN CANADA ———

From the above description of the environment, it can be observed that there is an overlap of factors between the general environment and the specific environment. An organization may have a specific market niche or set of consumers; but demographic changes in the general environment, such as an aging society, will certainly translate into changes to consumer tastes at the specific environment level. Similarly, as noted above, the government's aim to reduce trade barriers at a national level can translate into regulation within an organization's specific environment, or can result in increased competition within the organization's specific environment. This underlines the importance of understanding the impact of the general external environment or the specific environment of the organization. Let's revisit each of the external environmental forces with regard to the Canadian context of organization.

Economic Forces in Canada

What are some of the indicators of the current state of health of the Canadian economic scene? One indicator of the health of the economy is GDP — **gross domestic product**: the total value of a country's output of goods and services in a given year. The money that is earned from producing goods and services goes to the employees who produce them, to the people who own businesses and to the governments in the form of taxes. The general trend of governments worldwide is to reduce their share of GDP. Obviously, it is good for GDP to grow from 1979–1989: Canada's GDP grew about 3.2% annually. By 1999, growth in Canada's GDP reached 4.4%, and this level of growth was matched in 2000. Slower growth was experienced in 2001 with a 2.4% increase in GDP that year. While initial estimates for 2002 predicted more growth (in the 3.4% range), the unexpected downturn in the global economy in 2001, in addition to the devastating terrorist attacks in the United

---

LET'S TALK BUSINESS **1.2   THE ECONOMY AND TERRORISM**

[T]he damage caused by the first global slowdown in 25 years and the Sept. 11 terrorist attacks would take a heavy toll, Paul Martin, the Finance Minister, said yesterday. Economic growth would be kept to a meagre 1.3% this year (2001) and 1.1% in 2002 — well off robust growth of 4.4% in 2000.... "Indeed, for the first time in 25 years, we were in the midst of a slowdown that was happening concurrently in every major market of the world," Mr. Martin said. The Sept. 11 attacks exacerbated the slowdown, disrupting stock markets, air traffic and, most importantly for Canada, the flow of trade across the border with the United States.

Source: From Jacqueline Thorpe, "Heavy toll in 2002, says Martin. 1.1% growth next year: Fiscal stimulus, rate cuts and tax breaks to kick in" *Financial Post* (December 11, 2001).

States on September 11, 2001, led to much lower expectations for growth in the short term. (See Let's Talk Business 1.2.)

While recent years have reflected tougher economic times for Canadians, there are many indications that the future is bright. The future health of the Canadian economy, as in most economies, is continually the subject of speculation. It appears that economists are not necessarily more accurate in their predictions of economic well-being than are those looking into the proverbial crystal ball. It would seem crucial to understand what underlying forces are ultimately shaping the state of our business system in Canada. This amounts to distinguishing between short-term changes in the domestic economy and ongoing trends in the nature of the business enterprise system. It may be more manageable for us to consider what has been going on around us in recent years and assess what conditions will continue to persist in the coming years.

The unemployment rate increased sharply in the early part of the 1990s due to the severe 1991–1992 recession, and the steepest drop in economic activity since the Great Depression of the 1930s. The Canadian workforce remained at about 13.7 million from 1990–1996, with an official unemployment rate ranging from 7.5 to 11.8%. This meant that officially 1 to 1.5 million people were constantly out of work. The **real rate** is much higher that the quoted rate, because Statistics Canada does not include

- people who give up looking for jobs
- underemployed (i.e., part-time or temporary jobs)
- those who stay or return to school because they cannot find jobs at present

Even though GDP rose a significant 8% from late 1993 to early 1996, there was no net increase in the number of people working. Our economy got healthier, so to speak, without the added benefit of an increase in employment. We are actually just beginning to grapple with this new development — growth in the economy, as indicated by the GDP, without growth in jobs.

How can we produce more goods and services without requiring more employment? Consider the technological and globalization revolutions that have been occurring — we will

EXHIBIT 1.3	LABOUR FORCE, EMPLOYMENT AND UNEMPLOYMENT (1996–2000)				
	1996	**1997**	**1998**	**1999**	**2000**
			000s		
Population 15 years and over	23,030.7	23,359.3	23,671.1	23,969.0	24,284.9
Labour force	14,899.5	15,153.0	15,417.7	15,721.2	15,999.2
Employed	13,462.6	13,774.4	14,140.4	14,531.2	14,909.7
Full time	10,883.0	11,139.7	11,466.6	11,849.2	12,208.1
Part time	2,579.6	2,634.8	2,673.8	2,618.9	2,701.6
Unemployed	1,436.9	1,378.6	1,277.3	1,190.1	1,089.6
Not in the labour force	8,131.2	8,206.3	8,253.4	8,247.8	8,285.7
Actual hours worked	460,031.0	471,023.4	479,388.0	496,999.6	513,731.9
			%		
Employment to population ratio	58.5	59.0	59.7	60.6	61.4
Participation rate	64.7	64.9	65.1	65.6	65.9
Unemployment rate	9.6	9.1	8.3	7.6	6.8

Source: Statistics Canada, CANSIM, Matrix 3472 and Catalogue no. 71-528-XPB. (Last modified: June 21, 2001.)

discuss these issues in future chapters, but for now suffice it to say that changes in these areas have contributed to a reduction in the number of jobs in the whole industrialized world, including Canada. We have also witnessed massive job losses due to plant closings, record bankruptcy levels, and downsizings by both the private and public sectors. Some business shutdowns and layoffs have occurred due to company mergers or plants simply moving to the United States, Mexico or elsewhere to acquire cheaper labour. In the past, as the population increased, the number of people working in Canada increased every five years, despite recessions. But given the very heavy job losses in the early 1990s, the January 1996 figures showed no increase over 1990. Statistics Canada reported that only 88,000 net new jobs were created in all of 1995 in Canada, and most of them were not permanent or full-time jobs.

While much of the 1990s were not bright for employment, we have witnessed vast improvements in recent years. By 1999, the unemployment rate dropped to 7.6%, and in more recent years has hovered in the 6.8 to 7.1% range. (See Exhibits 1.3 and 1.4.)

Political Forces in Canada

The Canadian economic system has been described as a mixed system. This refers to the notion that while we possess a capitalist economy, government nonetheless plays an important role. In fact, historically, government has played a critical role in the Canadian econ-

| EXHIBIT 1.4 | EMPLOYMENT BY INDUSTRY, POPULATION 15 YEARS OF AGE AND OVER (1996–2000) |

	1996	1997	1998	1999	2000
			000s		
ALL INDUSTRIES	13,462.6	13,774.4	14,140.4	14,531.2	14,909.7
GOODS-PRODUCING SECTOR	3,487.8	3,585.5	3,691.3	3,785.7	3,867.8
Agriculture	425.5	417.7	428.2	410.1	372.5
Forestry, fishing, mining, oil and gas	292.6	299.1	294.7	267.5	283.2
Utilities	124.6	116.5	115.8	115.9	116.4
Construction	713.9	729.5	738.7	774.9	815.6
Manufacturing	1,931.2	2,022.4	2,113.8	2,217.3	2,280.1
SERVICE-PRODUCING SECTOR	9,974.7	10,189.0	10,449.0	10,745.4	11,041.9
Trade	2,103.8	2,128.7	2,156.2	2,248.3	2,318.1
Transportation and warehousing	674.4	697.9	716.5	744.5	779.8
Finance, insurance, real estate and leasing	868.9	874.4	854.3	863.0	867.0
Professional, scientific and technical services	702.2	779.7	849.3	905.1	945.8
Management administrative and other support	424.0	443.1	480.8	507.0	546.5
Educational services	908.4	914.1	934.9	982.6	974.8
Health care and social assistance	1,393.5	1,390.6	1,426.4	1,444.5	1,526.3
Information, culture and recreation	578.7	606.3	616.0	629.8	665.4
Accommodation and food services	854.4	874.5	922.9	924.7	960.6
Other services	656.5	684.5	710.7	721.6	695.8
Public administration	810.2	795.4	781.2	774.4	761.8

Source: Statistics Canada, CANSIM, Matrix 3472 and Catalogue no. 71-529-XPB. (Last modified: June 21, 2001.)

omy. In Canada, we have a long history of government involvement in business in the sense of promoting and protecting our industries. Tariffs on imported goods were designed to protect our domestic business by making the cost of foreign goods more expensive relative to those of Canadian goods. It can be argued that a large portion of Canada's industrial development is due to protectionism thorough tariffs first imposed in 1879 by Sir John A. Macdonald's National Policy. Eventually, the government also offered direct incentives for industrial and resource development. "Incentive programs" were established to encourage managers to conduct business in a manner desired by the government. What does this mean? It may be desirable for managers to, say, invest in a new product development, or engage in greater export activities, or to locate in an underdeveloped region. Consequently, government incentives will be offered to engage in such activities. Receiving government financial support or reward for such activities would influence decisions to engage in these activities. (See Let's Talk Business 1.3.)

LET'S TALK BUSINESS 1.3 GOVERNMENT AID TO BUSINESS

In Canada, recent issues concern the degree to which government can or should help businesses compete — whether in the form of direct subsidies, tax incentives or some other forms of protectionism. For example, one recurring controversy in recent years is the level of government subsidies to businesses operating in the global marketplace and government support for research and development programs. One recent controversy involved an ongoing dispute regarding government subsidies to Canada's aerospace giant Bombardier and its main competitor in the jet market, Embraer SA (Empresa Brasileira de Aeronautica SA.) of Brazil. The recent lumber dispute highlighted at the beginning of Chapter 8 is another example of the difficulty in establishing the degree to which government should aid business. In Chapter 9 we will assess some of the ways government can or should be involved in business activity.

Competitive Forces in Canada

When you think "Canadian business", what picture do you conjure in your mind? Looking back over Canada's past, it has been argued that we established a certain pattern for ourselves in terms of the type of business activity we emphasized here. During most of our existence, we have developed as a largely open economy, trading internationally, primarily, in resources. Specifically, Canada, for most of our existence, has focused on the extraction and processing of our natural resources. It has been suggested that our emphasis on the export of our natural resources, typically in a relatively unprocessed state, made us more akin to a simple supplier of raw materials, whether it has been logs and lumber, pulp and newsprint, unrefined minerals, agricultural crops, etc. In fact, it has been argued that our corporations are much more involved in the extraction and processing of natural resources than most other countries at comparable stages of economic development. This pattern has led critics to suggest that we have not developed the entrepreneurial and technological expertise of other nations, who used our "raw materials" and added value through their own technological resources. However, it would be unfair to suggest that this is the whole picture. The fact is, we have witnessed major changes in the nature of our economic sector, and we continue to see a major transformation in our economy, and in the types of business competitors we have created. As with any capitalist-based system, Canada views competition as an important part of the business enterprise system!

Imagine a situation where there is only one provider of an important good. If society requires this good, then they must be willing to accept whatever price the provider demands. There is also no assurance regarding the quality of the good. There is little incentive for the provider of this good to be efficient in operations — any high costs can be passed on to the consumer in the form of high prices. Similarly, there is little need to innovate or produce higher quality products for the consumer, given that there is no risk of losing this captive market. Consequently, competition is considered to be an important element: this entails firms competing with each other to provide better products at lower prices in order to increase sales and profits.

LET'S TALK BUSINESS 1.4   COMPETITION

How does the Canadian corporate landscape shape up in terms of the relative numbers of business competitors? Well, looking across industries, what we tend to see is domination by a relatively small number of firms. That is, we have a relatively small number of corporations in any particular industry. This has been referred to as "industrial concentration in the economy". Statistics Canada recently estimated that the largest 25 firms in Canada are responsible for about 25% of total profits generated in the business sector and own about 41% of the total assets. Of course, some industries are more concentrated than others. For example, we have relatively few large players in the brewery industry, in banking, and among department stores.

Pure competition, sometimes referred to as perfect competition, exists when there are many small firms producing an identical product, and consequently no single producer has the power to affect the price of the product. Traditionally, the agricultural industry is an example of this type of competition, given the identical nature of the products and the fact that no single producer can influence prices. In fact, these companies are forced to respond obediently to prices set in the market. Monopolistic competition involves a large number of small firms whose product or service is perceived as slightly different. As a result, each firm has some influence on the prices, such as may be the case with retail operations. An oligopoly exists where there are a small number of producers with a different product. For example, car manufacturers have significant control over prices, and yet competition does play a role in the prices set. Finally, a monopoly exists where there is only one seller or producer. (See Let's Talk Business 1.4.)

Our economic system is based on the assumption that sufficient competition exists among business enterprises to ensure that business provides the goods and services required by society at a fair cost. Competition is the "invisible hand" that ensures the market works in this manner. However, if an industry is relatively concentrated, then businesses can act as price setters, not price takers. Of course, with extreme concentration, as is the case with a monopoly, then business can set the price itself or collude with other businesses. Observers suggest that Canada has not taken as strict a stance on industry concentration as the United States, where legislation has been aimed at preventing industry concentration. In Canada, government legislated competition policy does attempt to discourage industry concentration, but also seeks to control the potential inequities created when a small number of firms dominate a particular market.

Technological Forces in Canada

Traditionally, Canada's economy has been resource based. This refers to our emphasis on industries like agriculture, mining, forestry, fisheries, minerals, and energy. Natural resources have constituted the bulk of Canada's exports. Given the nature of our primary industries, one important implication is that prices for the output of these industries are very much influenced by the world market. That is, these natural resource industries are highly affected by any fluctuations in the global supply and demand for these commodities. This suggests that many of our industries are highly sensitive to changes in the global or world markets. There has been a general criticism levelled at the Canadian business environment that we need to catch up in the area of technology and innovation rather than relying on our natural resources in largely unprocessed form.

However, the Canadian economy has been transforming. We have already seen significant changes in the sectoral composition of Canada's economy over the 20th century. At the beginning of the 20th century, there was a balance between employment in the primary sectors of the economy and the industrial and service sectors. What we mean by the primary sector is agriculture, mining, logging, fishing, hunting and trapping. The industrial sector is akin to the manufacturing or goods-producing sectors, while the service sector can include things like the hotel or restaurant industry. At the beginning of the 20th century, we had an abundance of employment in the primary sector, with most of this coming from the agricultural sector. However, even early in the century we witnessed a steady decline in agricultural employment right up until World War II — after which time this decline continued even more rapidly.

We have seen a clear shift in employment away from the agricultural sector. Why? A number of reasons have been offered. Perhaps one of the most obvious reasons for the decline in agricultural employment is a reduced need for human capital: that is, part of the reason is simply due to technological advances that have made human labour obsolete. Many areas have become increasingly mechanized and, consequently, require far fewer workers to achieve the same level of output. Parallel to this decline we have seen the increasing urbanization of the Canadian population: increasing numbers of Canadians continue to flock to cities from rural areas in search of employment, and it is the cities that attract the largest share of new immigrants.

If there has been a significant shift in employment away from the agriculture sector, the question is: Where has it shifted to? What we have seen happening in conjunction with that decline in Canada is great increases in the number of Canadians employed in goods-producing and service industries. The manufacturing sector produces tangible goods, such as clothes, oil, food, machines, and automobiles. The service sector includes things like banking, insurance, information, marketing, accounting, hospitality and food services, recreation and so on.

The shift to the manufacturing and service sectors was particularly striking in the first 15 years following World War II, after which growth in these areas slowed, although it certainly continued throughout the '60s, '70s and '80s. However, what is particularly striking in the later post-war period is the simultaneous rise in service sector employment, and at least since the 1950s, the rapid decline in goods-producing industries. We continue to witness this trend, albeit at a reduced rate. Consider this: in 1950, only 42% of Canadians were employed in service-producing industries; by 1993, the figure had risen to over 72%. Whereas at the turn of the century we shifted from an agricultural to an industrial economy, the second shift has been the transition from a goods-producing to a service-oriented economy. This shift is summed up in the observations in Let's Talk Business 1.5, and reflected in Exhibit 1.5.

Why are we moving away from the natural resources and the manufacturing sector to the service sector? What is driving this shift? Well, there is not really one accepted reason

LET'S TALK BUSINESS 1.5   INFORMATION TECHNOLOGY

Canada's information technology sector will replace rocks and trees as the dominant force in the economy over the coming decade, according to a study from the Toronto Dominion Bank. Despite the recent weaknesses in the New Economy industries, their growth will continue.... By 2010, Canada's economy is expected to be even less resource-based, more heavily wired and more service-driven than ever before.... By that time the New Economy is expected to reach 12.6% of gross domestic product, effectively closing the gap with the resource sector. Currently, these industries account for 8% of GDP, triple the amount in the early 1980s.... The bank defined the New Economy as eight industries in the area of information technology — four in manufacturing and four in services. Those in manufacturing include communications and electrical equipment; office and business machines; communications, energy, wire and cable; and scientific equipment. Services include telecommunications — both broadcasting and carriers — computers and software sectors. Meanwhile the resource sector, which includes oil and gas, agriculture, forestry, fishing and logging, and resource-based manufacturing, continues to decline, currently accounting for 14.5% of the economy, down from 17% two decades ago....

Source: From Marian Stinson, "New economy still seen as future" *The Globe and Mail* (May 31, 2001). Reproduced with permission from The Globe and Mail.

EXHIBIT 1.5   INDUSTRIAL OUTLOOK FOR CANADA

Projected annual average percent growth rates, 2001–2010.

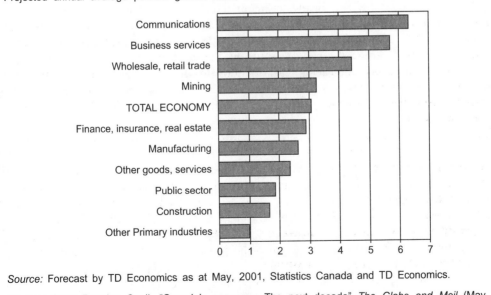

Source: Forecast by TD Economics as at May, 2001, Statistics Canada and TD Economics.

Source: From Douglas Coull, "Canada's economy: The next decade" *The Globe and Mail* (May 31, 2000), B7. Reproduced with permission from The Globe and Mail.

for this transformation to a service economy. But probably the most often cited reason is technology: just as mechanization of agricultural production decreased the need for human capital, more generally the increasing mechanization of manufacturing facilities has similarly reduced the need for human labour in this sector. We can produce comparable levels of output with far less labour than we did in the past. This is referred to as a productivity improvement. And as far as productivity is concerned, what we have seen is labour productivity growth in manufacturing outpacing productivity growth in services. Why?

Just consider the nature of many service-oriented jobs: social workers who counsel youths, waiters who serve customers, and medical caregivers who treat patients are not easily replaced by machinery. Productivity growth in this sector is thus much slower than in the manufacturing sector. The result of this difference in productivity growth rates is that more Canadians need to be employed in services in order to maintain the relative levels of service and manufacturing output.

Whatever the source, there is little question that services are playing a much greater role in our economy than they have in the past. However, one final question that we can ask related to all this is: **Is this shift a good thing?** Let's consider several implications of this transition.

On a personal level, anyone planning on entering the job market or remaining employable must consider their skill set. Obviously, our workforce must be better educated and capable of attaining the relatively higher skill levels required in the highly paying service sector jobs (in comparison to the manufacturing sector). The notion of the "knowledge worker", a relatively recent buzzword, underscores the increasing importance of higher education and the value of transferable skills. This is reflected in the observation of Let's Talk Business 1.6.

But in broader terms, is the service sector better for our economy? Or is manufacturing still very much a critical element? A number of observers suggest that we should say "good riddance" to the old, outdated manufacturing sector and welcome the growing service sector with open arms. For example, economist Nuala Beck referred to a "new knowledge economy" that is quickly replacing the old mass-manufacturing economy. Beck observed that these "knowledge workers" now make up 30% of North America's workforce, while only 10% are actually involved in production. Further, it is the more knowledge-intensive new industries (like the high-tech industries) that are creating most of the jobs and driving the economy. (See Let's Talk Business 1.7.)

Societal Forces in Canada

Demographics. What are some defining characteristics of our population? First, there are not many of us — relatively speaking. Canada's total population of approximately 31 million is among the smallest of the industrialized nations. It has been observed that our relatively small market has made it extremely difficult to develop more than a handful of domestic manufacturers of a stature capable of competing on the world markets. Moreover, it has been asserted that Canada has generated too many small operations that have been protected for too long by government. What are the implications of this? It underscores the fact that many businesses see an urgent need to expand their markets beyond Canadian borders.

LET'S TALK BUSINESS 1.6   THE LABOUR MARKET

[D]uring the 1990s a truly remarkable transformation of the Canadian labour market transpired. If you look at the period from the beginning of the last decade until 1997 (the year in which employment growth really began to accelerate), you will realize that from the start of 1990 until 1997, total employment in Canada grew by only about 500,000 — or about 70,000 per year on average. This is a dismal performance compared with any other seven-year stretch of our post-Second World War history. However, if you dig into the numbers, a very important different story unfolds. The number of new jobs created for those with university degrees was almost 600,000, which was an increase of over 30 percent between 1990 and 1997. Similarly, during that time period net new jobs for those with post-secondary certificates — but less than university degrees — rose by over 800,000. Therefore, in our economy that generated only 500,000 jobs total, those with post-secondary and university degrees generated about 1.4 million new jobs combined. Simple subtraction will tell you that those with only a high school diploma, or less, suffered huge job losses in the first seven years of the 1990s. Since 1997, the bulk of the new jobs created have been amongst Canadians with post-secondary and university degrees. The message, far from being ambiguous, is loud and clear: education and skills are essential elements of success in the current transforming Canadian economy. (And the popular notion that most of the new jobs are in menial, low paying service occupations is, simply, false. Most in service, yes; most in low paying, no.)

Source: From Lloyd C. Atkinson, "Canada: A remarkable story is unfolding" *Business Credit* (January 2001) 103(1).

Demographic (population) trends have a significant effect on business planning and activities. In the 20 years following World War II (1946–1966), Canada witnessed an unusual phenomenon. Large numbers of war veterans, aided by government grants, got married and acquired housing for their families. In addition, the hundreds of thousands of immigrants who were entering Canada annually also needed housing. Four children per family was the norm. These were **baby boomers**. This explosive growth in population and family formation led to a 20-year boom in many industries (e.g., housing, furnishings, children's clothing, etc.).

Today, other important demographic trends have emerged that will have a great impact on the next few decades. For example, consider the **aging population**. The demographics of the workforce have changed gradually over the years, and among these changes we have witnessed a graying or aging of the workforce. In 1921 the median age of the Canadian population was under 24 years; by 1993 it had risen to over 33 years. The median age continues to rise, and could be as high as 50 by the year 2036. In 1981, the largest age bracket was the group between 15 and 24. Population projections show that by 2006, the largest group will be the 40–49 age bracket, and by 2031 it will be the 70–74 age bracket. By 2011, the portion of the population over 65 and 75 will be about double what it was in 1981 (9.7%). At the same time, the portion of the population that is very young continues to decrease because of declining birth rates since the mid-1960s

---

LET'S TALK BUSINESS 1.7   REVOLUTION IN TECHNOLOGY

To be blunt, we are in the midst of a revolution — a technology-driven revolution — whose effects are every bit as profound as those delivered by the Industrial Revolution itself. Two aspects of the Industrial Revolution are worth recalling. First, the "front end" of that revolution was characterized by huge (some would say monstrous) economic and social upheaval and dislocation. People from the agricultural population poured into towns and cities in overwhelming numbers; and one after another, the many cottage industries that were the mainstay of the non-agricultural economy folded because they could not even come close to matching the production efficiencies and prices delivered by new, giant factories. But the painful upheaval wrought by the Industrial Revolution was not in vain. In fact, and this is the second critical aspect, in economies that successfully accommodated themselves to the realities of the Industrial Revolution, there occurred, in the "backside" of that revolution, increases in living standards the likes of which were then unfathomable.... In my view, we are still in the early stages — the "front end", if you will — of the technology revolution where, early on, all we appeared to see was social and economic upheaval. However, we are now beginning to see the generalized benefits that can be delivered to those who learn how to accommodate themselves to the realities of this revolution; this is evident in both the new kinds of jobs that have been created and in the recent bounce-up in productivity. And I suspect that 20 to 30 years from now someone will be writing about the astonishing improvements in living standards that resulted from accommodation to the realities of the technology revolution.

Source: From Fay Hansen, "Canada weathers the slowdown" *Business Credit* (April 2001) 103(4). Reproduced from Business Credit Magazine with permission from the National Association of Credit Management.

(e.g., in 1971 about 30% of the Canadian population was between 6 and 19; by 2001, it had dropped to about 20%). So businesses will cater to an older population: health care, recreation, travel are among the industries that are predicted to benefit from an older population. (See Let's Talk Business 1.8.)

One other major change in the makeup of the workforce: **women in the workforce**. The growing number of women in the workforce is another trend that will have a significant impact on business. In 1921 only 20% of the female population worked outside the home. By 1993 the figure had risen to about 60%. There are also some interesting patterns to observe within the workforce. In March of 1998 Statistics Canada published its major report on the labour force. Among the findings of this report, it was indicated that women were much more concentrated in part-time jobs than men. For example, in 1995, 12% of paid female workers worked part time, while only 4% of paid male workers worked part time. In terms of self-employment, it is also interesting to note the significant number of women who are self-employed. The Statistics Canada report also indicated that while the number of self-employed men increased by 29% over the past five years, the number of self-employed women rose by 62%. In addition to the increasing number of women in the workforce, we are also observing an increase in the cultural diversity of

---

LET'S TALK BUSINESS 1.8   AN AGING WORKFORCE

The challenges of dealing with a changing workplace demographic were also noted in a recent report by economist Bill Robson for the C.D. Howe Institute, entitled, *Aging Populations and the Workforce: Challenges for Employees.* The report suggested that over the next 20 years, both business and government will need to adapt numerous employment practices and social policies to meet the changing demands of an aging workforce, and a workforce that is more highly educated and largely female. Currently, the federal government has been initiating training and labour policy changes that recognize the aging of the workforce. Recently, the Minister of Human Resources and Development suggested, for example, that Canada accept more immigrants to replace retiring workers. According to the report, private-sector employers will also require new recruitment and training strategies to manage an older workforce and a greater immigrant population.

---

organizations — a greater heterogeneity of races and nationalities. The changing cultural mix of organizations demands that we place greater attention on efforts to effectively integrate the variety of cultures, along with men and women in the workplace.

Global Forces in Canada

The United States.   Clearly, our proximity to the United States is an element that influences the nature of our business environment. Keep in mind that the United States has a population that is approximately 10 times that of Canada. And though we possess one of the largest countries in terms of land mass, the bulk of our population lives within 200 km of the Canada–U.S. border. In fact, the U.S. presence in the Canadian business sector is a defining characteristic of our environment. Moreover, the trade agreements we have entered into with the United States have critical implications for our business sector (an issue we will deal with later in this book).

Importance of international trade.   Currently, Canada exports over 40% of its total annual production (GDP), compared to 25% a decade ago. This underscores the fact that Canada is considered to be a major trading nation. A key concern regarding our international business activity is whether we are selling more to other countries (exporting) than we are importing (buying from other countries). Other than the United States (our major trading partner, consuming more than 85% of our total exports), we have traditionally run a trade deficit with most other countries (i.e., our imports have outweighed our exports), as illustrated in Exhibit 1.6.

A number of issues regarding our trade status have received much attention in the last decade or so, not the least of which are the Free Trade Agreement and the North American Free Trade Agreement (NAFTA) and the consequent increase in the degree of openness to international trade. As mentioned earlier, Canada's traditional reli-

EXHIBIT 1.6	MERCHANDISE TRADE OF CANADA — BY PRINCIPAL TRADING PARTNERS

Seasonally Adjusted, $ Current

	2000	2001		Change from	
	April	March	April	March	Last April
	$ millions	$ millions		% change	
Principal Trading Partners					
Exports					
United States	28,552	30,559	31,902	4.4	11.7
Japan	863	884	800	−9.5	−7.3
European Union	1,744	2,093	1,960	−6.4	12.3
Other OECD countries[1]	762	1,067	666	−37.6	−12.6
All other countries	1,654	1,810	1,700	−6.1	2.7
TOTAL	33,576	36,412	37,028	1.7	10.3
Imports					
United States	22,144	22,104	22,333	1.0	0.9
Japan	1,002	816	1,053	29.0	5.1
European Union	2,830	2,857	3,089	8.1	9.2
Other OECD countries[1]	1,513	1,571	1,487	−5.4	−1.7
All other countries	2,573	2,784	2,733	−1.8	6.2
TOTAL	30,062	30,132	30695	1.9	2.1
Balance					
United States	6,407	8,454	9,570	—	—
Japan	−139	68	−253	—	—
European Union	−1,086	−764	−1,130	—	—
Other OECD countries[1]	−751	−504	−821	—	—
All other countries	−918	−974	−1,033	—	—
TOTAL	3,513	6,280	6,333	—	—

Notes:— Figures not appropriate or not applicable.
1. Includes Australia, Iceland, Mexico, New Zealand, Norway, Switzerland and Turkey.

Source: Statistics Canada, CANSIM, Matrices 3618, 3619, 3651 and 3685 and Catalogue no. 65-001-XIB. (Last modified: June 21, 2001.)

ance on trade in unprocessed natural resources (Exhibit 1.7) has received much criticism, and its current reliance on U.S. trade has been scrutinized, as reflected in Let's Talk Business 1.9.

Foreign ownership. How "Canadian" is Canadian business? In other words, what proportion of the corporations doing business in Canada are not actually controlled by Canadian sources?

| EXHIBIT 1.7 | MERCHANDISE TRADE OF CANADA — BY COMMODITY GROUPING |

Seasonally Adjusted, $ Current

	2000	2001			
				Change from	
	April	March	April	March	Last April
	$ millions	$ millions		% change	
Principal Commodity Grouping[1]					
Exports					
Agricultural and fishing products	2,147	2,400	2,497	4.0	16.3
Energy products	3,799	5,877	6,833	16.3	79.9
Forestry products	3,669	3,369	3,513	4.3	4.2
Industrial goods and materials	4,971	5,143	5,117	0.5	2.9
Machinery and equipment	7,744	8,214	7,539	−8.2	−2.6
Automotive products	7,746	7,329	7,565	3.2	−2.3
Other consumer goods	1,009	1,177	1,147	−2.6	13.6
Special transactions trade[1]	1,853	1,980	1,996	0.8	7.7
Imports					
Agricultural and fishing products	1,469	1,655	1,701	2.8	15.8
Energy products	1,468	1,726	1,635	−5.3	10.1
Forestry products	258	250	254	1.7	−1.2
Industrial goods and materials	5,901	5,595	5,609	0.3	−4.9
Machinery and equipment	10,119	10,031	10,052	0.2	−0.7
Automotive products	6,392	5,940	6,191	4.2	−3.1
Other consumer goods	3,331	3,582	3,603	0.6	8.2
Special transactions trade[1]	515	565	685	21.2	33.0

Notes:— Figures not appropriate or not applicable.
1. Figures not adjusted to balance-of-payments basis.
2. Mainly low-valued transactions, value of repairs to equipment and goods returned to country of origin.

Source: Statistics Canada, CANSIM, Matrices 3618, 3619, 3651 and 3685 and Catalogue no. 65-001-XIB. (Last modified: June 21, 2001.)

While the level of foreign ownership varies among different industries (e.g., about 67% in chemical product and textile manufacturers, and only about 9% in communications), the average level of foreign ownership is over 25%, relatively high by world standards. Annual foreign investment in Canadian companies means ownership of assets like factories, land, buildings, machinery, equipment and companies themselves. So, we have a pretty high level of foreign ownership, largely U.S.-based, in Canadian corporations — but what difference does that make to the nature of business in Canada?

LET'S TALK BUSINESS 1.9   THE UNITED STATES AND CANADA

... the critical importance that the United States holds for Canada as its largest trading partner, a relationship worth $1.3 billion a day in trade across the border.... Canada depends heavily on the United States as the prime market for its exported goods, and this dependency has increased in recent years. In 1995, the United States consumed 77.5 percent of all Canadian exports. By 1999, it accounted for 85.8 percent. Canada runs a large positive trade balance with the United States, but a negative trade balance with all other trading partners. If Canadian exports to the United States decline, Canada's overall balance of trade will slip into deficit territory.... Canada maintains relatively liberal trade policies and has provided favourable access to its markets for the least developed countries. However, high levels of protection still exist in some sensitive sectors, such as certain agricultural products and textiles and clothing. Eventually, Canada will have to accelerate the reduction of tariffs on these products and provide more duty-free access to improve resource allocation within Canada, and to end intermittent trade disputes with potentially important trading partners. With exports to the United States likely to decline, Canada will have to renew its efforts to build stronger trade relations with countries in the European Union and Asia, to stave off a downturn at home.

Source: From Fay Hansen, "Canada weathers the slowdown" *Business Credit* (April 2001) 103(4). Reproduced from Business Credit Magazine with permission from the National Association of Credit Management.

What are the implications of foreign investment? There is much debate about this topic. In fact, Canadians have traditionally been ambivalent when it comes to the issue of foreign investment. For some, interest in the Canadian economy is a good thing. On the one hand, we want to attract investors to our country in order to help generate more business and more jobs. The source of ownership shouldn't make a difference when the results are the same—more jobs for Canadians and more money invested in the Canadian economy.

What impact does foreign ownership have on the personality of our corporate sector? Keep in mind that these foreign-owned corporations are largely subsidiaries of U.S.-based "parent" companies. One important consideration is the activity that the corporation carries on in order to conduct its business—i.e., strategic planning, research and development, marketing, etc. Many foreign-owned firms, like the car manufacturers or the multinational oil companies, operate Canadian subsidiaries largely to produce or simply market the product. These products are typically designed outside Canada, usually using imported components. These Canadian subsidiaries, then, do not perform the complete range of functions in order to offer a product in the marketplace. These are the traditional so-called **branch plants**.

Some observers believe that we will continue to see the rapid spread of branch plants in Canada, with progressively less important activities being allocated to the Canadian subsidiary. This has led many critics to suggest that these subsidiaries are nothing more than "sales offices" for the U.S. parent company. Moreover, some critics argue that we have built up a dependence on foreign capital to supply us with the funds for business development. While this financial assistance was welcome, it brought a major cost with it — the establishment of these branch plants, and an economy that is approximately 30% foreign-owned. Moreover, it has been suggested that the presence of this branch plant economy has impeded the development of an innovative or entrepreneurial spirit in Canadian business. In other words, there is a sense that, historically, Canadian managers have not been challenged to do the strategic planning, to engage in the research and development and to develop the technological expertise to add value to the present supply of products or services. However, we are witnessing the increasing presence of Canadian-owned and global competitors, such as Bombardier and Nortel; it is important that Canada continue to move beyond its history and carve a bigger niche in the global environment.

CHAPTER SUMMARY

Understanding the context of business is the only way to get a sense of where we are headed in terms of future economic prospects. Whether you are currently a full-time student or in the workplace, an understanding of the context of organizations is a critical part of any intelligent person's portfolio. In many ways, the aim of the upcoming chapters is to shed more light on the internal and external contexts of organizations, and to consider the implications for the future of organizations. What are the prospects for business, and what are the challenges we must confront? This is the importance of the nature and context of business. This book takes an integrative approach with regard to the "inside-outside" framework. Rather than compartmentalizing the internal and the external issues affecting organizations, each chapter will consider both. Though some sections focus on the internal functions of organizations (such as Chapter 2, "Management Philosophies"), each chapter keeps the external context in mind. No organization operates in a vacuum, and so the real world surrounding the organization is also considered.

KEY TERMS

- general environment
- economic forces
- political forces
- competitive forces
- technological forces
- societal forces
- global forces
- gross domestic product (GDP)
- unemployment rate
- perfect competition
- monopolistic competition
- oligopoly
- manufacturing sector
- service sector
- knowledge workers
- demographics
- baby boomers
- international trade
- foreign ownership
- branch plants

CASE APPLICATION Sam the Record Man goes broke

Sam the Record Man, Canada's last remaining family-owned record store chain and a strong supporter of homegrown artists, announced yesterday it has filed for bankruptcy and will close 24 stores across the country. The news marks the end of a long struggle by the 53-year-old retail dynasty to stay afloat amid mounting pressure from newer rivals and upstart technologies. "We met with the accountants and the lawyers last week and said we just couldn't do it anymore," Sam Sniderman, the company's 81-year-old founder, said from his home last night. In its heyday, the chain had more than 100 locations and was Canada's leading specialty music retailer. Few retailers supported Canadian musicians like Sam's did.

The company never refused a Canadian artist shelf space, taking in the home-pressed discs of unsigned musicians and selling them, with few strings attached, for 60 days. "Every one of the stores has a section for Canadian artists," Mr. Sniderman said proudly. "We wouldn't have it any other way."

The family is the primary creditor for the corporation, Sniderman Radio Sales and Service Ltd., and is owed more than $8-million, according to bankruptcy trustee Peter Aykroyd, a senior vice-president of BDO Dunwoody Ltd. Other creditors, including the big record companies, are owed $9.5-million. "We will try to scale back and wind down the stock," Mr. Aykroyd said. "There is no bank here. It's a bit of a different situation. The family is its own bank."

Six stores owned by the corporation will remain open, including Sam's flagship Toronto outlet, and will be run by the trustee. The stores will be used to liquidate stock from the other outlets that are closing. The family hopes to restructure the company under a new name in the future, but it is unclear whether the remaining stores will survive that process.

Eleven franchises that operate under the Sam's name will also remain open. In the past half decade, the Sniderman family had poured $50-million to $60-million of its own money into the ailing chain, Mr. Sniderman said. His son Jason had whittled the chain down from more than 70 corporate stores in early 2000 to 30 as of yesterday, but the company continued to decline.

"Jason is heartbroken. He had a tough go of it, but he would have kept on going. It was an uphill battle," Mr. Sniderman said. "Everybody's selling records now, so they don't need us any more. And when they're not selling them, people are downloading music."

Jason, a musician, was valiantly opposed to Napster and other Internet sites offering downloadable music. The sites cut into artists' livelihoods by depriving them of royalties. Napster's effects on music retailers have been dramatic. Record sales dropped 7% last year in Canada, following a 7% drop in 1999. Sacramento-based Tower records pulled out of Canada this month, closing two unprofitable locations. Even Canada's biggest specialty record seller, British giant HMV, admitted the North American record market was soft this year.

Sam's and its competitors have also felt pricing pressure from the sheer number of large retailers, from Wal-Mart to Costco, now selling CDs at a steep discount. In the past three years, numerous other specialty retailers have begun offering CD selections for impulse buyers wanting to emulate the mood of the store, from Starbucks to Club Monaco's home furnishings chain, Caban.

Jason Sniderman tried to resuscitate the family business by selling the company wares online. He thought it would be an ideal forum to sell hit CDs and offer Sam's broad and unique selection — $8-million worth of rare merchandise — to customers outside of Toronto. The business failed to take off when it was run internally, so the family licensed its name last year to an e-commerce company, buying a 10% stake. Within months, Sams Online Inc. had shut down, one of the multiple casualties in the dot-com meltdown. Sam Sniderman said his family will continue to promote the Canadian music industry as philanthropists and through lobbying efforts. "One of the things [Jason] has made sure of is that no Canadian artists would get hurt by this," he said.

Source: By Hollie Shaw from *National Post* (October 31, 2001). Reproduced with permission.

QUESTIONS

1. What factors **inside** this organization may have contributed to the company's demise? That is, to what degree do you think that problems with the following areas might have caused the downfall of Sam's: internal management, decision making and organizational structure?

2. What factors **outside** the organization may have contributed to the company's demise? That is, to what degree do you think that problems with the following areas might have caused the downfall of Sam's: political forces, economic forces, global forces, technological forces, competitive forces, societal forces?

3. Which factor do you think played the greatest role in this bankruptcy: factors **inside** or factors **outside** the organization?

RELATED READING

"Top Ten List" for business

For executives of Canadian enterprises, the economic environment of the last few years has been about as good as it gets. The situation underscores the fact that an enterprise has to be really unlucky or really inept not to perform well when the economy is booming, and interest rates, the dollar and inflation are low. But there is a downside. Performance that comes too easily because of the good times can distract an executive from preparing for the bad times.

How well an enterprise rides out the bad times very much depends on the preparatory steps it has taken during the good times. A good economy should provide an enterprise with both the resources and breathing room needed to get ready for a slowdown. When our economy goes sour, as it inevitably will, my guess is that many executives will wish they had spent less time looking in the mirror admiring their own performance and more time focusing on the nitty-gritty of proper management practice. New Economy Executives should be under no illusion: The business cycle is alive and well; what goes up, also goes down.

A serious slowdown may not be far off. Regardless, right now is always the best time for executives to make preparations, and objectively answering 10 questions should aid in that task. Lamenting what was not done when times were ideal takes an executive nowhere. Prosperity always lies in doing what can be done now. Gardening enthusiasts say the best time to plant a tree is 20 years ago; the next best time is now. That analogy applies to the practice of management.

It is useful to consider just where we are in the business cycle. The only thing that is clear is where we have been. 1997 to 1999 were good, and things just kept getting better in 2000: almost five-percent real growth, with stable prices, a falling unemployment rate, aggressive business investment in equipment and machinery, strong consumer spending, and surpluses in both the current and government spending accounts. It is not often that the stars line up so perfectly! Reasons for our good fortune include the longest and strongest expansion in U.S. history (over one-third of our GDP is U.S. exports), a low dollar, low interest rates, technological revolution, rising productivity, a high level of pent-up consumer demand coming out of the much weaker early and middle years of the 1990s, low energy prices, deregulation, globalization and financial innovation.

With apologies to William Shakespeare (*King Henry VI, Part III*), the Canadian economic worm is turning. Seemingly overnight, the United States has gone from boom to slowdown. Moreover, U.S. interest rates could push the Canadian dollar significantly higher, putting our export sector at considerable risk. The technology sector is an earnings/demand/stock market wreck, and consumers are up to the gunnels in everything from cars to computer equipment. Energy prices are through the roof; poverty, labour, environmental and fairness problems are taking the sheen off globalization; and financial market turmoil is creating havoc for consumers and businesses. Add executive suites that in many instances have little or no experience with slowdown — let alone recession, persistently low commodity prices, and hugely indebted consumer and government sectors, and the potential is certainly there for things to get very ugly in Canada. The current economic malaise may be only a harbinger. We are clearly late in a business cycle with our best days behind us.

My guess is executives will soon be longing for the good old days of 2000. But regardless of what the economy does, executives have no control over it. What they do have control over is their own actions, how they position their enterprises. However late we are in the up part of the business cycle, there is purpose in asking the following questions.

1. IS THE STRUCTURE RIGHT?

To Alfred Pritchard Sloane Jr., the legendary architect of General Motors, the key to business success lay in getting people and other resources properly organized. Borrowing from the economist's jargon, the proper organization structure may not be a sufficient condition for enterprise success, but it certainly is a necessary condition. To Sloane, strategy followed structure. To add to Sloane, execution follows strategy, and performance follows execution. Over time, getting the structure right is crucial; only luck can save the chronically poorly structured.

Sloane's "decentralized operational management with central policy control driven by return on investment" surely belongs in the pantheon of contributions to management thinking. Every executive will find at least some value in Sloane's *My Years With General Motors*. Aficionados are referred to Sloane's lesser-known book, *Adventures of a White Collar Man*. Sloane was either president, CEO or chairman of General Motors from 1923 to 1956.

Structure is crucial, but it is rarely critical. As a consequence, it is easy to put off restructuring for another day. The trouble is that days become years. Enterprises can easily sleepwalk their way into becoming a structural relic that seriously impacts competitiveness and profitability and threatens survival. Fixing structure takes time, and it is best done in small bites after regular review. It should be on every executive's agenda. Structure is ideally tackled without the distraction of slowdown, falling stock prices, declining earnings, cutbacks and layoffs. Ideally, it is even tackled today.

2. IS THE BUSINESS MODEL SUSTAINABLE?

The business model is an enterprise's core strategy. It must be sustainable in the sense that it will indefinitely deliver competitive financial returns across the entire business cycle. Strategy that works over part or even most of the cycle is fatally flawed; the only issue is timing. No quality of the business model should be more important than its sustainability.

The business model should be continually tested and reviewed. For most enterprises, the greatest vulnerability is during the down part of the business cycle. That is precisely the worst time to find out that the business model does not work; options will be fewest and pressures will be greatest. Before slowdown is when executives should be asking if their business model is sustainable through slowdown. Testing a business model for cross-cycle sustainability is no easy task; even a good try is far better than no try at all. Experience, judgment, "what if" games, quantitative analysis and computer simulation are all useful business-model testing approaches.

Like a 10-step treatment program for a substance addict, fixing an unsustainable business model begins when the executive looks in the mirror and frankly admits that his/her model is unsustainable. Understanding and admitting that what you are doing is not sustainable is a precondition for fixing things. Such an admission may be hard on the ego, but it is surely good for the enterprise.

3. DO YOU WANT TO BE IN THE BUSINESS YOU ARE IN?

According to *U.S. News FY World Report* (May 8, 2000), the legendary management thinker and adviser Peter E. Drucker asked Jack Welch this question shortly after he became CEO of General Electric in 1980. Drucker's specific question was: "If you weren't already in this business, would you choose to get into it now?" Every CEO should be continually asking this question about every major business line. Prosperity lies in being unemotional and decisive when the answers are in the negative.

In the up part of the business cycle, judgment is likely to be clouded by how good things are. Yet that is when exiting a business will be easiest and most rewarding financially. During the down part of the cycle, pressures on earnings and cash flows can lead to hasty decisions that are later regretted. Perhaps Drucker's greatest strength is his ability to get to the core of an issue in just a few words.

4. IS EXECUTIVE SUCCESS IN PLACE?

In a slowdown, executives can be forgiven for thinking they have been singled out for a special application of Murphy's Law. With everything else going wrong, and seemingly at once, enterprises do not need the added burden and risk of abruptly replacing senior people in a no-succession-plan vacuum. Enterprises that have not thought about their next generation of management, at least to the point of the options available, usually find that slowdown brings those chickens home to roost, and hard. For example, decisions may be made too quickly, expectations of new executives may be excessive, integrating new executives fast may win out over doing it properly, and the executive team may fragment as individuals focus on their own interests that may or may not be the enterprise's.

All executives are important, but the most important by far is the CEO. The job of CEO is special. It is where vision, strategy, decision-making and execution come together. No enterprise can indefinitely survive bad leadership from its CEO. Slowdown heightens the already enormous pressures on the CEO and, hence, raises the chances of either resignation or termination. Enterprises will not regret the time and resources they devote to the CEO succession exercise. It is not an exercise best embarked upon in the down part of the business cycle. Thinking about the next CEO should begin on the current CEO's first day — the CEO job is that important. Poorly planned CEO succession inevitably disintegrates into a superstar search frenzy, something that is fertile ground for mistake.

5. DO YOU KNOW YOUR CUSTOMERS?

An enterprise's most important asset is its customers. They provide the revenues and, hence, the profits. In a very real sense, customers are the glue that holds an enterprise together. The problem today is that customer needs, wants, choices, characteristics and capacities are changing at a breathtaking pace, making the prospects bleak for enterprises that do not stay at the cutting edge of everything worth knowing about their customers.

You may not know your customers well, but you can be sure someone else does and is ready to pounce on them. This is particularly the case during slowdown, when overcapacity is highest and the chances of stealing customers are especially good. The science of customer research is developing as fast as any broad area of business inquiry, so it would not be surprising to find that an enterprise might have slipped on this important success dimension. The time to get serious about knowing your customer is not during slowdown, when the customer is cutting back and becoming increasingly price- and choice-sensitive. Executives who think knowing the customer is too costly should consider the cost of not knowing the customer.

6. ARE THE COSTS RIGHT?

Controlling costs is a vital executive function. Costs cannot get too far out of line without taking competitiveness with them; lose control of your costs and you lose control of pricing and profits. Costs are far more likely to get away from an enterprise during the good times, when the distractions are many and the consequences of being casual on costs seem minor. The more attention paid to costs during the good times, the less gut-wrenching and disruptive the cost-rationalizing-driven cutbacks and layoffs in the bad times. The "good guy" executive who lets costs go in the good times is not a good guy at all. That stark reality often only hits home when the economy goes bad. Controlling costs is a matter of continually comparing them with competitors', constant analysis and innovation, strong discipline and a relentless willingness to say no.

7. IS THE PRODUCT RIGHT?

The reason for knowing the customer and controlling costs (Nos. 5 and 6) is to have the right product available at the right price. In the process of asking about the customer and costs, executives should be asking about the product. Doing everything else right, and then seriously missing on the product, is not even a partial victory. Poor product management in the up part of the business cycle usually comes back to haunt enterprises in the down part.

8. DO YOU KNOW YOUR COMPETITION?

The competition is what beats you, and with globalization, technological change and deregulation, it has arguably never been so fierce. Not knowing what your competitors are up to is as dangerous as not knowing your customers. What your competitors are usually up to is finding ways to take your customers. The good times, when revenues and profits are easier, is when it is easiest to forget about the competition. Those who fall into that trap inevitably pay for it when things turn down. Slowdown is a bad time to discover that you do not know your competition. Knowing the competition involves everything from their products and customers to their policies and options. Corporate intelligence has never been more important.

9. IS THE BALANCE SHEET RIGHT?

Nothing exposes a too heavily indebted and/or too poorly matched balance sheet more than slowdown. Revenues needed to service providers of capital come under pressure during slowdown, and capital becomes more difficult to attract as lenders and investors raise standards. The best time to ask if the balance sheet is right, and fix it if it is not, is in the up part of the business cycle when confidence is high, the financial markets are buoyant and credit is easy. Those with too weak a balance sheet sometimes do not even make it out of slowdown. Key balance sheet issues are the debt/equity ratio, the debt maturity schedule, secure lines of credit and the regard in which the enterprise is held by the financial community.

10. WHERE ARE YOU ON TECHNOLOGY?

Slowdown is the worst part of the business cycle in which to be substantially behind the competition on technology. The reason is that slowdown diverts resources from technological competitiveness to the apparently more pressing needs of the day to day. If you are behind on technology going into slowdown, you will be the exception if you do not come out of slowdown even farther behind. Executives should commit to being technologically competitive across the business cycle. For executives today, the pace of workplace and product technological change is unprecedented. The faster the pace of technological change, the greater the consequences for the enterprise that lags. A cautionary note: Enterprises that are already cutting back on IT spending because they expect the economy to slip would do well to revisit their decision. After the fact, they may be glad they did.

Executives should use what is left of the up part of this business cycle to get ready for slowdown. The questions posed here will provide a focus in that regard. Executives should not misread their successes during the good times. A booming economy, low interest rates and a low dollar probably explain more than their own executive genius. A little humility in the good times will pay off in the bad times. Preparation will pay off even more.

Source: John S. McCallum from "As the economy turns: 10 questions for executives" *Ivey Business Journal* (May/Jun 2001) 65(5): 70–73. Ivey Management Services prohibits any form of reproduction, storage or transmittal of this material without its written permission. This material is not covered under authorization from CanCopy or any reproduction rights organization. To order copies or request permission to reproduce materials, contact Ivey Publishing, Ivey Management Services, c/o Richard Ivey School of Business, The University of Western Ontario, London, Ontario, Canada, N6A 3K7; phone (519) 661-3208, fax (519) 661-3882, e-mail cases@ivey.uwo.ca. Copyright © 2001 Ivey Management Services. One time permission to reproduce granted by Ivey Management Services on December 14, 2001.

QUESTIONS

1. According to the author, what are the key areas for business success?

2. How does each of these concerns reflect the elements of the context of business discussed in this chapter?

3. Do you think that possessing expertise in each of these areas guarantees success? Why or why not?

II

Looking Inside:
Managing Organizations

The Philosophy of Management

People are the most important asset of any organization. And how organizational members are managed will play a critical role in the ultimate success or failure of the organization. This chapter will introduce you to central ideas from a collected body of management knowledge. Specifically, in this chapter we will examine the roles of managers and the fundamental philosophies underlying different management styles. You will become familiar with the classical approaches and the behavioural approaches to management. This chapter also addresses the specific question: How do we generate a more highly motivated workforce?

LEARNING OBJECTIVES

By the end of the chapter, you should be able to:

1. Describe the types of roles managers play within organizations.
2. Identify three central philosophies of management within the classical school of thought.
3. Discuss the philosophies that comprise the behavioural school of thought.
4. Identify theories that address motivation in the workplace.
5. Contrast the differences between the classical and behavioural approaches to managing.
6. Outline central contingencies that influence the suitability of any management philosophy.

Organizational Insider

Managing the Workforce

At Radical Entertainment's new eight-storey building on the eastern edge of downtown Vancouver, taking care of employees gets as much consideration as taking care of business. That, says CEO Ian Wilkinson, is because the two are inextricably linked. A youthful 42, Wilkinson says the new digs are integral to the company's identity — and thus the success of its product, video games for clients like Sony Corp., Fox Interactive and Microsoft Corp. Working up a sweat on a stationary bike while he talks, Wilkinson says most of the people who work at Radical are just big kids, including himself. Nurturing that kind of energy and creativity is crucial to keeping the company competitive, he says. "We spend money when there is value to it, in human capital or revenue," Wilkinson says. "If creating a good place to work means that the people who work here will be inspired and that they will stay with us, then it's worth the cost."

Work. It soaks up more time and energy than just about anything else we do, and yet, for the vast majority of employees, it remains a tiresome necessity rather than a source of pride or satisfaction. Sure, many companies make an effort to offer help for the most common problems facing today's workers: high stress, low morale and difficulty balancing the demands of home and office. But employees — often rightly — tend to dismiss such programs as window dressing.

At Radical Entertainment, which was recently named one of the country's 50 best-managed private companies, the hours can be long but there are tangible — and unique — benefits for employees who give the job their best efforts. Besides the more predictable perks of flexible hours and enriched maternity leaves, there are innovations like new ways [of] dealing with intellectual property issues. Dreamed up by an employee who spotted a problem — that creative staff might be reluctant to float new ideas for fear they would lose the rights to them — Radical's system encourages employees to bring ideas forward by protecting their property rights. If an idea is not accepted, the employee still has the right to sell it to another company. "It's smart business for Radical because we get to see the best coming out of people," says art director Hamo Djoboulian. "And it's smart for the staff because there is something in it for them. There aren't many other companies who think this way."

Of course, software companies have become known for great perks and the royal treatment of staff, but what about other industries? Most people in full-time jobs don't expect to strike it rich through stock options or big salaries. The pay-offs they are looking for tend to be much more prosaic: greater control over their time and decision-making, the opportunity to do work they enjoy, enough time and energy to "have a life" when work is over. At the Royal Bank of Canada, a sea change in personnel policies has been underway for about five years, partly because senior managers began to realize that the traditional banking approach — rigid schedules, faceless hierarchies and inattention to people's personal preferences — was driving staff away and potentially compromising customer service. Now, the bank is in the forefront of change, offering its staff

40

job-sharing, telecommuting and compressed workweeks, among other innovative arrangements.

But creating a workplace culture where managers are flexible and empathetic towards their self-motivated, committed employees takes more than a few new rules for flex-time and telecommuting. Change must come directly from the top, points out David Stum, a senior vice-president with international human resources firm Aon Consulting, who has studied workplace issues for more than two decades. "The problem is not individual managers, as many people think," he says. "It's the whole system." The proper hiring and training of managers is the first step in achieving change at all levels. "Managers pick up from the culture whether they can be flexible in managing people," he says.

Faced with making changes or watching key resources head out the door, some businesses are rethinking almost everything about their work environment.

Work Numbers

According to studies:

- Productivity increases by about 20 percent after companies implement work/life balance programs.
- Staff turnover falls by up to 50 percent when employees are offered benefits such as child-care subsidies, elder-care programs and flexible hours.
- The cost of losing and replacing an employee can range from 50 percent to 150 percent of his or her annual salary.
- Forty-three percent of junior managers value home over work time, compared with 20 percent of top executives.
- Forty-eight percent of employees feel guilty when they leave on time.

(Source: *Values Shift: The New Work Ethic and What It Means for Business*, by John Izzo and Pam Withers.)

Source: Compiled from Patricia Chisholm, D'Arcy Jenish, Julian Beltrame and John Demont, "Redesigning Work" *Maclean's* (March 5, 2001). Reproduced with permission of Maclean's Magazine.

WHY STUDY MANAGEMENT THOUGHT? —————————

As the Organizational Insider illustrates, managing people is clearly central to an organization's success in today's context. What is the best way to manage people? Are there actually philosophies of managing?

Regardless of whether we are looking at a small business or a giant corporation, any type of organization must be managed. When we refer to the notion of "a manager", who are we referring to? A manager can be an individual at any level of the organization. For example, **top management** could include the chief executive officer (CEO) or president, along with vice-presidents; **middle managers** could include such figures as departmental or division heads, plant or branch managers, deans; **supervisors**, or first-line management, might include such titles as department heads, foremen, or supervisors. Individuals can take on formal or informal managerial roles. For example, a "team leader" may or may not be formally assigned a managerial role, though that person may have much of the responsibilities of a manager. Regardless of your profession, or your role in organizations, no doubt at some point in your career you will be required to apply some sort of management or leadership skills.

The field of management can, indeed, be systematically studied, and a consideration of it is of benefit to anyone who wishes to understand the philosophies that have guided managers for the past century. Below, we will consider the body of knowledge that attempts to identify principles employed by managers in their daily practice. However, before we embark, we need to ask a simple question: What do managers do?

WHAT DO MANAGERS DO? —————————

Before we talk about this body of knowledge of management thought, it makes sense to answer some more fundamental questions, including, what exactly does it mean to manage? What are the functions or roles of a manager?

Management has been defined in many ways, including:

> "The art of getting things done through people." (Mary Parker Follett)

> "Managers give direction to their organizations, provide leadership and decide how to use organizational resources." (Peter Drucker)

To be a little more systematic, management has also been described as:

> The process of administering and coordinating resources effectively and efficiently in an effort to achieve the organization's goals.

This last definition needs a little more explanation. The term **"efficiency"** refers to using the fewest inputs to produce a given level of output. The term **"effectiveness"** refers to the pursuit and achievement of goals that are appropriate for the organization.

We need to be a little more specific about what exactly it is that managers do. Here's a somewhat more detailed definition:

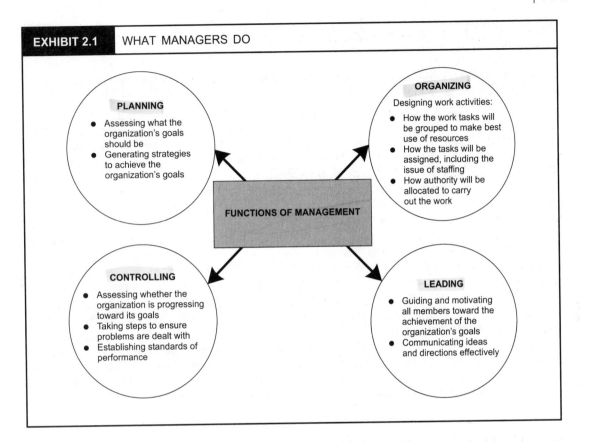

EXHIBIT 2.1 WHAT MANAGERS DO

PLANNING
- Assessing what the organization's goals should be
- Generating strategies to achieve the organization's goals

ORGANIZING
Designing work activities:
- How the work tasks will be grouped to make best use of resources
- How the tasks will be assigned, including the issue of staffing
- How authority will be allocated to carry out the work

FUNCTIONS OF MANAGEMENT

CONTROLLING
- Assessing whether the organization is progressing toward its goals
- Taking steps to ensure problems are dealt with
- Establishing standards of performance

LEADING
- Guiding and motivating all members toward the achievement of the organization's goals
- Communicating ideas and directions effectively

Managing includes the process of planning, organization, leading and controlling organizational resources in the effort to achieve organizational goals.

Exhibit 2.1 outlines each element of this definition — or what have commonly been considered the four central functions of management: planning, organizing, leading and controlling.

The Roles Managers Play in Organizations

Henry Mintzberg, a management scholar, conducted an in-depth study of managers in the 1960s. His observations have stuck with us today, and seem to present a useful account of the many roles that managers can potentially play. Among the interesting results of his study is the fact that Mintzberg's work contradicted the then dominant view of the role of managers.

The traditional view of the role of managers was that managers were able to reflect systematically on information before making decisions, and their job was relatively clear

43

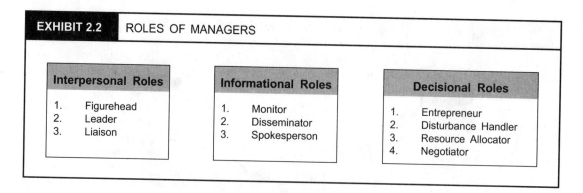

and narrow. Mintzberg's study of managers found that managers engaged in a variety of unpatterned short-duration activities, and the constant interruptions suggested that there was little time for systematic reflection. Most important, Mintzberg offered a classification of the various roles that managers play. (See Exhibit 2.2.) Let's consider briefly each of the roles that Mintzberg identified.

Mintzberg presented 10 roles classified within three broad categories: **interpersonal roles**, **informational roles** and **decisional roles**. Essentially, these reflect three key areas of managing: developing and managing interpersonal relationships, dealing with the transfer of information and making decisions.

Interpersonal Roles

Interpersonal roles include those managerial tasks that arise from the manager's formal authority base and involve relationships with either other organizational members or external parties. **Figurehead** roles are typically ceremonial or symbolic in nature. For example, in the role of a figurehead, the supervisor might hand out "employee of the month" awards at a company banquet. In the **leader** role, the manager may serve as a motivator, a communicator and a coordinator of his or her subordinates' activities. This might include conducting performance appraisals, offering training to a new recruit, etc. A final role within the interpersonal grouping is that of **liaison**, which includes those managerial activities that involve developing relationships with members of the organization outside the manager's area of authority. This could include anything from a sales manager's relationship with the production department to a university dean's networking relationship with the city council.

Informational Roles

Mintzberg's second broad category of managerial roles, referred to as informational roles, reflects the importance of managers as communication sources for the organization — whether this involves gathering or giving out important information to other organizational members, or to parties outside the organization.

First, we can consider the manager as a **monitor** of sorts. That is, managers must constantly monitor the internal and external environments of their organization in order to gather information that is useful for organizational decision making. For example, the marketing manager may be responsible for assessing consumer demand for a newly proposed product.

Second, managers are also **disseminators** of information. That is, they may share or distribute the information that they have gained in their role as monitors, for example. Obviously, managers must ensure that subordinates have all information that they require in order to perform their job effectively. This might include offering clear information regarding company expectations of performance standards and performance appraisal criteria.

Third, the manager may act as **spokesperson**. Managers can also transmit information to individuals outside their area of authority. For example, a marketing manager might provide the engineering department with the latest report of consumer preferences regarding product design. Or the company president may report to a government regulatory board regarding the company's environmental policy.

Decisional Roles

Mintzberg's final category is referred to as decisional roles, and highlights the fact that managers must process information and act as decision-makers. There are four classes of roles described here. First is the notion of the manager as **entrepreneur**. That is, the manager may, for example, develop and initiate new projects. This might include the personnel manager developing a new performance appraisal system, the marketing manager developing a new product, etc. Generating new projects and new ventures is a highly valued trait among today's managers.

Managers might also play the role of **disturbance handlers**. Dealing with and attempting to resolve conflict can include things like: resolving a dispute between two employees, dealing with a difficult or unco-operative supplier, etc.

A third role that managers can play is that of **resource allocator**. This involves deciding how resources (money, equipment, personnel, time) will be allocated. So, a department head might decide how to allocate a limited financial budget among the different areas. Deciding how much time the division should invest in a new project is also a decision about resources.

The final decisional role identified by Mintzberg is the manager as **negotiator**. Indeed, numerous research studies have underscored the great degree to which managers are engaged in some form of negotiation throughout their activities. Whether this involves negotiating with customers, employees or other departments, a manager often bargains over issues that affect the operation of his or her department, unit, or organization. For example, the production purchasing manager might negotiate with the supplier in an effort to speed up the supply of raw materials for the company's production department. A personnel manager might negotiate with a representative of the union to resolve a conflict.

Now that we have outlined the notion of managing and the roles of managers, in the next section we will take a more systematic look at how the role of manager is changing. We'll start with the oldest approach, and then consider more recent philosophies of managing people in organizations.

MANAGEMENT PHILOSOPHIES

If you have ever taken a trip to Disneyland, you will notice the great level of care and professionalism with which Disney employees (referred to as "cast members") conduct their jobs. In fact, Disney has even offered management training programs through its "university" for countless other organizations. What is so special about Disney's management approach that has helped it achieve worldwide fame and success? The answer — nothing is unique about its approach. However, what is rare is its ability to make sure the management philosophies employed are suitable for the nature of their organization. While a lot of what Disney is doing may make common sense, common sense alone won't get you very far when it comes to selecting and implementing a system of managerial practices that is suitable for today's organization. Clearly, not all organizations are created equal — from the McDonald's of the fast food industry to the Microsofts of the high-tech world, what works for one organization with regard to management philosophy may be deadly if applied in another environment. So the question is, what are the ranges of management philosophies that exist, and upon what principles are they based? Let's answer these questions as we consider the elements of two fundamentally different schools of management thought: the classical and the behavioural approaches.

CLASSICAL APPROACHES TO MANAGEMENT

The oldest of the formalized perspectives of management has come to be known as the classical school of management, and it arose during the late 19th and early 20th centuries. This view originated during a time of rapid industrialization of the U.S. and European business sector. Three streams that are central components of this school are:

1. **scientific management**
2. **administrative management**
3. **bureaucratic management**

Let's look at each of these perspectives, and attempt to understand the contributions they have made to the field of managing.

The Social Context

It is useful to consider the environment surrounding the evolution of management thought. Understanding the social context of that period sheds light on the logic of the management approaches that were generated.

One of the major driving forces behind the formalization of management thought was the **Industrial Revolution**. While management concepts have been around practically since the dawn of civilization, it was not until the 18th century, as a consequence of the intel-

| EXHIBIT 2.3 | MANAGEMENT PHILOSOPHIES |

I. Classical Approaches to Managing

1. Scientific Management
2. Administrative Management
3. Bureaucratic Management

II. Behavioural Approaches to Managing

1. The Human Relations Movement
2. Mary Parker Follett and Chester Barnard
3. Modern Behavioural Science and Motivation-based Perspectives

lectual and scientific accomplishments of the Renaissance period, that the systematic development of management principles and practices began.

The Industrial Revolution, as the name implies, was a major transformation in work processes that began in the 18th century with the replacement of hand production by machine and factory production. For example, a new energy source, the coal-driven steam engine, was created to run the machines. The introduction of new work processes and machinery culminated in the factory system of production that eventually led to the mass production processes. Certainly, the factory system brought with it many benefits, including a higher standard of living. It also brought with it extensive changes in management, given that work was no longer conducted in workers' homes, but in factories.

The philosophy that fuelled the Industrial Revolution was the notion of "**laissez faire**", a term used by the economist Adam Smith in his book, *The Wealth of Nations*. This term essentially meant that business or manufacturers should be free to make and sell what they please and, consequently, reflected the notion that government should not interfere with the economic affairs of business. Businesses should be allowed to pursue their own self-interest. The economic view of labour was a straightforward one — the employer buys the labour, and the employee provides the labour. There was no long-term obligation on either side. That reinforced the notion that employees were not valued. With a great supply of labour and jobs involving little skill, it became clear that all power rested with the employer. It was in such an environment that philosophies like Scientific Management eventually arose.

1.   *Scientific Management*

Frederick Taylor (1856–1915) was an American engineer who sought to help American industry deal with the challenges of improving productivity. Keep in mind that in Taylor's time there were no clear concepts of management and worker responsibilities. Taylor thought the problem was a simple one to solve — improve management practices, and you'll improve productivity. So, Taylor sought to better manage workers.

For most of his working life, Taylor was employed in steel mills, first as a labourer, eventually as foreman and, ultimately, as chief engineer. While working as a foreman at Midvale Steel Company in Philadelphia, and later as a consulting engineer at Pittsburgh's Bethlehem Steel, Taylor observed what he thought were significant inefficiencies in the conduct of work. The results of his observations and studies were eventually reported in a series of papers, *The Principles of Scientific Management*, published in 1911.

What was Taylor's philosophy? Taylor stated the fundamental objective of management: "Securing the maximum prosperity for the employer coupled with the maximum prosperity for each employee." This sounds reasonable; but what, specifically, does it mean and how do you go about achieving that apparently admirable objective? To answer the second question, Taylor believed that the way to improve things is through scientific management. What is scientific management?

There are at least three central features of Taylorism, or scientific management. Taylor proposed a number of important guidelines. Among them were the following principles:

(a) Standardizing the Work

During Taylor's days with Midvale Steel in Philadelphia, he made some interesting observations of workers whose task it was to shovel coal and iron during the manufacture of pig iron. He decided to experiment with different sizes of shovel, and varied the size of the load scooped in order to minimize fatigue. He also arranged for the workers to have varying work time and rest intervals so that he could experiment with recovery rate. Taylor closely analyzed the range of motions involved in shovelling. Based on his observations and recommendations, the average daily output of workers was tripled, and also the number of shovellers required for the job was reduced from 600 to 140! The science of shovelling was indeed born, and scientific management was a hit!

Scientific management, or Taylorism, then, was based on careful observation and measurement in order to determine the most efficient methods for performing a task. This essentially involves the scientific and systematic study of how work is done in order to improve the work process. Work can be studied objectively, and tasks can be broken down into their simplest steps. The scientific analysis of jobs required **time and motion studies**. This involved using a movie camera and a stopwatch to closely scrutinize the elements of performing a task. For example, bricklayers could be observed and timed in order to assess precisely which movements were most efficient for laying bricks.

All this was based on Taylor's belief that there is **one best method** for performing the job — and the job of management is to discover that method, and train workers and ensure that they employ that method. This resulted in **specializing** or **compartmentalizing** the job into its basic parts: breaking the job down into its most fundamental steps and, where feasible, allowing workers to perform the most basic tasks. This kept the job simple, made it easy and inexpensive to train workers, and ensured a cheap and ready supply of labour to perform the job. **Standardizing** the work meant that there were clear rules regarding how to perform it, which left little or no room for individual discretion. There is no better way of ensuring consistent performance than through the creation of strict guidelines.

According to Taylor, the purpose of managers, then, is to help set proper standards for work performance. Managers must also train the workers in these standards, and direct their performance in order to achieve the most efficient and least fatiguing manner of working. Other responsibilities of management include selecting workers with the abilities that make them most suitable for the job.

(b) Supervising the Workers

Taylor believed that a manager can't be expert in everything. He therefore suggested that managers take charge only of their area of expertise. As a first-level supervisor, you should be responsible for workers who perform a common function with which you are familiar. Of course, it is the supervisor or foreman who would do the planning, time motion studies, scheduling, etc. More generally, what Taylor did was make clear the separation of the mental work of managers from the physical work of the labourers. The managers directed workers to do the work according to the standardized manner. Keep in mind that Taylor's views arose at a time when American industry had at its disposal a vast supply of labour, with a huge segment of new immigrants who, it was felt, were not fully capable of managing themselves.

Taylor's views have been criticized as denigrating employees and treating them as machines. However, it has been, nonetheless, recognized that Taylor contributed to the creation of management as a "profession". Think of it: managers' skills now were not specific to the manufacture of the product; but rather, the skill of managers was to manage — regardless of the organizational context, managers could be trained to coordinate the activities of large numbers of people.

(c) Motivating the Workers

Taylor's philosophy about motivating the workers was quite simple: money motivates! While that may seem obvious to most of us, Taylor's views were interestingly consistent with the rest of his philosophy. In a sense, Taylor advocated a system that has recently been revisited by many different types of organizations. Taylor believed that compensation must be closely tied to performance. A paycheque for simply "walking through the door" is not motivating. It must be clear in workers' minds that they only get a "good day's pay" for a "good day's work". So, a **piece-rate system** was desirable whereby workers' pay was directly tied to their output. If you produced at a standard level of production, you received a standard rate of pay; if you produced above average, you were paid at a higher rate.

How far-reaching are Taylor's views, and does Taylorism exist today? Scientific management continues to influence the management of work. From the manufacturing sector to the service industry, this philosophy, in many ways, guided organizations for much of the past century. For example, consider the service industry and the teaching profession.

LET'S TALK BUSINESS 2.1   TAYLORISM — ALIVE AND WELL

Taylorism certainly remains alive and well across many different industries. You can probably think of some real-life organizations that are managed according to the principles of Scientific Management. For example, **UPS (United Parcel Service)** has built its success in the delivery service on the principles of Taylorism. This company designed time and motion studies to ensure that the work of its delivery team is based on maximum efficiency and performed under strict standardized guidelines. However, there is likely no better example of the modern application of scientific management than **McDonald's**. The success of McDonald's is obvious, and largely based on the duplication of its service across diverse areas. Their management system has been adopted not only by other fast-food chains, but has spread to retail and other industries. McDonald's achieved fame by making the dining experience reliable and predictable for consumers — by the application of the principles of scientific management. Standardization guaranteed that customers continually received what they expected — both in the design of the store and in the system. Employee jobs are compartmentalized and standardized: cooking and customer service are broken down into a series of simple, standardized tasks performed according to strict detail.

Source: Based on George Ritzer, *The McDonaldization of Society: An Investigation into the Changing Character of Contemporary Social Life* (London: Pine Forge Press, 1995).

Believe it or not, Taylor and the principles of scientific management had a profound impact on the education system. The industrial expansion of the early 20th century demanded a system of mass education that would educate huge numbers of formerly rural people, as well as new immigrants. The system required a rapid increase in the number of able though inexpensive teachers. Taylorism facilitated such a transition in the education system. Managers, who were typically male, became the supervisors or principals of the teachers, who were mostly women, and less powerful and less well-paid. The nature of teaching, too, became subject to the principles of scientific management. Remember the need to break the job down into its simplest components? Here, this meant that teachers were now specialized by grade and by subject; just as manufacturing work became **specialized** or **compartmentalized**, the task of teaching became **standardized** — what you taught and how you taught it were all part of a common plan. Clearly, then, Taylorism was adopted widely in industrial, as well as non-industrial, settings. Taylor's ideas also spread beyond North America to Russia, Japan, Germany, and elsewhere. (See Let's Talk Business 2.1.)

2.   *Administrative Management*

A second sub-school of the classical perspective of management is closely associated with the work of Henry Fayol (1841–1925). As the name implies, this approach focuses specifically on management and the functions that managers should perform. Fayol, like Taylor,

---

LET'S TALK BUSINESS 2.2   IS FAYOL ALIVE AND WELL?

Some of Fayol's assertions have gone out of vogue. For example, in today's environment many organizations do not view centralized decision-making authority as being as efficient as allowing authority to reside at lower levels in the organization. In addition, the rights of workers certainly are no longer subordinated to organizational goals, and considerable attention is placed on satisfying individual interests and needs at work. However, some of Fayol's principles are quite compatible with contemporary management views. For example, Fayol's notion of team spirit is certainly considered in many workplaces that are attempting to facilitate team work. Japanese management practices have been viewed as an application of many of Fayol's principles, including the emphasis on the collective good or general interest, as well as the emphasis on teamwork.

---

had some compelling views of how organizations should be managed. An engineer for a mining company in France, Fayol applied his principles with much success; revitalizing an ailing company certainly helped Fayol's management approach gain attention. However, whereas Taylor's work was largely aimed at guiding managers at the lower levels, Fayol's work focused on upper levels of administration. Fayol developed a number of principles of management that he believed could serve as universal principles that could be taught to managers regardless of their specific organizational environment.

Like Taylor, Fayol supported the notion of **division of work**: that is, by breaking work down into its simplest components and assigning these separate elements to workers, the work can be conducted more efficiently and productively. Similarly, Fayol believed that a manager's role is to give orders and to discipline employees. Fayol also advocated the notion of **unity of command**: that is, each employee should report to only one boss in order to avoid confusion and conflicting instructions. In addition, this authority should be concentrated at the upper levels of the organization.

Fayol believed that employees should **subordinate their individual interests to the common good** or general interest of the organization. In other words, it is the goals of the overall organization that must take precedence over any individual interests of employees. Finally, among Fayol's stated principles was the concept of *esprit de corps* — that is, team spirit and harmony should be encouraged among workers in order to generate organizational cohesiveness and unity. Are Fayol's views still with us? See Let's Talk Business 2.2.

3.   *Bureaucratic Management*

Max Weber, 1864–1920, was a German sociologist whose work became most closely affiliated with the school of thought eventually known as bureaucratic management. This perspective is broader in its focus than scientific and administrative management, in that Weber's focus is on the nature of the organization as a whole. As was the case with Taylor and Fayol, Weber's beliefs came from observations of his environment.

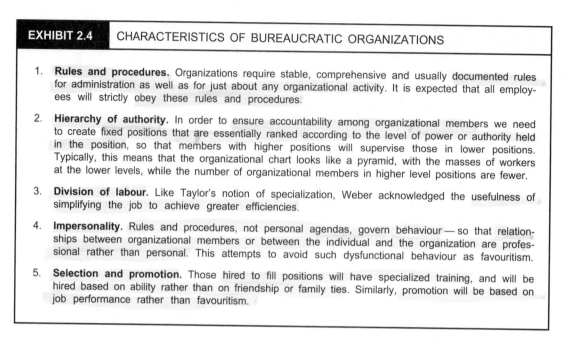

Weber observed that many 19th century European organizations were, in a number of ways, very poorly managed. One critical observation was that numerous organizations were managed on a personal basis, with employees guided more by personal loyalties to other individuals' agendas than by professional loyalties to organizational goals. This often resulted in the misuse of resources for personal means.

Weber believed that an alternative organizational structure was required, and this structure would improve the operations of the organization in a number of ways; this was the origin of the notion of the bureaucratic organization. Weber identified several fundamental elements of such an organization, including those in Exhibit 2.4.

What was behind Weber's principles? Consider what is potentially accomplished through these elements. Weber believed that an organization possessing these characteristics could best maintain consistent, dependable and reliable performance by its members. By having rigid rules and procedures and insisting on conformity to these guidelines, one ensures that the goals of the organization are perpetuated and are not dependent on the individuals who populate the organization at any one time.

The impersonality feature of a bureaucracy was also intended to avoid arbitrary and biased decisions of individuals that might be based on favouritism or personal agendas. Weber wanted to see an organization with a clear administrative structure so that employees would conform to these rules and regulations and understand that they must answer to the boss for their actions. Without these characteristics, Weber believed that organizational behaviour could be neither reliable nor predictable, and decisions might become arbitrary or biased. So, how much impact did Weber have? See Let's Talk Business 2.3.

LET'S TALK BUSINESS 2.3   IS WEBER ALIVE AND WELL?

Ironically, while Weber's work was based on observations of European organizations, his views (translated into English in the 1940s) had a profound impact on North American organizations. Certainly, we have witnessed, over a good part of the past century, the growth of bureaucracies. In fact, it is only more recently that we have come to question the utility of the bureaucratic organization with its emphasis on rules and regulations.

Rigid bureaucratic rules work well when the environment is stable: that is, where consumer needs are unchanging, where technology is fixed, and where other environmental factors, such as political and social forces, are relatively constant. In that type of environment, the need to have comprehensive rules and regulations governing organizational activity, to ensure that authority rests with well-trained managers, all make sense. However, business environments have increasingly undergone rapid change and, consequently, organizations have been moving away from bureaucratic structures and the traditional rules and regulations that might now be outdated. On the other hand, some of the features of bureaucracies remain as strengths for almost any organization. For example, the notion of applying rules and procedures equally to all individuals across the organization would appear to support fairness and dependable behaviour in organizations.

The Classical Approaches in Perspective

The three approaches discussed above (scientific, administrative and bureaucratic management), share a basic philosophy regarding what is required to manage effectively. The classical approaches all indicate a clear role for managers: the job of managers is to plan, control and direct the actions of their subordinates in order to obtain the greatest efficiency from their workers. Scientific management advocated the construction of tasks in a way that minimizes their complexity, and emphasized a machine-like approach to managing workers. The administrative management perspective highlighted the view that fundamental principles should guide the role of manager, regardless of the context. Finally, the belief in the benefits of bureaucracy reflects the view that organizations must be run according to a strict set of rules, with a clear hierarchy of authority to ensure accountability and adherence to the rules.

Now — the question is — **is this the best way to manage?** Let's reconsider the context within which this perspective was born. As mentioned above, these approaches arose at a time when industry was rapidly expanding, and relatively unskilled labour was in abundance. These approaches, in fact, all worked quite well from the time of their conception through the Great Depression of the 1930s. But times do change. And over time, the weaknesses of the classical approach became more and more apparent in some organizations. One major element absent in this approach is the role of human behaviour — the employee. These approaches assume that the worker will respond passively to his or her designated role in the workplace, and increasingly managers found that the assumption of the classical approach can break down in practice.

BEHAVIOURAL APPROACHES TO MANAGEMENT

What we observed during the early part of the 20th century was that employees were managed pretty much the same way as the company managed their physical or financial resources: as another piece of capital to serve the organization's objectives. Over this century, approaches to managing people have changed dramatically. What caused us to change our philosophy of managing? The impetus for change arose through a variety of sources. Some of the initiatives came from business itself, some from government, some thorough union action and some through broad social changes. Whatever the source, what we witnessed in the second and third decades of the 20th century was the beginning of a more humane way of managing — a recognition of employees not simply as another resource to be managed, but as individuals with certain needs that must be addressed.

The behavioural approaches focus on the nature of the employee and what factors encourage employees to maximize their effort. Consequently, the behavioural school ultimately has led us to a consideration of: What lies beneath the surface? That is, what is the driving force behind our decisions to put effort into our jobs or careers? What factors determine how much "blood, sweat and tears" employees are willing to expend in work performance?

The behavioural approach to management refers to managerial perspectives that consider the social or human side of organizations and address the challenges of managing human beings. This approach assumes that to achieve maximum productivity requires an understanding of the human factor of organizations and an ability to create an environment that permits employees to fulfill social, as opposed to simply economic, needs. As with the classical approach, the school of thought that has come to be known as the behavioural approach is actually composed of a number of different perspectives. In sum, this school of thought calls upon managers to consider at least two critical features of organizations:

1. Organizations are designed to produce a good or service efficiently and effectively (a view shared by the classical school).

2. However, unlike the classical school, consideration must also be given to the fact that organizations are **social systems** through which individuals attempt to satisfy their personal and social needs, as well as their economic needs.

We can consider three broad perspectives that constitute the behavioural approach: the work of Elton Mayo and the human relations perspective; the assertions of Mary Parker Follett and Chester Barnard; and, finally, another sub-school that has been referred to as modern behavioural science.

1.   The Human Relations Movement

Elton Mayo (1880–1949) conducted studies at Western Electric, in Hawthorne, Illinois, around 1924 that drew great attention to the importance of the social dimension of work. Among Mayo's studies was an investigation of the effects of lighting on worker productivity. To test the effects of lighting, Mayo chose one group of workers to be the experimental group: the "guinea pigs", so to speak. Here, a variety of lighting conditions were manipulated. A control group was also used whereby this group of workers worked under constant lighting conditions. If better lighting improved productivity, then the group of workers working under better lighting conditions should outperform the control group. The results were puzzling, however! For example, the productivity of both the control and the experimental group increased. In fact, even when lighting was worsened for the experimental group, their productivity nonetheless increased. How to explain these results?

Mayo had inadvertently discovered what came to be known as the Hawthorne Effect. The experimental results (the productivity increases) were not, in fact, caused by the intended experimental manipulation (the increased lighting), but by other factors — here, by "human nature". Specifically, Mayo uncovered that the true source of the great productivity increase was employees receiving some special attention. That is, all subjects realized that they were the focus of attention for this study, and that itself increased their motivation to do a good job.

Surprisingly, social factors had thus had a greater impact on productivity than did actual working conditions. The Hawthorne Effect had a major impact on management thinking; and, in fact, it has been viewed as marking the transition from scientific management to the human relations approach. This approach focuses on organizations as **social systems**, and not simply formal structures. It stresses the need for managers to recognize that managing involves social interaction — that "employees are people, too"!

2. Mary Parker Follett (1868–1933)

Mary Parker Follett was a social philosopher who made a number of significant contributions to the field of management in the first decades of the 20th century. Based on Follett's observations of real-life managers, she identified a number of elements necessary for effective management. Among the factors she emphasized as critical are coordination, self-management, and collaboration.

First, Follett argued that **coordination** was central to a manager's function. That is, Follett suggested that the manager's job of encouraging workers to maximize their productivity should come about not through force or coercion, but through involvement in coordinating and harmonizing group efforts. This requires the close involvement of managers with subordinates in the daily conduct of their work, rather than simply being people who make and enforce rules.

Second, Follett stressed the importance of **self-management** and **collaboration**. Follett felt that decisions regarding how the work is done can often be made by those performing the work, rather than by managers who may not be as familiar with the task. Consequently, subordinates should be involved in the decision-making process in matters that affect their work and how they should perform their work. Moreover, she felt that individuals would much prefer managing themselves than being led by a boss. Managers and workers should view themselves as collaborators or partners. Follett advocated her views at a time when Taylor was considered the leading management scholar. Follett's views were largely ignored, and have only gained acceptance in more recent times. Some observers suggest that the practice of management for the last 100 years might have looked very different had Follett been given more attention than Taylor.

3.   Chester Barnard (1896–1961)

Chester Barnard was a practitioner who served as President of New Jersey Bell Telephone Company. Like Weber, he was interested in organizational structure; but Barnard's view, unlike Weber's impersonal idea of organizations, considered them as social systems. Among Barnard's contributions were his notions of communication and authority. Barnard felt that the two most critical functions of managers are:

1. To establish and maintain a communication system with employees. Barnard felt that organizations, as social systems, require continual communication and co-operation among all members to be effective.

2. Management must clearly establish the organizational objectives and ensure that all employees are motivated to help attain these objectives.

In terms of the notion of authority, Barnard contradicted the then-popular view of traditional authority which reflected the notion that those in power have an absolute right to receive compliance from those at lower levels in the hierarchy. Barnard felt that authority of management over subordinates must be earned — that is, workers will only follow orders to the extent that:

- They understand what is required.
- They see how they relate to organizational goals.
- They believe that they will gain some benefit from accomplishing these goals.

Fundamentally, Barnard, like Follett, believed that a **collaborative** approach to management would be most effective for organizations.

4.   Modern Behavioural Science and Motivation-Based Perspectives

Another category of management theories that should be considered as an important part of the behavioural approach can be referred to as modern behavioural science. This school of thought arose largely in the 1950s, and continued the systematic study of the human element of organizations. Researchers came from academic backgrounds in sociology, psychology and anthropology, and became known as behavioural scientists and industrial psychologists. One underlying theme of this work is the issue of motivation. That is, rather than considering the primary role of management to be one of control (the classical approach), these theories consider the role of management as one that must foster a motivated workforce. Consequently, the underlying aim of much of this school of thought is to consider factors that influence the motivation of employees — a key issue for many of today's organizations. (See Let's Talk Business 2.4.)

Look around your workplace, and you will see some individuals who are completely committed to fulfilling the expectations and responsibilities of their employer. Continue looking, and you may also find someone asleep at his or her desk, or maybe surfing the web for interesting vacation sites, while the boss's back is turned. What distinguishes these

---

LET'S TALK BUSINESS 2.4   THE CONTAINER STORE

To the customer, the Container Store may look like it's just all about shelving, boxes, and storage units, but founders Garrett Boone and Kip Tindell organized the company around the employees who sell the merchandise. No small wonder that it was named the best company to work for in the U.S. by *Fortune* magazine. "Our core belief is that one great employee is worth as much as three merely good ones," says Melissa Reiff, vice president of sales and marketing at the Dallas-based retailer. "So we go to great pains in recruiting new employees and hold out for that great person." Reiff says the chain will happily pay twice as much as the industry average for a salesperson (many Container Store reps are hired on salaries of $45,000 or more) and receive twice the productivity in return. Whereas most retailers train salespeople seven hours each year, the typical Container Store worker gets 235 hours in the first year. Constant communication from management about sales and marketing goals, including day-after reports on sales every morning, Tuesday morning voice mails on weekend sales, store financial reports, and news of every corporate marketing description, is disseminated to every Container Store employee. The teamwork on display at each of the chain's 23 stores doesn't happen by accident. Corporate executives mingle with frontline employees regularly, often helping out with warehousing and customer service tasks. "This strongly relates to our low turnover," Reiff says, and it helps sales motivation, too, as Container Store salespeople aren't paid on commission. Rather, the company depends on employees who believe in the store's values. Being part of the team means wanting to sell more. "Since the chain launched in 1978, it has achieved revenue growth of more than 20 percent each year," Reiff says.

Source: From Mark McMaster, "The companies of the future: Why they'll succeed" *Sales and Marketing Management* (December 2001) 153(12).

---

two workers? Is it a personality difference? Is it a difference in work ethic? Is it pay? Is it the boss? Is it the work environment? What variables play a critical role in determining the level of effort or motivation that employees bring to the job? Clearly, this question is critical for any organization aiming to maximize the potential of its workforce. To help us grapple with these questions, we can consider what the management literature has found with regard to how people are influenced in terms of their motivation to work. Let's begin by looking at the issue of motivation, how it is defined, and what theories explain what is behind this somewhat elusive concept.

What is work motivation?   Work motivation has been defined as a processes that involves the arousal and maintenance of goal-directed behaviour or effort in a person's job.

Given the broad, complex nature of the construct of motivation, the literature has provided an abundance of motivational theories. These theories have been classified in a variety of ways. Clearly, the enormous number of theories precludes a detailed discussion within all areas. In this section, we will try to critically consider some of the major thinking in the area of employee motivation.

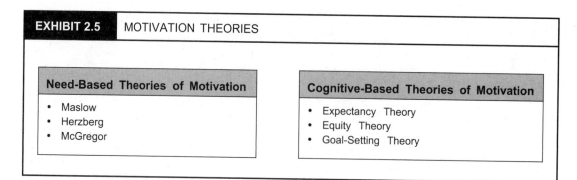

Employee Needs and Motivation

Abraham Maslow. One of the most widely cited motivation theories is the "needs hierarchy" proposed by a behavioural scientist, Abraham Maslow. Among Maslow's contributions was his examination of the factors that determine motivation of employees at work.

During the 1950s, Maslow developed a model that attempted to explain human motivation. It has come to be called **Maslow's Hierarchy of Needs**. This model asserts that all individuals are motivated to fulfill unsatisfied needs. Maslow's theory assumes that a person attempts to satisfy more basic needs (**physiological and safety needs**) before directing behaviour to satisfy upper level needs (**belongingness needs**, **social** or **self-esteem needs**, and **self-actualization**, or the sense of reaching one's full potential). The individual proceeds according to a satisfaction-progression principle: once a need at one level has been fulfilled, the individual then strives to fulfill a higher order need. Maslow's Hierarchy of Needs has for many years given us a simple, yet compelling, picture of the motivators: those needs we seek to fulfill. Maslow's work drew attention to the fact that employees are human beings who will be more motivated to accomplish organizational goals if these goals also allow them to fulfill psychological or social needs. The lesson for managers is to arrange the workplace in a way that permits employees to fulfill these needs; they will then be highly motivated to achieve an optimum level of performance. While Maslow's logic makes sense, his theory has **not** been supported by the field research studies. A general review of needs hierarchy studies revealed no consistent support for the five categories, or for the satisfaction-progression rule. Consequently, while Maslow's theory presents a general lesson in attending to employee needs, the lack of specification reduces the ability of this model to predict work behaviour and performance.

Frederick Herzberg. In many ways, Frederick Herzberg was also concerned with examining the relationship between employee needs and the nature of the job. He called one kind of need employees associate with their work **satisfiers**, and another kind, **motivators**. During the 1950s and 1960s, Herzberg closely examined the nature of work itself and how it motivated, or failed to motivate, individuals. Herzberg suggested that external factors that are part of the context of work — pay, work environment, supervision and working relationships — are hygiene factors. That is, they may be important, but they are part of the "context" of the job, not "intrinsic" to the job. Consequently, these elements could simply be considered **satisfiers**: their absence would lead to dissatisfaction with the job, but their presence alone does not guarantee a highly motivated workforce. On the other hand, factors that are inherent in the job were referred to as **motivators**: in other words, the degree to which the job allows a level of achievement, recognition or responsibility are factors that actually motivate people to do a good job. Herzberg's argument was based on the notion that people look for more than the hygiene factors in their job — if they do not find the work intrinsically motivating, then simply telling them to work harder will be futile. The message for managers is clear. To maximize worker motivation, employees should be given opportunities to receive challenging, meaningful work for which they can accept responsibility. Money alone may not be a true motivator.

Douglas McGregor. Douglas McGregor's work highlighted the importance of understanding employee needs — or rather, what they needed or derived from their jobs. According to McGregor, managers can impact the motivational levels of their employees simply by their view of what employees need or seek to gain from their job. In his well-known book, published in 1960, McGregor drew attention to what he believed were two different, important assumptions that managers make regarding their subordinates. He believed that these assumptions or beliefs carried with them important consequences. McGregor proposed two types of managers: **Theory X** managers, and **Theory Y** managers. Theory X managers perceive their subordinates as having little ambition, a desire to avoid responsibility and a need for direction. That is, they believe that it is human nature to avoid work; and, all else being equal, people would rather not work. Consequently, managers who possess this view will exhibit an authoritarian style of management: to achieve organizational goals, employees must be threatened, coerced or directed by managers. Theory Y managers, on the other hand, possess a very different belief regarding their subordinates. These managers believe that employees want to contribute to work and gain satisfaction from performing their job well. Employees actually desire responsibility, and have ambition to accomplish work goals and use their ingenuity and creativity on the job. Managers who subscribe to this view will likely display a more participatory style of management.

Employees' Thoughts and Motivation

The management literature currently emphasizes the value of cognitive-based approaches to understanding employee motivation. Cognitive theories attribute the causes of behaviour to individuals' processing of information. According to these views, behaviour results from decisions or action choices. In simple terms, these perspectives all try to consider what is going on within the minds of employees, in order to assess what factors motivate them.

Specifically, research into cognitive theories aims to model action choices. Let's focus on those theories that have attracted the largest research interest: expectancy theory, equity theory, and goal-setting theory.

Expectancy theory. Expectancy theory was formulated as a theory of work motivation by Victor Vroom. Many authors have provided extensions and refinements of Vroom's model, but the general underlying assumptions have not changed. The basic notion suggests that people choose tasks and/or effort levels that they believe will most likely lead to valued outcomes. In simple terms, this theory argues that a person will ask the following questions:

1. Will I likely be able to perform this job if I exert a given level of effort? (expectancy association — does effort lead to performance?)
2. After the job is done, will I get a reward for my performance? (instrumentality association — does performance lead to reward?)
3. How much do I value this reward? (valence association — what is the perceived value of the reward for job performance?)

Expectancy theory has been applied to the analysis of a wide range of phenomena, including occupational preference, job satisfaction and work motivation. How motivated will I be to join this organization? How motivated will I be to work hard at my job? These questions all involve answers to the above three questions. An illustration will clarify this:

> Imagine Joe has been hired for a summer job with an accounting firm. He feels that if he works hard, he can definitely perform the job well (strong **effort-performance expectancy**). He realizes that a good performance will likely result in being rehired the following summer (strong **performance-reward instrumentality**). He highly values this work experience because he is planning on pursuing a career in accounting (strong **positive reward valence**). Consequently, we expect that Joe will be highly motivated to do the job. If managers properly train Joe, they can maximize the performance-expectancy link. If managers make it clear in Joe's mind that better performers gain greater rewards, they can build the performance-reward instrumentality. And finally, if managers offer the types of rewards that Joe values, then they can optimize the reward valence perception.

Consider the three central beliefs or perceptions held by employees according to expectancy theory:

1. Individuals must believe their efforts will result in high performance.
2. They must perceive that high productivity will be rewarded.
3. Those rewards must be highly valued.

The lesson for managers from this theory is: How do I ensure that each of these three perceptions is strong? The first belief can be strengthened by ensuring adequate training. The second requires an adequate performance appraisal system that will recognize individual achievement. The third belief demands that managers understand the types of rewards, both monetary and non-monetary, that employees value.

Equity theory. Equity theory considers motivation as a consequence of perceptions of fairness or unfairness. That is, it posits that employees compare their treatment to that of others in similar situations, and they assess whether they are being treated fairly or unfairly in relative terms. Employees naturally are motivated by perceptions of fairness, and can be demotivated by perceptions of unfairness. The theory rests on three main assumptions:

1. People develop beliefs about what constitutes a fair and equitable return for their contributions.
2. People compare their own returns and contributions to those of others.
3. People react negatively to what they perceive as unfair treatment.

> Imagine you have been working for three years at an advertising agency. You have put in long hours and performed well. You inadvertently find out that your colleague, who started the same year as you, is earning a higher salary. How do you feel? Clearly, perceptions of inequity are likely to arise. What is your response?

Equity theory asserts that an individual is driven to maintain a balance between the ratio of his/her inputs/outcomes compared to similar others. The central message is that if an individual believes his/her ratio is lower than the "comparison other", that individual will seek to reduce this inequity through a variety of means. The theory predicts that individuals will choose a mode of inequity reduction that is personally least costly. (See Exhibit 2.6.)

A central lesson for managers suggested by equity theory is that managers must be aware that employees do make **comparisons** at work. Members of any organization assess their relative standing with regard to pay, status, responsibilities, etc. Where individuals perceive unfair treatment, they may react adversely. Consequently, managers must be very sensitive to any actions that cause imbalances in the perceived ratios that employees generate regarding their relative effort and their relative reward.

Goal-setting theory. Social scientists like Albert Bandura have for many years believed that people are neither driven by inner forces nor automatically shaped and controlled by the external environment. Rather, human behaviour is explained in terms of a model of reciprocality, in which behaviour, cognitive, and other personal factors, and environmental events all operate as interacting determinants on each other. The relative influence of these factors differs in various settings and for different behaviours; that is, there are

---

EXHIBIT 2.6	MECHANISMS FOR REDUCING PERCEIVED INEQUITIES

1. **Cognitively reducing the inputs or returns/outcomes.** This involves "mind games". In other words, a person may rationalize that they are not working as hard as their better-paid colleague.

2. **Changing one's own inputs or outcomes.** A person may become demotivated and decide to reduce their effort to be more in line with their perceived relative reward.

3. **Changing the person to whom the comparison is made.** Another form of "mind game" is to choose a different and, it is hoped, more favourable "comparison other".

4. **Leaving the situation where inequity is felt.** Commitment and loyalty can be adversely affected where an employee feels mistreated; they may choose to pack up and leave.

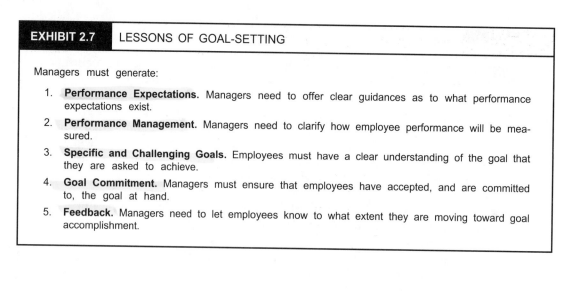

EXHIBIT 2.7   LESSONS OF GOAL-SETTING

Managers must generate:

1. **Performance Expectations.** Managers need to offer clear guidances as to what performance expectations exist.

2. **Performance Management.** Managers need to clarify how employee performance will be measured.

3. **Specific and Challenging Goals.** Employees must have a clear understanding of the goal that they are asked to achieve.

4. **Goal Commitment.** Managers must ensure that employees have accepted, and are committed to, the goal at hand.

5. **Feedback.** Managers need to let employees know to what extent they are moving toward goal accomplishment.

times when environmental factors exercise powerful constraints on behaviour, and other times when personal factors are the overriding regulators. That is, in the social learning view, people are neither driven by inner forces nor by environmental stimuli. Rather, psychological functioning is explained in terms of a continuous reciprocal interaction of personal and environmental determinants.

One such theory of motivation that considers this interaction is goal-setting theory. According to goal-setting theory, a goal is that level of performance the individual is trying to accomplish; it is the object or aim of behaviour. Goals affect performance by directing attention, mobilizing effort, increasing persistence, and motivating strategy development. Goal-setting theory holds that once a challenging task is accepted, the only logical thing to do is to continue to pursue it until the goal is achieved or until a decision is reached to lower or abandon the goal.

Formulated by Ed Locke, the theory postulates that there is a positive linear relationship between goal difficulty, specificity of the goal and task performance. Substantial evidence exists that **difficult goals**, if accepted, result in a higher level of performance than easy goals. It has also been found that **specific goals** lead to greater output than vague goals. The research further supports the view that goal acceptance and feedback are necessary to improve performance. The lessons of goal setting can be summarized, as in Exhibit 2.7.

THE BEST MANAGEMENT PHILOSOPHY?
A CONTINGENCY APPROACH

Now that we have considered two very popular schools of management thought, the question is: Where are we today? What approaches are guiding leaders in management of organizations? The approaches described above have both strengths and weaknesses.

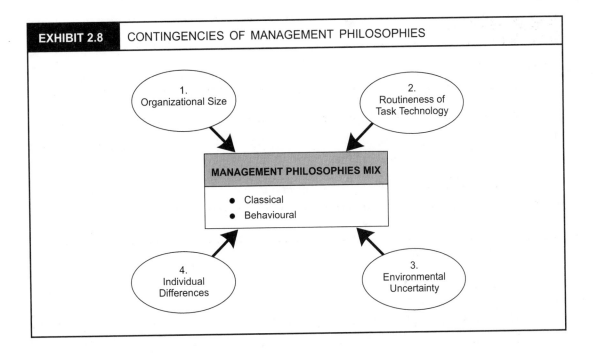

EXHIBIT 2.8 CONTINGENCIES OF MANAGEMENT PHILOSOPHIES

Experts agree that there simply is no one best way to manage. Instead, what has been advocated is referred to as the contingency approach to management.

As the name implies, this approach assumes that the best style of management depends on many contingencies: different conditions and situations require the application of different approaches or techniques. Essentially, this approach argues that there are few, if any, universal truths governing management techniques. Consequently, contingency management theories continue to examine different factors that dictate different requirements for managing people.

How to manage at UPS will differ from managing at Microsoft, which will differ from managing at a local hospital, etc. This is a central challenge for any manager — fitting their management philosophy to suit the organizational context. Think about the nature of different organizations and the type of work performed, and you will begin to see the importance of understanding the contingencies of management.

What are some contingencies of management philosophies?

1. Organizational size. Large organizations with hundreds of employees cannot be managed in the same manner as small organizations with few employees. The need for control and the challenge to achieve it in massive organizations may tend to encourage an approach that relies on elements of the classical school, such as the need for rules and regulations and the importance of an administrative hierarchy to ensure control. On the other hand, small, entrepreneurial organizations might function more effectively with a minimal number of rules and regulations.

2. Routineness of task technology. Some organizations may require employees to work in an assembly-line fashion, while their work is governed by machinery. Other jobs may not involve any significant level of technology: retail sales or being a bank teller are jobs that do not necessarily require technological expertise. These jobs are more easily subject to routinization — the standards advocated by Taylor, and the rules on which such workers can consistently rely. On the other hand, jobs that must continually adapt to changing technology require employees who are equally adaptive. High-tech organizations that employ "knowledge workers" are keenly aware that it is difficult to standardize the jobs of these workers, given the high rate of change within the present technology.

3. Environmental uncertainty. An organization that exists within a volatile environment must be prepared for continuous change. Change is the antithesis of the classical approaches, which emphasize stability and order. Consequently, organizations functioning in rapidly changing environments are less likely to find extensive application of the classical school useful in managing their workforce.

4. Individual differences. In any organization, employees differ with regard to their ability and motivation. Some people function better when given clear guidance: rules and regulations regarding how their job should be performed. Others perform better when the rules governing their performance are minimal. These differences suggest that a blanket application of either the classical or behavioural schools may risk ignoring the fact that the labour force is not homogeneous in terms of responses to the nature of work and management style.

CHAPTER SUMMARY

We have discussed the nature of managerial roles and considered what the job of a manager entails. This chapter also identified the central schools of management thought that have guided our thinking for over a century. Finally, we considered more specific theories regarding what it takes to generate motivation among the workforce.

In an effort to apply these management concepts to real life, you might consider the following questions:

1. Think of a real organization that implements elements of the classical school. What makes their implementation effective or ineffective?
2. Think of a real organization that implements elements of the behavioural school. What makes their implementation effective or ineffective?
3. What characteristics do you think make for the most effective manager? Why?

KEY TERMS

- interpersonal roles
- informational roles
- decisional roles
- scientific management (Taylorism)
- administrative management
- bureaucratic management
- time and motion studies
- compartmentalizing
- piece-rate system
- standardization
- unity of command

- *esprit de corps*
- The Human Relations Movement
- The Hawthorne Effect
- self-management
- modern behavioural science
- Theory X
- Theory Y
- Expectancy Theory
- Equity Theory
- Goal-setting Theory
- Contingency Approach

CASE APPLICATION How the workplace was won

[T]hese companies did make the fascinating discovery that improving working conditions and treating employees like human beings actually paid dividends (and kept union rabble-rousers at bay in the bargain). At four companies — Procter & Gamble, IBM, Hewlett-Packard, and Wal-Mart — enlightened leaders created workplaces that stood out during various epochs of the 20th century. Of course, we didn't discover a century of uninterrupted progress — even each of our fab four, and their workers have had their tough times....

Founded in 1837 as a soap and candle maker, Procter & Gamble was a model of exemplary employee relations at the turn of the 20th century. The driving force behind many of its pioneering policies was William Cooper Procter, grandson of a co-founder, who joined P&G as a low-level factory worker and quickly rose up the ranks. In 1887 he persuaded his father and uncles to introduce a profit-sharing plan to foster company loyalty. The plan was improved in 1903 by tying it to the purchase of company stock, and it stands today as the oldest known profit-sharing plan in continuous operation. In 1915, P&G workers were introduced to an "employee disability and death benefit plan," one of the first of its kind. After World War I the company gave factory workers an eight-hour day — long before any federal law required it and in 1923 it guaranteed 48 weeks of work per year. Barney Krieger, the first man hired by P&G, stayed for 47 years. While many employees have shown similar devotion, the rigid P&G bureaucracy that developed over the years — with its emphasis on controlling information, its obsession with memos, and the occasional snooping operation — has invited comparisons to the Kremlin. One sign of Perestroika: P&G employees can now wear casual dress.

IBM didn't become a corporate giant until the 1950s, but the ideals that built Big Blue took hold in 1914, when 40-year-old Thomas Watson Sr. ... joined a failing conglomerate called the Computing-Tabulating-Recording Co. Other manufacturers of the era emphasized reducing tasks to repetitive functions, but Watson made people the focus of his corporate culture. He borrowed money to fund in-house education programs, abolished piecework, spruced up factories, and paid above-average wages at all levels. Bereft of funds for generous benefit plans, he staged picnics (complete with band and theme song) to concoct company spirit. In 1934, IBM launched a group life insurance plan, and survivor benefits and paid vacations were added soon thereafter. Paramount within Watson's "human relations" mantra was his "open door" policy, whereby any employee could take a complaint to Watson himself. And since workers were ensured lifetime employment, even during the Depression, they were less afraid to speak their minds. But nothing good lasts forever: Watson's cherished no-layoff practice died in IBM's massive workforce cuts of the early 1990s.

Dave Packard and Bill Hewlett started their company in 1938, keenly influenced by the Depression and the importance of job security. Hewlett-Packard grew slowly — by 1951 it had just 215 employees — so Dave and Bill (they insisted on first names) got to know everyone personally. Maintaining those values as the company grew helped shape the now famous HP Way, a management style (codified in 1957) focused on sensitivity to employees. HP eschewed offices for cubicles, which allowed managers to manage by "walking around," as Packard demonstrates ... in the 1970s. The company's benefits plan was the envy of workers everywhere, and in 1973 HP became the first large American company to offer flex-time, a policy that Packard called the "essence of respect for and trust in people." Former CEO Lewis Platt once told FORTUNE that "in the HP environment, you really can't order people to do anything." That also meant it was hard to move the whole company in one direction — one reason Platt sought out Carly Fiorina from Lucent to succeed him as CEO. Fiorina has whipped up a whirlwind at HP, but she knows the HP Way is something she can't reinvent. The folks at HP call her Carly, proof that some things never change.

When Sam Walton joined J.C. Penney as a management trainee in 1940, he noticed that all the employees were called associates, a practice that dated back to 1902. Always quick to borrow from others, Walton instituted the policy at his growing discount chain in the 1960s. He also embraced Tom Watson Sr.'s open-door policy, and did HP's "management by walking around" one better by visiting every store. Where Walton broke new ground was by opening Wal-Mart's books to all associates, a strategy that made the corny Wal-Mart mantra — "Our people make the difference" — credible. Walton was notoriously chintzy on salaries, and his associates worked like dogs. But as at P&G years before, compensation included carrots like profit-sharing and stock-ownership plans for everyone. The company faltered after Walton's death in 1992, but it's back on track, and one visit to a Saturday morning meeting — a raucous business meeting-cum-pep rally — proves that Mr. Sam's legacy lives on.

Source: By Matthew Boyle from *Fortune* (January 8, 2001) 143(1): 139–46. Reproduced with permission. © 2001 Time Inc. All rights reserved.

QUESTIONS

1. Given the information in this article, and given your understanding of these organizations, in what ways do these companies implement elements of the classical school of management? In what ways do you think they implement elements of the behavioural school of management?

2. Which managerial role(s) would be most critical in managing at each of these companies? Why?

3. Which elements of which management approaches do you think are most accountable for the success of these businesses?

RELATED READING **Wanted: Good managers**

Ernst and Young is putting its managers under the microscope with a confidential employee poll.

The professional services firm is hoping to cull candid information from its workers to help its managers become more effective and help curb turnover.

"People leave managers. They don't leave organizations," says Keith Bowman, the company's director of human resources. "For the last five years, people have had an incredible number of work opportunities. They are more likely to look for other jobs and leave. The role of the manager is absolutely fundamental to keeping people from leaving."

Starting next month, Ernst and Young employees will be asked about their managers: "How well does the individual foster a positive work environment and help our people grow?" Staff can respond electronically to one of several preselected ratings, from not well to extremely well. All responses are anonymous.

This approach comes at a time when the working world is under siege by an employee retention crisis — one that observers say will only get more severe in the years to come as an impending labour shortage of almost one million workers is expected across all industries in Canada.

As a result, organizations are desperate to understand how to keep top talent from job-hopping.

Their desperation is well-founded, given that one in three workers will resign from his job in the next two years, according to a new survey by the Hay Group.

Ineffective managers are a major factor in the increasing rates of departure, says the research company, which interviewed over one million employees in 330 organizations around the world. "Poor managers have a huge impact on employee turnover. Management's inability to adapt to the times will continue to contribute dramatically to sustaining high levels of turnover," says Ron Grey, managing director of the Hay Group Canada.

"We have seen significant problems with senior managers who have not recognized the changing relationship with workers and continue to operate using historical methods," he says. As the workplace becomes more team-based and virtual, the role of managers must also change, Mr. Bowman says. "If you have the right people, you do not need to manage them. More work is team-based. More work is done from home. Managers should look for results and output, not whether their people are in the office at 9 a.m."

The Hay Group survey found the main reason workers left was that they felt their skills weren't being used. The second-most cited reason was the inability of top managers to be effective leaders. For instance, only 30 to 40 per cent of workers surveyed said they felt their bosses were eager to help advance their careers.

Managers were also criticized for tolerating workers who underperform — creating a key source of dissatisfaction among their peers, Mr. Grey says. Over half of the employees surveyed said their employers routinely accept poor performers who shirk responsibility. Many top workers respond by leaving.

To add insult to injury, Mr. Grey says, managers often don't understand why so many people are eager to leave and change jobs.

"Managers have a degree of blind loyalty that makes it difficult for them to understand the views of other employees." Mr. Grey says.

Workplace consultants urge managers to become better communicators, to treat employees as individuals and help foster career development.

KMPG's chief human resources officer, Lorne Burns, says many of the firm's employees leave because they are "cherry-picked" by their clients, not because of bad management. The company has started re-recruiting former employees who may want to return.

Still, Mr. Burns says, old-style management techniques that rely on close supervision, hierarchy and paternalistic methods are the most common reasons organizations are given for high turnover.

"People feel trapped. They are unhappy with the working relationship they have with their managers and want to get out."

Source: Natalie Southworth, "Managers crucial to curbing turnover" Special to *The Globe and Mail* (May 30, 2001). Reproduced with permission from The Globe and Mail.

QUESTIONS

1. What are some of the reasons for the dim view of managers as outlined in the article?

2. Does this article suggest that the classical or behavioural school is better suited to managing people?

3. Do you agree, or disagree, with some of the arguments presented in this report?

Decision Making in Organizations

Why do smart business leaders sometimes make foolish decisions? The success or failure of any organization ultimately is tied to the quality of the organization's decisions. This chapter is intended to offer a framework for understanding the process of decision making and to draw attention to the biases that influence the wisdom of decision-makers. We will begin our examination with a look at the classical model of decision making, and then consider more recent efforts at understanding how decisions are made. We will look at decisions made under conditions of risk or uncertainty, and identify those factors that influence our choice to take on risk or to avoid risk.

LEARNING OBJECTIVES

By the end of the chapter, you should be able to:

1. Describe the rational model of decision making.
2. Identify the assumptions and limitations of the rational model of decision making.
3. Explain how non-rationality enters into the decision-making process.
4. Define the notion of cognitive heuristics and their impact on decision making.
5. Discuss how non-rationality operates within decisions made under conditions of risk and uncertainty.
6. Explain the relationship between non-rationality and decision fiascos.

Organizational Insider

High-tech Decision Fiascos

In 1999 and 2000, Nortel rode the dot-com wave to unprecedented heights. The company's shares peaked in September, 2000 at $124.50, a spectacular increase of 300 percent in a year. At that point, the company dominated Canada's stock markets with a market value approaching $400 billion, making it Canada's most "valuable" corporation by far. At [its] peak, Nortel shares represented over 30 percent of the value of all Canadian-based companies traded on the Toronto Stock Exchange.... In the two years ending October, 2000, while Nortel Networks was enjoying its (short) honeymoon with stock speculators, the company announced 18 acquisitions of other high-tech firms — almost one per month — worth a grand total of about $45 billion.... The fact that Nortel hasn't made a dollar in bottom-line profit since 1997 hardly slowed down this spending spree, so long as the printing press kept running and the market kept buying.[1]

If the experience of Nortel Networks taught us anything, it is to beware the words "new paradigm." In recent years experts watching the phenomenal growth of technology and telecommunication stocks proclaimed that we were experiencing an entirely new paradigm, an age of sky-high growth and stock valuations that defied all conventional ratios....

... And to a great extent, this enormous mistake in forecasting isn't the fault of any particular company, including Nortel. It is the collective error of all those analysts, investment firms, technology gurus, business writers and excited investors who found it more profitable or just more exciting to believe the old ways no longer applied. The contrarians who insisted the technology sector was an empty bubble waiting to burst seemed like grumpy naysayers too unsophisticated to appreciate a brave new world. How vindicated they must feel now as Nortel and all its peers crash back to earth.

Yesterday, Nortel revealed it expects to lose $19-billion (U.S.) in the second quarter this year — a record Canadian corporate loss.... The company's shares, which peaked at $124 (Canadian) last August, closed yesterday at $15.17. And now it is increasingly clear that maybe there's no such thing as a new paradigm, but simply new technologies that grow explosively quickly and then are forced into dramatic restructuring as market demand stabilizes. It's worth remembering that North America also had hundreds of car companies in the 1920s, and most disappeared within a few years.

. . . .

Many other technologies have soared and then levelled, but it is uncommon to soar and crash as quickly as the fibre-optic market has this year. In a world of rapid change, it appears both the upswing and the downswing are accelerated. Nortel and its peers believed in the dawning of a new world order as much as any of their excited investors. The company's dramatic expansion, its huge acquisition program in recent years and its reluctance to lower growth forecasts as markets cooled are evidence that no one realized the need for prudence — although CEO John Roth admits that, in retrospect, the overbuilding of capacity was clearly unsustainable. Too bad no one considered that a year ago.[2]

Sources:

1. Quoted from Jim Stanford, "Dispatches from a meltdown" *Canadian Dimension* (May–June 2001) 35(3): 17–22.
2. Excerpts from "Seems the old rules apply to Nortel after all" *The Globe and Mail* (June 16, 2001), 1. Reproduced with permission of The Globe and Mail.

DECISION MAKING IN ORGANIZATIONS ——————

In recent years, we have seen numerous companies like Nortel struggle through unpredictable downturns. How should companies like Nortel approach decision making in such volatile environments? Managers are continually faced with the task of making decisions, both minor and major, on a daily basis. When do we schedule the next staff lunch? What approach do we take to the new product advertising campaign? Should we purchase another high-tech firm? Managers constantly make decisions. But how much do we know about how decisions are made? Is it possible to teach managers how to make "good" decisions? What can we gain from an examination of the process of decision making?

A definition. Decision making has been defined as a conscious process of making choices among one or more alternatives with the intention of moving toward some desired state of affairs.

We might be choosing between alternative courses of action in order to cope with a crisis, to solve a problem or to take advantage of an opportunity. We can identify two major characteristics of organizational decisions. How structured or unstructured is the context within which the decision must be made? How much risk or uncertainty is involved in the decision options?

Some decisions that we make in our workplace are likely to be quite routine. For example, an accountant deciding how to conduct the annual audit of a long-time client will make decisions that are relatively routine, assuming little has changed in their client's operations and in how they conduct audits. Or, consider a manager of a restaurant who decides to re-order more bottles of ketchup as the supply is reduced. What we have in both these cases are routine decisions that are made repeatedly using a pre-established set of alternatives. These types of decisions are referred to as programmed decisions.

On the other hand, you might face decisions that are one-time decisions and for which there are no ready-made solutions. In other words, imagine that you are in a novel situation, and somehow you must generate an adequate solution to a problem. For example, imagine that your company is about to merge with another large organization. Mergers don't happen every day and, clearly, the decisions made regarding how to ensure a successful merger require non-routine solutions. These types of decisions are referred to as non-programmed decisions. They are typically unstructured, or uncertain in the path followed to deal with the issues, and are more common at higher managerial levels. (See Exhibit 3.1.)

Clearly, the type of decision that you choose — programmed or non-programmed — will have different implications for the approach that you take to generate a solution. How, indeed, do you go about making decisions? Is the fundamental process of decision making the same, regardless of whether the decision is programmed or non-programmed?

THE RATIONAL MODEL OF DECISION MAKING ——————

What are we trying to accomplish through decision making? In broad terms, we attempt to make decisions that will maximize the attainment of our goals. That is referred to as rational decision making. For example: How do we increase our company's market share?

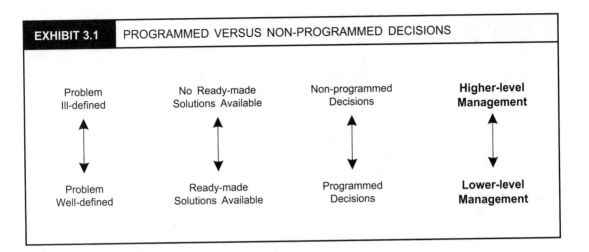

EXHIBIT 3.1   PROGRAMMED VERSUS NON-PROGRAMMED DECISIONS

Problem Ill-defined ⇕ Problem Well-defined

No Ready-made Solutions Available ⇕ Ready-made Solutions Available

Non-programmed Decisions ⇕ Programmed Decisions

Higher-level Management ⇕ **Lower-level Management**

Which new technology should be implemented in our production system? How can we better serve our clients? The answers to all these questions should involve decisions that maximize the goals we hope to attain — whether it is increased market share, maximizing productivity or better customer service. A rational decision is one that maximizes the attainment of goals — whether they are organizational goals, as in the example above, or personal goals.

Management scholars have, for many years, suggested that we can consider the process of decision making to be composed of a series of stages or steps. These steps are followed sequentially, and by addressing these steps we will have properly fulfilled the decision-making process. This model is based on a rational, economic view of individual decision-makers. The notion of rationality is evident when one considers the nature of the model.

This rational model of decision making outlines a systematic series of stages or steps that decision-makers resolve in the effort to achieve the best solution to a problem. Specifically, there are six stages in this model, as outlined in Exhibit 3.2.

Stage 1 — Identify Problems and Opportunities

A manager monitors the environment, and assesses information. The aim is to identify any potential gaps that exist between the current and the desired state of affairs. For example, ʰe results of recent surveys suggest that your company currently possesses 6% of the total ket of potential consumers for the company's product, and the desired level of market is 10%. You have now identified the problem or challenge. Perhaps you also recog-hat the additional market shared is due to a failure to market the product toward der segment of consumers. You have identified an opportunity; now you need to fig-ut how you can capture that market segment.

Assumptions of the Rational Model

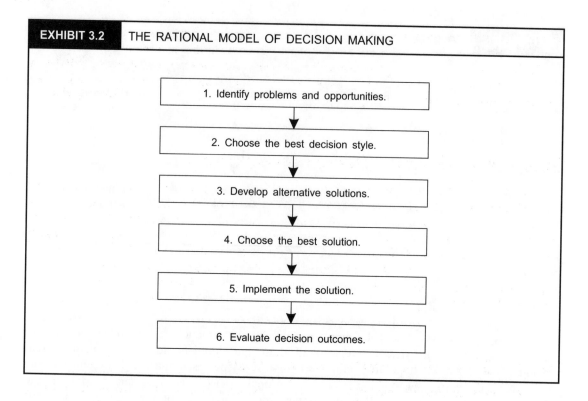

EXHIBIT 3.2   THE RATIONAL MODEL OF DECISION MAKING

1. Identify problems and opportunities.

2. Choose the best decision style.

3. Develop alternative solutions.

4. Choose the best solution.

5. Implement the solution.

6. Evaluate decision outcomes.

Stage 2 — Choose the Best Decision Style

Given that your aim is to figure out how to capture this additional segment of the market, you need to consider how you will determine your choice of action. Who will help you in your decision? How will you collect data to assess your options? If this is a programmed problem, then you would follow standard operating procedures. For example, if you discover that your inventory of Product X is low, you re-order the product. Standard decision procedure dictates the style or approach you will take to solve the problem. In the case of novel situations requiring a non-programmed decision, there are really no rules of thumb to follow here to solve your problem. So, you've got to search carefully for alternatives and identify appropriate solutions. How you capture that older segment of consumers is a non-programmed problem that requires a careful search.

Stage 3 — Develop Alternative Solutions

Before a decision is made, a range of alternatives is generated: these are potential solutions to the problem at hand. Consider the case of a sales manager who monitors sales, and discovers a downward trend. Say the source of this decrease is a poorly trained sales staff. How do we best upgrade the competence of the staff? The alternatives might include: increase on-the-job training and guidance; send staff off to an external consultant's training workshop retreat for one week; or provide in-house training workshops led by the company's senior sales managers. Programmed decisions will come with ready-made solutions; that is, routine business decisions will be dealt with according to clear policy or procedure. However, novel situations may require custom-made alternatives, so to speak.

Stage 4 — Choose the Best Solution

After having identified the problem or opportunity, we have to decide on how we will go about dealing with this issue; by generating a range of alternatives, we are in a position to choose the best solution. We reconsider what the goals or objectives of our decision include. We compare alternatives, and judge which one maximizes our benefits (i.e., which best achieves our desired outcomes) and which one minimizes any negative consequences. We systematically compare the advantages and disadvantages of each alternative. This might involve predetermined decision criteria, such as quality desired, anticipated costs and benefits, the risks or uncertainties associated with each alternative, etc.

Stage 5 — Implement the Solution

Once the best alternative has been chosen, it is implemented. For example, we may have decided that the best solution for our sales staff problem is to send our staff on a training retreat. Whatever the issue, we are now prepared to put into action our chosen alternative.

Stage 6 — Evaluate Decision Outcomes

Finally, the rational model argues that no decision process is complete until the consequences or the effects of the implemented decision have been evaluated. This includes re-examining where the company is in terms of its desired state. Has the gap been reduced, or closed, between the desired state of affairs and the current state of affairs? Clearly, this is an important part of any decision; obviously, there is a need to assess whether, indeed, the company's goals were achieved, or whether corrective action must be taken. There is also a need to understand whether the approach was wise or unwise: if we don't monitor the consequences of the decision, it is difficult to assess whether similar decisions or strategies should be undertaken in the future.

The notion of rationality is evident in the way this model conceptualizes the decision process: from systematically monitoring the environment and identifying all the problems or opportunities, to thinking carefully about the approach we will take to solve the problem; to generating and evaluating the range of alternatives; and, finally, choosing, and then evaluating, our decision. The clear, organized, systematic and rational approach of this model is why it has been referred to as a prescriptive model of decision making: it serves as a prescription for how organizational decision-makers **should** make decisions. However, the question is: Does it really explain how decisions are made in practice? This is an interesting question to address, because it forces us to consider how rational we really are when it comes to making decisions.

Are We Really Rational Decision-Makers?

There are numerous cases of organizations making decisions that clearly failed to achieve the intended objectives, and others that were outright fiascos. In such cases, do you think the decision-makers followed the six stages of the rational model? Think about some of the decisions you have made — career decisions, education decisions, personal decisions. Did all your decisions follow the six neat stages of the rational model? Clearly, the rational model of decision making, while perhaps an ideal approach, has a number of limitations in terms of its ability to explain how we actually go about making decisions in real life. Let's briefly examine the assumptions of this model, and its limitations, in order to more fully appreciate the rational and the non-rational side of the decision-making process.

Assumptions of the Rational Model

Why don't organizational decision-makers behave according to rational models of decision making? Researchers such as Kahneman and Tversky observed that the rational model has dominated the analysis of decision making under risk. March and Simon, in their critique of the rational model of decision making, also indicated the elements of this model and its weaknesses.

Essentially, a rational model of decision making assumes that all alternatives are known; that all consequences of each alternative are known; that all preferences are known; that there is a decision-rule for choosing alternatives. In essence, the rational model assumes that there is complete knowledge of all alternatives and outcomes to a decision. Further, it assumes that individuals are capable of fully processing all available information, in an objective manner, in order to come to a decision. Let's more fully consider some of the implications of the key assumptions of this model.

1. Bounded Rationality

There are at least two critical assumptions of the rational model. First, it assumes complete access to all information. That is, it assumes that decision-makers are able to gather all information necessary to make a decision. This assumption underlies the notion that we can identify clearly what, in fact, are the problems or opportunities that we must confront. And it assumes the ability to identify all possible alternatives or solutions to the problem.

Cognitively, we are limited in our ability to fully gather and process all available information. This reflects the notion of bounded rationality, a termed coined by Herbert

---

LET'S TALK BUSINESS 3.1   **BOUNDED RATIONALITY AND COKE**

In reality it is very unlikely that a manager is actually able to receive all necessary information in order to make a decision. Do we always know what the full range of alternatives are for us? How often have we made decisions without knowing all the options? The fact is, managers do not have the luxury of knowing everything — of receiving complete information nor of receiving completely accurate information. When Coca Cola decided many years ago to drop their original formula in favour of a new formula they clearly had no idea of the backlash they would experience, which subsequently forced them to re-introduce their original formula of Coke alongside the newer product.

Simon, an influential voice in the study of organizational decision making. In our effort to make sense of the problem, we need to simplify the situation, and may not consider all the complexities of the actual situation. This limitation might be due to time constraints in gathering data and making a decision. In addition, often the nature of the problem is ill-defined. So, our rationality as decision-makers has boundaries, or limits. (See Let's Talk Business 3.1.)

2.   *Satisficing*

A second fundamental assumption of the rational model is that decision-makers will choose the best possible solution to a problem or response to an opportunity. This is the notion that rational decision-makers will seek to maximize benefits in any decision that is made. Consequently, it assumes that people will also choose the best alternative to deal with a problem. We do not necessarily choose the best solution to a problem.

Herbert Simon argued that decision-makers typically will not optimize, but will "satisfice" in the decision-making process. What does it mean to satisfice? Satisficing means that once an alternative has been identified whose outcome is considered to be satisfactory, that alternative will be chosen. The search for other alternatives will be stopped once this acceptable alternative is found. Consider, for example, a personnel manager who is responsible for hiring a new employee. The notion of satisficing suggests that this manager will not sift through the thousands of applications received and systematically weigh all the relative strengths and weaknesses of each candidate, but might simply examine a number of applications and stop the search once a candidate has been identified who meets the acceptable criteria for the position. Has the best possible person for the job been chosen? Limited access to complete information, bounded rationality and the behaviour of satisficing suggest that while a satisfactory candidate may, perhaps, have been chosen, it is pretty unlikely that the best possible candidate will have received the job offer. How common is this? Well that is difficult to estimate, but according to Simon, satisficing decisions are more likely to be made than optimizing decisions.

NON-RATIONALITY IN DECISION MAKING —————

How do decision-makers actually process information to make judgments? The rational model of decision making indicated that, among the steps of the decision process, we generate a range of alternatives and evaluate these alternatives in order to choose the best one. While we would like to believe that we are purely rational decision-makers, there are a number of factors that limit our ability to generate the perfect solution. Let's consider cognitive or perceptual biases that we all possess that might distort our rationality in making a decision. We will specifically focus on several biases that can be referred to as cognitive heuristics. What are cognitive heuristics?

To understand what cognitive heuristics are, just think about the myriad decisions we face in everyday life: "Should I offer assistance to the new employee at the job?" "What should I order for lunch?" "How can I assess whether the boss is planning on promoting me or not?" "Can we develop a successful downsizing strategy?" Decisions and judgments are typical of all our lives, inside and outside of organizations. How do we cope with all these judgments about people, places and events? The notion of bounded rationality suggests that we cannot know everything, so we try to simplify things.

As opposed to the rational, economic view of decision-makers, there is a body of research based on a behavioural decision theory approach that essentially views individuals as "cognitive misers" who are subject to employing heuristics as a means to simplify decision making.[1] Specifically, this approach follows the view that individuals behave "economically" to accomplish goals by expending a minimum amount of time and processing resources (the "cognitive miser" notion). This tendency gives rise to heuristics, or cognitive "shortcuts", that facilitate information processing but often produce inaccurate judgments and biases.[2] Individuals' judgment processes often involve the use of heuristics that can create judgment biases. There is much research evidence to confirm the widespread use by decision-makers of cognitive heuristics as a means to simplify their decision making, and that doing so further results in non-rational biases.[3]

Cognitive Heuristics

Cognitive heuristics are simple rules or guidelines that we generate and employ to guide us through the decisions or choices that we must continually make. These can be thought of as "rules of thumb" that we rely on, particularly in decision making. Judgmental heuristics are rules of thumb or shortcuts that reduce the information processing demands for decision making. Such "cognitive shortcuts" allow for a reduction in the amount of information processed. Consequently, heuristics can be viewed as part of a cognitive data reduction process.

It is important to point out that the use of heuristics is not inherently non-rational. In fact, cognitive heuristics are employed as a coping mechanism. If cognitive heuristics are productively employed, they can act to reduce the time required to search for alternatives to a problem: they can help decision-makers access and effectively process data in an efficient manner. Indeed, some scholars have defined intelligence as based on an individual's capacity to use simplifying heuristics.[4]

When we act as decision-makers in ill-structured environments, we are essentially required to manage an almost limitless amount of information available for search, and discern which data is even relevant to our search needs. According to Kahneman and Tversky, one important way that decision-makers process information is to find ways of managing what might otherwise be overwhelming amounts of data. We, as decision-makers, may need to digest large amounts of information within short periods of time. Rules, or heuristics, can, in fact, be quite helpful; it is reassuring to have some rules to fall back on when trying to make decisions. However, reliance on these heuristics can also create impediments to rational decision making in cases where these heuristics encourage us to ignore valuable information and make less accurate decisions. Given the significance of these heuristics for helping or hindering the decision-making process, much of the general information-processing literature has examined the use of cognitive heuristics and how they may bias the decision-making process. Among the most commonly studied heuristics identified by Tversky and Kahneman are the **representative heuristic** and the **availability heuristic**.

Representative Heuristic

Tversky and Kahneman[5] suggested that individual decision-makers can be guided, unwittingly, by the representative heuristic. This heuristic is the tendency for decision-makers to generate broad, and sometimes detailed, generalizations regarding a target individual, group, organization or situation based on only a few characteristics of that target. This heuristic offers a guideline for estimating the probability of an outcome based on assessing how much a particular object resembles a class of objects. In a sense, the representative heuristic is a form of stereotyping by which small samples of occurrences are perceived as representing actual probabilities. For example, a male negotiator who perceives his opponent as a weaker, less aggressive negotiator because the opponent is female is relying on gender stereotyping. The individual is making generalizations about someone based on a few characteristics associated with that category of individual.

Statistically speaking, there is a "law of large numbers" that asserts that large random samples are more appropriate for making rigorous inferences about underlying population statistics. However, the representative heuristics reflect the fact that sometimes decision-makers generate such inferences not from large random samples, but from small, non-random samples — a less reliable source of inference. One such example of inferences or generalizations based on small, non-random samples is the use of personal experience.[6] Imagine that you purchase a product from Company X and you dislike the product. Later, you have an opportunity to purchase a different product from the same company, but you feel that all their products are not suitable for you. You have employed the representative heuristic in judging the suitability of Company X's products for you by generalizing characteristics of the company's products from a small sample.

People may overestimate the likelihood of an event or an incident occurring due to the use of less accurate information. An example offered by Tversky and Kahneman[7] illustrates the potential bias generated by the representative heuristic. In a study, the authors provided a description of an individual and then asked respondents to determine the profession to which the individual most likely belonged. For example:

> Steve is very shy and withdrawn, invariably helpful, but with little interest in people or the world of reality. A meek and tidy soul, he has a need for order and structure, and a passion for detail.

The authors presented a number of different professions and required respondents to indicate the profession to which Steve most likely belonged. The most common response listed Steve as a librarian. However, this response is based purely on the qualitative description of the individual, and one that reflects a stereotypical view of this job. It does not consider the popularity of different professions: the likelihood that any given individual will be a member of certain professions will be greater for more common professions than for others. The simple reality is that there are much fewer librarian jobs than, say, computer analyst jobs. Consequently, the response that Steve is most likely a librarian completely ignores the base-rate frequency of librarians when contrasted with other professions. This example illustrates the representative bias.

The tendency to ignore factual information like base rates when any other information about the event or person is provided is called the base-rate fallacy or the representative heuristic. Remember, we mentioned that cognitive heuristics are the simple rules we use. Here, the simple rule of classifying someone as a member of a certain group clearly is much less reliable than other, more valuable and accurate, information pertaining to the person. It illustrates how easy it is to ignore critical information in favour of less valid or less reliable information in common, everyday judgments. In other words, it is quite easy to become a non-rational decision-maker: non-rational in the sense that our decision process may being influenced by factors that distort the accuracy of our judgments — in this case, cognitive heuristics or rules of thumb.

Availability Heuristic

Decision-makers may sometimes generate probabilities based on their familiarity with a certain task, idea, or environment.[8] If we are trying to come to a decision, we may look to the past for assistance; particularly those situations that were successful. This can lead to bias when this heuristic encourages us to maintain a perception of the situation without a consideration that change could occur. In addition, this bias tends to stem from an over-reliance on easily retrievable, yet not necessarily accurate, information. When we employ the availability heuristic we are, essentially, assessing the frequency of a class or the probability of an event, according to the ease with which instances or occurrences can be brought to mind.[9] The dysfunctions arising from this heuristic are false assumptions generated by the decision-maker — presumed associations between events that are recalled, or assumptions of fact based on ease of recall.[10]

In the workplace. How might the availability bias operate in the workplace? Imagine that you have endured a recent conflict with an extremely unco-operative supplier that ended in breaking off the relationship with this supplier. You are now about to deal with another supplier and, perhaps, you are expecting a similar conflict with this supplier. Now, on average your company has had excellent relationships with its suppliers; but this recent information is very salient in your mind and easily retrievable. Consequently, this recent experience might cloud your judgments about other suppliers. Your relationship with this

---

LET'S TALK BUSINESS 3.2   LESSONS FOR DECISION-MAKERS

In general, should individuals endeavour to avoid cognitive heuristics? Is there a positive purpose in relying on the use of such heuristics under certain circumstances? The answer is — yes! Heuristics do not always lower the quality of our decisions. And if you reconsider how we defined heuristics, they do, in fact, potentially offer assistance with decisions. We often use broad rules to help us face complex decisions. Think of just about any profession. Don't we all generate and employ simple rules to help make judgments? Consider the doctor who, after identifying a series of symptoms, will rely on guidelines to suggest the possible source of the ailment without necessarily requiring the patient to undergo more rigorous tests. Consider the financial consultant who may rely on general guidelines to determine the best combination of an investment portfolio.

What, then, is so bad about cognitive heuristics? Consider the representative and availability heuristic that we identified earlier. Both these rules of thumb clearly can lead to inferior decisions because they discourage the decision-maker from seeking, gathering or processing all the information that is necessary for making an accurate judgment. If we ignore important information (like base rates), or over-rely on readily available information, we run the risk of engaging in poor decisions. Consequently, these cognitive heuristics also constitute cognitive biases that, potentially, interfere with our ability to make sound, rational decisions. A good example of the "double-edged sword" of cognitive heuristics can be seen when considering the use of such heuristics among real-life business people — entrepreneurs.

---

new supplier might be guided by this recent event, even though there is no rational reason to expect that this new supplier will behave the same way. Consequently, on occasions, inaccurate yet easily retrievable information can cloud our judgment about events or individuals.

Overconfidence heuristic.   Related to the availability heuristic is another cognitive bias referred to as overconfidence. Overconfidence, as the label implies, refers to the tendency for decision-makers to be overly optimistic in their predictive abilities upon receiving initial information.[11] This is most likely to arise when the decision-maker is relatively unfamiliar with the problem, or when significant uncertainty exists.[12] Overconfidence has also been considered as stemming from the anchoring and adjustment heuristic,[13] which we will discuss later. The notion that decision-makers can become overconfident in their initial assessments and, subsequently, slow to revise their initial judgments appropriately as additional information becomes available is certainly consistent with the notion of anchoring and adjustment.[14]

Cognitive Heuristics and Entrepreneurs

Recently, there has been interesting research conducted on entrepreneurial decision making. One central theme of entrepreneurship is the tendency for entrepreneurs to consistently engage in risky activities. Traditionally, the study of entrepreneurs seemed to include a characterization of this class of individuals as people who have a high propensity to take chances, and who are much more willing to endure risky activities. If you have ever met an entrepreneur, or read about the adventures of entrepreneurs, you get the sense that they are thrill-seekers willing to risk their time, money and commitment in order to pursue their dream. While there is clear evidence that such individuals, seeking to start a new business, face a huge amount of risk, there is little concrete evidence that entrepreneurs are actually more risk-seeking than the rest of the population.[15]

The paradox of entrepreneurs. Do entrepreneurs feel like they are taking on inordinate amounts of risk? There is evidence to indicate that entrepreneurs do not feel that they are necessarily embracing high levels of risk in the ventures that they pursue.[16] Researchers have been grappling with this odd paradox. Entrepreneurs invariably are willing to take on high risk, and yet they do not tend to exhibit higher risk preferences than the rest of the population.[17] How can this paradox be explained? If entrepreneurs take on more risk than other work arrangements, what accounts for this acceptance of risk, if not higher preferences for it?

Perceptions of risks. The answer to that paradox may lie in how entrepreneurs perceive risk. For example, some researchers[18] have found that entrepreneurs typically perceive their chances for success to be much higher than competitors starting in the same industries. It could be that entrepreneurs may tend to perceive less risk in their ventures because of the cognitive lens through which they perceive their situation.[19]

How do entrepreneurs deal with the high level of risk associated with initiating new ventures? It has been suggested that entrepreneurs apply cognitive biases and heuristics more extensively in their decision making and, consequently, fail to fully acknowledge the risk associated with starting their own businesses.[20] What types of cognitive biases might lead entrepreneurs to this perception?

The differential use of non-rational assumptions, or biases, might be a factor that explains the acceptance of risk among entrepreneurs. For example, recall Stage 3 of the rational model of decision making — the need to generate alternatives. It may be that entrepreneurs are much more willing to accept the cognitive limitations of that stage in the model. As we discussed earlier, bounded rationality limits the extent to which we can generate significant numbers of alternatives. Research has found that entrepreneurs may have a tendency to evaluate a small number of alternatives and to focus on only a few central aspects of the problem[21] based on a few personal biases and decision rules.[22] Decision-makers such as individuals in the start-up stage of their new business may apply the representative and overconfidence heuristic more than others.[23]

Representative heuristic. There is evidence that entrepreneurs may be more likely than organizational decision-makers to rely on the representative heuristic.[24] Why might they? That is, why might these individuals display a willingness to make general conclusions based on data from small, non-random samples? Consider the environment within which an entrepreneur may typically operate. Entrepreneurs have insufficient time, financial resources or institutional support to obtain massive, systematic data upon which to make decisions. In fact, a new venture may be based on little previous experience from which to draw data. Entrepreneurs may be forced to draw conclusions and make speculations simply from previous personal experience. For example, an entrepreneur might have personally observed a new business model or system that was successfully employed overseas. The entrepreneur may feel, based on this anecdotal evidence, that this business model will work for him/her.

Overconfidence heuristic. Overconfidence among entrepreneurs can tend to manifest itself in the simple belief that the probability of success is higher for the individual than for their competitors.[25] This confidence may stem from a need to cope with the massive uncertainty new ventures face; entrepreneurs are more likely to pursue new territory if they feel capable of meeting the challenge.[26] Overconfidence, is in this sense, a coping mechanism — a defence against all the obstacles that entrepreneurs face in the path to establishing a new business. A perception that failure is less likely, stemming from the overconfidence heuristic, might lead the entrepreneur to march forward with this idea, and perhaps face a level of risk that others who do not employ such heuristics may perceive as much higher. In fact, it has been suggested that individuals who don't possess such overconfidence would more likely be attracted to the security of larger organizations.[27]

How does the use of these heuristics help us understand the paradox cited above — the tendency for entrepreneurs to engage in riskier choices than the rest of the population? It has been suggested that, by being more willing to generalize from limited experience, and by feeling overconfident, entrepreneurs may oversimplify and conclude that their specific ventures are guaranteed success. In this sense, it is not a higher risk propensity, but differences in the ways entrepreneurs perceive risk, that distinguish them.[28] Cognitive

---

LET'S TALK BUSINESS 3.3   BIASED ENTREPRENEURS?

The puzzle of starting a new venture is usually very scrambled, and those individuals who use heuristics more extensively to assist in their strategic decision making are the only ones who are most likely to attempt such a start-up. Although there are no doubt shortcomings to an entrepreneur's clouded or naive perceptions of risk, such an approach may help explain why entrepreneurs are frequently able to transform an idea into a growing enterprise. In other words, it may be the naiveness of the risk involved that enables entrepreneurs to forge ahead with their new ideas. If entrepreneurs would carefully calculate all the risks involved in starting a new venture, most new ventures would never be started. (p. 330)

The use of biases and heuristics may also offer some help in explaining why entrepreneurs sometimes make bad managers.... Although the use of biases and heuristics can be very beneficial, it may lead to major errors in evaluating the riskiness of key strategic decisions. Although research has yet to establish performance implications, it is possible that the more extensive use of heuristics in strategic decision making may be a great advantage during the start-up years. However, it also may tend to lead to the demise of a business, particularly as a firm matures. (p. 333)

Source: Busenitz, 1999.

heuristics and biases can help simplify an otherwise complex and novel scenario of starting a business. (See Let's Talk Business 3.3.)

Why might entrepreneurs be more inclined to use more of these cognitive heuristics and biases? Entrepreneurs tend to function without the same set of decision-making guidelines that may be established within organizations.[29] Consequently, in the absence of such guidelines, entrepreneurs must employ their own decision-making guidelines or heuristics to guide their decision making. This helps the individual cope with the enormous uncertainty that surrounds their activities. Clearly, individuals who are less able to deal with ambiguity or uncertainty would be more comfortable functioning within an organization and within the decision-making guidelines set out for them. On the other hand, individuals who are comfortable with uncertainty and ambiguity tend to enjoy entrepreneurial ventures and are capable of generating their own decision rules. Organizations also would typically make available a greater set of resources with which to gather data and analyze, and consequently generate decisions under lower levels of risk. These resources are not as readily available for entrepreneurs and small business.

DECISION MAKING UNDER RISK AND UNCERTAINTY

Whether we are high level business executives, middle line managers or team members, we all tend to carry an image of ourselves as rational decision-makers. The question is: Do we always follow a rational process in the generation of decisions? Under what conditions might we depart from rationality? These are critical questions for any individual to ask, given that knowledge of our decision processes may save us from making blunders.

Earlier, we mentioned that the classical model seems to explain well the process of decision making when the situation is relatively routine, for **programmed decisions**. Think about it: making the same type of decision repeatedly probably could be well explained by the rational model. It involves a clear problem or problems, clear alternatives and clear judgment in deciding which alternative to choose. Organizational life is fraught with risk and uncertainty; it is not always clear to us what the problems or opportunities are. That is, many of the decisions you will confront in your professional lives will be **non-programmed decisions** for which the problems, alternatives and choices will be much less clear.

Decisions in organizations often involve a degree of risk; therefore, it is important to understand the process of decision making under risk. Moreover, decision making in modern organizations is characterized, more than ever, by elements of risk, uncertainty and ambiguity. The rapidly changing national economic scene and highly volatile global environment certainly highlight the critical issues surrounding risk, risk assessment and risk tolerance in organizations.

It is rare that decision-makers will possess complete certainty in a given decision situation; and so, some risk is almost always present in our decision-making process. Given the pervasiveness of risk and uncertainty in workplace decisions, it is worth considering what factors might potentially distort our judgment and force us to depart even further from the so-called rational model of decision making under conditions of risk and uncertainty.

LET'S TALK BUSINESS 3.4   GENDER AND RISK PREFERENCE

There is evidence that gender differences do exist with regard to risk preferences among decision-makers. The results of a number of studies suggested that females were more cautious in their decisions and less likely to take gambles compared to males. Why have many findings suggested that men are more risk tolerant than women?

There is no evidence to directly assert that risk preference is a trait and that there are biological differences. With regard to understanding why men and women might differ in risky decision making, it is useful to draw upon the sociological literature and, specifically, social role theory. The gender-role perspective asserts that gender differences in social behaviour originate from shared expectations or stereotypes about what is appropriate behaviour for men and women. Essentially, this model asserts that men and women experience different socialization processes whereby each learns gender-appropriate patterns of behaviour. Based on this view, through socialization at a young age, males are taught to be outgoing and achievement-oriented, while females are taught to be emotionally oriented and reserved in their interactions with others. Further, girls are generally socialized to respect male power and authority, and to refrain from expressions of aggressiveness or assertiveness. Boys, on the other hand, are typically socialized to be assertive and aggressive.

The differences in gender role socialization between men and women can be considered as one key source of variation in risk tolerance. Risk-taking can also be linked with the notions of aggressiveness and assertiveness in the context of managerial decision-making behaviour. Extending this line of reasoning, risk tolerance can be seen as being influenced by confidence or efficacy that managers, both men and women, possess in the domain of executive decision making. The literature suggests that women may be socialized to be more conservative in their risk preference. However, once in a managerial role, these gender differences in risky decision making may diminish.

Source: Karakowsky & Elangovan, 2001.

Many factors have been examined with regard to their influence on decision making. For example, Let's Talk Business 3.4 relates gender and the preference for risk.

Risk Preferences and Decision Frame

Among their research efforts, psychologists Daniel Kahneman and Amos Tversky[30] were interested in examining the methods individuals employ to make choices when faced with uncertain outcomes. Their theory, referred to as **prospect theory**, attempts to reveal patterns of behaviour that had been ignored by proponents of the rational decision-making model. This theory draws attention to the shortcomings of decision making under risk and uncertainty, and stands in clear contrast to the assumptions of the rational model. This theory offers a useful approach to understanding the source of decision dysfunctions and failures.

Prospect theory posits that decisions can be framed as a choice between losses and gains. Essentially, this theory suggests that, when faced with a choice of alternatives or prospects, the choice that we make will very much depend on how we have framed the alternatives. One way of framing alternatives is to think of them as choices between gains or choices between losses. Studies of framing demonstrate that decision-makers are systematically affected by the manner in which problems are framed, although the information may be objectively equivalent. For example, the research indicates that the actions of negotiators vary systematically with changes in the way contract information is worded.[31]

Kahneman and Tversky's research indicates that, when faced with a choice between options that have been framed as gains, people tend to become risk-averse: that is, we will choose a sure gain over a chance to receive a larger gain if that larger gain is not completely certain. On the other hand, people do not like sure losses; when we are faced with having to accept a loss or are offered the chance to avoid that loss, we tend to be more willing to accept risk. According to Kahneman and Tversky, the major driving force behind our preference for riskier choices is the notion of **loss aversion**. Prospect theory assumes the "certainty effect"— a given decrease in probability of an event will have most effect on judgment when the event is initially considered inevitable, rather than merely possible. This effect promotes risk-seeking in choices between losses.[32] Consequently, we tend to become risk-seeking when our choices are framed as choices between losses — a sure loss, or a chance to avoid that sure loss, along with a risk of incurring greater losses. In sum, then, according to prospect theory, decision-makers will tend to become risk-seeking when the decision is framed as a choice between losses, and they will become risk-averse when the decision is framed as a choice between gains.[33]

The rational or classical model of decision making, as discussed earlier, is an economics-based model of decision making. In contrast, prospect theory is essentially a behavioural decision theory framework. It attempts to reflect the behaviours that individuals actually display when faced with making decisions under circumstances of risk and uncertainty. In a sense, it attempts to describe the relationship between economic and psychological value. In addition, perceived losses have a greater psychological impact than perceived gains.

The rational model of decision making suggests that it is the consequences of decision options that determine the ultimate choice made. Prospect theory, on the other hand, suggests that how the decision-makers' choices are framed can influence the ultimate choice made. Specifically, how the decision-making situation is presented — either in terms of potential gains or potential losses (decision framing) — can influence an individual's ultimate decision.[34] Consequently, this is a **non-rational theory of decision making**. The theory explains the tendency for individuals to exhibit risk-averse behaviour when presented with the choice between a certain gain versus a higher but riskier gain. Individuals will exhibit risk-seeking behaviour when presented with the choice between a sure loss versus a chance to avoid the sure loss coupled with the risk of incurring greater losses.[35]

The following decision-making scenario illustrates a case where a decision-maker is faced with choices that are framed in terms of gains — in this case, gains are reflected in the notion of "jobs saved". What would be your decision in this scenario?

Decision-Making Scenario 1

Your company is preparing for an economic downturn that is expected to result in job losses for 600 employees. Two alternative restructuring programs are available to deal with this issue. The exact estimates of the consequences of the programs are as follows:

Option A: If program A is used, 200 jobs will be saved.

Option B: If program B is used, there is a 1/3 chance that all 600 jobs will be saved, and a 2/3 chance that no jobs will be saved.

Which program would you choose?

Now that you have thought about this first scenario, and have chosen either option A or B, consider the next scenario. The following decision-making scenario illustrates a case where a decision-maker is faced with choices that are framed in terms of losses — in this case, losses are reflected in the notion of "jobs lost". Would your ultimate choice differ from the first case?

Decision-Making Scenario 2

Your company is preparing for an economic downturn that is expected to result in job losses for 600 employees. Two alternative restructuring programs are available to deal with this issue. The exact estimates of the consequences of the programs are as follows:

Option A: If program A is used 400 jobs will be lost.

Option B: If program B is used, there is a 1/3 chance that no jobs will be lost, and a 2/3 chance that all 600 jobs will be lost.

Which program would you choose?

For many people, the choices made in Scenarios #1 and #2 differed, even though the options given remained the same. Option A is the same for Scenario #1 and #2, as is Option B. However, what may have influenced your choice was how these options were framed. Scenario 1 framed your choices in terms of gains, while Scenario 2 framed your choices as losses. According to prospect theory, we don't have consistent choices with regard to risk. When we are faced with a choice between gains — a sure gain or a possible additional, but risky, gain — we become risk-averse and choose the sure thing. However, when we are faced with a choice between losses — accepting a sure loss or risking the chance to wipe out the loss along with the chance of incurring more losses — we become risk-seekers. We will take our chances in order to avoid having to accept a sure loss or certain defeat. Kahneman and Tversky refer to the notion of loss aversion as the fact that humans are extremely averse to losses. Losses have a much more profound impact on us than do gains. That is, we will do more to avoid a sure loss than we will to seek a possible gain. The hurt of losing seems to be more powerful than the joy of winning, according to Kahneman and Tversky's research. Consequently, we tend to be more willing to accept risk in order to avoid a sure loss.

Prospect theory teaches us two important things about the non-rational side of decision making. First, we are not consistent in our choices among alternatives, even though the rational model implies that we are. Sometimes we are risk-seekers, and sometimes we are risk-avoiders. Second, prospect theory says that the decisions we make can be dependent on how we frame our options or alternatives. As we explained, if we frame our choices as choices between gains, we make more risk-averse decisions. If we frame our

---

LET'S TALK BUSINESS 3.5   FRAMING IN BUSINESS NEGOTIATIONS

One specific information processing strategy that has been found to produce biases in negotiators' cognitions is framing.[1] Recall that decision-makers are risk-averse when confronting potential gains, and risk-seeking when confronting potential losses. In the negotiation context, the risk-averse action is to accept an offered settlement, and the risk-seeking action is to hold out for more potential concessions.[2] In several studies, researchers have found that "positively framed" negotiators complete more transactions, and thus outperform "negatively framed" negotiators in a competitive market. However, "negatively framed" negotiators are able to complete transactions of greater value.[3] Essentially, then, those negotiators that frame the negotiation as a choice between losses are less likely to arrive at a negotiated settlement: they are more likely to risk an arbitrated settlement (i.e., hold out for concessions).

Based on the decision frame approach to negotiations, a number of predictions can be made concerning negotiator behaviour. First, negotiators who are risk-averse (positive frame) will be more likely to make concessions to avoid an impasse. Have you ever sold your home? Did the real estate agent make you feel that if you do not accommodate the prospective buyer you may lose the sale? This is all about risk aversion. Second, risk-seeking negotiators (negative frame) will be less likely to make concessions and more likely to risk an impasse.[4]

Source: [1] Kahneman & Tversky, 1979. [2] Northcraft & Neale, 1994. [3] Huber & Northcraft, 1987. [4] Neale & Bazerman, 1991.

---

choices as choices among losses, we tend to become more risk-seeking. This also underscores the importance of taking the time to think about how we have framed our alternatives. If you are ever faced with such a decision, consider how you may have framed your choices — as losses, or as gains, or as opportunities? Clearly, how you frame your alternatives will influence the choices you make. (See Let's Talk Business 3.5.)

DECISION FIASCOS

We began this chapter with a look at a prescriptive model of decision making: the rational model; that is, how we should make decisions. We then considered a number of factors that suggest we potentially depart from this rational process in practice. The presence of cognitive heuristics, or biases, along with the notion of decision frame, caution us to closely examine the sources of influence on how we go about making decisions.

Perhaps an even more potentially dangerous bias is the tendency to persist in a decision even after we have received information that suggests it is clearly time to abort that decision — whether it is the choice of a new product line, the decision to continue working for a certain company, or commitment to investing in the construction of a plant overseas. You may find yourself in a situation in which you fail to respond to information that suggests the decision is not productive and measures should be taken to opt out. What encourages us to sink more time, effort or money into something that clearly won't pay off? Consider the following real-life illustration, excerpted from *The Eatons: The Rise and Fall of Canada's Royal Family*:

> ... Eatons' most disastrous strategy: everyday value pricing.... Prior to launching everyday value pricing in the fall of 1990, George (Eaton) outlined the concept to a gathering of 150 key merchandisers.... Eatons marketing consultant, Martin Goldfarb, ... raised the alarm. "Everyday low pricing could never work" ... Canada was wracked by a recession; household income was shrinking. If Eatons held no sales, customers would go elsewhere.... By 1994 ... Eatons was light years behind the competition. For decades all Canadian retailers had hid behind the tariff walls. Following the launch of the Canada-US free trade agreement in 1989, three dozen US retailers invaded Canada, many of them category killers or big box stores such as Gap, Banana Republic, Talbots, Home Depot, Michaels and Wal-Mart. Grand old names began to disappear. The Bay took over Simpsons in 1991.... Woolworth closed 240 stores in 1993. Kresge was gone in 1994. Consumers Distributing went into receivership. "Eatons' response to such trends was to position itself where it had always been — everything to everybody, stuck in the middle in terms of price, merchandise, quality, assortment and service," wrote Donald Thompson.... "Eatons came to stand for nothing — not the lowest price, not the best depth in merchandise assortment and not the best service" ... No one could admit that everyday value pricing hadn't worked....
>
> Annual sales continued to fall by $100 million each year. After losing $50 million in the 1992–94 period, matters became worse. Eatons lost $80 million in 1995.... George oversaw a store-renovation plan, dubbed Eatons' 2000, that called for the expenditure of $300 million over five years. But the losses had increased debt and there was insufficient cash to service the debt and pay for all those upgrades, so in June 1995 Eatons put its real estate up for sale to raise money. Such a sell-off was a tragedy ... to dump prize assets at the bottom end of the real estate cycle....
>
> In 1995 everyday value pricing was officially and finally dumped.... For George the end was nigh. The economy was still slow and the money-losing retail arm could no longer be supported by real estate sales and profits from Eaton Credit Corp. At this rate, all assets would soon be gone, drained away by the sinkhole the stores had become. One-third of the chain's eighty-five stores were losing money....[36]

This illustration clearly outlines a commitment to a strategy, including this issue of "value pricing" even in the face of striking evidence that this was a losing course of action. Why were the signs of impending danger not sufficiently heeded? This is a question that can be levelled at any decision-maker. In fact, the organizational insider report on Nortel at the beginning of this chapter could be viewed in a similar manner. Why were any tell-tale signs of a slowdown in the high-tech sector ignored by so many organizational decision-makers? One answer suggests that this decision-making flaw, this non-rational behaviour, is not peculiar to Eatons or Nortel, but in fact is a phenomenon that can affect any decision-maker under certain conditions. In order to understand how this situation is, in fact, not unusual, we need to consider how decision-makers can depart from the last stage of the rational model of decision making.

The rational model of decision making suggested that the last stage is the notion of monitoring the decision: we want to see if the decision we implemented was successful or unsuccessful. Therefore we gather data or, perhaps, we simply receive feedback to assess the outcomes of our decision. If we have initiated a new product line, we want to assess sales in this new line and assess whether it indeed achieved the customer response we were hoping for. Obviously, if we receive negative feedback, the rational reaction would be to attempt to stop or reverse the decision. If sales on our new product line are extremely weak because there is no consumer demand for this product, then we should stop producing that line.

However, decision-makers may find themselves in a situation where they do not respond rationally to negative feedback. Imagine! There are actually cases where poor decisions are followed by more poor decisions — where a failing investment is continued, where more time and money is spent on a project that clearly is not effective. If this sounds rare, think again. We can find many cases of such situations or decision fiascos — where poor decisions were not rectified and, in fact, decision-makers grew more committed to their decisions even in the face of evidence that they should pull out of the situation, and continued to invest resources in the failing course of action. What is particularly striking about decision fiascos is the evidence that these executives received information early on that it was an unwise venture.

Researchers such as Staw and Ross have examined organizations with an eye to uncovering the elements and sources of influence on escalation, and have described the **typical escalation scenario** as situations where

- initial decision results in loss or negative outcome
- decision-maker commits more resources to the project
- further losses experienced

What is escalation of commitment to a losing course of action? Unfortunately, the newspapers are rife with examples of business bankruptcies and blunders. In recent Canadian history, the story of Eatons has become one in which critics, at least, have suggested that Eatons' "fall from grace" could have been prevented. While it is easy in hindsight to critique business decision-makers, the case of Eatons is interesting from an organizational perspective in illustrating the ease with which intelligent, experienced decision-makers can fall victim to decision biases. The excerpt above is a striking example of the potential for escalation of commitment to a failing course of action. (See Let's Talk Business 3.6.)

WHY DO WE ESCALATE COMMITMENT TO A FAILING COURSE OF ACTION?

Staw and his colleagues have identified a number of sources for escalation of commitment. These factors may be related to the nature of the project at hand, or related to the general nature of the organization, and can be broadly classified as social, structural and psychological determinants of escalation. We will briefly consider social and structural sources of influence on escalation, and then focus our attention on how psychological phenomena may lead us to escalate commitment to a failing course of action.

LET'S TALK BUSINESS 3.6   KNEE DEEP IN THE BIG MUDDY

Escalation theory focuses upon why individuals and organizations may continue to support failing projects. As one scholar observed:

> The mechanisms underlying escalating commitment may offer explanations of such diverse behaviours as shown by people who wait for an inordinately long time for a bus . . . the organization that sticks with a failing venture, and the nation that finds itself "knee deep in the big muddy" in an international conflict....[1]

Source: [1] Brockner, 1992: 39.

Social and Structural Determinants

Social determinants of escalation of commitment may hold an individual to a course of action, regardless of whether the person has lost faith in the possible success of the project or the utility of its purposes. For example, the notion of "saving face" reflects the potential to pursue the same course of action in order to maintain a certain relationship with others. A decision-maker may have found that the initial choice is failing. If the decision to abort is taken, the decision-maker may lose credibility with colleagues, consumers, employees. Consequently, there may be pressure for the decision-maker to avoid the appearance of "bailing out".

Structural determinants of escalation may include a variety of **economic, technical** or **political** obstacles to bailing out of a project. The structural features of an organization and its interaction patterns can influence how escalation situations are handled. For example, the political support for a venture may prevent decision-makers from abandoning the decision. The question for a business executive to consider is, who supports this decision? It could be the case that a decision to abort a plan of action may be viewed as an insult to those who initiated the decision. Depending on the power relationships, it may be difficult to step back and move away from a plan of action implemented by those who wield relatively greater power in the organization.

Another structural obstacle may stem from **administrative inertia**. For feedback to be effective, it must flow through the organization to those decision-makers responsible. However, the nature of the organization may be such that to turn around a failing decision is simply too difficult for a bureaucratic organization once the wheels are in motion. Further, the decision may be part of a series of institutionalized practices that cannot easily be overturned. Certain organizational practices can become institutionalized as legitimate and embedded in the mindset of the organization. In the case of decision making, it may be the case that though the prospects appear dim, the accepted practice of letting the decision continue may preclude any rational attempt to abort the decision. For example, the government's decision to give more money to the failing

Hyundai plant in Bromont, Quebec, several years ago, may have been considered politically acceptable, since the number of jobs at stake was high, and to withdraw support may have been viewed as unacceptable in the context of the government's role as protector of business.

Psychological Determinants

Decision-makers may be faced with the dilemma of stopping a failing investment and, consequently, being forced to admit defeat: that is, admission that the decision was poor. If decision-makers feel this sense of allegiance to carry out their initial decision, they will be less likely to pull out, even in difficult times. This is related to the notion of saving face — that is, maintaining public confidence in their ability as an effective decision-maker. All this suggests the need for self-justification: convincing oneself of the wisdom of one's choice even in the face of contradictory evidence. After all we all want to feel that we are wise, rational decision-makers.

Sunk costs. There is a traditional image of humans as being "prospectively rational". Under prospective rationality, the individual will process information and make decisions to attain a high level of outcomes. However, when ego defensiveness is dominant, individuals will behave in a retrospectively rational manner — i.e., they will re-evaluate alternatives and outcomes to make it appear that they acted rationally. The most critical element separating **prospective** from **retrospective rationality** is the individual's treatment of **sunk costs**. Under prospective rationality, resources are allocated, and decisions entered into, when future benefits are greater than future costs. Sunk costs (previous losses/costs that are not expected to recur) should not enter into decision calculations. Under retrospective rationality, there may be a motivation to rectify past losses, as well as to seek future gain.

Sunk costs will be considered to appear rational. This desire to recoup costs underlies much self-justification.[37] Clearly, this view also provides an understanding of decision dysfunctions and failures. Specifically, the need to justify sunk costs will impede decision-makers from objectively and critically examining the utility of the investment. However, if performance evaluation is based on process, clearly throwing good money after bad is not rational (retrospectively or prospectively). This view is in contrast to the traditional image of humans as prospectively rational (the rational model) which assumes individuals will process information and make decisions to attain a high level of outcomes.

Framing and decision fiascos. If you recall, prospect theory suggests that how we frame our choices can lead us to be risk-averse or risk-seeking in our decisions. Escalation inherently involves taking on more risk — becoming a risk-seeker. This suggests that those decision-makers who frame their choices as choices among losses are more likely to escalate commitment to failing course of action. Framing effects can explain the occurrence of decision failures or fiascos, because many of the decisions have a common structure. Decisions that lead to failures/fiascos are most naturally framed as a choice between two or more unattractive options. Further, the reference level suggested by the problem leads to the choice being interpreted as one between losses, rather than a choice between gains.

The decision to escalate commitment or to withdraw support can be seen as an example of a decision-maker under risk. Project abandonment is seen as accepting a certain loss, whereas escalation is perceived as possibly increasing losses combined with a chance that losses may be avoided. The belief that sunk costs are relevant in decision making creates the perception of a choice between losses. Escalating commitment is the natural consequence of negatively framing a decision about the fate of an entire course of action.

Avoiding Decision-Making Fiascos

This chapter has attempted to illustrate the potential pitfalls that decision-makers face in their efforts to engage in a rational process of decision making. In this section, we can turn our attention to some of the ways we can try to avoid the pitfalls that we outlined earlier. In other words, **what should we do to minimize decision errors?** Management scholars have offered many suggestions to avoid the cycle of project escalation and stop the outflow of money and resources. They advocate a number of ways to de-escalate commitment to failing projects, including the following:[38]

1.   Don't Ignore Negative Feedback

Decision-makers need to be aware of the human and societal biases that may encourage escalation. This demands a greater sensitivity toward recognizing the presence of negative feedback as warning signs that can aid in problem recognition. It is not uncommon for executives to convince themselves that a project will succeed, and that success is "just around the corner". This demands that decision-makers continually seek to **improve perceptual accuracy in decisions**. This may involve increasing awareness of cognitive biases and personal values, and questioning the mental model assumptions; for example, our discussion of framing illustrated that we can become prisoners of how we frame our choices in a decision.

Glen Whyte, a researcher in decision making, advocates the practice of multiple framing — that is, that we try to see a problem and its alternatives in different lights — to ensure that we are not being influenced simply by how our options are framed. Related to the notion of framing is the issue of sunk costs: our future decisions should not be driven by how much time, money or effort we have sunk into some project. That is, our decision to continue with an investment, for example, should not be led by how much money we have put in to this point. Rather, we should be led by our belief regarding what, realistically, will be the payoff of our investment. If the project is clearly a failing one, we should bail out, if we are being completely rational. Whyte's research suggests that when firms that are performing poorly engage in more risk, it simply increases the rate of organizational decline. We should treat sunk costs as just that — sunk. (See Let's Talk Business 3.7.)

LET'S TALK BUSINESS 3.7   STUDENT ESCALATION

Imagine the scenario of a university student who remains in a chosen program for several years after the student has perceived the program to be a "failing course of action" — the student believes he/she has entered the "wrong" program in university; they are uninterested in their course of study; they have no desire to enter that field as a professional after graduation. Why are they continuing with this program? Why not switch to another program? Their answer typically is: "I have invested too much time and money to turn back." Isn't that irrational? Shouldn't the choice of program be based on level of interest and desire to practice in that field? Choices are being driven by past costs rather than future benefits. One of the fundamental lessons of this notion of sunk costs is: They should not drive future decisions!

---

2.   Hire an "External Auditor" to Provide a More Objective Assessment

Given the personal biases that can arise and, consequently, encourage escalation, the use of an independent third party to provide an unbiased report on the decision is advisable. This individual would gather evidence that would ultimately support or refute the soundness of the decision, and this examination would occur free from personal attachment to the project. An external consultant can assess the severity of any problems and, potentially, help the executives responsible for these projects to extricate themselves and their organizations from failing courses of action. This may involve helping to facilitate the search for alternative courses of action. The biases we have discussed also highlight the importance of comparing our perceptions with those of colleagues: how I frame a problem may differ from your framing.

3.   Don't Be Afraid to Withhold Further Funding

One way to aid in withdrawal from a failing course of action is to discontinue the transfer of resources into that action. This also puts the project on hold until such time that an alternative course of action can be generated, or in gathering evidence to confirm the status of the original decision. The rational model suggests that organizations should encourage decision-makers to develop systematic procedures for any problem. While human cognition may have its limitations, the rational model advocates an organized, systematic identification of alternatives before decisions are made, and reminds us that the outcomes of our decisions must be monitored. Organizations can implement a formal ceiling on a decision, and funds can automatically be cut off if the decision continues to incur losses beyond a certain point. To avoid escalation of commitment, researchers have suggested that the organization have some kind of stop-loss routine — whereby the decision to abort a project, for example, is automatic beyond a certain point, rather than relying wholly on the decision-maker to choose the point at which he or she will pull out of the project.

96

4. *Manage Impressions*

The notion of face saving is a major influence on escalation. Clearly, the need to maintain a favourable public image would discourage a decision-maker from aborting their original path; it is akin to admitting defeat. Consequently, there is a tendency to want to continue a failing project in the hope of turning it around and saving face. If organizations were designed to accept failure and perceive it as a learning experience, there may be less emphasis on the need to persist in a failing course of action. Business decision-makers would be more likely to extricate themselves from failing courses of action when conditions permit them to manage impressions and save face in the process. Ego-defensiveness, self-justification and face saving all suggest the risk that decision-makers can focus on impressions rather than sound decisions. If the impressions of the decision-maker interfere with rational judgments, then it may be productive to separate the decision-maker from the decision-monitor or implementer. This suggests that those who monitor the consequences of the decision and have the authority to act on this feedback should not have any stake or commitment to maintaining the decision. It would avoid the potential pitfall of wanting to keep alive one's own pet project, or save face, or somehow feeling committed to maintaining a failing decision. If the decision-maker or chooser is separated from the implementer or monitor, there is little risk of ego-defence in reactions to negative feedback.

CHAPTER SUMMARY

Should we all strive to become rational decision-makers? From our discussions, one might easily conclude that the aim is to become a purely rational decision-maker. However, that is not really the aim of our discussions. It is hoped that you will think more critically about the potential biases you might fall victim to as decision-makers. However, it is important to note that the rational model is not necessarily the ideal one.

Many other models of decision making have been put forth. Some encourage things like creative and intuitive decision making, and, consequently, do not necessarily advocate a systematic, organized approach to making successful decisions. For example, there is a model that has been referred to as the intuitive decision-making model. This model actually focuses on experience and judgment rather than sequential steps in arriving at decisions. You have probably heard the term "gut feeling"; that is really what this model advocates. It considers managerial judgment as more important than the traditional, so-called rational, approach. For example, given the notion of bounded rationality — that is, the inability to collect, gather or process all available information — this model suggests that more emphasis be placed on intuition that comes with experience. If you consider some of the great entrepreneurial, artistic or scientific achievements of our time, they may arguably have been the product of intuitive, rather than rational, decision making.

Perhaps, then, the main lesson of this chapter is to understand how our decision process can operate in both rational and non-rational ways. We need to understand decision biases in order to avoid non-rational behaviour where it is dysfunctional. And, at a minimum, we need to understand the factors, rational and non-rational, that affect our judgments.

KEY TERMS

- programmed decisions
- non-programmed decisions
- bounded rationality
- satisficing
- cognitive heuristics
- representative heuristic
- availability heuristic
- overconfidence heuristic

- the paradox of entrepreneurs
- decision frame
- escalation of commitment to a failing course of action
- administrative inertia
- sunk costs
- retrospective rationality
- prospective rationality

CASE APPLICATION   High-tech decision making

In 1996, Gary Winnick hatched a plan to build the world's largest fibre-optic network — placing a multi-billion dollar bet that the growth of the Internet would translate into strong demand and huge profits for companies offering global data and phone services.

To achieve this ambitious goal, Global Crossing Ltd. spent US$20-billion to build a worldwide network of thousands of miles of underwater cables. Much of this spending spree was carried out using junk bonds, a financing vehicle intimately familiar to Mr. Winnick as a one-time associate of junk-bond king Michael Milken.

In theory, Global Crossing's business made a lot of sense.

If the Internet's growth came close to meeting the lofty expectations set out by experts like George Gilder, fibre-optic carriers like Global Crossing would be a crucial element.

This optimism propelled sales at equipment makers like Nortel Networks Corp. and JDS Uniphase Corp., and made fibre-optics companies investor darlings.

The harsh reality, however, is that Global Crossing made the wrong bet. The Hamilton, Bermuda-based company's vision that if it built the network, customers would come did not materialize. Instead, the Internet's growth — while still spectacular — has been far more modest than analysts expected.

As a result, the surge in demand and revenue Global Crossing was counting on never appeared. To make matters worse, Global Crossing was plagued by competition from a variety of carriers pursuing the same strategy.

"The short-term problem was that there [were] too many people chasing the market, and financing hit a brick wall," said Lawrence Surtees, an analyst with IDC Canada Ltd.

At the end of the day, Global Crossing's business was simply not viable. After much speculation, the company sank into bankruptcy yesterday, burdened with US$12.4-billion of debt and a stock price that has fallen to less than a US$1 from a high of US$64.25.

David Willis, vice-president of global networking strategy with the Meta Group in Plano, Tex., said that the long-haul market connecting global destinations has become a commodity business that will continue to see steady growth; regardless of whether companies like Global Crossing reduce prices to stimulate demand.

Instead, Mr. Willis said the key strategic element is the last mile — the final link between carriers and consumers.

This market, which hinges on the growth of high-speed connections using cable and phone networks, is still in its infancy. Until the last mile market reaches critical mass and consumers start buying services such as streaming video, there will be limited demand for global networking services from Global Crossing and its competitors.

In many ways, the global fibre-optic market is evolving much like the railway and automobile industries.

The industry pioneers make huge investments to establish new markets and, as a reward, get to experience the growing pains. The second-generation of entrepreneurs then arrive, and they pick up the assets at bargain-basement prices, and are able to build sustainable, profitable businesses with them.

In the case of Global Crossing, the second-generation is Singapore Technologies Telemedia Pte. Ltd. and Hong Kong billionaire Li Ka-shing's Hutchison Whampoa Ltd., which purchased a majority stake in Global Crossing for US$750-million.

Hutchison Whampoa is the biggest Asian investor in wireless telecommunications in Europe. It holds permits to offer wireless services in the United Kingdom, Italy and other countries.

Hutchison Whampoa also owns half of a Hong Kong phone venture with Asia Global Crossing Ltd., which is majority owned by Global Crossing.

In the final analysis, it could be argued that Global Crossing was perhaps ahead of its time by attempting to build [a] multi-billion dollar business without sufficient demand in the short-term to survive until the market eventually matures.

"Does it mean these guys were smoking something or had a bad idea?" Mr. Surtees mused. "I don't think so. If it was a bad idea, Hutchison Whampoa wouldn't have come and in and bought the assets for less than 10¢ on the dollar."

Source: Mark Evans, "Big bet went wrong when the horse fell. Internet let them down: Next generation of entrepreneurs waits to pick up the pieces" *Financial Post* (January 29, 2002). Reproduced with permission of the publisher.

QUESTIONS

1. How likely is it that the decision making in this case followed a rational model?

2. How might escalation of commitment and decision frame influence a decision-maker in this type of scenario?

3. What advice would you give decision-makers embarking upon risky ventures?

RELATED READING	Should we make big bets in business?

When Microsoft boss Steve Ballmer got up to speak about The Agile Business at the Rotman School of Management at the University of Toronto, much of what he had to say — in a very loud, forceful voice — was predictable. Successful companies like Microsoft need a clear vision and priorities, the agility to adapt, and strong leadership, he said. No one would disagree with that. But the man who founder Bill Gates hired as employee No. 30 in 1980, after he dropped out of Stanford Business School (Gates dropped out of Harvard), added a couple of surprising attributes.

The first was something that most managers would never dream of, the creation of employee excitement. Ballmer said that could be created by hiring smart individuals who were passionate about the changes technology can make to people's lives. The other key is a willingness to make "big bets." Though that strategy was not suitable for all companies, since failure could be cataclysmic, it was appropriate for Microsoft.

"If we get in a cycle where we're not making big bets, we're going to miss the next big trend in our business," he argued. Ballmer said his company had made three big bets in its history: on Windows, on NT technology, and on .NET, its gamble on the Internet. What he didn't say is that many observers criticize Microsoft for not making its bet on the Internet years ago.

Ballmer's description of Microsoft as "longer term and bet-focused" is intriguing. Certainly people who start and run small- or medium-sized businesses make substantial bets all the time, both because they are entrepreneurial and because of the risky nature of smaller businesses. But it's unusual for the CEO of a very large company to talk about making large gambles. As I listened to the rest of Ballmer's speech, I jotted down a list of Canadian companies — which, in general, have a reputation for being risk-averse — that have made big bets. (I didn't even try to list companies that create employee excitement, as opposed to the more familiar sullen resignation.)

Companies can make bets on products, as Microsoft has done, on mergers and acquisitions and on management, or they can try to reinvent what they do and what they stand for. Many Canadian high-tech companies have successfully made large bets on products. The most obvious, despite the downturn that started last September, are the bets that Nortel made on optical networking and JDS Uniphase on optical components. As a result, Nortel expanded its international reputation and JDS acquired one.

In financial services, our largest insurance companies reinvented themselves by demutualizing, or changing their owners from policyholders to shareholders. Because of this, for example, in less than two years Manulife has become one of the top dozen most profitable public companies in the country, with a market value of almost $20 billion. TD has been the boldest of the banks. Its biggest bet was not its successful acquisition of the widely admired Canada Trust, but its decision in the 1980s not to acquire an investment bank, which is what each of its competitors did. Instead, TD built up its own discount broker, and now TD Waterhouse is one of the world's largest and most successful discount operations.

Edgar Bronfman Jr. was widely criticized for the big bet he made in 1995 when he sold Seagram's 25% interest in DuPont, a proven money-spinner, in order to build up V.O.'s entertainment holdings. When he sold Seagram to France's Vivendi last year, the consensus was that he'd failed to establish a company with enough heft to compete against global giants like AOL Time Warner. The legacy of Bronfman's big bet was that the company his grandfather founded in 1928 no longer exists.

Source: By Douglas Goold from *Report on Business Magazine* (June 2001) 17(12): 13. Reproduced with permission from The Globe and Mail.

QUESTIONS

1. Explain the notion of "making big bets". What does this mean?

2. What is the argument here? Why should organizations make big bets?

3. Does this advice follow the view of rational, or non-rational, decision making?

III

The Landscape of Organizations

Assessing the Organizational Landscape

It is an obvious fact that we are a society of organizations — from our hospitals, to our schools to our multinational organizations, it is hard to imagine life without organizations. And, for better or worse, those very institutions and organizations that we have grown up with are continuing to undergo dramatic change. To understand what is going on out there, we need to first consider several things. What exactly are organizations? What constitutes the structure or anatomy of an organization? Why do different organizations have different structures? These are among the key questions addressed in this chapter.

LEARNING OBJECTIVES

By the end of the chapter, you should be able to:

1. Explain how metaphors lead our thinking about organizations.
2. Discuss the notion of organizations as open systems.
3. Identify the six elements of organizational structure.
4. Describe Mintzberg's classification of the organizational landscape.

Organizational Insider

Organizational Structure Is in the News: From Car Manufacturers . . .

GM is changing its organizational structure to become more competitive. The aim is to reduce bureaucracy and the rigid rules that impede innovation in car design. In the past, a new vehicle would start with designers who created the concept. Next, it would go to brand managers for their input. Then manufacturing bosses would take their turn and decide what chassis, platform, and parts to use. Finally, engineers would make a few more alterations. Little communication would occur among the parties in the various departments. The design would also involve huge delays as it made its way through the myriad of approvals required at various levels in the GM hierarchy.

Under the new organizational structure, GM can focus on making better vehicles, with those closest to the market making collaborative decisions regarding the model design. Of course, the success of this new structure will, in part, depend on the willingness of the different departments within the huge corporation to work together. Each new-vehicle program will boast a team of engineers, designers, accountants, researchers, and product planners working in concert. Under the new system, design moves to the forefront. For every vehicle idea, three teams will compete to create what will eventually make it to market.[1]

. . . to Marketing Firms

Mosaic Group, a direct marketer, said it will cut up to 10% of its staff and warned its earnings will fail to hit estimates. The Toronto-based firm — a provider of results-driven, measurable marketing solutions for global brands — said the layoffs are part of a massive restructuring, with 2001 revenue coming in at $755-million to $760-million.... Mosaic, which operates in Canada, the United States and Britain, will issue its 2001 year-end results by March 5. "The new organizational structure, leadership and other internal changes support our plan to simplify the business for our brand partners, the investment community and employees alike," said Marc Byron, chief executive. The reorganization is designed to divide the company's independent units into four business units, with three divisions focusing on North America — performance solutions, marketing and technology, and sales — and the fourth division to be dubbed Mosaic United Kingdom.[2]

Sources:

1. Based on David Welch, "At GM Bob Lutz maps a different route" *BusinessWeek* magazine (February 1, 2002).
2. From David Steinhart, "Mosaic plans layoffs, Profit to miss estimates" *Financial Post* (January 25, 2002). Reproduced with permission from the Financial Post.

THINKING ABOUT ORGANIZATIONS

The Organizational Insider tells the story of how organizations in many industries have been redesigning their organizational structure. This is not a new phenomenon. Consider recent events in the corporate world. Why, in the 1990s, did AT & T, America's largest telephone company, choose to split itself into three separate enterprises? Why did Toyota of Japan decide to eliminate three of its seven layers of management, and IBM Canada cut its levels from 10 to about four? Why have many of Canada's largest corporations radically redesigned their business?

Organizations in just about every industrialized nation have been undergoing change. Some companies reduced the number of levels in their hierarchy or laid off employees at all levels, others have undergone a concurrent change in their whole business process, while others have simply closed down. Fundamentally, what we have seen is a major rethinking of how organizations should be designed. Many observers have suggested that what we are witnessing is nothing less than a revolution in the corporate world! In order to understand what is happening and, more important, why it is happening, we need to understand more about the design or structure of organizations. The aim of this chapter is to offer an insight into the anatomy of organizations and ultimately to explain why organizations are being redesigned: in other words, what is behind the corporate revolutions we are witnessing.

What Is an Organization?

What do you think of when you think of an "organization"? We can identify three broad categories of organizations:

1. public/governmental organizations that provide goods and services without necessarily generating a profit;
2. private/non-governmental organizations, including voluntary organizations, that offer goods or services without necessarily generating a profit; and
3. private organizations that produce goods or services with the intent of making a profit for the benefit of their owners or shareholders.

Though we can observe such diverse organizations that operate in these very different sectors, we can also identify underlying characteristics that are common to all organizations. In fact, it is useful to consider a very fundamental question as a starting part in our examination of the nature of organizations. What is an organization? How do we define it? Nortel, GM, Microsoft, your high school, St. John Ambulance — what do all these entities have in common? Organizations may be large corporations or small non-profit organizations; they might be housed within a large skyscraper; or they could simply be composed of members who are spread across a wide location. What makes all these things organizations?

Using Metaphors to Describe Organizations

One helpful method of understanding the nature of organizations is through the use of metaphors. According to Gareth Morgan, a management scholar and author of *Images of Organization*, we can consider the notion of an organization as, essentially, a social construction. That is, we are giving a tangible name to something that we take for granted. Words, names, concepts, ideas, facts, observations, etc., do not so much denote external "things" as conceptions of things activated in the mind. They are not to be seen as a representation of a reality "out there", but as tools for capturing and dealing with what is **perceived** to be "out there".[39] Hence, we understand the usefulness of metaphors. A metaphor is often regarded as no more than a literary and descriptive device for embellishment, but more fundamentally it is a creative form that produces its effect through a crossing of images. A metaphor proceeds through assertions that "subject A is like B and . . ." Through the processes of comparison, between the images of A and B, we generate new meaning. The use of metaphors serves to generate an image for studying a subject. Different images of a subject guide and, ultimately, shape what is seen.

In more practical terms — what are the common features of these things that we call "organizations"? Why does this label fit a variety of entities, from non-profit to for-profit contexts? Metaphors are useful to help us describe and, ultimately, understand these social constructions. Consider dictionary definitions of the term "organization". The Oxford English Dictionary has defined it as a term used primarily to describe the action of organizing or the state of being organized, particularly in a biological sense. Also, the term has been considered as referring to "an organized body, system or society". The state of being organized in a biological sense was the basis of the metaphor of arranging or coordinating.

The term "organization" as a depiction of a social institution is relatively new, and creates a new meaning through metaphorical extension of older meanings. Ultimately, the importance of the metaphors we use to describe our hospitals, businesses, places of worship, etc., are important because they lead our thinking about the nature of these places, how they should be designed, and how they should function. Let's consider an example of how metaphors guide our thinking in the area of management philosophy.

In many ways, the different schools of thought with regard to organizational theories arise from insights associated with different metaphors for the study of organizations. Consider, for example, the theories of management, discussed in another chapter. The classical schools of management thought, including scientific management, administrative management, and bureaucratic management, can be viewed as arising from a specific conceptualization or metaphor of what organizations represent. Arguably, the classical school of management thought is based implicitly on a conception of organizations that employs a **"machine metaphor"**. Machines are perceived as entities that function in a prescribed, rational manner. They are devised to perform work toward specific goals, structure, and technology. Consequently, some organizational scholars, implicitly drawing on such a conception or metaphor of organizations as machines, emphasize an analysis and design of the formal structure of an organization and its technology. These scholars have explained the purpose of organizations as they would a machine — to function in an orderly, prescribed and controlled manner. The aim, then, is to design organizations as if they were machines. Taylor's notion of "economic man", and Weber's notion of the "faceless bureaucrat", are natural extensions of the principles of the machine metaphor of organizations. Scientific management encompasses the notions of control and efficiency — objectives well fitted to a machine metaphor of organizations. Of course, managers or management scholars whose philosophy is based on a machine metaphor will be led by such a metaphor. Consequently, the classical schools of management thought focused only on those issues

EXHIBIT 4.1	WHAT DOES "ORGANIZATION" MEAN TO YOU?

- Organization as machine
- Organization as living organism
- Organization as political system
- Organization as theatre
- Organization as sports team
- Organization as family

pertinent to this metaphor: rules, regulations, a bureaucratic structure, etc. Human needs had no relevance in such a metaphor or model.

Of course, management thought has also been affected by other metaphors. For example, the "organism metaphor" encompasses a conception of organizations as systems of mutually connected and dependent parts constituted to share a common life. This metaphor suggests that we can conceive organizations as living organisms that contain a combination of elements differentiated yet integrated, attempting to survive within the context of a wider environment. The open-systems approach of organizations, discussed below, is based on this metaphor. And with regard to management philosophies (see Chapter 2), the behavioural school of management thought is, in fact, based on this metaphor. Consequently, these schools are concerned with sustaining human motivation and treating organizations as social systems. In other words, the organizational metaphor implicitly underlies and, ultimately, guides thinking of how organizations should be designed and managed.

Certainly, we can apply myriad metaphors to try to advance our understanding of what organizations really represent. Among some of the more popular conceptions of organizations in terms of metaphors are: organizations as political systems;[40] organizations as loosely coupled systems;[41] organizations as theatres;[42] organizations as a collection of cultures.[43] (See Exhibit 4.1.) No one metaphor can capture the total nature of organizational life. New metaphors can be created for viewing and understanding organizations. Indeed, the very nature of the study of organizations and the field of organizational theory is metaphorical; that is, it is subjective in many ways. The notion of "organizations as systems" is one such metaphor whose implications we will explore in more detail below. This metaphor has guided organizational theories regarding structure and design.

Organizations as Systems

Scholars who have studied organizations have generated countless perspectives on the nature of these entities. One useful perspective involves the view of organizations as systems. How might the metaphor of an organization as a "system" guide our understanding with regard to how organizations operate and sustain themselves?

A system can de defined as interdependent elements working together to achieve a goal or goals. The interdependence of the elements creates an entity that is more than just the sum of its parts — something is achieved beyond the mere putting together of these separate components. The notion of organizations as systems is intended to guide our understanding of what organizations are all about and how they function and survive.[44] Specifically, the notion of an open system asserts that organizations are entities that are embedded in, and dependent on exchanges with, the environment within which they operate. In addition, organizations can be viewed as social systems, with people constituting the basic elements.

Interestingly, there have been times when organizations have been viewed as closed systems, with the belief that how organizations function and survive depends on their ability to remain divorced from their environment. Closed systems have been defined as fully self-sufficient entities requiring no interaction with the environment, and this clearly makes this metaphor difficult to find in practice. When observers first theorized about the nature of organizations, many scholars viewed these entities as closed systems. That is, they viewed the organization as, potentially, a self-sufficient entity. This guiding metaphor led much organizational thinking to focus on the organization's internal environment with regard to dealing with organizational functioning and survival. At the same time, this approach failed to recognize the role that the external environment can have in the operations of the organization.

It was only when the environment became sufficiently volatile and complex that theorists recognized the futility of viewing organizations as closed systems. It became necessary to embrace the open systems metaphor and further acknowledge the critical importance of the notion that organizations are embedded in their environment, requiring resources from and generating outputs to their environment. This also underscored the importance of further understanding the nature of the organization's external environment. (See Exhibit 4.2.)

An organization's environment represents all elements that exist outside the organization and that can, potentially, influence or affect the organization in some way. As mentioned elsewhere, the open-systems perspective of organizations emphasizes the importance of the environment and interaction with the environment. Clearly, organizations are dependent on the environment for their survival and success. Without obtaining the necessary environmental inputs, whether they are suitable employees or the raw materials for production, organizations cannot function effectively. Similarly, if organizations fail to generate the types of products or services sought by the environment, then, too, these organizations will cease to exist. As suggested earlier, organizations are created in response to societal or environmental needs; and ultimately, it is the environment that will determine the organization's fate.

So What Is an Organization?

Given the implications of the systems approach to organization, we can generate the following definition of organizations:

1. **Organizations are social entities.** Clearly, all the examples cited above have at least one common element — they are made up of people! They are entities that have been generated and are maintained by people. They involve some level of human interaction.

EXHIBIT 4.2 ORGANIZATIONS AS OPEN SYSTEMS

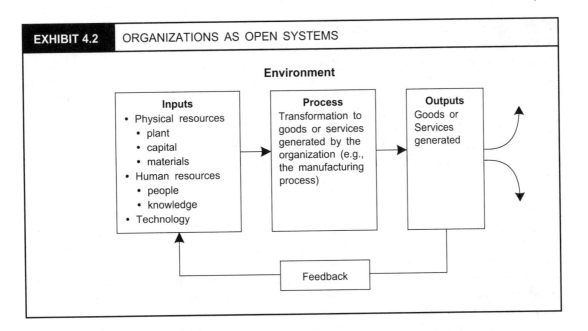

2. **Organizations interact with the environment.** Can you think of any organization that is not somehow linked to its external environment? Think about it. An organization obtains inputs from its environment, whether in the form of people, raw materials, technology or financial capital. All these inputs are transformed by the organization and become outputs: the goods, services or knowledge that the organization generates.

3. **Organizations are created to achieve goals.** That is, they are goal directed. Whether it is a profit-making organization or a non-profit organization, all organizations have some kind of goal or objective they were designed to achieve.

4. **Organizations possess some sort of structure.** All organizations need some kind of structure to ensure the work is properly allocated and coordinated. Of course, it is not so straightforward, defining precisely what organizational structure is. What do we mean when we say that organizations possess a structure? How are organizations structured? We will address these questions below.

THE ANATOMY OF AN ORGANIZATION ———

What is organizational structure? The image of an organizational chart might come to mind for some of you. And, in fact, the organizational chart is a reflection of the underlying structure of an organization. However, there is a more specific notion of organizational structure. Organizational structure has been defined as a deliberately planned

EXHIBIT 4.3	THE SIX DEFINING ELEMENTS OF ORGANIZATIONAL STRUCTURE

1. Work Specialization
2. Chain of Command
3. Centralization
4. Span of Control
5. Formalization
6. Departmentation

network or pattern of relationships that exists among individuals in various roles or positions. This includes the formal hierarchy of authority, the distribution or grouping of work (for example into departments), and the rules or procedures that control and coordinate behaviour in the organization. However, we can move beyond this definition and attempt to examine more systematically the dimensions along which organizational structure can be described (Exhibit 4.3).

What Constitutes an Organization's Structure?

1. Work Specialization

One fundamental question that must be addressed in designing organizational structure is, how are we going to divide up the work that must be done to achieve organizational goals? **Horizontal differentiation** represents the degree of differentiation between horizontal (as opposed to vertical) units of the organization, based on things like the orientation of the members, the nature of their jobs and their education or training. The greater the number of occupations in an organization that require specialized knowledge and skills, the more complex the organization. One obvious dimension of horizontal differentiation is job specialization. The term specialization, or division of labour, refers to the degree to which organizational tasks are subdivided into separate jobs. There are fundamentally two different kinds of specialization: functional and social specialization. **Functional specialization** refers to the division of jobs into simple, repetitive tasks. If you recall the discussion (in another chapter) of Frederick Taylor's scientific management, his philosophy of managing advocated a high degree of job specialization; that is, Taylor argued that to maximize worker efficiency, jobs should be divided up into their smallest components, so that workers perform simple, specific and repetitive tasks. More recently, there has been a dramatic shift in beliefs regarding the degree of job specialization that should be implemented at work. Approaches to job redesign, like job enrichment, essentially advocate a low degree of job specialization: that is, rather than performing one narrow task, employees in some organizations perform a wide range of tasks. Job enrichment involves provid-

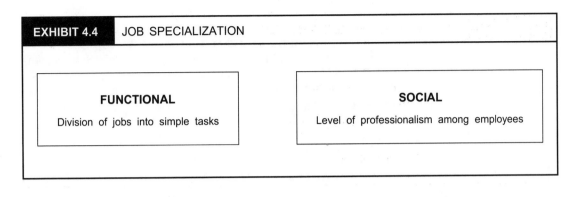

ing employees with more challenging and meaningful work largely by allowing them to increase the variety of work they perform, and the level of autonomy or freedom they have in performing the work.

Social specialization refers to the specialization of individuals, rather than the specialization of jobs. Social specialization is accomplished through the employment of professionals whose skills cannot be easily routinized. For example, an accountant who performs an audit does so through the application of specialized, trained skills. Similarly, engineers, nurses, doctors and professors are specialized professionals whose skills have been developed in a specific area or specialty.

2. *Chain of Command*

The notion of chain of command addresses the question: "To whom do employees report?" That is, we need to consider what kind of authority structure will be put in place to ensure work is coordinated and controlled. The chain of command refers to the line of authority that extends from the top of the organization to the lowest level. This is the administering function of the organization. Each managerial position is given a place on this chain with a corresponding degree of authority.

As with the notion of job specialization, the philosophy regarding the chain of command has also changed dramatically over the 20th century. Again, if we think back to the days of Frederick Taylor and the Industrial Revolution, there was a strong belief in the principle of unity of command. That is, management philosophy in the earlier part of the 20th century reflected the view that there should be an unbroken chain of command or line of authority. What this principle suggests is that an employee should have only one supervisor or boss to whom he or she is directly responsible. Why was that considered to be such an important principle? The view was that, in addition to keeping the job simple for employees (for reasons we discussed earlier), there should also be a clear and simple line of authority. The subordinate should know who is giving the orders, and he or she should not be confused by potentially conflicting demands of more than one boss. Later in the 20th century, the principle of the unbroken chain was given much less consideration. For example, the notion of worker empowerment is a move toward shifting much greater levels of responsibility back to employees, so that, in a sense, they are at least partly their own bosses. One popular example of the trend toward less emphasis on one boss is the use of self-managing work teams. These essentially are collections of workers who work together on a project or task and largely manage themselves. Some organizations that have employed self-managing teams include GM's Saturn division, Motorola, Frito Lay, Shell and Microsoft, to name but a few. The need to have one all-powerful boss is no longer considered the best way of designing organizations.

3.   Centralization

Where does authority rest within the organization? That is, what level in the organizational hierarchy has decision-making authority? This raises the question of centralization-decentralization.

Fundamentally, decision-making power can rest at the top of the organizational hierarchy. For example, if top management makes all the important decisions, with little or no input from lower levels of the organization, this would be considered a highly centralized decision-making structure. On the other hand, if decision-making authority is not concentrated at the top level, but rather is spread to the lower levels, this is referred to as decentralized decision making. As with the other elements we have discussed to this point, the 20th century also witnessed great changes in the relative concentration of decision-making authority. Essentially, many organizations chose to move from centralized to more decentralized structures. Largely, this move was intended to make organizations more efficient and speedier in their decision-making ability. Centralized organizations typically require longer time frames for decisions to be made. For example, it takes much longer for the head office of a geographically diverse operation to make decisions about its operations in another corner of the world than it would if that operation had authority to make its own decisions.

4.   Span of Control

How many levels of those in charge do we have? To address this issue, we can consider the notion of hierarchy of authority. The hierarchy is very much connected to something called the span of control. The span of control refers to the number of employees reporting to a supervisor. Obviously, it can vary from organization to organization, depending on how many subordinates it is felt a manager can effectively direct.

The span of control is important because it really determines the number of managers and levels there are in the organizational hierarchy, something also referred to as **vertical differentiation**. How does the span of control determine the number of managers and levels? Consider the following examples. (See Exhibit 4.5.)

Imagine two organizations with the same total number of seven members, but with different spans of control; so that in Organization X, there is an average span of control of two and it has three levels of hierarchy (the president, two managers and four subordinates). In Organization Y, which also has a total of seven members, the span of control is six — there are only two levels in the hierarchy. (This organization might be considered as having one central leader, with all employees as one self-managing team who only report to one boss: the president.)

We can describe Organization X as having

- a relatively narrower span of control (two) compared to Organization Y, which has a wider span of control (six).
- a taller hierarchical structure (three levels of hierarchy), compared to Organization Y, which is relatively flatter (two levels of hierarchy). That is, the span of control clearly determines how "flat" or how "tall" an organization is.

In general terms, a narrow span of control tends to reflect a tall organization; while a wide span of control tends to reflect a flat organization. What difference does it make how many subordinates a supervisor oversees? What difference does it make how many levels of hierarchy exist within an organization? First, it has been argued that maintaining small or narrow spans of control improves a manager's ability to manage. Think about it — a manager who oversees, say, a handful of employees is much more capable of maintaining close supervision than a manager with a wide span of control who is responsible for a large number of employees. However, there are also downsides to the narrow span of control: they are costly! Why? Quite simply, because they add layers of manage-

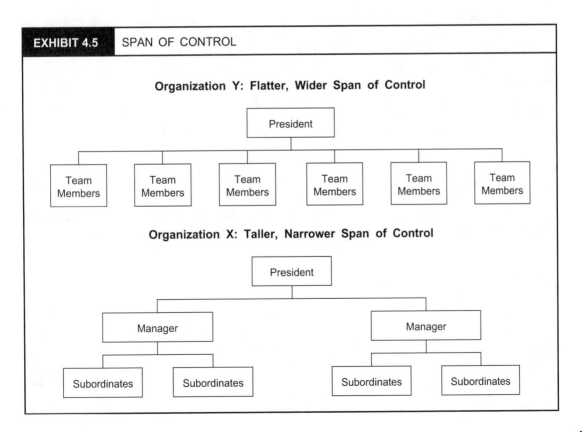

EXHIBIT 4.5 SPAN OF CONTROL

Organization Y: Flatter, Wider Span of Control

President

Team Members | Team Members | Team Members | Team Members | Team Members | Team Members

Organization X: Taller, Narrower Span of Control

President

Manager | Manager

Subordinates | Subordinates | Subordinates | Subordinates

LET'S TALK BUSINESS 4.1   DECISIONS MADE IN A JIFFY

Jiffy muffin and biscuit mixes, produced by Chelsea Milling of Chelsea, Mich., have become so familiar that it's easy to overlook how amazing the brand's success really is. Recent market data indicate that Jiffy is the leader in the $230 million muffin-mix category, with 30.6% of the market as measured by revenue and 55.3% share as measured by unit sales. This performance is particularly impressive given that Chelsea Milling is a family-run operation competing with such corporate giants as General Mills and Pillsbury. Just how has Chelsea Milling beat the big players at their own game for more than 70 years? Part of the secret of their success is in their organizational structure. The firm is a simple operation that replaces corporate bureaucracy with lean efficiency. The decision-making process of their larger competitors is considerably more complicated. In this company, it's done by three or four people, as opposed to three or four departments. Most of Chelsea Milling's 350 employees are in manufacturing. The company mills and stores its flour, and everything except the printing of the little boxes is done on-site.

Source: Based on Paul Lukas, "Jiffy's Secret Recipe" *Fortune Small Business* (December 3, 2001).

---

ment, and more management means more expenses to cover. Second, a narrow span of control (or tall structures) makes vertical communication more time consuming. Why? Again, consider what a narrow span of control creates. It creates more levels in the hierarchy, so that any information that must be transmitted from the top of the hierarchy to the bottom takes longer than it would to communicate if there were fewer levels. One other potential disadvantage of narrow spans of control, or tall structures, is that the close supervision they encourage also tends to discourage employee autonomy and self-management.

We have seen changes in the span of control in organizations over the past century. Certainly, the trend in recent years is to widen the span of control or, in other words, flatten the organizational hierarchy. From IBM to Toyota, we have seen significant de-layering of organizational hierarchies. Why? This has occurred for most of the reasons cited above: cutting costs and speeding up the communication or decision-making process. (See Let's Talk Business 4.1.) Typically, widening the span of control or flattening the hierarchy includes spreading decision-making authority down to the lower levels of the organization.

5.   *Formalization*

To what degree will rules or procedures be employed to guide organizational members? The answer to that question is addressed in the notion of formalization. The level of formalization in an organization refers to the degree to which rules, regulations, procedures and the like govern how work is performed. In other words, formalization reflects the degree to which jobs within the organization are standardized. A high level of formalization means highly standardized work — i.e., clear rules regarding how the work should be performed. Highly standardized work, or work that is very much rule-directed, suggests that there is little individual discretion in how it can be performed. In this regard, high formalization is what scientific management advocated in its assertion of standardizing work. And, if you recall, this was intended to ensure that performance is consistent and reliable — i.e., workers know what is expected of them and how, exactly, they should be performing their jobs. In addition, the greater the degree of formalization, the less reliance on individual discretion.

Can you think of any organizations that are highly formalized? Where you have an organization that has explicit job descriptions, numerous rules or procedures governing the work process, you've got a highly formalized organization. Like the other elements of structure, attitudes toward formalization in organizations changed dramatically throughout the 20th century. Essentially, what we have witnessed in many organizations is a shift from high formalization and standardization of work practices to less formality. Why? Given the need to adapt to the rapidly changing external environment, organizations have found they must be willing to scrap the old way of doing things in favour of methods that better accommodate the changing demands of their environment, whether the sources of change come from competitors, consumers, technological changes, etc.

6. *Departmentation*

Recall the definition of organizational structure: a deliberately planned network or pattern of relationships that exists among individuals in various roles or positions. This includes the formal hierarchy of authority, the distribution or grouping of work (for example, into departments), and the rules or procedures that control and coordinate behaviour in the organization. The notions of hierarchy, rules and control and coordination were issues addressed within these five elements. However, one other part of this definition suggests that the distribution or grouping of work is also a central feature of structure. That is, in the design of almost any organization, we must address the question: On what basis will jobs be grouped together? This is the notion of **departmentation** — the dividing or grouping of major functions or work activities into separate units. How does an organization go about departmentalizing? That is, on what bases can organizational activities be grouped or divided? There are a number of ways that organizations can form groupings of work activities, and we will examine some of the most popular ones.

Functional departmentation. The most traditional and, perhaps, most common form of departmentation is to group workers together who carry out the same type of functions on behalf of the organization. Hence its name, functional departmentation. In other words, employees who have common or similar skills or expertise will be grouped together in one unit or department. A simple example:

> Company X has a production department, a finance department, a marketing department, an accounting department and a human resources department. As you can clearly see, each of these departments is based on different functions provided to the organization, and so each is staffed with employees who share that area of expertise: accountants in the accounting department, marketing specialists in the marketing department, etc.

LET'S TALK BUSINESS 4.2   FUNCTIONAL DEPARTMENTATION

What does this form of departmentation contribute to organizational structure? Among the **strengths** are the following:

1. Achieves economies of scale. This refers to the notion that by having all members of one function together, all resources for that function can be centralized and all expert knowledge is concentrated in one place, rather than being dispersed throughout the organization. This is akin to the notion of "power in numbers".
2. Skill development. Skills are developed in depth, and employees can progress within their department with experience. In other words, people benefit by being grouped with all other organizational members who shared their interests and maintain expertise in the same functional area.
3. Finally, this form is best suited for companies that are small to medium sized, with relatively few products or services.

It is equally important to note the challenges that this form of departmentation creates for organizations. Among the **weaknesses** are:

1. Difficulty in horizontal coordination. In other words, sometimes we find that different departments tend to become isolated from each other. And where this leads to poor communication or coordination, it can also lead to other inefficiencies.
2. Slow in responding to environmental changes. An organization may not respond fast enough to environmental changes because its departments are failing to coordinate their activities fast enough.

Divisional departmentation. Another possible method is to group or organize employees based on the products or services produced by the organization. This is referred to as product or divisional departmentation. For example, a company that produces computer hardware and software may have separate divisions for these products along with their own research and development (R & D) division, marketing division, and production division. Clearly, these functions vary greatly among the hardware and software items, so each department will specialize in those functions. This form of departmentation is particularly useful to organizations that produce a large number of different types of products or services. There are, of course, variations of the divisional form of departmentation. For example, an organization may want to focus on the needs of its different customers; and so, by grouping activities on the basis of those needs, it can better service its customers. This is the notion of **customer departmentation**. A drug manufacturer may departmentalize its activities based on its consumers in the medical community, as well as on its consumers in the general public. **Geographic departmentation** involves the grouping of work activities and resources in a way that serves customers in different geographical areas. A multinational organization may thus find it most efficient to group functions based on different geographical regions in order to be most responsive to the customer needs of those regions.

Hybrid. It is important to briefly note that there are numerous organizations that do not contain "pure" forms of the functional, divisional, customer or geographic departmentation, but rather, employ a combination of the characteristics of these different forms,

---

***LET'S TALK BUSINESS* 4.3   DIVISIONAL DEPARTMENTATION**

The **strengths** include:

1. The product form is actually well suited to unstable, changing environments, because each product is a separate division; it is very much focused on customer needs and is driven by a product focus rather than a functional focus.
2. Horizontal communication across functions is now achieved more readily, because all these functions are now working for a common division.
3. Speeds up decision making: decision making in the functional form tends to be centralized, with top decisions made at head office, so to speak. However, because the divisional form is driven by its product base, each division has authority over its own functions.
4. Best in large organizations with several products, because of its product focus.

Among the **weaknesses** of the product structure are the following:

1. Eliminates economies of scale in functional departments: for example, instead of 20 researchers working within one common R & D department, they are now spread across different product divisions, each of which requires separate resources. It does not concentrate common areas of expertise within one unit. This also tends to create additional costs, given the duplications of some functions in different divisions.
2. While horizontal communication is better served within a division, this form leads to poor coordination across product lines. Again, each operates as an autonomous unit, and so there may be difficulties in communicating across product divisions.

---

referred to as a **hybrid** structure. For example, although Air Canada, as we mentioned earlier, can be considered a functional structure, in fact, it also has geographic or regional departments (domestic, U.S. and overseas services, for example).

Matrix.   In addition, there are some organizations that combine the functional and divisional forms to create a **matrix** departmentation. This form of departmentation combines the divisional and functional forms in order to exploit the strengths of each. In organizations that use this form, both product managers and functional managers have equal authority in the organization, and employees report to both of them. So, for example, the functional departments of marketing, production and R & D have their own functional leaders; but mapped onto that are project managers, each of whom is responsible for a different product and each of whom must lead employees of each department to service the needs of that product. Consequently, employees in the three functional departments are responsible to both their functional leader and to the product or project leader. In effect, what happens is that specialists from different parts of the organization are coordinated or brought together to work on specific projects or products, but still remain part of their functional area. This form of departmentation was developed in the aerospace industry at companies like McDonnell Douglas and NASA. It is now also quite popular in areas as diverse as banking and the education system. Essentially, it attempts to maintain the strengths of the functional form (economies of scale, expertise, etc.) while also achieving the coordination, innovation and adaptiveness of the product form.

THE ORGANIZATIONAL LANDSCAPE: A CLASSIFICATION

In addition to the anatomy of organizations that we addressed above, we can consider a classification scheme of organizations developed by the well-known management scholar Henry Mintzberg. Mintzberg offers a closer look at the types of organizational structures we can observe in the real world, and what components actually comprise an organization. According to Mintzberg, we can think of an organization as being composed of five different components, as follows: the operating core, the strategic apex, the middle line, the technostructure, and the support staff. (See Exhibit 4.6.)

1. The **operating core** refers to those individuals who perform the basic work related to producing the products or providing services to clients for the organization. These could include anybody from a salesperson to a machine operator, to an assembly-line worker, to a doctor or nurse.

2. The **strategic apex** includes the top-level managers whose responsibility it is to oversee the whole system. This might be the CEO, the president, or the board of directors.

3. The **middle line** is composed of managers who form a hierarchy of authority between the operating core and the strategic apex. This could include people like plant managers, district sales manager, supervisors, etc.

4. The **technostructure** is essentially made up of analysts. These analysts also perform administrative duties, but of a different nature from that of the managers mentioned above. That is, while they are concerned with planning and controlling the work of others, their job is more outside the hierarchy of authority. For example, this could include the strategic planning staff, the controller, personnel training officer, etc.

5. The **support staff** are those people who provide indirect support services for the organization. This could include anything from legal counsel to cafeteria services, to mailroom, to payroll staff, to reception.

Using these five basic components, we can consider how organizations are fundamentally different with regard to structure. Mintzberg suggests that any one of these five components can dominate an organization. Based on this notion, Mintzberg suggests that what we can discern in the world of organizations is essentially five different basic structural forms or organizational configurations, each related to the domination of one of the five components.

Let's briefly identify Mintzberg's five configurations, and then we will talk in a little more detail about the nature of each configuration: simple structure, machine bureaucracy, professional bureaucracy, diversified, adhocracy.

1. The simple or entrepreneurial structure. As the name implies, this is the most basic form of organization, perhaps with one boss and one or more employees: a strategic apex with no middle line, no support staff or technostructure, and a small operating core. So, essentially, the strategic apex is dominant: we see an organization whose control or

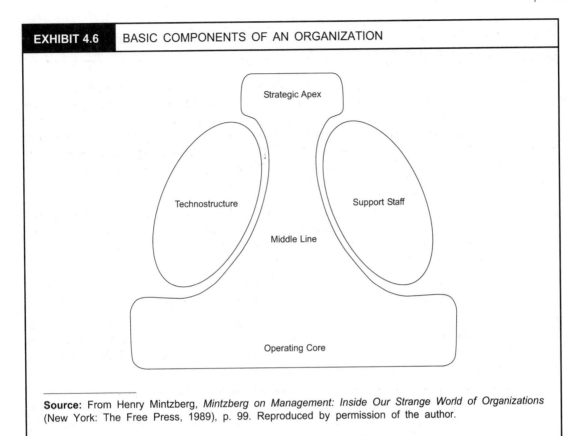

EXHIBIT 4.6 BASIC COMPONENTS OF AN ORGANIZATION

Strategic Apex

Technostructure

Support Staff

Middle Line

Operating Core

Source: From Henry Mintzberg, *Mintzberg on Management: Inside Our Strange World of Organizations* (New York: The Free Press, 1989), p. 99. Reproduced by permission of the author.

decision-making authority is very centralized, and the organization is a simple structure. You might think of a small retail business, a restaurant or a small consulting firm as a simple structure: it has one boss, or owner, who largely runs things. Typically, it is a new, relatively small, organization. Clearly, this is a flat organization with basically everyone reporting to one person.

Probably the greatest strength of this configuration lies in its simplicity—i.e., no layers of hierarchy to bog down the decision-making process. Instead, what you've got is lean, fast and flexible organization with few costs to maintain. There is one clear line of authority, and so accountability is easily maintained. A leader, particularly a strong leader with a vision, can often clearly convey this to his staff, given his or her close proximity to the operating core.

Are there any weaknesses in this organizational type? Why doesn't every organization look like the simple structure? Consider growing or large organizations. While it may be fine for the owner of a corner convenience store to avoid any managers and simply manage his or her own staff of one or two, what happens if this business becomes very successful, and the owner decides to expand and buy three other locations? As an organization grows, the simple structure eventually becomes inadequate. Decision-making authority may need to become decentralized when operations become large and spread apart.

2. The machine bureaucracy. When the technostructure dominates, we have a machine bureaucracy. What is the connection? As mentioned earlier, the technostructure is the technical support staff — those areas focused on control and supervision, but not through the direct line of hierarchy. In other words, this is a body that is concerned with generating standards for performance. Frederick Taylor and scientific management advocated time-motion studies: the consultants who performed this work could be considered the technostructure. The planners, budgeters, controllers, all are concerned with maintaining the organization like a machine, running smoothly and efficiently. A machine bureaucracy, as the name implies, is all about standards and standardized methods of work. The machine bureaucracy relies on standardized tasks, formalized rules and regulations. It is akin to what has been called the mechanistic structure.

The central strength of this configuration is its efficiency. As we mentioned earlier, this form is distinguished by its emphasis on standardization, rules and regulations: all elements employed to maximize efficiency in the performance of work activities.

Ironically, it is this strength that also contains the sources of its potential weakness. Those very same rules, regulations and standardized work practices that offer clear guidance to employees can also tend to make the organization less responsive to any changes in its environment. You may have heard the expression "bureaucratic red tape". It reflects the view that too many rules can bog down an organization. Add that to the tendency for these organizations to be centralized, and you have a slow-moving dinosaur when quick decisions need to be made. Consequently, while the machine bureaucracy works well in stable, unchanging environments, it tends to be less effective in volatile environments, where rules and methods for conducting work need to be frequently revised.

3. Professional bureaucracy. The main feature of this configuration is that the operating core is composed of professionals. Such is the case with organizations like hospitals, universities, or accounting firms, for example. And when control or decision-making authority lies with the operating core, this would be considered a professional bureaucracy: decisions are decentralized.

With the operating core being dominant and granted such authority, we can see the "professional" part of this organization; but why the "bureaucracy" reference? In this type of organization, power is permitted to rest with the operating core because they have the central skills that the organization requires, and they are provided the autonomy, through decentralization, to apply their expertise. In other words, this organization has substituted work that is specialized (as in the machine bureaucracy) for individuals who are specialized — i.e., they have trained skills; standardization is achieved not through rules and regulations applied to the work, but by the fact that these individuals will have standardized skills from their training. For example, a library, a hospital, an accounting firm are composed of individuals who have been trained to apply standardized skills. Hence, the professional bureaucracy (through standardized professional skills) combines the standardization of a bureaucracy with decentralization accorded to professionals.

The major strength of this form lies in the professional skills that populate this organization. So, with these standardized skills they, like the machine bureaucracy, achieve the goal of high efficiency in the performance of their work. However, as opposed to the machine form, the professional bureaucracy gives over decision-making authority and power to the operating core of professionals, who need this autonomy (decentralized decision making) to do their jobs. The potential weaknesses of this form are the same as that for the machine. The professionals who are guided by their own rules and regulations might sometimes similarly be bogged down by the inflexibility of such rules.

4. Diversified/divisional. What do General Motors, Canadian Pacific, DuPont, and Procter & Gamble all have in common? They are all based on a divisional structure. Recall our discussion of divisional or product departmentation: the notion is essentially the same. In this case, the dominant component is the middle line. In other words, decision-making authority is decentralized among middle managers, as is often the case with organizations that have a number of largely autonomous diverse divisions. Typically, each division is a machine bureaucracy that runs itself; the division managers have significant control.

The strengths of this form are somewhat similar to the advantages of the product or divisional departmentation that we discussed earlier. For large organizations with diverse products or services, the notion of spreading authority to autonomous units or divisions allows the organization to be much more responsive to its environment — customers, clients, and changes in that environment. The divisions can focus specifically on their concerns, while head office can focus on broader strategic planning issues. This decentralization is a key strength of this form. The potential weaknesses of this structure are also analogous to the weaknesses of the divisional or product form of departmentation that we considered earlier. Among them are the fact that it can be costly to maintain many separate, autonomous divisions. It may also be difficult to coordinate or facilitate communication among these independent divisions.

5. Innovative organization, or the adhocracy. It is difficult to define this configuration or type. Perhaps the clearest explanation involves explaining not what the adhocracy possesses, but what it doesn't possess. In contrast to the bureaucracies and divisional structures, it does not possess an established hierarchy (middle line), no permanent departments, little if any formalized rules, and few if any standardized procedures regarding how work is conducted; and, unlike the simple structure, it tends to be decentralized. Which component dominates its structure? Well, none dominates, exactly. This type of configuration has also been referred to as an "organic organization". Organizations that thrive on innovation and creativity, like advertising agencies or a film production company, might be called adhocracies. Many organizations in the electronics and aerospace industries reflect this configuration.

This form is also reflected in team-based organizations where there is less emphasis on formality, authority, rules and standards, and more emphasis on innovation and creativity. Clearly, where such qualities are desired and where the environment is extremely volatile or dynamic, this form is able to adapt swiftly to the changing demands of the environment. In this regard, it is the antithesis of the machine bureaucracy. However, by the same token, it may not achieve the efficiency of the machine bureaucracy: there are no standardized ways of doing things, and so there is much less certainty regarding reliability or consistency in the performance of work activities.

CHAPTER SUMMARY —————————————————————

The discussion above indicates that there is a clear purpose behind organizational designs. Any organizational structure must consider: the organization's goals — what are we trying to accomplish?; the fundamental forces acting on the organization — what are the central challenges we face? The ultimate organizational structure will serve the organization's goals and suit the nature of the organization's environment. It is useful to examine factors that influence the type of organizational structure that is generated. This issue will be more fully addressed in the next chapter, along with some of the most pervasive changes we have recently observed with regard to organizational structure.

KEY TERMS

- open systems
- work specialization
- horizontal differentiation
- chain of command
- centralization
- span of control
- vertical differentiation
- formalization
- departmentation
- operating core

- strategic apex
- middle line
- technostructure
- support staff
- entrepreneurial organization
- machine bureaucracy
- professional bureaucracy
- diversified organization
- adhocracy

Great Harvest Inc. is an organization made up of a head office and 137 franchises, which are Great Harvest bakeries. These retail bread bakeries make and sell to the general public soft-crust bread from whole wheat that's freshly milled in each bakery. Great Harvest Inc. is a franchiser; that is, it sells its various bakeries to interested buyers (franchisees), who in return for ownership of one bakery will pay a franchise fee and give annual royalties to Great Harvest Inc. headquarters. Each store is staffed with several employees, including bakers and sales staff, in addition to the franchise owners.

While Great Harvest is a franchised organization, it is not designed like the traditional franchise organization. While most franchisers dictate everything about their franchisees' operations in order to ensure a predictable experience for customers everywhere, Great Harvest doesn't even require that its franchisees use the same bread recipes, nor must they paint their stores the same colours; nor must they use the same promotions. Instead, Great Harvest sets its franchisees free after a one-year apprenticeship to run their stores in the time-honoured "mom-and-pop" way, however they choose. Be unique, the company tells them; be yourselves, and experiment with your bakery and with the people you hire.

As part of the training given to the new bakery owners (franchisees), the Chief Operating Officer, Tom McMakin, gives information on how to market the products, as well as much information on running their bakery. However, he does not simply train the owners; he often adapts the goals of the overall organization to their suggestions. For example, one of the bakery owners suggested the implementation of a promotional campaign called "Baker for a Day". This involved choosing a "needy group" in their community, opening the bakery on a Sunday (when Great Harvests are normally closed), donating the ingredients and labour, and handing over the day's sales as charity. The community group would promote the event, help staff it, and bring attention and new people to the store. Consequently, this idea was implemented on a store-wide basis. Great Harvest headquarters prides itself in adopting such ideas from owners and employees. Is there anything more important to a business these days than making good ideas spread? Imagine capturing the ideas of each employee and exposing them to the collective, enabling each notion to prompt whatever reactions it will, to spark rounds of fresh thoughts by other employees. Such a company would almost run itself, naturally and with the market's demands.

And therein is Great Harvest's fundamental philosophical principle: the conviction that command-and-control is wrong, that the company's real product is its offer of freedom to run a bakery as the owner sees fit. In other words, Great Harvest says to its bakery owners, "Do whatever you want"; except in one respect, which makes all the difference: every owner in the chain is encouraged to be part of Great Harvest's "learning community". Those who join (and most have) must share information, financial results, observations, and ideas. If asked questions, they must give answers. They must keep no secrets. They must, as McMakin describes it, "let things go." The result is what academics would call an intentionally created "learning organization".

Great Harvest headquarters, who basically oversee the performance of the 137 bakeries, also try to facilitate communication among them so that they can learn from each other's successes and failures. For example, head office provides each franchisee bakery with a list of the 10 best-performing bakeries. If a bakery has a problem controlling labour expenses at their store, they can simply call up the bakery owners who've got that figured out and get their advice. There is also a Best Measures report, which gives bakery owners a benchmark or standard for identifying their own store's strengths and weaknesses and comparing their employees' performance. Finally, to help motivate each store's owners and employees, headquarters has established a website. This "Breadboard site" contains announcements ("Slicer for sale," "New baby in Dallas!"), discussion threads for ongoing electronic chats among owners on a wide variety of subjects (new recipes, notes on maintaining particular ovens). According to management at head office, this makes everyone feel like part of a community, and their overall contribution to the Great Harvest organization does make a difference!

Source: Based on Michael S. Hopkins, "Zen and the Art of the Self-Managing Company" *Inc magazine* (November 1, 2000).

QUESTIONS

1. Using the frameworks for describing organizational structure, the six elements, describe the organizational structure and the potential benefits of this structure for this business. Because not all elements of the structure are explicitly indicated in this case, make assumptions about the structure given the nature of this organization, and state those assumptions.

2. Using Mintzberg's notion of configurations, how would you describe this organization?

3. What types of management philosophies do you think are being applied in this organization?

Bigger and better?

[A] majority of mergers — about two-thirds involving U.S. companies — fail to deliver value. In fact, according to Salomon Smith Barney, for companies acquired since 1997 in deals for $15 billion or more, the stocks of the acquirers have generally underperformed the S&P 500 stock index by 14 percentage points after the deals were announced; they've also underperformed their peer groups by four points. Other studies from the last several years, cutting across every industry, confirm this conclusion — and show that no one is immune.

Yet against this ever-mounting empirical evidence that says don't do it, CEOs continue to say yes to mergers at a record-breaking pace that has quadrupled since 1995. Why?

For struggling dotcoms or fledgling companies in volatile sectors, consolidating is a matter of survival. But can the standard arsenal of strategic reasons CEOs use to justify a merger — such as the need to develop new distribution channels, to serve broader customer wants, to take advantage of changing technology and legislation, to integrate vertically, to eliminate overcapacity, and to reduce risk — explain this behaviour? No. So what's different today? What's driving this merger mania?

. . . .

GLOBALIZATION AND THE PATHOLOGY OF BIGNESS

A number of factors have aided globalization: the fall of the Berlin Wall and communism, NAFTA, changes in the law, the liberalization of global markets, the proliferation of technology, and customers who demand global service. Mike Campbell, CEO of Arch Chemicals, explains that many of his customers, who were once located only in the United States, have opened international plants that Arch Chemicals must serve in order to keep them as customers. "The trend toward global customers has accelerated," he says, "much more so than five years ago." To compete globally, Campbell has turned to M&A [mergers and acquisitions] options, as have many other companies. According to Charles Elson, Woolard Professor of Corporate Governance at the University of Delaware, globalization is the No. 1 reason for the record-breaking M&A activity.

Once global competitors emerge in a given industry, Elson believes, consolidation follows. Academics refer to these patterns of consolidation as a "follow-the-leader" syndrome, or herd behaviour, where CEOs either want to be with or hide in the herd. Robert B. Lamb, clinical professor at New York University's Stern Graduate School of Business, confirms, "Time after time, you see follow-the-leader patterns. If an industry is consolidating, companies feel compelled to follow."

Campbell contends that this mentality takes discipline to avoid, but not all CEOs are so quick to agree. Even though, as retired Texaco CEO Alfred DeCrane admits, "There's a kernel of truth there," it depends on the situation. Using the oil industry as an example, he explains, "As the industry is changing, you have to decide what tier of this industry you want to be in." If you want to be a supplier, that's one segment, but if you want to be actively searching for new oil reserves, it means greater risk and capital investment, and a merger is often the answer. (Chevron is currently negotiating a $35 billion deal to acquire Texaco.)

One theme is consistent: With the perceived need to compete globally, we have become caught up in the relentless drive for strategic bigness. When you stop growing, you start dying. "We're swept up in bigness," admits retired Olin CEO John Johnstone.

Just scan the newspapers — the bigness pathology is evident. Former Texaco chairman Peter I. Bijur was quoted in The New York Times last fall: "It's apparent now that scale and size are important as the supermajor oil companies have come on the scene. We want to do the right thing for our shareholders and create a U.S.-based company that can compete worldwide." And a recent Harvard Business Review article quotes Whirlpool CEO David R. Whitwam: "The market is more global than ever and growing more so every day. Global barriers are rapidly deteriorating. So you have to integrate all your operations into a total global strategy." Even Joel Klein, the feared former antitrust chief of the Department of Justice, appears convinced that bigger is better, saying in the Times recently, "We understand that companies have to be of sufficient size and scope to play in the global marketplace."

REVENUE GROWTH OR BUST

An obsession with top-line growth, with both CEOs and investors fixated on revenue and earnings figures, also fuels merger mania. Sometimes CEOs publicly commit themselves to a certain goal, and if they can't make it by means of internal growth, they will achieve it through acquisition. Take the case of retired AlliedSignal CEO Lawrence A. Bossidy. Early in his tenure, he proclaimed that he would grow the company's revenue to $20 billion by the year 2000; "20 in 20" even became a company slogan. As the date approached, he found himself short. Only a big M&A deal would allow him to save face, so AlliedSignal acquired Honeywell in 1999, boosting revenue to $24 billion. Bossidy could retire knowing he had not failed.

He is only one of many who have fallen into this trap. "With large companies in some industries, their drive toward growth requires them to merge because the organic opportunities are not there," confirms Melissa Berman, former senior vice president of research for The Conference Board. Correspondingly, when bigger companies become more active in seeking growth opportunities, the market witnesses more mega-mergers, sharply driving up the total value of M&A deals.

This bias toward aggressively growing revenues and earnings rather than concentrating on profit margins is due not only to CEO ego, as could be argued in Bossidy's case, but also to investors who want to see bigger and bigger numbers. Investors love increased market share and geographic expansion, while companies with flat sales are punished mercilessly. "With unrelenting pressure for sales and earnings gains, CEOs will seek opportunities everywhere," concludes management consultant Thomas M. Grubb, co-author with Robert Lamb of *Capitalize on Merger Chaos: Six Ways to Profit From Your Competitors' Consolidation and Your Own.* After a merger, regardless of whether productivity goes down and profit margins shrink, Grubb points out, "CEOs can report record sales and earnings." And the record-breaking CEO is a hero on Wall Street.

·   ·   ·   ·

FEAR AND LOATHING IN THE EGO

You can't talk about the quest for bigness without discussing ego, which has played a role since the beginning of time. So what's different today in the land of ego that's driving today's merger mania? Big Money and Celebrity Status.

. . . .

While we've always had flamboyant business figures, from J.P. Morgan to Ross Perot, today's CEOs, more so than ever, are celebrities. They're on magazine covers, they're recognized on the street. "Many retiring CEOs are searching for a legacy as they leave their companies," says Grubb, who believes CEOs are often ego-driven. And, in driving mergers, he says, "Fear is such an underlying factor." Today's CEO doesn't want to be remembered as the one who let the company be acquired, absorbed, or vaporized. Lamb calls it the "psychology of victors." The acquiring companies are the victors; the acquired are the weak losers that couldn't make it on their own.

. . . .

In the final analysis, CEOs are caught in a catch-22: They are under intense pressure to deliver strategic growth to shareholders, but in doing so through mergers and acquisitions (often their only choice), they will most likely destroy shareholder value. Therein lies the root cause of fear and loathing in the executive suites.

Source: Excerpts from *Across the Board* (May/June 2001) 38(3): 22–27. Copyright Conference Board, Inc. May/June 2001. Reproduced by permission of Peter Krass.

QUESTIONS

1. What is the author's central argument regarding the proliferation of mergers?

2. Does the author suggest that a "bigger organization" is a "better organization"?

3. How do you think organizational structure changes as the organization grows larger?

The Organizational Revolution

Organizations have largely moved away from the traditional bureaucratic organizational design. In this chapter we will examine some of the recent approaches that organizations have adopted with regard to structure and design. Specifically, this chapter will consider some of the central changes to the nature of organizations, including: re-engineering, downsizing, and going virtual. We will also examine the reasons behind these changes, and consider more generally the question: What determines how an organization is designed?

LEARNING OBJECTIVES

By the end of the chapter, you should be able to:

1. Identify four broad trends in the changing nature of organizational design.

2. Discuss the central determinants of organizational structure.

3. Explain the concept of re-engineering.

4. Describe the notion of the virtual organization.

5. Identify the methods, objectives and potential results achieved through downsizing.

6. Explain why downsizing may fail to achieve the anticipated results.

Organizational Insider

Outsourcing the Medicine Man

You probably wouldn't know much about the company, tucked away as it is in a nondescript low-rise in Mississauga, on the western periphery of Toronto. Still, chances are good that you've popped one of its products in the past month or two. Chances are better that you've at least heard of some of its spawn — Aspirin, NeoCitran, Theraflu, to name a few. But Patheon (TSE: PTI) doesn't actually own these brands; rather, it's on the leading edge of the latest trend to sweep the pharmaceutical industry: outsourcing. All told, the company manufactures more than 400 products — everything from anti-inflammatories to AIDS drugs — for 125 clients, including industry heavyweights like Pfizer, GlaxoSmithKline and Johnson & Johnson. In the process, Patheon itself has become somewhat of a financial big hitter — and, more importantly, may have developed a nearly recession-proof business.

Even at 5 p.m. on a Friday, the company's 184,000-square-foot plant in Mississauga — one of nine factories it owns in Canada and Europe — is humming. A group of technicians garbed in air-purifying respirator suits are cleaning a mixing machine that will blend tomorrow's batch of liquid drugs. Assembly lines churn out bottles of anti-inflammatories, while buckets of sedatives are perched on pallets, ready to be shipped. A lab-coated worker watches over a machine as it spits out pink pills with machine-gun-like precision.

But unlike many outsourcing firms, there's more going on at Patheon than run-of-the-mill manufacturing. Behind the windowed walls of its drug development lab, a group of scientists are hunched over microscopes, flanked by test tubes burbling with solutions. Their challenge: to help determine the most efficient way to make pills dissolve in the stomach. The scientists are key to Patheon's new business strategy of working with big pharmaceutical companies to not only make drugs, but to design products to be as effective as possible once they've been ingested. It's what Patheon CEO Robert Tedford calls "serving the innovators," and it could give his company a big chunk of the growing US$375-billion pie that makes up the world market for prescription and over-the-counter drugs. So far, Patheon has invested $5 million in the new research arm and plans to add 1,600 employees to its current staff of 2,400 by 2003.

Despite that new initiative, outsourcing has been the real star for not only Patheon, but for high-tech in general in the past couple years. Toronto-based Celestica Inc., which manufactures electronics components for companies like Sun Microsystems and Nortel Networks, raked in almost US$10 billion in 2000, even as its biggest customers took huge hits on the stock market. The pharmaceutical industry, by contrast, has dragged its feet, despite the fact that outsourcing can save manufacturers both time and money. "Big pharmas are the last set of dinosaurs," says Bob Leshchyshen, a special situations analyst with Toronto's Northern Securities Inc. who has been following Patheon for four years. "They've been very slow to accept outsourcing."

. . . .

Lately, Patheon has been on a tear, buying up manufacturing plants in suburban industrial parks around the world. Last year alone, it acquired sites near Milan, London and Lyon, France. But the real prize — a base of operations in the US, as opposed to the US distribution of its products — has been elusive, as pharmaceutical giants in the US seem to be reluctant to sell their plants. Analysts like Leshchyshen suspect that middle managers at many large pharmaceutical companies are resisting outsourcing, even though they know it's more cost-effective. "Big pharma's manufacturing department doesn't want to give up making the drugs," says Leshchyshen. "The company wants to get away from manufacturing, but it still has people to deal with. When it outsources, people can lose their jobs." But their days may be numbered anyway. Outsourcing is changing the industry, which means Patheon is even facing some competition in its own backyard. ... Montreal-based PanGeo Pharma Inc., which started back in 1987, has contracts with Shoppers Drug Mart Ltd. and Obus Forme Ltd., though it had sales of just $5.6 million last year (compared with Patheon's $256 million) and operated at a loss. "There might be a little bit of competition there, but PanGeo is really a poorer cousin to Patheon, which has been around longer and has more money," says George Mahmourides, a biotech analyst with Montreal-based Groome Capital. "It has critical mass in the marketplace." So sure, Patheon has little to no profile in the eyes of Canadian consumers, and its rise in the global marketplace has been downright stealthy. But if it continues to grow its critical mass, Patheon might just turn out to be the best little drug company you've never heard of.

Source: By Raizel Robin from *Canadian Business* (June 25, 2001) 74(12): 40–41. Reproduced with permission of Canadian Business Magazine.

THE CHANGING NATURE OF ORGANIZATIONS

Patheon is a great illustration of the power of organizational structure, and the benefits of adapting structure to the environment. How are structure and the issue of outsourcing benefiting Patheon and countless other companies? This is an issue we will explore further in this chapter.

We began the last chapter with a description of the tremendous change and turmoil that we have witnessed across the organizational landscape. From the massive reductions in the workforce of many well-known organizations like IBM, AT & T, and Bell Canada, to changes in how organizations are designed and operated — fundamentally there has been a rethinking of how organizations should be designed. Organizational theory has been trying to make sense of the revolution we have observed in the organizational world.

Some observers have suggested that what is going on is a shift away from the classical, traditional, bureaucratic model. Recall our earlier discussion of perspectives of management and Weber's notion of the bureaucratic organization: a central stream of classical management thought. This philosophy of organization design guided many of our organizations for most of the 20th century. The traditional, bureaucratic organizational structure emphasizes factors such as job specialization, a formal hierarchy of authority, a clear system of control, and rules and regulations to guide behaviour.

Why do we need the bureaucratic design? Because it achieves the fundamental goals of organizations: predictability and reliability — rules and standardized jobs ensure workers are doing what the boss wants; and control — the formal hierarchy ensures that how the work is conducted is clearly controlled. Ironically, these very strengths of the bureaucratic structure can also become weaknesses when the environment changes. For example, increasing competition, demands for better products and services, improved customer service, and more sophisticated processes of generating the product all suggest that the stability of bureaucracies impedes any chance for innovation. The philosophy of organizational structure that emphasized job specialization, the narrow division of labour, standardization, rules and the like is simply not suitable to a changing environment.

The traditional or classical approach to organizational structure was still relatively firmly entrenched up until the 1980s. Believe it or not, this old philosophy that arose in the time of the Industrial Revolution dominated our thinking about the nature of organizational design right up until the 1980s. It was not until then that organizations began to realize that the bureaucratic structure needed to be replaced with new designs. It seems that most of the shifts in organizational design essentially aimed to move away from the bureaucratic paradigm. Among the important trends in the redesign of organizations, the adjectives identified in Exhibit 5.1 best describe the new approaches and the shift away from the bureaucratic design.

1. Flatter Organizations

If there is any consistent pattern in the sweeping changes to corporate architecture, it has been the de-layering of organizational hierarchies. If you recall our discussion of span of control, it was noted that tall organizations have narrow spans of control and flat orga-

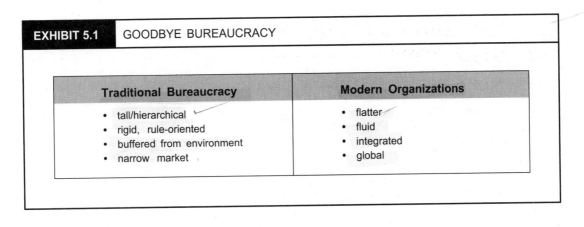

EXHIBIT 5.1   GOODBYE BUREAUCRACY

Traditional Bureaucracy	Modern Organizations
• tall/hierarchical	• flatter
• rigid, rule-oriented	• fluid
• buffered from environment	• integrated
• narrow market	• global

nizations have wider spans of control. The shift we have observed in organizational redesign has been from the former to the latter. Certainly, one of the most pervasive phenomena to hit the organizational landscape since the 1980s has been downsizing, which often involves flattening the organizational hierarchy. We will address this issue in more detail later in the chapter. It is difficult to read the newspaper without reading some report on an organization flattening its hierarchy through downsizing. As mentioned earlier, Toyota eliminated three of its seven layers of management, and IBM Canada cut its levels from 10 to about four, in the 1990s, and these trends continue today among many organizations.

Flattening the hierarchy accomplishes a number of things. Among the benefits are increased speed of decision making: decisions and information take much less time to travel across levels of bureaucracy. This allows organizations to react much faster to the demands of a changing environment. In addition, the de-layering of layers of management means that much more responsibility and self-management is coming from the lower levels of the organization, so that employees and those who are closest to serving customers or producing the product are now more involved in the decision-making process.

2. Fluid Organizations

The bureaucratic organization is obsessed with control and facilitates control largely through strict adherence to rule and standards for how work is done. Again, think back to our discussion of the purposes of organizational structure. When organizations exist in dynamic environments, being able to adapt to change is critical. Bureaucratic rules tend to impede such adaptiveness, given that rules must be changed to fit new circumstances. The organic organization that we identified earlier derives some of its strength from its ability to avoid being bogged down in rules that govern how work must be performed. Later in this chapter we will examine a very fluid or organic form of organization — the virtual organization.

LET'S TALK BUSINESS 5.1   THE FLUID ORGANIZATION

Lifetime employment was once a goal that both companies and individuals hoped for, but today the idea is dead. Few people will ever achieve it. In fact, prospective employers are suspicious of candidates who possess a recent, lengthy tenure. If a "lifer" loses a job, he or she must counteract doubts about his or her ability to adapt quickly to a new workplace environment. As it is, many individuals in their 20s are changing jobs every year and would apparently have it no other way. Employees and communities were once critical factors in companies' long-term strategic decisions. Moving factories and jobs to another area of the country was unthinkable because of the damage it would do to the local community. In recent years, thousands of companies — including UPS, J.C. Penney, and Boeing — have moved their headquarters or operations from cities where they had deep roots. The old business structure — with a dominant CEO, a largely ceremonial board of directors, and employees willing to put the goals of the company first — is nearly extinct.

Source: From John A Challenger, "The transformed workplace: How can you survive," *The Futurist* (Nov./Dec. 2001) 35(6): 24–28. Originally published in the Nov./Dec. 2001 Issue of *The Futurist*. Used with permission from the World Future Society, 7910 Woodmont Avenue, Suite 450, Bethesda, Maryland 20814. Telephone: 301/65608274; Fax: 301/951-0394; <http://www.wfs.org>.

Fluidity or flexibility in the functioning of an organization has been reflected in other ways, such as the notion of just-in-time inventory, which emphasizes the ability to generate inventory as needed through flexible manufacturing/supplier relationships, and consequently minimize costs. These **just-in-time inventory principles** have also been applied to the work relationship where we now have a just-in-time labour pool, so to speak. That is, organizations have recognized that they no longer need to maintain a fixed supply of labour. If revenues at any time are diminishing, so too the labour pool can be diminished via downsizing, and that pool can be increased when revenues increase. Consequently, by the 1980s and throughout the 1990s we witnessed growth in temporary or contract-based employment. This adds immensely to the fluidity of an organization, since a temporary workforce can be easily adjusted to meet the upswings and downturns of a less predictable environment. This fluidity has, of course, profound implications for individuals within organizations, because it also underscores attitudes toward the permanence or lack of permanence of jobs within the "new" workplace, as observed recently in Let's Talk Business 5.1.

3.   Integrated Organizations

The traditional bureaucratic organization advocates clear lines of authority and control. However, the newer organizational designs are less focused on the need for unity of command and clear lines of authority. It is unimportant to maintain distinct boundaries between levels in the hierarchy, between individuals and departments, and between organizational members and individuals external to the organization. In fact, just the opposite is now emphasized — aiming to create more integration among the formerly disparate units in the organization. For example, the new approaches to organizational design typically focus on teams of workers rather than on individuals. Cross-functional teams are quite popular work groups that bring together members from various parts of the organization.

Typically, work teams are given the power to manage themselves and make decisions without the approval of formal management — hence the name self-managing work teams. Thus, GM's Saturn plant brought individuals from the legal department to marketing, to engineering, in order to be involved in the production of the Saturn car. Shell Canada has achieved much success with their use of self-managed teams, as have numerous other companies. Information sharing is a big part of this team-based approach — that is, having management give over information that once was solely their domain. This is much more common in today's organization than in the traditional bureaucratic model, where those in power held the information and did not share it with the lower levels.

The integration of units or members within the organization is one major trend. Another trend includes integration of the organization with players outside its boundaries. Organizations are increasingly building closer connections with their external environment. For example, an organization may attempt to establish close relationships with suppliers, integrating them into the manufacturing process, and generally creating an interdependent relationship. Other organizations are even creating alliances with other companies in order to develop new products or services. There are even cross-functional teams that include participants from outside the organization, such as suppliers, or distributors, or even competitors.

The Japanese term for networking of major enterprises is **keiretsu**. These are loosely affiliated collections of companies, and have been quite common in industry and banking in Japan. Creating an organization out of a network of organizations is an issue we will address later in this chapter.

Of course, not all integration of organizations has been of such a loosely coupled nature. We have also witnessed recently the trend toward building collections of organizations through mergers and acquisitions. The spate of mergers and acquisitions that occurred in the 1990s seems to be continuing in the new millennium, as noted in Let's Talk Business 5.2.

4. Global Organizations

Perhaps the most profound recent trend in the changing nature of organizations is the drive to "go global". Many organizations in today's world must focus on the global environment. The issue of globalization of business will be discussed in detail in a later chapter. Globalization can be considered one of the leading forces behind organizational change since the 1980s and 1990s. Globalization has brought with it many implications, including the increase in competition and greater access to more markets. Industries that were traditionally "protected" by tariffs, such as auto manufacturing, faced intense competition from foreign competitors for the first time, and with serious consequences. Chrysler almost went bankrupt, and General Motors was forced to cut over 70,000 jobs in 1991, in one of the largest downsizings conducted.

LET'S TALK BUSINESS 5.2   MERGER MANIA

The 1990s business environment could be characterized, in part, by the "bigger is better" philosophy. Merging with other companies had a particularly high profile in sectors such as auto manufacturing, forest products manufacturing, finance, retail trade, and high-technology-related businesses. In theory, mergers allow companies to take advantage of new synergies and improved purchasing power, as well as reducing duplication in head-office functions and marketing. "Merged with another company" was identified by 20 percent, or 10 companies, that restructured in the 1980s. During the 1990s, 28 percent, or 34 companies, experienced a merger. Companies have also "moved to fewer but larger establishments." About one-quarter of companies that restructured in the 1990s did this.

Source: From Carolyn C. Kwan, "Restructuring in the Canadian economy: A survey of firms" *Bank of Canada Review* (Summer 2000): 21.

Just about every sector of business is no longer insulated from competitors, customers or suppliers outside of their home country. Consequently, the notion of integration or networking can include relationships with suppliers, or even competitors, outside of local boundaries. Moreover, these members may exist in other countries. An organization may have networks of members across the world. For example, Canadian Company X might be selling a product they had designed by their team in Sweden, engineered in the United States and manufactured in Japan. In the global marketplace, businesses are also selling to customers all over the world. Consider, for example, Bata Ltd. whose head office is in Toronto. This is a company that has approximately 6,000 shoe stores in about 65 different countries. Given its large size, it is a challenge for Bata to ensure it is flexible and responsive to local market needs. Consequently, it employs a geographic form of departmentation, with independent divisions operating in Europe, Africa, South America and the Far East. Just think about the challenges this company faces in terms of responding to the variety of consumer preferences within these different locations. For Bata, decentralized decision-making authority is required to permit these divisions to focus on and quickly respond to local market needs.

WHAT DETERMINES ORGANIZATIONAL STRUCTURE? A RATIONAL PERSPECTIVE

The classification of five broad types of organizations discussed in the previous chapter suggested that different forms offer different strengths for meeting the challenges or forces facing organizations. Now, in broader terms, we can consider why organizations take on

| EXHIBIT 5.2 | MECHANISTIC VS. ORGANIC ORGANIZATION |

	Mechanistic	**Organic**
1. Division of Labour	narrow	wide
2. Adherence to Clear Chain of Command	strict	flexible
3. Span of Control	narrow	wide
4. Centralization	centralized	decentralized
5. Formalization	high	low
6. Departmentation	functional	divisional

different structures, and we can consider other sources of influence on organizational design in general. To simplify our discussion, we can consider the two extreme opposites, in terms of the organizational configuration identified in the previous chapter: the machine bureaucracy, and the adhocracy, or innovative organization. These organizational types have also been given the labels of mechanistic and organic organizations, respectively. Each can be defined using the six elements of structure. (See Exhibit 5.2.)

Organic and mechanistic organizations are polar extremes in every one of these six elements. Machine bureaucracies, or mechanistic organizations, maintain jobs that are highly specialized, with a clear chain of command and a narrow span of control (tall organization), and are, typically, highly centralized and highly formalized. On the other hand, organic organizations tend to have jobs low in specialization (with a broad variety of tasks or responsibilities), no clear chain of command (team-based approach) and a wide span of control, and are highly decentralized with a low level of formalization. While there are a variety of influences on the design of organizations, perhaps among the most significant sources of influence on the structure of organizations are strategy, size, technology, and environment.

1.   Strategy

Clearly, an organization's structure is intended to help achieve its organizational objectives or strategy. In other words, structure should follow strategy. For example, if an organization's central mission is to be innovative, to pursue new product designs or services, then its structure should help achieve that goal. Clearly, from what we have discussed earlier, the characteristics associated with the organic organization would best suit that objective. Few rules, decentralized decision making, and a wide span of control encourage

EXHIBIT 5.3	STRATEGY AND STRUCTURE	
	Types of Organizational Strategies	
Elements of Structure	**Focus on Innovation**	**Focus on Cost and Efficiency**
1. Division of Labour	wide	narrow
2. Adherence to Clear Chain of Command	flexible	strict
3. Span of Control	wide	narrow
4. Centralization	decentralized	centralized
5. Formalization	low	high
6. Departmentation	no specific preference	no specific preference

flexibility and adaptiveness to environmental demands. And these are, consequently, useful for encouraging innovation. If, on the other hand, efficiency or cost-minimization is a central strategy, then the mechanistic organization is the better-suited structure. (See Exhibit 5.3.)

2.   Organizational Size

If you observe the organizational landscape, it is hard not to see some kind of connection between the size of an organization and its structure. We mentioned earlier than an entrepreneurial structure is suited to small business, but is not well suited to larger organizations that tend to require, for example, more rules and regulations to substitute for the individual leadership that is present in an entrepreneurial organization. In terms of our organic-mechanistic classification, there is a tendency for larger organizations to shift more toward a mechanistic structure — largely because of the need to control and coordinate many more employees. When you have masses of employees whose performance must be directed, it would seem beneficial to standardize or specialize work, to departmentalize into units that can be supervised by managers. It is difficult to maintain the informality of the organic structure when organizations grow. However, that is not to say that many large organizations do not try to retain an organic structure, even in the face of significant growth. For example, although Microsoft is a large organization, it prides itself in innovation, and has attempted to divide itself into manageable units where team-based approaches are employed and where informality frees up the entrepreneurial spirit. Similarly, Johnson & Johnson prides itself in being a decentralized empire that has had 166 separately chartered companies. The top managers are given much decision-making power

EXHIBIT 5.4	ORGANIZATIONAL SIZE AND STRUCTURE	

Six Elements	Small Organization	Large Organization
1. Division of Labour	wide	narrow
2. Adherence to Clear Chain of Command	no specific preference	no specific preference
3. Span of Control	wide	narrow
4. Centralization	centralized	decentralized
5. Formalization	low	high
6. Departmentation	functional	divisional

for their units, and there is a great effort to maintain a flat organizational structure, even though the company itself is quite large. Exhibit 5.4 illustrates the relationship between size and the elements of structure.

3. Technology

Technology essentially refers to how an organization transforms its inputs, such as financial capital and physical and human resources, into services or products. For example, the assembly-line approach has been used to produce output in the car manufacturing industry. Among classifications within technology is how routine or non-routine that technology is. Routine technology refers to automated and standardized operations typical of mass production operations, while non-routine technology is not standardized, and might include anything from conducting genetic research to custom-made furniture. As you might have guessed, standardized, mass production technologies are more compatible with mechanistic structures where such standardization is part of the main objective. Non-routine technologies, on the other hand, are better suited to the innovative, organic structures that do not allow formality and rules to govern activity. The following observation has been made with regard to the significance of technology and how it has transformed the way companies operate:

> ... The personal computer revolution brought power to the desktop that was unimaginable in the 1980s. A powerful array of technologies — cell phones, e-mail and the Internet, e-commerce, and business-to-business exchanges — rapidly emerged to transform business practices. Economic alliances and supply chains were destroyed and then recreated. Big computer makers like IBM lost their dominant position because of an onslaught of competition from companies like Apple and other companies making PC clones. IBM announced the second-largest downsizing of the 1990s, with 63,000 let go in July 1993.[45]

LET'S TALK BUSINESS 5.3   DYNAMIC DEREGULATION

The deregulation of protected industries in the 1980s and 1990s created competition for companies where none had previously existed. The telecom, banking, energy, and aerospace industries were roiled by the change. As the dominant companies in these sectors were forced to compete in an open market, they started letting sizable numbers of people go. The breakup of the Bell System into AT&T, Lucent, and the seven Baby Bells unleashed a surge of technology inventiveness. It was not surprising that telecom, financial services, and aerospace dominated the list of industries experiencing the heaviest downsizing in the early to mid-1990s.

Source: From John A Challenger, "The transformed workplace: How can you survive" *The Futurist* (Nov./Dec. 2001) 35(6): 24–28. Originally published in the Nov./Dec. 2001 Issue of *The Futurist*. Used with permission from the World Future Society, 7910 Woodmont Avenue, Suite 450, Bethesda, Maryland 20814. Telephone: 301/656-8274; Fax: 301/951-0394; <http://www.wfs.org>.

---

4.   Environment

Among the main elements we might consider as composing an organization's environment are: suppliers, customers, competitors, the government, and the general public. When might an organization's structure be affected by its environment? Again, if we can use a broad classification, you can think of an organization's environment in two broad classes: **dynamic** or **static** environment. Static environments, as the name suggests, exhibit little if any change — no new competitors, no new technologies, no government regulatory changes, etc. In such an environment of certainty, the mechanistic structure would be quite suitable: it generates rules and methods of performance based on environmental needs and, once established, does not change. A dynamic environment contains much uncertainty and undergoes much change. Clearly, an organic structure is much better suited, given its higher adaptiveness, to change. Competition alone has accounted for much change in the environment of business. Such competition has accelerated largely through the forces of globalization and deregulation, issues discussed elsewhere in this book and briefly mentioned in Let's Talk Business 5.3.

Each of these factors are useful to keep in mind when considering the range of changes we have witnessed in recent years.

The Importance of the Environment

In order to understand why organizations are designed in a certain way, it makes sense to consider the environment within which they operate. There are numerous theories and models that have attempted to identify those factors that determine the structure of organizations. Contingency theory is a natural outgrowth of systems theory,[46] and it recognizes that all organizations are open systems that can only survive through continuous and successful interaction with their environment.

What factors influence whether a tall bureaucratic organization or a simple flat structure is suitable? In what contexts does a centralized decision-making structure, as opposed to a decentralized structure, make sense? Contingency theory focuses on the contextual factors that can influence the structure and management of organizations, with a particular emphasis on organizational design. Why do some organizations benefit from centralized decision making? Why do some organizations require a high level of formalization with regard to employee job responsibilities? Contingency theories seek to explain what factors in the organization's environment influence these organizational design choices.

A central philosophy underlying contingency theory is that there is no one ideal way to organize. That is, there are no universal principles of what constitutes the best form of organization. The optimal organizational structure is dependent on, or is contingent on, the nature of its operating environment. Consequently, this implies that managers should seek to achieve a fit or alignment among the major elements of their organization's environment and its internal organizational design. Therefore, while contingency theory suggests that there is no one best way to organize universally, it does assert that there is one best way to organize, given a specific type of operating environment or organizational context.

Contingency theory is based on the assumption that organizations are able to adapt to changing environmental conditions. Given the need for organizations to design their structure in reference to their environment, successful organizations must adapt to any changes in that environment via structural change. This also assumes that organizations behave as rational entities that are able and willing to make internal structural changes to achieve a compatibility with their environment as a means for survival and success. According to contingency theory, there are a number of specific contingency factors that can influence organizational design. One of the most widely studied factors is the notion of environmental uncertainty.

Environmental uncertainty has been defined as the rate at which market conditions and production technologies change. There is no doubt that environmental uncertainty is an important dimension that may vary among organizations and industries. For example, some organizations operate within relatively static environments — few, if any, new competitors, unchanging technology, few changes in governmental regulations, etc. Other organizations may exist in very dynamic environments — constantly new competitors, rapidly changing technology, new governmental regulations, etc.

Researchers by the names of Burns and Stalker were among the first, in the 1960s, to systematically study the influence of the environment on organizational structure. Among their studies was a comparison of organizations existing in two fundamentally different environments: one set of firms operated within a dynamic, changing industry; another set operated in a stable, established industry. The researchers found that there were a number of significant structural differences in these two sets of organizations. (See Exhibit 5.5.) In essence, the results of this research suggested that an organization's structure is dependent, or contingent, on the type of environment within which the organization operates.

Lessons for managers. The contingency approach presents some important lessons for managers. Among these lessons is the need for managers to take great caution in the

EXHIBIT 5.5	DYNAMIC VS. STATIC INDUSTRY	

Organizational Characteristics	Static Industry	Dynamic Industry
Rules and Procedures	• reliance on formal rules and procedures to carry out most organizational activities	• relatively fewer rules
Decision Making	• highly centralized	• more decentralized
Levels of Administration or Supervisory Control	• greater number of levels	• fewer levels

way they interpret the organization's environment. Managers must accurately define those environmental factors that have significant impact on their organizations in order to generate a suitable organizational structure — one capable of responding to environmental demands and the characteristics for which it was designed. By the mid-1980s, managers found that their assumptions about the environment largely no longer held. Organizational characteristics regarding the different kinds of hierarchies, organizational practices and strategies developed in the past were suddenly incapable of dealing with changes in the organizational environment.

RE-ENGINEERING

A management consultant by the name of James Champy was asked to observe the operations of an insurance company in an effort to improve its efficiency. Among his observations, Champy discovered that it took 24 days to obtain a policy after the client purchased it. Champy was curious to understand what work was done on these insurance policies during the 24 days it took to reach the purchaser. After following the trail of these policies, Champy found that only about 10 minutes of work was actually performed on these policies during that 24-day period. The additional time arose because the policies were transferred through 14 different departments. Was this necessary? Champy discovered that while there was no real need for policies to travel through this long and winding road, it nevertheless had become a tradition: "This is how we do things here." There had been no assessment, however, of whether, indeed, this method was still necessary.

James Champy and one of his colleagues, Michael Hammer, engaged in many more observations of different types of organizations, and they, along with a number of other experts, advocated a rethinking of organizational design, detailed in their best-selling book, *Re-engineering the corporation*. Re-engineering became one of the hottest business buzz-words of the 1990s; but what exactly is it? Fundamentally, re-engineering asks the question: "If I were creating this company today, if I could start over, given what I know and given current technology, what would it look like?" A more systematic definition includes the following elements:

> **The fundamental rethinking and radical redesigning of business processes to achieve dramatic improvements in measures of performance (cost, quality, service, speed).**[47]

In examining the definition of re-engineering, we can understand its essence and its basic contributions to organizational design. Let's consider each element of this definition.

1. Fundamental rethinking of the organization's structure and functions. Re-engineering involves a critical examination of the traditional method of structuring work. An organization will examine how it performs its functions in order to assess whether, indeed, this method makes the most sense. This examination of work processes is done with a focus on how to best serve customer needs. Two fundamental questions that any re-engineering effort must ask are: "How do we improve quality of our product/service?"; and, "How can we reduce costs?" One central aim is to eliminate any company practice that is not adding value to the process of generating a product or service for the customer. The notion of focusing on the company's "core competencies" implies that the aim is to concentrate on what the company does best and eliminate unnecessary functions or practices.

2. Radical redesign of organization processes and structure. The thrust of re-engineering is to "re-invent" the organization according to the current objectives. Hammer and Champy suggested that a lot of organizations that claim they are making changes to become more efficient are really just trying to do "worthless tasks" more efficiently. What re-engineering advocates is a "quantum leap". However, it is important to note that while the radical redesign of an organization is the fundamental rationale behind re-engineering, it is difficult to achieve in practice.

Accomplishing the goal of redesign typically involves organizing around process rather than functions. For much of the 20th century, beliefs about organizing focused on specializing jobs, compartmentalizing them into the simplest elements, therefore ensuring work was standardized (as advocated in scientific management and Weber's notion of bureaucracy). Re-engineering advocates the collection of individual tasks into more whole jobs. This relates to the distinction between process and functions. It is reflected in the notion of moving away from a focus on specialized tasks to a focus on process. Consider an example offered by Hammer and Champy, the case of a credit agency, in Let's Talk Business 5.4.

The illustration reflects the notion of organization around process — in other words, designing the organization in a way that considers the actual jobs that need to be performed. This is in contrast to a blanket approach to organizational design that would simply advocate the creation of different departments within which jobs will be organized. Often the bureaucratic structure becomes preoccupied with administrative levels of hierar-

---

LET'S TALK BUSINESS 5.4   THE CREDIT AGENCY

This organization found that the task of processing a credit application was extremely slow and inefficient, taking anywhere from six days to two weeks to complete. After a credit request was received by phone it was recorded on a piece of paper. This paper was then passed along to credit checkers, pricers (who determined what interest rate to charge), and to many other individuals who performed single, compartmentalized tasks. Credit applications typically were bounced around to different areas before they were properly completed. Now after much scrutiny, it was discovered that the time actually required to complete such an application shouldn't take more than 90 minutes! Consequently, it was time to re-engineer — "scrap" the traditional method organized around specialized, compartmentalized tasks and redesign the work around the process itself of completing a credit application. This did not require numerous specialists but simply required few generalists. That is, one person could process an entire application without passing it on to others. So this work was re-engineered, resulting in a decrease to the four-hour application time, an enormous increase in the number of applications processed, and fewer employees required to do the job.

---

chy, rules and regulations. The machine bureaucracy and the professional bureaucracy are examples of these popular forms of organizational design. What re-engineering advocates is to move away from a preoccupation with organizing work based on tasks, jobs, departments and administrative levels of hierarchy, and instead to focus on processes — the activities required to transform inputs into outputs. This fundamental logic of re-engineering was recently observed, as shown in Let's Talk Business 5.5, by management scholar William Kettinger.

With regard to the nature of the job, re-engineering also advocates combining several jobs into one. This, too, was reflected in the credit agency example above. This is akin to the notion of job enrichment: that is, enriching the responsibility and challenge of jobs by allowing workers to do more of the task rather than one narrow, highly specialized piece of the work. Certainly technology has helped facilitate the integration of jobs and the ability of fewer people to perform a greater variety of tasks. In fact, it has been observed that among the leading factors contributing to the proliferation of re-engineering activity in the early 1990s were advances in information technology. Technologies including shared databases, client-server architecture, and imaging could be efficiently applied to facilitate processes that cross different functional departments.[48]

The above suggests that re-engineering may result in the view that work can be performed efficiently with fewer employees. Typically, re-engineering means **cutting** the size of the workforce, and often involves flattening the organizational hierarchy. Examples abound, including organizations like Pepsi-Cola North America, which cut seven layers of its hierarchy to four in order to focus on designing itself around serving customers rather than simply maintaining a hierarchical bureaucracy. This also presents a major challenge for

---

LET'S TALK BUSINESS 5.5   LESSONS IN RE-ENGINEERING

Typically in an early lecture in one of my classes, I ask a student to come to the board and draw a picture of a company where she or he has worked. Inevitably, they draw a hierarchical organization chart — the student is typically on the bottom, and the bosses are on top. I respond that if this is a picture of a company, then where are the customers, and how do products and services get produced, delivered, and improved? This pushes them to draw a horizontal, or process-based representation, of the company which explains these relationships. Soon the board is covered with every conceivable business process — order fulfillment, product development, quality assurance, and on and on. These students quickly see that a business process is nothing more than logically related tasks that use the resources of a company to achieve a defined business outcome. This is a simple, but powerful, concept! Within a few classes, these students have internalized a process view (or "process think," as we refer to it) that helps them conceptualize new ways to improve operations, satisfy customers, and make the best use of the latest information technologies. Similar to the way these students learn process thinking, employees at all levels have grown to incorporate a process view into all aspects of their work. As process thinking has become mainstream, re-engineering has lost its radical tone. We have seen reconciliation with more incremental process change methods such as TQM. Today we recognize that we must broaden the business change tent to accommodate radical business objectives, incremental implementations, and both top-down-driven and bottom-up-driven process change.

Source: From Varun Grover, William J. Kettinger, and James T.C. Teng, "Business process change in the 21st century" *Business and Economic Review* (Jan.–Mar. 2000) 46(2): 14–18. Reproduced with permission of the authors.

---

organizations attempting to re-engineer: the threat of job loss for many employees. As management scholar Varun Grover recently observed:

> Perhaps the biggest challenge associated with the success of the re-engineering phenomenon may be that of selling such a major change to the employees of the organization and getting them to "buy into" the strategic changes that must be undertaken for the firm to survive and prosper. For example, outsourcing activities that don't contribute to core competencies or technology to other firms that can perform them better may be a legitimate outcome of a good re-engineering effort. It would lead to work force reduction, but only with the purpose of making the firm leaner and more responsive. Time-based competition and the creation of "agile" corporations may not even be possible without such changes in work force size and composition. As companies emphasize the notion of capturing and leveraging "knowledge" as a source of value, a broader focus on process change management may perhaps be the only way to avoid skill obsolescence of employees and encourage horizontal career paths. The extent to which top level management can sell such a vision of change and its impact on the employees is critical. We found that often information technology problems are considered critical before the project, but it's the management of people and change that really makes the difference.[49]

TOWARD A VIRTUAL ORGANIZATION

If downsizing has become one of the most feared business buzzwords in recent years, a much more benevolent yet popular buzzword is the "virtual organization". How does an organization become virtual? And equally important: Why would an organization want to become virtual? The virtual organization underscores how far we have come from the traditional notion of organizations. According to our old philosophy, the bureaucratic structure is typically large. The virtual organization, on the other hand, is not dependent on size for its functions. In fact, the virtual organization attempts to maximize its fluidity, flatness and integratedness with the environment — i.e., building off of many of the structural trends we identified earlier. Let's consider the ways a virtual organization attempts to achieve these characteristics.

Outsourcing. Outsourcing (or contracting out) involves hiring external organizations to conduct work in certain functions of the company. For example, payroll, accounting, legal work can be assigned to outsourced staff. The organization typically will retain its core functions or competencies — that is, those areas that it is in business to conduct. In other words, it sticks to what it does best and outsources functions that it doesn't wish to focus on. While the buzzword "outsourcing" may seem relatively recent, the practice of outsourcing has, in fact, been with us for many years. Consider the extensive list of "suppliers" of expertise to industry — lawyers, public accountants, independent insurance adjusters, contractors, appraisers, health care professionals and independent medical specialists. Perhaps what is also more recent is the trend toward building businesses with a consideration of which activities are required "in-house" and which functions can simply be outsourced. For example, CIBC recently outsourced a major portion of its Human Resource administrative functions to Electronic Data Services (EDS). The move is consistent with the philosophy of outsourcing: shedding business activities that do not reflect the organization's core competencies. Obviously, managing human resource functions, such as payroll or pension plans, are not part of CIBC's core competencies. These functions can be outsourced to a company whose core competency is in such areas. EDS specializes in these areas. CIBC gains by having an expert company deal with these functions, and at the same time they have cut costs through the elimination of almost half their Human Resources department in 1999–2000.[50]

A good example of the potential benefits and, often, necessity of outsourcing is found in the popular trend of outsourcing the payroll function. There are a variety of reasons for choosing to outsource the payroll function, including dealing with increased human resource demands that may be caused by employee population growth, mergers, acquisitions, spin-offs, consolidations, and downsizing. As Heather Erickson points out in a recent article, outsourcing can often be used to help in special or unique circumstances. As an illustration, Erickson offers a number of possible circumstances that have encouraged the outsourcing of the payroll function in Exhibit 5.6.[51]

Networking. We have increasingly been observing organizations limiting themselves to fewer activities in which they have expertise and assigning specialists to handle all other functions. This is also associated with the notion of integrated or networked organizations that we identified earlier. That is, organizations can engage in co-operative relationships with suppliers, distributors or competitors. The aim is to improve their efficiency and flexi-

---

EXHIBIT 5.6	OUTSOURCING PAYROLL: WHY?

1. **Mergers:** Following consolidation, the payroll function may be outsourced in order to permit the HR function and accounting function to focus on making changes that reflect the pay and benefit policies of the new corporation.

2. **Foreign acquisitions:** When a foreign buyer acquires a Canadian company, the unique nature of tax laws may not mix well with the new parent company's payroll system. Outsourcing the Canadian subsidiary payroll function avoids this conflict.

3. **Closing down a division:** In cases where a company is shutting down a division, complex severance packages paid over an extended period of time to a diverse group of former employees may be required. The demanding nature of these packages may not be efficiently dealt with by the internal payroll function, but may be better served by being outsourced to an external party while allowing the internal payroll department to focus on existing employee accounts.

4. **Confidentiality:** Salaries are typically a sensitive issue requiring high security. Some organizations may prefer to outsource the work done on particularly high security salaries, such as for senior executives, and on performance and incentive compensation plans in order to ensure that no organizational member becomes privy to this information.

5. **Entrepreneurial firms:** Small companies that are experiencing rapid growth in numbers of employees may find that outsourcing can offer a faster, more cost-effective way to manage the increasing demands of payroll. The outsourcing of the payroll function allows the business managers to focus on managing business growth and the core functions of the business rather than becoming preoccupied with the peripheral yet demanding function of payroll. For example, a small business that grows rapidly from three employees to 150 in 12 months found that when there were only the three owners to pay, writing cheques was easy. On the other hand, at 150 employees, the owners realized it was a function they no longer had time to manage. By outsourcing, the owners avoided hiring a full-time payroll person, and consequently the cost was much less than the cost of salary and benefits for a new full-time employee.

---

bility in meeting new consumer needs. For example, a close relationship with a distributor might offer the supplier company more information about the changing needs of customers. The Japanese version of networked organizations called keiretsu could, in fact, really be considered the first form of the virtual organization.

Typically, a keiretsu involves a large bank or financial institution, a large industrial organization, and a number of smaller firms. This integrated network of relationships allows the large industrial organization to produce the product with financial assistance from the bank. The role of the smaller firms may be to supply parts to the manufacturer, conduct research or, perhaps, distribute the final product. What we observe in virtual organizations are only those activities that are central — they are kept in-house, so to speak, and all other functions are outsourced to separate companies or individuals who are typically coordinated by a small head office. Or, each company is simply involved in some kind of network where each brings their own expertise to the collection of companies.

Shed non-core functions. The outsourcing aspect, again, is a central feature of the virtual organization. Clearly organizations can become more "virtual" by shedding some of

---

LET'S TALK BUSINESS 5.6   GOING VIRTUAL

Toyota Canada Inc. in Toronto outsources selected portions of their application management functions. Bell Canada is another of many Canadian companies involved in outsourcing functions. Bell started with the outsourcing of its mainframe services in 1996, and later outsourced application development and maintenance, in addition to help desk and desktop support. Bell Canada's choice to outsource reflects the fundamental philosophy — Bell transferred Information Technology functions that were not part of the organization's core competencies to organizations that have those core competencies. Similarly, Xerox Canada and Air Canada found a win-win gain from an outsourcing arrangement. They engaged in a $25 million, seven-year agreement for Xerox Global Document Services to provide document management services to Air Canada. These outsourced services include printing, distributing materials, paper supplies and managing Air Canada's national copier fleet. Air Canada viewed this arrangement as offering improvements in cost savings and document process productivity.[1]

Source: [1] Denise Deveau, "The source of service" *Computing Canada* (July 13, 2001) 27(15): 14–15.

---

the non-core functions of the company and outsourcing these to affiliated organizations. Companies that use information technology (IT) need to become as flexible as the virtual organizations, given the rapidly changing face of technology and its applications. For organizations whose core competency is not IT or all its elements, there is much to be gained from partnering with other organizations, in the virtual sense. A growing number of IT departments are considering outsourcing models to address all or part of their needs. "Small component" or discrete outsourcing service providers include such specialized offerings as storage and Web hosting. Application management has become a high growth area in outsourcing service markets in Canada. Those seeking such services have a range of services to choose for outsourcing, including desktop or infrastructure services to various business functions. Network management can be outsourced, along with backup and recovery, as well as data centre services. Such examples are noted in Let's Talk Business 5.6.

A virtual organization might be composed of simply a small group of business executives who form the core of the organization. Their responsibility is to oversee and coordinate the activities that might be done in-house as well as those functions that are outsourced — which might involve coordinating relationships among the companies that develop, manufacture, market and sell their products. Many more companies have found that they can become quite profitable without actually having to own their entire operation. Certainly, the traditional bureaucracy is structured so that production occurs in company-owned plants, research and development are conducted by in-house experts, sales and marketing are performed by the company's own sales and marketing department. This is not the case for the virtual organization that doesn't believe you need to own everything. For example, Dell Computer owns no plants, and simply assembles computers from parts whose manufacture has been outsourced. Similarly, Apple Computer sub-contracted the manufacture of its first notebook to Sony as a means to speed entry into the market.

Companies like Nike and Reebok have achieved success by focusing on what they do best — designing and marketing their products. They outsource almost all their footwear manufacturing to outside suppliers. Obviously, the virtual organization doesn't just outsource the peripheral function of the company; they outsource whatever costs less than conducting it in-house.

There are a number of **gains** potentially achieved by going virtual:

1. **The cost savings are significant.** A virtual organization need not own its own plants, employ its own research and development teams, nor hire its own sales staff. This means the virtual organization also doesn't need to hire the extra staff to support all these functions — such as personnel specialists, company lawyers, accountants, etc. The virtual organization can outsource most of these functions, and focus on what they do best. So there is little, if any, administrative overhead, so to speak, because work activities are largely contracted. Costs savings arise in areas such as training, purchasing of work-related tools, benefits, downtime, and educational requirements. All these requirements are typically obtained with the arrival of the external or "outsourced" experts.

2. **The virtual organization is a great alternative for entrepreneurs.** That is, individuals seeking to start up a new business or venture may face huge start-up costs. The network of arrangements can exploit the expertise of different companies while not requiring the initiator of the business to buy everything and start a business from scratch.

3. **For a mature company, going virtual can be a fast way to develop and market new products.** Relying on the expertise of partners means that no huge investment is required to enter a new product or service territory.

4. **Fast and flexible are adjectives to describe the virtual organization** — the flexible arrangements of those parties involved can be of a temporary nature to produce a good or service. Resources can be quickly arranged and rearranged to meet changing demands and best serve customers. Management isn't getting bogged down in peripheral functions, but is simply focusing only on central functions.

Among the **risks and challenges** of becoming virtual are the following:

1. **Probably the biggest sacrifice is the notion of control.** Control has traditionally been a key goal of any organization. The structure of the bureaucratic organization is fundamentally based on the notion of control — control through standardization of work, control through hierarchy of authority, control through rules and regulations, control through clear division of labour. However, the virtual organization doesn't provide such control. Think of it — how can you monitor all activity when it may not even be occurring within the walls of one building? Among the fears of going virtual and outsourcing is that we are "hollowing out" the organization and making it extremely dependent on external sources. The employees are not all ours; outsourcing to independent contractors doesn't carry with it the same level of control as staffing our own employees to do the work. Difficulties in control can particularly occur when a variety of subcontractors are involved in the work. This lack of control may also generate a lack of control over costs — once a company

becomes dependent on a supplier, it may be unable to refuse an increase in the supplier's prices.

2. **Another potential disadvantage is the lack of employee loyalty.** If our organization is largely composed of temporary workers and subcontractors, who is really committed to perpetuating the goals of this company? Can a virtual organization really develop a sense of identity or culture that is the "glue" that binds everyone to a common purpose? This is an issue that virtual organizations must deal with. In fact, turnover in many virtual organizations tends to be high, because employees are committed only to the task for which they are hired, and in addition, employees may be working under temporary contractual arrangements and could be dismissed in favour of another contractor.

3. **A final significant risk in going virtual is the potential to sacrifice competitive learning opportunities.** Outsourcing involves the strategic decision to "let go" of some aspect of the organization — the decision could be to permit the manufacture of the footware, as in the case of Nike, while retaining the core competencies (such as the marketing function, also, as in the case of Nike). The question is: Is there a danger in "letting go" of functions that may currently appear peripheral, but could become important functions of the organization should the organization's strategy change in the future? Clearly, if a function is outsourced, the experience or learning of this function as a skill is lost to the internal organization. Is there an inherent danger in such a situation? That is: Is there a danger in outsourcing, given the risk of losing key skills that could be needed for future competitiveness? Read Let's Talk Business 5.7 for the risks of outsourcing.

DOWNSIZING

In terms of business buzzwords, probably the most dreaded buzzword of the 1990s was the term "downsizing". While the 1990s have been referred to as the "lean, mean 90s", the trend toward leanness via downsizing has not gone away in the new millennium. In recent years, across Canada, thousands of workers have been losing their jobs. In August 2001, Canada's unemployment rate rose to 7.2% (its highest level in two years). Downsizing has also cut across all industries, from high-tech, to manufacturing, to banking. CIBC slashed hundreds of jobs in 2001.[52] The large fibre-optics organization JDS Uniphase Corp (based in Ottawa and San Jose) announced plans for 16,000 layoffs in 2001, while Nortel cut thousands of jobs. In the same year, General Motors announced the closing of its assembly plant in Ste-Thérèse, Quebec, with the consequent loss of 1,400 workers. Of course, following the terrorist attacks in September 2001, airlines suffered huge losses, with organizations like Air Canada announcing 12,500 layoffs and American carriers cutting over 100,000 jobs.[53]

In broad terms, downsizing refers to the planned reduction in the breadth of an organization's operations. Typically, it entails terminating relatively large numbers of employees and/or decreasing the number of products or services the organization provides. It seems that if you think of just about any large corporation, they have likely experienced some kind of downsizing: from AT & T to Bell Canada, to Air Canada, to IBM, to General

---

LET'S TALK BUSINESS 5.7   THE RISKS OF OUTSOURCING

[O]utsourcing can result in the unintended transfer of the most significant part of an industry's experience curve. Even in the closest of outsourcing relationships, the partners will always remain potential future competitors, and in such cases, the one with the most efficient learning capability across the partnership interface may prosper at the ultimate expense of the other. For companies like Hewlett Packard and Apple, the strategy to outsource some high-level components to Canon may make sense, if the learning afforded by the manufacture of today's laser printer engines is marginal to the development of their own core competencies. However it can be notoriously difficult to know when particular opportunities to learn in the present might be more crucial to future competitiveness than they now seem. For example, several years ago Eastman Kodak decided to exit the camcorder business altogether when there was little prospect of its ever becoming a major commercial activity for the company. Years later it came to look back at this decision as a lost opportunity to develop skills in key components of the camcorder with potentially much wider future applications.

In the same vein, few in the 1970s could have foreseen how many of the key competencies on which the future of the computer industry came to be built would have passed so quickly from those of IBM and Digital to those of the upstream suppliers like Intel and Microsoft. This is always a risk in outsourcing. The dilemma facing any company attracted to such a strategy is the risk that it helps its supplier-partners to deepen their competencies at its own expense, which, in the competition for learning opportunities today, will be crucial in the competition for tomorrow's key markets. In short, outsourcing companies need to consciously think through not just which parts they can outsource with profit today, but what learning opportunities they may be foregoing, and which competencies they may be fragmenting in the process. This kind of caution will be crucial if long-term competitiveness is not to be carelessly sacrificed for short-term advantage.

Source: From Brian Leavy, "Outsourcing strategy and a learning dilemma" *Production and Inventory Management Journal* (1996) 37(4): 50–54.

Motors, to Northern Telecom — all have experienced massive cuts in their workforce. Consequently, most of us associate downsizing with the reduction of the workforce. However, we can be more specific, given that organizations can downsize in a variety of ways. For example, does reducing an organization's ownership of assets amount to downsizing? Does a reduction in the number of employees constitute downsizing?

> One definition of downsizing that has been offered is: "downsizing is a set of activities undertaken on the part of management and designed to improve organizational efficiency, productivity, and/or competitiveness. It represents a strategy implemented by managers that affects the size of the firm's work force, the costs, and the work processes."[54]

Based on this definition, there are three fundamental types of strategies for downsizing: workforce reduction, work redesign, and systematic change. Workforce reduction typi-

153

cally involves a short-term strategy that is aimed at reducing the number of employees through such programs as attrition, early retirement, voluntary severance packages, layoffs, or terminations. It has been observed that downsizing approaches have largely been directed at workforce reduction rather than the more detailed and longer-term strategies of job redesign and systematic change.[55] Below, we can more clearly identify the common approaches to downsizing. That is, we can be more specific about what exactly an organizational downsizing may entail. This will allow us to briefly identify the potential benefits as well as potential pitfalls of an organizational downsizing.

Methods of Downsizing

Management scholar Martin Evans has provided a summary of the forms of downsizing, and he also identified the potential benefits and consequences of these different approaches to it. The most common forms of downsizing include any one, or a combination, of the following strategies:

1. **Across the board cutbacks.** Cutting a fixed percentage of the workforce across all departments or units.

2. **Early retirement and voluntary severance.** Those nearing retirement take early retirement, voluntary as opposed to a forced leave — typically as the first stage in a downsizing process.

3. **De-layering — cutting a level or levels of the organization.** Termination or reassignment of the middle managers who are not replaced, flattening the organizational hierarchy by removing horizontal slices.

4. **Contracting-out (also referred to as outsourcing).** Lay off staff in areas that perform specialized functions and contract out this work to agencies that can staff those areas with temporary workers. Types of activities that are typically contracted out include payroll, data entry, public relations and clerical work, as opposed to the core activities of the organization.

5. **Dropping product lines.** Discontinue some programs or product lines provided by the organization.

Exhibit 5.7 offers an identification of the pros and cons of each of these approaches to downsizing.

Consequences of Downsizing

The strategy of downsizing that started in the mid-1980s has now become commonplace. In the early stages, downsizing strategies were viewed as a panacea for the ills of organizations, providing organizations with a method of cost reduction, productivity and profitability improvement and, consequently, a higher competitive ability. Unfortunately, there is vast evidence that the anticipated benefits of corporate downsizing have largely failed to materialize. It is of interest to reconsider the anticipated benefits of downsizing and in

| EXHIBIT 5.7 | POTENTIAL BENEFITS AND RISKS OF DOWNSIZING |

Potential Benefits

1. **Across-the-Board Cuts.**
   - "Shares the pain", spreading it across the organization — all levels are equally affected.

2. **Early Retirement and Voluntary Severance.**
   - Concentrates the terminations among those who are willing to leave.
   - May help achieve the reduced cost objective by encouraging the more senior and more highly paid staff to leave.

3. **De-layering.**
   - Because the organization is cut horizontally, all areas are equally affected, and the "pain" is shared across all departments.
   - To the extent that decentralized decision making is desired, this approach allows the shift of responsibility to the lower and, perhaps, more appropriate levels in the organization.

4. **Contracting-out.**
   - Immediate costs savings.

5. **Dropping Product Lines.**
   - Decide what areas may not be productive to continue to maintain.
   - A closer connection to long-term strategic planning compared to other approaches.
   - Concentrates the disruption in one or a few business units, as opposed to the entire organization.

Potential Risks

1. **Across-the-Board Cuts.**
   - Efficient parts of organization are hurt. This form of downsizing ignores how well or how poorly managed are the units.
   - Typically conducted when there is no strategic plan — it simply cuts staff throughout the organization.

2. **Early Retirement and Voluntary Severance.**
   - Not necessarily guided by a strategic plan.
   - Encourages voluntary exits from all parts of the organization.
   - "Loss of corporate memory" — that is, a company may lose highly experienced, valued members who have been an intrinsic apart of what this organization is all about.

3. **De-layering.**
   - A loss of corporate memory with the removal of middle managers. There may also be an overload of responsibility to top management, who now may need to fill the role of some middle management as well.
   - There may be significant costs attached to the transition from a taller organization to a flatter one where lower level employees must be trained to take on additional roles and responsibilities.

4. **Contracting-out.**
   - Difficulties of dealing with the new suppliers of this labour and avoiding future cost increases.
   - The general loss of control with these temporary workers.

5. **Dropping Product Lines.**
   - Pain is concentrated and not shared across the entire organization — a few people will carry the burden of this type of downsizing.

LET'S TALK BUSINESS 5.8   RESULTS OF DOWNSIZING

Why does an organization engage in a downsizing? A survey of over 1,000 downsized companies conducted in the early 1990s by the Wyatt Company identified the following short-term goals of downsizing: to reduce costs, to increase profitability, and to increase productivity. In terms of long-term goals, the following were identified: improve product quality, increase customer service, improve competitiveness. These are in fact quite commonly identified aims of a downsizing. The key question is: What percentage of these companies achieved these goals after their downsizing? The results of this specific study are discouraging. Out of the approximately 1,000 companies surveyed, 61% achieved reductions in their costs of operation. However, that is where the good news about the downsizing appears to end, based on this survey. For example, only 37% of these companies achieved increases in profitability; only 40% achieved increase in productivity; in terms of long-term goals: 45% saw improvements in product quality; only 31% showed an increase in customer service; and only 17% felt they had improved their competitiveness.

---

what way these benefits have not been realized. Let's Talk Business 5.8 illustrates some of the reasons for engaging in downsizing.

As the Wyatt report and numerous other studies have indicated, there are a host of benefits that organizations feel they can achieve through engaging in downsizing, including: reduced bureaucracy, lower overhead costs, improved decision making, improvements in productivity, and a stronger ability to innovate. However, there is an abundance of empirical evidence that indicates that the anticipated benefits of downsizing typically fail to materialize. For example, does downsizing contribute to a better "bottom line"? That is, does this activity enhance the organization's financial performance? There is research evidence that suggests that a downsizing or layoff announcement often leads to a drop in the organization's share price, particularly if that announcement was related to financial concerns or a massive and permanent cutback of employees.[56] There is also evidence to suggest that investors respond negatively to layoff announcements.[57]

Does downsizing improve organizational performance as measured by return on assets and common shares? There is research evidence indicating that organizations that engaged in an employee downsizing (i.e., termination of at least 5% of the workforce combined with little change in plant and equipment costs) did not outperform other organizations in their industry.[58] Similarly, a 1994 study by the American Management Association found that less than 35% of downsized firms reported significant improvements in productivity, and 44% reported significant increases in operating profits. Ironically, the study reported that almost one-third of the downsized firms experienced productivity decreases during the same period. Similarly, a CSC Index survey found that less than 33% of all downsizing initiatives had achieved their anticipated productivity or profitability goals.

In a large-scale study conducted in Canada, data were collected from 1,907 Canadian organizations with at least 75 employees. This study examined how a permanent workforce reduction affects employer efficiency, employee satisfaction, and employee–employer relations. The findings indicated that a permanent workforce reduction was associated with negative consequences. This echoes the findings in the United States and elsewhere, and underscores the consistent failure of downsizing to live up to its expectations.[59]

Added to the lacklustre results of downsizing is the wealth of evidence of the costs of downsizing in terms of human consequences. Needless to say, those individuals who are victims of a downsizing can be subjected to intense psychological trauma. However, there is also ample research evidence to indicate that the survivors of a downsizing may experience trauma. According to numerous studies conducted, survivors of a downsizing typically report greater levels of stress, burnout, reduced self-confidence and self-esteem, and lower job satisfaction.[60] Studies have also found that a downsizing can have adverse effects on employee commitment to the organization, performance, customer and client needs, and reduced morale and trust.[61]

Why Has Downsizing Failed to Achieve Anticipated Results?

If the cost reduction results are inconsistent, if there is no evidence that productivity, profitability and competitiveness improve as a result of downsizing: What is going wrong? There are at least three fundamental issues that have been repeatedly linked with the failure of downsizing. These issues reflect shortcomings in the planning for and execution of organizational downsizings, rather than an outright condemnation of the practice itself.

1. Lack of strategic planning. Many downsizings have not been guided by a long-range strategic plan, but rather have been a short-term response to environmental pressures. The poor performance of downsizing has been associated with the tendency of downsizing programs to be hastily formulated and not linked with the strategic plans of the organization.[62] While downsizing is by no means going away, by the end of the 1990s organizations were looking more critically at downsizing as a method of organizational change, and many reconsidered its role without the broader framework of organizational planning. Moreover, a *Fortune* magazine article expressed the growing sentiment that downsizing by itself provides no answers for organizational ills without a strategic plan. That sentiment is reflected in the observation made in Let's Talk Business 5.9.

2. Lack of concern for, and involvement with, employees. Many downsizings do not involve those who are affected in the planning stages. That is, those in charge of the downsizing do not expect to get objective feedback or advice from those who will potentially be terminated, and so many employees are cut off from the actual planning of the organizational downsizing. It is important to note that the adverse effects of a downswing may be mitigated through suitable communication of the downsizing to employees,[63] employee participation in the planning of the downsizing, a thorough analysis of tasks, and perceived employee support from the organization,[64] as well as through advanced planning and coordination of outplacement services.[65] Attention needs to be given to both the terminated employees and those remaining. However, research evidence has suggested that insufficient attention has been given to the survivors of a downsizing. For example, evi-

---

LET'S TALK BUSINESS 5.9   STRATEGIC PLANNING

As previously hot tools such as re-engineering and total quality management cool off, other approaches rise to take their place. The latest surveys show that tool preferences are shifting away from cost-reduction techniques toward tools for retaining customers, outsmarting competitors, motivating employees, and accelerating innovation. Today 90% of managers report that they want to improve performance through revenue growth, not downsizing. To accomplish that, they are implementing strategic planning systems, and 87% are polishing up their mission and vision statements — making these the two most popular tools. Slightly more than three-quarters admit that their company's managers have been focused on operations at the expense of strategy.

Source: From Darrell K. Rigby, "What's today's special at the consultants' café?" *Fortune* (September 7, 1998). © 1998 Time Inc. All rights reserved.

---

dence gathered from downsizing in the 1990s found that nearly 80% of surveyed organizations provided structured services for departing employees, while only 45% provided structured services for survivors.[66]

3. Careless removal of corporate memory. Downsizings can eliminate individuals who are a central part of the organization's knowledge base — the notion of corporate memory. While intangible, the cost of corporate memory loss to an organization can be very significant. This can go beyond simply losing the expertise of a valued, experienced employee. This significance has been expressed by many observers:

> Downsizing devastates social networks. When a person is laid off, an entire personal network of internal and external relationships is lost as well. Downsizing destroys informal bridges between departments, disrupts the information grapevine, severs ties with customers, and eliminates the friendships that bond people to the workplace.[67]

It has also been suggested that the loss of corporate memory can be particularly devastating to the organization's ability to innovate, as an article in *The Economist* points out in Let's Talk Business 5.10.

For better or worse, downsizings continue to reshape the corporate landscape; and, given that they are unlikely to disappear in the very near future, one can only hope that they will be planned carefully in order to bring about some of the improvements for which they are intended. To this point, the results of downsizing do not appear to be largely positive for many organizations, and yet we have witnessed the pervasive acceptance of downsizing as a legitimate organizational practice. The question naturally arises: Why have so many organizations agreed to adopt a practice that is not proven to be effective? If there is no significant proof that downsizing offers the results organizations are struggling to achieve, the question arises: Why does downsizing continue to be per-

---

LET'S TALK BUSINESS 5.10 MEMORY LOSS

... IBM's personal-computer unit has suffered because the company has got rid of staff who worked on previous generations of PCs. A similar loss of "design memory" has also hampered Ford's Taurus. The original car was a hit because it met the needs of big-car buyers better than most rivals. But the latest Taurus, a product of a constantly re-engineered "global" design effort, has failed to capture buyers' imagination. In losing its design memory, it seems, Ford forgot what customers wanted.... Service companies are especially vulnerable to amnesia. Numerous downsized banks, insurers and retail chains have seen their customers' satisfaction plummet. One insurance group, having slimmed its claims department, found that it was settling big claims both too swiftly and too generously. Belatedly, it discovered that it had sacked a few long-term employees who had created an informal — but highly effective — way to screen claims. It was eventually forced to reinstate them.

Source: From Anonymous, "Fire and forget?" *The Economist* (April 20, 1996) 339(7962): 51.

---

formed? In order to make sense of why organizations engage in restructuring themselves, it is useful to consider why organizations adopt such trends as downsizing. In terms of a rational explanation, the evidence is weak. Consequently, researchers have also considered non-rational approaches to explaining the phenomenon of downsizing. This requires an understanding of how non-rationality can influence organizational structure.

Downsizing as a Non-rational Approach to Organizational Structure

How can organizational structure be non-rational? A perspective of organizations called **institutional theory** argues that organizations are driven to incorporate practices and procedures defined by current concepts of work and those accepted or institutionalized in society. Institutional acts, or the rules that govern organizational activity, are simply taken-for-granted means of "getting things done". They represent shared norms or expectations within or across industries. These rules dominate thinking with regard to how organizations should be designed. The implications are that accepted norms or rules, rather than necessarily, any set of rational reasons based on clearly identifiable and measurable objectives, can encourage the creation or maintenance of organizational structures and processes. Institutional rules have little to do with efficiency, but give organizations that conform to them a sense of legitimacy. That is, organizations can have, embedded in their structure, elements that are simply taken-for-granted ways of doing things — which may not, in fact, be accomplishing any specific organizational goals.

According to institutional theory, organizations may conform to institutionalized beliefs as a means to achieve legitimacy, resources and survival capabilities. The shared beliefs provide order through their institutionalization into organizational procedures and their direct influence on the behaviour of individuals. Consider such diverse organizations as IBM, Ben & Jerry's, McDonald's, Procter and Gamble, and Bell Canada. All these organizations have risen within society. They have gained success and longevity through their ability to adapt their operations to the needs of society. Specifically, the organization becomes filled with various cultural forces: e.g., political rules, occupational groups and professional knowledge. In other words, as these organizations have grown, they have instituted acceptable ways of conducting business.

The ideas generated from institutional theory draw attention to the notion of the forces that act on an organization and encourage the adoption and maintenance of those activities that are viewed as legitimate. This perspective suggests that organizational structures and processes can arise not simply due to rational objectives for control and coordination, but because of adherence to non-rational, but institutional or socially accepted, rules. Meyer and Scott described a "continuum" — from organizations dominated by technical criteria (e.g., manufacturing organizations) to those dominated by institutional criteria (e.g., schools). What we have seen since the mid-1980s is a questioning of many of the fundamental institutional rules governing how organizations should be designed. In other words, at one time, the machine bureaucracy was the socially accepted structure for most organizations. Recently, this rule has been called into question, and increasingly the phenomenon of re-engineering, downsizing and going virtual seem to be the established trend in organizational design.

The continued use of downsizing by organizations, even though it has not lived up to its reputation, appears to be non-rational. Organizations do not, in fact, always act purely rationally. Institutional theory asserts that organizational structures and policies can become institutionalized and persist, even when they are no longer efficient.[68] This theory emphasizes the fact that an organization's functions can become established or embedded in social networks. These functions, whether they are how organizations are designed or simply how they behave, are affected by the pressures of conformity and legitimacy, which arise from the organization's environment.[69] Meyer and Rowan[70] defined institutionalization as "the processes by which social processes, obligations, or actualities come to take on a rule-like status in social thought and action".

By the early 1990s, downsizing became an entrenched corporate ideology. For example, it was reported that between 1987 and 1991, more than 85% of the *Fortune* 1000 corporations downsized their white-collar staffs.[71] The notion of downsizing has come to represent more than a reduction in an organization's workforce. It has come to reflect a longer-term, organizational evolution. Numerous organizations, by the 1990s, felt obligated to downsize given the intrinsic connection between being "lean-and-mean" and being highly competitive. Institutional theory offers some insight. Such institutional theorists suggest that the spread of corporate downsizing has been facilitated through: conforming to institutional rules that define legitimate structures and management practices; copying the actions of industry leaders; and responding to the legitimization of downsizing practices as accepted management practices via the media and popular press.[72] Why do organizations persist in conforming to the "rules" of downsizing?

Addressing this question can be accomplished through addressing the question of why organizations conform to institutional rules. At least three social factors have been cited. These factors include the notions of: **constraining**, **cloning** and **learning**. We can briefly consider each factor in order to get a better understanding of how they influence adherence to the institutional rule of downsizing. In this regard, we can understand how these factors can make organizations follow rules or ideas that are not necessarily rational.

1. *Constraining Forces*

These forces represent those practices that come to define what are perceived as legitimate management structures and activities and that consequently place pressure on organizations to conform to these institutional rules. An example given[73] involves the relationship between large U.S. corporations and the stock market. Interestingly, studies have found that layoff announcements made by large corporations that were undergoing restructuring and consolidation were followed by increases in share prices. In other words, we have seen the tendency for public reactions to downsizings to be favourable — the notion of becoming "leaner and meaner" has become an accepted business strategy, and one apparently favoured by shareholders. Consequently, since the markets respond positively to such news, organizations have become constrained to perceive downsizing as a positive outcome and one to be sought. Of more interest is the finding that this constraining force was found to be even stronger when executives' compensation packages and bonuses were linked to share values.

2. *Cloning Forces*

These are forces or pressure for organizations to imitate the behaviours of industry leaders. Revisiting the downsizing example, some observers have suggested that organizations have been "jumping on the bandwagon". That is, many organizations downsize to demonstrate they are in tune with modern business trends, and consequently downsizing has been viewed as a way of "keeping up with the corporate Joneses".[74] This action represents a clear reduction in rationality — i.e., a move away from objectively defined criteria for downsizing and toward strict adherence to institutional rules. It has also been found that downsizing among industry members is more likely to occur when industry leaders downsize. The risks of failure are obvious given that this approach lacks a careful evaluation of the costs and benefits of this strategy.

3. *Learning Forces*

These forces are the result of institutionalized management practices. The lessons we teach future managers and businesses leaders are embedded in the courses taught in universities and professional associations. Researchers like McKinley and his colleagues[75] point out, as an example of the biases generated in business schools, the case of cost accounting techniques used in business strategy education. From a purely cost accounting perspective, the practice of outsourcing appears infinitely superior to maintaining a full-time workforce. Specifically, the method of allocating overhead costs clearly draws attention to the cost efficiencies gained by outsourcing; and by definition, those units remaining as a permanent fixture for the organization appear more costly. According to McKinley, this perceived cost reduction gained from outsourcing increases the preference to outsource and can, consequently, become the driving force for a series of outsourcings and downsizings. This, then, is an example of how an emphasis on certain approaches toward business strategy that are spread through business education can come to play a role in rationalizing downsizing as a legitimate activity.

CHANGING STRUCTURE AND CHANGING CAREERS

Given the ever-changing nature of organizations, a compelling question is: Where do we fit into all this organizational change? What awaits us, as employees, in the changing organizational landscape? And specifically, how do the organizational changes we have identified already suggest changes in the very nature of the work that we perform within these organizations? A number of authors, including Jeremy Rifkin in his book entitled *The End of Work*, as well as author William Bridges, have talked about how the nature of work itself is changing. That is, the nature of work or the type of work we will perform in the future may be dramatically different from that we did for most of the 20th century.

These authors argue that the job itself is becoming an artifact, and the task of organizations is to create the "post-job" organization. How will the job disappear, and why should organizations shift away from jobs? Well, though this sounds mystifying, much of this can be understood in the context within which we have explained many of the changes to organizational design. To clarify, the authors are not actually referring to disappearing jobs in terms of the number of jobs lost or job losses in certain industries, but rather the very notion of the job itself is becoming outdated. In the future, certainly, people will continue to work, but not within the familiar envelopes that we call jobs. And in fact, many organizations are already becoming "de-jobbed".

The authors argue that what we think of as a job is really a social artifact. That is, it is based on an idea that emerged in the late 19th century to package the work that needed to be done in the growing factories and bureaucracies of industrialized societies. Before that time, people worked just as hard, but at shifting clusters of tasks, depending on the needs of the day. In a sense, Taylor and scientific management helped build our concept of jobs — as compartmentalized, specialized tasks that we are trained to perform. However, the conditions that created this notion of the job have changed dramatically over 200 years: mass production and large bureaucratic organizations are vanishing. Technology allows us to automate the assembly line, so masses of unskilled labour are much less needed. Large firms are outsourcing much of their activities, as we discussed earlier. So, given that the conditions under which jobs were created have changed, we are redefining not just organizational structure, but also how work should be performed — not in the traditional jobs that led our thinking for most of the 20th century.

If you consider some of the issues we identified in this chapter, virtual organizations, downsizing, re-engineering, outsourcing — it is understandable that with so much change occurring around us, clearly the very nature of the type of work we perform within these organizations must also somehow be changing! For example, in place of jobs, we are seeing more and more temporary and part-time work situations. That is simply one manifestation of a greater underlying change: the fact is, organizations are essentially moving away from a structure built for the performance of jobs into simply a field of work needing to be done. In other words, the specialization or division of labour encouraged us to become preoccupied with filling jobs and positions rather than simply focusing on performing the work that needs to be done.

In a relatively stable environment, rigid jobs are fine for performing the work; however, the increasingly dynamic nature of our environment seems to almost continuously rewire new skills and new combinations of work; a philosophy that is wedded to a jobs mentality is simply too slow to adapt. This is the new, post-job, world. An example is given of a fast-moving organization like Intel. Here, an individual is hired and assigned to a project. This project changes over time and, consequently, the person's responsibilities and work change with it. Of course, this person may also be assigned to other projects requiring other responsibilities and skills. Getting work done efficiently within these evolving projects requires skilled project teams, not a formal hierarchy of authority with masses of workers who are working under a formal job description. No supervisor, nor any job description, can sufficiently guide a worker through these continually changing projects and demands. Workers must simply focus their efforts on the work that needs to be done and that changes as the requirements change. In this sense, the individual has filled a specific job (as we traditionally think of the term job). It is a package of skills or capabilities drawn upon at various times, depending on current needs.

In other words, we are moving as far away from the early 20th century conception of work as we can: the conditions that created bureaucracies and the highly specialized, narrowly defined jobs are disappearing. Consequently, the nature of work itself is changing. And it is following the lead of the new organizational structures. Just as virtual organizations are throwing away the rules of the traditional bureaucratic organization by only focusing on getting the key activities done and outsourcing or networking with other companies to do other work, so too, at the individual level, we are beginning to redefine how we should work: we should not be led by narrow definitions or job descriptions, but continually adapt to the changing demands of our organization. The fact that organizations are being downsized with a dramatic reduction of middle management also suggests that workers are becoming much more responsible for decision making and involved in organizational strategy. Teams and team leaders are replacing managers and subordinates. This, too, underscores the need to redefine how work is performed and move away from the narrow definition of the job.

We have identified the dramatic types of changes occurring in organizations, and now we have suggested that how we work within these organizations is also undergoing fundamental changes. What does this suggest for us in the new workplace? There are at least two important implications for us, as members of the workforce, to keep in mind:

1. **Our careers will look very different from those of earlier generations.** It is no longer the case that you find a job and join the company when you are in, say, your twenties, and retire from that job in that company 20 or 30 years later.

2. **In the new workplace, it may not be permanent jobs per se that we will be seeking.** We can no longer depend on one job for our entire career. What we can focus on is building a portfolio of skills that we can move with from company to company and from career to career, and rely on this skill set in a variety of settings.

LET'S TALK BUSINESS 5.11 A NEW EMPLOYMENT MODEL

Contemporary organizational structures and environments require a new employment model. Under the old model, employees were expected to fit into the corporate culture, work hard, and remain committed and loyal to the organization for long periods of time. In return, the organization offered extended employment, promotion opportunities, and rewards for long-term tenure. Under the new model, organizations no longer promote "lifetime" employment. Instead, they offer employees learning opportunities and development options, as well as career coaching and assessment tools. In return, employees accept responsibility for steering their own careers and, simultaneously, commit their time, effort and loyalty to the organization for at least several years — as long as they are learning and growing. Thus, the new employment model emphasizes mutual responsibility for skill development and professional growth, and fosters the "employability" of the individual, both inside and outside the present organization.

...This shift away from employment and toward employability represents the key psychological differentiator of the new employment model. To be successful, this shift will require a significant change in managerial thinking to ensure that employees become more able to leave, but also more motivated to stay. Thus, as organizations move toward employability as a conceptual model, they must find alternative programs and strategies to develop skills and to retain and motivate employees.

Source: From Jeffrey E. Lewin and Wesley J. Johnston, "The impact of downsizing and restructuring on organizational competitiveness" *Competitiveness Review* (2000) 10(1): 45–55.

In other words, the notion of flexibility, that seems to underscore the changes we have been witnessing at the organizational level, is probably the same notion we need to carry with us throughout our careers. We need to be flexible in our attitude toward work and in the ability to adapt to different work environments and changing demands. Read Let's Talk Business 5.11 regarding advice for both employees and managers.

CHAPTER SUMMARY

If you recall our discussion of **contingency theory** in the previous chapter, you will remember that contingency theory asserts that organizations continually adapt to "fit" the environment. This implies that organizations will respond to changes in economic and environmental conditions by looking for alternatives to the traditional hierarchical organizational structure. The 1990s certainly were marked by increasing threats to the survival of many organizations stemming from sources such as technological change, global competition, and the emergence of a knowledge-based economy. And in response to these threats, many organizations attempted to redesign and initiate fundamental changes in their organizational forms and management practices. According to many observers, the accumulation of changes in the organizational environment has demanded a shift in thinking with regard to organizational design. This shift has involved the movement away from the traditional large, rigid, bureaucratic structure. Current practices now include outsourcing, re-engineering, going virtual, and downsizing.

KEY TERMS

- de-layering
- fluid organizations
- integrated organizations
- cross-functional teams
- keiretsu
- organic and mechanistic organizations
- dynamic environment
- static environment
- environmental uncertainty

- re-engineering
- outsourcing
- networking
- downsizing
- corporate memory
- institutional theory
- constraining forces
- cloning forces
- learning forces

Lexmark breaks away

The parent company declares that your organization is not part of the core business and unceremoniously dumps it into a marketplace of much more established competitors. That was what happened when International Business Machines Corp. cut loose its ugly duckling printer business in 1991, creating Lexmark International Group Inc. The managers of the new company seemed to have more headaches than common sense. "Some of us have said if we had known how big a challenge it would be, we might not have started," says Lexmark chairman and chief executive officer Marvin Mann. But the challenge was tackled and overcome. Lexmark has paid off the vast majority of the $1.5-billion (U.S.) debt it incurred when a group of venture capitalists took it over from IBM.

The company has steadily gained a foothold in the corporate laser printer market, which is overwhelmingly dominated by Hewlett-Packard Co. of Palo Alto, Calif., and it has launched a successful and growing consumer inkjet printer business. The result is a case study in how to handle the dreaded spinoff. "It's the classic story of how something that is not regarded highly, and in fact was thought to be a loser within IBM, becomes a winner outside of IBM," says Robert Djurdjevic, president of Phoenix-based Annex Research Inc., which tracks IBM and its competitors. The strategy adopted by Lexmark, based in Lexington, Ky., was to attack its rivals one market at a time. It targets a sector, such as banking and financial services, and develops products aimed directly at that segment. In the United States, the retail branches of nine of the top 10 banks now use Lexmark laser printers, Mr. Mann says. The company has forged a similar strategy to dominate the retail pharmacy business, and it is targeting about eight other segments. The result: Lexmark has become the No. 2 player in the worldwide corporate laser printer business. Its 12-percent market share is still miles behind Hewlett-Packard's 70 percent, but it has opened up a big lead on other competitors, such as Apple Computer Inc., Canon Inc. and Brother Industries Ltd.

In Canada, Lexmark's printer revenue [has] risen to over $800 million (Canadian). Recently, Lexmark International went public offering shares on the stock market. Some observers suggest that Lexmark's problem at the N.Y.-based IBM was lack of management attention. "Within a huge IBM, the printing operation was something that was relegated to the back burner. It was not important, not considered glamorous." And the spinoff freed Lexmark's otherwise capable management to concentrate on printers alone, and not on mainframe or personal computers.

Lexmark's challenges at the outset were quite fundamental. "We had an organization that wasn't really a company," Mann recalls. Indeed, the company had product development and manufacturing departments, but no marketing, sales or corporate structure. "We couldn't write an invoice, collect an invoice, make a payroll," Mr. Mann says. "We didn't have systems to do any of that." Lexmark started putting the nuts and bolts of an independent organization into place, while dealing with employees' shock at being sold off by IBM. It also had to try to build greater market share. "We recognized our competitors were many times our size, that they had been in the business a long time, that they were good at what they did, and that we had limited resources," Mr. Mann says. The first thing Lexmark's senior managers had to do was communicate with a rattled workforce about what challenges lay ahead and how the company would proceed. This process was tough because the management team was a very contentious group. "People were debating across boundaries about what should be done, what customers' needs were and what were the right solutions," Mr. Mann says. "People having different objectives were pulling against one another."

The managers concluded that they had to change the way they behaved if the company was to survive. Eventually, they wrote down, single-spaced on two pages of paper, their key initiatives — all the things that had to be done for the spun-off company to succeed. These included the following: Streamline the corporation. Within six months, some 2,000 employees were laid off, cutting Lexmark's manufacturing and support structure in about half. Speed the development of new products: Lexmark threw away its book on development processes and started over, studying how other companies worked. It switched to a small, integrated team approach to development and design. Teams now spend more time in the concept stage, which has cut design time in half. Suppliers are also brought into the process early. Become cost competitive and responsive, quickly: Lexmark was restructured into four business units, each with a worldwide responsibility for development, manufacturing, pricing, forecasting, business planning and financial functions. A number of layers of the management structure were removed. In terms of culture, Lexmark needed to build employee trust after the trauma of being sold by IBM. It cut stifling bureaucracy, encouraged teamwork, and implemented training and education programs. All 5,000 employees have [been] placed on an incentive plan that measures the performance of their specific business unit or the employee's team and rewards accordingly.

Source: Geoffrey Rowan, "Lexmark tames the dreaded spinoff: the printer company was loser under IBM, but it's gaining market share on its own" *The Globe and Mail* (August 20, 1997). Reproduced by permission of The Globe and Mail.

QUESTIONS

1. How would you describe the "old" versus "new" organizational structure with regard to Lexmark (i.e., before and after the spin-off)?

2. What advantages does Lexmark gain from its new organizational structure?

3. How is the re-engineering concept applied here?

RELATED READING — The outsourcing question

For Canadian companies, outsourcing is like exercise. They know they should do it. They really want to do it. But they're just not sure how to do it.

Outsourcing is all about hiring others to do the daily things required to run a company. And like exercise, it is all about reducing — costs, in this case, not waistlines.

And, according to a new study from Accenture released yesterday, reducing costs is now the single biggest priority of Canadian executives.

The study asked 304 companies and government agencies about their use and perceptions of outsourcing. It says executives acknowledge outsourcing can help achieve their cost-cutting goals, but they fear the changes it brings to their corporate culture and the loss of control it creates.

"Like exercise, it comes down to commitment. It's easy to talk about it but when you have to lace up the skates or the running shoes it's an entirely different thing," notes Blake Hanna, a partner in Accenture's communications and high-tech practice.

Accenture, a giant management and consulting organization, is using the survey results to promote its own outsourcing practice.

Almost all Canadian firms polled by Accenture said they have first-hand experience with outsourcing, but most feel they are novices at managing the outsourcing relationships that can bring real value.

"Companies have been outsourcing non-core functions for years — parking lot attendants, cafeteria services, security guards — but once they focus on outsourcing things core to their business, they get nervous," Mr. Hanna notes.

"That kind of outsourcing has to be part of a vision-led strategy within an organization, at the executive management level."

Companies most adept at outsourcing core business functions are in financial services, telecommunications and high-tech sectors; they're also the ones that have been fastest to adopt technology into their businesses.

Nortel Networks Corp., for example, announced yesterday it will divest its global outbound logistics operations management business to Kuehne & Nagel International AG. K&N will manage the performance of all of Nortel's logistics services providers, with the goal of improving its supply chain and its service to Nortel clients.

This is the kind of outsourcing that brings real value — and requires the highest amount of trust and executive management.

Geoffrey Moore, technology guru, partner at venture capital giant Mohr, Davidow, and author of *Crossing the Chasm* and *Inside the Tornado*, says companies need to re-examine every function their company is performing, and outsource everything that does not contribute to their market worth.

That requires an overhaul in corporate culture.

Corel Corp., for example, almost never went outside for anything when it was run by founder Michael Cowpland. Advertising, product design, marketing, public relations were all done by Corel employees and personally approved by Mr. Cowpland.

Under Corel's new chief executive, Derek Burney, the company has taken its first steps to outsource some non-core functions. It has hired a marketing agency, a public relations firm and other outsiders to cut costs and improve performance. While it's not clear how far Mr. Burney will take this new model, he has already taken a critical first step.

Accenture says almost half of the companies it surveyed outsource their information technology management and payroll. A smaller 38% use other firms to manage customers. Just over half of government departments outsource some IT, and that number is growing — witness the mini-boom that the massive federal Government Online project has created among IT services firms in Ottawa.

As Canadian companies get more comfortable with outsourcing, they'll rely on it more for core functions. Research firm IDC predicts that Canadian spending on IT outsourcing alone will amount to $3.6-billion this year, and $4.4-billion in 2005.

That's some serious reducing program.

Source: Jill Vardy, "Outsourcing cuts too close to the bone. Managers know they should be doing it, but they fear change" *Financial Post* (February 1, 2002). Reproduced with permission of the publisher.

QUESTIONS

1. What is the author's central argument regarding the proliferation of outsourcing?

2. Do you think outsourcing is beneficial to business? To employees? To society?

The Entrepreneurial Landscape

Small businesses play a vital role in the Canadian economy. This chapter is intended to identify the nature of entrepreneurship and small business ownership and the challenges facing entrepreneurs and owners of small businesses. Entrepreneurship is typically associated with the creation of a new business, or business "start-up". Consequently, it is useful to consider the requirements of, and the obstacles facing, individuals who are engaged in the process of new venture creation. This chapter also identifies the potential avenues or modes through which individuals can enter entrepreneurial ventures.

LEARNING OBJECTIVES

By the end of the chapter, you should be able to:

1. Define the nature of small business and the notion of entrepreneurship.
2. Describe the typical characteristics of entrepreneurs.
3. Discuss the challenges of new venture creation.
4. Explain the modes of entry into entrepreneurship.

I am grateful to Professor Jon Kerr, York University, who served as first author in the writing of this chapter.

Organizational Insider

Ad Agency Takes Great Leaps

It sounds like a David and Goliath story with an ad biz angle. Two Canadians and a Swede launch an oddly named Amsterdam-based advertising business called StrawberryFrog and beat much larger agencies for global clients.... Brian Elliott, one of the agency's Canadian partners, offers his much-repeated metaphor about "the nimble frog beating out the lumbering, soon-to-be extinct dinosaurs" of the advertising world.

For global clients such as Sprint, Ford, Motorola, Europcar and Credit Suisse, however, the reason for using the firm may be more concrete. StrawberryFrog gets the message out quickly and efficiently, and has found a way to help traditional clients feel comfortable with non-traditional advertising. StrawberryFrog sells an approach to marketing and brand building that combines a lean organizational structure with innovative ways of reaching consumers, through both traditional media and the more aggressive channels of guerrilla and [virtual] marketing.

Housed in an old warehouse in the centre of Amsterdam, StrawberryFrog has maintained the trappings of a New Economy business. After many years at traditional agencies, including a stint at J. Walter Thompson in Toronto, partner Scott Goodson believes that agency politics interfere with creativity and make the work suffer. "Understanding the market and the consumer is important; having layers of account management is . . . not productive," he says. StrawberryFrog's multinational 30-member team brings cultural, creative and linguistic perspective to the agency's work. According to Mr. Elliott, the benefit to clients is that it "enables the agency to customize campaigns with specific national twists."

. . . .

In order to keep the machine lean, StrawberryFrog outsources many functions, using graphic studios in Amsterdam, San Francisco, Brussels, and Sydney, and freelance writers and media placement organizations in various countries. Its hands-on, non-traditional approach seems to resonate with corporate clients....

. . . .

Staying independent while expanding its client base is StrawberryFrog's goal. But it's a tough task. Neil Silverzweig, chief financial officer of the San Francisco office of agency giant McCann Erickson, explains: "The lure of a small creative shop is undeniable, but with clients consolidating their business, do smaller players have the power to build a brand around the world? It may be hard for a smaller shop to grow if that's their goal."

Source: By Lee Jacobson. Excerpts from Special to *The Globe and Mail* (September 28, 2001), M1.

DEFINING ENTREPRENEURSHIP ————————————

StrawberryFrog is a prime example of the potential power of entrepreneurs and small businesses. Given the ability of small business to play a prominent role in the business landscape, it is certainly worthwhile to consider more fully the nature of these organizations, as well as the kinds of individuals who populate entrepreneurial organizations.

Despite the fact that research in entrepreneurship continues to grow each year, as does the creation of the new business ventures that are typically associated with the entrepreneurial process, there is still no succinct* definition of entrepreneurship. From an historical perspective, the noun "entrepreneur" was derived from the French verb *entreprendre*, and was translated into the German verb *unternehman*: both verbs meaning "to undertake". In the early 16th century, entrepreneurs were those people engaged in military expeditions. Contemporary definitions, however, relate entrepreneurs to business activities and, combining the old with the new, tend to encompass the notion of undertaking a venture that has some element of risk and demands some level of innovativeness.

*brief, concise

In trying to answer the question, "What is entrepreneurship?", the majority of business leaders and academics will determine whether a situation is entrepreneurial by considering what entrepreneurship might entail as well as the personality characteristics and abilities commonly associated with entrepreneurs. In this regard, the aspects of entrepreneurship that are most frequently cited in the literature are opportunity recognition, organization creation, innovation and risk-taking.[76] How each of these should contribute to the definition of what constitutes entrepreneurship is at the root of the ongoing debate.

Opportunity Recognition

Kirzner, an early economist, suggested that entrepreneurship involves seizing the knowledge that might otherwise remain unexploited, and his definition of entrepreneurship was "alertness to profit opportunities".[77] He believed that entrepreneurs realize a profit because they are proactive, moving on opportunities before they occur. In fact, according to Kirzner, this distinguishes an entrepreneur from a manager. "If people know that a gap needs to be filled, and that it is worthwhile filling, the task is no longer entrepreneurial in as much as it can be handled by competent managers through routine production methods." So, entrepreneurs must be able to spot unique opportunities; they must be good strategists.

Organization Creation

The term "entrepreneur" is usually applied to the founder of a new business and, not surprisingly, the creation of an organization is the most frequently encountered theme associated with entrepreneurship.[78] According to this criterion, the entrepreneurial process involves the harnessing and integration of the resources necessary for a business start-up. Interestingly, under this definition, anyone who buys an existing business or manages the growth or turnaround of an existing business is not an entrepreneur. Many business managers and proprietors might beg to differ!

Innovation

One of the reasons for the heightened interest in entrepreneurship is the role it is perceived to play in advancing an economy through innovation. Entrepreneurial activities are often viewed as being those that involve doing something new, such as a new product, service, or application of technology. In fact, it has been suggested that 50% of all innovations and 95% of all radical innovations since World War II have come from new and smaller firms.[79] According to Schumpeter, "the carrying out of new combinations we call enterprise, with the individuals carrying them out called entrepreneurs." He regarded entrepreneurs as a destabilizing force in any economy, and entrepreneurship as a prime socio-economic force.[80] But, using innovation as the determinant of whether a situation is entrepreneurial or not would mean that the majority of new ventures must be excluded, as most simply imitate tried and tested business practices.

Risk-Taking

Entrepreneurial activities are also frequently associated with risk,[81] which involves not only financial risks, but includes career opportunities, family and social relationships, and the entrepreneur's physical and emotional well-being. While it seems reasonable that bearing some risk is requisite to entrepreneurship, implicit is the assumption that the risk is measured and managed by the entrepreneur. We can also look to the assumption of risk to exclude certain activities from being entrepreneurial. Specifically, individuals who assume only financial risk are not entrepreneurs: they are investors.

A Definition

For the purposes of this chapter, our discussion will focus on the most common of these entrepreneurial attributes: organization creation. That is not to suggest that any of the other attributes are of lesser importance. Instead, it is a matter of convenience and is consistent with the tenor of other textbooks on the subject. Before moving on, however, consider for a moment that, even among these four attributes, there appears to be room for differing degrees of entrepreneurship.[82] For example, if you consider innovation, is not introducing a new product to a new market more entrepreneurial than introducing a new product to an existing market? Possibly we have here some further fuel for the entrepreneurship debate.

Regardless of which of the four attributes one might favour, the critical aspect of entrepreneurship appears to be "doing": that is, recognizing, creating, innovating and risk taking, all of which are consistent with the original definition, "to undertake". And, today, more and more individuals are "doing", by undertaking the creation of new ventures. Over the past two decades, there has been a reawakening of interest in entrepreneurship and small business, as evidenced by the number of new firms being created, and this has been coined "the entrepreneurial revolution".

THE ROLE OF SMALL BUSINESS AND ENTREPRENEURSHIP ——————

Today, small businesses account for 99% of all businesses in Canada. They also account for 38% of the gross domestic product, and 10% of total exports; and small businesses create a disproportionate share of employment and innovations when compared to larger businesses. Accordingly, the economic and social contributions of small businesses cannot be denied. Perhaps that is why a recent survey suggests that the majority of influential North Americans indicate that they believe that entrepreneurialism will define business in this, the 21st century.[83]

Defining Small Business

Small business is said to represent a significant portion of the Canadian business community, but there is little agreement as to what, exactly, constitutes a small business. Most organizations interested in small business use different measures when defining them. While this may seem trivial, consider the implications. At the macro-level, government policy-makers use small business statistics to provide support or rebuttal for divergent positions. Imagine it — with no standard measure for small business, it is possible for one government department to report growth in the small business sector, while another reports decline!

For practitioners and entrepreneurs, understanding what constitutes a small business is a more practical concern. Specifically, it is critical in the benchmarking process and for establishing sponsorship program eligibility. Benchmarking refers to the process of comparing one small business performance to that of other, similar businesses. For the process to be valid, the data must be comparable. Accordingly, agencies such as Statistics Canada, which collect the data, must ensure that they are using a constant and meaningful definition of small business. Operating and financial data for incorporated and unincorporated businesses, classified by revenues, is available on-line from Statistics Canada.

The other reason to understand small business definitions is to determine eligibility for the various public and private sector sponsorship programs that are available, including financial, marketing and technical assistance. These can be major contributors to a new venture's success, and certain of the criteria commonly employed by different Canadian government agencies are identified in Exhibit 6.1. Other criteria include the value of the firm's assets, the volume of bank deposits and the type of management and ownership structure present in the business.

Numbers of Businesses

There is conflicting data available on the number of small businesses in Canada. This is due, partly, to the inconsistent definitions of what constitutes a small business. But there are also many businesses that go unreported as part of Canada's underground economy. The Bank of Canada estimates that as much as 15% of business dealings are part of this underground economy.[84] So, bear that in mind as you consider the following statistics.

EXHIBIT 6.1	MEASUREMENTS COMMONLY USED TO DEFINE SMALL BUSINESS

Measurement Criteria	Government Agency Examples
1. Number of Employees	• The Department of Industry, Science and Technology specifies a small business as one that employs fewer than 100 in manufacturing and less than 50 employees in non-manufacturing industries. • Statistics Canada usually classifies businesses as "small" when there are fewer than 500 employees. • The Business Development Bank considers businesses with less than 75 employees to be eligible for its Counselling Assistance for Small Business Program.
2. Total Revenue	• The Ministry of State for Small Business considers $2 million in revenue as defining a small business. • Eligibility under the Small Business Financing Act is restricted to businesses with revenues of less than $2 million.
3. Profitability	• Revenue Canada has established a net operating profit of $200,000 to define which businesses qualify for the Small Business Deduction, which presently equates to an effective tax rate of 19%.

EXHIBIT 6.2	NUMBER OF CANADIAN BUSINESSES BY EMPLOYMENT LEVELS

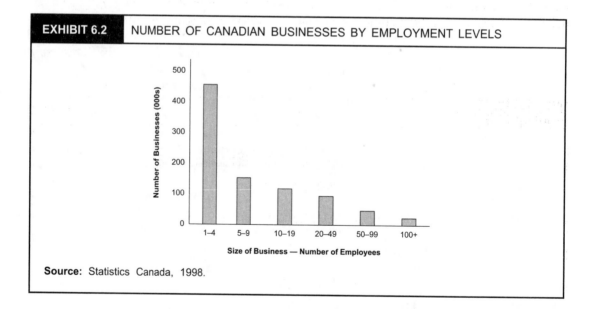

Source: Statistics Canada, 1998.

Statistics Canada estimates that 97% of the nearly 930,000 existing businesses in Canada had fewer than 50 employees.[85] The distribution of these businesses, classified on the basis of employment levels, is illustrated in Exhibit 6.2. In addition, in 1998 there were 2.5 million self-employed individuals, representing 17.4% of the Canadian workforce (up from 13.4% in 1983).[86] If the number of self-employed individuals is added to the number of business enterprises in Canada, the total is in excess of 2 million. Simply put, 99% of all businesses in Canada have fewer than 50 employees.[87]

Among the businesses identified above, it is important to note that small firms are not represented equally in all industry segments. Larger firms tend to dominate in capital-intensive industries such as financial services, telecommunications, pharmaceuticals and aircraft manufacturing. These industries tend to present barriers to entry that smaller firms cannot overcome. Instead, small business is growing most rapidly in the services industry, with business services, such as consulting, showing the greatest rate of growth.[88] It should also be noted that small business activity, while present in all provinces and territories, is highest in British Columbia, followed by Alberta and Ontario.[89]

The Economic and Social Contributions of Small Business

We have seen that firms with less than 50 employees account for 99% of all businesses and employ 53% of the labour force, but this emphasis on the number of small businesses may distort the overall importance of small business. A more accurate picture of the economic role of small business in Canada is portrayed in Exhibit 6.3. Small business provides 38% of the country's gross domestic product[90] and contributes approximately 10% to the nation's exports.[91] Interestingly, small businesses appear to be more efficient than their

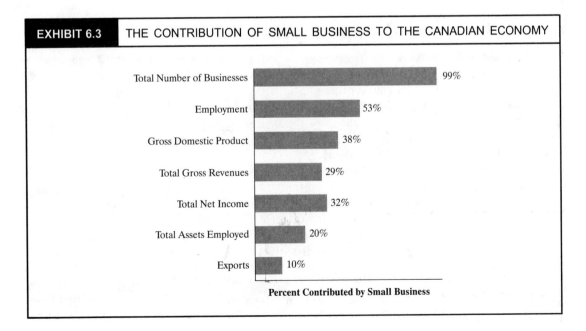

EXHIBIT 6.3   THE CONTRIBUTION OF SMALL BUSINESS TO THE CANADIAN ECONOMY

Total Number of Businesses	99%
Employment	53%
Gross Domestic Product	38%
Total Gross Revenues	29%
Total Net Income	32%
Total Assets Employed	20%
Exports	10%

Percent Contributed by Small Business

larger cousins, producing 32% of all business profits, while accounting for only 29% of gross revenues.[92] Finally, approximately 20% of all business assets are owned by small businesses.[93] This reflects big business's domination in the capital-intensive industries.

Job Creation

In terms of job creation, small businesses create a vastly disproportionate share of net new jobs. Three-quarters of all job growth between 1989 and 1997 was accounted for by small business and, between 1986 and 1996, growth in self-employment was four times that of paid workers. Over a 15-year period, firms with less than 20 employees boosted employment at an average annual rate of 8%, versus a 0.2% gain for firms with 20–49 employees and a 1% decline in employment in larger firms. This trend is likely to continue as we move into the 21st century, with massive layoffs at large corporations such as Nortel Networks and Canada 3000.

Interestingly, among the firms with less than 20 employees, jobs created by small business births are nearly three times as plentiful as those created from small business expansion.[94] This reflects the soft underbelly of this employment data. While small firms create new jobs at a much higher rate than larger firms, they also destroy them at a higher rate. For example, in one study, the one-year survival rate for all jobs was shown to increase with firm size, such that 81% of jobs in small firms survived for one year, while 92% survived in larger firms.[95] The net effect of this is that there appears to be greater job "churning" in the small business sector; and this has raised questions about the quality of these jobs. However, research indicates that employees feel that small companies are better places to work than larger ones.[96]

Innovation and Competitiveness

Small businesses and their employees have also been responsible for a disproportionate share of inventions and innovations. In a survey of all industries, small firms were observed to generate 36.2 significant innovations per one million employees, compared to 31.0 innovations per million employees in larger firms.[97] Further, small firms are superior innovators in both increasing-employment and decreasing-employment environments. So, while the innovations of large firms may overshadow the innovations of smaller firms, the latter's contribution cannot be denied.

Many economists have expounded on the role of competition in advancing an economy, and it is central to Michael Porter's models of industry attractiveness.[98] Fierce competition forces businesses to improve through innovation and productivity. While conventional wisdom has been that economies of scale favour larger firms in terms of productivity, there is evidence to the contrary, such as the higher profitability realized by smaller firms. Certain of the attributes of successful corporations that Peters and Waterman identified in their best seller, *In Search of Excellence*, are also found in small businesses.[99] For example, small, entrepreneurial firms tend to possess a bias for action, and they are typically unfettered by complex or bureaucratic organizational structures that might slow their response to competitive forces.

Social and Personal-level Impact

Beyond their role as employers, small businesses provide many Canadians with the opportunity to realize their entrepreneurial dreams. Approximately 99% of the small businesses in this country are Canadian-owned and, accordingly, the nation may possess in excess of two million active entrepreneurs. Further, these individuals are also very involved in their communities, and appear to have higher levels of community involvement than do employees of larger corporations.[100]

WHO ARE ENTREPRENEURS?

Similar to their attempts at defining entrepreneurship, scholars and researchers have also offered numerous and widely diverse descriptions of that creature they call an "entrepreneur". However, understanding an entrepreneur's motivation is simple. Thus, if small business does contribute to the economy as believed, knowledge of the factors associated with entrepreneurial inclination could be of immense practical importance. For example, it might be used as a career guidance tool for students. We could screen potential entrepreneurs and provide appropriate support to those with potential while weeding out those with none.

A common response to the problem has been to do research on entrepreneurs to learn who is an entrepreneur. To summarize the findings, such studies have determined that the typical entrepreneur is male, and is in his thirties, which has allowed him to gain experience, establish a track record and accumulate some savings. He is the first-born, and is from a family with entrepreneurial inclinations, which exposed him to role models and experience. He's married, with children, and his wife works, providing for an alternate source of income. And, despite the fact that we have all heard of the high school dropout who made it big in the business world armed with an education from the school of hard knocks, research paints a different picture. Our entrepreneur has an above average education of 14.6 years. In fact, the probability of him pursuing the entrepreneurial lifestyle appears to increase with each year of formal education.

Obviously, such a well-defined entrepreneurial population does not exist. Today, those participating in the entrepreneurial revolution come from all walks of life, and the entrepreneurial revolution knows no boundaries relating to gender, ethnic background or age. (See Let's Talk Business 6.1.)

ENTREPRENEURIAL INCLINATION

Are entrepreneurs born, or are they made? Are they endowed with certain traits or qualities that differentiate them from others? These are the questions researchers have asked, and many studies have shown significant differences between founders and non-founders with respect to personal characteristics. One school of thought, the "great person" school, portrays entrepreneurs as charismatic leaders. Some of the most frequently mentioned

179

LET'S TALK BUSINESS 6.1   THE MANY FACES OF ENTREPRENEURS

Female Entrepreneurs. While the number of self-employed men is more than triple the number of self-employed women, women are increasingly joining the ranks of small business operators. Between 1989 and 1997, the number of self-employed women increased by over 40%.[1] North American women are leading the way, with greater entrepreneurial involvement than the average for other industrialized nations. Presently, women own approximately 35% of all small businesses.[2]

Immigrant Entrepreneurs. Among industrialized nations, Canada and Germany have the highest proportion of immigrant entrepreneurs, accounting for approximately 16% of all business start-ups. If this is traced back one generation, then the number of Canadian entrepreneurs who are immigrants or the children of immigrants account for over one-quarter of all small businesses, the highest in a survey of 11 industrialized nations.[3]

Young Entrepreneurs. While the average age of the owners of Canada's fastest growing small businesses is reported to be about 40,[4] there is increasing interest among young Canadians in entrepreneurship as a career alternative. Approximately 23% of the nation's self-employed are under the age of 35.[5] Also, entrepreneurial interests are being piqued at earlier ages. Over the past decade, the number of students involved in the Junior Achievement program has doubled to 188,978.[6]

Part-Timers. It is estimated that 43% of entrepreneurs have only part-time involvement with their ventures. One distinguishing feature of part-time entrepreneurship is that it affords the individual the opportunity to attend to other aspects of their lives, possibly including a full-time job. There are, however, certain disadvantages to the part-time entrance strategy. Because it is part-time, there may not be the level of commitment to the business that is necessary, and this can cause the entrepreneur to overlook critical requirements for success.

Source: [1] Industry Canada and Statistics Canada, 1998. [2] Statistics Canada, 1998: 9. [3] Thompson, 1986–87. [4] "The Young and the Restless" *Profit Magazine* (June 1993): 48. [5] Statistics Canada, 1997: 16. [6] As taken from the Junior Achievement Website, December 2001.

---

traits of entrepreneurs, according to this school, are identified in Let's Talk Business 6.2. While it seems reasonable that successful entrepreneurs would exhibit at least some of these traits, is it not just as reasonable that possessing such desirable characteristics would lead to success in any line of work?

A second school of thought, the "psychological school", focuses on personality factors. While findings of empirical studies on psychological traits are not homogeneous, there is a commonality among the dimensions most frequently associated with entrepreneurial inclination. Specifically, personality characteristics commonly associated with entrepreneurs include a high need for achievement, a propensity for taking risks, a tolerance of ambiguity, and an inner locus of control. If these traits do, in fact, contribute to entrepreneurial inclination, they are worthy of further discussion.

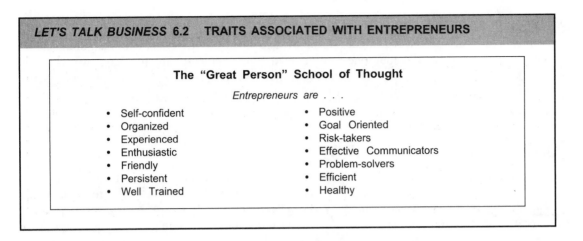

LET'S TALK BUSINESS 6.2   TRAITS ASSOCIATED WITH ENTREPRENEURS

The "Great Person" School of Thought

Entrepreneurs are . . .

- Self-confident
- Organized
- Experienced
- Enthusiastic
- Friendly
- Persistent
- Well Trained

- Positive
- Goal Oriented
- Risk-takers
- Effective Communicators
- Problem-solvers
- Efficient
- Healthy

High Need for Achievement

A high level of need for achievement among entrepreneurs is supported by the bulk of research. Entrepreneurs have a higher level of need for achievement when compared to the general population, and a high need for achievement seems invariably present among successful entrepreneurs.[101] These individuals set challenging goals, and value feedback as a means for assessing goal accomplishment, with profit and growth data serving as objective means of providing such feedback. In a study by David McClelland, a Harvard psychologist, of the participants in a course for entrepreneurs, 75% with above average need for achievement had started a business within two years of completing the course, while only 46% with below average need for achievement had established their own businesses.[102]

A Propensity for Risk

tendency

It has been observed that entrepreneurs exhibit only moderate risk-taking propensities, although entrepreneurial activities are frequently associated with risk. This observation has been tied to the entrepreneurs' need for achievement, and it is suggested that they avoid low-risk situations because there is a lack of challenge, and they avoid high-risk situations for fear of failure.[103]

Everyone sees things differently, and risk, like beauty, is in the eye of the beholder. So, while entrepreneurs are risk-takers, each one's perception of risk may differ. Few successful entrepreneurs forge ahead without planning, with the expectation being that if they have more information about a situation, the outcome is more predictable and the associated risk more easily measured and managed. So, if an individual wanted to open a restaurant, they could establish risk by determining how many restaurants fail in their first year statistically. However, this is rarely done. Rather, people's judgments are influenced by cognitive heuristics, such that a person who read about a restaurant closing in the morning paper will perceive a higher level of risk involved in opening a restaurant than someone who hasn't read about one closing in a long time. Or, an individual who knows of two local restaurants that have failed may perceive a lower likelihood of failure than the person who knows that thousands fail nationally each year.

Tolerance for Ambiguity

Ambiguity refers to situations that are doubtful or uncertain, and that frequently emanates from novelty or complexity. Research suggests that entrepreneurs are comfortable with ambiguity, see ambiguity as a challenge, with uncertainty serving as a motivational catalyst that may foster entrepreneurial success. Inasmuch as uncertainty implies risk, if entrepreneurs are risk-takers, then it seems reasonable that they also are tolerant of ambiguity. In fact, it has been suggested that tolerance of ambiguity is proportional to risk-taking propensity.[104]

Internal Locus of Control

Another aspect relating to tolerance of ambiguity is that entrepreneurs have been shown to have an internal locus of control. That is, they perceive themselves to possess an ability to influence events in their lives. They are self-confident and give little credence to "external" forces, such as destiny or luck. While an internal locus of control may distinguish entrepreneurs from the general population, it does not appear to be a valid discriminator of entrepreneurs and managers, implying that it is a poor measure of entrepreneurial inclination. However, in a longitudinal study of business owners, those that survived exhibited a higher internality than those that failed.[105] Accordingly, internal locus of control may be a variable involved in success.

MAKING THE ENTREPRENEURIAL CHOICE ⸻

A recent survey by Ernst & Young found that nearly two-thirds of Canadians believe that entrepreneurs are happier than employees. It is not surprising, then, that 40% of those surveyed indicated that they intend to start a business at some point in time. Their decisions are influenced by a variety of factors, which might be characterized as either "push" or "pull" factors.

Push versus Pull Factors

Push factors carry with them certain negative connotations. Individuals "pushed" into entrepreneurship are those faced with limited choice, either through job retrenchment, job dissatisfaction or the relative unattractiveness of known employment opportunities. One

| EXHIBIT 6.4 | THE LURE OF ENTREPRENEURSHIP |

- A desire to control one's destiny
- The potential for profit more than salary
- For personal interest
- A desire for challenge
- The opportunity to develop one's self

report found that 12% of self-employed individuals were pushed into entrepreneurship due to the lack of available jobs.[106] Professor Russell Knight, of the Ivey School of Business at the University of Western Ontario, has labelled those individuals who are pushed into entrepreneurship as "refugees".[107]

Individuals who are pushed into entrepreneurship would appear to have lower opportunity costs, at least in terms of foregone employment. There is also empirical evidence that supports the hypothesis that the lower the opportunity costs of an individual, the more likely they are to undertake entrepreneurial activities. It is not surprising, then, that there is an increase in entrepreneurial activity during times of higher unemployment. Interestingly, inasmuch as career opportunities are frequently connected to education, experience and competence, it may also be reasonable to assume that those people who are pushed into entrepreneurship are less educated, experienced and competent than those who are free to choose. If so, then this could explain, in part, the high failure rates reported for new ventures.

Pull factors, on the other hand, are more positive and imply freedom of choice. Some of the more common motivating factors that "pull" individuals into making the entrepreneurial choice are seen in Exhibit 6.4.

Windows of Entrepreneurial Opportunity

Among those deciding to start a business, there appears to be a number of critical junctures in their lives where becoming an entrepreneur is most appealing. Plaschka and Welsch describe these junctures as "strategic windows", and suggest that they follow a predictable pattern.[108] Specifically, they identify six strategic windows where individuals are most likely to pursue entrepreneurial opportunities. These windows are:

1. after attending college or university.
2. when a functional expertise has been developed.
3. after having held a position of authority.
4. when industry expertise has been gained.
5. once "financial freedom" has been achieved.
6. upon retirement.

183

LET'S TALK BUSINESS 6.3 BARRIERS TO ENTREPRENEURSHIP	
Reason Cited	**% of Sample**
1. Lack of finances	50
2. Restraints	31
3. Lack of readiness	26
4. Change in employment	21
5. Too risky	12
6. Too much time involved	7
7. Poor economy	4
NOTE: multiple responses were permitted.	

Other researchers have expanded upon this, and identified the strengths and weaknesses individuals possess at each strategic window. For example, they have proposed that the energy and enthusiasm of the college or university graduate, at one extreme, gives way to the experience and resource base of the retiree at the other end of the continuum.[109]

Notwithstanding the fact that 40% of those surveyed by Ernst & Young indicated that they intended to start a business at some point in time, many of them will not. The reasons for not proceeding with these intentions are many, but one study found that the lack of finances is the most common.[110] Other barriers to the entrepreneurial life identified in the study are summarized in Let's Talk Business 6.3. Several of these relate to risk, and the risk assumed by the entrepreneur in terms of capital and time can be staggering, with the median commitment being $55,000 and 60 hours per week, respectively.

It is interesting to note that while 50% of individuals in the sample cited lack of finance as a reason for non-continuance, only two percent complained that they were unable to obtain funds from a financial institution. This casts doubt on the prime expressed reason for many non-starters, and suggests that they may have negative feelings toward funding the cost of start-up themselves.

Two other reasons for not starting are of interest, and both relate to opportunity costs. The first, restraints, reflects family commitments and lack of support. The second relates to employment. It is interesting to note that when faced with the commitment that would be needed in self-employment, many intenders found that their present job had now become more desirable. Also, it appears that for many individuals, the process of considering self-employment is simply part of a process to redirect their lives: if not into self-employment, then toward some other change in their employment status.

Developing Entrepreneurial Abilities

Regardless of whether the requisite skills can be taught, studies show that entrepreneurs frequently have no formal plan for learning. Where plans do exist, they tend to be loosely structured, somewhat long-range, and a bit vague.[111] Nevertheless, self-development is important to entrepreneurs, and there are effective strategies for learning. While approximately 60% of entrepreneurs rely on workplace experience for their entrepreneurial education, other learning strategies include simulated events, such as case studies or project work, lectures and reading books on the subject.

Surprisingly, only a small fraction of entrepreneurs turn to formal education for their entrepreneurial training. Perhaps this is because of the cost, or perhaps because it has only been relatively recently that universities have recognized the big training needs of small business. There is no doubt that entrepreneurs need knowledge in the functional areas of business, and this knowledge is of significant importance for success. Specifically, we have seen that knowledge is needed in marketing, finance and management, and a survey of entrepreneurs indicates that most believe that these skills can be taught and suggest that traditional teaching methods, including instruction and testing, are most appropriate.[112]

Another study by Hood and Young, of the University of New Mexico, provides some interesting insights into other skills that are required. In a survey of successful entrepreneurs, the top three skill requirements identified were leadership skills, oral communication skills and human relation skills[113] — a mix of entrepreneurial and managerial skills discussed by Wesley Balderson of the University of Lethbridge.[114] Again, these entrepreneurs strongly believed that each of these skills could be taught. Development of them can be accomplished in a variety of ways. Examples could include a leadership program, such as one offered through a university or Outward Bound. For oral communication skills development, an aspiring entrepreneur might choose to join Toastmasters International.

Finally, consideration must be given to an entrepreneur's personality. Whether or not the personality traits most frequently associated with successful entrepreneurship can be taught is subject to debate. However, the general consensus among entrepreneurs is that they can't be, at least in the context of conventional entrepreneurial education. These personality traits are typically thought to be acquired during youth, learned over time and influenced by family, friends, teachers, the church, etc. By the time most individuals consider entrepreneurship, these traits are stable and not easily changed. This may suggest that the focus of entrepreneurship education should be at the early ages.

Entrepreneurial Skills versus Managerial Skills

Before deciding whether entrepreneurship can be taught, there must be an understanding of what skills are required of successful entrepreneurs. In this regard, Balderson distinguishes between entrepreneurial skills and managerial skills.

Entrepreneurial skills are those that are required to start or expand a business, and include creativity, innovativeness, risk-taking and independence. Entrepreneurs are idea-oriented, and those who have a high tolerance for ambiguity tend to think and plan with a longer-term perspective. Among the founders of new businesses, Balderson identifies two types: artisans and promoters. The artisan founder has technical or operational expertise that they bring to the business, while promoters usually identify product or market opportunities and then team up with an artisan to assist with either financial or marketing expertise.

Managerial skills are appropriate for maintaining the smooth running of an existing business, and include skills in strategic and general management and in each of the functional areas, such as finance, marketing and human resource management. Managers are effective communicators, and require strong team-building skills. These managerial skills are fundamentally different from the entrepreneurial skills necessary for start-up. However, if an entrepreneur expects to move the business beyond start-up, sound managerial skills are also required. Unfortunately, one of the problems often associated with entrepreneurship is that those who posses strong entrepreneurial skills lack strong managerial skills, and vice versa.

NEW VENTURE CREATION

Entrepreneurship is most often associated with the creation of a new business, or "business start-ups". This involves building a business from the ground up: that is recognizing the opportunity, refining the business concept, creating the organization, implementing the plan and managing through growth and stability. From this perspective, start-up is the entrepreneurial process!

Despite the extensive initiative and planning that is required by the start-up strategy, it appears to be the most desired of all the modes of entry. Over two-thirds of Canadians who decide to pursue entrepreneurial activities elect to do so by establishing their own businesses. This is lower, however, than the international average. Start-ups are favoured because of their many advantages over the other modes of entry. Principally, in creating a brand new venture, the start-up entrepreneur has no historic artifacts from a previous business with which to contend. It is a fresh start and, subsequently, there is a great amount of personal freedom and room for creativity. The start-up entrepreneur selects the product, location, equipment, marketing mix, etc.; and, depending on the nature of the business concept, may have greater control over costs and resource requirements than with other modes of entry.

Start-ups have their disadvantages, however, and many of the more frequent problems encountered during the entrepreneurial process are discussed below. So, while the start-up mode of entry offers higher profit potential than other entry strategies, the statistics on small business failure also suggest that it entails the greatest amount of personal risk.

The Small Business Life Cycle Model

The central proposition of any small business life cycle model is that development follows a predictable pattern of sequential and progressive stages. As the business moves from stage to stage, it faces different sets of internal and external challenges. From the perspective of the entrepreneur, understanding this entrepreneurial process can serve as a useful framework and alert them to strategic and operational issues at each stage. One such model is presented in Exhibit 6.5, and identifies three stages of development: formation, expansion, and stability.

| EXHIBIT 6.5 | A SMALL BUSINESS LIFE CYCLE MODEL |

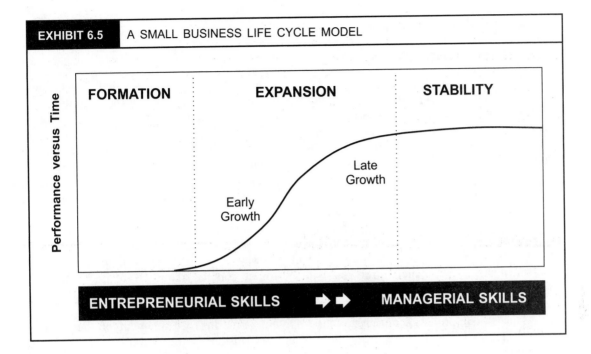

The formation stage is initiated with the idea for a new business, and culminates when products or services based upon that idea are sold to customers in the marketplace. During this period, the entrepreneur develops the business plan, identifies markets, builds financial support and harnesses the other resources necessary to establish the business.

Expansion is the growth stage, and the viability of the business and movement to this stage is contingent upon gaining sufficient customer acceptance. Expansion can be considered to consist of two sub-stages: early, exponential growth; and later, slowing growth. The early growth stage requires an iterative management approach, with the entrepreneur reacting to market demands and conditions. Later, growth will slow as the gap between the active market and potential market narrows and competitors respond to the firm's presence.

Finally, the venture will stabilize and the day-to-day operating practices will become routine and institutionalized. This may lead to a more bureaucratic environment, and sales often decline if the entrepreneur is unable or fails to respond to market conditions and competitors.

Within this model, two trends are of particular interest. First, as the firm evolves, entrepreneurial activity generally decreases, while the management or administrative responsibilities of the founder increase. This observation gives rise to a concept widely used in small business research: that of the owner-manager. Moving from entrepreneur to owner-manager can be a difficult transition. The second theme to be conscious of relates to the different sets of internal and external variables impacting the organization at each stage of development. These variables pose challenges to the entrepreneur, and further the entrepreneurial and management skills required at each stage of development.

Common Problems Encountered by Small Businesses

In order to succeed, entrepreneurs will have to overcome the problems frequently encountered by small businesses, and understanding the problems that arise at the various stages of development can aid in assessing current challenges and help with anticipating future requirements. While it is reasonable that not all firms will have the same major problems, there is a recurring trend in the research. The problems most frequently encountered are typically classified as marketing-related, management-related or finance-related; and there are significant changes in the nature of problems encountered as the business moves from formation to stability. The relative frequencies with which these problems are encountered by small businesses are seen in Exhibit 6.6.

Among the marketing-related problems, a difficulty in assessing the market and contacting the customer through sales and promotional efforts prove to be the greatest challenges. As expected, as entrepreneurs gain knowledge of the market, problems with assessment abate. Subsequent problems with customer contact frequently relate to advertising, promotion and personal selling, and can be compounded by product timing issues, such as premature market entry, or by product design issues.

Management problems during formation relate primarily to refinement of the business concept. These problems ease, but continue into expansion as the entrepreneur undergoes the iterative process of incorporating feedback from the marketplace into further refine-

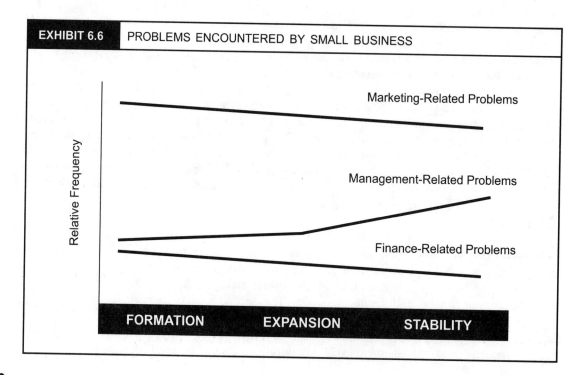

EXHIBIT 6.6 PROBLEMS ENCOUNTERED BY SMALL BUSINESS

Relative Frequency

Marketing-Related Problems

Management-Related Problems

Finance-Related Problems

FORMATION EXPANSION STABILITY

ment of the business plan. Other common management-related problems are the issues of organizational design and personnel management. This should come as no surprise, as they are generally overlooked during the organization creation process.

Of those problems that are finance-related, undercapitalization and locating financing sources, referred to here as financial planning, are the most frequently encountered prior to the creation of a new venture, and will likely persist throughout its life. It should be noted that while one in three businesses is undercapitalized, failure to anticipate financing needs can be reduced through a well thought-out business plan. During expansion and stability, cash flow problems predominate, and can only be exacerbated by undercapitalization.

Finally, recognize that these function-related problems are not all encountered with the same frequency. The most frequently cited problems are marketing-related, and this is consistent throughout the business life cycle. Next most frequent are management-related problems, which increase as the business evolves. Surprisingly, finance-related problems are the rarest, although financial difficulties are perceived to be a major contributor to business failures.

Small Business Failures

According to the small business life cycle model presented earlier, subsequent to creation, new ventures enter an expansion stage, leading to stability. Clearly, the model overlooks the obvious reality that many new ventures fail. How many fail, exactly, is not clear, and efforts here are complicated by the facts that it is not easy to define and identify failures, and reliable statistics and databases are not available. As a result, it is not uncommon to hear pronouncements such as, "In their first year 50% of all new businesses fail, and by the tenth year, between 80 and 90% have failed." The accuracy of such pronouncements is suspect. Yet, they reinforce people's perceptions that failure rates are quite high, and this can be a serious obstacle for aspiring entrepreneurs.

The problem is compounded by the negative connotations of the word "failure". In terms of small business, failure does not necessarily mean bankruptcy. The credit rating agency Dunn & Bradstreet attempts to bring some structure to the problem by differentiating between discontinuance and failure. When an entrepreneur or owner ceases operations, the process is referred to as discontinuance. Businesses that are discontinued are classified as failures only if there is a loss to creditors. Using this definition of failure, a Dunn & Bradstreet survey found that only one percent of all businesses fail annually.[115]

Discontinuance

Determining when and why an entrepreneur will decide to discontinue operations are complex problems that are compounded by the fact that entrepreneurs are reticent to discuss what they may regard as failure. One school of thought relates this to the entrepreneur's personal level of satisfaction. Overall, it is suggested that satisfaction is the fundamental measure of success for individual entrepreneurs and may bear on decisions about whether to invest more time and money or whether to close down. Further, there

EXHIBIT 6.7	COMMON CAUSES OF SMALL BUSINESS FAILURE

Cause	Frequency
General management problems	73%
Finance-related problems	71%
Economic downturn	68%
Marketing-related problems	49%
Competition	47%
Problems with customers	44%

Source: Statistics Canada, *Failing Concerns: Business Bankruptcy in Canada*, 1997.

appears to be a significant relationship between satisfaction and the gap between an entrepreneur's expectations for their business and actual business experiences. Quite simply, the greater the reality-expectation gap, the less satisfied an entrepreneur will be, and the higher the probability of discontinuance.[116]

Earlier it was suggested that entrepreneurs look to growth and profitability as objective measures of performance. If growth and profitability fail to meet expectations, a reality-expectation gap exists. So, factors that impair growth and profitability may be one and the same as those that cause discontinuance or failure. A summary of those factors often cited by entrepreneurs as the reasons for their business's demise is provided in Exhibit 6.7. Note that multiple responses were permitted.

In general, there are two paths to discontinuance: the business can be sold, or it can be folded. If it is sold, whether the owner realizes a gain or a loss on its sale will be correlated to profitability, among other things. If it is a successful business, the owner might expect a gain. If it is producing marginal returns, as is frequently the case with ma-and-pa type operations, it may be sold for a profit or a loss, depending on the circumstances. And, if the business is experiencing losses, it will likely be sold at its asset value and at a loss.

The probability that a business will be folded rather than sold increases as profitability declines. Accordingly, a business experiencing losses is more likely to be folded than a successful one. The process of folding a business involves selling off its assets and paying off its creditors. In general, the value received for the assets on disposition will be negatively influenced by the urgency of the situation, but enhanced by the owner's involvement in the process. Accordingly, owners should be proactive, and not wait for a third party, such as a bank, to initiate the process.

On a final note, there are costs associated with discontinuance. At the very least, there is potential for a loss of capital by the owner. In many cases, these financial losses may be significant and lead to personal bankruptcy. Beyond this, there was time invested and foregone opportunities. Researchers have also identified a variety of human tragedies that often coincide with, or result from, failure. They have uncovered affairs, divorces, suicides, and even murder. There are also costs to society, such as the underutilization of resources or the elimination of goods and services that the market wants. No doubt, many entrepreneurs experience some form of personal loss in the process of discontinuance, but the experience gained can be invaluable.

MODES OF ENTRY INTO ENTREPRENEURSHIP ———

Although building a business from scratch represents the most common form of entry into entrepreneurship, there are alternative entry strategies. These are discussed below, and differ from start-ups in terms of risk, resource requirements and suitability for individual entrepreneurs.

Buying an Existing Business

Twenty-five percent of Canadians enter into entrepreneurship through the process of acquiring an existing business. While purchasing a business may not seem as "entrepreneurial" as a start-up, this depends on both the nature and state of the business being acquired. If the business being acquired is a strong, flourishing one, the purchaser is able to avoid many of the typical problems encountered in start-ups, such as developing a market, hiring effective employees, and generating sufficient revenues. However, individuals might acquire businesses that are failing in one way or another and, as a result, face many of the same issues confronting individuals who opt for the start-up mode of entry. Either way, there is risk involved, and finding a business and negotiating its purchase requires great initiative.

Provided that the many critical issues associated with acquisition are positively resolved, this mode of entry can present many advantages. Because the business is already established, certain of the time-consuming concerns that are faced by individuals who start their own business from scratch are avoided. Therefore, entry into business can be relatively quick. In addition, an acquired business already possesses many of the essential business relationships, such as clients and suppliers. They also have an existing infrastructure, including personnel. The existence of these critical components typically means that the new owner/manager can quickly generate positive revenues from the business. Acquisition ventures are also advantageous in that the owner can draw upon previously acquired knowledge from the business, including the use of past financial information, to forecast its growth potential. And, because the acquired business comes complete with existing assets and cash flow, it is often easier to obtain the necessary financing for an acquisition than it is with the other modes of entry. Finally, as many businesses that are up for sale are in the midst of difficult times, with an acquisition there is the potential for a lower start-up cost than might be possible with one of the other entry strategies. Although, in these cases, there is clearly greater risk.

Acquisitions are obviously not without their disadvantages. With an acquisition, the new owner not only inherits business relationships, a location, an infrastructure and personnel, but also the image of the business in the marketplace. That is, they do not start with a clean slate, and any unfavourable aspects may not only limit the operation of the business, but also its potential for development and growth. It can also be quite costly to maintain the business and update the various technologies that are essential to its competitive positioning. The financing of this can also be a time-consuming and complex issue, and take away from the owner/manager's ability to attend to essential operational issues. A final disadvantage of acquiring an existing business is that, as an individual who is new to the business and quite possibly new to the industry as a whole, the new owner is often unable to foresee potential changes to the industry.

Having painted a rather bleak picture, it is interesting to note that the general consensus among venture capitalists is that would-be entrepreneurs should buy, rather than build, a business. Their focus is on cash flow, but they also stress that when shopping for a company, prospective purchasers must observe due diligence. That is, they must do their homework. While this is an endeavour that can take a great deal of effort and time, it is the only way of ensuring that the business to be acquired fits the purchaser's capabilities and objectives. During the due diligence process, the information that might be collected includes:

- General, historic issues, such as the age of the business, its ownership history, its reputation, its recent successes and failures, and so on
- Industry issues, such as the stability of the industry, the legal requirements of the industry, and the industry's future
- Product or service issues, such as the potential market for the product or service, the potential for product or service development, and the long-term demand for the product or service
- Competitor issues, such as who the competitors are, how many of them there are, and the relative competitiveness of the other businesses in the industry
- Operational issues, such as the location, the state of the equipment, and access to current technologies
- Employee issues, such as the effectiveness of the employees, their satisfaction, their training and education, their pay, and whether or not they are part of a union

In general, one of the most critical criteria on which an individual bases the decision to buy an existing company is the actual monetary value, both present and future, of the prospective acquisition. In this regard, there are various valuation methods. These are summarized below.

Discounted cash flow: The expected annual after-tax operating cash flow of the business is forecast for a discrete time frame. This is added to the projected residual value of the business at the end of that time frame, and used to establish the overall dollar value of the business in present value terms.

Earnings multiple approach: The value of a business is estimated using some number of years of historical and/or projected earnings. The average earnings are multiplied by a factor determined by the risks associated with the venture and the desired payback period.

Net asset approach: Also known as the book value approach, this method calculates the value of a business by simply subtracting the total value of the business's liabilities from the total value of its assets.

Replacement cost approach: The value of a business is determined by the cost to replace all of the assets of the business, including its land, buildings, equipment, inventory, and so on, ensuring that it is consistent with the age and state of the business and its facilities.

Market approach: The value of a business is established by simply comparing it to similar businesses in the industry that have recently been sold.

Franchising

Franchising is a method of distribution or marketing whereby a parent company (the "franchisor") grants to an individual or another company (the "franchisee") the legal right to sell its products or services. For its part, the franchisor receives a fee, or royalty. In return, the franchisee gains exclusive rights to a particular area or location for a specified period of time, but must conduct business in a prescribed manner, using registered trademarks, uniform symbols, specific equipment, standardized services and products, and so on, as governed by the franchise agreement. For individuals who are willing to accept the sometimes-strict operating policies of a franchisor, there is great potential for success with this mode of entry.

The initial success rate for franchising is among the highest of all of the modes of entry. There is roughly an 80% success rate for franchises over the first five years of operation.[117] It is this very high success rate that continues to attract would-be entrepreneurs to this entry strategy. Over the past two decades, franchising has grown at a rate of approximately 20% per year, and this trend is expected to continue. In addition, franchise sales continue to grow at a rate of approximately 10 to 15% annually, and there is no evidence to suggest a decline in this general trend, either. It is also interesting to note that 45% of retail sales in Canada are generated by franchises despite the fact that franchises make up only about five percent of all of Canada's retail businesses.

It is important to note that growth of franchising has not been limited to a single class of franchise. Most types of franchises have grown steadily, and are expected to continue to do so. However, not all franchise types are expected to offer continued growth into this century. Certain markets are becoming, or have already become, saturated. As such, these markets promise both a higher risk to the franchisee and a lower probable rate of return. This is particularly true for the more traditional franchise types, such as automobile dealers, petroleum service centres, and soft drink distributors—which, despite accounting for nearly 75% of all franchise sales revenue, are on the decline.

Because franchising involves myriad rights, responsibilities and obligations on the parts of both the franchisor and the franchisee, a formal contract is central to all franchising endeavours. Although there is no standard franchising agreement, a typical franchise contract contains clauses that outline the obligations of the franchisor and the franchisee, the fees or royalties due to the franchisor, both at start-up and as the business progresses, the cost to the franchisee of building construction or equipment purchased, the territorial restrictions or exclusivity of the franchise, etc.

Despite the legal aspects of franchising and its many contractual obligations, this mode of entry into entrepreneurial business offers many advantages. In buying a franchise, the entrepreneur enters into business with a proven product or service and a well-established identity in the market. As such, their chances for success are significantly higher than if the start-up mode of entry is pursued. Further, as the success of an individual franchisee contributes directly to the success of the overall franchise, franchisors generally offer their franchisees an array of professional assistance and training programs. They also detail prescribed and proven operating procedures for the entrepreneur. Finally, franchising can be advantageous in that banks are often more willing to supply capital to entrepreneurs associated with well-known and established franchises than they are to supply capital to entrepreneurs who act independently. All of the above are forms of external support that are frequently inaccessible to other entrepreneurs, and have motivated many individuals to opt for franchising.

While the legal contract is an essential element of the franchising strategy, it confers upon this mode of entry some disadvantages that can be a source of great personal disappointment and a cause of business failure. (See Exhibit 6.8.) In agreeing to the conditions of the franchise contract, the franchisee agrees to work under a previously established name and under rather strict operating procedures. As such, many franchisee entrepreneurs feel that they lose the independence and sense of personal identity that they had hoped to establish by venturing out on their own. In addition, a franchise contract generally requires that the franchisee pay to the franchisor an up-front franchise fee and ongoing royalty fees as a percentage of the gross sales, as well as fees to cover the cost of local, regional, and national advertising. The contract may also stipulate that the franchisee purchase from or through the franchisor all products and services that are essential

---

EXHIBIT 6.8	FRANCHISEES BEWARE OF . . .

1. The history of the franchise. This should include checking the business backgrounds of the principals, and checking the reputation of the franchise by contacting the Better Business Bureau or the local Chamber of Commerce.

2. The size and extent of the franchise, including the number and location of each of its outlets. If possible, it is also desirable to obtain the names and phone numbers of each of the franchisees — these individuals can provide insightful information regarding the operation of a franchise, the supportiveness of the parent company, their satisfaction with franchising, and so on.

3. The present financial status of the franchise and its forecasted financial position. Many companies will make readily available their most recent financial statements, while with others it may be necessary to rely on information from banks or other creditors.

4. The business controls that the franchisor is entitled to exercise in order to maintain uniform standards from each of the franchisees.

5. The purchase fees, royalty payments and any other costs, such as the cost of ongoing advertising, or the cost of any required management or training programs.

6. The location and layout of the franchise, including its decor and the equipment that is required. And in cases where a new building must be constructed, the costs and availability of financing.

7. The territory covered by the franchise, and the protection and exclusive nature of this territory.

8. The availability and extent of assistance programs, such as management and operations training and advertising programs.

to the operation of the business, even if they can be obtained elsewhere at a lower price. As such, purchasing a franchise can be an extremely expensive proposition. It is not uncommon for purchase and start-up costs to run well into the six figures. One final disadvantage of the franchise mode of entry is that, as a franchisee, an individual will be directly affected by all activities undertaken and decisions made by the franchisor, including any mistakes that might adversely affect the good name of the company.

CHAPTER SUMMARY

Entrepreneurship involves recognizing opportunities, taking calculated risks, innovating and creating new ventures; and the growth in the number of entrepreneurial ventures over the past decade has been referred to as the entrepreneurial revolution.

The pursuit of entrepreneurial activities knows no boundaries relating to gender, race or age, and Canada leads most industrialized nations in terms of the number of small businesses owned by women, immigrants and young entrepreneurs. While some are pushed into entrepreneurship by lack of attractive alternatives, others are pulled by the desire to control their own destiny, personal freedom and the potential for profit. Among the successful entrepreneurs, researchers have identified certain common personality characteristics, including a high need for achievement, a propensity for risk, tolerance of ambiguity and an inner locus of control. Beyond this, there are certain entrepreneurial and managerial skills needed for success.

Small business development follows a predictable sequence of progressive stages, beginning with an idea and ending with stabilization of day-to-day operating practices. As a new venture moves through its life cycle, it encounters many common problems, with marketing-related problems predominant. A venture's ability to overcome these problems influences the entrepreneur's decision to carry on or to discontinue the business; and discontinuance rates are high. However, the success of new ventures is influenced by diligence in the planning process, and having a formal plan correlates with success. But ventures should go beyond functional area plans, and consider developing a sound business strategy focusing on competitive advantage.

Business start-ups might be the most traditional mode of entry into entrepreneurship, but other modes, including buying a business and franchising, are increasingly common.

KEY TERMS

- entrepreneurship
- innovation
- benchmarking
- need for achievement
- a propensity for risk
- tolerance for ambiguity
- internal locus of control

- small business life cycle
- formation
- expansion
- stability
- small business failures
- discontinuance
- franchising

CASE APPLICATION — Canada Pure comes home

"People ask how we do it," Tracy Tavares remarks, eyes twinkling. "A mother-and-daughter team going up against the big boys with multi-million dollar marketing and advertising budgets."

Tracy, 29, and her mom Anna, 49, are the dynamic executive board of Canada Pure, a beverage that's been perking up the taste buds of American school kids since its U.S. introduction in 1996. They have achieved double-digit sales growth without fancy marketing, choosing instead to reach their target market — moms with young children and calorie-conscious teens — via state-run school lunch programs across the U.S. Now, the blue-hued bottles of fruit juice and sparkling spring water are making their first splash in Ontario's main food retailers, including Loblaws, Fortinos, Zehrs and Sobeys.

The Tavares are breaking into the Canadian market with a solid reputation. Their products have barely touched the shelves, but their packaging has already won two major awards from the Packaging Association of Canada. Canada Pure won silver in the brand marketing (new brand/product introduction) 2001 category, and another silver for merchandising in the paperboard packaging 2001 segment.

"We were totally surprised by it all," smiles Anna. "There we were surrounded by the biggest and the best in the beverage industry — Nestle, Coke, Pepsi — what an amazing sense of achievement going to the podium when our name was announced. But we also knew many in the audience were thinking, 'Who are these people? How did they get here?' Mom and I smiled and thanked everyone."

Little did the audience know that the Tavares have been around since 1991, when Tracy's father began the Toronto-based beverage operation. In 1994, he decided to return to his first love — telecommunications. Says Tracy Tavares: "My mom, who ran a furniture-making business for many years, seized the opportunity, taking the helm of Canada Pure. We saw the explosive growth of the alternative beverage category, a $9.6 billion industry in North America, and knew that our formulation was a sure bet to gain a following."

The Tavares's first strategic drive was to tackle U.S. school lunch programs. Increasing the line to seven flavours — raspberry, wildberry, strawberry, black cherry, peach, lemon lime and orange — they pursued lucrative contracts with district school boards.

"This was the best way, we believed, to raise awareness of the brand and to build a loyal consumer base," explains Anna Tavares. "Our target demographic is moms with young children and teenagers wanting a healthier drink, one that's low in carbohydrates, with 41% less calories than other fun beverages without using artificial sweeteners, and is fortified with vitamin C. Canada Pure meets the nutritional requirements of the American School Food Service Association."

The tactic worked. The slightly carbonated bubbly beverage won the hearts and stomachs of dozens of school districts and is now the #1 selling sparkling spring water approved for sale in U.S. schools.

In just five years Canada Pure has doubled its volume over 1994 figures. In 1996, Canada Pure was sold to over 10 million students in the U.S. And sales continue to grow, according to Tracy Tavares. "We projected a 15% increase in sales volume in 2001 over 2000, but we're currently growing at 24% — not including the [Canadian] retail sales now embarked on."

The company's expansion approach remains measured, methodical. "We get it right with one market before focusing on the next area of distribution," stresses Tracy Tavares. "Now that we've secured space on retail shelves throughout Ontario, we will roll out the program across the country over the next 12 months. Once our distribution channels are anchored here, our sights will turn south again, going after major U.S. retail chains. How will we do it? Watch us."

Source: By Jack Kohane from *Profit Guide Magazine* (December, 2001). The story originally appeared in *Profit-X*, the e-newsletter division of Profit Magazine published by Rogers Media in Toronto. Reproduced with permission of Jack Kohane.

QUESTIONS

1. What characteristics do you think these individuals share with the typical entrepreneurial profile?

2. Given the ideas generated in this chapter what advice or caution would you give to these entrepreneurs and why?

3. Do you think this venture is risky? Why or why not?

A sweet business

Larry Finnson and Chris Emery have been best buddies since they met in Grade 10 at Oak Park High School in Winnipeg.

Not much has changed in the 17 years since then.

Larry has a wife and two kids, with a third on the way this summer. In his spare time, he coaches his six-year-old son's squirt hockey league. Chris, who is single, is still a drummer in a local rock band, inspired by Pink Floyd.

But they're still just a couple of hyperkinetic dudes who hang out together for most of every day. It's just that instead of drinking beer — their preferred former pastime — they're doing business.

And it's not just any business. Chris and Larry want to strike it rich in the cutthroat world of candy. In North America, it's a US$24-billion industry dominated by large multinationals that control display and distribution. Prime shelf space can cost thousands of dollars in "fees" paid to retailers. Hershey Foods has a lock on 35% of the market.

But against all odds, their six-year-old company, Krave's Candy Co., is thriving. They employ 15 people full time, with the payroll tripling during peak production periods.

Annual sales growth has averaged 40% and in 2000 they grossed about US$2-million. Chris & Larry's Clodhoppers are available in Wal-Mart, Zellers, The Bay, Costco, Shoppers Drug Mart, Safeway, Overwaitea and Loblaw stores across Canada.

WestJet Airlines Ltd. recently started serving packets of the candy — a mixture of graham crackers, cashews and either peanut butter, vanilla or chocolate fudge — on all flights. And Dairy Queen Canada has developed a Clodhopper version of its Blizzard ice cream dessert.

No one is more surprised that the venture has survived — and flourished — than Chris and Larry. The company has suffered several near-death experiences brought on by the strains of uneven seasonal demand, flawed packaging, inadequate financing and spurts of rapid growth.

"If we'd known anything at all, we probably wouldn't have done this," admits Chris.

Neither partner had any business background — let alone a business plan — when they decided to commercialize a family recipe developed by Chris's grandmother, Edith Baker.

Larry was working for his dad in northern Manitoba building ice bridges and winter roads. Back in Winnipeg, Chris was answering phones at his dad's office, playing drums and dreaming of ways to become a millionaire. "The fact that both our dads were entrepreneurs gave us the example and inspiration to try it ourselves," explains Larry. "And living and working the way I was, I didn't exactly have a lot of downside."

After scraping up $20,000 from savings, family and friends, they rented a derelict 700-square-foot industrial space. Larry transformed a couple of old kettle cookers and some packaging equipment into a makeshift production line. They had the capacity to churn out 80-pound batches, packing the Clodhoppers into large plastic jars. The first year they sold about $60,000 worth.

With no insight into marketing, they haunted local craft fairs and retailers. They tirelessly handed out samples in malls and stores in Winnipeg.

After knocking on doors with limited success, they finally talked their way on to the shelves at a local Wal-Mart outlet. That renegade act — all purchases are supposed to be cleared through head office in Toronto — swiftly brought them to the attention of Wal-Mart Canada's chief buyer, Pat Whitehall, who became one of their biggest supporters.

Once they had scaled the ramparts of Wal-Mart, other retailers were more receptive. Zellers decided to carry Clodhoppers for the 1999 Christmas season. And after participating in a Wal-Mart Canada vendor show in Toronto, they caught the eye of Lee Scott, president and CEO of Wal-Mart Stores Inc., the U.S. parent. He agreed to stock their products — which they were by then packaging in expensive laminated and embossed boxes — in 400 U.S. stores for the Christmas 2000 season.

As they scrambled to keep up, they were also grappling with the urgent need to upgrade their ancient equipment and finance their expansion. No matter how strong their sales, they found they were always broke. "We had no margin at first," says Larry. "We had big growth in revenues but we were bleeding like stuck pigs."

Three years ago, as family members were finally tapped out, they managed to secure a line of credit from a chartered bank and a $100,000 loan from the Business Development Bank. They even borrowed money from a lender-of-last resort ("I guess you'd have to say he was actually a loan shark," says Chris) at 30% interest.

Part of the problem was the expensive laminated and embossed boxes. "We thought that we could compete by targeting the high-end of the market," says Larry. "We aimed at Lindt and the other truffley-type imports."

Another was the seasonal nature of demand. The company was swamped with orders over Christmas but had limited sales the rest of the year. That meant that even though they had increased their capacity to 3,000 pounds of candy, production wasn't achieving the necessary operating efficiencies.

So Chris and Larry repositioned the product. Having built a level of consumer awareness, they decided it was time to let their distinctive personalities rip. "People like the fact we aren't a big faceless corporation. We're two real guys from Winnipeg," says Chris. "The story has a grassroots appeal and we needed to capitalize on that."

They replaced the fancy boxes with funkier plastic bags adorned with cartoon images of themselves. They rebranded the candy as Chris & Larry's Clodhoppers, sidelining the original name Krave's Candies. They also set to work to develop a single-portion bag suitable for convenience stores and gas stations — an increasingly profitable distribution point for candy merchandisers.

They also talked their way on to the "snack schedule" for NorthWest Airline's first-class service. The airline had committed to a US$400,000 contract to purchase one million packages. That had the effect of smoothing seasonal demand and reaching potential new consumers. But NorthWest was hard hit by Sept. 11 and it cancelled the deal.

"Sept. 11 also caused us to chew our fingernails down because of our new export sales to the U.S.," Larry notes. "We were terrified our shipments would be delayed and that we'd miss our deadlines for Christmas display."

That was an especially important issue this year: Wal-Mart had finally agreed to sell Clodhoppers in 2,700 of its U.S. stores.

Given the significance of the lost contract with NorthWest, Chris and Larry decided to pitch a little closer to home. Late last year, WestJet began serving Clodhoppers on Canadian flights. Discussions are now under way with several other Canadian carriers.

The deal to supply Canadian Dairy Queen outlets with Clodhoppers is also crucial. Chris and Larry plan to break into the massive U.S. Dairy Queen market using a typically unorthodox plan. Last year at a charity auction for DQ franchisees, they paid US$6,500 to spend the day with Chuck Moody, CEO of Dairy Queen U.S. In April, they'll bring him to Winnipeg to tour their facility and listen to their pitch.

As for financing future growth, a new venture-capital partner, Ensis Management of Winnipeg, is helping to ease the process. Although the chunk of equity taken by Ensis in exchange for a $500,000 cash infusion clearly chafes, Larry acknowledges the relationship is bringing higher standards to administration and planning.

By next year, Clodhopper production is projected to double from the current level of one million pounds a year. Within four years, the target is 20 million pounds.

Another target is to sell the company for big bucks. "We want to build more value before we sell — the longer we hold out, the bigger the price tag," says Larry.

They may eventually succumb to a takeover or they may take the company public. "You got to figure the shareholders are already out there — they're the ones eating the Clodhoppers," says Chris.

Whatever the future holds, the partners insist they have remained best friends throughout the wild ride. "It's not unlike a marriage," says Larry, the one who knows. "The rough spots break you up or pull you closer together."

"Totally," agrees Chris.

Sweet stuff — even for a couple of candy guys.

Source: Deirdre McMurdy, "Building future on sweet idea. Entrepreneurs are anything but Clodhoppers" *Financial Post* (February 11, 2002). Reproduced with permission of the author.

QUESTIONS

1. Do you think that these individuals fit the entrepreneurial profile?

2. Do you consider these individuals to be high risk-takers? Why, or why not?

The Non-profit Organizational Landscape

There is little doubt that our society owes much to the presence of non-profit organizations amid the organizational landscape. The aim of this chapter is to shed more light on the nature of the non-profit sector. What types of organizations make up this sector, and in what ways do they contribute to society? We will address these questions, and look more closely inside and outside non-profit organizations. How are they typically designed and governed, and what environmental factors play a critical role in their functioning?

LEARNING OBJECTIVES

By the end of the chapter, you should be able to:

1. Identify the role of non-profit organizations in society.
2. Explain the notion of non-profit organizations as open systems.
3. Describe the environment of non-profit organizations.
4. Discuss the issue of governance and leadership in non-profit organizations.
5. Discuss major challenges facing non-profit organizations, including the acquisition and management of financial resources.

I am grateful to Professor Agnes Meinhard, Ryerson University, who served as first author in the writing of this chapter.

Organizational Insider

The New Face of Corporate Charity

As Canada suffers from a drought of volunteers, corporate volunteering is on the rise. One in four companies is encouraging workers to donate their time by giving them paid days off or modifying their work hours, according to a recent Statistics Canada survey. While corporations continue to donate cash, supporting staff to volunteer is part of a growing trend among employers across the country.

Lisa Davies, who works for American Express Canada Inc., is one of these new worker volunteers. Just recently, her company gave the 10-year cancer survivor a six-month paid sabbatical to volunteer at the Hearth Place Cancer Support Centre in Oshawa, Ont. "They encourage you to volunteer within your own community," says Ms. Davies, who works in customer service at American Express. At Hearth Place she helped with fundraising and peer support groups. Andrea Shaw, director of Hearth Place, says companies that help employees volunteer on work time are sending a clear message to the community. "They're putting their money where their mouth is," she says. "You'll always get from your community what you give to the community."

Employer-supported volunteering increased to 27 percent of all volunteer work in Canada last year from 22 percent in 1997, according to the National Survey of Giving, Volunteering and Participating, led by Statistics Canada. The study showed that Canada has one million fewer volunteers today than it had four years ago, mainly because people are pressed for time. Employee volunteering "is definitely on the rise," says Kristin Smith, a spokeswoman for Volunteer Canada, a non-profit agency. It most commonly takes the form of companies allowing staff to use corporate equipment, such as fax machines and photocopiers, for charitable causes. And although many firms don't have formal volunteering programs, they are slowly developing them, she says.

For companies, volunteer support can be a recruitment and retention tool or a chance to equip their staff with new skills. There is a "real thirst on the corporation level" to get employees volunteering and engaged in their communities, says Louis de Melo, vice-president of resource development at the United Way in Ottawa. Many United Way branches across the country have a loan representative program, where employees are assigned to various campaigns for 15 weeks. The number of employees in the Ottawa program has risen to 32 this year from 17 in 1997. The employees are paid their regular salaries by their employers. Companies often use the program as a chance to fast-track select employees, who gain management experience and hone their public speaking skills along the way, Mr. de Melo says.

Often company volunteer efforts are initiated by staff. Employees at Suncor Energy Inc., for example, approached their employer two years ago asking for financial help in organizing a team to pursue volunteering initiatives. Suncor responded by giving employees who want to volunteer extra days off with pay. Last year, 30 percent of the Calgary-based office donated their time to 15 non-profit organizations, according to Greg MacGillivray, a company employee.

"Employees can make a difference and give something back," he says. "It's a [way] for Suncor to show how it does care about the communities . . . and it's a win for the community." Other companies, such as Manulife Financial Corp., are taking volunteering a step further. The Toronto-based insurer already has an active volunteer program, which includes team initiatives and citizenship awards. But now, the company is in the process of developing a retiree volunteer program. A group of former employees are calling agencies to find out what their needs are, and encouraging other retirees to volunteer. "If we can facilitate, making it easy for the employees and retirees, they really embrace the idea of volunteering," says Sharon Cobban, Manulife's manager of employee volunteerism. The firm hopes to launch the program this year.

For Ms. Davies of American Express, a paid sabbatical at the cancer centre was fulfilling. The 34-year-old had been volunteering there for a few years after her battle with cancer. And although she can no longer be at the centre five days a week, she still stops by to help out in her free time. In addition to the paid sabbatical, American Express also gives money to charities that employees volunteer at, and has a day set aside for staff to assist in various projects, such as planting trees. "It's a core part of being a great employer," says Steve Gould, vice-president of human resources at American Express in Markham, Ont. To apply for the sabbatical, employees have to have worked at the company for 10 years or more. They also have to be strong performers and produce a letter of acceptance from the non-profit organization where they want to volunteer. The length of the sabbatical ranges from 12 weeks to a year. American Express believes the program gives it a broader edge. "Many people these days are more interested in investing in companies that are socially responsible," Mr. Gould says. "We feel that both from our employees' standpoint and shareholders' standpoint, everyone benefits. And the community agencies get something out of it as well."

Source: By Caroline Alphonso from *The Globe and Mail* (September 10, 2001): M1. Reproduced with permission of The Globe and Mail.

THE NON-PROFIT AGENDA ──────────────

As the Organizational Insider highlights, the profit objective is not the only goal that exists within our working society. Non-profit objectives are increasingly visible on the organizational landscape. Organizations are our society's primary instruments to accomplish social, political and economic goals. For a long time, social, economic and political scientists have divided society into two sectors: the private sector and the public sector.[118] Private sector organizations produce, process and market goods and services for consumers, while turning a profit for themselves. Public sector organizations sustain the framework of our society: by providing protection against foreign attackers, criminals, unsafe products, unhealthy air and water; by building and maintaining roads and airports; by educating our children; and by providing health and social services to those in need. A public organization is any organization controlled and run by government.[119] In Canada these include schools, hospitals and universities, as well as various governmental departments.

There is a third category of organizations: private, non-governmental organizations performing myriad services that cannot be adequately provided directly through the open marketplace or by the state. They are organizations that serve the broader public interest, bodies that rely heavily on private donations of money, government grants and volunteer labour, and that are involved in a high degree of civic engagement. Only recently have these organizations been recognized as constituting a separate and significant sector of the economy. This "Third Sector", or "Voluntary Sector", or "Non-profit Sector", or "Independent Sector", as it has variously been called,[120] can be defined as constituting all those organizations that are:

- private, non-governmental
- formally incorporated
- independent of government coercion
- prohibited from distributing profits to their stakeholders
- governed by a board made up of volunteers[121]

A subset of non-profit organizations is registered charities. Registered charities differ from non-profit organizations in that they have the ability to provide their donors with tax receipts. They are also subject to more stringent regulations. Non-profit organizations that aren't registered charities may raise funds, but cannot provide receipts. Their main source of funding is from governments, foundations, United Way-type federated funding, user fees and commercial activities.[122]

In Canada, an estimated 200,000[123] non-profit, non-governmental organizations deliver crucial social (Covenant House Toronto), health (The Victorian Order of Nurses), educational (Frontier College), economic (Daily Bread Food Bank), cultural (Clans & Scottish Societies of Canada), research (Social Planning Council of Metropolitan Toronto; The C.D. Howe Institute), funding (The United Way of Canada) and advocacy (National Anti-Poverty Organization) services to all segments of the Canadian population. They range from food banks, children's aid societies, and immigrant service organizations to opera companies and sporting societies. The value set that tends to guide and distinguish this "third sector" from private business and the public sector proper is the one that includes altruism and mutuality.[124]

Of the estimated 200,000 non-profit organizations, approximately 75,000 are registered charities.[125] Together they account for 12% of the GDP, and 13% of job growth.[126] Eight percent of Canada's labour force works in the non-profit sector. This paid labour is augmented by voluntary service that is equivalent to half a million full-time, full-year jobs.[127] The dollar value of this voluntary activity has been estimated to be worth $13 billion.[128]

Why Are There Non-profit Organizations?

The question of why there are non-profit organizations and why they have multiplied has intrigued researchers. The earliest non-profit, non-governmental organizations were charities formed to provide relief to the poor, sick and indigent.[129] Later, organizations advocating political and social change were created to influence government policy. These organizations did not seek to make a profit; so, although they were definitely private organizations, they were not part of the for-profit sector. In the last half century, the growth of non-profit organizations has been exponential.[130] Following are some of the theoretical explanations propounded by researchers.

The most prevalent explanation attributes the rise of non-profit organizations to the **failure of the market and public sector**. According to this theory, voluntary organizations emerge to provide people with services that they are unable to get from public institutions or private companies.[131] Private, for-profit companies provide only goods and services that enough people are willing and able to pay for. This would leave many people wanting for services because of their inability to pay. Public institutions provide some of these services, but they are limited to services that are deemed to be for the common good, as consensually agreed to by the general population. Thus, in Canada we have public hospitals, public education, public prisons and the like, but our public institutions are not always given the mandate to supply shelter for the homeless and abused women, for example; or to supply food for the hungry, or special services for the handicapped. Neither are they given the mandate to provide us with art museums and opera houses, institutions that are not supported by the for-profit sector because they are unlikely to generate enough profit.

A second explanation points out that voluntary organizations are **instruments of political and social action for special interest groups**.[132] According to this thesis, non-profit organizations form the very heart of the democratic system. Voluntary associations give voice to groups of people who may be in opposition to the government of the day, or its policies. They provide people whose interests are not represented by the ruling establishment, be it government or private industry, with a vehicle for collective expression and advocacy. These organizations are independent of government and market, hence the term "independent sector".

The phenomenal growth of the non-profit sector since the end of World War II is explained by the unique **partnership between government and non-profit** organizations that was fostered during this period. Governments, reacting to the ravages of the Great Depression, felt obliged to provide social-welfare services to their citizens. Although they provided some services directly, most were channelled through non-profit providers. This kind of partnership was deemed the most efficient and effective way of ensuring that citizens receive the services they need. Small organizations, more in touch with their constituents, are more innovative and effective in providing services. But they are not good at raising money. On the other hand, governments are good at raising money (through taxation), but not in providing services.[133]

Finally, some researchers explain the growth of non-profit organizations as being a response to a deep-seated conviction that the impersonal nature of market forces precludes the kind of care necessary in the provision of social services. Basic values in our society lead us to balk at the idea that someone may make a profit from the miseries of others. Charitable motives for helping people are more trusted than profit motives. Therefore, in situations where there are no clear measures of service quality, such as in human and social services, non-profits will be seen as **more trustworthy** deliverers of care and service. Non-profit organizations represent "social capital" that generates civil society and mitigates the impersonal forces of the marketplace.[134]

THE NATURE OF NON-PROFIT ORGANIZATIONS

Non-profits as Open Systems

As with other organizations, the most informative metaphor to use to explain the basic nature of non-profit organizations is the open systems model. Non-profit organizations, like others, take inputs from the environment, transform these inputs, and export the new product to the environment. Inputs for non-profit organizations would be human resources (workers, volunteers, clients), financial resources (loans, grants, donations), equipment, energy, knowledge and information. The transformation process would involve some kind of counselling, teaching or helping behaviour that is given to the client by a professional or volunteer. The output would be the client who has been helped in some way. To be successful, organizations must be sensitive to feedback by monitoring the services they are providing and adjusting them appropriately. Although the basic organizational processes are similar in non-profit and for-profit organizations, there are some key differences that have implications for organizational management.

Perhaps the most conspicuous difference between non-profits and for-profits lies in their mission, their reason for being; for, despite what a for-profit organization states as its mission, be it to manufacture a product or to give a service, underlying these activities is the goal of making a profit for the owners of the company. For non-profit organizations, the mission is what they state. There is no profit motive underlying the organizational activity. If there is an underlying goal, it is to make the world a better place to live in for all.

Another key difference is the way in which non-profits and for-profits interact with their environment. All organizations rely on the environment both for their resources (inputs) and the acceptance of their products or services (outputs). Without resources, they cannot continue their operations, and without acceptance of their product or service by the environment, they cannot generate the financial resources necessary for their continued operation. On both the input side and the output side, organizations must compete with other organizations. On the input side, they compete for resources that other organizations may also want; on the output, side they compete with other organizations that are providing the same or a similar product or service. Non-profit organizations differ from for-profit organizations in the focus of their competition.

A for-profit manufacturing organization, for example, has to buy the raw materials needed to manufacture its product. If many other organizations seek the same materials, then there will be increased competition for these resources. However, in manufacturing organizations, the competition is greatest on the output side of the equation. They compete with other organizations selling the same or a similar product. If they fail to compete successfully, they will not be able to garner the revenue necessary to continue their operations. In for-profit service organizations such as banks, insurance companies, dental clinics or daycare centres, the situation is the same. The competition will be stronger on the output side. It is the sale of their services that generates the revenue that enables the organizations to continue.

In non-profit organizations, on the other hand, most of the competition is on the input side. The most important resource for non-profits is financial support for their operations. Even organizations charging user fees rely on outside financial aid, as user fees cannot cover all their expenses. There is usually far less competition on the output side, since non-profit organizations are niche players, concentrating on providing services to a particular group in need. Even if they are not the only providers, other providers will be few, and probably all of them are needed to fill the demand.

To ensure their survival, for-profit organizations have to compete successfully in selling their product or service. Non-profit organizations, on the other hand, have to compete successfully for their financial resources in the form of grants and donations. The environmental changes that have taken place in the past two decades have made the acquisition of these resources more difficult for the non-profit world.

The Environment of Non-profit Organizations

The last two decades of the 20th century bore witness to many revolutionary changes in the environment, starting in the areas of technology and communications. These breakthroughs facilitated the movement of goods and the concomitant expansion of markets, as world commerce became more global. Globalization, in turn, has wrought many social, cultural, political and economic changes, which have had an impact on organizations and citizens around the world. Governments are bowing to the demands of free trade and open commerce by changing, sometimes quite radically, social and economic policy. These policy changes are having a tremendous impact on the non-profit sector.[135]

The Changing Social Climate in Canada

In the economic expansion that followed the end of World War II, and with the memory of the Great Depression still fresh in people's minds, the federal and provincial governments in Canada launched an ambitious social welfare program. Governments at all levels encouraged the formation of voluntary organizations to partner with them to provide services to all citizens, and to help erase inequalities. By the mid-1970s in Canada, the federal and provincial governments had largely completed the construction of the social welfare system. This system involved a matrix of programs and services that were delivered by both the public sector and the voluntary sector. Under this structure, non-profit organizations were part of an elaborate system that extended specialized services to the public that the government was uninterested in or unable to provide. Not only did voluntary organizations receive funding from government sources; but, more important, they gained legitimacy to represent and serve their various constituencies.[136]

Since the mid-1980s, the political philosophy in Canada has been changing from a pluralist, social welfare conception of the state to a neo-conservative philosophy.[137] Proponents of this philosophy believe that market forces should dictate the formation and survival of all organizations, including non-profit organizations. Funding for non-profit organizations should come from private charitable support and user fees, not from government. Funds from government to provide social services should be tendered to the lowest bidder, be it a non-profit or for-profit organization. The voluntary sector is only now beginning to feel the impact of this neo-conservative policy.

In tune with this new philosophy, there has been a steady erosion of government-non-profit partnership, as both the federal and provincial governments have been withdrawing from direct service provision in several areas of social welfare. In response to global forces, they have been slashing their health, education and welfare budgets, including grants to the voluntary sector, by billions of dollars.[138] At the same time, they were expecting voluntary organizations to pick up the slack. Voluntary organizations in Canada are being forced to change their strategies, and often their structures, in order to meet the new challenges.

With the general acceptance of free market principles, non-profits have been pressured to adopt "business-like" practices, which include marketing, entrepreneurial initiatives, increasing efficiencies and streamlining management.[139] Government funders and private donors are requiring greater accountability and insisting on performance indicators. Without the benefit of tangible indicators such as profit, or number of products sold, it is difficult to gauge the true performance of non-profit organizations. Much of their impact is long-term and unmeasurable. One unfortunate side effect of this demand for performance measures is changing service goals to measurable outcomes. Thus, programs that help individuals in the long term, through intensive one-on-one care, are often dropped for ones with more immediate, tangible goals. For example, a program to teach the handicapped to be more independent, allowing them to eventually find meaningful work, has been modified to include only those whose short-term prospects are good. The most vulnerable people, those who are most in need of intervention, are now left out in order to improve job placement numbers.

Forces for Change

Generally speaking, for non-profit organizations the forces for change are to be found less in the area of technology, and more in the area of demographic, social, political, philosophic and economic environments. For example:

- New statutes may expand or contract an organization's jurisdictions;
- Changes in government often bring new policies;
- Changes in the economy or politics may result in diminished or increased resources;
- New taxation laws may affect non-profits;

- Advances in professional procedures often require structural changes in organizations;
- Demographic shifts often lead to changes in needs;
- Public attitudes, client needs may change;
- Stakeholder demands for improved performance, greater accountability.

Technology and Change

A caveat is in order before proceeding with this discussion. Although the discussion seems to be a condemnation of technological progress, it is not. Rather, it is a brief summary of the concern of several writers about the exploitation of whole classes of people in the wake of rapid technological advances.

The world we live in today is very different from the one we lived in a quarter of a century ago. Some theorists[140] present very persuasive arguments that the political, philosophical and economic upheavals that have occurred in the past 25 years have been fuelled and driven by the technological revolution in information and communications. This has truly shrunk the world into a "global village", where some multinationals disregard political boundaries in their competitive thrusts to become richer and more powerful. In order to remain competitive in this globalized world, organizations must be more efficient than their rivals. Since labour costs are the most expensive aspects of running an organization, technology has been developed to replace human resources. In Canada, this trend has resulted in a chronic unemployment rate, hovering around 10%, with an additional 15% of Canadians underemployed part-time workers. Even many of those employed full time are used as mere extensions of technology: for example, workers in call centres, or data entry operators. Only a few people actually control technology. Corporations are reaping unprecedented profits from this "jobless economic growth". This "technology mystique" has been embraced in all areas of life, including government and the public services, so that while thousands of public service workers are being laid off, all levels of government have been spending hundreds of billions of dollars on technology in their quest for efficiency.

The medium has truly become the message. The technological imperative that we are accepting blindly is fundamentally changing our society, our culture and our civilization. It is polarizing society into people who control technology and those who are controlled by it. It is resulting in the devolution or downloading of health care and welfare services to private providers who are "wired in" to this new technological network, in the privatizing and selling out of education to high-tech manufacturers, and the abdication by governments of citizen protection.

Attempting to respond to this, non-profit, non-governmental organizations are struggling to maintain the concept of a civil society where people come first. Individual organizations are trying to adjust, but there is also an attempt at a collaborative response to these societal upheavals. This is not a new phenomenon. It happened in the Industrial Revolution as well, until laws were passed to protect the worker. The protections that were initiated then, and expanded since, are now being threatened. It seems that in the name of the new technology, the trend today is to dismantle many of these protections. It almost seems as if the only collective voices against what is happening are raised by non-profit organizations that are themselves in the throes of change as a result of these new societal trends.

GOVERNANCE OF NON-PROFIT ORGANIZATIONS

The governance of non-profit organizations differs significantly from for-profit organizations. Structurally, they look the same. There is a board of directors responsible to the owners, a chief executive officer or executive director, responsible to the board, and different levels of staff members who are ultimately accountable to the CEO or executive director (ED). Despite this structural similarity, the role of the board, the composition of the board and the relationship of board to staff are very different.[141]

The first major difference between non-profit and for-profit governance is ownership. It is easy to know who owns a for-profit organization. Whether privately or publicly owned, the for-profit organization carries out the wishes of its owners. The owners can communicate directly with the board of directors. The board is accountable to the owners. As a matter of fact, the directors themselves are part owners of the organization. In the case of most types of non-profit organizations, it is difficult to ascertain ownership. For example, who owns a non-profit organization teaching reading skills to illiterate adults? The people whose idea it was to form such an organization? They may not be there anymore. The funders who give money to the organization? There may be many funders, including government, but none of them have legal rights to influence the organization. The people whom they serve? Society at large? To whom, in the end, is the board accountable? All the above mentioned, as well as others who in some way are connected to the organization, are all stakeholders who have to be satisfied, but there are no clear owners. This fact places even more onus on the board, because they are then responsible to the broad "common good". Their decisions must not only abide by legal regulations, they must also adhere to the moral and ethical standards of the community/society that they serve. The governing boards of non-profit organizations are made up of volunteer members who are legally prohibited from obtaining any financial gain from their membership on the board. This legality is a distinguishing feature of voluntary organizations. As a matter of fact, the term "voluntary organization" refers not to the fact that all members of the organization are volunteers, but rather to the fact that the directors of the governing boards of these organizations are volunteers.

This stipulation means that the executive director, who is a paid staff member of the organization, cannot be a member of the board, and has no vote or authority on the board; whereas, in for-profit organizations, the CEO is often the chair of the board, and thus has full authority. Thus, in principle, there is a clear separation of board and staff in non-profit organizations. But, in reality, there are different types of non-profit boards. (See Exhibit 7.1.)

Functions of Boards

With respect to the public, the board is the legitimate connection between the community and the organization, and therefore is legally and morally accountable to its consumers, the general public, and clients. The main function of the board is to manage the affairs of the organization by providing direction and ensuring that the organization meets its legal obligations. In order to do this, an effective board must perform a number of functions, as outlined in Exhibit 7.2.

EXHIBIT 7.1   TYPES OF BOARDS

There are three main types of volunteer boards:

Working boards are where board members do the organization's work or work closely with the staff to carry out the operations of the organization. Working boards are characteristic of newly created organizations where: a) board members are the founders of the organization and have a passion for the mission of the organization, so that they wish to be a part of the day-to-day operations of the organization; and/or b) the organization has insufficient resources for paid staff persons to carry out the operations of the organization. In some organizations, there is little distinction between the organization and the board. Board members are merely organizational members who have taken on added duties.

Policy boards focus on strategic planning and decision making, rather than on the day-to-day operations of the organization. Policy boards also set limits for their executive directors and paid staff. This type of board is more characteristic of mature organizations, where board members are solicited for their expertise in different areas of importance for the organization. Even in policy boards, it is impossible to completely disentangle the strategic and operational roles and responsibilities in an organization. Some policy boards function merely as rubber stamps for the decisions taken by the organization's executive director.

Mixed boards are a characteristic of many non-profit organizations, especially smaller ones. Board members are responsible for the strategic direction of the organization, but they also participate in the day to day operations of the organization. This model can result in considerable role confusion and conflict. However, if the board members and the staff are comfortable with ambiguity and are conscious of when a mixed board is performing operational duties and when it is performing governance duties, this contingency model can be quite successful.

Sources: Murray, 1995; Carver & Carver, 1997.

EXHIBIT 7.2   FUNCTIONS OF BOARDS

- Keeps the mission of the organization as the central focus of activities by judging all functions and decisions against it.
- Guards the values of the organizations through explicit deliberation and discussion.
- Keeps the organization focused externally on the needs of its stakeholders.
- Assures the performance of staff and the continuous quality improvement of the organization.
- Concentrates on the future by providing strategic leadership for the organization and defining its vision.

Sources: Murray, 1995; Carver & Carver, 1997.

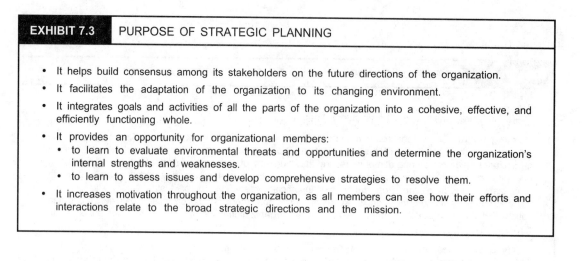

EXHIBIT 7.3 | PURPOSE OF STRATEGIC PLANNING

- It helps build consensus among its stakeholders on the future directions of the organization.
- It facilitates the adaptation of the organization to its changing environment.
- It integrates goals and activities of all the parts of the organization into a cohesive, effective, and efficiently functioning whole.
- It provides an opportunity for organizational members:
  - to learn to evaluate environmental threats and opportunities and determine the organization's internal strengths and weaknesses.
  - to learn to assess issues and develop comprehensive strategies to resolve them.
- It increases motivation throughout the organization, as all members can see how their efforts and interactions relate to the broad strategic directions and the mission.

Strategic Planning

Strategic planning is a process by which an organization creates its own future. Instead of beginning from a point of, "What we have to do given the realities of our situation," strategic planning begins from the point of, "What is our real purpose, and how can we build the organizational capacity to fulfill that purpose?"[142]

The process of strategic planning is as important as the actual plan itself, and fulfills a number of important goals, outlined in Exhibit 7.3.

Strategic planning is a function of the board, but participation in the planning process does not have to be limited to members of the board, nor does it have to include all board members. The important thing is that key organizational members be involved. These may be people who are at the boundaries of the organization and have a clearer view of environmental demands; these may be people who are creative and innovative; they may be people with specific skills or knowledge. Although the ultimate decisions rest with the board, there is no reason why staff members cannot be full participants in the planning process. The involvement of staff members in the process will reduce resistance and assure better implementation.

The strategic planning process entails an organizational stock-taking and an environmental assessment. This is best accomplished using a SWOT analysis, which looks at the internal strengths (S) and weaknesses (W) of the organization, and the external opportunities (O) and threats (T). In light of this analysis, the strategic planning team should re-examine the organization's mission statement and endorse it or revise it.

Official goals or mission statements are extremely important for a voluntary organization. Not only do they **represent the reason for the organization's existence** and **define its function in society**, they also **provide** a sense of **legitimacy, direction and purpose** to the organization. They help to **reduce uncertainty** within the organization, and **justify its activities to the outside world**. They serve as a source of **cohesiveness** for organizational members, and are also important **recruitment devices**.

Once the organization's mission is clearly defined, the planning process begins with carving out a shared vision of the future through the systematic consideration of three questions:

- What is the desired future for the organization?
- What will be needed in the organization's future?
- What will the organization be capable of doing in the future?

Based on the mission and vision, specific operative goals must be defined. These operative goals describe the future desired results toward which present efforts are directed. Organizational goals are "those ends that an organization seeks to achieve by its existence and operation".[143]

There are two types of goals:

- **Official goals**, which express the general aims of the organization and are primarily intended to show the purpose of the organization.
- **Operative goals**, which are more specific and measurable, pertain to the primary tasks an organization must perform, and are used to guide behaviour and evaluate performance.

Operative goals are the means to achieve the ends defined by the official goals, which are vague and symbolic. They provide direction and motivation to organizational members and act as guidelines for decision making. Because they are measurable, they outline criteria for performance evaluation of both the organization and its individual members. Although operative goals should ideally reflect the official goals, this is not always the case. They may displace official goals even as they take on a life of their own. For example, the official goals of a prison, as stated in the mission, emphasize rehabilitation, but the operative goals, evident in budget allocations, hiring practices, etc., reinforce only custodial functions.[144]

Priorities should be determined on the basis of the interplay between external opportunities and threats that the organization faces and the strengths and weaknesses of the organization in dealing with them. In other words, priorities should be set within the context of a SWOT analysis.

The implementation of the strategic plan is carried out by staff in organizations with policy boards, and by board members in organizations with working boards. Proper implementation requires good communication, wise task assignment and a reward system that will motivate volunteers and staff alike to carry out the plans. Timely feedback and follow-up are essential. Once the new goals are achieved, their outcomes should be evaluated. This may result in a renewed strategic planning process.

Most non-profit boards don't engage in strategic planning, for several reasons. Cost is one factor; strategic planning requires both time and money, which many boards don't have. Also, in many organizations, there are so many operational crises, it hard to get into a strategic frame of mind. Another, often unconscious, reason organizations avoid strategic planning is that the process results in a sharing of power between the board and the staff at the same time as it forces a clarification of boundaries and roles.

Legal and Ethical Obligations of the Board

The concept of ethics is usually applied to the behaviour of individuals. However, as organizations are made up of groups of individuals, at another level, ethical terms may also be applied to organizations. Ethics in organizations refers to the moral character of organizational actions and the extent to which these actions represent "good" or "bad" conduct. Ethical decision making involves making choices based not only on narrow problem-relevant criteria, but also on a broader set of principles used by society to judge the morality of conduct.[145]

Members are both influenced by and influence the organizational values and codes of behaviour that can be said to make up the ethics of an organization. They also act in accordance or in conflict with those same values and codes of conduct. These values and codes of conduct may be seen by society as either positive or negative. Recently, as more attention is paid to the importance of the non-profit sector, the ethics of non-profit organizations are coming under greater scrutiny. Activities and behaviours that until recently were considered acceptable, such as letting volunteers have first pick of free goods at a church rummage sale, are now viewed as illegal and immoral.

As society's expectations of ethical behaviour of non-profits have changed, the law has also changed and codified those expectations. All independent, incorporated, non-profit organizations and charities must be governed by boards under the laws of Ontario and most other provinces in Canada. Board members are called directors, and considered fiduciaries — those who accept and hold a "public trust". Public trust is the obligation placed on directors to maintain, preserve and further develop and expend resources, and to ensure that the organization's activities remain in the public domain to benefit this and further generations. It refers to the obligation placed on directors to provide governance and management of the organization, and to implement programs and services for the benefit of the organization's public. In the case of incorporated non-profits, this trust is to their members and/or their donors, to carry out the mission of the organization. The interests of a non-profit that is not a charity are private.

In the case of charities, the public trust is to the public at large, and is governed by specific laws and regulations. Directors of charities are accountable to the courts and to the Attorney General. Some organizations may think that they are not a charity, as they are not tax registered. However, if the purposes of the organization are wholly and exclusively charitable in law, then they are a charity. The law defines a charitable purpose as: advancement of education, advancement of religion, relief of poverty or the benefit of the public in general. There are also many unincorporated non-profit associations whose directors and members have fewer legal restrictions, but a much higher degree of personal risk.

As all incorporated bodies are treated as a person, the board of directors is viewed, under the law, as acting for the corporation's person. Directors must safeguard the interests of the corporation. They are also, individually or jointly, held accountable for the actions of the corporation.

The leaders of non-profits play a strong role in creating the ethical guidelines for the organization. It is the founding board that determines the initial values of the organization that underlie the ethical codes of behaviour. Non-profits, especially charities, are, in a sense, charged with operating at a higher ethical level than are organizations in the private sector. The owners of charities are actually the general public, rather than specific shareholders. As well as obeying the classic prohibitions against lying, stealing, drunkenness

---

LET'S TALK BUSINESS 7.1   ETHICS FOR NON-PROFIT ORGANIZATIONS

Non-profit organizations are value intensive; that is, the promotion of specific values is often a major purpose of many non-profits. Therefore, there is a demand on their members to ensure their behaviour is consistent with the values the organization is trying to foster. Non-profit organizations often have workers who face complex ethical decisions as a routine part of their jobs. The use of volunteers brings additional ethical issues that are not present in the for-profit sector, or even in the public sector, where there is a monetary exchange for labour performed. With volunteers, there is no such exchange. Labour is performed with the expectation of furthering the goals of the organization, and the organization is ethically bound to use volunteer labour appropriately. Other ethical obligations of non-profits are due to the vulnerability of clients served and the high degree of societal responsibility assumed. Many charities work with and for clients who hold a weak, disadvantaged position in society. In some cases the vulnerability is not readily visible, but creates an ethical obligation nevertheless, due to the power imbalance between the client group and the organization.

---

and sexual and other forms of harassment, non-profit organizations are expected to "do things the right way, to do good for the greatest number of people while protecting individual rights and ensuring everyone is treated equitably". (See Let's Talk Business 7.1.)

Board-staff Relations

Board-staff relations are traditionally viewed as hierarchical in nature, with the board of directors as the ultimate source of authority and responsibility. As such, the board is expected to oversee programs and establish standards. The chief executive is hired to assist the board in accomplishing this. According to this model, the board plans and reviews, hires and fires, and revises the organization's mission when necessary. In other words, it is the board that steers the organization. This clear separation of functions (between board chair and executive director) creates a situation of dual leadership, which can, and often does, lead to conflict. The skilful steering of board-staff relations is an important function of non-profit boards.[146]

The traditional model. The traditional model of board-staff relations stems from the legal requirements demanded of the board. Canadian law requires that a non-profit board be held ultimately responsible for the affairs and conduct of the organization. As such, the board has to maintain control over the actions of its members. Coupled with this legal requirement is the moral assumption that the board of directors makes sure that their organization operates toward a mission, and in a manner that reflects and serves the interests of the broader community. This, too, requires board control over members' activities.

Because of its ultimate legal and moral responsibility to the community, the board is the final arbiter of mission and policy. It is the board that

- articulates the mission of the organization
- makes major policy decisions
- controls financial policy
- has final jurisdiction over staff

The executive director provides information and expertise to the board and implements its policies. Thus, we see that in the traditional model, a strict distinction between policy and administration is maintained.

John Carver, who is perhaps the best-known commentator with respect to non-profit boards, advocates this traditional model by using an end-means distinction to describe board-staff relations. In his model, the board's role is to specify the ends or outcomes that the organization is striving toward. It is the role of the ED and the staff to select the means to achieve the board's specified ends. The board, however, must set limits to the ED's discretion in choosing the means. The board also monitors the extent to which the ends have been achieved, and makes sure that the means used do not transgress organizational and community values.

In the traditional model, the hierarchy of decision making and liability is clearly defined. In reality, the distinction between board and staff roles and functions is not nearly so clear-cut. In their founding stages, many non-profit organizations start with a vision that focuses on the practical. Governance and management are entwined in a hands-on, action-oriented process at the board level. The board is thus accountable for its own actions. As the organization grows and recruits professional staff, management is delegated to the executive director, who is directly accountable to the board. However, many board members are still "working in the trenches", functioning as volunteers, doing staff work or providing expertise to staff as they do their work. Sometimes this happens because an organization is new and has few staff. Sometimes it is the result of a need for a particular board member's expertise, and sometimes it is a result of the board member being unable to stay out of the operational workings of the organization. Whatever the reason, this mixing of roles often can lead to conflict.

"The greatest source of friction and breakdown in voluntary organizations of all types, sizes, ages and relative degrees of sophistication and excellence relates to misunderstandings and differing perceptions between the voluntary board president and staff directors."[147] Problems arise because the EDs, who remain while board chairs rotate, have more information and greater expertise than do the board members, who are the final arbiters of policy.

An alternative model.   Robert Herman and Richard Heimovics[148] offer an alternative to the traditional, hierarchical model. This alternative model does a more realistic job of depicting how the board and staff function in a non-profit organization. In their research, Herman and Heimovics found that board members, staff, and the EDs themselves all attributed both successful and unsuccessful critical events in the organization to the executive director, thus effectively pointing to the ED as the *de facto* leader of the organization. Their model recognizes the central role of the chief executive in the organization. After all, because the work of the organization is more central in the lives of the EDs than in the lives of the board members, many of whom hold other jobs and may not be longtime board members, EDs have access to more organizationally relevant information, and also have greater expertise in areas relevant to the organization. Therefore, realisti-

---

LET'S TALK BUSINESS 7.2   PARTNERSHIP IN NON-PROFIT ORGANIZATIONS

Partnership is key in decision making and policy formulation as well. "The worst illusion ever perpetrated ... is that the board ... makes policy and the staff carries it out."[1] Boards are generally reactive, not proactive. They work best when they can respond to specific issues presented to them by management. But even on occasions when the initiative comes from the board, they should formulate policy and work in close collaboration with staff members, until they hammer out a policy that can be implemented by the organization.

Source: [1] O'Connell, 1985: 44.

---

cally, it is the EDs who ensure that the governance function is properly organized and maintained.

In this alternative model, as in the traditional model, the NPO's board of directors is, ultimately, legally responsible. The moral assumption of serving the community is also retained as an ideal for the board to strive toward. But in this model, it is recognized that public stewardship is "likely to occur if, and only if, the chief executive helps the board to understand and carry out this responsibility as well as its legal responsibility".[149] Thus, the legal and moral responsibilities of the board are the foundations of this model as well; but given the realities, these responsibilities can be met by the board only in partnership with the executive officer. (See Let's Talk Business 7.2.)

The fundamental difference between the prescriptive traditional model and the alternative model is that "the latter no longer puts the board at the centre of leadership in non-profit organizations".[150] Executive directors are expected to provide board-centred leadership, not usurping the board's role, but working with them, not only on decision making and policy formulation, but also in providing criteria for evaluation of programs and individual performance. The board still has the ultimate authority to hire and fire staff, and therefore, even in this alternative model, ultimate power lies in the hands of the board.

The board is responsible for ensuring a high quality of work life in the organization. This means fair compensation, benefits, work hours, work environment, and human resource policies that ensure equitable treatment of staff and volunteers. These policies should include a performance management system for staff and volunteers and other mechanisms to enable the board to receive feedback on organizational productivity. As the employer, the board is often the final court of appeal in employee relations matters.

Organizational Control

Organizational control involves a balance between the need for accountability to the board and a need for flexibility and creativity in carrying out the organization's mission.[151] How is control maintained in organizations that empower their employees? How do organizations reconcile the conflict between creativity and control?

As discussed above, the board must set the ethical tone for the organization by communicating the organization's core values, belief systems and mission to all levels of employees in an inspirational way in order to draw their attention to the key tenets of the organization. The principal purpose is to inspire and promote commitment to the organization's core values. If these statements truly reflect the company's deeply rooted values, they will be very effective.

In the absence of clearly articulated core values, people are forced to make assumptions about what constitutes acceptable behaviour, and often these assumptions prove inaccurate. Thus, the board must set the boundaries as well. These boundaries should be defined by what **not to do**, rather than by what **to do**.

Telling organizational members what to do discourages creativity. Telling them what not to do allows freedom of action within certain clearly defined limits. These clearly articulated boundaries serve as the organization's brakes. Empowerment should never be interpreted as a blank cheque. In an organization, pressures to achieve often collide with strict codes of behaviour, so boundaries have to be clearly articulated. Boundaries are especially important in organizations where temptation is great.

From this brief overview of the governance of non-profit organizations it is evident that the voluntary board plays a larger and more significant role in the organization's activities than does the for-profit board. Thus, management of non-profit organizations cannot be studied without a full understanding of the role of the board.

LEADERSHIP IN NON-PROFIT ORGANIZATIONS

In organizations, leaders have two roles: symbolic and substantive. The **symbolic role** involves providing explanations, rationalizations and legitimizations of organizational activities and decisions both to the organization's members and to outside stakeholders. The **substantive role** involves strategic planning and decision making that leads to concrete outcomes. Both of these roles subsume the ability to influence other group or organizational members to work toward the achievement of defined group or organizational goals.[152]

Important components of the exercise of leadership are organizational knowledge and leadership skills. A leader must be knowledgeable with respect to the formal and informal power structure of the organization. He/she must understand the input, transformation and output processes of the organization. He/she needs insight into the organization's culture and its role as aider or hinderer of innovation and change. He/she must understand the importance of the symbolic function as well as the substantive function of leadership.[153]

As in all organizations, effective leadership is key for the success of a non-profit organization. Although many of the functions of the leader are similar in for-profit and non-profit organizations, leadership in non-profit organizations has certain unique challenges. (See Exhibit 7.4.)

Recently, scholars have identified two distinct types of leadership roles: transactional and transformational.[154] The **transactional leader** manages exchanges within a basically stable and knowable framework. His/her role is organizational maintenance, ensuring that the

EXHIBIT 7.4	LEADERSHIP CHALLENGES

- There is a dual, interdependent, and legally unequal leadership shared between the volunteers and the paid professional executive director. This chief executive-board relationship is critical to effective leadership in non-profits. Boards have legal and hierarchical authority over the executive director, while the executive director typically has greater information, expertise, personal passion and personal identification with the organization. In reality, it is the executive director who typically wields the greatest influence over the organization, and the challenge of the board is to provide leadership to the executive director.

- Leaders in the non-profit sector are in the position of having to use non-monetary rewards. Some of their "staff" are actually volunteers. Also, non-profits provide a lower level of compensation than does the private and, often, the public sector. As they cannot use many rewards available in the other sectors, leaders in the non-profit sector tend to rely more on their referent and expert power to strengthen their legitimate power.

- Because the public is the "owner" of a non-profit organization, leaders in the non-profit sector are held to a higher level of public scrutiny than are leaders in the private sector.

- Leaders in the non-profit sector are faced with conflicting organizational goals: fiscal restraint and quality service to all in need. They have a collective responsibility to integrate the realms of mission, resource acquisition and strategy formulation. They have to guard against mission displacement as they define and redefine strategy. Securing resources necessary to achieve the mission must be consistent with the values of the organization and the achievement of the mission.

- A turbulent environment that is changing the very nature of the sector. This implies that leaders of non-profit organizations have to be able to steer their organizations through change processes. The talents and skills necessary for leadership in times of change are different from those that are needed in times of stability.

various units in the organization or departments function in an integrated and coordinated manner. He/she uses legitimate reward and power bases to facilitate and direct employees toward accomplishing tasks and organizational objectives.

The **transformational leader** goes beyond management by communicating a vision and inspiring employees to strive for that vision. He/she commits people to action, and converts followers into leaders.[155] Transformational leadership is most important in times of organizational change, when both the symbolic and substantive functions of leadership are critical. The creation of a strategic vision (substantive role) and its communication (symbolic role) are paramount in managing change. Transformational leaders instill feelings of confidence, admiration and commitment in their followers by performing a number of key functions, as outlined in Exhibit 7.5.

Successful change in organizations requires transformational leadership, as opposed to transactional leadership, which preserves the status quo. Transformational leadership is the preferred leadership style in most non-profit organizations for two reasons. First, non-profit organizations are in a period of turbulence that requires strong, visionary leadership. Second, because non-profit organizations do not have the necessary financial resources to reward their paid staff generously, and because many of them rely on volunteers, their leaders have to be able to motivate both staff and volunteers without recourse to tangible rewards. This latter is a very difficult task. Executive directors of non-profit organizations

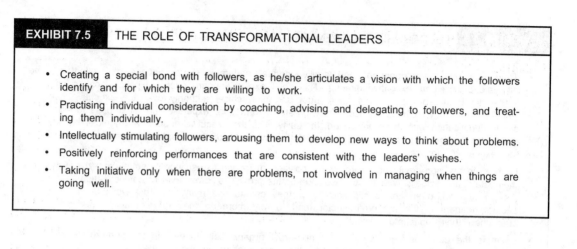

EXHIBIT 7.5   THE ROLE OF TRANSFORMATIONAL LEADERS

- Creating a special bond with followers, as he/she articulates a vision with which the followers identify and for which they are willing to work.
- Practising individual consideration by coaching, advising and delegating to followers, and treating them individually.
- Intellectually stimulating followers, arousing them to develop new ways to think about problems.
- Positively reinforcing performances that are consistent with the leaders' wishes.
- Taking initiative only when there are problems, not involved in managing when things are going well.

have to be able to create special bonds with their workers. They have to know how to make them feel valuable, both to the organization and to the accomplishment of the cause. However, this is a veritable balancing act, because with limited human and financial resources, both staff and volunteer workers dedicated to the cause will be inadvertently exploited, and they will end up burned out. The problem, therefore, is not so much how to motivate staff and volunteers, rather how to prevent burnout. (See Let's Talk Business 7.3.)

LET'S TALK BUSINESS 7.3   LEADING VOLUNTEERS

One of the most pressing issues for organizations that use volunteer labour is the recruitment and retention of volunteers. Of the two, retention is by far the more difficult. Motivations for volunteering are many. The most frequently cited reasons given for voluntary affiliation are "helping others",[1] and identifying with a "good cause".[2] However, more probing investigations suggest that altruism is not a major motivator.[3] In fact, affiliation can best be explained by the pursuit of tangible rewards offered by the organization to potential members.[4] These tangible rewards include participating in friendship and professional networks,[5] as well as acquiring skills and experience.[6] With most volunteers, the motivations for joining an organization are a mixture of all of these. Thus, the voluntary organization must understand the wide range of motivations involved in volunteering, and provide the volunteer with opportunities to meet these conditions. Traditional transactional leadership will not suffice to help the volunteer understand the organization's vision and make him/her feel needed and become a true contributor to the organization and its cause. Transformational leadership is more appropriate in this case.

Sources: [1] Duchesne, 1989; Carter, 1975. [2] Kramer, 1981; Duchesne, 1989. [3] Lang, 1986; Gluck, 1985; Smith 1982. [4] Olsen, 1965. [5] Flynn & Webb, 1975; Gluck, 1975. [6] Clark & Wilson, 1961; Flynn & Webb, 1975; Masi, 1981.

ACQUIRING AND MANAGING FINANCIAL RESOURCES

Since non-profit organizations do not generate their own income for carrying out their mission, they are ultimately accountable to those individuals and organizations who provide them with funds. There are many types of resources available to non-profits in Canada, including government grants, individual and corporate donations, made-in-kind donations, matching grants, volunteers, investment planning, fee for service, special events, commercial activities and partnerships with corporations. The resources used by an organization can range from purely philanthropic to purely commercial.[156]

At the purely philanthropic end of the continuum, the organization is mission driven, and appeals to the goodwill of donors and funders based on its social value. An example would be a grassroots organization that charges nothing for service, depends on donations and grants to fund all its activities, is run by volunteers and depends on made-in-kind donations for any needed supplies, equipment or other capital expenses.

At the midpoint of the continuum, the organization is driven by mixed motives, both mission and market. It secures its resources by appealing to both the social and the economic value of what it does. For example, a store selling second-hand clothes as a source of revenue for a hospice receives its stock as donations, pays subsidized rent and is staffed predominantly by volunteers, with one paid staff. This non-profit charity sells the clothes at varying prices, depending on what the individual can pay.

At the purely commercial end of the continuum, the organization is market and self-interest driven. It receives resources in exchange for economic value. An example would be a non-profit horticultural business set up to provide employment for the mentally ill. This organization has to survive purely on what the marketplace will pay for its products and services. It buys its stock at the going rate, charges competitive prices and pays competitive wages. It is still a non-profit, as there are no shareholders, and it provides a social good, employing those who would otherwise be unemployed. As such, it is driven by a desire to keep the organization alive and growing.

In the past, the majority of non-profit organizations, especially charitable organizations, were at the purely philanthropic end of the continuum. With government support radically decreasing, more and more organizations are now involved in revenue diversification, which includes charging user fees and engaging in commercial activities. Non-profit organizations are increasingly taking on entrepreneurial ventures to generate additional resources. However, fundraising is still the primary means of acquiring resources.

Fundraising and Marketing

We are all familiar with appeals for donations from charities, and other non-profit institutions such as universities and hospitals. In recent years these appeals have become more and more professional in nature. With a growing number of charities appealing to citizens and corporations for support, organizations feel a need to engage in marketing activities to attain strategic advantage in the fundraising game.

Traditionally, non-profit organizations have not operated within a marketing framework. They relied on the belief that if the cause is good, people will give. This strategy is no longer viable. The growth in the number of non-profit organizations has increased competition for the same dollars. Donors feel over-solicited as organizations compete for the same audiences. They are also more selective with respect to the causes they support.[157] Given the increased competition, selectiveness and sophistication of donors, voluntary organizations have to be more strategic in their appeals.

Marketing can be defined as "the process of planning and executing the conception, pricing, promotion, and distribution of ideas, goods, and services to create exchanges that satisfy individual and organizational goals".[158] However, marketing is much more than that, especially in the context of non-profit organizations. Marketing provides

- tools to gain knowledge of client satisfaction
- ways to identify potential client group
- ways to sell the organization to potential staff and volunteers
- tools to assist in the development of linkages, partnerships, and collaborative activities with other non-profits, for-profits and governments
- tools to convince potential donors and funders

Marketing activities may be used to support and enhance fundraising through assisting in answering the following questions: Who should be approached for funding? Which solicitation method should be used? and, Who should do the asking?

People are potential funders for many reasons, including personal, social, negative, rewards, stimulations and situations. Corporations give to fulfill their social responsibility goals. Foundations give when the request matches their current purposes and priorities. The art and science of fund development involves matching the organization's needs, mission, purposes, and priorities with the appropriate revenue sources.

There are many ways of soliciting funds, as outlined in Exhibit 7.6.

EXHIBIT 7.6   SOLICITING FUNDS

- Advertising is a very public mode of communication that confers an aura of legitimacy on the product presented or the organization sponsoring the communication.[1] However, the communication is impersonal, and the audience does not feel obliged to respond. Otteson suggests that advertising is useful for developing awareness, which is an essential step in initiating donating behaviour.[2]

- Direct marketing, which includes direct mail and telemarketing, can be personalized and can include a customized appeal.[3] While telemarketing is relatively low cost, it is also a personal approach that does provide an opportunity to respond immediately to target audience concerns.[4]

- Personal selling is the most expensive contact tool, even when volunteers are used, because of the costs of recruiting, training and motivating them. The benefit of a personal appeal is that it makes the buyer feel obliged to respond.[5]

- Spokespersons, particularly celebrities, are often used by voluntary organizations because they may be respected, and credible experts in the field are viewed as trustworthy.[6] Choosing the right celebrity is critical, because of the transfer of the spokesperson's qualities to the organization.[7] However, spokespersons can be distracting, undermining attention to the message and reducing learning.[8] There is also evidence to suggest that audiences are becoming bored with celebrity spokespersons.[9]

Sources: [1] Kotler & Turner, 1995. [2] Otteson, 1977. [3] Kotler & Turner, 1995. [4] Novelli, 1981. [5] Kotler & Andreason. [6] Sternthal, Dholakia & Levitt, 1977; Graig & McCann, 1977. [7] Rein, Kotler & Stoller, 1987. [8] Ogilvy & Raphaelson, 1982. [9] Lipman, 1990.

Entrepreneurial and Commercial Alternatives

Because of the uncertainties entailed in relying on donations and government grants, non-profit organizations are increasingly trying their hand in entrepreneurial and commercial ventures.

Entrepreneurial ventures can be defined as "activities which involve selling products or services for the purpose of making a profit that supports the provision of the non-profit services of the 'mother' organization".[159] Organizations embark on entrepreneurial ventures for many reasons, among them: to replace lost sources of funding, to gain leverage with funders, to offset rising costs, to counterbalance lower donated revenue resulting from higher competition, to be better equipped for increased competition from for-profits entering the traditional non-profit sectors, and to be more resilient in responding to changes in government policy, in societal norms and in the economy.

Entrepreneurial ventures in non-profits can take various shapes.[160] They may seek new markets for their existing services and products, they may offer new services and products to both old and new markets, and they may diversify their service and product range. These strategies may be beneficial to the organizations, in that the new revenue sources will allow the organization to survive and, even, enhance its original mission. The addition of new services and products can lure more highly skilled members to the organization, leading to greater organizational success.

On the downside, however, the entrepreneurial ventures can divert organizational energy from their original mission (mission displacement). They can also drain organizational capacity. Moreover, the addition of commercial ventures may change the public's perception of the organization and may turn donors away. All of these may lead to the eventual demise of the organization.

Embracing commercial activities is fraught with risks, not only for the individual organization, as elaborated above, but also for the client/consumer and the sector as a whole. With so much attention focused on the commercial aspect of the organization, the client may be shortchanged in services. The sector as a whole may suffer. Claims of unfair competition are already voiced by for-profits when non-profits encroach in their area, selling products at lower prices, because they are exempt from paying taxes. This may lead to changes in the tax laws, which may impinge on the viability of the non-profit. More serious may be the deterioration of the public's trust in the sector, as non-profits become more profit oriented. Finally, the blurring of lines between non-profit and for-profit organizations may lead to the disappearance of non-profit organizations in certain mixed economy situations, such as the provision of daycare, homecare and nursing homes.

Partnerships with For-profit Organizations

More and more non-profit organizations are entering into partnerships with corporations as a means of increasing their revenue potential. Historically, corporate involvement with the third sector has been minimal. In Canada, donations to charitable organizations account for only one percent of the total funding received by charitable agencies.[161] Recently, however, for-profit organizations, realizing the potential market benefits of supporting social causes, have begun to engage in a variety of exchanges with non-profit organizations.[162] These range from straight philanthropic exchanges, where the non-profit agency receives no-strings-attached donations, to complex commercial partnerships that involve common strategic planning.[163]

While full partnerships between non-profit and for-profit organizations are still relatively uncommon,[164] the engagement of the for-profit sector in socially responsible activities is certainly growing. Citizens are looking beyond governments for solutions to pressing social issues. They expect business firms to become full social citizens with shared responsibilities for maintaining, or even improving, social welfare.[165] At the same time, for-profit organizations are seeking new ways to connect with their customers beyond solely buying and selling goods and services. Involvement in highly valued social causes is seen as a means of gaining the loyalty and trust of customers. Some of the reasons corporations enter partnerships are: a sense of social responsibility, improving public relations, improving employee relations, fulfilling organizational mandates, and improving potential for profit.

Non-profit organizations enter these partnerships for different reasons: increasing revenues, helping fulfill client needs, increasing networking possibilities, improving public relations, developing services, developing new skills, and garnering media attention.

Six different types of partnerships have been identified:[166]

- **Commercial partnerships:** for-profit purchases goods or services for the non-profit, or they use the non-profit name to sell their goods or services in exchange for a percentage of profits. For example, in 2002, McDonald's announced their plans to hold a "World Children's Day", which included raising funds for local children's organizations (including such non-profit organizations as UNICEF) throughout their locations worldwide.
- **Sponsorships:** for-profit organization pays a sum of money to the non-profit in exchange for the right to display their name or logo at an event or in conjunction with some program.
- **Policy marketing:** for-profit organization helps non-profit lobby for support of a particular social or political cause. For example, Crayola helped lobby for government funding of arts in education.
- **Donation of equipment:** for-profit provides equipment free of charge to an organization. For example, Bell Canada providing telephones for Kids Help Line.
- **Civic partnership:** for-profit is one of a group of for-profit organizations donating resources to a project run by a non-profit organization. For example, the Special Olympics.
- **Philanthropic partnership:** for-profit donates resources without restrictions on how the resources are used and without expectation to benefit from the donation.

There are risks involved in these partnerships for the non-profits, as outlined in Exhibit 7.7.

THE PAST AND FUTURE OF NON-PROFITS —————

The most salient point of this chapter is that non-profit organizations are not only different in many respects from for-profit organizations, but they also exist in a very different environment, one that is driven by government social and economic policy. In terms of the

EXHIBIT 7.7	THE RISKS OF PARTNERSHIPS

- **Wasted resources:** Building a partnership requires time and effort that cannot be recouped if the venture fails.
- **Mission displacement:** Using limited resources may detract from the main mission.
- **Loss of donors:** Knowledge of partnership may make people think the organization is getting enough funding.
- **Loss of flexibility:** Corporation may impose restrictions.
- **Tainted partners:** e.g., corporate partners for child welfare programs may be using child labour abroad.
- **Antithetical marketing:** e.g., Quaker helped American Heart Association to produce a "heart smart" pamphlet, using two-thirds of the booklet for coupons.
- **Overwhelming success:** more funds than organization can handle properly. May require a change of mandate.
- **Structural atrophy:** non-profit may rely excessively on corporation, or devote resources to supporting the alliance instead of pursuing other goals.

Source: Andreason, 1996.

third sector, the 20th century can be divided into three separate periods, reflecting very different government policies with respect to the role of the sector and the role of government in supporting it.

Reviewing the Past

In the first half of the century, citizens were expected to perform their civic duty by supporting their children and their aging parents. Where families weren't able to provide support, informal neighbourhood and community groups lent a helping hand. Charitable and religious organizations were also involved, particularly with alms for the poor, the widowed and the orphaned. Thus, the channelling of care was predominantly direct, without the involvement of intermediaries.[167] Cultural and recreational activities were also, for the most part, informal community events.

As the century progressed, the growing urbanization of the country weakened family and community networks of support. Individuals were no longer tightly connected to a network of friends, extended family and acquaintances. More people were exposed and vulnerable to poor working and social conditions. With the help of volunteer labour and donations, institutions such as churches and charitable organizations were better able to ensure that services reached those in need. Thus, individuals funnelled their help and donations through institutions. At this time, the state started moving more directly into the provision of universal benefits, such as education and the support of cultural and recreational activities.[168]

It wasn't until the Great Depression that governments at all levels became seriously involved with the welfare of Canadians. The prevailing philosophy before the Depression was free-market capitalism; that is, the market would benefit all by providing the basis for full employment. The belief was that those who were poor and unemployed were so because of their own lack of motivation. The Great Depression, during which unemployment rose tenfold, from 1.7% of the workforce in 1928 to 19.3% in 1933, shattered this myth.[169] Unemployment could clearly no longer be blamed on the individual. With massive numbers of unemployed, and farmers rendered destitute by falling wheat prices, local governments and charitable organizations could no longer care for the needy. The federal and provincial governments had to step in forcefully. As a result, social services shifted from the private/charitable domain to the state, and provision changed from voluntary and non-professional to bureaucratic and professional.[170]

The second clearly identifiable period comprised the 35 years following World War II. During this time, Canada, like other liberal democracies, began to implement Keynesian economic policy.[171] This was based on the belief that the economy could move toward full employment through judicious government intervention in spending, taxation, and the setting of interest rates. Still in the shadow of the Great Depression, Western governments felt they could afford to become more heavily involved in the social welfare of their citizenry, especially in light of the unprecedented economic growth that characterized the three decades after the war. In this period the voluntary sector grew exponentially. During a single decade, between 1970 and 1980, more non-profit organizations were created than during the 70 years preceding.[172] A vigorous partnership was created between the state and the voluntary sector in an integrated model where welfare benefits emanate from the government but responsibility for delivery is shared.

This all changed in the past two decades. With diminished transfer payments from the federal government, and under the changed funding formulas, programmatic retrenchment occurred in most provinces. Provincial governments reduced social spending, dropped programs, tightened eligibility requirements in remaining programs, and expected the voluntary sector and community networks to fill the vacuum, without increasing their grants. These cuts "seriously reduced the capacity for voluntary agencies to provide services".[173] Paid positions were lost, recruitment and training had to be curtailed, and competition was increased, which undermined communication and information sharing. Forced commercialization, introduction of fees for service, adoption of business practices, and marketing and fundraising strategies led to mission displacement. A sense of vulnerability temporarily reduced the role of advocacy and networking for policy changes.[174]

A Glimpse of the Future

The new millennium marks a crossroads for the non-profit sector. Although the future is unknowable, some trends are emerging that may give us a glimpse. The third sector has clearly had an impact in many ways on our lives as Canadians. Although human and social service organizations form the bulk of the sector, recreational and cultural organizations, as well as advocacy groups, have also served to enhance the quality of our lives. Yet, there is fear that the sector will cease to be a distinct entity, as boundaries between private for-profit enterprise and private non-profit service blur.[175] This is happening mainly in three ways: the commercialization of non-profits in search of funding, the encroachment of for-profit organizations into areas previously served only or mainly by non-profit organizations and, finally, the pursuit of efficiency for its own sake.

Commercialization: In the previous section we have discussed the growing popularity of commercial ventures by non-profit organizations. We have also discussed the risks involved in such ventures. Despite this, commercialization is a growing trend in the future as organizations scramble to find ways to ensure their survival.

Encroachment: With the emphasis on saving, government provision of operating grants to non-profits has been replaced by contract tendering for specific projects. These contracts are awarded to the lowest bidder, be they non-profit organizations or for-profit ones. In Ontario, this has resulted in an influx of for-profit home care service providers into a domain hitherto served predominantly by non-profit organizations. A recent call for bids to provide nursing homes for Ontario's aging population resulted in 60% of the contracts being offered to for-profit organizations. Such blurring of boundaries in social and human services provision is undermining the unique role of the non-profit sector in helping the needy and underprivileged.

Efficiency: But perhaps it is the juggernaut of the cult of efficiency that will be most damaging to a sector previously devoted to human caring and the fostering of a civil society.[176] In the relentless pursuit of efficiency and the demand for accountability, the focus on providing the best care and service for the client is subverted. Unlike in the profit sector, where competition is purportedly the guarantor of quality, and consumer choice is plentiful, in the non-profit human and social services realm competition is for attracting funders, not clients. Client choice is limited.

Thus, the related policies of contracting for service through the tendering of bids and the push to efficiency are eroding the quality of care and the unique role of the non-profit sector in human services. Underfunding and the push for efficiency is also affecting recreational and cultural services, as programs are being shut down. This is, indeed, a bleak picture. In a recent survey of 645 executive directors of non-profit organizations from across Canada, 71% reported being pessimistic about the future of the sector.[177]

There are signs, however, of new initiatives. The Canadian government has sponsored a series of round-table discussions with sector representatives to work out a new formula for government-sector relations. It is the first time that the sector is actively involved in policy formulation. It is to be hoped that the new social contract will stabilize funding and clearly define the role of the sector. Another good sign is that the sector is still growing. Organizations representing and providing special services to various immigrant and minority groups are sprouting. The advocacy role of non-profit organizations has come to the forefront, representing the interests of those whose voices are weak, thus strengthening democracy. Perhaps the role of the sector is changing. As boundaries between organizations blur in the social services domain, the sector is redefining its role in society as a guardian of values. Non-profit organizations are partnering with powerful corporations to advance their message and cause. Moreover, worldwide there is a groundswell movement of local, national and international non-governmental organizations joining forces in combatting the relentless pressures for globalization.

CHAPTER SUMMARY

There is no question of the contribution of this sector to Canadian society, both from a service perspective, fulfilling societal needs that aren't provided by either of the other sectors, and from an economic perspective, providing fiscal growth and job opportunities. Despite this, until recently, very little research has focused on this sector, and textbooks have not devoted separate analysis to the organizations in this sector. This neglect is unfortunate, because many graduates will be finding work in non-profit organizations, and many more will be dealing with non-profit organizations. Understanding them, their role in society and in the economy, will enrich our understanding of the organizational world. It is hoped that this chapter has offered insight into the nature of the non-profit sector, the role it plays in Canadian society, and the challenges these organizations face in the future.

KEY TERMS

- private, non-governmental organizations
- profit organizations
- open systems
- governance
- working boards
- policy boards
- mixed boards
- strategic planning

- SWOT analysis
- official goals
- operative goals
- board-staff relations
- transactional leader
- transformational leader
- commercial partnership
- sponsorships

CASE APPLICATION   Making money, and a difference

After selling his technology company to a venture-capital company last year, Greg Habstritt was looking for a fresh start. Young, bright and used to thinking big, he wanted to use his money-raising skills to make a significant social contribution. So, with partner Grant Doyle, he launched Calgary Renaissance Corp., which will attract high-powered speakers to town to raise money for non-profit organizations.

Mr. Habstritt says he was overjoyed when the first person he invited — Bill Clinton — agreed to appear. He will speak on Nov. 8 to a crowd of 1,500 who are paying $2,800 per table of eight (or up to $1,000 for a VIP ticket). "I think he realized, and his people realized, it was more than just a speaking engagement," says Mr. Habstritt. "We put in a fairly lengthy proposal and included a lot of elements of what we were trying to accomplish."

Calgary Renaissance is part of an innovative trend in fundraising called venture philanthropy or social entrepreneurship, which challenges the notion that doing good and making a profit are mutually exclusive. Venture philanthropy promotes money-making projects in the non-profit sector or, at the very least, self-sustaining ventures that require fewer donations. "Clearly the world is changing and it's becoming more and more difficult to raise money, and charities have to be more creative and innovative in their approach," says Mr. Habstritt. "This idea takes $1 [charities] normally would have spent and uses it to earn $5 back."

For example, one of the groups that will be funded by Mr. Clinton's appearance is the Canadian Paraplegic Association, which will use the money to lend out equipment for people with disabilities that otherwise they would have to buy. Barry Lindemann, spokesman for the association, says the attraction of projects like this one is that it frees up time and resources to focus on activities other than fundraising. Mr. Doyle adds that the involvement of CRC makes business sense: "A lot of charities don't have the knowledge and resources to make money. We give the tools and the management. We don't want to just throw blind dollars down a hole."

The University of Alberta has established a Canadian Centre for Social Entrepreneurship to monitor and promote the development of venture philanthropy. "These entrepreneurs bring the language of business to the philanthropic discussions, as, for example, in the creation of 'social venture capital' funds or in discussions of social return on investment. They don't want to 'donate' to a worthy cause, they want to 'invest' in sustainable social initiatives," says the institute in a recent paper.

Brad Zumwalt became involved in venture philanthropy after selling his Calgary company, EyeWire Inc., for US$37-million to Getty Images, a U.S. graphics software giant. He launched Social Venture Partners last year, using a model that has more than 10 U.S. chapters. The Calgary unit has 50 members who donate $5,000 in exchange for a tax receipt. They also volunteer time and skills to ensure the money is well spent. "It's very similar to the venture-capital model," he says. "We form a standard type of limited partnership and we all chip in some money. We sit around the table and pick the deals we want to be involved in, taking into consideration whether anyone around the table has the industry experience to help out."

Investment banker Brett Wilson, managing director and president of FirstEnergy Capital Corp., which contributes to a number of charities, says venture philanthropy has been evolving informally for a number of years, but the approach taken by groups such as Social Venture Partners takes the model to a higher level. Long-time volunteer leader Brian MacNeill, chairman of Petro-Canada and retired chief executive of Enbridge Inc., says he hopes the venture philanthropy injects new blood into the sector, which includes 175,000 Canadian charities and non-profit organizations. From 1997 to 2000, a million volunteers left the sector, a drop of 4%. The trend must be reversed because the voluntary sector accounts for 12% of GDP by engaging the efforts of 7.5 million volunteers and employing 1.3 million Canadians, he says.

And venture philanthropy can give as much as it gets, Mr. Zumwalt observes: "It's so humbling for a guy to walk out of a business meeting and into the foyer of a homeless shelter and see what is going on. Those kind of experiences change people and the work they are doing." Terri Adair, who with her husband runs a real-estate company and is a partner in SVP, had one of those experiences last spring during a visit to a Calgary project for street people. She met a woman carrying an infant, her grandchild, who told her a remarkable story. Her daughter, unable to care for the child, sent the infant from Regina to Calgary on a Greyhound bus, leaving the driver and the passengers to care for the baby. "It was one of those huge eye-openers for people who live in a world of more wealth and affluence," she says. "This woman was a good example for us of someone stepping forward and doing what had to be done." SVP also decided to step forward and fund a daycare centre in downtown Calgary for the homeless and the poor.

Source: By Carol Howes and Claudia Cattaneo from *Financial Post* (October 29, 2001). Reproduced with permission of National Post.

QUESTIONS

1. How do these organizations combine elements of entrepreneurship with a non-profit orientation?

2. Do you think these organizations have more in common with profit-oriented, or non-profit oriented, organizations? Explain.

3. How important do you think these types of organizations will be in terms of strengthening the non-profit landscape?

Helping non-profits

An enthusiastic cheer recently rang out from the country's charity fundraising offices and it was joined by wealthy philanthropists with juicy stock portfolios. The cause for this celebration was the announcement by Paul Martin, the Minister of Finance, that the Canada Customs and Revenue Agency intends to make permanent the tax rules that allow for a reduced capital gains inclusion rate for making charitable gifts of publicly listed securities that have appreciated in value.

This tax reduction opportunity was originally introduced in 1997 as a five-year trial measure (originally set to expire on Dec. 31) to see if, in fact, it would result in an increase in gifting of securities as charitable donations. Both the government's own research and the planned giving associations' surveys have confirmed that this experiment has been a resounding success. One such organization claimed "this has been the greatest success since the introduction of the charitable tax receipt."

Now that this gifting tax strategy has become a perennial financial planning opportunity, charities, financial planners and potential donors should all take a moment to fully understand how the strategy works.

The rule is relatively simple: when giving a registered Canadian charity a gift of publicly listed securities (this can be in the form of stocks, bonds, mutual funds or segregated funds), the disposition is subject to a lower capital gains inclusion rate of 25%, as opposed to the regular rate of 50%.

This means that, tax-wise, it is more beneficial to gift securities of appreciated value than selling these same securities and gifting the resulting cash. If you gift the securities, you save on your capital gains inclusion rate in addition to benefiting from the usual charitable donation tax credit for the market value of the securities.

This non-refundable tax credit is limited to 75% of your net income in the year of the gift plus 25% of the taxable capital gain. Unused charitable tax credits can be carried forward for up to five years should you exceed your limits for the year.

The limit is increased to 100% of net income in the year of death (and the year preceding, if required), which is another good reason to gift securities to a charity through your will if you are interested in spreading the wealth while at the same time using an efficient tax strategy to reduce taxes at death.

Potential donors of a large gift with substantial gains should be aware, though, that they might be subject to the alternative minimum tax (AMT). The AMT calculation will take the non-taxable portion of your capital gain and add it to your income. This may require more sophisticated tax-planning strategies such as structuring the gift over a number of years.

Whatever approach is used, it is clear that the gifting of securities can form one of the charitable donation tools of choice. While the opportunity for soliciting or donating these potential securities may seem to be at an ebb at present (given last year's decline in market values), significant capital gains will resurface and the government's decision to extend this lower tax incentive means donors will once again part with their appreciated securities for the benefit of all.

Source: John Archer, "Gifting tax strategy to be permanent. Reduced capital gains inclusion rate on charitable gifts" *National Post* (January 3, 2002). Reproduced with permission of the author.

QUESTIONS

1. What are the implications of this tax strategy for non-profit organizations?

2. Do you think that business would assist non-profit organizations if they did not receive something in return?

IV

Looking Outside:
The Context of
Organizations

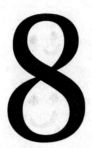

Globalization: Threats and Opportunities

What are some of the fundamental sources of influence on the decision to engage in global business? In addition to addressing this question, this chapter will identify the different **types of global business activity**. We will examine one of the central controversies of globalization: **the multinational corporation**. This chapter will also explain why nations desire, or do not desire, to promote international **trade**, including an examination of the pros and cons of Canada's free trade agreement with the United States.

LEARNING OBJECTIVES

By the end of the chapter, you should be able to:

1. Define the notion of globalization.
2. Identify factors that have encouraged the globalization of business.
3. Describe the central channels or forms of global business activity.
4. Discuss the importance and consequences of multinational and borderless corporations.
5. Explain the purpose of protectionism and its relationship with international trade.
6. Identify the types of regional economic integration.
7. Discuss the purpose of NAFTA and its consequences.

Organizational Insider

Hollywood's Case against Canada

No sooner had Prime Minister Jean Chrétien departed Los Angeles last week than a group of angry Hollywood film hands denounced Canada's movie subsidies. They had a point. Mr. Chrétien, who as Canadians know does not suffer criticism, told U.S. gripers to stuff it. "We're competitive. That's what the world is all about." Actually, Canada is not competitive in the movie business. We make very few films that people want to watch, in Canada or anywhere else. When U.S. movie studios produce films in Canada — films called "runaway productions" by grumpy Americans — they come north because of the enfeebled Canadian dollar and enormous provincial government subsidies.

Canadians who defend themselves against the "runaway production" charge point to beautiful scenery and skilled film technicians to explain why U.S. firms head north. They are, of course, kidding themselves. British Columbia offers spectacular mountain scenery, but so does the United States. Toronto is a perfectly nice city — too nice for some U.S. filmmakers who need to dirty up the streets to make them look American — but the same streetscapes and architecture can be found in dozens of U.S. cities.

As for the technical skill of Canadians, it is no better than what Hollywood or New York boast in their own back yards. No, the pathetic loonie is what lures the Americans north. It's one crutch on which the movie industry leans. The other one is the provinces' tax codes. The U.S. protesters may lose on points of law, since U.S. states also offer incentives to the film industry. They're correct in point of fact, however, since Canadians always scream when other countries' subsidies exceed their own, as in agriculture.

The U.S. protesters are disproportionately drawn from Hollywood's unions, whose members are displaced when work follows the Canadian dollar and subsidies north. The Hollywood studios, for their part, are silent because they like filming in Canada. The bedraggled loonie and the provincial subsidies cut their costs of production, thereby increasing their profits.

The side effect of these Canadian crutches is the further enfeeblement of the country's domestic film industry, because so much Canadian energy and talent flows into making U.S. films for U.S. audiences. Or, to be more precise, the energy and talent flows into making U.S. films about U.S. stories that Canadians then watch.

This colonization of the Canadian mind is far advanced anyway in popular culture. English-speaking Canada is largely a cultural appendage of the United States, as any glance at the movie listings or popular television programs reveals. For the better part of three decades, Canadian governments have spent billions of dollars trying to encourage Canadian popular cultural products that Canadians will consume. The dollar-per-eyeball ratio has been, and remains, discouraging at best, pathetic at worst.

There are years when Canadians could hardly be blamed for not wanting to witness their country's most "popular" films, since these were centred on chopped-up bodies buried in back yards, a bus filled with children sliding down a cliff, necrophilia, serial killers and sundry other story lines from the "kinder, gentler" nation. Television is almost as discouraging. The CBC tries its best to produce popular entertainment; the private networks barely try. Figures released earlier this year — and not contested by the private networks — showed them delivering paltry amounts of Canadian dramatic programming. Global's record was abysmal, CTV's barely better. The private networks deliver Canadian sports and news, but when it comes to popular culture, they remain conveyer belts for U.S. programs. That's where they make their money.

Last week, Charles Dalfen became the latest chairman of the Canadian Radio-television and Telecommunications Commission, an agency whose efforts to get more and better Canadian domestic production of popular culture have largely failed. The CRTC has consistently proved to be a tiger without claws in dealing with the privates. Whether it will so remain under Mr. Dalfen, only time can tell.

The protesting Americans don't know how Americanized Canadians really are in popular culture. They care only about some jobs slipping north, and they have every right to be mad. Sure, Canada takes only a small portion of total U.S. filmmaking dollars, but it's the way the money is being taken that galls — a cheapening currency and government subsidies. Hardly the stuff of genuine competition, as Mr. Chrétien pretended.

Source: By Jeffrey Simpson from *The Globe and Mail* (December 4, 2001): A23. Reproduced with permission from The Globe and Mail.

WHAT IS GLOBALIZATION?

The Organizational Insider highlights the new business world — one that involves many more players than local business and its domestic market. The case of Hollywood versus Canada underscores the increasingly tangled web of players in the global business context: domestic and foreign competitors, workers, industries, governments, national cultures and economies. How business is conducted in light of trade agreements and global arrangements is a key issue for our entire society. And this is a theme we will explore more fully in this chapter.

While you may have heard or read about this popular buzzword, many of you may not be completely familiar with what it represents and its implications. What is globalization? While there is no one, universal definition, it is useful to consider this concept as a process.

Globalization is a process involving the integration of world economies. The presence of trade blocs reflects the accelerating pace with which nations are integrating their economies. For example, NAFTA, the North American Free Trade Agreement, discussed later in this chapter, is a free-trade bloc consisting of Canada, the United States and Mexico. The EU (European Union) groups 15 countries, while APEC (Asian Pacific Economic Co-operation) consists of 18 nations forming a free-trade zone around the Pacific.

Globalization is a process involving the integration of world markets. This reflects the notion that consumer preferences are converging around the world. Whether it is for products made by McDonald's, Sony, The Gap or Nike, organizations are increasingly marketing their goods and services worldwide. Though local modifications may be made to tailor the product to the local consumers, there is a push toward global products. On the other side, production is increasingly becoming a global affair. Businesses will set up operations wherever it is least costly to do so.

In sum, the recurrent themes raised in any discussion of globalization tend to include elements of the following:

- Globalization can be considered as a process that is expanding the degree and forms of cross-border transactions among people, assets, goods and services.
- Globalization refers to the growth in direct foreign investment in regions across the world.
- Globalization reflects the shift toward increasing economic interdependence: the process of generating one, single, world economic system or a global economy.

SOURCES ENCOURAGING GLOBAL BUSINESS ACTIVITY

Why have we witnessed a tremendous surge in business activity on an international scale? From giant multinational corporations to small businesses, in recent years the drive toward global business has accelerated. A number of fundamental factors have encourage the move to "go global". Some factors can be considered "pull" factors, and are reasons a

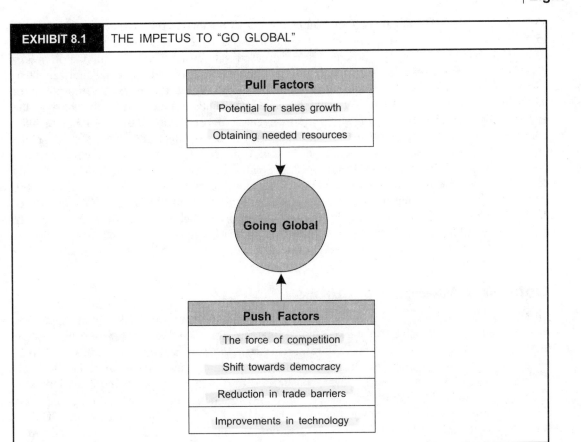

EXHIBIT 8.1 THE IMPETUS TO "GO GLOBAL"

Pull Factors

Potential for sales growth

Obtaining needed resources

Going Global

Push Factors

The force of competition

Shift towards democracy

Reduction in trade barriers

Improvements in technology

business would gain from entering the international context. Other factors are "push" factors—these are forces that act upon all businesses to create an environment where competing successfully means competing globally. (See Exhibit 8.1.)

Pull Factors

Potential for Sales Growth

A fundamental reason for engaging in global operations is to help a business expand its markets. Increased sales are typically the central aim behind a company's expansion into international business. A significant portion of sales among the world's largest firms are generated from outside the home country. For example, U.S.-based specialty coffee chain, Starbucks Corp., in 2001 started planning to open dozens of outlets in Vienna and compete against the traditional coffee houses there. The chain that serves approximately 15 million customers a week, and includes 4,300 shops in 23 markets, is taking its global strategy to Vienna. While the potential for increased sales was clearly a pull factor, a key question was: Will consumers in this European culture be attracted to this American business? Starbucks' aim is to provide a more modern version of the relaxed atmosphere of the Viennese café in order to attract this new consumer segment. Clearly, having the world as your market offers almost limitless potential beyond domestic consumers. Having access to foreign consumers also may mitigate the negative effects of domestic downturns in demand for the businesses' product or service. Consider, for example, the case of Avon Products Inc. This organization faced declining sales in North American markets, largely due to its traditional marketing channel (door-to-door sales), which failed to address the increased entry of women into the workplace and away from the home. On the other hand, Avon was able to successfully transfer its approach globally to over 20 emerging markets, including China, Brazil, South Africa and Mexico.

Obtaining Needed Resources

Businesses may choose to engage in global business activity in order to obtain resources that are either unavailable or too costly within the domestic borders. Acquiring foreign imports is a case of obtaining needed resources. It could be the case that a textile manufacturer imports its raw materials from a foreign supplier because these materials are not available locally. The decision to locate businesses or plants in developing or underdeveloped nations may be a means to access inexpensive labour. For example, to access less expensive energy resources, a number of Japanese businesses have located in China, Mexico and Taiwan, where energy costs are not as high. Both Canadian and U.S. firms continue to expand their operations overseas because they can achieve higher rates of return on their investment, largely due to lower labour costs.

Push Factors

The Force of Competition

Many domestic economies have become inundated with competing products or services. Typically, a business that seeks to grow needs to consider the markets beyond its domestic borders: this is where new, and potentially untapped, market opportunities still exist. Ironically, domestic economies are increasingly being filled with foreign competitors in many industries. The fact is, a business may find that it must compete against not merely domestic competitors, but foreign competitors as well. By default, a business may be **pushed** into becoming a global business by the simple fact that it is forced to compete with a foreign competitor. Moreover, for some businesses it seems foolhardy not to combat the foreign competition by attempting to go after the competitor's market overseas. In other words, the drive to "go global" may be a response to competitors' actions.

In addition, other domestic competitors may be expanding their markets overseas, which creates additional incentive for the business to follow suit. The notion of **first**

mover advantage is a philosophy that underscores the benefits of being among the first to establish strong positions in important world markets. Later entrants into a foreign market may have more difficulty establishing themselves, and may even be effectively blocked by competitors.

Shift toward Democracy

The shift toward democracy among many societies that were formerly economically and politically repressed has contributed to the creation of new market opportunities. Numerous totalitarian regimes have been transformed in Eastern Europe and Asia, for example, which has created new economic opportunities for businesses in other parts of the world. Countries like Russia and Poland have shifted toward a more capitalistic and democratic approach. Perhaps one symbol of this acceptance was the success of the North American McDonald's in entering the Russian marketplace years ago. Similarly, there has been a great interest in foreign investment in China since its move toward privatization — reduction in government ownership — in many areas.

Reduction in Trade Barriers

In recent years it has been observed that global business activities have been growing at a faster rate than in previous years, and in comparison to growth in domestic business. This acceleration may be largely due to the general push toward freer trade. In fact, probably the most powerful source of influence encouraging increased international business is the reduction in trade and investment restrictions. For example, the North American Free Trade Agreement (NAFTA) was established as an agreement to remove trade barriers between Canada, the United States and Mexico. This agreement essentially aimed to produce a common market among the members. Later in this chapter we will consider in more detail the nature of NAFTA, as well as a number of other important trade agreements.

Improvements in Technology

Another fundamental source of influence on globalization has been technology. Advancements in technology have more efficiently facilitated cross-border transactions. Innovations in information technology, as well as advances in transportation, have made it increasingly easy to transfer information, products, services, capital and human resources around the world. E-mail, the Internet, teleconferencing, faxing, and transatlantic supersonic travel were among the activities that were not available until the late part of the 20th century.

Electronic commerce, e-commerce, has been relatively free from government control, and this flexibility has contributed to the rate of globalization and the generation of virtual global organizations. Virtual organizations increasingly exist at the global level, where the geographic sources of the product or service and the location of the workforce are unimportant.

CHANNELS OF GLOBAL BUSINESS ACTIVITY

There are a variety of ways that businesses engage in global business. While practically any connection a business has with a foreign country essentially constitutes a form of global business, the degree of involvement of a business with a foreign country can vary. Below, we highlight various channels or forms within which businesses operate in the global sense. At a lower level of interconnectedness, a business can simply export or import goods or services to or from other countries. At a somewhat higher level, a company may choose to outsource some aspect of its business operations; it may choose to license some aspect or, perhaps, even arrange for franchise operations in foreign territory. Forming a strategic alliance or creating a joint venture with a foreign company requires the business to become more fully entrenched in the global context via directly investing in a foreign country. This can take the form of a merger or acquisition and the creation of a subsidiary in foreign territory. Each of these possible channels is discussed below. (See Exhibit 8.2.)

EXHIBIT 8.2	CHANNELS OF GLOBAL ACTIVITY

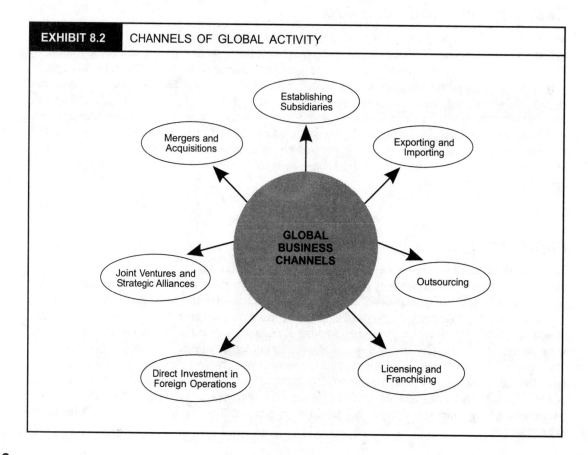

Exporting and Importing

Businesses that engage in international business are more likely to be involved in importing and exporting than in any other type of global business activity. In addition to selling our goods or services to other countries, Canadian businesses may also purchase goods or services from foreign countries for resale to Canadians. Merchandise exports are tangible goods transferred out of the country, while merchandise imports are goods brought into the country. On the other hand, businesses might deal in service exports or imports of services. For example, banking, insurance or management services can be performed at an international level. Another type of service export or import can involve the use of a company's assets, including things like patents, trademarks, copyrights or expertise. The use of such assets constitutes a service rather than the provision of a tangible good, and is typically arranged through a licensing agreement. This channel of global business is discussed below.

Exporting certainly offers much additional profitable activity for businesses. The business opportunities available through exporting are significant. While there are about 30 million potential customers within our Canadian borders, there are over 6 billion potential customers across the world, increasing by about 95 million people annually. Many Canadian businesses have taken advantage of the benefits of exporting. Canada exports over 40% of our production, making us a major trading nation. (See Exhibit 8.3.)

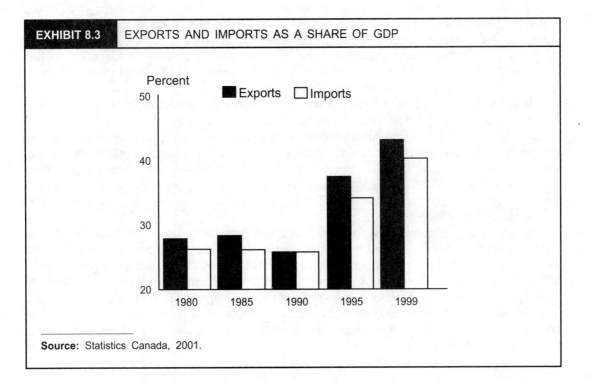

| EXHIBIT 8.3 | EXPORTS AND IMPORTS AS A SHARE OF GDP |

Source: Statistics Canada, 2001.

LET'S TALK BUSINESS 8.1   WHO EXPORTS?

It is interesting to note that in the years 1993 to 1995, about 21% of Canada's exports came from only five companies. In other words, these five Canadian companies exported an average of about $48 billion worth of goods in each of those years. This list included GM, Chrysler, Ford, IBM Canada and the Canadian Wheat Board. The next 45 biggest Canadian exporters accounted for about another 24% of all exports. So we have a relatively small number of large companies driving our export business.

On the other hand, our numerous small businesses (accounting for about 52% of private sector jobs) have been slower to enter the international market, with only about 10% of small businesses exporting. However, more and more small businesses are entering the international market. Overall, Canada continues to experience growth in our exports.

Recent Statistics Canada reports indicated that as of 1995, Canada was the world's seventh largest exporter. Among those ahead of us in terms of the amount of exports are the United States, Germany, Japan, France, Britain and Italy. We are among the top 10 nations that together account for over 60% of global exports of goods. However, added to all this good news are some cautionary notes. Observers have noted that the bulk of our exports are to the United States. The United States is by far our major trading partner, purchasing almost 80% of our exports. While they purchase the bulk of our exports, it should equally be noted that the bulk of our purchases (i.e., our imports from outside our border) is from the United States — over 60%. To some critics, this underscores a large economic dependence on the United States and a need to expand our trade with other countries. In addition, traditionally four of our major trading companies, identified earlier, have head offices in the United States: again underscoring the degree of economic dependence of our export sector on the United States.

The bulk of our exports to the United States, according to a recent Statistics Canada report, includes autos, trucks and parts, and that has been the case for some time. Of course, our traditional major area of exports has been our natural resources, including things like pulp and paper, agricultural products, energy, fish products, and lumber, all of which constitute almost half our exports. Canada is still relatively weak in exports from the high-tech industries, like telecommunications, computers and the like, with some exceptions like the Canadian-based Nortel and Bombardier companies, who are major exporters in the high-tech sector.

Another area of concern is Canada's ability to export service-related work. While the service industry contributes about two-thirds of Canada's GDP, only approximately 10% of the roughly $470 billion exports in 2000 were derived from the export of services (about $55 billion). Some observers have commented that, even with the presence of NAFTA, Canadian service providers have had difficulties entering U.S. territory. For example, while it has been relatively easy for U.S.-educated engineers to work in Canada, Canadian-educated engineers, who choose to practise in the United States, must be certified in the United States. Service companies also tend to face a relatively greater set of regulatory and other barriers to entry.[178]

Outsourcing

Contracting out, or outsourcing, was discussed in an earlier chapter of this book. As you may recall, outsourcing involves hiring external organizations to conduct work in certain functions of the company: so, for example, payroll, accounting, and legal work can be assigned to outsourced staff. The organization typically will retain its core functions or competencies: that is, those areas that it is in business to conduct. Nike is well-known for its use of outsourcing on an international basis. Nike has typically entered into contractual arrangements with manufacturers in developing nations to produce its footwear while it focuses largely on marketing its product. In fact, this has been a major underlying source of controversy with regard to businesses "going global" — the fear that relatively higher paying North American jobs will be lost as business decides to outsource manufacturing functions to cheaply paid labour in Third World countries. Countries can be contracted for the production of finished goods or component parts, and these goods or parts can subsequently be imported to the home country or to other countries for further assembly or sale.

Licensing and Franchising Arrangements

The licensing agreement is an arrangement whereby the owner of a product or process is paid a fee or royalty from another company in return for granting permission to produce or distribute the product or process. How could this be a type of global business activity? For example, a Canadian company might grant a foreign company permission to produce its product; or conversely, perhaps a Canadian company wishes to distribute a foreign-made product in Canada and requires a licensing agreement.

Why might a business enter into licensing agreements? Essentially, companies that don't wish to set up actual production or marketing operations overseas can let the foreign business conduct these activities and simply collect royalties. Whether it is for licensing fees or for management consulting services between two companies from different countries, the fees paid to foreign firms in return for the performance of a service would constitute service imports. Fees earned by businesses through providing such services would constitute service exports.

Franchising shares some of the advantages of licensing, in that both are relatively lower risk forms of global business. Franchising is, of course, a common type of business activity in Canada and elsewhere. This becomes a global business activity when the franchises are scattered in different locations around the world. While franchising is discussed elsewhere in this book, it is sufficient to note here that franchising involves drafting a contract between a supplier (franchiser) and a dealer (franchisee) that stipulates how the supplier's product or service will be sold. The franchisee is the dealer (usually the owner of a small business), who is permitted to sell the goods/services of the franchiser (the supplier) in exchange for some payment (e.g., flat fee, future royalties/commissions, future advertising fees). Probably one of the best-known international franchises is McDonald's, which licenses its trademark, its fast-food products, and operating principles to franchisees worldwide in return for an initial fee and ongoing royalties. In return, McDonald's franchisees receive the benefit of McDonald's reputation, its management and marketing expertise.

Direct Investment in Foreign Operations

Foreign direct investment (FDI) involves the purchase of physical assets or an amount of ownership in a company from another country in order to gain a measure of management control. Capital can be invested in factories, inventories, and capital goods or other assets. Control of a company can be achieved without necessarily owning 100%, or even 50%, interest. A direct investment can be done through acquisition of an already existing business in the host country or through a start-up built "from scratch", so to speak. The choice may be dependent on a number of factors, including the availability of suitable businesses in the host country. If a suitable business already exists in the host country, it may prove more efficient than starting up a business there from scratch. It is no surprise that the vast majority (about 90%) of all FDI stems from developed countries, given that business in these countries will more likely have sufficient resources to invest overseas.

Data for the first quarter of 2001 (from Statistics Canada) indicated that in a ranking of ownership of the largest Canadian corporations by foreign enterprises, more than 13,000 corporations residing in Canada are controlled by foreign interests. The United States controls 6,825 of this total. Exhibit 8.4 shows the sources of the remainder of the foreign-controlled firms. With regard to the U.S.-controlled firms, about 59% (4,021) have their head offices in Ontario, followed by Quebec (14%, 942), Alberta (11%, 724) and British Columbia (9%, 612). The remainder (7%) are located in the other provinces and territories.

Throughout the 1990s, we observed a growth in foreign ownership in the Canadian business context. (See Exhibit 8.5.) Toward the end of the 1990s, foreign firms controlled about 22% of assets in Canada, which is a modest growth from 20.5% in 1994. In 1998, foreign firms accounted for 31.7% of all corporate operating revenues, compared to 29.4% in 1994. The majority increase in foreign control of Canadian assets has occurred in the non-financial sector, largely because government regulation in the finance and insurance sector has maintained a high level of control by Canadian corporations. Other sectors

EXHIBIT 8.4	TOP 10 FOREIGN OWNERSHIP RANKING BY COUNTRY OF CONTROL

	Country of Control	Number of Enterprises Owned
1	United States	6,825
2	United Kingdom	1,219
3	Germany	942
4	France	591
5	Japan	585
6	Hong Kong	490
7	Switzerland	436
8	Netherlands	318
9	Australia	168
10	Liechtenstein	88

Source: Statistics Canada, 2001.

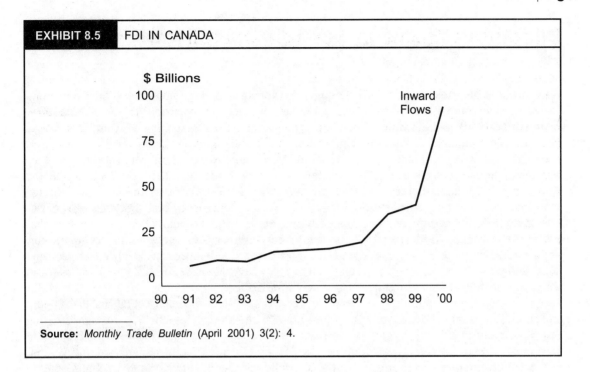

EXHIBIT 8.5	FDI IN CANADA

\$ Billions

Inward
Flows

100

75

50

25

0

90 91 92 93 94 95 96 97 98 99 '00

Source: *Monthly Trade Bulletin* (April 2001) 3(2): 4.

where government has limited the amount of foreign ownership include cable, telecommunications and satellite providers, where foreign ownership is limited to 47.6%. There is also a restriction on ownership of private newspaper companies to no more than 25% ownership. However, it is interesting to note that the majority of FDI into Canada in 1999 included telecommunications equipment and communications industries.

By 1998, U.S.-based corporations were responsible for about 69% of the foreign-controlled assets, while the European Union-based firms controlled 18%. Sectors where foreign control has been particularly high (over 50%) include chemical products, textiles and transportation. In 1998, the majority of increases in foreign control were largely due to mergers and acquisitions. In the period from 1995 to 1999, the share of FDI stemming from the United States increased from 67.2% to 72.2%, and most of this additional FDI was from cross-border mergers and acquisitions. In 2000, FDI more than doubled, reaching \$93 billion, and this too was largely the result of mergers and acquisitions. The United States invests significantly more in Canada than Canada invests in the United States. The view is that a strong domestic performance in Canada has continued to attract additional U.S. FDI.

What about Canada's FDI in other countries? While the United States has traditionally been the main destination for Canadian outward FDI, its share decreased from 61% in 1990 to 51.1% in 2000. The European Union's share has also decreased, while the share of other countries has been increasing. Specifically, during the 1990s, non-European countries, like the Asia-Pacific region, have become greater targets for Canadian outward FDI.

Why would businesses wish to engage in foreign direct investment? Controlling companies can obtain access to a larger market or needed resources via the FDI. Earlier in the process of globalization, direct investment was, in a sense, a substitute for trade. That is, while companies traded commodities that they had in abundance or that they could produce more competitively, they would also directly invest in countries where they needed to secure their source of raw materials or to manufacture their products inside the domestic market and, thereby, avoid tariffs or other import barriers. In that way, foreign investment occurred as a substitute for trade. More recently, however, with the liberalization of trade, foreign investment exists alongside trade. This is clearly seen in the fact that about one-third of world trade is conducted between members of the same organizations — i.e., between a parent company and its subsidiary, and between two subsidiaries of the same company. For example, a foreign subsidiary may require resources or supplies from the home country and, consequently, will import them.

It is interesting to note that a recent report indicated that most FDI in the United States in fact came about through mergers and acquisitions, rather than through creating new businesses (1997 *Survey of Current Business*). Consequently, although FDI increases in a country, employment levels do not necessarily rise because of this increased investment. For example, mergers often result in the consolidation and elimination of some common functions: this can entail layoffs and, therefore, reduced employment levels. This relates to a more general concern about FDI: Does it benefit, or harm, the host country? That question continues to be debated. (See Let's Talk Business 8.2.)

LET'S TALK BUSINESS 8.2   DO WE WANT FOREIGN INVESTMENT?

The issue of foreign investment in Canada has been a controversial one for years. A specific case of concern over FDI arose recently with the purchase of an interest in Canada's McClelland & Stewart Publishing by a German-based company, Random House. Governments tend to intervene in FDI where there is a potential threat to domestic culture and domestic businesses. This is a case in point.

Interestingly, the results of a recent poll reported in the *National Post* indicated that while Canadians are opposed to foreign control of companies, they do not fear foreign investment. Sixty-two percent of the respondents were in favour of foreign investment, viewing foreign capital as a benefit to the Canadian economy. On the other hand, only 24% of respondents opposed increases in foreign investment, compared to 77% in 1987 (at a time when the debate over whether to sign a free trade agreement with the United States was at its peak).

Source: Based on James Baxter, "Majority against foreign-owned media: poll Decima research: But study finds foreign investment not opposed" *Southam News* (July 6, 2001).

Joint Ventures, Strategic Alliances

A joint venture involves an arrangement between two or more companies from different countries to produce a product or service together, or to collaborate in the research, development, or marketing of this product or service. This relationship has also been referred to as a strategic network. These organizations develop an arrangement whereby they share managerial control over a specific venture, such as seeking to develop a new technology, gaining access to a new market, etc. For example, Canadian-based Northern Telecom has formed strategic alliances with numerous foreign-based organizations, like Daewoo in Korea, Mitsui in Japan and Ascom Hasler in Switzerland. Strategic alliances often aim to: extend or enhance the core competencies of the businesses involved; obtain access to the expertise of another organization; and generate new market opportunities for all parties involved. The level of ownership and specific responsibilities can be unique to that particular joint venture created among the partners. It has been observed that a high number of international joint ventures have failed largely due to the inability of the partners to find a proper "fit" with regard to their approaches and managerial styles. As in any relationship among partners, it must be given special attention, particularly when the partners are culturally diverse.

A typical arrangement may exist between a multinational corporation (MNC) and a local partner, since this facilitates the MNCs quick entry into a new foreign market through the joint venture with an already established local business. Consequently, the international joint venture has proven to be an efficient way of entering foreign markets rapidly and easing entry where local requirements have been implemented with regard to a degree of domestic ownership and participation in the production or distribution of the good or service.

Mergers and Acquisitions

A Canadian-owned company could actually merge with a foreign-owned company and create a new jointly owned enterprise that operates in at least two countries. The newspapers have been littered with reports of mergers and acquisitions on a global scale. It makes sense that, to the extent that globalization is a process of increasing the connectedness among economies, there is a further consolidation of markets and companies. For example, the Montreal-based commercial printing and book-publishing business, Quebecor World Inc., was able to expand rapidly in Latin America in recent years, largely through acquisitions and partnerships with local companies in Argentina, Chile and Peru. In the mid-1990s, the U.S.-based company Nike acquired the Canadian-based Canstar, which produced major lines of hockey equipment, including brands such as Bauer and Cooper.

Why do such mergers occur? A number of factors typically generate the drive to merge, including the goal of obtaining new markets for the business and the effort to obtain new knowledge and expertise in an industry. The notion of achieving economies of scale in production may also be a source of influence on the decision to merge. Companies that merge on a global scale may be doing so in order to generate world-scale volume in a more cost effective way. Specifically, economies of scale in production are obtained when higher levels of output spread fixed costs (overhead, plant, equipment, etc.) over more produced units and, consequently, reduce the per unit cost. It is, in a sense, the ability to achieve cost efficiency through larger scale production that is made possible through the creation of a bigger organization.

Establishment of Subsidiaries

Another well-known type of global business activity is the creation of subsidiaries or branch operations in foreign countries, through which the enterprise can market goods and services. Where possible, a business may choose to maintain total control of its product or service by either establishing a wholly owned subsidiary or by purchasing an existing firm in the host country. Acquisitions of local companies have become increasingly popular. These types of acquisitions allow efficient entry into a market with already well-known products and distribution networks. On the other hand, establishing a subsidiary from scratch in the host country may also be a viable option. For example, shortly following the import quota placed on Japanese cars in the 1980s, Japanese-based car manufacturers set up operations in North America and captured an even greater segment of the consumer market. Toyota, Honda and Nissan are among the companies that have successfully employed this strategy.

What are the benefits of such types of global arrangements? If the foreign country is a high source of sales for the enterprise, it may make sense to establish a presence in that country, in order to be more responsive to local consumer needs. Among the risks is the fact that much more is at stake when the company has invested in a wholly owned subsidiary: they have invested time, effort and expense to create this operation. Subsidiaries may face the threat of political instability, as evidenced in the past in places like China or South Africa. Subsidiaries may also face adverse environments that might turn hostile toward foreign ownership. For example, Toyota's presence in Canada has not been without controversy. In recent years Toyota's Canadian subsidiary argued that it was being unfairly slapped with import tariffs on parts, making it more difficult to compete with North American-based car manufacturers.

THE MULTINATIONAL CORPORATION ———————

In terms of global types of business activity, the multinational corporation is a type of global business that has been receiving increasing attention, for better or worse. What is a multinational corporation, and why are we seeing its presence increasing across the globe? Observers have noted that such corporations are breaking down borders among countries and creating, in essence, borderless corporations. What are the implications of multinationals in terms of the costs and benefits they bring to the countries in which they set up business? We will address these questions in this section.

LET'S TALK BUSINESS 8.3   THE BIG GUYS

The divisions of large MNCs can operate either as relatively independent subsidiaries, like IBM Canada or IBM Tokyo, or as elements of a closely integrated global network. The former typically have an in-depth knowledge of the local culture and can adapt swiftly to changes in local market conditions. In addition to the large size of MNCs, there has recently been a string of international mergers that have continued to increase the size of many MNCs. For example, in 1998, the world's largest firms created mergers in excess of $1 trillion. Many powerful multinational organizations have grown so large that they have, in effect, reduced the power of their central headquarters and found that they must decentralize decision making among their various geographically dispersed branches. For example, Coca Cola, IBM, Sony, and Ford, to name a few, have reduced the responsibilities of their head offices to act largely as a coordinating mechanism for all the locally managed activities of their global businesses.

The first place to start is to offer a definition. What exactly are multinational corporations, and in what way are they "global business"? A global business is a business that engages directly in some form of international business activity, including such activities as exporting, importing or international production. A business that has direct investments (whether in the form of marketing or manufacturing facilities) in at least two different countries is specifically referred to as a multinational corporation (MNC). In other words, **multinational organizations, or MNCs, are business enterprises that control assets, factories, etc., operated either as branch offices or affiliates in two or more foreign countries**. A MNC generates products or services through its affiliates in several countries, and it maintains control over the operations of those affiliates, and manages from a global perspective. MNCs may also be referred to as global companies when they operate in myriad countries across the world.

Typically, MNCs are very large organizations and, in terms of their relative role in the world setting, it has been estimated that the 600 largest MNCs account for about one-quarter of the activity in the world's economies. Technically, it may be more accurate to refer to such organizations as MNEs (enterprises), given that such organizations could, in fact, possess partnership status, for example, rather than being incorporated: a business can be multinational without being a corporation per se. Further, MNEs can be divided between those businesses that are globally integrated and those that are multi-domestic. Globally integrated companies are companies that integrate their geographically diverse operations through decisions centralized at head office. Consequently, all areas might be given the task of developing and selling a single global product; or perhaps each region is contributing to the manufacture of a certain product. A multi-domestic company, on the other hand, permits its geographically diverse components to operate relatively autonomously. For example, the Canadian division will focus on its market, and the U.S. division will focus on its market. (See Let's Talk Business 8.3.)

So who, exactly, creates these organizations?   Most MNCs have headquarters in developed countries — the **home** country. More specifically, over half of the MNCs have head-

---

LET'S TALK BUSINESS 8.4   WHAT'S THE THIRD WORLD?

With regard to the globalization debate, it is useful to note that the term **Third World** was originally intended to describe the poor or developing nations of the world. In contrast, the first and second worlds were composed of the advanced or industrialized countries. The developed worlds were viewed as including: the United States, Canada, and most of the countries of Eastern and Western Europe, as well as Australia, New Zealand and Japan. Within the broad territory described as the Third World, there are actually countries that are developing either rapidly (e.g., Brazil, Hong Kong, Israel, Mexico, Singapore, South Africa, South Korea and Taiwan) or modestly (including many countries of Africa, Asia and Latin America, in addition to India, Indonesia, Malaysia, and China) and others that have remained underdeveloped (e.g., Somalia, Sudan, sub-Sahara Africa). According to recent estimates, the Third World contributes most to the world's population growth, but is able to provide only about 20% of the world's economic production. A major controversy with regard to global business revolves around the fate of these underdeveloped nations: will they be purely exploited for the economic gain of MNCs, or will they benefit from the presence of increased industry?

---

quarters in the United States. France, Germany, the United Kingdom, and Japan are among the other countries that are home to headquarters for most of the remaining MNCs. MNCs maintain branch plants or subsidiaries in two or more foreign countries — these are the **host** countries, and they are either developed, developing or Third World countries. (See Let's Talk Business 8.4.) Among some of Canada's well-known MNCs are Bata Corp. which operates footwear manufacturing and distribution facilities in about 60 countries. Bombardier Inc. similarly is very much a part of the global market. This company has operations that include transportation equipment and aircraft production. While its head office is in Montreal, nearly 90% of its sales are made in markets outside of Canada. It has production facilities in locations including Canada, the United States, France and Austria; and it markets products on five different continents.

The Borderless Corporation

Anthony Spaeth commented in a recent *Time Magazine* article: "The machinery of globalization is already integrating financial systems, dismantling territorial frontiers and bringing people closer together." This comment is perhaps best illustrated in the new term for MNCs — borderless corporations. In some ways, it does seem the next logical step in the globalization of business.

The increasing ability of MNCs to ignore international boundaries and set up business just about anywhere reflects the title "borderless corporation". In fact, more and more MNCs are taking on the appearance of borderless corporations. Many of today's organizations that operate globally are, perhaps, less accurately referred to as MNCs than as TNCs, or transnational corporations; and in fact, these two terms are often used inter-

---

LET'S TALK BUSINESS 8.5   THINK GLOBAL, ACT LOCAL

There is no better way of serving the needs of a geographically diverse market than by locating in the different geographical regions. This is reflected in the motto well-known among today's MNCs: "Think global, act local!" It has been suggested that many MNCs, such as Coca Cola, Sony, Motorola, and Nestle, have decentralized decision making among their geographically dispersed locations. For example, in IBM each subsidiary has its own local management, its own culture and its unique market focus. What this does is ensure that, for example, a Canadian client of IBM Canada sees the company as, indeed, IBM Canada, and not as simply a subsidiary of another U.S. MNC. This same philosophy is increasingly being employed by just about every MNC. Consider Nestle, which is headquartered in Switzerland, and yet which seems to many to be a U.S. company. Consider also the car industry — is a Ford car an American car? Well, not exactly, if you can imagine that it might be assembled in Brazil with parts from Europe and the United States. Also, consider the entertainment industry: for example, MTV broadcasting, by the mid-1990s, was being transmitted to more than 70 countries, using different formats and languages adapted to the local markets. Is MTV American? Like many other MNCs, in the new global economy the idea is to think global but act local. Regardless of where they operate, they aim to reflect the local market tastes.

---

changeably. The term TNC, as well as the term borderless corporation, is also being applied to MNCs, given the increasing tendency of not simply setting up branch plants in foreign countries but of organizing management, investment, production and distribution as if the world were one country.

The term multinational is a bit inaccurate, given that many of these companies do not claim any specific nationality but, in fact, gear their planning and decision making to global markets. For example, goods could be designed in one country, raw material obtained from a second country, manufactured in a third country and shipped to consumers in another country. Consequently, top management can be composed of international members reflecting the international composition of the organization. The headquarters of MNCs can often be quite irrelevant. For example, while Nestle Food Corp. is headquartered in Switzerland, fewer than 5,000 of its over 200,000 workforce are actually working in the home country. Nestle has manufacturing facilities in over 50 countries and owns suppliers and distributors all over the world. Other similar examples of borderless or stateless corporations would include Coca Cola, which although headquartered in the United States operates independent facilities around the world. In fact, Coca Cola has seen the bulk of its profits generated in the Pacific and Eastern Europe rather than in the United States, as have companies like General Motors. Other companies are equally transnational and almost borderless: like Phillips, Nissan, and Canada's Northern Telecom (Nortel), which has increasingly moved beyond the title of being a "Canadian business".

The term borderless corporation, as opposed to multinational, emphasizes the notion that an enterprise can be a global company without any clear nationality. (See Let's Talk Business 8.5.) Often, the company has international ownership and international management. Headquarters do not necessarily belong to one home country, but are located simply

---

LET'S TALK BUSINESS 8.6   THE BORDERLESS CORPORATION

The slogan "think global, act local" is perhaps best achieved by the borderless corporation: it simply sets up business where it is profitable, rather than creating a branch plant whose head office is in another corner of the world. Decision making is local and decentralized. This underscores the focus of the borderless corporation in addressing the local needs of the market within which it operates.

Many factors, like the reduction in trade barriers, permit a much freer flow of labour, goods, services and capital across borders. This facilitates the rise of borderless corporations, and allows them to be very mobile across international borders. Goods could be designed in one country, raw material obtained from a second country, manufactured in a third country and shipped to consumers in another country. The process is made easy when transfers are not impeded by trade barriers or tariffs. On the other hand, borderless corporations can be equally effective in circumventing any trade barriers. For example, countries refusing to conduct trade with another country may not view a borderless corporation as a problem.

---

for convenience. Consequently, there is typically no allegiance to any one country or location. Rather, business is simply set up wherever profits can be maximized. These companies are very mobile across borders with regard to the transfer of financial capital, materials and other resources. (See Let's Talk Business 8.6.)

Currently the rapid rise of these MNCs, or TNCs, or borderless corporations, is raising many questions that have not yet been satisfactorily addressed. For example, at a time now when many countries are concerned with their competitiveness on the international market and their status in terms of trade, should we be concerned with who is generating the bulk of our exports? Does it matter what a company's nationality is, as long as it is providing jobs? Which government, and whose set of rules, will govern the behaviour of MNCs, or borderless corporations? These questions are serious concerns raised by those who view the globalization of business as bringing with it as many threats as it does opportunities. (See Exhibit 8.6.)

INTERNATIONAL TRADE

The globalization of business may be a relatively new buzzword, but one of its fundamental forms has been around for a long time: the notion of international trade. International trade essentially involves the purchase, sale or exchange of goods or services across countries. This can be distinguished from domestic trade which involves trade, between provinces, cities or regions within a country.

Certainly, the trend of globalization has included the gradual reduction in trade barriers among many nations of the world as a means to promote greater international trade. You have probably heard about the Free Trade Agreement and the debates surrounding

| EXHIBIT 8.6 | THE POTENTIAL BENEFITS AND THREATS OF MNCs |

Potential Benefits

- Encourages economic development.
- Offers management expertise.
- Introduces new technologies.
- Provides financial support to underdeveloped regions of the world.
- Creates employment.
- Encourages international trade through their access to different markets: it is relatively easy to produce goods in one country and distribute them in another country through their subsidiary or foreign affiliate.
- Brings different countries closer together.
- Facilitates global co-operation and worldwide economic development.

Potential Threats

- MNCs do not have any particular allegiance or commitment to their host country.
- Profits made by an MNC do not necessarily remain within the host country but may be transferred out to other locations depending on where the MNC feels the funds are most needed.
- Decision making and other key functions of MNCs may be highly centralized in the home country, so that even though other operations are performed in the host country, they do not necessarily include things like research and development and strategic planning.
- Difficulty in the ability to control and hold MNCs accountable can create serious ethical concerns for the host country. (See Let's Talk Business 8.7.)

| LET'S TALK BUSINESS 8.7 | THE ETHICS OF MNCs |

Nike manufactures many of its products though outsourcing arrangements: that is, it contracts companies in about six Asian nations for much of its production. Wages are very low, and typically plants have been used as sweatshops, with very poor working conditions. Nike has attempted to respond to these criticisms and improve arrangements. MNCs typically want to locate their plants where labour is inexpensive. However, critics argue that they still have an ethical obligation not to ignore the working conditions where their products and profits are made.

Nike has been accused of failing to rely on U.S.-based labour to produce their shoes and, instead, have relied on cheap foreign labour. Similarly, a number of years ago we observed the famous case of GM closing their automobile plant in Flint, Michigan in favour of setting up operations in Mexico. Shutting down operations in their home country in order to set up operations in another country where costs of labour are cheaper, and consequently profits can be further maximized. The exodus of both U.S.-based and Canadian companies to Mexico when free trade began proved to be another illustration of this pattern among critics. Nike and GM further underscore the view that MNCs are motivated by greed and self-interest, and are extremely difficult to control.

it, but perhaps you are not very familiar with the issues. What are the implications of promoting freer trade across nations, and what are the implications of barriers to trade?

In order to understand some of the critical implications of free trade, it is useful to consider the nature of international trade. Why might countries want to trade? Why might countries want to engage in protectionism? Below, we will consider a brief history with regard to the issue of international trade.

The Logic of Trade

One fundamental argument is that since some countries can produce certain goods or services more efficiently than others, global efficiency and, hence, wealth can be improved through free trade. Clearly, it is not advantageous for citizens of a country to be forced to buy an inferior quality, higher-priced domestic good if they can purchase a superior, lower-priced, foreign produced import. Consistent with this view is the belief that trade should be permitted to continue according to market forces and not artificially restricted through trade barriers. Freer trade would allow countries to trade as they deemed appropriate, rather than trying to produce all goods domestically. Consequently, each country can specialize or focus on producing those goods or services in which it maintains an absolute advantage, and simply trade with other countries to obtain goods or services that were required, but not produced by domestic suppliers.

Free trade is based on the objective of open markets, where a level playing field is created for businesses in one country to compete fairly against businesses in other countries for the sale of their products or services. The aim reflects the fundamental principles of comparative advantage. Each country expects to take advantage of each other's strengths, and thereby be permitted to focus on their own strengths. In simplistic terms, it is relatively inefficient for Canada to try to grow coffee beans or bananas, given the climate. Rather than wasting effort and money, these items can be imported from countries more suited to such endeavours, while Canadians can focus their efforts in areas where they can produce relatively more efficiently.

Mercantilism

The trade theory underlying economic thinking from the period ranging from about 1500 to 1800 is referred to as **mercantilism**. Specifically, the fundamental view was that a country's wealth depends on its holdings of treasure, typically in the form of gold. Mercantilism, essentially, is the economic policy of accumulating this financial wealth through trade surpluses. **Trade surpluses** come about when a country's exports exceed its imports and, consequently, more money is entering the country (from foreign consumers buying these exports) than is leaving the country (from domestic consumers buying foreign imports). This policy was particularly popular in Europe from about the late 1500s to the late 1700s, with the most dominant mercantilist nations including Britain, France, Spain, and the Netherlands.

Countries implemented this policy of mercantilism in a number of ways. Foremost, the government would intervene to ensure a trade surplus by imposing tariffs or quotas, or by outright banning of some foreign imported commodities. Typically, the governments would also subsidize domestic industries in order to encourage growth in their exports. Another strategy employed by mercantilist nations was colonialization: acquiring less developed regions around the world as sources of inexpensive raw materials (such as sugar, cotton, rubber, tobacco). These colonies would also serve as markets for finished products. Trade between mercantilist countries and their colonies resulted in large profits, given that the colonies typically were paid little for their raw materials but were forced to pay high prices to purchase the final products. Obviously, the colonial powers benefited to the detriment of the colonies. In addition, mercantilist countries aimed to become as self-sufficient as possible with regard to domestic production of goods and services. This also served to minimize reliance on foreign imports.

Given this brief historical description, it is easy to see why, today, countries that endeavour to maintain a trade surplus and expand their wealth at the expense of other countries are accused of practising mercantilism or neo-mercantilism. Japan has often been viewed as a mercantilist country because of its typically high trade surplus with a number of industrial nations, including the United States.

Trade Protectionism

Essentially, trade protectionism is about protecting a country's domestic economy and businesses through restriction on imports. Why might imports be a threat to a country's business and economy? Well, two fundamental reasons can be considered:

1. Low-priced foreign goods that enter the country could compete with goods already produced here and, in effect, take business away from domestic producers. The ultimate consequence may be loss of sales and loss of jobs for domestic industries that are unable to compete with these lower-priced imports.

2. A country that imports more than it exports will have a negative balance of trade, or a trade deficit — which often results in more money flowing out of the country (to buy the imported goods) than flowing in (for our exports).

Among the best-known government responses to address these potential risks are the imposition of tariffs and import quotas. A **tariff** is essentially a tax placed on goods entering a country. Specifically, protective tariffs are intended to raise the price of imported products in order to ensure that they are not less expensive than domestically produced goods. This, of course, discourages domestic consumers from buying these foreign imports by making them more expensive to purchase.

Another common form of trade barrier or restriction is the **import quota**, which limits the amount of a product that can be imported. The reasons for this restriction are the same: to help ensure that domestic producers retain an adequate share of consumer demand for this product. For example, in the 1980s, both the U.S. and Canadian governments were concerned with the growing popularity of Japanese-made cars in Canada and the United States. These cars were higher quality and cost less than the three big North American car manufacturers. After pressure from the automakers, both the U.S. and Canadian governments negotiated deals with the Japanese government and the Japanese

---

LET'S TALK BUSINESS 8.8   THE FUTILITY OF PROTECTIONISM

Restrictions on imports can be self-defeating, given that other countries will act in a similar manner and reduce their imports. Consider the case of Canada, where a large portion of our raw materials are exported. Can it restrict imports from countries who are similarly purchasing our exports?

The Great Depression of the 1930s was largely due to the protectionist policy passed by the U.S. government at that time. The government placed tariffs on many goods entering the United States in order to protect U.S. industry. However, the result was that many other countries raised their tariffs and caused a sharp drop in U.S. exports and, in fact, hurt trade among almost all countries.

---

automakers to "voluntarily" restrict the number of vehicles they would export to Canada and the United States for the next three years. Ironically, this strategy was short-lived, given that Japanese automakers eventually built auto plants in Canada and the United States and achieved an even greater share of the North American market (about 35%).

What's Wrong with Mercantilism and Protectionism?

A trade surplus, as opposed to a trade deficit, certainly seems like a desirable aim, and is, in many respects, a benefit for any nation. The issue, though, is whether a policy of mercantilism is feasible, given its dependence on restriction of foreign imports. Perhaps the most significant criticism of mercantilism is that the central assumption upon which this policy is largely based is inherently flawed. Mercantilism assumes that trade involves a **zero-sum gain** — that is, the world's wealth is a fixed pie, and a nation can only increase its share of the pie by forcing other nations to reduce their shares of the pie. Based on this logic, one can understand the drive to minimize imports while maximizing exports. The flaw in this logic, however, is readily apparent. The practice creates a **"one-way street"** of trade, so to speak. That is, a mercantilist country aims to maximize the goods/services it sells to other countries, yet it expects to restrict the goods/services that these same countries attempt to sell to it. Even in the time of colonialism, the policy was ultimately self-defeating: colonies that receive little payment for their raw material exports could not accumulate sufficient wealth to afford the high-priced imports that the mercantilists offered. (See Let's Talk Business 8.8.)

Promoting International Trade

Whether it is tariffs, or quotas, or other forms of protectionism, we have seen a gradual lifting of trade restrictions as part of the wave of globalization. Most countries are endeavouring to eliminate trade barriers.

One of the most ambitious programs designed to encourage free trade was established way back in 1948 with the founding of GATT, the **General Agreement on Tariffs & Trade**, which was an agreement among approximately 100 countries to reduce the level of tariffs on a worldwide basis. And it did encourage a gradual reduction in trade barriers. In 1995 the **World Trade Organization** (WTO), in effect, took over the management of the global trade system from GATT. Its mandate is, essentially, to develop and administer agreed-upon rules for world trade, and discourage protectionist laws that restrict international trade.

Other organizations exist whose purpose is also to assist nations of the global economy. For example, the **International Monetary Fund** (IMF) was established after World War II to provide short-term assistance in the form of low-interest loans to countries conducting international trade and in need of financial assistance. The **World Bank** was established at the same time to provide long-term loans to countries for economic development projects. Typically, the World Bank will borrow funds from the more developed countries and offer low-interest loans to underdeveloped Third World nations. So, both these organizations, by assisting less prosperous nations, help to facilitate trade and investment between countries.

Countries themselves have been pursuing trading blocs and other forms of economic integration as part of the general thrust toward a more integrated world economy. This issue of economic integration is discussed below.

Facilitating Global Business: Regional Economic Integration

Regional economic integration means bringing different countries closer together by the reduction or elimination of obstacles to the international movement of capital, labour, and products or services. A collection of countries within such an integrated region is typically referred to as a regional trading bloc. Why do countries endeavour to integrate? It is, largely, a logical conclusion to maximizing the benefits of international trade, as discussed earlier, with regard to greater availability of products, lower prices and increased efficiency or productivity. Trading blocs increase international trade and investment, with the central aim of improving their economy and living standards for their citizens.

Regional integration can occur at different levels of intensity, so to speak. These include, from the lowest to the highest levels of integration: free trade areas, customs union, common market, and economic union. It is worthwhile to briefly examine each form.

1. Free trade area. This form of economic integration involves the removal of tariffs and non-tariff trade barriers (i.e., subsidies and quotas) on international trade in goods and services among the member countries. Given that this form involves the lowest degree of regional economic integration, there is greater member autonomy with regard to such issues as how it chooses to deal with non-members and what types of barriers it should construct against non-member countries. Examples of this form are the North American Free Trade Agreement and APEC, both of which are discussed later in this chapter.

2. Customs union. This form of economic integration involves the removal of trade barriers on international trade in goods and services among the member countries. How-ever, given that this form involves a somewhat greater degree of economic integration, there is less member autonomy with regard to such issues as how it chooses to deal with non-members, and what types of barriers it should construct against non-member countries. Members will typically generate a uniform policy regarding treatment of non-members. One example of this type of integration is the MERCOSUR customs union, which is a major trade group in South America. This customs union was established in 1991, and its partners include Argentina, Brazil, Uruguay, and Paraguay; it grants associate status to Chile and Bolivia. By 1996 the members had eliminated tariffs on goods accounting for 90% of trade between the member countries and, eventually, largely abolished trade barriers. In 1995 MERCOSUR implemented a common external tariff: which, by defini-tion, makes it a more highly integrated trading bloc than NAFTA. These countries repre-sent an attractive market for foreign companies because of the large population and high proportion of middle-class consumers. However, tariffs for non-members have ranged from 16% to 32% and, consequently, have made it challenging for outsiders. Countries like Canada and the United States are awaiting further agreements like the FTAA (The Free Trade Area of the Americas) that would allow greater access to the Latin American mar-kets for North American exports.

3. Common market. This form of economic integration builds on the elements of the two previous forms, including the removal of trade barriers and the implementation of a common trade policy regarding non-members. In addition, members of a common market will typically also generate a freer flow of labour and capital across their borders. Given the requirement of co-operation in economic and labour policy, this level of economic integration is, consequently, more difficult to achieve than the previous two levels. The European Union, discussed below, is one such example of a common market arrangement.

4. Economic union. This form of economic integration builds on the previous three forms and, in addition, involves a coordination of economic policies among the member countries. It requires a higher level of integration than a common market, because it involves the harmonization of fiscal, monetary and tax policies. In addition, it often includes the creation of a common currency. Consequently, member countries in such an arrangement maintain much less autonomy compared to the lesser forms of economic inte-gration. In the following discussion of the EU, it can be noted that the members are moving toward greater integration of economic and political policies, which would, essen-tially, move them closer to a genuine economic union.

A significant portion of total world trade occurs within three regional trading blocs, also referred to as the Triad market of North America, Europe and Asia. Given the importance of these trading blocs, it is worthwhile to highlight each. Following is a rela-tively brief description of the trading blocs in Europe and Asia, followed by a lengthier discussion of the North American trade agreement and its implications for the Canadian business environment.

European Union (EU)

In 1992, 12 nations of Europe established a common market, called the European Community (EC); and in 1994, after adding several new members, it became known as the European Union (EU). The European Union is a common market with a single currency, a free flow of money, people, products and services within its member countries. Technically, there are 15 member states within the EU, with 11 members also adopting a common currency (the Euro) and monetary policy. The members include: Denmark, Sweden, Finland, Netherlands, France, Austria, Germany, Belgium, Luxembourg, Britain, Ireland, Italy, Greece, Spain, and Portugal. Many other countries have recently been invited to join, including Poland, Hungary and the Czech Republic. In total, the EU is currently the largest integrated common market in the world, with approximately 400 million consumers

Common market is a term that refers to a group of countries who remove all tariff and non-tariff barriers to trade. Indeed, the aim of the EU is to create a borderless Europe, so to speak. In fact, the bulk of the advanced regions of Europe exist in essentially one giant market, with the free movement of goods and services, as well as people and financial capital. Businesses that operate outside the boundaries of the EU can achieve the benefits of membership if they have a subsidiary in at least one member country. For example, U.S.-based companies like 3M, Hewlett-Packard and GE had already established a European presence, and consequently enjoy the same benefits as businesses who are part of the member European countries. Those not yet established in Europe are developing strategies to exploit this large market. The EU can be a double-edged sword for non-members. It can generate protectionist policies for its members, like tariffs or quotas, to bar the United States or Japan from entry, for example. On the other hand, the EU could also create opportunities for non-members — they comprise a huge market for North American exports, for example. A number of U.S.-based companies have chosen to engage in joint ventures with European-based companies as a means of obtaining some kind of presence in the European market. Does this common market matter to Canada? It certainly does. The EU is one of Canada's most important trading partners. Clearly, this large market cannot be ignored. Aside from the United States, six of Canada's top 10 export markets are in Europe. Consequently, observers view Europe as a potentially strong market for Canadian goods, if tariff and non-tariff barriers can be reduced. In addition, many critics feel that there is currently too high a reliance on one market (the United States) for Canadian exports (approximately 85%), and increased trade with other markets is preferable. (See Let's Talk Business 8.9.)

Asian Trading Bloc

Another region of growing importance to Canada has been the Asia-Pacific region. This region has a total population of about two billion — approximately twice that of the European community. In addition to the drive for greater economic integration and free trade in Europe and North and South America, Asia has also sought to create trading blocs. Singapore, Hong Kong, Taiwan and South Korea (also referred to as the Four Tigers), together with the relatively dominant partner, Japan, have grown to become an increasingly integrated economic region.

LET'S TALK BUSINESS 8.9   TRADING WITH THE EUROPEAN UNION (EU)

A recent report issued by the trade sub-committee of the House of Commons called for the Canadian government to push for free trade negotiations with the European Union. While Europe is the second-largest economy in the world after the United States, Canada does less than 5% of its trade, or just $20 billion a year, with the European Union. On the other hand, more than 85% of Canada's trade is with the United States. The report said the government should "rapidly develop a business case for a free trade agreement with the EU and undertake an aggressive campaign both in Canada and in Europe to promote its findings to key decision-makers". Ironically, while there has been a push to increase trade with the EU for some time, Canada's exports to the EU have fallen from 10% to approximately 6% of the total over the past decade. In the year 2000, approximately 5% of Canadian merchandise exports were sent to the EU. According to Statistics Canada, Canada exported $21 billion of goods and $9 billion of services to the EU in the year 2000, while goods and services imports from the EU were $33.6 billion and $10.3 billion, respectively.

Source: Based on Ian Jack, "Ottawa told to push for free trade with EU Sub-committee report" *Financial Post* (June 7, 2001).

ASEAN. The **Association of South East Asian Nations** (ASEAN) was established in 1967 and became the first major free-trade bloc in Asia. Its aim was to promote greater co-operation in areas such as industry and trade among the members, including Singapore, Malaysia, Indonesia, Thailand, Viet Nam, the Philippines and Brunei. At the same time, member countries are protected by trade barriers from non-members. There is a move to create a greater East Asian trade and economic grouping, consisting of the Association of Southeast Asian Nations (ASEAN) countries, plus Japan, China and South Korea.[179] The process of creating a trading bloc has been slower in Asia partly because, unlike NAFTA and the EU, there is a very wide disparity between the economic infrastructures and the GDPs of Japan, South Korea and China. While disparities exist among members in the EU, they are not as great. For example, a number of current EU members, like Portugal and Greece, have remained behind such members as Germany, France and Britain. In addition, much of Mexico's southern region lives in essentially Third World conditions. However, the disparities in the economies of China, South Korea and Japan are much greater. For example, per capita income in Japan is near US$24,000, compared to about US$8,000 in Korea and US$800 in China. Large areas of inland China, including Tibet, remain underdeveloped. All this contributes to a greater difficulty in integrating the regions for trade purposes.

APEC. The Asia-Pacific region has also set out to facilitate greater economic co-operation and freer trade through the establishment of the **Asia-Pacific Economic Co-operation** (or **APEC**), formed in 1989. Among the members of APEC are the People's Republic of China, Hong Kong, Japan, Indonesia, Malaysia, South Korea, Canada and the

United States, to name some of the 18 members. It is viewed as a significant economic force, given that its members generate over 50% of the global output and about 50% of its merchandise trade. APEC was established to promote economic co-operation among members in the areas of trade and investment. Its relatively diverse mix of countries is, in effect, an effort to counter the narrower regionalism of such arrangements as the EU and NAFTA. In fact, APEC includes three of the traditionally largest economies — the United States, China and Japan. NAFTA was included in APEC largely as a means to forge stronger economic links between North America and Asia.

How important is APEC to Canada? Canada's central aim in joining APEC was to expand trade opportunities with the region. This region has a total population of about two billion — approximately twice that of the European community. This represents a large market for Canadian exports. Next to the United States, Japan has been one of Canada's largest trading partners; and Japan, along with other member nations, represents a high potential as consumers for our exports. The suggestion is not necessarily to decrease the level of trade and investment that Canada has established with the United States; but rather, to pursue similar levels of access to other major regions, such as Asia. (See Let's Talk Business 8.10.)

LET'S TALK BUSINESS 8.10 APEC AND CANADA

The Asia Pacific Foundation of Canada (2000) Report indicated the following:

- Since the Asian economic crisis in 1997, Canada's involvement in the Asian economies has been lagging.
- Canada desperately needs to expand its trade activities beyond its current concentration on the United States, which makes it vulnerable to change based on the status of the U.S. economy.
- Focus on the United States has been at the expense of developing a closer relationship with Asia. This is seen as unwise, given that Asia has been the fastest growing segment of the global economy over the past two decades. Canada's share of the major Asian markets has dropped from about 2.7% prior to NAFTA to less than 1% by 1999.
- Canada needs to increase its presence in the Asian economies to take advantage of their eventual growth.
- One obstacle facing Canadian businesses, in this regard, is the general difficulty of raising capital in Canada for investment outside the familiar environment of North America.
- The report was particularly critical of Canada's banks with regard to Asian investment.
- The report accuses banks of merely claiming to seek international stature, while neglecting to take advantage of opportunities in Asia. During the Asian crisis, the Royal Bank shut down half its offices in Asia, for example. On the other hand, all the world's leading banks have offices in Asia, and can finance investments by Canadian businesses operating there.
- Canadian banks may fail to exploit the rapid growth in Asia if they do not maximize their presence.
- In general, Canada's direct investment in Asia (DIA) has been relatively flat since 1994. Between 1990–1994, Canadian investment in Asian APEC member economies rose significantly, and represented 5.9% of Canada's worldwide portfolio of foreign investments by 1994. However, since that time, investment in these economies has only risen by about 4% annually, compared to the 12.8% annual growth rate in Canadian global investments.

North America Trading Bloc and NAFTA

The Canada–U.S. Free Trade Agreement (FTA) came into effect January 1, 1989, and was largely aimed at reducing, and eventually eliminating, tariff barriers on almost all goods and services traded between Canada and the United States, as well as at further facilitating cross-country investments. Among the other provisions of the agreements are rules regarding government subsidies, the imposition of countervailing duties, standards of health and safety, and the environment. Essentially, for Canadian exporters this agreement offered better access to the huge American market for Canadian goods and services. In 1994, the North American Free Trade Agreement (NAFTA) was established and this, similarly, was an agreement to remove trade barriers between Canada, the United States and Mexico. This agreement that replaced the FTA essentially aimed to produce a common market among the members. There has been much written regarding the impact that NAFTA has had on Mexico, the United States and Canada. Before we identify some of the major arguments supporting or condemning free trade, let's consider some of the more tangible results that have been connected with the implementation of this free trade agreement. (See Exhibit 8.7.)

NAFTA's Impact on Trade

- The most obvious outcome of NAFTA and FTA is that they have achieved their most fundamental objective: to increase the level of trade between Canada and the United States. Canada and U.S. trade has increased by about 75% since the establishment of the FTA. Of course, the United States continues to be Canada's major trading part-

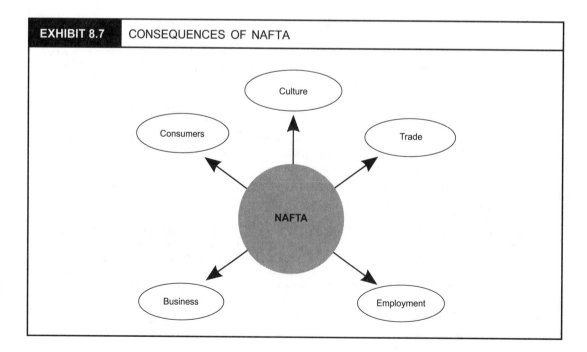

| EXHIBIT 8.7 | CONSEQUENCES OF NAFTA |

ner, accounting for almost 80% of Canada's total trade. In 1994 Canada's exports to the United States increased by over 20%, and exports to Mexico increased by 22%. (Similarly, U.S. exports to Canada increased over 19% in that same year.)

- In the period between 1993 and 1996, overall trade among the United States, Canada and Mexico increased by about 43%, from approximately $290 billion to $420 billion. Canada's merchandise trade with the United States increased by 80% in the first five years of the NAFTA, and Canada's trade with Mexico increased by 65%, reaching $271.5 billion and $1.4 billion in 1998. U.S. investment in Canada reached $147.3 billion in 1998, up 63% from 1993, and Mexico's investment in Canada reached $464 million in 1998, tripling from 1993. Since the inception of NAFTA, the proportion of Canada's domestic product attributable to trade with the United States has increased consistently, as illustrated in Exhibit 8.8.

- One measure of the relative significance of trade to a country is to observe the volume of an economy's trade relative to its total output (percentage of GDP). Exports of Canadian goods to the United States were approximately 17% of GDP in the 1980s, prior to NAFTA. With the implementation of NAFTA, exports and imports

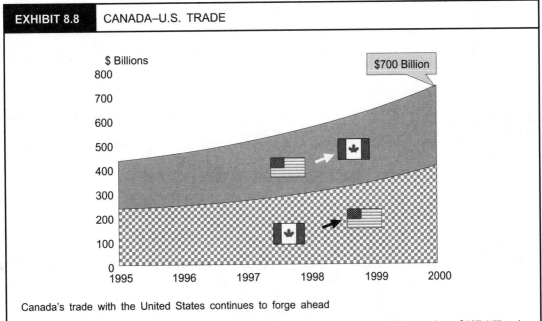

| EXHIBIT 8.8 | CANADA–U.S. TRADE |

Canada's trade with the United States continues to forge ahead

- Total Canada–U.S. trade (goods and services) reached $700 billion in 2000, up from $427 billion in 1995.
  - Exports reached $393 billion and imports $307 billion in 2000, increases of 15.4% and 7.3%, respectively, over the previous year.
  - $1.3 million dollars worth of goods and services cross the Canada–U.S. border every minute.

Source: *Monthly Trade Bulletin* (March 2001) 3(1): 3.

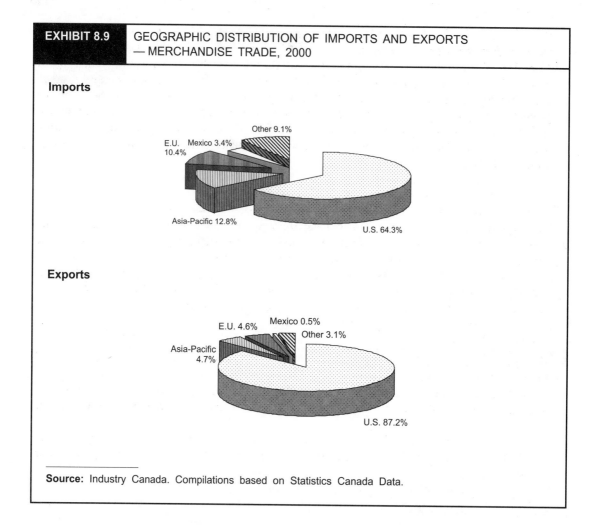

EXHIBIT 8.9   GEOGRAPHIC DISTRIBUTION OF IMPORTS AND EXPORTS
— MERCHANDISE TRADE, 2000

Imports

Other 9.1%

E.U. 10.4%   Mexico 3.4%

Asia-Pacific 12.8%

U.S. 64.3%

Exports

E.U. 4.6%   Mexico 0.5%

Asia-Pacific 4.7%   Other 3.1%

U.S. 87.2%

Source: Industry Canada. Compilations based on Statistics Canada Data.

grew significantly over the period from 1990 to 1999. Specifically, as a proportion of GDP, exports grew from 25.7% to 43.2%, while imports grew from 25.7% to 40.3%. In contrast, for the 10 years prior to the Free Trade Agreement, exports and imports as a proportion of GDP were practically constant. Total Canada–U.S. trade in both goods and services rose from $425 billion in 1995 to $700 billion in 1999. In 2000, exports to the United States reached $393 billion, while imports from the United States were $307 billion, giving Canada a trade surplus or positive trade balance. Interestingly, while Canada has maintained a positive trade balance with the United States, Canada has a negative trade balance with all other trading partners. (See Exhibit 8.9.) In 1995 the U.S. share of Canadian exports was 75%, and this share rose to 82.9% by 2000. During this same period, the U.S. share of our imports has remained relatively constant at about 72%.

- Ninety percent of Canada–U.S. trade is in goods, with 10% being trade in services. With regard to Canada's dependence on the United States, we observed that while Canada's merchandise exports to the United States grew by 79.4% over the period of 1995–2000, exports to the rest of the world dropped by 3.2%. By the same token, it can be noted that Canada is the largest trading partner of the United States. A major strength of Canada's exports is currently in transportation equipment, accounting for nearly one-third of merchandise exports to the United States. The manufacturing sector was the only one of the three sectors to increase its share of trade between 1990 and 1999.

NAFTA's Impact on Canadian Employment and Business

NAFTA's impact on employment and wages has not been clearly determined to date. Different groups have offered different information as to whether jobs have been lost or created as a result of free trade. The key controversy surrounding NAFTA is the issue of jobs. Do open trade and increases in foreign presence in a country result in job creation or job loss? If countries allow products or services to freely enter their borders, what happens to the domestic producers of such products or services?

Advocates of free trade say:

- Foreign competition forces domestic businesses to improve their operations and improve their products or services.
- Protecting domestic business amounts to discouraging competitiveness and innovation and, ultimately, will lead to job losses, given the inability to remain competitive in world markets.
- Free trade encourages countries to abort inefficient operations and focus on the relatively stronger commodities or services in which they have a competitive or comparative advantage.

Critics of free trade say:

- Many Canadian manufacturers cannot compete with U.S. imports, and will be forced out of business.
- Job losses could arise from U.S. companies deciding to shut down their Canadian subsidiaries and exporting their tariff-free goods to Canada.
- Many manufacturing jobs will be lost to Mexico, given that country's relatively cheaper labour and, hence, lower-priced goods.

NAFTA's Impact on Canadian Culture

Advocates of free trade say:

- The agreement is not signing away Canada's cultural heritage, any more than the European Community forced European nations to lose their individual cultures.
- According to Statistics Canada, Canadian cultural exports exceed $4.5 billion, and more royalty money for music is coming into Canada than is leaving. (See Let's Talk Business 8.11.)

LET'S TALK BUSINESS 8.11 CANADA'S MAGAZINES

Perhaps the fear of losing Canadian culture in the onslaught of big multinationals has been made most salient in the magazine industry. The potential for U.S.-based magazines to eventually monopolize the Canadian magazine market was an issue in recent years. This stemmed from a concern that split-run magazines (U.S. magazines produced cheaply in Canadian versions) would attract more Canadian advertisers because of their cheaper advertising rates and consequently force Canadian-based magazines to lose advertising revenues. This reflects a concern among media-based businesses that they will fall victim to foreign competitors who may not be as well equipped to communicate and perpetuate Canadian culture. Critics also remind us of the large level of foreign ownership in Canada — about 45% of Canada's manufacturing sector is foreign owned.

Critics of free trade say:

- Free trade will encourage the destruction of a unique Canadian culture.
- Increasing foreign domination of the Canadian economy will transform Canada into a pure economic subsidiary of the United States.
- Publishing and broadcasting industries are threatened by American competitors and the increasing presence of American-based media.
- The presence of the United States in areas like the Canadian entertainment industry would pose a serious threat to the transmission of Canadian culture.

NAFTA's Impact on Canadian Competitiveness and the Canadian Consumer

Advocates of free trade say:

- One of the central objectives of the FTA was to encourage Canadian businesses to become more competitive through exposing Canadian businesses to greater competition from American business.
- Canadian consumers are given more choice and exposed to competitive products with free trade. That is, they will have access to potentially less expensive goods or services — whether they come from the United States, or from increasingly competitive Canadian businesses.
- Canadian companies that require inputs from U.S. businesses can now obtain them more cheaply, and pass these savings on to the consumer.
- Canada cannot afford to ignore the U.S. market. If Canadian companies wish to become more competitive, they also need to serve a larger market — and the United States certainly offers a huge market for Canadian goods. Free trade gives Canada greater access to selling goods and services to this market through the reduction of trade barriers.

Critics of free trade say:

- NAFTA has not encouraged any increase in productivity. Canadians have been unable to match U.S. productivity rates for the past 20 years, and have produced at rates that are equal to about 80% of the output of workers in the United States.
- Productivity rates in the United States have increased at approximately twice the rate of Canadian productivity increases in recent years.
- Free trade failed one of its central objectives — to improve Canada's competitiveness.
- The success that Canada has experienced in international trade has been achieved largely through our relatively weak dollar.
- Just as Canadian businesses became complacent when tariffs protected them from foreign competition, so the weak Canadian dollar is artificially making Canadian businesses seem competitive. According to a report by Industry Canada, the depreciation of the Canadian dollar (by 22% over 1990–1998) was completely responsible for Canada's improved labour cost position in the 1990s.
- What is needed, arguably, is real improvements in productivity coming from things like updating equipment, retraining workers, and building competitiveness.
- Our good record of exports has come about largely because the relatively low value of the Canadian dollar has made our goods cheaper. In other words, it is not that we are producing cost-efficient goods, but rather it is an artificial reduction in the value of our dollar that has made them cheaper on foreign markets. Consequently, a higher Canadian dollar might result in decreased exports, given that Canadian goods would then likely be more expensive in foreign markets.

CHAPTER SUMMARY

There is little doubt that the phenomenon of globalization will have profound effects on businesses and societies across the world. In this chapter we tried to make sense of this phenomenon — what it entails and what are its implications. Specifically, we considered why organizations may "go global", and we identified the different types of global business activity. We examined the significance of multinational and borderless corporations. We also considered why nations desire, or do not desire, to promote international trade, including an examination of the pros and cons of Canada's free trade agreement with the United States. Is all this good or bad? That is, will the trend toward an increasingly integrated world economy benefit societies, or generate greater harm? What are the challenges and opportunities for managers in the global workplace? It is hoped that the material in this chapter has encouraged you to think more critically about these questions.

KEY TERMS

- globalization
- exporting
- importing
- outsourcing
- direct investment in foreign operations
- multinational corporation (MNC)
- borderless corporation
- international trade

- mercantilism
- trade surpluses
- trade protectionism
- tariff
- free trade area
- customs union
- common market
- economic union

CASE APPLICATION   Good-bye to another Canadian retailer

Future Shop, one of Canada's merchandising success stories, has been bought by giant U.S. retailer Best Buy Co. in a $580-million all-cash deal that headed off an expensive showdown between the two chains. Future Shop shareholders will get $17 a share — a 53 percent premium over the chain's closing price on the Toronto Stock Exchange over the last 20 days — a deal that came together relatively quickly.

As recently as a month ago, Future Shop said it planned to fight Best Buy's announced expansion into Canada by adding 30 stores to its 88-outlet countrywide chain. The deal will see the widely recognized Future Shop name disappear within three years, although executives from both firms say consumers will see few other changes because the two big-box chains have similar sales philosophies.

Best Buy is the biggest American retailer of consumer electronics and appliances, with 60,000 employees at 1,800 stores. Best Buy plans no layoffs among Future Shop's 7,000 employees and promised more hiring as the chain expands. Future Shop, founded by Iranian **emigre Hassan Khosrowshahi**, grew from one Vancouver store in 1982 to become Canada's largest retailer of home electronics, computers and appliances with sales of $2 billion in fiscal 2001. The company went public in 1993 and Inwest Investments Ltd., Khosrowshahi's family owned holding company, owns 70 percent of the shares.

Best Buy, with 1,800 U.S. stores selling under Best Buy and other brands, posted revenues of $15.3 billion US in the last fiscal year. The Minneapolis-based retailer was poised to move into Canada, opening 65 stores in the first phase of a planned global expansion. Best Buy chairman **Richard Schulze** said Tuesday he first put out feelers to Khosrowshahi a year ago for a potential buy-out. But after being refused, Best Buy began developing its own expansion plans, signing leases to open up to a dozen Canadian stores by next year. But as its plans began to materialize, Schulze said Best Buy recently renewed contact with Future Shop through intermediaries to see if anything had changed. "The response we got was clearly an interest in discussion," said Schulze. "Over the course of the last three or four weeks we came to the conclusion that together we could accomplish infinitely more." Schulze said the takeover gave Best Buy a faster, but not necessarily cheaper, entry into the Canadian market. "It was going to cost us something close to $600 million Cdn to do what it was we planned to do up here," he said.

Khosrowshahi, expressed little regret at turning over his operation. "It is a bittersweet decision but . . . at the end of the day it's a business decision," he said. "I believe the offer we received from Best Buy was fair, it was in the interest of our shareholders, it was in the interest of our employees, it's going to be in the interest of consumers." Retailing analyst George Hartman of Dundee Securities praised Khosrowshahi as a shrewd businessman who forced Best Buy to negotiate this buy-out by locking up prime store locations for its own planned expansion. "It was probably more advantageous to talk to Future Shop if Future Shop went ahead and tied up a lot of good real estate," Hartman said from Toronto.

Schulze told investment analysts on a conference call the acquisition should boost Best Buy's profits between one and two cents a share this fiscal year, adding five and 10 cents in fiscal 2003 and 2004, respectively. The impact on Future Shop's rivals is not yet clear. The chain competed across product sectors, from computers to music CDs and kitchen appliances, which put it up against everyone from record chains such as HMV to furniture stores like The Brick, department stores such as Sears Canada and regional audio chains such as Quebec's DuMoulin. A&B Sound, a Vancouver-based chain with 21 stores in Western Canada, is not scared by the takeover, said president Tim Howley. "I think it will make it more of a challenge," Howley said from Calgary, on the way to open a new store in Winnipeg. "There are strong [specialty] regional players that have not only done well, they have thrived when a Best Buy comes to town because they've figured out how to differentiate themselves and make themselves that much closer to their customer base."

Future Shop will operate as a separate Canadian subsidiary of Best Buy and there are no plans to change the signs on the stores "to begin with," said Schulze. "Our intent has always been that Best Buy would be a global brand," he added, noting the two chains are very similar. The brand change will take place somewhere between one and three years, Schulze said. He acknowledged Future Shop's name recognition on the Canadian market but "but we're pretty proud of Best Buy." One change for employees, said Layden, will be a gradual shift from Future Shop's commission-based wages to straight salaries used at Best Buy outlets. Schulze said there is no cost advantage in moving away from commission-based sales but it has enabled Best Buy to offer higher levels of service. Layden also said Future Shop's head office now will review Best Buy's Canadian leasing deals to see which mesh with expansion plans. "There are some sites Best Buy has signed up for that will make excellent Future Shop locations," he said.

Source: Steve Mertl, Canadian Press, "Best Buy to acquire top Canadian electronics retailer Future Shop for $580M" *National Post* (August 14, 2001). Reproduced with permission from the Canadian Press.

QUESTIONS

1. How does this case reflect themes of globalization?

2. How are the following parties potentially affected by this takeover? Discuss both the potential benefits and negative consequences that each may experience as a result: Best Buy, Future Shop, Canadian employment, the Canadian consumer, the Canadian economy, Canadian competitors in this industry, global competitors in this industry.

3. "The Canadian government should protect Canadian business from both foreign competition and takeovers." Discuss the merits of this statement.

Global Skies

Sir Richard Branson isn't sure about the crab cakes. Or the pesto chicken breast, or even the sauteed calf's liver. As our waiter at the Café Victoria in Toronto's King Edward Hotel lingers patiently, the British billionaire scans the luncheon menu, baffled by the offerings. "Just get me anything low in cholesterol," he finally relents.

I'm impressed by how quickly he's digested Canadian culture. Here only a few hours — to prep the market for the June launch of Virgin Atlantic Airways' Toronto-to-London route — he's already learned that in these parts, choice can be a pain. But is this the same Richard Branson who descended on Toronto in his trademark red chopper last November, sporting a hockey uniform, to announce that he would convince the federal government to give Virgin a crack at Canada's domestic market as well — Just like he'd done in Australia and South Africa. Since then, Ottawa has told Branson to take off. The reason, says Brian Carr, Transport Canada's director of international air policy, is that when it comes to airlines, only our own kind need apply. That, he explains, is because of regulations as old as air service itself — "from an era of economic nationalism" — that grant airlines special status. Like broadcasters, publishers and bookstores, airlines supposedly represent part of our "cultural identity."

Branson doesn't buy it. "Airlines have nothing to do with national culture," he says. (And remember, this guy happens to own a few broadcasters, publishers and bookstores himself, along with other holdings.) Pretending that it is, Branson argues, "hasn't benefited the other 99.9% of companies in the country — it hasn't benefited the consumer and it actually hasn't benefited the flight carriers themselves." You need look no further than Air Canada, which is running about as smoothly as a Paris air show.

Maybe Branson's right. Maybe airlines aren't an essential strand in the Canadian cultural fabric. But Air Canada suggests some people are concerned that a foreign carrier would exploit major routes and leave far-flung Canadian towns out to dry (though nothing stops it from doing the same). Realistically, Branson argues, "the high costs of Air Canada, years of unions pressing for higher salaries, means they are less capable of operating the thinner routes than a newcomer." Besides, if the government were really worried about smaller markets, it would be better to subsidize any airline that wanted to serve them.

All this so-called protectionism, Branson says, doesn't protect us at all. It doesn't even protect shareholders. (Besides Air Canada's notorious inefficiencies, being an impossible takeover target keeps shares undervalued.)

"Protectionism is just a euphemism for protecting the status quo," says Branson. "People in positions of power are often there because of the status quo. They don't want to upset things." So when agents of global change like Branson fly into town with a planeload of capital and a cargo of fresh ideas, we don't roll out the first-class treatment. We just close the airport.

True, we don't need foreign airlines. We'll survive with the meager competition that allows Ottawa to pretend Air Canada really has to work hard to win customers. But in today's global economy, we will not survive with legislators who don't embrace innovation

—wherever it's from. Bucking the status quo, says Branson, "takes brave ministers—but without them, a country just stagnates." After all, how much faith can we put in Ottawa's vow to connect Canadians with high-speed Internet access when it can't even connect them with efficient air travel? Globally, warns Branson, "your country is at a disadvantage."

Yet another cultural subtlety picked up on. After only a few months, our government has proven to be more stubborn than Australia's or South Africa's—and has succeeded in driving the brave knight away. "Realistically, I think the government here isn't going to open up the skies for the time being," Branson confides. "I think we'll take our investments elsewhere." Then the waiter arrives with our food. It looks like fish, though Branson doesn't even bother asking what kind. "I'm happy to eat whatever's put in front of me," he says, tucking in. Boy, this guy's a fast learner.

Source: Kevin Libin, "Take off, hosers" *Canadian Business* (April 16, 2001). Reproduced with permission of the publisher.

QUESTIONS

1. How is the issue of globalization related to this article?

2. What is the author's point regarding foreign entry into this Canadian industry?

3. What is your opinion?

The Government–Business Relationship

The traditional relationship between government and business is clearly undergoing change. In this chapter, we will examine how government can intervene in business activity while fulfilling its role as both guardian of society and guardian of business. We will consider current and critically important trends regarding the shift toward reduced government involvement in the business sector. Specific attention will be paid to the issues of deregulation and privatization.

LEARNING OBJECTIVES

By the end of the chapter, you should be able to:

1. Describe the fundamental nature of the Canadian business enterprise system.

2. Discuss government's relationship with business with reference to government's guardianship of society.

3. Identify the functions of the Competition Bureau.

4. Explain the notion of government as guardian of the private business sector.

5. Discuss government's role with regard to global business.

6. Describe the objectives and consequences of deregulation and privatization.

Organizational Insider ───────────────────────

A Hard Case of Softwood

The softwood lumber dispute waging between Canada and the United States represents the most important economic challenge facing Ottawa today. The battle puts tens of thousands of jobs at stake as a result of dishonest harassment by the Yanks. And underlying this latest attack against Canada's lumber exports, involving a 19.3% duty, is a piece of new legislation that is nothing more than state-sanctioned theft in contravention of standing trade agreements. It's a threat to all Canadian exporters and to free trade itself.

The duty against softwood lumber was imposed after the United States argued that Canada's lumber producers are essentially subsidized because they cut down trees on publicly owned land and pay lower royalties than U.S. lumber producers whose trees grow on private lands. However, this argument is totally dishonest. If it's true, then why aren't U.S. forestry companies going after their Canadian pulp and paper counterparts — whose trees come from the same publicly owned lands? And why aren't U.S. mining companies going after Canadian miners who extract metals and minerals on public lands? Why aren't they after Canada's oil producers, who operate on mostly public lands, for that matter?

Why? Because the public lands argument is a crock and that's the reason U.S. regulators aren't using that argument in other sectors or with other products. What really angers the U.S. regulators behind the softwood duty dispute is that Canada's lumber producers are the first group in Canadian business history to out-compete the United States significantly in the U.S. marketplace. And the United States doesn't like it, even though it represents its business community as the champions of competition.

Canada's lumber guys have captured an unheard of 34% market share south of the border because of their superior product and service. This has never been accomplished by any other Canadian sector and the success has come at the expense of hundreds of little, inefficient U.S. sawmill and wood lot owners. U.S. regulators are being dishonest because they aren't making the same subsidy argument against other resource outfits operating on public lands. This is because nobody there cares about other industries at the moment. After all, pulp and paper sales south of the border are minuscule in terms of market share. Metals, minerals, oil and natural gas sold in the United States don't replace U.S. supplies. The United States doesn't have enough of these commodities, and it is happy to let Canadian producers export to them in whatever quantities they wish to sell. Lying is bad enough but what's most worrisome, in my opinion, about the softwood lumber situation is that for the first time the United States is stealing as well as being downright dishonest.

New legislation passed last year instructs that the billions of dollars in duties collected from Canadians must be handed out proportionally to U.S. lumber producers — not retained by the federal government, as has been the practice in the United States and everywhere else in the past. In other words, Washington is now going to subsidize U.S. businesses by confiscating proceeds from their most successful foreign competitors. If Canada had similar legislation, we could impose a 20% duty on Microsoft products and distribute the proceeds to rival Canadian software companies because Microsoft dominates the market. We could skim 20% of revenue earned in Canada from Hollywood films and hand millions of dollars over to struggling Canadian film producers. But such redistribution would constitute an illegal subsidy in contravention of all trade agreements. Canada would have to sue in world courts and attack the legislation in trade courts, too. Instead, Ottawa has been attacking only the decision to impose duties against softwood lumber. I think that some kind of political negotiation should resolve the softwood dispute. This has happened before. It is unfair, but is a form of managed trade. The legislation must be attacked because it is a de facto subsidy and is patently illegal. Unchallenged, this law threatens to escalate the problem for Canada and other trading nations and to involve other sectors and products. That's because it will encourage harassment. Any individual or group who has lost market share to imports can simply hire expensive attorney after expensive attorney until a case for injury is made. Once successful, they can then become subsidized, and have their legal costs covered by the foreign competitors they took to task — even if their loss of market share is their own fault.

What it means is that Canadians are free to sell their goods in the United States, but not successfully. Even worse, the new law means that the U.S. government will steal the profit of any hugely successful Canadian exporter and use the funds to subsidize less successful U.S. competitors. This new law is neither free trade nor fair trade nor managed trade. It's trade theft.

Source: Diane Francis, "Softwood duty a tax on success: Lumber law just subsidizes weak U.S. competitors" *Financial Post* (September 4, 2001). Reproduced with permission of National Post.

THE CANADIAN BUSINESS ENTERPRISE SYSTEM: FUNDAMENTAL FEATURES

The Organizational Insider highlights the significance of government's role in business activity. In fact, historically, government has played a critical role in the Canadian economy. From our very beginning as a nation, the government has taken responsibility for the success of business. It is useful to briefly consider the nature of our economic or business enterprise system, within which all business operates. The Canadian economic system has been described as a mixed system. This refers to the notion that while we possess a capitalist economy, government nonetheless plays an important role.

All developed countries have some sort of economic or business enterprise system that essentially determines:

1. What goods and services are produced and distributed to society.
2. How the goods and services are produced and distributed to society.

What kind of business enterprise system we have determines how or by whom these decisions are made. For example, the two decisions above might be made purely by business, or they might be determined by government, or perhaps by a combination of the two. To understand the basis of our Canadian business enterprise system, it is necessary to understand the nature of capitalist economic systems. So let's briefly explain what capitalism is.

Capitalism is a type of economic system that is based on a number of fundamental principles, including:

1. **Rights of the Individual.** The notion of capitalism is based on the view that it is the individual who takes precedence in society, as opposed to institutions, or the overall society. This implies that the individual has every right to pursue their own self-interest, which includes seeking to make profits from business enterprises. The notion of the individual as the most important element of society is not entirely representative of the ideology present in Canadian society. There are limits placed on individuals' right to pursue their self-interest. Government regulations enforce rules that affect how business owners conduct their affairs. For example, government guidelines regarding job candidate selection criteria may affect who is hired for a job, and place emphasis on certain groups in society over others.

2. **Rights of Private Property.** As opposed to state ownership, capitalism asserts that individuals have the right to own land, labour and capital. In Canada, certainly, individuals are permitted to own their means of production, whether it is land, labour or capital. However, because there has been an uneven distribution of wealth in society, the government has intervened in a number of ways. For example, taxation is one approach that can be partly aimed at redistributing wealth among members of society. Much of the natural resources in Canada have still been retained by federal or provincial governments. The government may also decide that where a product or service is of a national interest, this product or service should be nationalized — e.g., government control of health care.

3. **Competition.** Capitalism advocates competition. The belief is that sufficient competition among business enterprises will ensure that business provides the goods and services required by society at a fair cost. Competition is the "invisible hand" (in the words of economist Adam Smith) that ensures the market works in this manner. In Canada, the notion of "perfect competition" does not exist in practice — there is no guarantee that an adequate supply of competitors exists across all industries.

4. **The Role of Government.** The view of government is reflected in the French term *laissez faire*, which means "let people do as they choose". This suggests minimal government interference in the business enterprise system. This notion of capitalism has also been referred to as the "free enterprise system", reflecting the notion of the right to private ownership of property, competition, and restricted government involvement.

Of course, the polar extreme of capitalism is another economic system referred to as **communism**. Whereas the capitalist system allows individuals or businesses the responsibility for the allocation of resources, the communist system, on the other hand, places the responsibility for the allocation of society's resources into the hands of the government. There really are no societies today that are purely capitalist or communist. Canada has been referred to as a "mixed economy" because, while it is primarily a capitalist-based economy, government does play a role in the business enterprise system. In Canada, government does intervene in the affairs of business. Business is not left entirely to conduct its own affairs. When Canada first came into existence as a country, the federal government was granted the power to "regulate trade and commerce". And the fact is, throughout our history, the government has played a major role in fostering industrial development, and continues to provide significant support to the business sector.

GOVERNMENT AS GUARDIAN OF SOCIETY

Exhibit 9.1 illustrates the variety of ways government can influence business activity: issues that we explore in the sections below.

Collecting Taxes from Business

Government plays many roles in relation to business. The most obvious role, and perhaps the least popular one, is that of government as tax collector, whether it is at the federal, provincial or local level. There are two broad forms of taxes: revenue taxes and regulatory or restrictive taxes. The intent of revenue taxes is to collect money in order to help fund government services and programs. **Revenue taxes** include individual taxes as well as corporate income tax, along with property tax and sales tax. **Individual income taxes** have provided the largest source of revenue for the federal and provincial governments. Individual income tax is levied on the income of individuals or on the net profits of proprietorships and partnerships. **Corporate income tax** has provided the second largest source of

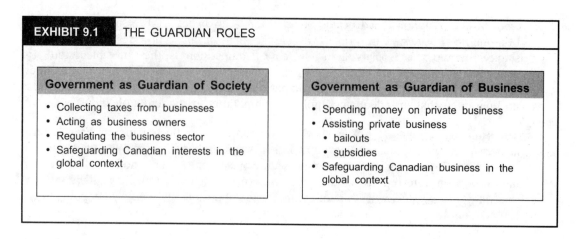

EXHIBIT 9.1   THE GUARDIAN ROLES

Government as Guardian of Society

- Collecting taxes from businesses
- Acting as business owners
- Regulating the business sector
- Safeguarding Canadian interests in the global context

Government as Guardian of Business

- Spending money on private business
- Assisting private business
  - bailouts
  - subsidies
- Safeguarding Canadian business in the global context

revenue for the federal government. Corporations are taxed on their net profit at a combined federal and provincial rate that can vary among provinces, and are subject to change based on government policy. Government policy may include an agenda of manipulating taxation to stimulate government investment or to raise more revenues.

Sales taxes are an important source of revenue for most provinces, as well as for the federal government. This tax is paid through retail stores, which act as collection agents when they sell their goods to consumers. The Goods and Services Tax (GST) that came into effect in 1991 provides substantial funds to the federal government. It is a value-added tax — a tax that is paid at each step of the manufacturing process. Consider, for example: a producer buys raw materials from a supplier, and the GST is charged by the supplier. The producer may then work on the raw materials and produce a part for sale to a manufacturer, who is then charged GST on that purchase. Everyone involved in the goods or services production pays GST, but only the final consumer, obviously, cannot pass the tax on to another party.

Finally, another well-known form of taxation is **property taxes**, which have been the largest revenue source for municipal governments. The revenue gained from this form of tax is typically used to fund the operating costs of the municipal government and the services that it generates.

As mentioned earlier, the second broad form of taxation is referred to as **restrictive or regulatory taxes**. There are two main types of regulatory taxes, referred to as excise taxes and customs duties or tariffs. Restrictive taxes are primarily aimed at controlling or curbing the use of specific products or services. **Excise taxes** typically are applied to goods or services, the purchase of which the government desires to restrict, such as products deemed to be potentially harmful (including tobacco and alcohol products). It has also been considered a deterrent to potential excesses, so to speak. In fact, way back in 1976, the federal government actually levied an additional tax on gasoline to discourage overuse in order to help conserve what was then a product in very short supply. Whatever the source, excise taxes are, essentially, a selective sales tax. **Tariffs** are also a form of restrictive taxes, and the purpose of tariffs is detailed elsewhere in this book.

Acting as Business Owner: Crown Corporations

What is a Crown corporation? A Crown corporation or public enterprise is an organization accountable, through a minister, to parliament for its operations. Crown corporations may be federal (e.g., Canada Post, the Canadian Broadcasting Corporation (CBC), the Canadian Wheat Board) or provincial: the Liquor Control Board of Ontario (LCBO), for example. (See Exhibit 9.2.)

Whether federal or provincial, why are Crown corporations established? Governments establish Crown corporations for a number of possible reasons:

- **To implement public policy that includes protecting or safeguarding national interests.** For example, federal Crown corporations, such as Air Canada and Petro-Canada, helped facilitate government policy in the area of cross-Canada transportation and Canadian ownership in the domestic oil industry.

- **To protect industries deemed to be vital to the economy.** The Canadian Radio Broadcasting Commission was established by the Canadian government in 1932 to administer a national broadcasting service in order to prevent Canadian broadcasting becoming inundated with material originating in the United States. Similarly, this was a reason for taking control of the Canadian National Railways. The CNR originated in 1919 in order to "safeguard the government's large investment in the railways" and "to protect Canada's image in foreign capital markets". While few municipal governments have traditionally held significant corporate holdings, they have been owners of public transit systems, recreational centres and other facilities that are intended to enhance the quality of life in society.

- **To provide special services that could not otherwise be made available by private business.** For example, Trans Canada Airlines (Air Canada) was established in the 1930s, after observing that no private business was willing or able to provide domestic air services. Consider also the Bank of Canada. The Bank of Canada, created in 1935, was established to first serve as a control agent for the chartered banks: for example, requiring the banks to report regularly on their operations and to hold deposit reserves with the Bank of Canada. Second, the Bank of Canada is responsible for developing monetary policy and regulating monetary operations in Canada.

- **To nationalize industries that were considered to be "natural monopolies", including the generation and distribution of electricity.** It is not hard to imagine that in the early days of Canadian society the private sector was too small to undertake the creation of a national electricity supply grid. On the other hand, government was capable of raising the necessary capital and, consequently, it took on the establishment of public utilities, including things like water supply, sewage treatment plants, and electricity generating plants, in addition to road construction and the like. In some cases, there were companies capable of building their own private utilities, which then became subject to government regulation, as we will discuss further below.

Each Crown corporation is a legally distinct entity wholly owned by the Crown, and each is managed by a board of directors. The recent range of Crown corporations has been relatively diverse, with corporations operating in a variety of areas of the economy. Naturally, the corporations differ with regard to their public policy purpose, as well as in their size and in their relative need for government financial support.

EXHIBIT 9.2	PARENT CROWN CORPORATIONS

Agriculture and Agri-Food

- Canadian Dairy Commission
- Farm Credit Corporation

Canadian Heritage

- Canada Council
- Canadian Broadcasting Corporation
- Canadian Film Development Corporation
- Canadian Museum of Civilization Corporation
- Canadian Museum of Nature
- Canadian Race Relations Foundation
- National Arts Centre Corporation
- National Capital Commission
- National Gallery of Canada
- National Museum of Science and Technology Corporation

Finance

- Bank of Canada
- Canada Deposit Insurance Corporation
- Canada Development Investment Corporation
- Canada Pension Plan Investment Board
- Petro-Canada Limited

Fisheries and Oceans

- Freshwater Fish Marketing Corporation

Foreign Affairs

- International Development Research Centre

Industry

- Business Development Bank of Canada
- Enterprise Cape Breton Corporation
- Standards Council of Canada

International Trade

- Canadian Commercial Corporation
- Export Development Corporation

Natural Resources

- Atomic Energy of Canada Limited
- Cape Breton Development Corporation

Public Works and Government Services

- Canada Lands Company Limited
- Canada Mortgage and Housing Corporation
- Canada Post Corporation
- Defence Construction (1951) Limited
- Old Port of Montreal Corporation Inc.[1]
- Queens Quay West Land Corporation
- Royal Canadian Mint

Transport

- Atlantic Pilotage Authority
- Canada Ports Corporation
- Federal Bridge Corporation Limited, The
- Great Lakes Pilotage Authority
- Laurentian Pilotage Authority
- Marine Atlantic Inc.
- Pacific Pilotage Authority
- VIA Rail Canada Inc.

Treasury Board[2]

- Public Sector Pension Investment Board

Notes

1. The Old Port of Montreal Corporation Inc., a wholly owned subsidiary of the Canada Lands Company Limited, has been directed by Order in Council (P.C. 1987-86) to report as if it were a parent Crown corporation.
2. President of the Treasury Board. The Public Sector Investment Board commenced operations on April 1, 2000.

Source: Treasury Board of Canada, *2000 Annual Report to Parliament — Crown Corporations and Other Corporate Interests of Canada.* Online: <www.tbs-sct.gc.ca/report/CROWN/00/cc-se1_e.htm>. (Last accessed: 01-07-18.)

EXHIBIT 9.3	EMPLOYMENT IN CROWN CORPORATIONS

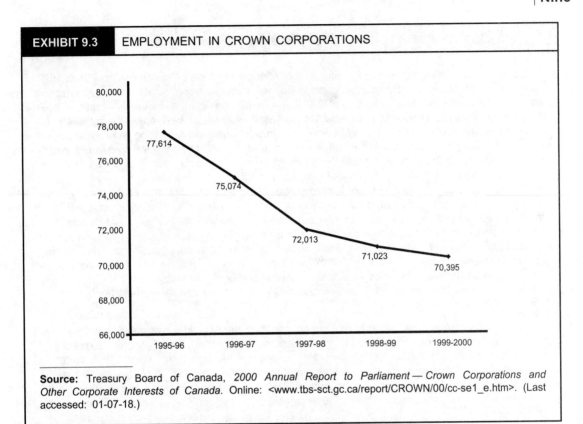

Source: Treasury Board of Canada, *2000 Annual Report to Parliament — Crown Corporations and Other Corporate Interests of Canada.* Online: <www.tbs-sct.gc.ca/report/CROWN/00/cc-se1_e.htm>. (Last accessed: 01-07-18.)

Employment in Crown corporations has been steadily decreasing, though at a somewhat lower rate than in earlier years. For example, the total number of Crown employees was 70,395 in 1999–2000, a decrease of 0.9%, compared to a 1.4% decrease over the previous two years. This trend is illustrated in Exhibit 9.3.

Many observers suggested that, traditionally, there has been a great reliance on Crown corporations in the Canadian context. For example, by the late 1980s there were 53 parent Crown corporations (at the federal level) and 114 wholly owned subsidiaries, employing about 180,000 people, and maintaining assets worth approximately $60 billion. By 2000, the number of parent Crown corporations stood at 41.

The LCBO is a provincial Crown corporation in the sense that it is owned by the province of Ontario. Technically, it is also an agency of the Ministry of Consumer and Commercial Relations. It receives its purchasing directives from the Cabinet's Management Board Secretariat, and it abides by the same regulations, laws and trade agreements that govern purchasing for all provincial government departments. For many years, the Liquor Control Board of Ontario (LCBO) has been the largest single retailer (and the largest buyer) of alcoholic beverages in the world. By 2000 it had established five regional warehouses and was supplying 602 stores across Ontario with over 7,000 products. In the year

---

LET'S TALK BUSINESS 9.1   TOASTING THE LCBO?

The LCBO was named Innovative Retailer of the Year by the Retail Council of Canada in 1997 and 1998. For some observers, the combination of award-winning retailer and government agency seems unusual. In addition, to critics, it seems paradoxical that this organization is both a government regulator and at the same time a highly successful business. The question, for some, is: In what ways do the public benefit from this organization remaining as a state-owned corporation? Certainly, one benefit includes the fact that the LCBO generates over a billion dollars in revenue for the provincial treasury. In addition, one can argue that it operates in a purchasing environment that private retailers might find difficult to operate within. In fact, while there has been traditional criticism of Crown corporations as inefficient, the LCBO has typically been run like a successful, profitable private business. Consequently, criticism of the LCBO tends not to focus on its business acumen but rather focuses on the philosophical debate over whether state-owned enterprises should be operating in the domain of the private sector. In blunt terms, critics view the LCBO as another case of an unnecessary government-run monopoly. In fact, critics have asserted that improvements in their operations and continued expansion are aimed at preserving their monopoly power and avoiding privatization, rather than being aimed at helping the consumer. These sceptical views of the LCBO were summarized in an article by Terence Corcoran:

> With a few exceptions, nobody in Ontario can buy beer or liquor at any other retail outlet, not at corner stores nor in supermarkets. All alcoholic sales, therefore, must pass through an expensive system that keeps prices high and wages high and deprives entrepreneurs of the right to enter the business unless they join the large black market. The number of jobs that could be created by opening the market to competition is substantial. When Alberta privatized liquor retailing, employment in the industry tripled.... The monopolies also impose significant hidden costs on consumers. Even with the recent increase in the number of retail locations, buyers must make special trips, often involving many miles of travel and wasteful expenditures of time — costs that are not measured in the already high mark-ups....[1]

Source: [1] Terence Corcoran, "Ontario: Monopoly's Friend" *The Globe and Mail* (November 18, 1997).

1999–2000, it delivered approximately 283 million litres of alcoholic beverages to Ontario consumers. Net sales were $2.55 billion in the fiscal year 1999–2000, and as of March 1999, the total estimated value of Ontario's beverage alcohol market was $6.6 billion. (See Let's Talk Business 9.1.)

As Let's Talk Business 9.1 indicates, Crown corporations have both their advocates and critics. The state-owned liquor outlet of the Societe des Alcohols du Quebec receives the same type of praise and criticism as the LCBO. It has been viewed as a well-managed business with excellent customer service. On the other hand, critics also argue that private food retailers would like to be allowed to enter the alcohol sales industry more fully, given that the potential for profits is very lucrative. This sentiment also argues for privatization — the expansion of private industry into what has traditionally been the domain of the public sector.

There are other examples, globally, of state-owned corporations that are struggling to avoid privatization as well as to compete with private businesses. For example, according to recent reports,[180] European post offices are making great efforts to upgrade themselves because their two basic businesses — delivering letters and delivering parcels — are both threatened by e-mail and competition from U.S. market leaders Federal Express Corp. and United Parcel Service Inc. At stake is the state post office's concern for control of Europe's $27 billion fast-growing parcel service. Observers note that Europe's big postal bureaucracies have continued to lose ground, and are also losing their domestic letter monopolies in 2003 because of European Union deregulation. Below, we will discuss in more detail the issue of privatization and deregulation.

Regulating the Business Sector

Government economic regulation has been defined as "the imposition of constraints, backed by the authority of a government, that are intended to modify economic behaviour in the private sector significantly".[181] As Exhibit 9.4 indicates, there has been a relatively wide scope for government regulation in business activity: for example, regulation focused on consumer protection, regulation aimed at environmental protection and regulation regarding the nature of competition. One obvious set of regulations exists fundamentally to protect the consumer, and the Canadian government has initiated a number of programs designed for consumer protection, many of which are administered by the Department of Consumer and Corporate Affairs — a body that plays a major role in regulating business in Canada. Among the numerous regulations, there is, for example, the Food and Drug Act, which was designed to protect the public from potential risks to health as well as from fraud or deception as it relates to food, drugs, cosmetics and the like. Similarly, the Hazardous Products Act serves to protect public safety by either banning products because they are deemed dangerous or requiring warning labels on products that might be considered hazardous. Ecological regulations are designed to protect the environment, and include things like the Environmental Contaminants Act, which creates regulations to limit any dangerous by-products of industrial production that could be harmful to individuals' health.

Why does the government need to intervene in the functioning of the business enterprise system? Consider the notions of competition and the public interest, discussed below.

Imperfect Competition

One fundamental shortcoming in the market system — the presence of imperfect, as opposed to perfect, competition — suggests the need for government involvement. If you recall our earlier discussion of the nature of the business enterprise system, we identified it as a system that essentially determines what goods and services are produced and distributed to society; and how they are produced and distributed. Ideally, such a system produces all the goods and services a society wants at a fair price. In very basic terms, on the demand side, decisions are made by individuals regarding their tastes or preferences for certain goods or services. On the supply side, businesses aim to meet the demands

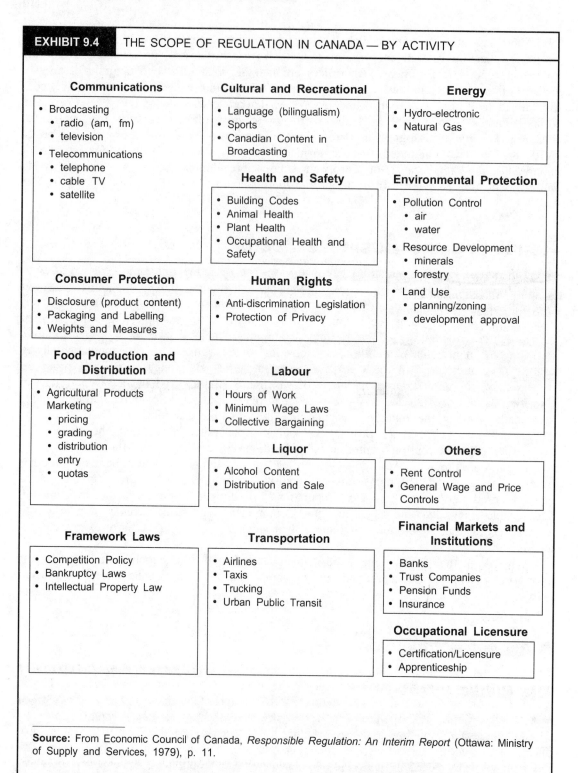

EXHIBIT 9.4 THE SCOPE OF REGULATION IN CANADA — BY ACTIVITY

Communications

- Broadcasting
  - radio (am, fm)
  - television
- Telecommunications
  - telephone
  - cable TV
  - satellite

Cultural and Recreational

- Language (bilingualism)
- Sports
- Canadian Content in Broadcasting

Energy

- Hydro-electronic
- Natural Gas

Health and Safety

- Building Codes
- Animal Health
- Plant Health
- Occupational Health and Safety

Environmental Protection

- Pollution Control
  - air
  - water
- Resource Development
  - minerals
  - forestry
- Land Use
  - planning/zoning
  - development approval

Consumer Protection

- Disclosure (product content)
- Packaging and Labelling
- Weights and Measures

Human Rights

- Anti-discrimination Legislation
- Protection of Privacy

Food Production and Distribution

- Agricultural Products Marketing
  - pricing
  - grading
  - distribution
  - entry
  - quotas

Labour

- Hours of Work
- Minimum Wage Laws
- Collective Bargaining

Liquor

- Alcohol Content
- Distribution and Sale

Others

- Rent Control
- General Wage and Price Controls

Framework Laws

- Competition Policy
- Bankruptcy Laws
- Intellectual Property Law

Transportation

- Airlines
- Taxis
- Trucking
- Urban Public Transit

Financial Markets and Institutions

- Banks
- Trust Companies
- Pension Funds
- Insurance

Occupational Licensure

- Certification/Licensure
- Apprenticeship

Source: From Economic Council of Canada, *Responsible Regulation: An Interim Report* (Ottawa: Ministry of Supply and Services, 1979), p. 11.

they face. The "invisible hand" of competition transforms these decisions of demand and supply into a system that uses scarce resources in the most efficient manner. In other words, business supply will be responsive to consumer demand: those products and services that are needed most will demand increased production, while those no longer in demand can only be sold with a drop in price; or, ultimately, businesses that do not serve any demand would go bankrupt. If a resource becomes scarce, its price will increase, and this may lead consumers to shift their preferences to a less costly alternative. In this sense, by allowing individuals and businesses to follow self-interest, the market system is responsive to consumer needs and to the capability of the environment. However, the system does not work flawlessly and, in fact, there are challenges to the effective functioning of this system. One such challenge is the notion of **imperfect competition**.

Generally, businesses aim to reduce competition as a means of succeeding and prospering. The fewer the competitors, the more secure a business becomes. Of course, on the consumer's side, the ideal scenario is perfect competition: where, essentially, there is an optimal number of competitors in any given industry to ensure fair pricing and distribution of the goods or services at the highest possible level of quality. In such a situation, those businesses unable to compete will be replaced by more efficient competitors. Imperfect competition is, quite simply, the case where fewer than the optimal number of competitors exist to ensure this type of situation. Where there are an insufficient number of competitors, there is less pressure on businesses to offer the best possible good or service at the lowest possible price. Businesses that are not worried about competition are also not worried about innovating, managing their operations at peak efficiency, improving product/service quality, or offering their product/service at competitive prices. Consequently, inefficient businesses will remain, and consumers will be forced to accept those types of products or services, at prices dictated by those businesses. Overall, society is, then, offered fewer of the goods and services citizens really want than they would be in the situation where competition was stronger. This also leads to a less efficient use of society's resources, than in the case of perfect competition, where resources are divided among various activities in a manner that would generate the optimal combination of goods and services desired by consumers. For example, industries that lack sufficient competition may choose to restrict their output as a means to maintain higher prices, as opposed to the case of perfect competition, where businesses must accept prices determined by the market.

It is relatively easy to see, with an understanding of the notion of imperfect competition, that the market system itself will not necessarily guarantee the best and most efficient use of resources to generate the optimal mix of products and services for consumers at fair prices. Consequently, this is one fundamental rationale for government intervention in business.

The Public Interest

One of the central objectives of government regulation is to protect the public interest. Instead of having to establish their own public enterprise, government can control the operations of a private enterprise through regulations. Consequently, what we see in some areas of business is government regulation of businesses through commissions, tribunals, agencies and boards. National regulators include the **Canadian Transport Commission**, which judges route and rate applications for commercial air and railway companies. In terms of provincial regulatory bodies, for example, like the provincial liquor boards, provincial boards or commissions will assess and judge proposals from private business. Liquor boards, for example, are responsible for approving any price changes proposed by breweries within their province. The **Canadian Radio-television and Telecommunications Commission** (CRTC), under the auspices of the Department of Communications, regulates the telecommunications industry and its carriers, such as Bell Canada, and its traditional responsibilities have included accepting or refusing requests for rate increases among these carriers. Exhibit 9.4 summarizes the scope of regulation in Canada.

The government has also established a competition policy to control the nature of competition in the business sector. Earlier, we identified the importance of competition in our economy, given its ability to encourage the production and distribution of goods and services at the lowest possible cost. Consequently, the competition policy, set out in the Competition Act, is intended to stimulate open competition and eliminate any restrictive business practices with the aim of encouraging maximum production, distribution and employment opportunities. The role of the Competition Bureau is discussed in Let's Talk Business 9.2.

We have, for example, government regulation in the area of public utilities, such as an electric power company or a telephone company. The government has regulated this

---

LET'S TALK BUSINESS 9.2   THE ROLE OF THE COMPETITION BUREAU

Competition policy is aimed at creating equity in the marketplace among all the different and potentially competing interests, including: consumers and producers; wholesalers and retailers; dominant players and minor players; the public interest and the private interest. The Competition Bureau (under the auspices of the Department of Industry or Industry Canada) is responsible for enforcing and administering the Competition Act, and it has four main functions:

1. The Bureau informs companies of what they can and cannot do under competition law. It also informs consumers with regard to their rights.
2. The Bureau takes on an advocacy role in promoting greater competition in the business sector. For example, the Bureau has been actively involved in the deregulation process of the telecommunications sector, including its numerous appearances before the CRTC to urge regulators to take the least restrictive action possible so as to minimize the level of regulation, and therefore maximize potential competition.
3. The Bureau closely reviews mergers prior to their occurrence in order to ensure that they do not lead to undue concentration that would limit competition.
4. The Bureau seeks to rectify anti-competitive activities, including: the use of suasion (warning letters, visits, interviews, etc.); enforcing compliance by obtaining injunctions, consent orders, adoption of voluntary codes; or prosecuting for violations of the Competition Act.

Source: Based on Statement by Konrad von Finckenstein, Q.C. Commissioner of Competition Bureau to the "Meet the Competition Bureau," Forum Insight Conference, Toronto (May 3, 1999).

industry because there has traditionally been an absence of competition there. Consequently, the public utilities boards or commission that regulates the industry will monitor the performance of the company, as well as assess requests for rate increases and changes in the types of services provided. Consider, for example, the CRTC, which, among other things, regulates the Canadian broadcasting system. The CRTC is responsible for issuing broadcasting licences, and can require companies seeking such a licence to conform with standards regarding the type or content of programming they will provide. Their responsibilities extend far beyond broadcasting, and also govern the nature of competition in the telecommunications and media industries. For example, in the telecommunications industry, there are regulations regarding the permissible amount of foreign ownership. Specifically, non-Canadians are not permitted to own more than 20% of voting shares in telecommunications and media companies, or 33.3% of holding companies. In 2001, the government's Broadband Task Force released a report recommending the Chrétien government change foreign ownership rules to permit greater foreign investment and, consequently, increase competition in that industry. Part of the aim for this initiative was to encourage the supply of high-speed Internet service to all communities in Canada as soon as possible. Companies such as AT & T have been lobbying the Canadian government and the CRTC to relax foreign ownership regulations in this industry and to force Bell to offer access to its wires to competing service providers at wholesale prices. The argument is that such deregulation would stimulate needed competition in Canada's telephone, cable and Internet providers, and avoid potential monopolization by Bell Canada Enterprises.[182]

Safeguarding the Interests of Canadian Society in the Global Context

An Example: U.S. Magazines in Canada

The notion of preserving national identity or culture has been an argument for limiting the extent of foreign ownership in the Canadian business context, particularly where such businesses are involved in cultural activities, such as the television media and popular press. One such example was the recent controversy with dual-run U.S. publications in Canada, which has lasted for several years. The controversy centres on split-run magazines — which are essentially U.S.-produced magazines like *Time* or *Sports Illustrated* — whose Canadian edition carries Canadian advertising, but little in the way of Canadian editorial content, and which offer very inexpensive advertising rates in this "Canadian edition" of the magazine. Because split-run magazines have no additional editorial or design costs, the publishers can offer advertising at a rate well below the price required by Canadian produced publications.

The WTO initially ruled that it would be unfair for Canada to ban outright these split-run magazines. In June 1999, a compromise deal between Canada and the United States was reached that gave U.S. split-run magazines limited access to the Canadian advertising market (American publishers will eventually be able to sell up to 18% of their ads to Canadian advertisers). The United States threatened $3 billion in trade sanctions if Ottawa went ahead with proposed magazine legislation designed to keep split-run magazines out of Canada.

Canadian publishers of such magazines as *Maclean's* and *Canadian Business*, among many others, have argued that this will create an unfair advantage for U.S. publishers, who can offer much lower advertising rates because they are producing this split-run in much larger quantities. Consequently, these U.S. competitors will take away critical advertising revenues and could, in fact, threaten the survival of Canadian publishers. The threat is that eventually Canadian advertisers would stop advertising in Canadian magazines in favour of the cheaper advertising rates offer by these U.S. split-run magazines. Opponents argue that the U.S. publishers simply want to exploit the Canadian market for advertising profits, and are not interested in investing in Canadian versions of their magazines. Canadian publishers have continued to demand that these magazines be banned. The U.S. magazine industry requested a threshold as high as 40% of Canadian advertisements before they would be required to include Canadian content. It has been estimated that more than 80% of newsstand sales of magazines in English Canada are U.S.-owned publications.

The question raised by many observers in this case was: Should the Canadian government impose restrictions on U.S. split-run publications? Should the power of competition and consumer demand dictate which businesses survive? Should the Canadian government protect Canadian business? However, this case suggests that the most critical question is: Must the government intervene because the businesses involved here are intimately connected to Canadian culture and identity? The argument is that the government needs to consider the impact of U.S.-owned businesses taking over an industry that reports about the nature of Canada and tells stories that involve the Canadian heritage.

It is not uncommon for governments to restrict trade in goods and services as a means to achieve cultural objectives, including preservation of national identity. The earlier discussion of globalization suggested that international business and trade brings with it a mingling of different cultures. This can create a sense of attack on a domestic culture. Many countries have, for example, enacted laws to protect their media programming as a means to help preserve national culture.

GOVERNMENT AS GUARDIAN OF THE PRIVATE BUSINESS SECTOR

Government Expenditures in the Private Sector

Government may play the role of "customer" and acquire goods or services from the private sector in order to fulfill its duties. In fact, in Canada, the largest consumer of goods and services is the government. The expenditures of federal, provincial and municipal governments together have amounted to over 40% of our Gross National Product. This includes expenditures on things like purchasing goods and services, salaries, and grants.

Traditionally, the federal and provincial governments have used their purchasing power to favour Canadian firms. Government contracts with private business would typically go to a Canadian, rather than a non-Canadian, company. However, NAFTA and the general push to freer trade with the United States are modifying the practice of this policy. In addition to the traditional favouring of Canadian over non-Canadian firms for government business contracts, the provincial governments have, similarly, favoured firms in their own region, which has encouraged the generation of trade barriers between provinces.

Government Assistance to Private Business

In Canada, we have a long history of government involvement in business in the sense of promoting and protecting our industries. For example, tariff and non-tariff barriers on imported goods were designed to protect our domestic business by making foreign goods more expensive relative to Canadian goods. In fact, it can be argued that a large portion of Canada's industrial development is due to protectionism through tariffs first imposed in 1879 by Sir John A. Macdonald's National Policy. Eventually, the government also offered direct incentives for industrial and resource development. Incentive programs were established to encourage managers to conduct business in a manner desired by the government. For example, it may be desirable for managers to invest in a new product development, or engage in greater export activities, or locate in an underdeveloped region. Consequently, incentives will be offered to engage in such activities. Receiving government financial support or reward for such activities would influence decisions to engage in these activities.

For example, provincial and municipal governments can encourage new employment opportunities by offering incentives to industry for locating in their areas. The municipal government might offer property tax incentives to attract industry to their jurisdiction, and the provincial government might even offer an outright grant to attract large-scale industry. Governments at all levels have provided both direct and indirect assistance for businesses, in the form of grants, loans, information, consulting advice, etc. Among the better known and largest forms of government assistance to a business occurred in the 1980s, when both the Canadian and U.S. governments provided a loan guarantee to banks of over $1 billion in an effort to prevent the Chrysler corporation from bankruptcy. Why the high level of assistance? If Chrysler had collapsed, hundreds of thousands of jobs would have been lost in both Canada and the United States.

The government also has tried to offer assistance to those industries deemed to be of particular importance. Industries with leading edge technology, or those providing highly skilled jobs, or oriented toward exports, might be among the more likely recipients of government aid. The federal and provincial governments have also provided financial incentives in an effort to dissuade companies from moving their operations outside of Canada. For example, Pratt & Whitney Canada Corp. was given an $11.7 million interest-free loan from the Quebec and federal governments to encourage them to retain the development of a new aircraft component within Canada.

Bailouts

Bailouts may involve a one-time financial assistance to combat significant financial troubles that a business may be experiencing. This financial assistance could also take the form of a loan or loan guarantee, for example. Bailouts were relatively common in the 1980s, involving such companies as Dome Petroleum, Chrysler Canada and Massey Ferguson. By the 1990s, while complete bailouts became rare, the government nevertheless did not refuse to offer some assistance in a bailout arrangement, as evidenced in the 1992 bailout of Algoma Steel, which involved government loan guarantees.

Subsidies

Government assistance to business in the form of subsidies has significant implications in the global business context. Subsidies have been identified as either cash payments, low-interest loans or potentially reduced taxes. Specifically, subsidies in the global context are intended to assist domestic industry to compete against foreign businesses, whether in the home country or through exports. One central argument against subsidies, whether in the domestic or global context, is that businesses should be required to manage their costs without external help, or "hand-outs", from the government. This is part of the requirement of fair competition, according to the critics. In addition, it is argued that consumers essentially pay for these subsidies. The government collects revenues through income and sales taxes, and it is these funds, collected from the general public, that are used to help some businesses. The question is: Are subsidies to business an unfair drain on public funds? There is no clear resolution to this ongoing debate.

From the global perspective, there is a second central criticism aimed at companies that receive subsidies from their local government. The criticism asserts that subsidies are not merely harmless forms of assistance to businesses; rather, they constitute a form of trade barrier, just like tariffs, and they create unfair competition. Why are subsidies viewed as non-tariff trade barriers, and how do they amount to unfair competition? Recently, the WTO has dealt with numerous international cases of allegedly unfair subsidies. The question is: Why should government subsidies to private industry be considered unfair? If the government deems it necessary, why shouldn't a domestic business receive some financial assistance? The answers to these questions have been subject to much debate. In the next section, we consider the issue of subsidies in the global context.

Government as the Guardian of Business in the Global Context

The pervasiveness of globalization has demanded that governments reconsider the extent to which they feel obligated to maintain a relationship with the private business sector. Thomas Friedman, in his book, *The Lexus and the Olive Tree*, asserts that globalization is, in fact, increasing the importance of government while changing the roles that it plays:

> The ability of an economy to withstand the inevitable ups and downs of the herd depends in large part on the quality of its legal system, financial system and economic management — all matters still under the control of governments and bureaucrats. Chile, Taiwan, Hong Kong and Singapore all survived the economic crises of the 1990s so much better than their neighbours because they had better-quality states running better-quality software and operating systems.[183]

EXHIBIT 9.5 GOVERNMENT AS GUARDIAN OF BUSINESS IN THE GLOBAL CONTEXT

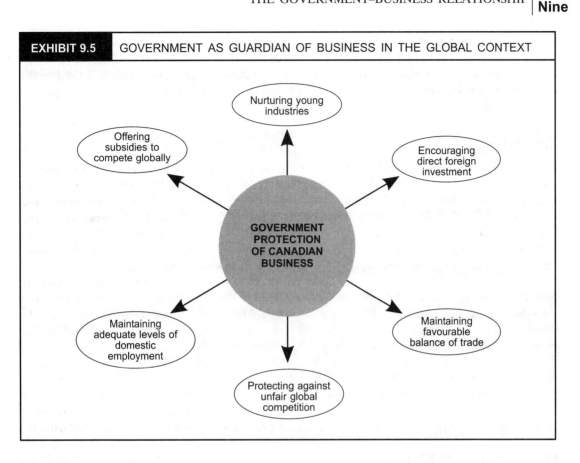

Consequently, while governments may find their role increasingly challenged, and in some ways compromised, by the onslaught of multinationals and globalization, the need for government involvement in certain ways may be increased in this new, global context. In the following sections, the roles governments play in the global business scene are discussed. (See Exhibit 9.5.)

1. Nurturing Young Industries

The notion that government must play a role in nurturing domestic industry was raised earlier in this chapter. The infant-industry argument asserts that the government should help a young industry to grow and develop by ensuring that the industry maintains a dominant share of the domestic market until it is mature enough to compete against foreign competition. Consequently, this philosophy is still applied, particularly, among developing countries. The rationale is that the infant industry may be less competitive, particularly because of initially high output costs; however, with maturity, the production will become more efficient, and protection will no longer be necessary.

293

At least two risks have been associated with this form of government influence:

1. Such protection can discourage domestic industry from increasing competitiveness and engaging in innovation. This is an argument that has been levelled at Canadian business.

2. There is a question as to whether consumers are better or worse off from such practices. Not all Canadian parties want the Canadian steel industry to receive this type of protection from foreign rivals (see below). In fact, Canadian purchasers of any good or service arguably would want the lowest-cost supplier to be accessible and, consequently, may not appreciate the protection of infant industry if it comes at the expense of blocking access to cheaper foreign goods or services.

2.   *Encouraging Direct Foreign Investment*

The action of reducing foreign imports may result in the foreign business directly investing in the target country instead. That is, a foreign company can decide to set up business in the target country if they wish to gain access to this country's consumer market and they are unable to achieve that with imports. Of course, from the domestic country's viewpoint, this foreign investment may be desirable if it increases job opportunities, contributes to the growth of industry and adds to the amount of capital.

3.   *Maintaining Favourable Balance of Trade*

Government may seek to influence the relative status of exports and imports to avoid running a trade deficit. (The chapter on globalization expands the discussion with regard to the importance of trade and the issue of trade surpluses and deficits.) **Trade surpluses** come about when a country's exports exceed its imports and, consequently, more money is entering the country (from foreign consumers buying these exports) than is leaving the country (from domestic consumers buying foreign imports). A trade deficit is the reverse — when a country imports more than it exports. Traditionally, governments intervened to ensure a trade surplus by imposing tariffs or quotas or by banning outright some foreign-imported commodities. Typically, the governments would also subsidize domestic industries in order to encourage growth in their exports.

4.   *Protecting Domestic Business from Unfair Competition*

There is a concern among some businesses that foreign competitors will offer their products at extremely low prices as a means of monopolizing their share of the target country's market. The ultimate consequence would be that domestic producers could potentially be driven out of business and replaced by the foreign imports. A foreign competitor who manages to export the products at such low prices may be accused of **dumping** — which is pricing the product below cost or below the cost of the target country. In other words, a foreign supplier who sells the product at a loss or for less than the price of the seller's domestic market would be considered guilty of dumping.

The newspapers recently reported the case of dumping in the steel industry. Steel companies have been among the most avid users of anti-dumping legislation in Canada and the United States. Hamilton-based Dofasco Inc. lodged a dumping complaint against steel mills in Asia and South America. The aim was to seek government assistance, which in this case resulted in a decision by the Canadian federal government to place anti-dumping tariffs on low-cost imported steel from these foreign suppliers. In total, these anti-dumping tariffs were aimed at blocking the dumping of steel shipments from nine countries. This echoes similar action taken in the United States. Steel producers in both the United States and Canada have blamed the increasing foreign imports of steel for reducing demand for their product domestically and, consequently, reducing product prices and revenue. It is interesting to note that while Canadian steel producers welcome such government intervention, other domestic players are not happy with the implementation of anti-dumping tariffs, which effectively raise the price of these cheaper goods. Specifically, western Canadian manufacturers have claimed that the protectionist measures will reduce their ability to compete with Ontario steel manufacturers. Many western steel businesses argued that they will lose access to these cheaper foreign sources and now be forced to rely on costlier steel sources in Ontario. The argument of these businesses is that they feel that they should have access to the lowest cost sources of steel, whether these sources are from Canada or from foreign producers. In this regard, they are opposed to the government's protectionist policy of imposing anti-dumping tariffs.

5. *Maintaining Adequate Levels of Domestic Employment*

A government knows that society holds it responsible for ensuring the unemployment rates are not high. Imports that come to dominate an industry bring the threat of causing domestic industries to go bankrupt. Consequently, where businesses claim they are under threat of bankruptcy due to foreign competition, the government is forced to consider what action it can take to combat this threat. In the past, the government protected Canadian business and employment from the risk of foreign competition via the implementation of tariffs, as discussed in the previous chapter. Clearly, such an option is complicated by the fact that reducing imports is not necessarily feasible, for reasons also described earlier. Protectionist policies are not compatible with the sentiments of free trade, and thus governments are sometimes placed in the unenviable position of balancing the needs of the domestic economy with the need to honour the rules governing global business. A case in point is the issue of government subsidies.

6. *Offering Subsidies to Compete Globally*

Whether it is for the purpose of maintaining employment levels or of assisting businesses in the global marketplace, the issue of government subsidies to business has become much more controversial in the context of globalization. Whether it is cash payments, low-

---

LET'S TALK BUSINESS 9.3   HELPING BOMBARDIER

One recurring controversy regarding government subsidies to businesses operating in the global marketplace involves government support of research and development programs. For example, the U.S. government has effectively subsidized McDonnell Douglas and Boeing via financial assistance in research and development for military aircraft with commercial applications. In Canada, one recent controversy involved an ongoing dispute regarding government subsidies to Canada's aerospace giant Bombardier and its main competitor in the jet market, Embraer SA (Empresa Brasileira de Aeronautica SA.) of Brazil. In addition, in 2001, the Canadian government offered low-interest loans worth up to $1.7 billion to assist Bombardier in winning a $2.35 billion contract to construct regional jets for Air Wisconsin Inc. Officials said that they had proof that the Brazilian government was offering their businesses high subsidies, and this measure allegedly was intended to maintain a "level playing field". The Canadian government argued that while the loan arrangement with Bombardier breaches WTO conditions on the surface, international trade rules allow a country to match a subsidized offer. Brazil has challenged this position. Canadian trade officials maintained that the Canadian government must "fight back against Brazilian cut-rate financing that is costing Bombardier business". In June, 2001, the WTO ruled that Brazil's financing program did not, on its face, break international trade rules. That is, the WTO ruled that Brazil's subsidy program for jet buyers was not illegal as long as it followed the rules established. These rules include rules about minimum allowable interest rates for governments to offer, as well as maximum terms of loans. Earlier, Brazil had breached those rules when they offered Air Wisconsin Airlines Corp. financing over 16 years. The Canadian government matched those terms and, ultimately, Bombardier won the US$1.5 million contract. Brazil complained to the WTO about this; however, Canada's defence has been that they have simply matched the competitor's terms.

Source: Based on Heather Scoffield, "WTO ruling seen as win-win" *The Globe and Mail* (June 23, 2001), B2.

---

interest loans or tax breaks, such financial assistance is referred to as a subsidy. And in the case of the global context, such subsidies are intended to help domestic industry deal with global competition. In recent years, the WTO has been involved in many international disputes regarding whether a local government has given their domestic industry an unfair advantage through some form of subsidy. The risk of such subsidies, in addition to the potential conflicts they create with regard to facilitating free trade, include the notion that competitive industries should be able to absorb such costs themselves rather than relying on the government for these hand-outs. The lumber dispute highlighted at the beginning of this chapter (see Organizational Insider) is an example of the difficulty in establishing the degree to which government should aid business in the global context. Other examples abound with regard to government aid to business in the global context. (See Let's Talk Business 9.3.)

SHOULD GOVERNMENT "MIND ITS OWN BUSINESS?"

Government intervention in the economy has traditionally been greater in Canada than in the United States. For example, government expenditures as a percentage of GDP are typically higher in Canada than in the United States, and public sector employment in Canada has been as much as 30% greater than the United States. However, Canada has been following the trend of reducing government's involvement in the business sector. Why are we witnessing this reduction in government involvement, and what are the implications of this trend? These questions are addressed in the sections below. (See Exhibit 9.6.)

Deregulation

Earlier, we discussed the issue of government regulation. And, as we mentioned, government regulates the operation of businesses through commissions, tribunals, agencies and boards. Whatever the form, the government directly regulates about one-third of the economy through more than 600 organizations. However, what we have witnessed since the 1980s is a trend toward deregulation. Deregulation, as the name suggests, involves a reduction in the number of laws or regulations affecting business activity. It also suggests a reduction of the powers of government enforcement agencies and other forms of government control or influence.

In recent years, the process of deregulation in the Canadian economy seems to have accelerated, particularly in industry sectors such as transportation, telecommunications, financial services and energy services. While the telecommunications sector maintains varying degrees of regulations in different areas, it has created an increased level of competition through deregulation in areas such as overseas calling, domestic long distance, local,

EXHIBIT 9.6	QUESTIONS TO BE ADDRESSED

Why has the government deregulated certain industries?

Why has the government engaged in privatization?

What areas of business has the government chosen to deregulate or privatize?

What are the benefits of deregulation?

What are the benefits of privatization?

What are the risks of deregulation?

What are the risks of privatization?

THE NATURE OF MANAGEMENT AND ORGANIZATIONS

wireless and other services. In the Canadian electricity sector, deregulation has recently been applied, particularly in Alberta and Ontario.

We have witnessed economic deregulation among many industries in a number of countries, including: airlines, trucking, railroads, financial markets, energy and telecommunications. At the same time, there has been an increase in regulations that are intended to govern such areas as health and safety and the environment. In order to understand the implications of economic deregulation, it is useful to briefly reconsider why, in fact, there is a need to regulate any industry at all.

As explained earlier in this chapter, regulation is aimed at correcting market failures and inequities that may arise for a variety of reasons, including the case where insufficient competition exists in an industry. However, just as the market can fail, so, too, the government policy of deregulation may not always achieve the goals for which it was intended. While it may be an oversimplification, the significant consequences of deregulation fall into two categories: potential benefit and potential risk.

What's the potential benefit?

- The benefit to consumers of increased competition arising from the reduction of regulations that have formerly restricted the entry of new competitors.

What's the potential risk?

- The risk to consumers of exploitation — e.g., reduction in quality of product or service, increases in consumer fees or price increases as a result of the reduction in laws governing their operation.

The question is: Will deregulation accomplish the central objective of sufficiently loosening constraints in order to encourage the entry of more competitors? On the other side, the question may be: Will deregulation fail to encourage adequate competition, and will this loosening of constraints instead permit current competitors to abuse the system and exploit consumers in some way? (See Let's Talk Business 9.4.)

Research evidence from U.S.-based studies has offered strong support for the benefits of deregulation among a variety of sectors, including railway, trucking, airline, telecommunications and financial industries. Comparisons have been made of the U.S. and Canadian railway industries between 1956 and 1974, when the U.S. railway industry was more heavily regulated than the Canadian. While both industries had access to the same technology, productivity growth was much greater in the Canadian (3.3%) than in the U.S. railroads (0.5%). Studies have indicated that unit costs in the U.S. trucking industry decreased significantly in the period following deregulation in 1983. Similarly, the airline industry managed to reduce costs by 25% in the period following deregulation.

The U.S. telecommunications industry has also benefited from deregulation, according to recent studies. For example, by 1996 long-distance telephone rates in the United States had dropped by over 70%. A number of studies have also suggested that deregulation encouraged much more innovation, as reflected in the emergence of such profitable services as cellular telephony and voice messaging. It is interesting to note that the concept of cellular phones was discussed as early as the 1950s, and the technology had become available by the early 1970s, yet the Federal Communications Commission did

---

LET'S TALK BUSINESS 9.4   THE BENEFITS OF DEREGULATION

A number of studies have attempted to measure the economic benefits of deregulation. For example, studies conducted in the United States in the early 1990s suggested that eliminating entry restrictions and freeing prices to market levels resulted in gains of between $35 and $46 billion, with consumers gaining approximately $40 billion in lower prices and better services, while producers gained about $3 billion a year from increased efficiency and lower costs.[1] Researchers have acknowledged the difficulty of quantifying the consequences of deregulation. For example, while the impact of deregulation on innovation is often overlooked, it has been estimated that innovation sparked by deregulation has led to reductions in operating costs by one-fourth to more than one-half in different industries.[2]

Source: [1] Winston, 1993. [2] Guasch & Hahn, 1999.

---

not issue licences until 1983 — an illustration of the inhibiting effect of regulations on innovation.

Deregulation in the financial industries, including securities, investment and banking sectors, has also yielded some positive support from U.S.-based studies with regard to its consequences. For example, it has been estimated that partial deregulation of the banking and savings and loan industry contributed to a 300% increase in productivity, while deregulated brokerage fees resulted in a 25% decrease in rates.

Comparative studies have supported the benefits of deregulation. For example, by 1999, in industries such as the airline industry, the United States was clearly maintaining a significantly higher level of deregulation than many European countries. Advocates of deregulation have asserted that the benefits of deregulation were reflected in the fact that European airline fares were about twice as costly as U.S. airfares, while European companies were neither as efficient nor as profitable as the U.S. carriers. Consequently, supporters of deregulation claim that eliminating price and entry restrictions would increase competition and, ultimately, benefit consumers through lower airfares and better service. Comparisons of the relative differences in levels of regulation between Europe and the United States by the late 1990s drew similar conclusions. It was estimated that many European companies were paying about 50% more for their electricity than their U.S. counterparts. For example, the high level of regulation in Germany's electricity market, including the requirement to purchase electricity from regional producers rather than less expensive alternative sources, was viewed as inhibiting efficiency and productivity. In contrast, the U.K. greatly benefited from energy deregulation with regard to productivity gains, estimated at 70% subsequent to deregulation. A recent article in *BusinessWeek* noted the following impact of deregulation in the energy industry, as reported in Let's Talk Business 9.5.

While the findings above certainly point to the potential benefits of deregulation, there is no doubt that support for deregulation is far from universal. While advocates claim that beneficial impact on consumers and businesses outweighs any costs, opponents

---

LET'S TALK BUSINESS 9.5   UTILITY DEREGULATION

What's going on here? In a nutshell, utilities aren't the staid monoliths they once were. In the old days, utilities were local monopolies that basically generated power and delivered it to customers. But when states began to deregulate electricity markets, opening the door to competition, utilities had to think about ways to retain and attract new customers. The companies started pursuing widely disparate strategies. Today, a look at the Dow Jones utilities index reveals companies that explore for and produce natural gas, generate and sell power in deregulated markets in Europe and elsewhere, and trade a variety of commodities, such as paper, coal, chemicals — even fibre-optic bandwidth.

Source: *BusinessWeek*, 2001.

---

suggest the reverse — that the risks of deregulation are too high to enter into this venture. There is likely no area more mixed with regard to the reaction to deregulation than in its impact on developing countries. Nonetheless, there is, again, evidence that is very supportive of the policy of deregulation. For example, deregulation in the telecommunications industry among some Latin American countries has greatly encouraged private sector involvement and led to increased efficiency in services. By the late 1990s, telephone user rates were reduced by about 50% following the deregulation of entry requirements in the long-distance telephone market in Chile. At the same time, studies have pointed out the negative consequences of maintaining regulation in various sectors within developing countries. For example, in the late 1990s Brazil and Argentina's transportation regulations forced businesses to ship largely by road, even though the costs were significantly higher than rail charges.[184]

Example #1:
Deregulation in the Transportation Industry

As mentioned, the main objective of government regulation is to protect the public interest. The railroad industry was among the very first to have regulations applied, with the deal made in 1895 between Prime Minister Wilfrid Laurier and the CPR. Essentially, the government promised the CPR the financing it needed to complete a transcontinental line if the CPR would carry wheat produced by western farmers for shipping on a regular basis at a negotiated rate. Many years later, the National Transportation Act created the Canadian Transport Commission (in 1970), whose job it was to regulate and control the various means of transportation in Canada, including motor, air, water transport and railways, among other things. However, on January 1, 1988, the new National Transportation Act came into effect, and brought with it a new era of deregulation. What did this new legislation contain, and how did it bring about deregulation in the transportation industry? Well, just consider its impact on the trucking industry.

This act brought with it the passage of the new Motor Vehicle Transport Act. Prior to that time, anyone wanting to enter the trucking business was required to appear before the provincial licensing board and prove there was a public need for their service in order to get a licence to operate a truck. However, under the new act the prospective trucker must simply present proof that they are insurable and can pass some minimal safety criteria. So what is the result of all this? One of the major benefits of the reduction in requirements for new entrants was increased competition: more truckers entered the industry. Shippers gained from a wider choice of trucking services and more competitive rates. Following the passage of this Act, shippers could negotiate the level of service and price of any domestic movement with any carrier. Consequently, consumers benefited in terms of reduced costs arising from increased competition in highway carriers. In fact, a central aim of this deregulation was to encourage greater efficiency in Canada's over $2 billion transportation market. In a more recent report of the trucking industry in Canada, the following observation was made:

> What has emerged is a new breed of Canadian trucker — one that is more efficient, value-priced, eager to customize to shippers' needs and adept at filling specialized niches in a North American market dominated by huge and efficient American carriers.[185]

In the related railway shipping industry, recent reports have indicated that shipper rates dropped by 35% since deregulation, and were considered lowest in the world — 60% below the international average.[186] However, there has been a downside for some. With increased competition, some trucking companies have been unable to compete effectively and have gone bankrupt, resulting in the loss of hundreds of jobs. In fact, in 1990 about 130 trucking companies declared bankruptcy — over twice as many as those in the previous year. A major threat has come from U.S. trucking companies, which have lower labour, equipment and tax costs and, consequently, lower operating costs. So there are winners and losers in the trend toward deregulation, and the issue of competition lies at the heart of this. Reducing regulations welcomes more entrants and creates more pressure on existing Canadian companies. During the years following deregulation, the Canadian carriers admitted that they were slow to adapt to new technologies such as electronic data interchange, bar coding and satellite tracking of trailers. For example, by 1997 almost all U.S. truckload tractors were equipped for satellite tracking, while only 50% of Canadian tractors were equipped.[187]

Example #2:
Deregulation in the Insurance and Banking Industry

In the financial services industry, deregulation permitted banks to enter the brokerage business and allowed them to sell insurance. This has not yet received widespread approval. A case has been made for deregulating the insurance industry to allow banks to enter.[188] The banks have long served as an example of an industry with inadequate competition and that, consequently, requires rigorous government regulation. In fact, the recent pressure exerted on the government by banks to allow them to merge was faced with a public fear of the creation of a greater monopoly situation and the negative consequences of such a situation. Interestingly, on the other hand, there has been an opposite sentiment with regard to allowing banks to expand their services into the insurance industry through their branch networks.

Critics assert that the insurance industry and, specifically, the current insurance distribution system fail to meet the requirements of the Canadian consumer. Relatively lower sales and a distinct lack of insurance availability suggest the need for more competition within the insurance industry. The argument is that allowing banks to enter the insurance industry would be a great service, particularly to lower-income Canadians, who currently cannot afford proper insurance coverage. With present government regulation, banks are not permitted to enter the insurance field. However, as with the general notion of deregulation, permitting the bank to enter the insurance industry would, allegedly, result in less costly, more comprehensive insurance service for Canadians, and create a more competitive, stronger, financial services industry.

In addition, advocates of deregulation in this industry offer examples of similar practices in other countries. For example, allowing integration of insurance services has occurred in France, where banks are allowed to sell insurance policies in their branches. The average expense ratio for bank insurance policies was under 5%, compared with almost 14% for other companies selling insurance. The lower cost structure contributes to lower policy costs for consumers of insurance obtained through the banks. Combining banking and insurance services for French consumers allows banks to offer small, standardized policies for low-income persons that under normal circumstances, would not generate sufficient commissions for a typical insurance agent. The advantages of permitting banks to enter the insurance industry are also evident in New Zealand, where there is evidence that competition from the insurance subsidiaries of banks led to falling prices for term life insurance. Consumers also valued the convenience of one-stop shopping. Benefits in the Canadian context are noted in Let's Talk Business 9.6.

LET'S TALK BUSINESS 9.6   DEREGULATING INSURANCE

A Canadian example of the benefits of allowing banks to sell insurance is provided by the Caisses Desjardins of Quebec, which is a not a chartered bank but, rather, is governed by provincial regulation and, consequently, is not restricted by the insurance regulations. Allowing this bank to sell in-branch insurance policies in Quebec has made the purchase of such policies much more accessible. In Quebec, 60% of insurance policies are purchased by people with annual incomes of less than $30,000, compared to 44% in the rest of Canada. In fact, critics note that Canadians overall are underinsured. Recent reports indicate that approximately 17% of all Canadians have no life insurance, and 25% feel they require more life insurance than they can afford. The assertion is that by permitting banks to enter the insurance industry, they would significantly increase access through their network of more than 8,000 branches and 12,000 automated banking machines. In sum, advocates of deregulation believe that the insurance industry will improve its treatment of consumers if they are faced with competition from the banks. It would also improve the quality of service and, arguably, result in reduced costs.

Example #3:
Deregulation in the Airline Industry

Deregulation in the airline industry actually started around 1984. The passage of the new National Transportation Act in 1988 eliminated many restrictions in the airline industry, including restrictions related to routes, frequency of flights and type of aircraft. Among the loosening of restraints, airlines could offer any combination of scheduled and chartered services on their current routes, and were no longer restricted in offering discounts. Once again, the effects of deregulation made it easier for new players to enter the industry, as well as allowing existing airlines greater ease in expanding routes and increasing or reducing fares. In 1990, measures were taken to remove Canada–U.S. government-imposed restrictions. The "open-skies" agreement completed in 1995 permitted Canadian and U.S. airlines to fly across the border on any routes they think will be profitable and, essentially, create one North American market for air travel.

Now, why did all this deregulation occur in the airline industry? Well, for essentially the same reason that it may occur elsewhere — to encourage increased competition. The Canadian government initiated deregulation because it felt that Canadian companies needed to learn how to compete internationally. The government had been observing large numbers of Canadians taking advantage of lower airfares in the United States. It has been argued that deregulation was, in a sense, a push to force Canadian carriers to be much more competitive. Of course, as was the case with the trucking industry, consumers of the service also are winners: more choice of carriers, and more competitive prices. However, deregulation also means much more difficult times for carriers that must now contend with more competition. Deregulation, like the reduction of trade barriers, has forced many companies to become more competitive in order to survive in a more crowded marketplace. Of course, the hope is that the Canadian airline industry will increase their competitiveness, and benefit the consumer with lower prices and better products and services.

To date, the positive results of deregulation do not appear to have materialized in the Canadian airline industry. The deregulation process initiated by the National Transportation Act encouraged fierce competition between Air Canada and Canadian Airlines, with each offering identical fares, seat sales, etc. However, by the latter part of the 1990s, still only the two airlines remained as dominant competitors in the industry, accounting for about 80% of industry operating revenues. By 1999, only Air Canada dominated the industry, after acquiring Canadian Airlines. Consequently, in February of 2000, Canada's Ministry of Transport announced some degree of re-regulation of the airline industry. The proposed legislation was intended to increase the power of the Competition Bureau and Transport Canada to control fares, among other issues.

The Canadian press has carried many stories reporting the criticisms of Air Canada, an airline that is about 13 times larger than its closest competitor. Relatively smaller competitors have been viewed as not big enough to mount any real threat to Air Canada's monopoly power in Canadian skies.[189] Does it really matter that there is only one big player in the Canadian airline industry? Critics suggest that, as with any monopoly, consumers ultimately suffer from a lack of real competition. Consequently, critics also relate overbooked flights, air rage and high air fares as the consequences of the Air Canada monopoly.

Air Canada was once a Crown corporation, privatized in the late 1980s. Critics encouraged such privatization in order to improve efficiency by taking this airline out of

303

the hands of "inefficient bureaucrats". Ironically, many critics suggest that those same inefficiencies are back because of the power of private ownership in a monopoly situation. So, what, if anything, should the government do to combat what critics view as unwieldy monopoly power? The government could engage in regulating the behaviour of Air Canada. It could force Air Canada to agree not to overcrowd routes, to fly certain routes at certain times. Some regulations have been re-imposed on Air Canada. However, in a climate of deregulation, this is not a popular choice. Consequently, in line with the philosophy of deregulation, the Transport Minister also recently warned, in a 2000 speech, that if domestic competition does not increase in the short term, U.S. airlines would be permitted to serve domestic routes in Canada, even though foreign airlines traditionally have been barred from owning more than 25% of a Canadian airline.

Example #4:
Deregulation in the Electricity Industry

The past 10 years or so have seen a great interest in deregulation in the energy sector: specifically energy supply, with Britain and Scandinavia largely initiating this practice since the early 1990s. Traditionally, electricity costs have been higher in Europe than in North America. After a number of European governments privatized the public utilities, the cost of electricity dropped in those regions. Deregulation also welcomed much more competition, and this competition forced the power companies to become more efficient and improve customer service.

It seems that the Canadian government, drawing on the European experience, decided to initiate privatization and deregulation in the energy sector in Canada, beginning with Alberta in 1995. Unfortunately, the reaction to this transition has been mixed, with some observers criticizing the 1995 deregulation process in Alberta's electricity industry, and others adding that the purchase of electricity has become more complicated with the advent of deregulation. (See Let's Talk Business 9.7.)

Ontario has followed Alberta's lead in electricity deregulation, although they have proceeded somewhat more slowly, and, according to some, more cautiously. By 2001, Ontario Power Generation (the government-owned utility, formerly part of Ontario Hydro) provided 85% of the province's electricity, while it is expected that by 2005 it will sell off 40% of its generating capacity to private enterprise. In January 2001, the government of New Brunswick announced its plans to deregulate its electricity system. While advocates of deregulation feel that, ultimately, the benefits of increased competition will prevail, those opposed to deregulation believe that public ownership should continue to exist for essential services in order to ensure that all members of society will be guaranteed access to the same service at a reasonable price.

Privatization

What does privatization mean? In broad terms, privatization refers to the divesting of government involvement in the operation, management and ownership of activities. Typically, privatization involves the transfer of activities or functions from the government

---

LET'S TALK BUSINESS 9.7   DEREGULATING ELECTRICITY

Three years later the province is suffering from a critical shortage of power and a free market is still nowhere in sight. The promised benefits of deregulation — better service and cheaper rates — have yet to materialize for either industry or citizens.... Economists all agree that deregulation makes sense when the benefits exceed the costs. In theory those benefits can include lower prices, better generators, new products, energy efficiency and more green power.[1]

Buying electricity used to be so simple for householders. There was one supplier whose price was set by government regulators. Deregulation complicates this issue to no end. Door-to-door salespeople now offer consumers a bewildering array of choices and hardly anybody has enough information to make an informed decision.[2]

Source: [1] "Bright lights, big mistake" *Canadian Business* (December 11, 1998): 81.
[2] *Canada and the World Backgrounder* (March 2001), 66(5): 8–11.

---

to the private sector. Privatization might involve selling off a Crown corporation to the private sector. For example, Air Canada, formerly a Crown corporation, was sold to the private sector in 1988–1989. In 1988, the government sold Teleglobe Canada Inc., a handler of overseas satellite calls for the telephone and telecommunications companies, to private business. Privatization might also involve contracting government jobs to private companies. For example, in some provinces private businesses contract to manage hospitals and other health care institutions previously managed by government employees. Other services that can be contracted out are things like garbage collection and road construction. In addition, public institutions have also contracted out services such as data processing and food and janitorial services to private sector corporations. The closing of some postal stations and the franchising of postal services in retail businesses is yet another example.

In recent years there has been a significant transformation of the organizational landscape across the world, as numerous state-owned monopolies, agencies and other public organizations are privatized. Government ownership in areas from airlines to electricity has been sold to either domestic or foreign investors. Over 15,000 enterprises were privatized during the period from 1980 to 1992. By 1997, worldwide privatization proceeds reached $153 billion.[190] Privatization has been implemented not only in advanced countries like the United States, Canada, the U.K., Australia, France, Germany and Japan, but also in transitional countries like Poland, Chile, Brazil, Mexico and Argentina. In addition, developing countries have also been implementing privatization, including countries like Nigeria, Tunisia and Zimbabwe. It is also expected that privatization will continue to progress around the world and in most economic sectors over the coming decade.

Global privatization accelerated in the 1990s, with a significant portion coming from Western Europe, with developing countries accounting for about one-third of the annual funds raised by privatization. In the economies of Eastern Europe, the transition to private from state ownership has reflected a particularly significant political transition, as recently observed:

The development of a large-scale privatization program is also a highly political act. Almost by definition, privatization represents an ideological and symbolic break with a history of state control over a country's productive assets. Nowhere is this symbolism more apparent than in the economies of Eastern Europe and the former Soviet Union, where privatization of state-owned enterprises has come to signal a nation's transition from communism to democratic capitalism. In Russia, the privatization of enormous petroleum (Lukoil), natural gas (Gazprom) and telecommunications (Syazinevest) companies represented a fundamental break from socialist state ownership.[191]

Why Do Governments Privatize?

Why have we observed the increased divestiture of government in business activities, including the sale of Crown corporations? What are the reasons for reducing the level of government ownership in business enterprises? Let's consider some of the popular arguments for privatization.

Reasons for Privatization

Belief in the power of competition as a control mechanism. Privatization is considered to be an expected outgrowth of the free enterprise system. That is, private enterprise should be allowed to expand into areas that were once monopolized by the government. Moreover, privatization programs are typically guided by the view that the force of market competition is best suited to fostering efficiency and innovation in an industry. Specifically, the view is that privatization of a state-owned monopoly will open an industry to competition and, consequently, encourage innovation, growth and efficiency. Moreover, where privatization opens an industry to foreign competition, this permits consumers to have access to goods or services developed in other parts of the world, and will stimulate innovation among domestic firms operating in the industry. In addition, opening an industry to foreign investors may also provide access to needed financial and technological resources, and create growth in the industry.

Belief that private business can operate more efficiently. A second, common view, is that transferring the management of organizations to the private sector will result in increased productivity. Studies conducted in a variety of countries have found evidence that the private production of goods and services is typically more efficient than public production. Why should this be considered to be true? Well, think back to our discussion of why Crown corporations were established: a central reason for their establishment was not a profit, but a social policy consideration — i.e., serving public interests. Consequently, many observers feel that it is difficult for government-owned enterprises to reconcile the social goals of the enterprise with the economic efficiency goals that must be of concern to any business. Moreover, efficient operation may be difficult given that there are political interests to be considered. Removing the political element of an enterprise allows it to focus on efficiency and avoid potential conflicts of interest. The Ontario government announced that its main goal for privatization is to improve economic efficiency of the underlying organization, as reflected in reduced prices and improved customer service.

No longer need public involvement in some sectors. Air Canada was established as a Crown corporation at a time when no private company had the resources to develop a transnational airline. In more recent times, there are both domestic and international airlines more than capable of conducting such business and, consequently, there is little need for government ownership in such sectors. Where the enterprise is no longer required by the government to achieve its initial public policy goals, then ownership can be handed over to the private sector. If private industry is willing to offer the same product or service in a reliable and cost effective manner, why not allow them to do so? As we discussed above, in Canada's earlier days, the creation of Crown corporations was deemed necessary, in part, by the "natural monopoly argument" in industries such as public utilities or communications, given that low unit costs of production could be attained only if output is sufficiently high. Consequently, a large government monopoly or a regulated, privately owned monopoly was acceptable and, perhaps, necessary. This argument has weakened in more recent times, when globalization has introduced large, worldwide competitors who may be bigger and more efficient than federal or provincial Crown corporations.

Financial benefits from selling government-owned assets. Another reason for selling off government-owned enterprises is that the money can be used on other, more needed, areas. Certainly money received from sales of Crown corporations or partial disposition of Crown-owned assets has been applied to government deficit reductions. In addition, opening an industry to private investors may attract, for example, an influx of foreign capital. Maintaining a Crown corporation can be an increasingly costly venture, particularly when high subsidies are made to inefficient state-owned enterprises. Privatization can remove this unnecessary financial burden from government and taxpayers. For example, in the U.K. over $16.8 billion (U.S.) was raised between 1990 and 1995 through the privatization of two power generating companies, the 12 regional electricity companies and the National Grid. Similarly, Argentina raised over $4 billion (U.S.) through the partial disposition of government-owned electricity assets and cut its level of debt. Similarly, the financial incentive for privatizing Ontario Hydro was based on estimates of a corresponding provincial debt reduction of at least $8 billion (Cdn). The initial public offering of shares in CNR in 1995 was Canada's largest stock market flotation in Canada at that time. However, during the 1980s and 1990s, privatizations in Canada were most likely to have been conducted through sales to private businesses rather than public share offerings. Revenues from sales of Canada's 10 largest federal corporations amounted to $7.2 billion in the period between 1986 and 1996. Proceeds to the federal government were over $3.8 billion from the sale of shares in CN and Petro-Canada alone.

Challenges to "Going Private"

Stakeholders and objectives. Governments in Canada began to privatize their corporate holdings in the mid-1980s for many of the reasons cited earlier, including: efficiency objectives, financial concerns and the capability of the private sector to fulfill public policy objectives.

It is useful to point out that while these may be objectives of privatization, they are not held equally by all parties affected by a privatization. The objectives of various stakeholders in the privatization of a Crown corporation may be different and potentially conflicting. Consider, for example, the stakeholders affected by the privatization of public utilities, which may include, among others: government owners, other government parties (i.e., other levels of government), creditors or bondholders, future shareholders of the organization, the unionized and non-unionized employees of the corporation, the regulators, the taxpayers, the consumers, and other existing or potential competitors in the industry.

Employees' objectives.   In effect, the objectives of privatization mentioned above could all be considered as objectives of the government owners, but some may conflict with elements of the enterprise itself. For example, after initiation of the privatization plan for Ontario Hydro, the senior management of Hydro was also agreeable to the province's plan for privatization. In fact, their view was that rapid privatization was necessary in order to face the increasing competition from the United States and from other provincial utilities in the Ontario electricity market, since deregulation began to open up the market for competition. However, within Hydro there has been much disagreement — culminating in a number of strikes by employees opposed to the government's plans.

A possible cost of privatization is massive layoffs of public employees, particularly in developing and transition countries. For example, the privatization of Argentina's national rail company in 1991 involved laying off almost 80% of the company's total workforce as part of the restructuring. However, numerous studies suggest that aggregate employment remains largely unchanged subsequent to privatization efforts.

The public's objectives.   Another possible conflict is between the objectives cited above and the public's concern for their "protection". For example, in the case of Ontario Hydro, some citizens are concerned that private competitors may be less likely to serve the public's interests than a government-owned enterprise. Consequently, some fear that privatization will bring higher rates and safety concerns. Other issues may relate to foreign ownership. For example, there were no foreign ownership restrictions placed on the privatization of Canadian National Railways (which involved a public offering of a majority of shares) and, consequently, 40% of the $2.3 billion share issue was sold outside Canada, and largely to U.S. organizations. For some critics, this sale left too much power out of Canadian hands, and there was some question whether the newly controlled enterprise would keep Canadian interests high on their agenda. On the other hand, the government did not restrict foreign ownership, given the view that the Canadian market was not large enough to allow for complete privatization in one attempt. There were, however, other restrictions, including: no investor could own more than 15% of the shares, and that CN must remain headquartered in Montreal.

While privatization has been viewed as a means to generate higher levels of entrepreneurship and efficiency in an industry, simply transferring ownership to the private sector does not guarantee efficiency gains. At least one important qualification is the level of competition that exists subsequent to the privatization. For example, critics suggest that although Air Canada was privatized in the late 1980s, clear efficiency gains and benefits to the user did not readily materialize, because Air Canada continued to operate in an environment that lacked sufficient competition and, consequently, maintained its monopoly status.

Ironically, the technical responsibilities of the government may increase after privatization, because governments are shifting from owning and managing individual companies to potentially regulating an entire sector or industry. Critics have asserted that if the government fails to implement effective regulation over the new private sector owners, then

LET'S TALK BUSINESS 9.8   PRIVATIZATION AND REGULATION

The government is facilitating the transition from private or public monopolies in certain industries to ones that will ideally foster competition through deregulation. This has naturally changed the mandate of the Competition Bureau from being solely a watchdog of business. The following basic roles for the Competition Bureau and industry regulators have been emphasized as the atmosphere of deregulation and privatization spreads:

1.   Ensure Regulators Promote Competition
The Competition Bureau encourages specific regulators to play a clear role in promoting competition. The benefit of providing regulators with a role to promote competition is illustrated in the telecommunications industry. The Telecommunications Act is ultimately aimed at nurturing increased reliance on market forces. Consequently, the Act encourages the industry regulator, the CRTC, to open new areas of the telecommunications industry to competition, such as local telephone service and pay phones in recent years.

2.   Implement Regulatory Control over Excessive Pricing from Monopolies
Even in deregulated markets the Bureau recognizes the need for regulators to monitor industries in transition and, potentially, regulate excessive pricing due to the market power held by a competitor. For example, during the initial stage of deregulation in the telecommunications industry, the CRTC continued to regulate long distance rates of telephone companies until the establishment of sufficient competition in the market. Similarly, the Bureau has continued to support regulatory control over Ontario Hydro Generation Company's electricity prices until such time as the Ontario generation market becomes sufficiently competitive.

3.   Support Regulatory Control Concerning Essential Facilities
The Bureau advocates regulatory control over essential facilities in an industry — that is, any facilities that businesses require in order to compete in a market, and for which there is no effective competition. Examples of such essential facilities include: transmission and distribution systems in electricity and natural gas, and interconnection to the public switched telephone network by competitive long distance and local exchange carriers. An industry regulator is present in such cases in order to prohibit excessive pricing of essential facilities due to any monopoly power.

4.   Establish a Framework for Deregulation
It is recognized that where regulation is not productive for the industry, the aim becomes one that is geared toward creating mechanisms to remove that regulation. Such would be the case where an industry is clearly approaching the perfect competition ideal; that is, when the level of competition is sufficient to prevent any market participant from establishing or sustaining a significant and permanent price increase. On the other hand, even where a lower level of competition exists, deregulation may also be a goal if the costs of maintaining regulation outweigh the benefits.

Source: Based on Lafond, 1999.

many of the benefits associated with privatization will not materialize. (See Let's Talk Business 9.8.) This risk may be most apparent in the case of government transfer of ownership of natural monopolies like electricity or gas utilities to a single private owner who takes over the monopoly. This was a criticism levelled at the British government when a number of utilities were privatized, yet monopolistic industries were not consistently restructured to facilitate competition. Consequently, some privatized utility companies continued to operate under monopolistic conditions.

CHAPTER SUMMARY

We have noted the shift toward reduced government involvement in the business sector, reflected in the trends toward deregulation and privatization. Observers suggest that what we are witnessing is a marked decrease in government involvement as public preferences shift toward a more purely private market system. It seems that many observers view the decrease in the level of government influence in business as a positive change. However, some individuals believe that there is good reason for advocating a continued and, perhaps, increased role for government in business. What kind of role should government play in the business sector?

The question of government involvement in business has been debated for years. Certainly, the trend toward reduced government in terms of deregulation, privatization and elimination of tariff barriers seems to reflect the ideology that "less government is better". However, scholars such as Michael Porter suggest that the government still has a critical role to play in the health and well-being of business. For some, the answer lies in the government's ability to work with industry in order to develop a long-term industrial strategy to lead the country out of its current problems and ensure a more secure future for working Canadians. Consequently, rather than simply taking a "hands-off" approach, it may be argued that what is required is a clear rethinking of the different types of roles that government can play, or how it may play its current roles in a different manner.

KEY TERMS

- business enterprise system
- capitalism
- revenue taxes
- restrictive or regulatory taxes
- Crown corporations
- government regulation

- imperfect competition
- Competition Bureau
- bailouts
- subsidies
- deregulation
- privatization

Buy Canadian books

"Buy Canadian this holiday season," is the theme of an ad campaign initiated by Michael Redhill and Esta Spalding in *The Globe and Mail* on Saturday. Paid for entirely by Canadian writers, it explains to book readers that by "purchasing books published by Canadian companies, book-buyers can play a real role in keeping these publishers in business and helping to end their year on a much more positive note."

Mr. Redhill's Martin Sloane, you'll remember, was one of this year's six Giller-shortlisted novels. Esta Spalding, American by birth, is an admired poet and the author recently, with her mother Linda, of the novel *Mere*. They have, together, raised $14,000 more than the $6,000 they were asking for. Clearly, cultural nationalism is alive and well and living in Canada.

Now, I don't want to be a spoiler, but I can't help wondering how Mr. Redhill would feel if, having recently sold Martin Sloane in the United States and Britain, those countries' writers were to embark on a campaign of such [a] protectionist aspect. Buy British for a Better Book. Read American, Do Your Part in the War Against bin Laden. Books, and the rights to books, are just like any other products contributing to the GDP. What if Americans were to begin regarding our lucrative system of grants — not just to writers, but to publishers and distributors — as forms of subsidy, slapping a tariff on Canadian novels at the border, perhaps?

Don't get me wrong. I am as interested as the next reader in the writing of the region we call Canada, but I am wary of taking this predilection to the point of nationalist chauvinism. What worries me is that, true to custom, our failure to be robust — to behave, instead, dependently — means once again we are missing the opportunity that the plummeting dollar also presents. You could restore 15¢ to the loonie immediately, I figure, if Canadians felt an appropriate sense of alarm, and tapped into the ingenuity that, elsewhere, accompanies fear in a capitalist market. Instead, we remain a nation paralytically dependent on the subsidy — from writers, to airline carriers, to the CEOs recently polled by this paper, who are as guilty as anybody of looking for the easy way out (by pegging the loonie to the American buck). Why, oh why, are Canadians so hopelessly lacking in market savvy — in courage? The truth is we are at a turning point in the history of Canadian publishing. Our miserable dollar, hovering at its all-time low, means Canadian writers and publishers need next to no help at all, domestically anyway. An American hardback novel, note, whose Canadian equivalent might cost $35, will now set you back $10, even $15 more — if the book makes it across the border at all.

At an exchange rate of $1.60 and climbing, we have already arrived at the point where it may no longer be economically viable for U.S. publishers, in particular, to market their products here. Canadian book readers are on the verge, for the first time, of making perfectly rational decisions about cultural and educational matters based on cost. We will "buy Canadian," good or bad, because we cannot afford to do otherwise. Welcome to the new, provincial, Canada.

On the other hand, if economic theory holds, the publishers and writers who stand to prosper from our economic downturn will be Canadian. If we are honest with each other, and reach beyond the many plaudits we accord ourselves, they have been doing so already. For the truth about the "success" of many Canadian mid-list writers in particular is that it is as dependent as car parts on the wavering fortunes of the loonie.

Consider the business of rights: A publisher's fiction catalogue will require, biannually, so many thrillers, first novels, soapy stories, multi-generational sagas, etc. (Non-fiction is more regionally particular.) An American publishing house, therefore, can buy the work of a young U.S. writer acclaimed as the next Amy Tan, for US$100,000, let's say, or publish Canadian author Madeline Thien, writing the same stories of second-generation immigrant life, broadly applicable across the continent — for what? $60,000, maybe. The next novel by Camilla Gibb, an extremely talented writer whose first novel, *Mouthing the Words*, was picked up in the United States, also addresses a demand for gay literature nicely — and it comes at a discount. Do you really think agents don't talk like this?

As far as the distribution of Canadian books in the United States is concerned, some of our small presses — Arsenal Pulp Press, Beach Holme, ECW and Insomniac come to mind — are seizing the economic opportunity. They are not blaming a bad year on the Chapters merger or the world's most popular excuse: 9-11. Instead, they are concentrating their efforts on the American market. Consider, for instance, that in the realm of children's literature — a far more cost-competitive arena than what is so-called "literary" fiction — a Beach Holme children's book will set you back a mere $10. In the United States, that's six bucks, roughly the price of a hamburger. Nearly a third of Arsenal Pulp Press' revenues are now derived from American sales. These companies know, as a dear French-Canadian friend of mine used to say, "what side of the butter the bread she's on."

None of this is to denigrate the affecting, if somewhat earnest, sentiments of the writers who feel so alarmed on their publishers' behalf — but their focus is wrong, and it diverts the industry's attention from the problems — and opportunities — at hand.

It's time to stand on our own, and to find some other solution than yet more special pleading.

Source: Noah Richler, "Our books need readers, not subsidies" *National Post* (November 26, 2001). Reproduced with permission of author.

QUESTIONS

1. "The Canadian government should protect the Canadian book industry from foreign competition." Discuss the pros and cons of this statement, and make reference to other examples (from this chapter) that also illustrate the pros and cons of government aid to business.

2. In what specific ways does the "buy Canadian books" campaign, and the low value of the Canadian dollar conflict with the notions of globalization and NAFTA (see Chapter 8)? How do these factors potentially affect the Canadian publishing industry and the U.S. publishing industry?

3. With reference to the external forces that act on organizations (see Chapter 1), in what ways might each of these forces impact Canadian book publishers?

Let Air Canada manage itself

I was involved in the initial decision to privatize Air Canada, as Deputy Minister of Finance in 1988 and as chief of staff of the prime minister when the last 57% interest was sold to the public in 1989.

In retrospect, it seems a strange contradiction to have launched this corporation into the private sector while hobbling it with restrictions on where it must keep its maintenance bases and head office, and who should own it.

At the time, the political imperative seemed to be to convince Canadians little would change: If the people owned the airline indirectly beforehand, we would ensure, through the Air Canada Public Participation Act, that the broadest public ownership was achieved. The idea that it might not be appropriate for small investors to own stock in a volatile, cyclical industry was overwhelmed by the conventional wisdom that it would not be popular if ownership of the airline fell into too few institutional, corporate or foreign hands.

The constraint on the location of bases and offices creates duplication of costs that cannot be rationalized in difficult times. The requirement to observe the Official Languages Act (which normally does not apply to companies in the private sector) costs Air Canada millions of dollars a year in extra training when downsizing triggers bumping, which leaves bilingual posts held by unilingual personnel.

The knee-jerk tendency to impose political obligations on Air Canada despite its status as a commercial business continued in 1999, when Air Canada was finally allowed to rescue a faltering Canadian Airlines. In exchange for taking on CAIL's obligation to employees (and their 17,000 families) and creditors ($3-billion still remained outstanding after Canadian's restructuring), commitments were extracted regarding fares (no increase in prices for the first year, despite soaring fuel costs), employment (no layoffs until March, 2002) and service to small communities (routes cannot be abandoned until 2003).

The Competition Bureau required that Aeroplan points be made available to competitive carriers below a certain size and that access to gates, slots and counter space was to be offered to competitors. The Competition Act was amended to impose on Air Canada the concept of "avoidable costs," forcing the airline to dominate by redeploying resources it would rather mothball. Air Canada is the only corporation in Canada to which this legislative provision applies.

Under the regulatory framework where both the Canadian Transportation Agency and the Competition Bureau have jurisdiction, Air Canada is variously criticized for price gouging when it raises fares and predatory pricing when it lowers them, sometimes on the very same route!

What is wrong with this picture? If one believes the principal justification for privatization is that the private sector can manage and finance competitive businesses better than the government, we need a consistent policy: hands off Air Canada except for laws and regulations of general application.

The private sector is a demanding taskmaster — stock prices and credit ratings are the keys to being able to access capital. Failure to perform results in the harsh discipline of the business world — lower sales, reduced ability to finance, loss of office for the corporation's leaders.

So why should Air Canada get assistance from the federal government to help it through the consequences of the tragic events of Sept. 11? Is this a private-sector solution? To be fair, the airlines in the United States, which are very much private-sector businesses, asked for and received US$15-billion because of the unforeseen nature and the massive implications of the terrorist attacks and the shutdown of civil aviation. Moreover, airlines in Canada need comparable assistance with airport security, air marshals and insurance if this country's industry is to remain competitive with the United States.

But beyond relief for calamitous events, Air Canada should be free to manage its business. The airline should be able to lay off and relocate staff, pick its routes the way its competitors do and offer a more modest schedule. It is gratifying to learn that, to help Air Canada find new capital, the Minister of Transport announced yesterday he is prepared to eliminate the constraints on individual shareholdings.

The decision to privatize was the right one. The government's political standing would not benefit from a return to publicly owned, taxpayer-financed status for Air Canada. The last thing the government wants is for every lineup, every lost bag, every delayed arrival and every instance of imperfect customer service to be laid at the doorstep of the Minister of Transport.

To those who point to Air Canada's current problems as having been created by Air Canada itself, I say why not let Air Canada manage its own destiny and see whether things get better?

Source: By Stanley Hartt from *National Post* (October 24, 2001). Reproduced with permission of Stanley H. Hartt.

QUESTIONS

1. Is the author of this article arguing for or against government involvement in Air Canada? Discuss.

2. Should government offer aid to important Canadian companies like Air Canada? Why, or why not?

3. Do the tragic events of September 11, 2001 alter your opinion with regard to government assistance to businesses like Air Canada? Explain.

10

Business Ethics and Social Responsibility

Do business and ethics go together, or are they a contradiction in terms? This chapter begins by addressing the challenge of defining business ethics. We will examine models of ethical reasoning in organizations. We will look at the issue of corporate social responsibility, and analyze the debate regarding what role business should play in this area. The purpose of this chapter is to draw attention to the ethical dimension of business, and to encourage a more critical understanding of the ethical issues that you will no doubt confront at some time in your career.

LEARNING OBJECTIVES

By the end of the chapter, you should be able to:

1. Understand the challenges of defining business ethics.

2. Explain the models for judging the ethics of decisions.

3. Discuss how organizations may contribute to unethical behaviour at work.

4. Define corporate social responsibility.

5. Analyze the debate for and against the relevance of corporate social responsibility.

Organizational Insider

Profiting from September 11?

Some Toronto hotels raised their rates after learning of the arrival of 25 U.S.-bound flights which were diverted following the terrorist attacks in New York and Washington, D.C. ... Citing the principles of supply and demand, hotels near Toronto's Pearson International Airport decided to hike their room rates by as much as $100 after being informed of the unexpected guests.

"They told us to double the rates. I thought it was crazy — I mean, $275? It's not right," a front desk employee, who did not want to be identified, at one airport hotel that is part of an international chain said yesterday. "I couldn't believe it. It's gouging people. It's just pure greed."

A standard single-occupancy rate at the 445-room hotel runs from $130 to $150, but with occupancy approaching 100% on Tuesday afternoon the employee said the decision was made to more than double the rate. "I've been giving people [the rooms] for $118 a night [the special rate for federal government employees]," said the employee. "I'm probably going to get in trouble for it — but it's just not fair. I mean, it's been like a refugee camp in here."

Doug Kreiser, who was to return to his Chicago home yesterday, tried to check in to the hotel Tuesday afternoon and was quoted the heightened $275 rate. "The woman behind the desk was saying, 'Is that the price? Is that right?' to the woman next to her," Mr. Kreiser said. "They offered to knock it down a few dollars because I had a business discount card, but I was so appalled I just walked out and got a room next door."

The hotel's general manager denied that any rates had been altered, explaining that there were some talks yesterday about raising rates, but no action was taken. "Something like a worldwide conference where all Toronto is full or if the World Series or Super Bowl were in town — that would be a good reason," he said. "But something like this. It's not demand — it's a catastrophe." Other hotel employees acknowledged that price hikes were at least considered as hundreds of travellers scrambled for rooms. Some had jacked their rates as high as $279, but most had returned them back to normal yesterday. "We were a little bit higher yesterday but then we decided to drop it back down," Suzette Edwards, the assistant manager of [Carlingview] Airport Inn, said yesterday.

Mike Harris, the Premier of Ontario, vowed to take action against hotels that gouge stranded U.S. travellers by publicizing their names and fired off a letter to the Greater Toronto Hotel Association citing "disturbing phone calls" he had received regarding price hikes. Rod Seiling, president of the GTHA, said in a statement he was "extremely dismayed by allegations of 'gouging' at Toronto's hotels," and stressed that they were "completely unfounded."

Meanwhile, consumers in the American Midwest swarmed gasoline stations to pay up to $6 a gallon for fuel amid rumours of an imminent gasoline shortage. "We're having to assign officers to convenience stores to direct traffic and break up fights," said Sgt. Wayne Allen of the Tulsa Police in Tulsa, Okla. A 78-year-old man in Topeka, Kan., was arrested for aggravated assault for allegedly pulling a pellet gun on another customer for access to a pump. Lineups for gasoline stretched two and three blocks long in Bucyrus, Ohio, prompting the mayor to shut down the small town's nine gas stations on the night of the disaster.

The owners of R & L Texaco — a small station in Oklahoma City — offered refunds to customers yesterday after hiking their prices to $5 a gallon for two hours on Tuesday. The national average price of unleaded gasoline was $1.538 a gallon on Monday, the day before the attacks. The station's prices returned to $1.599 yesterday morning after Spencer Abraham, the United States Energy Secretary, said there were no supply disruptions to justify gasoline priced at $5 a gallon. Several companies froze their wholesale prices to retailers yesterday. Gas price spikes to $4 and $5 a gallon in Illinois led Jim Ryan, the state's Attorney General, to prepare two consumer fraud lawsuits against two stations. State officials throughout the United States are also investigating complaints of unethical price gouging.

Investigators in Wisconsin probed allegations of price gouging. "It is unAmerican to take advantage of Wisconsin citizens at a time of such tragedy," said Gov. Scott McCallum. Michigan's Lt. Gov. Dick Posthumus urged motorists to bypass stations "capitalizing on the fears of many people and raising their prices."

Source: Brad Mackay and Mary Vallis, "Hotels accused of hiking rates for the stranded. Harris vows to take action: Citing 'supply and demand,' some rooms go for $279" *National Post* (September 13, 2001). Reproduced with permission of the National Post.

THINK ABOUT BUSINESS ETHICS ————————

Is Business Unethical?

The Organizational Insider raises the question: What constitutes ethical or unethical business behaviour? In addition, should businesses be required to look beyond their profit objectives in order to help society? Unethical behaviour may be directed against the organization itself, or it may be consistent with the organization's goals, but inconsistent with commonly accepted ethical principles. Whether unethical behaviour comes in the form of subtle discrimination against other employees, "padding" expense accounts, paying or accepting bribes, questionable advertising or other forms of fraudulent activity, there is little doubt that the costs of such behaviour eventually accumulate.

The media has increasingly reported a concern over the erosion of business ethics, and unethical activities in organizations are estimated to cost industry billions of dollars a year.[192] It seems that much of what has been written in the popular press and reported in the news has tended to reflect poorly on the ethics of business. The recent phenomenon of corporate downsizings and massive layoffs has certainly contributed to the dim view of business. Other recurring issues that raise questions about the ethics of business include things like: misuse of natural resources, too close a relationship with government, not treating employees properly, and corporations being too big and too powerful. All these perceptions, whether accurate or inaccurate, reflect a commonly held view that business and ethics do not go together.

Some scholars have suggested that there is a crisis of confidence in a variety of corporate activities.[193] The Enron scandal in 2002 drew further attention to it. This scandal involved a large U.S. corporation that misled employees and shareholders with false reports and claims regarding its financial viability. (See Let's Talk Business 10.1.)

LET'S TALK BUSINESS 10.1 THE ENRON SCANDAL

Only the other day Kenneth Lay was heralded as a business genius. Now he is dismissed as a villain. This week, Enron's boss further burnished his reputation for villainy, first by refusing to appear before two congressional committees and then, when faced with a couple of subpoenas, turning up and — like any Hollywood villain in such circumstances — exercising his Fifth Amendment right to remain silent.

Does Mr. Lay's fall from grace presage a wider change in attitudes to business? Many think so. Ralph Nader, a veteran anti-corporate crusader, points out that the Enron affair has all the right ingredients for galvanising opinion: identifiable villains such as the shifty Mr. Lay and the unbearably arrogant Jeffrey Skilling; poor working stiffs who have been bilked [out] of their pension; and plenty of collusion and corruption in high places.

Source: From "The businessman as villain" *The Economist* (February 14, 2002).

318

LET'S TALK BUSINESS 10.2 BUSINESS ETHICS???

There is a perplexing disdain among these business students for business and a cynical attitude about their decision to pursue it as a career. Feeling very much as if they have sold their souls by going into business in the first place, they are resigned to, and comfortable with, myriad forms of immoral conduct as a routine part of business. It's as if they have concluded: If you are going to rob a Seven-Eleven convenience store, what difference does it make if you get a speeding ticket during the getaway? ... A recent survey of MBAs found that 73 percent would hire a competitor's employee to obtain trade secrets. The same survey found that only 60 percent of convicts would. One student's response when asked if he would leave a note if he hit a parked car in a parking lot was, "You mean a note with my name?" ... They have the yearnings of the liberal heart.... That businesses cheat is a given for them and they are cynically resigned to participation. Such is the result of this generation's students schooled amidst a curriculum and academy aligned against the evils of capitalism and comfortable avoiding the judgmentalism of right versus wrong.

Source: From Marianne M. Jennings, "What's happening in business schools?" *Public Interest* (Fall 1999) 137: 25–32.

Who Cares?

There is a growing view that corporations must be accountable to society for their behaviour. For example, in a recent survey[194] of over 1,000 CEOs from around the world, 68% agreed that ethical business practices are central to the profitability of any company. Similarly, the Canadian Democracy and Corporate Accountability Commission's poll[195] indicated overwhelming support for increased attention to ethical business behaviour. Of the respondents, 74% agreed with the statement that, "Executives have a responsibility to take into account the impact their decisions have on employees, local communities, and the country as well as making profits." In addition, 80% of the respondents want corporations to establish clear standards of social responsibility and require companies to report on their activities in this area.

Business ethics is not simply a societal concern — it has increasingly become an organizational issue that demands urgent attention. Managing ethical behaviour in business organizations requires an in-depth understanding of the many factors that contribute to employees' decisions to behave ethically or unethically. For those of you who are pursuing careers in business, it is useful to consider the ethics of your career. For students currently enrolled in business programs, their ambivalent view of business and ethics is captured in Let's Talk Business 10.2.

Defining Business Ethics

Before we begin to consider the issue of business ethics, a definition would clearly be helpful. Unfortunately, as one writer on business ethics recently put it: defining business ethics is like nailing Jell-O to the wall. However, what we can do is examine what constitutes the topic of business ethics, and we can identify the models that people employ to try to judge what is ethical and what is unethical behaviour. A major weakness of much of the scholarly literature on the topic of business ethics is a failure to adequately define the construct of ethics. Often, ethics have been defined differently by theorists. Beauchamp and Bowie wrote that ethics is the "inquiry into theories of what is good and evil and into what is right and wrong, and thus is inquiry into what we ought and ought not to do". Others have, quite simply, defined ethics as "the study of morality", the right standards of behaviour between parties in a situation,[196] and activity that we should or should not do.[197] Ethics is the study of morality or moral judgments, standards and rules of conduct.[198] The notion of business ethics has been considered as comprising the rules, standards, principles, or codes giving guidelines for morally right behaviour in certain contexts.[199]

A situation can have an ethical dimension, where the consequences of an individual's decision affects the interests, welfare, or expectations of others.[200] Unethical behaviour has been defined as behaviour that in some way has a harmful effect on others and is "either illegal, or morally unacceptable to the larger community".[201]

Ethical Behaviour as a Social Phenomenon

One central implication is that ethical behaviour, by its very nature, occurs within a **social context**. That is, it is a social phenomenon and, consequently, must be evaluated in terms of the relationships among a potential network of players. The social aspect of ethics is also reflected in theories of ethics such as Kant's **Categorical Imperative**.[202] Kant asserted that actions, to be moral, must respect others — to function in society, individuals recognize that they must restrict their actions, just as they expect others to restrict theirs.

As many scholars have observed, behaviour, in its abstract interpretation, has no values or ethical component. Therefore, what is defined as ethical or unethical behaviour represents a judgment based on a referent structure. It is further difficult to define what constitutes ethical or unethical behaviour within an organization. In very broad terms, business ethics requires the organization or individual to behave in accordance with some carefully thought-out rules of moral philosophy. While the term itself is not easily definable, one can readily think of examples of activities that could be considered unethical business practices, based on our views of what constitutes ethical or unethical behaviour. For example, types of activity that may be considered unethical behaviour include: misrepresenting the worth of a product or a business; engaging in forms of corporate spying; deciding to launch an aircraft that does not meet strict safety requirements; employee theft.

Certainly, behaviour that is illegal is, by definition, unethical; however, the reverse is not true: what is legal is not necessarily ethical. It is this latter issue that makes the study of business ethics much more compelling. That is, grappling with the "grey areas" of business presents a major challenge. What are the examples of behaviours that might be considered acceptable business practices, but might otherwise be considered unethical? Keep in mind that unethical behaviour may be directed against the organization, or it may be an activity that is consistent with the organization's goals but inconsistent with commonly accepted ethical principles. Later in this chapter we will identify these types of behaviour.

Business Ethics as Managing Interests

For the purpose of this chapter, we can consider one of the broader definitions of business ethics. In general terms, we can think of business ethics as the standards/rules/ principles used to judge the rightness or wrongness of behaviour. Mark Pastin, a writer on business ethics, notes that: "Managers today manage interests as much or more than they manage people or assets." That is a useful observation from a business ethics perspective. In fact, the workplace can be viewed, in Pastin's terms, as a "tangled web of conflicting interests vying for scarce resources". A manager is required to balance the interests of many different parties: shareholders, employees, customers, creditors, etc. And a basic issue of business ethics is really all about balancing these interests, many of which may be competing.

MODELS FOR JUDGING THE ETHICS OF DECISIONS

The literature on ethics is extensive, and exists across a variety of disciplines, including philosophy, anthropology, sociology, and psychology. However, until recently there have been few attempts to apply this theoretical framework to the specific area of business ethics. As Pastin[203] pointed out, the challenge to scholars in the field of business ethics is "to apply what appears to be esoteric, philosophical concepts to the real concerns of business organizations".

Business ethics is typically examined using normative theories — theories of how individuals should ideally behave. There are a variety of ways theories of ethics have been grouped. Among these classifications is the grouping of theories as utilitarian (consequential) or single-rule (non-consequential). We can consider two central models that have been used to describe the basis of judging the ethics of organizational decisions:

1. Utilitarian, or end-point ethics.
2. Rule ethics.

These two models identify potential methods of resolving conflicting interests within organizations. The models identify the logic or rationale a manager might employ in dealing with organizational issues that possess ethical implications.

End-Point Ethics

A major model of ethics used in the literature is end-point ethics. The dominant form of this view was articulated in John Stuart Mill's *Utilitarianism*, as a response to the Industrial Revolution. Utilitarianism asserts that to determine whether an action is right or wrong, one must assess the likely consequences, including: tangible economic outcomes (profit for shareholders), or intangible outcomes, such as happiness or friendship. For example, "What does it mean to be an ethical business person?" Utilitarianism posits that

321

an ethical person acts so as to produce the "greatest ratio of good to evil". Consistent with this view, an ethical manager would ensure the owners, employees and customers all share fairly in the business's gain. Utilitarianism asserts that an action is ethical if it produces, or if it tends to produce, the greatest amount of good for the greatest number of people affected by the action.[204] In other words, actions themselves are neither ethical or unethical; rather, ethics are judged based on the outcomes of such actions. That is, ethical behaviour is a behaviour that results in total benefits or utility exceeding total costs, or negative consequences. In this regard, utilitarianism ideally requires an examination of the fairness of the outcomes,[205] given that the consequences experienced by all affected parties ultimately determine whether or not an action is ethical. The "modern" counterparts of end-point ethics are cost-benefit and risk-benefit analyses.

The Consequences of Our Actions

In sum, end-point ethics is a model for ethical decision making that states that a person, organization or society should engage in that activity that results in the greatest balance of good over harm for all. In other words, where we have a number of different interests at play, we need to consider what action will benefit most of the parties. The focus is on judging the ethics of an action by considering its outcome for all potentially affected parties. It is not the process of the decision or the behaviour to achieve the outcome that are considered, but the outcome itself. As mentioned, the concept of end-point ethics is also referred to as utilitarianism. Why this strange name? Well, because we are talking about maximizing utility, or usefulness, of a decision for all stakeholders — those potentially affected by the decision. It is an ethical analysis that considers the relative gains and costs for all parties affected by a decision or action. If the benefits outweigh the costs, then we go ahead with the decision — or choose the decision that gives us this outcome.

In other words, according to utilitarianism, an ethical person will make a decision or act in a way that produces the greatest ratio of good to evil, so to speak. From a business perspective, this might suggest that an ethical manager will ensure that owners, employees and customers, for example, all share fairly in business gains. Now, how do we compare the relative benefit and harm to each stakeholder? That is difficult to answer. In broad terms, we compare the costs and benefits to each stakeholder by considering a number of possible factors, which might include: social (i.e., how it affects society or the public as a whole), human (psychological or emotional impact) or economic (for example, what is the dollar impact of our decision?).

Limitations

Clearly, a major problem with this approach to ethical reasoning lies in the difficulty of estimating and comparing relative benefits and costs or harm to the stakeholders. Consider an example. Many Canadian businesses are increasingly conducting business globally. Should we be concerned if our Canadian business people are conducting business with a foreign country that has a record of human rights violations? For example, the Prime Minister of Canada has led trade missions to a number of countries with an infamous record of human rights violations in order to establish business relations. Is this ethical?

Well, consider what end-point ethics suggests. Do overall benefits exceed overall harm? There are great potential gains for Canadian business by expanding their reach to foreign markets. This means potentially more jobs in Canada and a healthier economy. What harm arises? Those supporting such ventures argue that there is no harm generated and, consequently, they can ethically support such business. Those opposed might argue that we might be supporting oppressive regimes. So how do we judge whether, indeed, there are more benefits than harms arising from such business ventures?

A second fundamental problem with the end-point ethics approach is that, as the name implies, it looks just at the end-point, or result, without considering the implications of what it takes to achieve those results. It does not ask us to consider whether or not the manner in which the outcomes were achieved is ethical. This is the notion of the "ends justifying the means". So even if end-point ethics helped generate a solution that resulted in a maximization of the greatest good for all those affected, it ignores what happens "in-between", that is, to get to that point or outcome. End-point ethics says: start with a consideration of the consequences to judge the ethics of a decision. This involves asking at least two key questions:

1. Who will be significantly affected by this decision?
2. What is the impact of this decision as perceived by each of the affected groups?

In sum, end-point ethics gives managers a tool for analyzing business decisions. This line of thinking basically asks us to consider: Who counts most in our decision, and how are they affected by it? However, it doesn't tell us to examine the process or what to do about strategy.

Rule Ethics

A second major method of ethical reasoning is referred to as rule ethics. Deontological theories of ethics (that is, theories of ethics arising from the study of duty) refute the utilitarian assertion that the ethics of an action is based on its outcomes, and suggest that the ethics of an action are independent of the outcomes or consequences. Rule ethics is essentially the fundamental deontological perspective, which considers actions as ethical or unethical based on their relation to the rules and principles that guide behaviours.[206] Based on this perspective, ethical behaviour is behaviour that can be deemed as morally right regardless of the consequences. In the Western world, for example, Judeo-Christian religious and moral rules or values have played a major role in defining morality in society.[207] Of course, even within Western society, there are a variety of beliefs or rules regarding what is ethical, and society has tended to permit rules to change in many areas of behaviour.

Right versus Wrong

Rule ethics is the view that there are basic rules that determine the "rightness" or "wrongness" of actions. Stated quite simply, rule ethics asserts that an individual should do what is required by valid, ethical principles, and should not do anything that violates those principles. These are the fundamental notions of right and wrong. Given the diverse nature of society there is no one clear set of rule ethics that is followed by all individuals. This is, perhaps, one of the central problems in assessing whether behaviour can be deemed ethical — whose rules should apply?

Both utilitarian and rule ethics consider the social aspect of ethics: unethical behaviour is behaviour that has a harmful effect on others, and is "either illegal, or morally unacceptable to the larger community".[208] How do these two models of ethical reasoning operate differently? Let's consider a business issue, and see what each model offers with regard to resolving a problem.

Applying the Models: A Scenario

You are a business person trying to win a $22 million contract for your company with a major corporation overseas. You learn that in order to gain the contract, you need to offer a substantial monetary gift to the CEO of the major corporation. **What would you do?**

This question is one that managers must increasingly ask themselves as we continue to conduct business on a global scale. And certainly, as many observers have pointed out, attitudes and customs regarding ethical business practices can vary widely among different countries.

From an End-Point Ethics Perspective

From this perspective we could not get any universal agreement as to the ethics of such a practice. Clearly, many countries have no problem with bribery. Reconsider the principles of end-point ethics: Do we achieve the greatest balance of good over harm for all potential stakeholders? First, who gains from a bribe? Well, clearly your company will benefit from getting the deal and, consequently, you benefit as well. Who is harmed by such a transaction?

You might consider three potential losers:

1. Does the bribe compromise your ability to do business with companies like this one in the future — will the perception of your company be negative?
2. Competent competitors who are otherwise deserving of the contract may lose because they refused to offer this bribe.
3. The bribe might permit inferior products or services to be purchased simply because the supplier bribed those in power to help get the product or service to market. Consequently, consumers may be harmed.

If, indeed, these three stakeholders are harmed in this way as a consequence of our decision, end-point ethics would likely guide us away from such a decision. However, end-point ethics does not necessarily condemn such behaviour as unethical. If the product or service is not inferior — that is, if the bribe helps us conduct business and sell a good product that is fairly priced — then consumers are not harmed. If the CEO will likely receive a bribe from some other supplier, regardless of whether you choose to bribe or not, then end-point ethics suggests that no one is "worse for the wear", so to speak, by having received the bribe. Depending on how it is applied, end-point ethics potentially could justify the giving of a bribe. Certainly, it does not uniformly condemn such a decision. Rather, the result depends on how rigorously the decision-maker has identified all potential stakeholders, and carefully weighed the relative costs and benefits (both tangible and intangible) that arise from this action.

From a Rule Ethics Perspective

What guidance does rule ethics offer us in considering whether or not to bribe the CEO of this foreign corporation in order to gain the contract? Again, consider what rule ethics says. It says that we should do what our ethical codes or beliefs tell us to do. Now, in North America, at least, there are many organizations that have instituted strict codes of ethics that prohibit giving or accepting gifts of any kind. Perhaps that would be a guiding rule for some decision-makers. On the other hand, perhaps an individual's personal or religious beliefs dictate honesty in all aspects of life; and this may also serve to act as a rule prohibiting engaging in a bribe. It may be our belief that no business person should pay a bribe to any company official, even though the ethical codes of some other countries do, indeed, tolerate bribery.

Does rule ethics generate a negative response to the question of gift-giving? Once again, this model does not generate universal responses to problems. For example, perhaps we have rules that advocate such gift-giving, and these rules guide our behaviour. Do we have any obligations that override our ethical prohibition of bribery? What if your company's survival depended on securing business with this foreign company? What if thousands of jobs would be lost in your company if the business was not obtained and that could not be obtained other than through the bribe? Could these issues offer compelling reasons to follow a rule that "all is fair in business"? Rule ethics may dictate overriding the general prohibition against bribery because of the greater urgency to protect the company and jobs. Consequently, even rule ethics does not provide a blanket condemnation of bribery. Modern society, it seems, has lost its ability to provide clear rules or guidelines to individuals that will enable them to resolve conflicting interests.

Lessons?

What lessons do we learn from an understanding of end-point ethics and rule ethics? Perhaps the greatest value of these models lies in what they demand of us. Both models are inherently flawed, as we discussed above. They are limited by the degree of rigour that the user (decision-maker) employs in their use. End-point ethics demands that we question the ethics of our actions in the following ways:

- Which stakeholders have we identified, and which not identified?
- Have we clearly acknowledged the harm, as well as the benefits, that may arise from our decisions?
- How have we determined the relative importance of each of the stakeholders?

- How have we determined the relative weight of the benefits and harms that will potentially arise from our decisions?

Similarly, rule ethics suggests we need to think more critically about what rules we employ in making decisions:

- Where did the rules that guide our behaviour and choices come from?
- Do we use these rules consistently, or only when it is convenient?
- Do we apply separate sets of rules to govern our professional and our personal lives? Why?

As you can see, the value of considering the models we use to make decisions is in demonstrating the fact that our decisions often have an ethical dimension. Without an understanding of the motivation behind our decisions, we may fall victim to making decisions on purely a business basis, even though they may have ethical implications.

DO ORGANIZATIONS MAKE US UNETHICAL?

The two models of ethical decision making outlined above help give us an understanding of the ways we may resolve conflicting interests in the workplace. Neither model guarantees we will make a sound, ethical decision. That depends on the level of rigour with which we analyze our choices and the impact of our choices. When faced with decisions that involve ethical implications, why might we not "do the right thing"? Why do some individuals choose to engage in unethical behaviour, while others do not? There are countless theories that attempt to answer that question. Among the theories are suggestions that self-interest is a major influence on unethical behaviour. For example, based on **agency theory**, it is argued that when agents (employees) possess more information than principals (employers), and their goals conflict, agents may behave in accordance with their self-interest and, thereby, such individuals may deceive the principal.[209] Other scholars have accused individuals (human agents) of being "pure egoists"[210] whose behaviour typically reflects a desire to maximize their own utility.[211] This sentiment is also expressed in neo-classical economics and social exchange theory, which assert that individuals will engage in unethical behaviour if it is in their best interest to do so.[212] As an example of this self-interest connection, there is some research evidence to suggest that if individuals receive a personal gain or reward from giving a bribe to another party, they are very likely to engage in this form of unethical behaviour.[213]

From a normative perspective, business ethics advocates that individuals should be motivated by more than a complete focus on self-interest.[214] Some scholars have pointed out that a rational, economic focus on self-interest can be irrational — "rational agents approach being psychopathic when their interests are solely in benefit to themselves."[215] Certainly this criticism of self-interest makes sense from a social perspective. We live in societies where co-operation is expected, and a purely economic, self-interest focus would prove dysfunctional for society.

For many years researchers have attempted to discern the relative role of the individual's and the organization's characteristics in encouraging unethical behaviour in the workplace: the notion of distinguishing "bad apples or bad barrels".[216]

Managing ethical behaviour in business organizations requires an in-depth understanding of the many factors that contribute to employees' decisions to behave ethically or unethically. One key question that needs to be addressed is: Under what conditions will individuals, within their role as employee, engage in behaviour that does not conform with commonly accepted standards of ethical behaviour?

What factors in the workplace might create an environment where unethical behaviour is acceptable? That is, when do employees willingly engage in what otherwise would be considered unacceptable behaviour? For example, why may an individual willingly engage in corporate "spying", or why may an individual willingly misrepresent a product's quality to a customer? The research and theory has acknowledged that organizations can present unique challenges to ethical behaviour for their constituents. Organizational factors play a role in ethical decision making and behaviour at two points: establishing moral intent, and engaging in moral behaviour.

Exhibit 10.1 summarizes the framework adopted to explain the impact of organizational context. The elements that play a critical role in individual ethical behaviour in the organization are: culture, organizational de-coupling, routinization of work, organizational

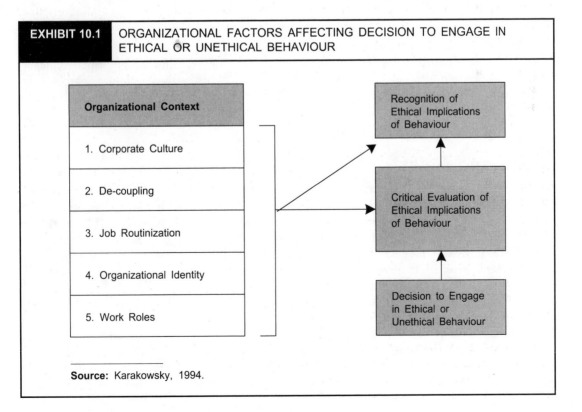

EXHIBIT 10.1 ORGANIZATIONAL FACTORS AFFECTING DECISION TO ENGAGE IN ETHICAL OR UNETHICAL BEHAVIOUR

Source: Karakowsky, 1994.

identity, and work roles. The influence of these factors on behaviour arises through their impact on

- perceptions or recognition of the ethical dimension or ethical implications of the work situation
- critical evaluation of the ethical implications or consequences of work behaviour
- final decision to engage in the behaviour

The elements of this framework are delineated below.

1. Unethical Behaviour as a Consequence of Corporate Culture

Business morality is essentially a social reality, as opposed to a physical reality, and therefore cannot be fully understood apart from the social system and organizational culture that are conceptualizing it.[217] What is organizational culture, and how can it impact my decision as an employee to engage in ethical or unethical behaviour?

Organizational culture has been defined as the bond or glue that holds an organization together. It encompasses a set of shared beliefs regarding how members of the organization should behave and what goals they should seek. In this sense it is an intangible, abstract component of any organization. There is an IBM culture, a Nortel culture, a McDonald's culture and a Harvard University culture. Every organization contains some kind of culture.

The notion that norms influence ethical behaviour has been suggested for many years. Specifically, organizational culture provides an organizational reality within which ethically relevant actions are discussed, judged and legitimized. For example, culture, through its transmission of organizational beliefs, can provide employees with **legitimate** (sanctioned) or **non-legitimate** approaches to ethical decision making and behaviour.

Rituals and Myths

Organizational researchers who consider culture to be a system of publicly and collectively accepted meanings also suggest that an organization is filled with organizational "rituals and myths".[218] Organizational rituals and myths contain messages that provide a shared experience and reinforcement of values for members of the organization. Myths specifically contain a narrative of events, often with a "sacred" quality attached. Both ritual and myth play a crucial role in the continuous processes of establishing and maintaining what is legitimate and what is unacceptable in any organizational culture.[219] The "myths" and "rituals" are simply the organization's established products, services, techniques and policies or rules that employees adopt/conform to.[220]

Organizational myths could be, for example, legends of corporate heroes and their deeds within the organization, which can provide guidance (positive or negative) for employees facing ethical decisions in similar circumstances.[221] This may permit individuals to legitimize their actions in ethical dilemmas.[222] That is, the culture, through its transmission of myths, can provide employees with legitimate (sanctioned) or non-legitimate approaches to ethical decision making and behaviour. Indeed, Gatewood and Carroll[223] suggested that the socialization of ethics, which occurs through a process of internalization of organizational ethical standards, is fundamental to the ethical conduct of organizational members.

What's the Connection to Ethics?

How can managers generate a culture that encourages ethical behaviour? It has been suggested that a strong ethical culture can be generated through the areas of selection (choosing employees whose beliefs are consistent with those of the organization), socialization (conveying the organization's goals and norms effectively), and training and mentoring (reinforcing the organization's culture through training and personal role models).[224] Gatewood and Carroll[225] suggested that the socialization of ethics, which occurs through a process of internalization of organizational ethical standards, is fundamental to the ethical conduct of organizational members. Other authors have provided similar suggestions for encouraging ethical behaviour in organizations, including the development of corporate ethical codes of conduct,[226] and public discussions of ethical issues through formal meetings.[227] This sense of open confrontation and discussion of ethical concerns must be institutionalized before it becomes an effective means of resolving moral conflict. Corporate codes of conduct are one of the most common methods used by the business community as an attempt to improve ethical conduct. These rules are intended to reflect the general values of society. Codes of ethics are one means of "institutionalizing" ethics in corporations.[228] This involves incorporating ethics formally and explicitly into daily business life.

Corporate Codes of Conduct

Ethical codes are necessary because laws cannot prescribe the standard of ethical conduct for all situations.[229] However, it should be noted that many critics have suggested that these codes may become nothing more than "window dressing" — a means of appearing ethical that does not necessarily reflect actual practice. For example, it has been suggested[230] that the lack of reinforcement of ethical behaviour reflected in management's "results orientation" can encourage employees to behave unethically. "Good guys finish last" is the sentiment that propels this attitude in business. In other words, organizations that do not reward ethical behaviour are sending out the message that such behaviour is unnecessary. This can happen regardless of the presence of formal corporate codes of conduct.

Bureaucratic Cultures

Research support has been provided for the notion that moral atmosphere affects moral reasoning and moral judgment.[231] A number of research studies have attempted to explore this concept within the organizational context. Findings have indicated that when an informal or formal organization policy was present, ethical behaviour increased and unethical behaviour was deterred.[232] Weber[233] examined the effects of size of the organization on a manager's stage of moral reasoning. The results of Weber's study indicated that managers in smaller organizations appeared to be operating at a higher stage of moral reasoning.

329

Weber suggested several reasons for these findings. Larger organizations often exhibit cultures with more complex bureaucracies and greater control over their employees through rules and regulations. Therefore, managers feeling isolated from the central decision-making authority will tend to rely on more immediate peers or supervisors for support or approval of their behaviour. On the other hand, smaller organizations tend to be less bureaucratic and possess fewer rules to govern employee behaviour. Subsequently, managers in this environment feel a greater sense of control over the decision-making process, along with a greater need to conform with social laws as means to protect themselves from conflict with other stakeholders (i.e., customers, public, etc.). This reflects a higher stage of cognitive moral development. In other words, a democratic culture may encourage members to take responsibility for their actions, while an authoritative culture may dictate rules that replace individual discretion and, thereby, suppress development of ethical decision making.[234]

2. Unethical Behaviour as a Consequence of De-coupling

Organizations sometimes try to cover up inefficiencies by separating or de-coupling the behaviour from its evaluation. Specifically, "avoidance", "discretion" and "overlooking" of inefficiencies are acts that maintain the assumption that people are acting in good faith. This encourages confidence in the myths that legitimize an organization's activities. Organizations can protect themselves from public scrutiny by ensuring that any questionable activities are "de-coupled" from external evaluation in this sense.[235]

Corporate Language

The notion of de-coupling suggests that organizations can conduct themselves in ways that hide activities that would otherwise be considered unacceptable if they were subjected to closer scrutiny. Among the most infamous examples of conformity with organizationally legitimized, yet unethical, behaviour were the crimes of the Nazi Party during World War II. While a variety of theories have been applied to attempt to explain the atrocities committed by the Nazis, one can consider how the Nazis de-coupled behaviour from its evaluation. The use of accepted or legitimized symbols or practices can help to de-couple actual activity from evaluation of that activity. For example, the use of euphemisms by the Nazi perpetrators de-coupled actual behaviour from evaluation of that behaviour — the victims were not murdered, according to Nazi language, they were "selected". This language provided a sense of legitimacy to what would otherwise be viewed as inhuman behaviour. The ability to de-couple deeds from evaluation or scrutiny supported the notion that legitimized beliefs, perpetuated through the use of symbolic language, could help maintain conformity and allegiance to a brutal cause.

Meyer and Rowan argued that to maintain external legitimacy organizations adopt commonly accepted rules on the surface and incorporate them into their structure. However, these rules may, in effect, be unrelated to how the activities are really conducted. The selective use of language to label various work practices is one method of disguising the unethical implications of workplace behaviour. For example, the unethical practice of corporate spying may be symbolically legitimized (to the organization and its employees) as a form of market analysis — a term that gives a sense of legitimacy to what would otherwise be considered unethical business practice. This use of corporate language or labels can de-couple the behaviour from moral evaluation of the behaviour. Consequently, this suggests that employees will be encouraged to engage in unethical behaviour where that behaviour has been legitimized through the adoption of the behaviour as accepted business practice, and where behaviour and evaluation of that behaviour are de-coupled.

3. Unethical Behaviour as a Consequence of Work — Routinization

McDonald's is the most famous example of routinized work: that is, work that is governed strictly by rules and regulations, as scientific management advocates. However, McDonald's is not the only organization dependent on routinized work practices; in fact, to a degree, most jobs have some element of routinization. A number of scholars have recognized the pervasive existence of routinized work practices, or habitual routines, in organizations. This phenomenon has been described as concrete behaviour that is not governed by rational deliberation but, rather, by routinized performance programs.[236]

The notion of adopting routinized performance programs as accepted ways of doing work can be thought of in terms of institutionalizing behaviour on the job. For example, consider the airline pilot who follows clear procedures with regard to flying the plane, or the auditor who follows strict guidelines with regard to performing an audit. Clearly, both these jobs require a high degree of professional judgment or discretion. However, both also rely on some standards and commonly accepted methods for performing the work, also referred to as habitual routines. Gersick and Hackman[237] suggested that behavioural norms that evolve in groups pressure individuals to adhere to habitual routines. That is, once a routine has been established in a group, the behaviours involved in executing the routine will submit to normative control. Management scholars have suggested that once a behaviour is accepted as a legitimate means of accomplishing the work, its actual effects (efficiency or otherwise) are not readily questioned.

Habitual Routines

The legitimization of acceptable behaviour can extend to the actual job itself — how the work is performed. The organization may generate routinized work procedures that are viewed as legitimate since they follow an acceptable set of rules. For example, following the written guidelines of conducting an audit is viewed as a legitimate method of auditing. The proliferation of technical guidelines to govern work methods enhances the perceived legitimacy of the work. However, in actuality, these routinized work methods may be neither the most efficient, nor the most effective, way of conducting the work. Gersick and Hackman[238] identified both functional and dysfunctional consequences of routinized or habitual behaviour. A major advantage of habitual routines is that they save time and energy, since they don't require active management: in this respect, they should improve efficiency. How much of our work constitutes simply "going through the motions" — that is, that portion of our work that does not demand constant mental scrutiny but, rather, can be performed with minimal attention to detail? Among the disadvantages identified were the tendency for routines to permit a misinterpretation of the situation to occur. That is, if a group fails to recognize a novel stimulus situation, or if changes to familiar situations occur, then invoking a habitual routine will be inappropriate. What is the impact of such habitual routines on ethical behaviour in organizations?

Reduction of Critical Thought

A fundamental characteristic of habitual routines, the inability of habitual routines to adapt to change, has important implications for ethical behaviour in the workplace. For example, consider a situation involving an engineer who habitually performs a safety check on the construction standards of a building plan. The engineer performs all the checks in accordance with the professional or legal requirements, while neglecting to consider non-routine indicators of potential risk in the construction. Certainly, there is an ethical or moral dimension to decisions or practices that can affect the well-being of others: the duty of care in performance that exists beyond strict legal requirements can be considered an ethical concern. In the case of the engineer, strict adherence to habitual routines permits unethical behaviour to occur due to the failure to critically analyze the ethical implications of a workplace behaviour — i.e., to consider the welfare of all parties potentially affected by the behaviour.

4. Unethical Behaviour as a Consequence of Organizational Identity

Jackall argued that the bureaucratization of organizations has influenced "moral consciousness". According to Jackall, this transformation heralded:

> the decline of the old middle class of entrepreneurs, free professionals, and independent businessmen — the traditional carriers of the old Protestant Ethic — and the ascendance of a new middle class of salaried employees whose common characteristic was and is their dependence on the big organization.[239]

According to this view, corporate America destroyed ethical values. The Protestant Ethic emphasized the "stewardship" responsibilities associated with the accumulation of wealth. However, as Jackall argued, "the very accumulation of wealth that the old Protestant Ethic made possible gradually stripped away the religious basis of the ethic, especially among the rising middle class that benefited from it." In addition, organizational bureaucracies created their own "internal rules" and "social context" to guide individual conduct. Jackall argued:

> Bureaucracy ... breaks apart the older connection between the meaning of work and salvation. In the bureaucratic world, one's success ... no longer depends on one's own efforts ... but on the capriciousness of one's superiors and the market....[240]

Is Bureaucracy to Blame?

Based on this perspective, modern organizations encourage unethical behaviour largely as a result of the demise of the Protestant Work Ethic through the bureaucratization of these organizations. Why blame bureaucracy? Bureaucracies are considered guilty given their characteristics of requiring the subjugation of personal belief systems to the beliefs or goals of the organization. This is reflected in the notion of "working for the boss" — our futures are dependent on our ability to fulfill our organizational responsibilities, regardless of the consequences. To the extent that individual identities continue to become intrinsically bound up with organizational identities, the ethics of an individual employee may be tied to the ethics of the organization with which they identify. To the extent that our personal identity is bound up with our organizational identity, what organizations demand of us may dictate the ethics that we live by.

Social identity theory[241] posits that individuals classify themselves and others into social categories (e.g., organizational membership, age, gender) that are defined by the typical characteristics abstracted from the members. Organizational identification is a specific form of social identification.[242] Individuals can identify with elements of the organization that have been reified — i.e., that have become embodiments of the characteristics perceived as typical of its members: "I work for IBM", "I am a lawyer", etc. These are all statements of identity based on an organization or a profession. For example, an individual can identify with his/her membership as a professional accountant. What are the consequences of this process of social or organizational identification? One consequence of social identity is the tendency of the individual to support the values and actions of the group, and to internalize the perception of the group as more desirable compared to other groups.[243] Group members can enhance self esteem by increasing the desirability associated with their social categories.[244] The consequences of identification with the organization also have implications for ethical behaviour of group members.

In the Name of the Boss

When we identify with our organizations, we tend to become less critical of its policies and behaviour. The notion that identification with the organization restricts or discourages evaluations or perceptions that might reflect poorly on the organization has clear ethical implications. For example, Ashforth and Mael[245] suggested that identification can provide a mechanism whereby an individual can continue to believe in the integrity of the organization despite wrongdoing by senior management. An individual who maintains a strong organizational identity will not critically evaluate his/her behaviour on its own merits (i.e., actual consequences), but will judge behaviour based on perceptions of the social category to which he/she belongs. For example, a public accountant who identifies strongly with his/her firm or professional body may avoid critical evaluation of his/her conduct when he/she perceives themselves as acting on behalf of that firm or professional body, which upholds professional standards. Indeed, at the extreme, there is research to suggest that employees will engage in unethical behaviour at the request of authority figures.[246] In addition to the influence of authority figures, the research has explored the effects of peers on ethical behaviour. In fact, many researchers have suggested that unethical behaviour is learned in the process of interacting with persons who are part of intimate personal groups or role-sets:[247] those employees who have learned through differential association in their role-sets to be unethical and have the opportunity to engage in unethical behaviours will be more likely to do so.

5. Unethical Behaviour as a Consequence of Organizational Roles

Organizational role theory proposes that individuals in organizations occupy positions or roles that involve a set of activities, including interactions with others, that are required or expected as part of the job.[248] Individuals fulfill role requirements based on internalized expectations concerning the responsibilities of the role. Roles have a psychological reality to individuals occupying them.

The presence of incompatible expectations of attitudes, beliefs and behaviours inherent in social roles will generate an ambivalence known as role conflict.[249] Kahn et al.[250] identified several forms of role conflict, including inter-role conflict, which refers to the competing demands of two or more roles that an individual occupies. For example, the demands associated with the role of employee may conflict with the demands associated with the role as family member. How do individuals resolve the inherent conflict of organizationally situated roles or identities? Ashforth and Mael[251] summarized the methods individuals employ to cognitively resolve role conflict, including: denying role conflict, compartmentalizing roles or identities, and prioritizing roles.[252] These types of coping mechanisms suggest that individuals do not necessarily engage in a critical, objective evaluation of competing role demands.

Role Conflict

What are the implications of organizational roles for the ethical behaviour of individuals occupying those roles? More specifically, what are the implications of these conflict resolution strategies for ethical behaviour? Consider the case of an employee in the role of salesperson who must decide whether the role responsibility of reaching the sales target at all costs should take priority over his/her role as honest citizen. The individual may rationalize that he/she is responsibly fulfilling role obligations, even though the behaviour required to fulfill the role of salesperson might be ethically unsound. Consistent with Ashforth and Mael's[253] summary of responses to role conflict, the individual can resolve the role conflict by compartmentalizing or prioritizing role demands as a means to rationalize the behaviour. That is, the employee can adopt a different set of standards to judge what constitutes appropriate salesperson behaviour as contrasted with appropriate honest citizen behaviour. Essentially, this suggests that ethical conflicts among competing role demands can effectively be ignored by the individual through this cognitive process.

Conflict Resolution

What effect does the organization have on role conflict resolution? How an individual chooses to resolve the multiple role conflicts will depend largely on the organizational context. Returning to the previous discussion, the institutional elements, including culture, identity, de-coupling and routinization, will impact the individual's reactions to role conflicts and demands. For example, if the organizational culture ignores an ethical dimension to role requirements, individuals will not attempt to reconcile their role performance with ethical considerations; if the organization institutionalizes habitual behaviour and suppresses analytical thought, then evaluation of the ethical implications of role responsibilities and role conflicts will similarly be reduced. Clearly, organizational context will significantly influence how an individual resolves role conflict.

CORPORATE SOCIAL RESPONSIBILITY ——————

Much of our examination to this point has focused on business ethics in relation to the individual: whether an employee, boss, etc. Now we can step a bit further back, and think more generally about the nature of business itself as an entity. How a business, as opposed to an individual, behaves with regard to other parties, including its members, its customers, its investors, its competitors and to society in general, is an issue captured in the concept of corporate social responsibility (CSR).

The historical "ethical yardstick" for business has been profit — the "bottom line". Scholars such as economist Milton Friedman[254] argued that the workings of the free and competitive marketplace will "moralize" corporate behaviour. Therefore, business need only be concerned with the profit motive, since the "invisible hand" of the free market will produce a "systematic morality". Similarly, John Kenneth Galbraith[255] argued that corporate responsibilities should be purely rational and economic. However, according to Galbraith, it is the regulatory hands of the law and the political process, rather than the invisible hand of the marketplace, that turns these objectives to the "common good". Both views reject the exercise of independent moral judgment by corporations as actors in society. On the other hand, most scholars concerned with the study of business ethics[256] implicitly reject these views, and instead argue that it is the responsibility of business organizations to develop a "moral conscience" and exercise ethical judgment or social responsibility.

The term social responsibility refers to those obligations or responsibilities of an organization that involve going beyond

- the production of goods/services at a profit
- the requirements of competition, legal regulations or custom

Social responsibility involves an obligation to create policies, make decisions, and engage in actions that are desirable in terms of the values and objectives of society.

Consider recent observations of companies that have attempted to save their employees from job losses in Let's Talk Business 10.3.

All companies mentioned in Let's Talk Business 10.3 made an effort to save their employees from termination. There are numerous other examples of businesses going "above and beyond" the profit objective to pursue socially responsible goals. For example, Levi Strauss & Co. has tried very hard to maintain strict work standards to protect employees in operations in different parts of the world. In addition, they are consistently lauded for their efforts in the social sphere, an effort summarized recently in an article:

LET'S TALK BUSINESS 10.3 BEING SOCIALLY RESPONSIBLE

Alberta Energy Co. (AEC) has been in business for 26 years and has never laid off a single employee. At a time when blizzards of pink slips are raining down on the Canadian economy, that's an accomplishment of which few businesses can boast. Certainly not Nortel Networks Corp. (with 49,500 workers laid off this year) or JDS Uniphase Corp. (down 16,000). Calgary-based AEC, with a market capitalization of about $8-billion and a staff of 1,700, is among a handful of North American companies whose record for never downsizing is a point of pride. The benefits — fierce employee loyalty and increased productivity — are clear-cut, though in lean times it's not an easy ideal to achieve. What is remarkable is that [at] AEC there is no formal policy prohibiting downsizing. The firm has just always found ways to avoid it. For example, in 1986, a major downturn hit the energy sector, prompting AEC to introduce a program called the Extra Mile: Employees were asked to come up with ways to save their jobs. And that's exactly what they did....

The Sept. 11 terrorist attacks have prompted the largest plunge in consumer confidence since the 1992 Persian Gulf War. Billions of dollars worth of business has been lost and layoffs across both Canada and the United States have rocketed to a nine-year high. But while the airline sector has been particularly hard hit in recent weeks, there is one company where that won't happen. Southwest Airlines — survivors of numerous rises in jet fuel prices, recessions and the Gulf War — has not laid off a single worker in 30 years. Its advantage: about US$1-billion in cash and no debt. James Parker, the airline's chief executive, recently told Business Week, "We are willing to suffer some damage, even to our stock price, to protect the jobs of our people."

While many North American companies go the route of the pay cut, shorter work week and cutting expenses to the bone to avoid job losses, none compares with auto parts giant Magna International Inc. of Aurora, Ont. Even as the car sector gets slammed, Magna offers an unusual corporate culture where layoffs are avoided at all costs. With a workforce of 60,000 worldwide, Magna ... has never experienced downsizing in its 40-year history. "Our unique culture makes those who work for us stakeholders in the company," said Belinda Stronach when she took over from her father as chief executive seven months ago. "It makes employees the decision makers on their futures."

Source: From David Steinhart, "Where pink slips are not part of corporate culture: Workers' champions" *Financial Post* (October 5, 2001). Reproduced with permission of National Post.

Besides patching together jeans, Levi Strauss has a long history of funding projects that help patch together groups of people. Project Change, an independent nonprofit originally funded by the Levi Strauss Foundation (and still closely associated with it), combats racism in communities where the company has manufacturing operations. There are now sites in Albuquerque, El Paso, Knoxville, and Valdosta, Ga. In Albuquerque..., research showed that people of colour were twice as likely as whites to be denied home loans, regardless of their income. Project Change established a Fair Lending Center to help customers comparison-shop among local banks and to encourage banks to lend in poor New Mexico neighbourhoods. In Valdosta, the project talked nine banks into funding mortgages for low-income first-time home buyers.[257]

This is certainly admirable corporate behaviour, but let's ask a question: Is it necessary? That is, does Levi's have an ethical obligation as a business to do this? While we applaud the efforts of companies like Levi's, AEC, Magna, Southwest Airlines, should we demand such behaviour from all organizations? And more generally, does business have a moral responsibility to us — whether we are employees, customers, creditors, or society in general?

The CSR Debate

There is much diverse opinion regarding the degree to which business should practise social responsibility. Some argue that, at best, business should have very limited social responsibilities, while others argue that the social responsibilities of business should be extensive. What are the arguments for believing that business should take on extensive social responsibilities, and what is the rationale used by those who believe business should not be required to take on the mantle of social responsibility? Let's consider the cases for, and against, social responsibility.

The Case Against CSR

1. Business Is Business

Probably one of the best-known arguments against social responsibility for business comes from the work of economist Milton Friedman, who argued, quite simply, that profit maximization is the primary purpose of business, and to have any other purpose is not socially responsible! Friedman points out that in a free enterprise, private property system, a manager is an employee of the owners of the business and, consequently, is directly responsible to them. In other words, Friedman and others argue that a business's primary responsibility is to the owners or shareholders. Clearly, owners and shareholders want to maximize profit, and so this should be the highest priority of the business.

EXHIBIT 10.2	THE CSR DEBATE

Against Social Responsibility	For Social Responsibility
1. Business is business.	1. Business should conform to societal expectations.
2. Business plays by its own rules.	2. CSR is a practical strategy.
3. Business should not dictate morality.	3. Must acknowledge network of stakeholders.
4. Organizations cannot be held accountable for their actions.	4. Long-term benefits.

LET'S TALK BUSINESS 10.4 WHAT'S A COMPANY TO DO?

Thomas J. Bata opened the plant in 1939 on the banks of the Trent River, about 100 km east of Toronto.... The company made four million pairs of shoes and boots a year, which were sold across Canada and around the world. Bata owned all the land within the town, 480 hectares, and built cookie-cutter bungalows for the workers to rent, adding schools and churches for the families. Workers played on Bata baseball and hockey teams and shopped at the company-owned grocery store.

But then labour became cheaper overseas and work at the Batawa plant started to dwindle — as did the jobs. "It's no secret it costs a lot less to produce a shoe in China than it does in Canada," says Graeme Spicer, director of international communications at Bata. "And the economy is not set up to support jobs for life. The day of the company town is gone." In its last decade, Bata lost $32 million on the plant, which had been manufacturing less than one percent of the company's total output. Bata now has 55 factories worldwide, including the one in Zlin, which it reopened in 1991.

Source: From Tanya Davies, "Letter from Batawa: When the jobs go" *Maclean's* (August 14, 2000). Reproduced with permission of Maclean's Magazine.

It has been argued that a regard for ethical values in market decisions might lead businessmen to confuse their economic goals with altruistic goals so that they fail to fulfill the basic business function of operating efficiently. While most scholars in the field advocate one form or another of corporate responsibility, they also acknowledge the difficulty of adopting an ethical corporate objective. Albert Carr[258] argued that no company can be expected to serve the social interest unless its self-interest is also served, either by the expectation of profit or the avoidance of punishment.

Consider an example: the case of Bata. Here was a company, Bata Ltd., a Canadian-based national company, known for its socially responsible behaviour — including establishing a plant where no community formerly existed. Yet, recently, it chose to shut down its Ontario plant, and move operations overseas. (See Let's Talk Business 10.4.)

Is it socially responsible for a company to take away the jobs that it initially created? On the other hand, given the significant drop in annual profits, if the company did not move production overseas, where costs were much cheaper, the company would be in dire straits. Consequently, jobs were shifted from Canadian workers to those in China, where labour was much cheaper. Is this socially responsible? If you consider Bata's responsibility to its owners and its creditors, they would argue that it would have been irresponsible not to move production abroad.

2. Business Plays by Its Own Rules

This sentiment suggests that business cannot be judged by the same set of rules or standards of moral conduct that we apply outside of business. Carr, in a famous article written for the *Harvard Business Review*, raised the question of whether, indeed, we should expect that business managers apply the same ethical standards we might apply in our personal lives. Carr suggested that "bluffing" (i.e., lying), which may be viewed as an unethical practice in social relations, can be viewed as legitimate behaviour within the boundaries of business activity. Carr[259] compared corporate activity to a poker game, whereby ethical standards within the boundaries of the "game" may differ from societal standards. The "players" (business executives), therefore, may engage in activity that is acceptable within the "rules" of business, even though this activity may be viewed as unethical by the public (those outside the "game" of business). Therefore, individuals may employ ethical standards in business that differ from those generally employed in their non-working lives. That is, where "business bluffing" has been accepted as a form of business conduct, members come to believe in this behaviour as an accepted way of doing business. For example, union and management negotiations are subject to negotiator tendencies to demand more than what might otherwise be equitable, as a means of bargaining. Similarly, a company may convince customers that its product is worth significantly more than the cost of producing it, as a means to accrue a high profit. Members of organizations will engage in behaviour compatible with accepted beliefs, although these behaviours might otherwise be viewed as unacceptable.

Given this, why should we expect businesses to be good citizens in the same way that we expect of individuals? We might expect that a business will try to advertise its product in a manner that suggests it may be of much higher quality than it really is. That's part of the rules of business — which are largely focused on profit maximization, and not necessarily on seeking the truth in advertising, for example.

Is business a game? Do you accept the notion that business is like a game, and should be played by its own rules? Is it acceptable to leave our moral standards at the door, so to speak, when we enter the workplace? Recall the scenario earlier of the CEO and the gift in order to achieve the $22 million contract. Would you give the gift? Why, or why not? If this is considered a bribe and therefore unethical, why would you give the gift? The common response is because it is part of the "rules of the game". This is the expectation that, in business, this is a legitimate, commonly accepted practice. However, there is a danger in de-coupling behaviour — in avoiding scrutiny of business behaviour. First, it makes an assumption about what is and what is not acceptable in business. In this case, for example, businesses are increasingly frowning upon giving gifts to clients or customers. Consequently, what is acceptable for business and society is not necessarily a stable factor. In addition, for some individuals, it is unacceptable to trade off one's ethics in the "line of duty". The question becomes: What is acceptable for you?

3. Business Should Not Dictate Morality

Given that business enterprises are fundamentally responsible to the owners or shareholders, their mandate is to maximize profit, and that is their area of expertise. They are economic institutions, and they should leave the issue of social policy to the jurisdiction of government. Managers are simply not skilled in the area of social policy, and consequently should not be held responsible to carry out duties of social responsibility. If businesses enter the area of social policy, they are, in effect, expanding their power. How? Well, a corporation that is engaging in extensive social programs is essentially performing a political function in addition to its economic purpose. Some critics suggest that allowing business to have both economic and political power in its hands is potentially dangerous. As an article in *The Economist* argued:

> It is no advance for democracy when public policy is "privatized", and corporate boards take it upon themselves to weigh competing social, economic and environmental goals. That is a job for governments, which remain competent to do it if they choose. And when it comes to business ethics, it is worth remembering that managers do not, as a rule, own the companies they are directing. Their first duty is to serve the people who are paying their salaries, so long as they stay within the law and the canons of ordinary decency. In the political arena, the chief executive of the biggest multinational has just one vote — and that is how it should be.[260]

Consequently, those opposed to businesses venturing into the social sphere, for this reason, argue that government can simply enforce regulations to ensure that business is socially responsible rather than allowing business to take it upon itself to judge matters of social responsibility.

4. Organizations Cannot Be Held Accountable

While society may judge somewhat cynically the ethics of "big business", who exactly is to be held accountable for the actions taken by individuals on behalf of their company? It is not always easy to place blame when the entity responsible for an action is not an individual but, rather, a corporation. Many scholars have asserted that rather than observing organizations, it is the corporation's leaders and their constituents whose behaviour must be studied. Following this line of reasoning, Carroll[261] argued that unethical business behaviour is the result of two ethical standards — personal and business. Carroll's research suggested that individuals under pressure compromise their personal standards in order to achieve the goals of the organization. Similarly, Carr[262] argued that "the ethic of corporate advantage invariably silences and drives out the ethic of individual restraint."

Can we hold organizations responsible for their crimes? Should IBM be somehow held accountable for its alleged involvement in the Holocaust, as reported in Let's Talk Business 10.5? What responsibility do organizations have to ensure their products are not misused? Do businesses have a responsibility not to associate with countries that are violating human rights? Or, on the other hand, should business strategy be guided purely by profits?

The Case For CSR

Now that we have looked at some of the more common sources of support for ignoring social responsibility, let's consider the counterargument. Why should business be concerned with the issue of social responsibility? Why might business be obliged to take on social responsibility? Why should business go beyond its legal requirements or industry standards?

1. Conform to Societal Expectations

Scholars in the field of business ethics have argued that business and society need not be seen as distinct entities but, rather, that business plays a role within society: fundamentally, businesses are created to serve public needs. It is for this same pragmatic reason that a

---

LET'S TALK BUSINESS 10.5 IBM AND THE HOLOCAUST

A recent book by Edwin Black, entitled *IBM and the Holocaust*, offers compelling evidence that IBM played an important role in some of the most horrific events of the 1930s and 1940s in Europe. Specifically, IBM's production of hundreds of Hollerith machines, the precursor to the computer, played a central role in the first racial censuses conducted by the Nazis. Beginning in 1933, the Hollerith machine was used by the German government to identify its intended targets. As Black comments in his book:

> Nearly every Nazi concentration camp operated a Hollerith Department ... in some camps ... as many as two dozen IBM sorters, tabulators and printers were installed ... [I]t did not matter whether IBM did or did not know exactly which machine was used at which death camp. All that mattered was that the money would be waiting — once the smoke cleared.

The author suggests that IBM's involvement with Nazi Germany helps explain one mystery of the Holocaust — how so many people were killed in so little time. With the knowledge of top IBM management in the United States, IBM's European subsidiaries actually perfected the means for the Nazis to quickly collect census data for its murderous plans. Hitler awarded IBM chairman Thomas Watson a medal for his company's work.

Source: Based on Edwin Black, *IBM and the Holocaust: The Strategic Alliance between Nazi Germany and America's Most Powerful Corporation* (New York: Crown Publishers, 2001), p. 375.

---

business will not act in any way that will reduce its legitimacy in the eyes of the public. Given that the very existence of business enterprise is largely dependent on acceptance by society, there is an obligation not to violate societal beliefs regarding socially responsible behaviour — particularly if such violations would undermine the credibility of an enterprise's role in society. Scholars have suggested that the doctrine of corporate social responsibility can also be understood as part of an effort to reconcile the intentions and results of capitalism. Advocates of corporate social responsibility understand the importance of the profit motive; however, they view this as only part of the social responsibility of business.

2. Adopt CSR as Practical Business Strategy

A second, even more pragmatic, reason for businesses to be socially responsible is to avoid public criticism or scrutiny that might inadvertently encourage more government involvement or regulation. For example, we have recently witnessed a number of organizations accused of unfair business practices and attempting to create a monopoly. Other organizations, like Nike, have been heavily criticized for shutting down operations in America in favour of setting up business where labour is cheap, and in some cases where sweatshop-like conditions exist among the factories of the foreign contractors. A lack of concern for social responsibility may invite public scrutiny.

3. Acknowledge Membership in a Broader Network of Stakeholders

What are stakeholders? Stakeholders refer to any individuals or groups who bear some type of risk as a result of the corporation's actions. Stakeholders might have financial, physical or human stakes or interests in the corporation. Who are the potential stakeholders in business activity? Among the list of stakeholders and the corporation's responsibilities to them, we can include those identified in Exhibit 10.3.

Among some of the other potential stakeholders in a business are **suppliers**, the **government** and **society** in general — each of whom may also be affected in some way by corporate activity and, consequently, must be considered in conducting business. In any actions a business takes, the argument, then, is that business should consider the impact on any party that has a stake in its operations: that is affected by its behaviour. Aside from ethical considerations, there are practical reasons to attend to all the stakeholders' interests, even when they conflict: if management focuses on only the concerns of a minority of stakeholders, such as the owners, other stakeholders may withdraw their participation with and support for the enterprise and consequently, can harm the business. Thus, to suggest that business need not be socially responsible is to ignore the fact that business enterprises regularly interact with, and affect, numerous stakeholders.

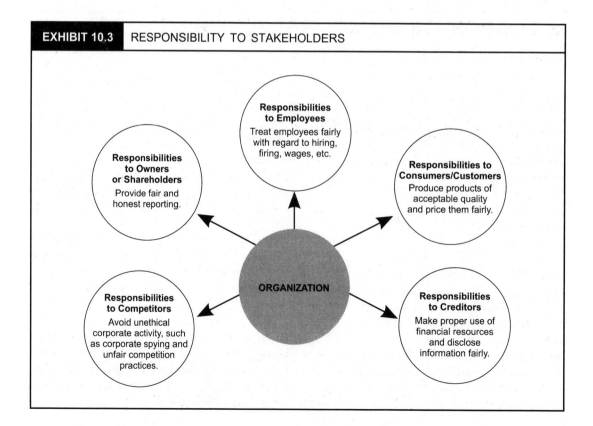

EXHIBIT 10.3 RESPONSIBILITY TO STAKEHOLDERS

4. Gain Long-term Benefits of CSR

Advocates of corporate social responsibility suggest that even if an action does not result in immediate benefits for the enterprise, engaging in socially responsible behaviour is wise from a longer-term strategic perspective. This, perhaps, connects to the first point made — regarding the relationship of business with society. A business that fosters this relationship will more likely continue to receive acceptance from, and be considered legitimate by, the public. The notion of building and maintaining goodwill with the public and a positive image are certainly influenced by social responsiveness. For example, Johnson & Johnson, the maker of Tylenol, was faced with major disaster in the 1980s after a number of tragic deaths were found to be the result of poisoned Tylenol capsules. While the cause was later found to be tampering at the retail location, not at the manufacturers' site, Johnson & Johnson took complete, extensive responsibility in withdrawing all their Tylenol capsules from the market (retail value of over $100 million) and urging the public not to use them by running television commercials and establishing telephone hotlines. And this also prompted Johnson & Johnson to re-introduce the product in tamper-proof packages. While their social responsibility was costly, they made up for that loss by restoring public confidence in their reputation.

IS CORPORATE SOCIAL RESPONSIBILITY ON THE RISE?

The central arguments that support the case against business enterprises taking a more active role in the area of social responsibility were outlined above. One remaining question is: Where are we now? That is, how have the views of corporate social responsibility changed over the years? What philosophy are more and more businesses adopting currently with regard to social or moral obligations? According to some observers, we are undergoing a gradual transformation that increasingly involves shaping organizations to reflect higher levels of social responsiveness. There is an increasing push for organizations to balance the profit objective with goals of social responsibility. In other words, business enterprises have begun to make greater efforts to recognize and balance the needs of different stakeholders.

Of course, how business responds to different stakeholders may be represented on a continuum from a purely pragmatic, self-interest approach to a socially responsible approach. The traditional pragmatic approach has been one that focuses on strategies that consider only the objectives of the owners or shareholders. It places emphasis on the needs of one group of stakeholders — the owners or shareholders. This reflects the notion that the primary orientation of business is to fulfill economic, as opposed to social, interests. On the other hand, there is a drive to adopt a more socially responsible approach. This approach does not ignore the responsibility of business to owners or to shareholders to maximize profits; however, this should not be accomplished at the expense of other stakeholders. Managers are challenged to use ethical principles to guide managerial actions when faced with competing interests among different stakeholders.

Judging the Ethics of Organizations

Earlier in this chapter, we considered two central models of ethical decision making, endpoint ethics and rule ethics. These prove to be useful models for critiquing the ethics of our everyday decisions. Can we judge the ethics of organizations as entities? That is, can we critique the nature of the organizational arrangements under which we function as employees? There is another ethical tool or model that speaks very directly to the nature of organizations and the question of the conditions under which organizations conform to or violate ethical principles. One such tool for considering the ethical dimension of organizational issues is **social contract ethics**.

Social Contract Ethics

One version of rule ethics, social contract ethics, was articulated by John Locke.[263] This model posited that the rules by which people live are those that they would agree to live by if given the opportunity to make a choice based on reason or knowledge. Locke's idea of the social contract provided a basis for a new model of organizations that views them as networks of contracts. Immanuel Kant[264] added that only rules that apply equally to everyone are ethical.

Taken together, the social contract model of ethical reasoning views the ethical rules that we live by as products of an implicit contract. The social contract is an implicit agreement regarding basic principles of conduct. These social contracts are harboured by the cultures of groups or organizations and by our society. Organizational social contracts represent the ground rules regarding conditions of employment, rewards and performance expectations. Organizational management researchers have viewed organizations as a web of implicit contracts (Pastin) — every time you enter a new organization you are entering a web of contracts. Of course, the question is: Are these contracts or ground rules sound?

A contract is sound if all parties entering into it have entered into it freely and fairly. That is, parties enter into them voluntarily. And fairness involves the notion that, regardless of your position, you would view the contract as equally fair from all perspectives. **It is not unbalanced** in favour of some interests over others. According to social contract ethics, then, an individual should do what a fair, voluntary contract would dictate: that is, the ethical guide for dealing with any issue. Social contract ethics is essentially about assessing the ethics or fairness of an organizational arrangement — whether that is how people are hired or fired; how they are evaluated; or how they are rewarded, among other things. Social contract ethics offers a test for assessing whether a contract is sound — and that test is rather simple: the contract is sound if all parties in the contract have entered into it freely and fairly. So, any member of an organization attempting to address that test would ask at least three questions: Do I really agree with this contract, or am I just tolerating it? If I occupied a different position in this company, would I accept this contract?

An Example: The Ethics of Downsizing

Let's consider a pervasive issue that continues to affect the business landscape: organizational downsizings. What might the social contract model say about the ethics of downsizing? Consider the recent observations of a writer, who commented on the "new deal" between workers and the organizations in Let's Talk Business 10.6.

LET'S TALK BUSINESS 10.6 LEANER AND MEANER?

Free agency is over. Layoffs are back. Since January, announcements of job cuts have come rapid-fire: 26,000 at DaimlerChrysler; 16,000 at Lucent; 9,600 at P&G; 8,500 at Cisco; 8,400 at Sara Lee; 4,000 at Disney. The list is long and getting longer; some companies, including Nortel, Dell, and 3Com, recently announced a second round of cutbacks only a few months after their first. Hardly any company is immune. John Challenger, CEO of the outplacement firm Challenger Gray & Christmas, calls the carnage "instant, no-fault job loss." In the old manufacturing economy, blue-collar unemployment always rose and fell in lock step with factory inventories; now a similar thing is happening to the mostly white-collar workers in the sleek offices of the new economy. Morgan Stanley estimates that 81% of layoffs in March and April were white-collar.

   If this sounds like deja vu all over again, it is — sort of. The 1990–91 recession introduced the notion of equal-opportunity job loss; back then, college-educated workers were among the first to be laid off. Debate raged in Washington about how to retrain white-collar workers and ready them for the new job insecurity. Companies began getting very explicit in their warnings to employees: Jobs were not for life. Harvard professor Rosabeth Moss Kanter was one of a chorus of academics and consultants arguing that since companies could no longer provide job security, they should do more to give workers "employability security" through training and skills counselling. All this prompted a 1994 Fortune cover story called "The New Deal" that said legions of white-collar workers were encountering the "widespread replacement of the job compact of the previous era, the one that traded loyalty for job security. That deal is virtually dead."

Source: From Betsy Morris, "White-Collar Blues" *Fortune* (July 23, 2001). © 2001 Time Inc. All rights reserved.

We could consider the implicit contract between a number of different parties, but let's just consider the implicit agreements among employer and employee. Many critics have argued that what we have seen with the downsizing phenomenon is a violation of a number of implicit rules existing between employer and employee. No longer is there an implied agreement that you enter a company in your twenties, work hard, and retire some 20 or perhaps 30 years later. Throughout the 1990s we witnessed massive layoffs of employees who felt they kept their end of the social contract by working hard for their organizations, yet were terminated in an organizational restructuring or downsizing.

   This view of a violation of the social contract was expressed in a recent article in *The Globe and Mail* entitled, "One day you're family, the next day you're fired." This article recounted the events that preceded the termination of about 300 employees of a Canadian company as part of a downsizing. The author recounts how those terminated were locked out of the building and only permitted back inside under the supervision of security guards who watched closely as they collected their personal belongings and were escorted out of the building again. These kinds of stories were pervasive throughout the 1990s and, unfortunately, continue today.

What does the future hold? Will we see a decreased, or increased, emphasis on social responsibility? Well, we have been experiencing much turbulence in the corporate world in recent years. Part of the chaos, including the infamous spread of corporate downsizing, has left many people sceptical of the morality of business. On the other hand, there is a strong belief that business will place increasing emphasis on the recognition of the needs of different stakeholders. That is, many observers believe that more and more businesses will need to place more emphasis on their social responsiveness to maintain legitimacy and acceptance from the community at large.

CHAPTER SUMMARY

This chapter attempted to underscore the ethical dimension of organizational decisions and behaviour. How managers balance the different needs of stakeholders demands knowledge of the ethical implications of otherwise typical business decisions. Ethics is central to the managerial task. Management educators have been expanding the realm of management literature to consider the relationship of ethics and management. An understanding of the social responsibility of business organizations and their constituents may help create a more productive and trusting relationship between business and society.

KEY TERMS

- business ethics
- Categorical Imperative
- utilitarian or end-point ethics
- rule ethics
- agency theory
- de-coupling
- organizational identity

- corporate codes of conduct
- habitual routines
- social identity theory
- organizational role theory
- corporate social responsibility (CSR)
- stakeholders
- social contract ethics

CASE APPLICATION The ethics of drugs

DRUG INDUSTRY UNDER FIRE

The global drugs industry, accused by critics of profiting from AIDS in Africa and bioterrorism in the United States, faces a rough ride at world trade talks in Qatar this week. Executives were on the offensive at an industry conference in London yesterday, warning of a "slippery slope" as developing countries and health activists stepped up a campaign to secure broad rights to override patents on life-saving drugs.

The US$300-billion-a-year industry sees a profit threat in demands by 60 developing countries, led by Brazil and India, for a loosening of the World Trade Organization's agreement on Trade-Related Aspects of Intellectual Property Rights (TRIPS). Poor countries argue that TRIPS rules, guaranteeing 20-year patents on medicines, make it hard for governments faced with HIV/AIDS and other epidemics to get access to drugs. Drugmakers say the system is vital to reward innovation.

The controversy has been complicated by threats from Canada and the United States to override patents on Bayer AG's antibiotic Cipro, in order to protect citizens against anthrax, leading to accusations of double standards. George Poste, former research head at SmithKline Beecham, who heads a consultancy firm, said the row highlighted the "populist politics" the industry now had to contend with. "The issue of AIDS drugs pricing, the Canadian government's wish to impose compulsory licensing on ciprofloxacin [Cipro] and the recently negotiated U.S. deal with Bayer are symptoms of a rather slippery slope that could all too easily overtake a broader product portfolio," he told the conference.

No one believes the provision of cut-price — or even free — AIDS drugs in Africa will seriously dent drug company profits. But surrendering intellectual property in one part of the world would undermine the system of commercial incentives vital for the development of tomorrow's medicines, according to Hank McKinnell, chairman of Pfizer Inc. Without the protection of patents, drug companies would never have developed the 64 AIDS drugs on the market and the hundreds more in development, he argued. "Critics say we should abrogate all intellectual property protection in the developing world and this will solve the problem of people in sub-Saharan Africa having access to necessary medicines. Nothing could be further from the truth," Mr. McKinnell told the conference.

The key proposal by developing nations states that "nothing in the TRIPS agreement shall prevent countries from taking measures to promote and protect public health." The United States, Britain, Germany and Switzerland — all states with large pharmaceutical industries — fear this would dramatically weaken WTO protection for intellectual property. Health campaigners, however, think the tide is turning their way, helped by the recent controversy over anti-anthrax drugs.

Source: Ben Hirschler, "ANALYSIS — Drug industry under fire at World Trade meeting" *Reuters* (November 6, 2001). Copyright 2001 Reuters Limited.

WHO SHOULD WE PROTECT?

Generic firms have long argued that these "draconian" laws not only give the big firms an unfair monopoly on the market, but they keep cheaper drugs off store shelves. But the companies that invent the medications say the exclusivity laws are fair because of the time, effort — and money — they invest in developing the drugs.

The conflicting arguments are not limited to Canada. Mr. Rock's blunder has already dominated talks at the World Trade Organization, where representatives of poorer countries have accused Health Canada of a double standard. When countries dealing with AIDS epidemics suggested relaxing international patent laws in order to supply the sick with cheaper drugs, the response from North America was lukewarm.

"Now they're saying, 'Listen Canada, the minute you get into trouble you say you want to break the patents, whereas you're telling us Third World countries that we shouldn't break the patents when it comes to AIDS,'" said Jim McIlroy, an international trade lawyer who specializes in intellectual property rights.

Source: Excerpts from Michael Friscolanti, "Pressure builds to change drug patent law" *National Post* (October 27, 2001). Reproduced with permission of National Post.

QUESTIONS

1. In what ways are the issues presented here issues of business ethics?

2. In what way is corporate social responsibility an issue here? Should these companies be forced to be socially responsible? Why? Why not?

3. Are patent laws in this industry ethical? Consider rule ethics, end-point ethics and social contract models.

The ethics debate

READING I: DO GOOD AND YOU'LL DO WELL

NEW YORK — The tone and emphasis of this year's World Economic Forum, which ended here yesterday, was remarkably different from years before.

This was in large measure due to the realization that the globalization of business was dramatically linked to geo-politics, a notion that came home in horrifying fashion on Sept. 11 when terrorists harboured in decrepit Afghanistan obliterated part of Wall Street and killed more than 3,000 people.

"The two cultures have come together. If we are to have a peaceful world, we must have a world that is responsible," said James Wolfensohn, the president of the World Bank who led a panel discussion on corporate responsibility with CEOs from around the world.

Protesters surrounded the Waldorf-Astoria for most of the five-day Forum, chanting, marching and holding up signs attacking corporate greed. They were not invited in, but their presence were nagging reminders that critics are ready to pounce on bad business practices.

Mr. Wolfensohn said business has become the engine of development, replacing governments. In 1990, overseas assistance to developing countries totalled US$60-billion and private-sector investment US$30-billion. By 1998, private-sector investment totalled US$300-billion and outside development assistance US$50-billion.

Pressure from critics has forged new business practices, agreed the panelists, not out of altruism, but as a result of enlightened self-interest. Anyone with a "brand name" to protect must invest and behave ethically, lest criticism damages the asset.

"To be a good corporate citizen pays," said Rolf-Ernst Breuer, a spokesman for the Deutsche Bank. "The function of the CEO is to be in charge of corporate citizenship. Now people who aren't shareholders are asking tough questions. Ten years ago that never happened."

For instance, after Sept. 11, the bank reversed a decision to finance a pipeline project in Latin America after becoming convinced that ecological damage would result.

David Komansky, chairman and chief executive of Merrill Lynch & Co., noted the new "moralizing" that's taking place in boardrooms.

"We have been looking at financing the Three Gorges [hydro-electric] project in China. It has some unappealing consequences, such as the burial of historical relics 200 feet below water and the displacement of one million people. Then there is the fact that the project will stop flooding, which causes damage and displacement. Suddenly, we're put in a position that we're not qualified to be in. Now we have pressure to make moral judgments on the validity of financings. This is something new we are grappling with," he said.

Bill Gates, who remains Microsoft Corp.'s chief architect and chairman, is also busy giving away his personal fortune of US$40-billion to health and other social projects around the world.

349

"There is a new moralism," he said, adding that if you have a brand name and need partners "success is coupled" with responsibility.

Mr. Gates, whose business practices at home were successfully attacked by anti-trust officials in recent years, said that legislative interventions into business behaviour, such as the Foreign Practices Act and prohibitions against the apartheid regime in South Africa, were good developments.

Concern about brand name protection is also leading to a new, higher ethical standard of quality, said Taizo Nishimuro, chairman of Toshiba Corp. in Japan. His company's cars worldwide meet the highest pollution standards even when made or sold in countries where there are no such standards.

Don Evans, the U.S. Secretary of Commerce who left his business career to serve in the Cabinet, urged businessmen to do public service and "have the courage to get into the game."

"You cannot separate good investments from social responsibilities," he said. The linkage is that responsible investments lead to economic growth, which leads to higher living standards and eventually to human freedoms.

Another incentive to do well by doing good was suggested at a prior panel comprised of clergy from around the world. Said George Carey, Archbishop of Canterbury: "I delivered a sermon on Sunday at a Wall Street church and told the attendees that you cannot go to church on Sunday and to hell for what you did on Monday."

Source: Diane Francis, "Do good and you'll do well. Business must now grapple with moral judgments" *Financial Post* (February 5, 2002). Reproduced with permission of the publisher.

READING II: THE HARM IN CORPORATE SOCIAL RESPONSIBILITY

... CSR is a flawed doctrine with the potential to do significant harm.

According to the doctrine, the combination of changed economic conditions and pressures from public opinion require businesses to take on a new role — to play a leading part in reshaping the world by embracing the notion of corporate citizenship. They should run their affairs, in close conjunction with an array of different stakeholders, so as to pursue the goal of sustainable development. Sustainable development is said to have three dimensions — economic, environmental and social. Hence companies should set objectives, measure their performance and have that performance independently audited, in relation to all three. They should aim to meet the "triple bottom line" rather than focusing narrowly on profitability and shareholder value.

Only by acting in this way, the argument goes, can businesses respond to society's expectations. In this lies the key to long-run commercial success for individual firms, since profits depend on reputation, which in turn depends increasingly on being seen to act in a socially responsible way. Thus, taking the CSR path will, in fact, be good for enterprise profitability. Further, its adoption by businesses generally is necessary to ensure continuing public support for the private enterprise system as a whole. Capitalism has to be given a human face.

.   .   .   .

This consensus is misguided. For one thing, neither sustainable development nor the means to achieve it are either well defined or universally agreed upon. It is not the case, as CSR supporters typically assume, that such policy issues involve well-specified problems with known solutions. Goals such as eco-efficiency or social justice are ill defined and questionable. They form a poor basis for redefining the scope and purpose of modern business.

The notion of society's expectations is likewise open to question. It is doubtful that most people expect businesses to pursue sustainable development and the triple bottom line, which could well result in higher costs and prices for the products and services.

Often, CSR advocates are global salvationists. This accompanies alarmist views on the state of the environment and the damage done to it by business-related activities, a belief that fateful choices now have to be made on behalf of humanity and the planet, and a distorted view of globalization and its effects.

Contrary to the salvationists, globalization has not brought social exclusion, nor has it marginalized poor countries. It has not brought disproportionate benefits to multinationals in particular, nor has it increased their power to influence events while reducing that of governments. To the contrary, governments retain their capacity to act, while privatization, deregulation and the freeing of cross-border trade and capital flows have reduced the economic power of businesses by making markets more open and competitive. The idea that businesses now have to take on new and wider social responsibilities because they have become more powerful, while governments have become weaker, has no basis.

CSR doesn't just rest on dubious or false assumptions. Carrying it into effect is liable to do actual harm.

Within businesses, the adoption of CSR carries with it a high probability of cost increases and impaired performance. Managers have to take account of a wider range of goals and concerns and to involve themselves in new and time-consuming processes of consultation with outside stakeholders. New systems of accounting, monitoring and auditing are called for. On top of all this, the adoption of more exacting self-chosen environmental and social standards is liable to add to costs, all the more so if firms demand observance of these same standards by their partners, suppliers and contractors.

Such adverse effects on enterprise performance make everyone poorer. Nor is it clear there will be offsetting gains. Contrary to what is often assumed by supporters of CSR, it is not the case that progress necessarily results from the adoption of higher norms and standards. There are many instances where insistence on these has brought higher costs for small or dubious benefits. There is an obvious risk that, in the name of CSR and in response to society's expectations, firms will mark out a path of over-regulation of economic life. This, too, would reduce welfare.

Insofar as socially responsible businesses find their new role is bringing with it higher costs and lower profits, they have a strong interest in having their unregenerate rivals compelled to follow suit, whether through public pressure or government regulation. The effect of such enforced uniformity is to limit competition and hence to worsen the performance of the economy as a whole. The systemic effects of CSR, as well as the enterprise effects, will tend to make people poorer.

The greatest potential for harm of this kind arises from attempts, whether by governments or by businesses in the name of CSR and global corporate citizenship, to impose worldwide norms and standards. Since circumstances differ widely across countries, such regulatory actions would restrict the scope for mutually beneficial trade and investment flows. In particular, they would hold back the development of poor countries by suppressing employment opportunities within them.

Prominent businesses which have adopted CSR have lent their support to dubious corporatist notions of global governance in which business joins hands with governments, international agencies and leading NGOs to raise standards across the world. Besides carrying with it the danger of over-regulating the world economy, this confers on organizations that are not politically accountable powers and responsibilities that do not rightly belong to them.

. . . .

All the same, it is quite wrong to think profit-making is something largely separate from the contribution business makes to the general welfare. In a competitive market economy, firms make profits, and can only make profits, by providing products people wish to buy of their own free choice, and by being enterprising and innovative in doing so. The best way to ensure businesses contribute to the general welfare is to extend the scope and improve the functioning of markets.

CSR advocates want to remake capitalism. They show little awareness that the case for private business depends on its links with competition and economic freedom. Instead, they see defence of the market economy in terms of making businesses more popular and respected, through meeting society's expectations, which they identify with current radical programs for change.

Like sustainable development, corporate social responsibility is an appealing notion. But the current widely held doctrine of CSR is deeply flawed. It rests on a mistaken view of issues and events, and its general adoption by businesses would reduce welfare and undermine the market economy.

Source: Excerpts from David Henderson, "The harm in CSR. Corporatist global governance confers on organizations that are not politically accountable powers and responsibilities that do not rightly belong to them" *National Post* (February 2, 2002). Originally published in *Misguided Virtue: False Notions of Corporate Social Responsibility* (London, England: The Institute of Economic Affairs, 2001).

QUESTIONS

1. What are the main arguments of Reading I?

2. What are the main arguments of Reading II?

3. Which argument do you find more compelling? Why?

V

The Future

11

Organizational Strategies in a Changing World

Almost every area of business is undergoing some kind of change. Consequently, it is fitting that we devote specific attention to a discussion of the nature of change. What does change entail? What are the forces for change? We will examine the concept of change at both the organizational level and the individual level. For example, the concept of the "learning organization" will be examined. In addition, we will consider how organizations may facilitate or impede change and development. The chapter ends with a discussion of the issue of technological change.

LEARNING OBJECTIVES

By the end of the chapter, you should be able to:

1. Identify the forces encouraging change in organizations.
2. Explain the relationship of organizational learning with organizational change.
3. Identify the three phases of managing organizational change.
4. Discuss barriers to change and ways of reducing resistance to change.
5. Identify the role of technology and its impact on change.

Organizational Insider

The Next Big Thing: Nothing

[T]irelessly future-focused technologists only want to talk about ... what is coming next. Here is the answer: Nothing. And it is about time. No, it is not that nothing is coming for the economy. Most technologists are magnificently naive about macroeconomics, but few if any are anything but blissfully optimistic for the super-bounce coming in the impending recovery. Instead when technologists fret about what is coming next, they are worrying about which new technology will set the world afire, the way the Web browser did in the 1990s or perhaps the way computers, spreadsheets and the word processor did in the 1980s.

And what do technologists point to? There is a cacophony, but they point to next-generation cellular phones or perhaps some iteration of personal digital assistants like the Palm. Or better yet, maybe wireless networking. Not the much-maligned Bluetooth variety, of course, but the better-faster-stronger 802.11b standard. And in the background lurks a witch's brew of science projects, from nanotechnology, to the fruits of proteomics and genomics.

All of these horses for courses have punters placing bets that they'll be the Next Big Thing. These innovations have the requisite characteristics, techies argue. They make older technologies obsolete; they change the way people behave; they are premised, in part, on new companies that can upset the existing order. These are all part of an implicit orthodoxy, a founding myth of chained logic in the world of technology. Things Change Fast. The Small and Nimble Will Unseat the Large and Slow. New Technologies are Wildly Profitable for the Winners. But here is a secret: the founding myth, that chain of logic, is a lie. To the extent that there have ever been killer applications — and that is a debatable point — they have been unpredictable, generally unprofitable for the first-mover and only identifiable in retrospect through a heroic exercise in revisionism.

It doesn't matter whether you look at the personal computer market where Altair beat the PC clone-makers by years with the first personal computer, only to vanish; or the spreadsheet market where Visicalc and a range of others beat current incumbents by ages, only to disappear in a sea of red ink. Or, more recently, the giggling mess that was Netscape Communications, a supposed purveyor of killer applications that was going to unseat bad, sad, slow Microsoft. All of these companies, these vendors of killer applications, the poster-children for the Killer App Orthodoxy, failed. And failed quickly. And unprofitably, many without generating a penny of profit. As far as market magnets go, these killer apps seem more like twinned Scylla and Charybdis than a useful target.

So why does no one in an industry badly in need of some perspective concede this to be true? Why does no one, even sotto voce, concede that one of their founding myths, that of the killer application that will give order to all that came before, is blatantly false? It is, of course, for the same reason any failing religion refuses to change. Because it can't. It is so intimately tied up in the mosaic of myths that got it to where it is, it wouldn't know where to begin if it were to change. To insiders, the killer-application tenet is no more questionable than faith in Jimmy Jones, belief in the addled musings of Reverend Sun Myung Moon or, better yet, [faith that] the Flat Earth Society's ideas will one day be borne out. Those beliefs, however flawed, are what make these people what they are.

Technologists are staunchly forward-looking people who motivate themselves, and a legion of parrots in the popular and trade media, by talking endlessly about the future. ... But what happens when the myths fall apart? Because the collapse of the Internet as the Next Big Thing put a little fear into the blue-eyed believers, as did the corresponding collapse of the startup factories pumping out dime-a-dozen Standard Industrial Classification-code-killer startups in every e-commerce category. But it has left most believers more than a little confused, frantic in their search for the next thing that will change the world.

The trouble is, while the flow of useful new products is unceasing, few new technologies can have the impact old ones did. We are like a market iceberg, with more and more technology fused beneath the waterline. It isn't as easy as it once was to run around disrupting things with killer applications — there is too much invested in what went before. More and more, prior killer applications looked like youthful flings had by a young technology market, not some pre-ordained paroxysm that unseats the existing order. And consumers and corporate buyers bear that out. They are putting their feet down, doing a kind of buyer's boycott, saying they don't really care what gets flogged next, because they're still trying to make money off the last round of goods they were sold....

Source: By Paul Kedrosky from *National Post* (November 28, 2001). Reproduced with permission of Paul Kedrosky.

CHANGE AND MORE CHANGE

The Organizational Insider suggests that predicting the new technological breakthroughs for business is futile. The way technology changes business, and who ultimately profits from these innovations, are questioned. While speculating on the next big change may be futile, sensible questions may be: What are the sources of change directed at organizations? How do these changes affect the nature of organizations and work? In every chapter in this book, from management thought to business ethics, we have, often, recognized that just about every important area of business is undergoing some kind of change. How is the organizational environment changing? Consider a number of issues addressed in this book, including issues like globalization, free trade, deregulation, privatization, the changing emphasis on corporate social responsibility. Much of what we have addressed involves issues that are undergoing dramatic change. In terms of planned organizational change, there are at least three central targets: organizational structure, technology and people. (See Exhibit 11.1.)

Forces for Change

While we have previously considered the changing nature of organizational structure, we will now consider how technology is both a target and a tool for organizational change, and we will also consider how the nature of the individual's role in the workplace is changing. However, before we consider this area of change, we will briefly outline the elements of the environment that can act as triggers for change.

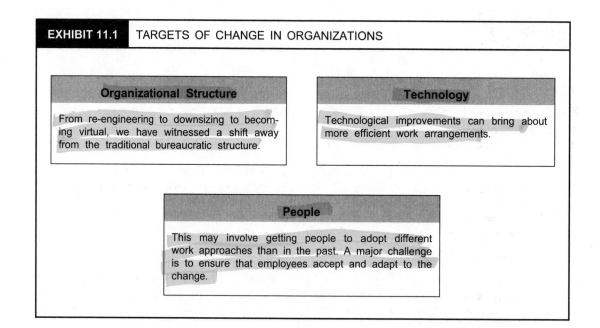

EXHIBIT 11.1   TARGETS OF CHANGE IN ORGANIZATIONS

Organizational Structure

From re-engineering to downsizing to becoming virtual, we have witnessed a shift away from the traditional bureaucratic structure.

Technology

Technological improvements can bring about more efficient work arrangements.

People

This may involve getting people to adopt different work approaches than in the past. A major challenge is to ensure that employees accept and adapt to the change.

EXHIBIT 11.2	FORCES FOR CHANGE

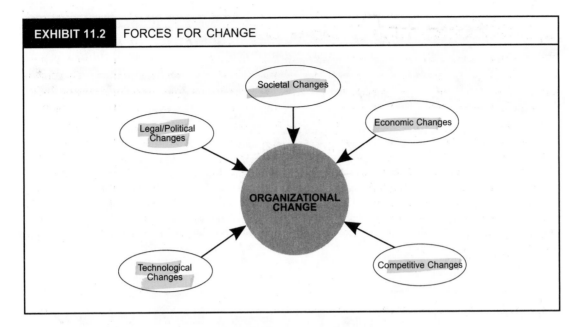

John Challenger, in his article entitled, "The transformed workplace,"[265] highlights a number of environmental factors that are transforming the nature of organizations. He suggests that the combined forces of technology, globalization, and deregulation are changing the social contract between the individual and the organization. Below, reference is made to Challenger's interesting assertions within the framework of environmental factors. (See Exhibit 11.2.)

1. *Economic Changes*

Is the economy healthy, or weak? Clearly, organizations must adapt to changing economic conditions. Downsizings are more likely to occur in lean times than in rich. Organizational expansion cannot occur in an economic vacuum, as the following indicates:

> We have watched what the new workplace rules mean in periods of economic expansion. The decade long boom of the 1990s occurred just as downsizing became de rigueur at American companies. The greater efficiency with which companies allocated their human resources spurred enormous gains in economic growth and productivity. Companies hired contract consultants who could deliver specific expertise on a project, and they hired temporaries to handle the surge periods of the business day.[266]

This quote alludes to a few of the changes that resulted from changing economic circumstances. Certainly, such changes have also facilitated changes to the nature of the employer–employee relationship. Lifetime employment appears to be a thing of the past.

359

Consider the 1950s or the 1970s: these were actually times where employment meant security. The dominant model was long-term employment — stability. However, a change to this implicit employment contract occurred sometime in the 1980s. And as we identified in an earlier chapter, the age of downsizing began — with large, secure organizations beginning to lay off employees. Part-time and temporary work arrangements have become much more common than in the past.

> Organizations are typically responding to this challenging new organization world by becoming preoccupied with improving performance and bottom line results while losing sight of the importance of a people/performance balance in achieving lasting success. In these organizations, slashing costs, continuous restructuring, downsizing, trying endless quick fix programs and solutions, announcing new visions, values, and goals that everyone is expected to embrace, and lots of well intended talk about the importance of people and values is becoming common place. It is a push, cut, slash, slice, talk, quick fix management mentality and strategy that places a high emphasis on performance and a low emphasis on people and often creates an illusion of doing well while the organization is regressing and in some cases unraveling! It appears to employees to be a "built to sell or built to fail" strategy that assumes that you can manage or shrink your way to success.[267]

We have also witnessed a change with regard to the pattern of career movement within an organization. Traditionally, employees attempted to move up the corporate hierarchy throughout their career. However, the flattening of many organizational hierarchies has tended to substitute horizontal or lateral career movement for the former vertical movement, so that you might move around an organization into different areas rather than directly up the hierarchy. The following quote reflects the new era of the "free agent":

> Employees and workers must view their careers in terms of what skills they can offer. As individual identity has become uncoupled from a particular company, people have focused on functional career areas, such as law, human resources, financial, sales and marketing, and manufacturing. In the 1990s, professional associations and functional groupings have seen explosive membership gains. More and more people have sought community and networking opportunities in the company of like-minded career professionals.[268]

2.   Competitive Changes

Globalization, as discussed elsewhere in this book, opened the floodgates for competitors. Clearly, the number of competitors and the nature of competition will dictate changes in organizational design and strategy.

> Employees and communities were once critical factors in companies' long-term strategic decisions. Moving factories and jobs to another area of the country was unthinkable because of the damage it would do to the local community. In recent years, thousands of companies — including UPS, J.C. Penney, and Boeing — have moved their headquarters or operations from cities where they had deep roots. The old business structure — with a dominant CEO, a largely ceremonial board of directors, and employees willing to put the goals of the company first — is nearly extinct.... Several primary forces created systemic change in the American economy in the 1980s and 1990s, leaving the former system in shambles. One such factor was globalization, which

forced the United States out of its isolation. Companies began to look for new markets overseas. Coca-Cola and McDonald's spread throughout the world. NAFTA, GATT, and free trade brought down barriers that had prevented the flow of goods and services and human resources around the world. The law of unintended consequences worked its way into the American economy. Protected industries such as auto manufacturing faced serious competition from overseas for the first time, with devastating consequences. Chrysler almost ceased operations, and General Motors cut 74,000 jobs in December 1991, one of the largest downsizings ever.[269]

Competition, both domestic and foreign, certainly has demanded an acceleration in innovation among firms in many industries. Organizations, to compete effectively, must continually create new and better methods of serving customers. While globalization has opened up larger markets for businesses, it has also facilitated much higher levels of competition.

3. *Technological Changes*

Technology, as we discuss below, is both a continuously changing variable and one that permits and demands organizational change. As one scholar observed:

> In recent years, there has been considerable discussion of whether the development and application of information and communications technology have changed the ... economy in a fundamental way, promising a golden future of rapid growth, low unemployment and inflation, perpetual economic expansion, and a booming stock market. The change is sometimes called the "Information Revolution"; more commonly, it is called the "New Economy." ... As the economy absorbs any new technology, what typically happens first is that existing economic activities are performed at lower cost. E-commerce is no exception...Only a few firms have gone through the deep organizational changes needed to become web-based organizations, but those that have done so have achieved remarkable results, like cutting administrative costs by 75 percent.[270]

Technology has been a double-edged sword for members of the workforce — bringing both benefits and threats. Benefits from technology have included the ability to gain more flexibility in work arrangements such as the practice of telework.

> The idea of telecommuting isn't new, but companies still have a long way to go to fully exploit the benefits of a networked economy. Indianapolis pharmaceutical company Eli Lilly and Co. lets all its knowledge workers work from home occasionally, and a formal telework program lets a smaller number of employees keep their primary offices at home. Such telecommuting generally had been considered a concession to work-life balance, but these days, the company is also thinking about it as a means to drive productivity, says Candi Lange, director of workforce partnering. "We bring in such smart people who are responsible for so much important work in the company," she says. "Why not let them control their own schedules as well?"[271]

Part-time work has increased dramatically in recent years, and we also continue to see the increasing use of compressed workweeks and flex-time — all in all, this means that the 9-to-5 job is certainly no longer a fixed rule.

4. Legal/Political Changes

Deregulation and privatization, discussed in an earlier chapter, are clear examples of the importance of considering governmental changes on business strategy. Are legal regulations facilitating, or restricting, certain strategies? The legal environment of business can dictate changes in how business competes, what services it offers, and how they can be offered.

> The deregulation of protected industries in the 1980s and 1990s created competition for companies where none had previously existed. The telecom, banking, energy, and aerospace industries were ruled by the change. As the dominant companies in these sectors were forced to compete in an open market, they started letting sizable numbers of people go. The breakup of the Bell System into AT&T, Lucent, and the seven Baby Bells unleashed a surge of technology inventiveness. It was not surprising that telecom, financial services, and aerospace dominated the list of industries experiencing the heaviest downsizing in the early to mid-1990s.[272]

In the workplace, we have witnessed an increasing emphasis on organizational justice — how employees are treated. This has translated into more laws governing fairness in the workplace. One such area that has been dramatically affected is compensation. Pay equity has been among numerous issues involved in redressing inconsistencies in pay treatment among men and women, for example. We have also witnessed an increasing emphasis in merit-based pay, and pay-for-performance, which all attempt to more closely link actual effort to performance instead (versus seniority-based pay, which bases pay on the number of years you have been with the organization).

5. Societal Changes

Business must respond to society: consumer tastes change, for example, and business must adapt to such changes. Similarly, the types of organizations that service societal demands can change. The aging population suggests greater emphasis needs to be placed on such industries as the health care sector.

> The growing number of people with advanced educational degrees is another force hurtling knowledge forward at a higher rate. As more people become educated, knowledge expansion increases geometrically simply because there are more people to move the cutting edge of knowledge ahead. Geniuses emerge who could not have appeared in past eras because they did not have access to the then-current state of knowledge necessary to push the thought boundaries. Unprecedented numbers of people today are working at the cutting edge of research in a variety of fields. And the glass ceiling is breaking apart because young women are achieving the advanced degrees necessary for economic and social advancement.[273]

The increasing education level of the workforce has also generated changes to the nature of work. As we discussed in an earlier chapter, there has been, for some time, a movement away from high job specialization, where jobs are broken down into simple, distinct packages. The trend has been to generate jobs that demand employees be multi-skilled in order to handle more challenging and enriched work. Consequently, employees are also tending to work more in teams, and are responsible for a larger piece of the work, so to speak. Knowledge work (as we will discuss later in this chapter) demands a more highly educated workforce.

ORGANIZATIONAL CHANGE AND THE LEARNING ORGANIZATION

A view among many management scholars is that organizations that effectively change or adapt to changes in their environment are ones that have first "learned" — they have learned how to recognize the need for change, and they have learned what actions are necessary to adapt. This notion of the central role of change is reflected in one of the many definitions of a learning organization: "an organization that facilitates the learning of all its members and consciously transforms itself and its context."[274] Learning, in this sense, involves a three-stage evolution in which the highest stage incorporates three aspects of learning:

- adapting to their environment
- learning from their people
- contributing to the learning of the wider community or context of which they are a part

Organizations, like individuals, need to develop and grow — not necessarily in size, but in their capacity to function effectively. Clearly, this demands organizational change. Organizational development has been defined as:

> a process of planned system change that attempts to make organizations (viewed as social-technical systems) better able to attain their short- and long-term objectives. This is achieved by teaching the organization members to manage their organization processes, structures, and culture more effectively.[275]

Chris Argyris and Donald Schon[276] made a tremendous contribution to the management literature and to the topic of organizational change through their examination of the issue of **organizational learning**. How do organizations learn? Do organizations learn from their mistakes? This seems to be an abstract notion, and yet it is a very real topic. Argyris and Schon suggested that organizational learning represents the collective experience of individuals within the organization and comes about when organizational procedures change as a result of what has been learned. In this sense, organizational learning has been defined as the detection and correction of error.[277] Organizations can learn through individuals acting as agents in an effort to critically examine the methods and functioning of their organization. Argyris and Schon make a distinction between two types of learning: single-loop learning and double-loop learning. It is the latter that constitutes genuine organizational learning, and that leads to significant organizational change. (See Exhibit 11.3.)

Single-loop learning simply involves the correction of errors that employees may find in organizational methods of performance in order to keep the system working. This

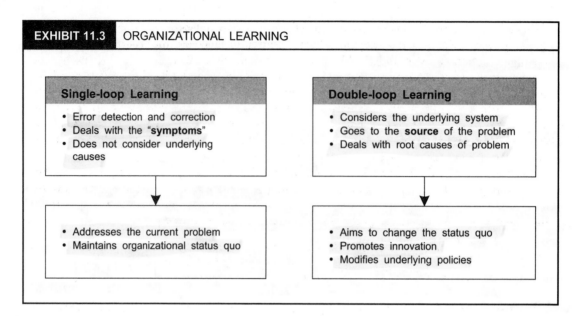

approach assumes that the organization has the right systems established but simply needs to fine-tune the present system. For example, an organization may find that downsizing permits it to be more flexible with lower costs. However, does reducing the workforce achieve flexibility? Individuals engaging in single-loop learning or adaptive behaviour are essentially functioning within the boundaries or constraints of the presented problem. Single-loop behaviour typically results in making **incremental** improvements, and improving efficiency. Such behaviour involves, at best, the modification of strategies or assumptions underlying the strategies in ways that maintain the existing organizational approaches to problems. That is, single-loop learning results in the organization continuing its present policies or achieving its current objectives.

Double-loop learning requires that individuals assess whether an error or problem exists in an organization because the systems themselves need to be changed. Changing organizational systems or assumptions requires a deeper level of examination, and typically is a precursor to significant organizational change. For example, if an organization wants to achieve "flexibility", is this achieved simply through a reduction in the workforce? Perhaps the objective itself of "flexibility" needed to be re-evaluated.

Double-loop learning leads to the organization modifying its underlying policies or goals. The double-loop learning process requires innovation and involves challenging the status quo within an organization. Individuals engaged in double-loop learning are not bound by the constraints of the presented problem. Rather, double-loop learning involves an examination of the assumptions and values underlying an organization's functioning. This critical examination culminates in fundamental changes to the present system and in the recognition of new problems to be solved. These new problems and new solutions will ultimately transform current strategies and assumptions.

Single-loop learning results from addressing the "**symptoms**" of a problem, while double-loop learning results when individuals attempt to uncover the **root causes** of the problem — questioning why the problem arose in the first place.

What type of learning is dominant in most organizations? Many scholars have suggested that most organizations, at best, encourage single-loop, but not double-loop, learning. Moreover, it has been suggested that organizations typically create systems that inhibit double-loop learning. For example, the bureaucratic nature of most organizations encourages employees to be methodical and disciplined, and, consequently, less likely to question the basic assumptions of most organizational practices.

How do organizations change? According to Argyris and Schon, change is accomplished through double-loop learning. This demands that individuals increase their awareness of the nature of the status quo, and of those elements that deserve and require change. What is the ultimate goal? As one scholar commented:

> [The] ultimate goal [is] to help individuals unfreeze and alter their theories of action so that they, acting as agents of the organization, will be able to unfreeze the organizational learning systems that also inhibit double-loop learning.[278]

Argyris and Schon[279] assert that people tend to adopt a single-loop learning approach in organizations rather than developing double-loop learning skills. Argyris stated that: "We strive to organize our individual and organizational lives by decomposing them into single-loop problems because they are easier to solve and to monitor."[280]

Is the job of management one that demands learning? This is an interesting question. Some critics suggest that management, with its emphasis on concrete results (typically measured in profits, dollars, costs, etc.) has traditionally de-emphasized the importance of learning as a necessity of proper management. (See Let's Talk Business 11.1.)

Why don't organizations encourage double-loop learning and, consequently, innovation? Clearly, innovation is a desirable objective and yet, organizations tend to manifest rules and regulations that facilitate consistency and stability — qualities needed to function effec-

---

LET'S TALK BUSINESS 11.1 THE LEARNING MANAGER

As management scholar Steven Henderson noted:

> Why is it that managerial work is not generally as scientific, or learning-oriented, as it could be? In many ways, the process of scientific thinking would appear to be significantly different to that of management thinking, since managers rarely set knowledge as the prime target of their activity. Indeed, the so-called learning curve or learning effect is seen as a consequence of carrying out managerial activity (typically production) rather than prerequisite. Organizations structured along the lines of a "learning laboratory" remain isolated exceptions.

Source: From Steven Henderson, "Black swans don't fly double loops: the limits of the learning organization?" *The Learning Organization* (1997) 4(3): 99. (Note omitted.)

tively on a day-to-day basis. Ironically, it is innovation and the ability to change that are the skills necessary for long-term survival. Unfortunately, organizations do not tend to encourage double-loop learning. If organizations are guilty of inhibiting genuine learning (double-loop learning) and, consequently, failing to generate real change, what are the sources of this dysfunction? We will consider the sources next.

Do Organizations Encourage or Discourage Learning and Change?

Peter Senge,[281] in many ways, popularized the concept of the learning organization as one where there is an encouragement of all employees to engage in the learning process through dialogue, experimentation and learning from each other. It has been acknowledged that "learning organizations" cannot exist without "learning employees".[282] That is, organizational learning and development are facilitated through individual learning and development. The ability of organizations to adapt to, and change with, a changing environment is dependent on the ability of their members to change and adapt.

Individual change is really about learning — learning new skills, learning or developing new perspectives and new ways of dealing with everyday challenges. Do organizations facilitate individual learning and development? Can organizations provide a learning environment for their employees whereby employees can grow and develop throughout their careers? Given that the traditional bureaucratic organizational structures are rapidly being replaced with more organic structures, it would seem critical to similarly shift greater attention to a more adaptive, innovative type of employee, better suited to the changing needs of the new organization, and capable of changing and developing along with the organization.

Can Employees Learn?

Workplace experiences comprise a significant portion of people's lives and, consequently, it is understandable that the manner in which individuals experience their workplaces will have a considerable impact on their growth and development.[283] Adults continue to learn throughout their lifetimes, and their past experience can help or hinder this learning.[284] A number of developmental theorists have emphasized the presence of challenge and stimulation in the environment as a means to encourage learning and development. Environments or experiences that challenge individuals will help bring about development.[285] The workplace is an important element in adult development, with the power to foster or impede development of its members. For example, organizations that encourage self-exploration, and information-seeking, will facilitate individual growth and development.[286] The workplace is a significant influence on individual development, given its ability to promote individual challenge and critical reflection through the introduction of new tasks and responsibilities.[287]

What is adult learning development?   There is not one all-encompassing definition of adult learning or development. Among the streams of thought in adult learning and development theory is the notion that development grows out of the interaction of both internal/psychological events and external/social events.[288] Adult development is based on change rather than stability, and this change or growth occurs at a predictable rate and sequence.[289] Individuals can learn from their experience if they can effectively see what changes are involved and how they can be accomplished.[290]

Based on the views cited above, learning from experience essentially involves changing both what one does and how one see things. As we identified earlier, according to Argyris and Schon, learning in organizations involves the process of detecting and correcting "error".[291] When individuals begin to question or confront the underlying organizational norms and goals that relate to this process of error detection and correction, this constitutes double-loop learning. The questions of interest in this regard are: Do organizations contain elements that encourage, or impede, challenge, confrontation and enquiry as a means to facilitate double-loop learning among individuals? A consideration of the "institutional" nature of organizations offers some insights in this regard.

Bureaucracies and Roles

To understand the ability of organizations to influence individuals in the manner described above, it is useful to consider a theory of organizational behaviour that considers the institutional nature of organizations: **institutionalization theory**.[292] In order to determine what institutionalization theory has to offer in terms of understanding the influence of organizations on adult learning and development, it is necessary to understand what this theory says about the nature of organizations and their influence on individual behaviour.

Institutionalization involves the processes by which shared beliefs take on a rule-like status. Institutionalization has been defined as a social process through which individuals create a shared definition of what is appropriate or meaningful behaviour.[293] Meyer and Rowan suggested that organizations that incorporate societally legitimated elements in their formal structures maximize their legitimacy and increase their resources and survival capabilities.[294] Essentially, this perspective acknowledges that organizations often generate "accepted practices" that tend to govern how things are done. These practices may continue even when they are no longer functional, simply because they have become an "ingrained" part of the organization.

Single-loop learning would seem to be a natural consequence of adherence to institutionalized structures. Single-loop learning is emphasized in organizations governed by institutionalized structures — following organizational policy without critically examining behaviour or the policy that dictates behaviour. This is reflected in the image of the "mindless bureaucrat" who follows rules and regulations without considering the necessity of such rules. On the other hand, when individuals are not forced to conform with myriad rules and regulations, they are more likely to engage in thoughtful consideration of the utility of workplace policy in order to determine whether such policies are effective or ineffective. Consequently, organizations where institutionalized structures are deeply entrenched are less likely to provide an environment conducive to adult learning and development.

Cognitive Scripts

Organizational policy can discourage employees from thinking "outside the box", so to speak. This is also reflected in the notion of **cognitive scripts**. What are cognitive scripts? They are scripts we all carry with us in the performance of our jobs. Though they are not concrete or tangible, they are very real. That is, any organization possesses shared meanings regarding how its members should conduct themselves in the performance of their duties.[295] Cognitive scripts or schema have been described as mental pictures (most often unconscious) that serve to organize knowledge in some systematic fashion. Essentially, organizational members can function efficiently in organizations through the use of scripts or schema, to reduce the mass of information to be processed as a means to guide their performance. That is, they may guide thought and behaviour, and are based on beliefs about people, situations, or behaviours. A script is a type of schema that serves to help understand and enact dynamic patterns of behaviour. A script provides knowledge about expected sequences of events, and guides behaviour for a given situation.

What are the implications of organizational scripts for learning and development in the workplace? Cognitive learning is one learning domain that assumes that people have characteristic ways of making sense of the world by organizing it into abstract categories.[296] These categories change with age and, ideally, should be in the direction of growth. How do organizations impact cognitive learning? Individuals, within social settings, form and use categories in such processes as perception, decision making and conceptualization. As explained earlier, this categorization is intended to reduce the cognitive complexity of the environment. In other words, individuals within organizations often rely on pre-programmed methods of conduct (scripts) and cognitive pictures of their environment. In effect, scripts internalize a routinized approach to performance on the job. Similarly, the use of scripts to guide behaviour in the workplace can potentially discourage individuals from critically examining events and situations each time performance is required.

The reliance on cognitive scripts and schema in the workplace reduces the need to continually question and confront environmental cues. Rather, a pre-programmed approach to dealing with others in the workplace seems to be developed. To the extent that reliance is placed on these scripts and schemas, confrontation and change will be discouraged, and consequently, learning and development will be impeded.

Employees can differ in the degree to which they rely on scripts or pre-programmed performance guidelines to govern their work conduct. Work behaviour that is largely scripted discourages employees from engaging in critical evaluation of how their work is conducted. Through their need to maintain reliability and consistency in employee performance, cognitive scripts that we use to function in our jobs can actually generate obstacles to individual-level change and learning. Organizations that encourage a critical evaluation of these scripts are more likely to motivate learning and development among members than are organizations that discourage the critique of established methods of work.

MANAGING ORGANIZATIONAL CHANGE

The urgency of change seems to be accelerating, given the abundance of environmental changes. This urgency is illustrated in the following comments:

> How fast and how much management practice must change to assure a good chance of enterprise prosperity may be up for debate, but what is driving the process is not. Behind most of the action is a blizzard of speed, technological change, globalization and complexity. Stunning advances in microelectronics, genetics, optics, materials,

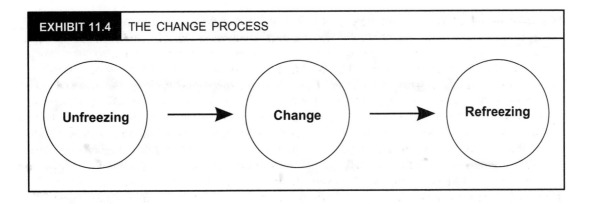

EXHIBIT 11.4   THE CHANGE PROCESS

lasers, communications and the organizational sciences are turning workplaces, work processes and products upside down at a breathtaking pace. We are living in our very own industrial revolution and it is every bit the rival of its steam/textile/paper-money and electricity/internal-combustion-engine/assembly-line driven predecessors. The case is so compelling that the pace of future technological advance will make the present look like a period of tranquillity. Growing open-market capitalism, more commonly known as globalization, has ramped up the competitive environment abruptly and spectacularly.... The business world has become mind-bendingly complex seemingly overnight. Executives are supposed to see the big picture, but when each of the little pictures presses the limits of comprehension in their own right, that is no small challenge. For executives, the speed/technology/globalization/complexity cocktail is something to behold. Small wonder a revolution in management practice has appeal.[297]

Let's now examine conceptually what organizational change is all about. To do that, we should first identity conceptually what change is. The well-known psychologist Kurt Lewin referred to change as involving: **a sequence of organizational events or a psychological process that occurs over time**. Lewin also suggested that any **planned** effort on the part of organizations to implement change can be viewed a as process consisting of three distinct phases, which he referred to as unfreezing, changing and refreezing. Let's describe briefly what these three phases entail. (See Exhibit 11.4.)

Three Phases of Managing Change

1.   *Unfreezing*

A responsibility of managers in paving the way for change is to facilitate the "unfreezing" of the current situation. In other words, for any change to occur, the first phase involves a recognition that the current state of affairs is inadequate. Consequently, the challenge for a manager may be to disconfirm existing attitudes and behaviours in order to generate a feeling that change is, indeed, required. Now, unfreezing might occur through environmental pressures: for example, the awareness that globalization has resulted in significant increases in competition. Unfreezing might also stem from the recognition that performance is declining or, indeed, from simply seeing that a problem does, in fact, exist.

While the notion of unfreezing is simple, obtaining it in practice is not so easy. In fact, organizational researchers refer to the tendency for some organizations to avoid change as the **"boiled frog" phenomenon**, which is a metaphor for failure to unfreeze. The metaphor asks one to imagine a study (albeit a somewhat gruesome one) that involves placing a frog in a pan of hot water. The argument is that the frog will jump out immediately. However, this imaginary experiment also informs us that the frog will **not** jump out of the pan if the water is heated slowly. In other words, organizations, like some creatures, can fail to detect environmental changes that are occurring slowly — and they may, simply, never respond until it is too late. The warning to managers is clear. You must continually monitor the environment, recognize changes in the environment, and sense the need for change.

2. Change

The change phase, of course, involves some action. That is, it occurs when some program is implemented to move the organization and its members to a more adequate state. This might involve changing things like technology, the type of tasks performed, or the people who perform the work; or, perhaps, it involves changing the structure of the organization. Whether the change is effective or ineffective often depends on how well the situation has been prepared for the change.

3. Refreezing

The final phase of the planned change process is, in fact, refreezing. This occurs when the newly developed behaviours, attitudes or structures become an enduring part of the organizational system. In other words, refreezing is aimed at making the desired change and its benefits long-lasting. This phase involves evaluating the progress or results and assessing the costs and benefits of the change.

Lewin's three-step model of change, when you consider it, is really based on the notion of change as an episodic activity. In other words, change is viewed as having a specific starting point, a process and, finally, an outcome that ideally constitutes an improvement over the starting point. That is, change is really a break in the status quo and, eventually, results in establishing a new status quo or state of equilibrium, so to speak — accomplished through re-freezing. However, it has come to be viewed as a continuous process in today's turbulent environment. That is, this process is viewed as ongoing — the status quo may not remain in an organization for very long.

Why Do Individuals Resist Change?

Consider the facts of two separate real-life disasters that both involved teams engaged in wilderness firefighting — one occurring in 1949, in which 13 firefighters lost their lives; and the other in 1994, when 14 firefighters died under very similar circumstances. In both cases, the firefighters were overrun by exploding fires when their escape was significantly slowed largely because they failed to drop the heavy tools they were carrying. In an examination of these tragedies, an organizational researcher by the name of Karl Weick, in an article written for the *Harvard Business Review*, asked an interesting question: Why, in the face of a clear need to change their strategy in order to survive, did these firemen fail to "drop their heavy tools"?

Now, at the risk of trivializing this tragedy, Weick uses this case as a striking example of the fact that even when individuals are required to change — that is, even when an individual's life depends on change — resistance can be overpowering. There are, unfortunately, many examples of cases where people fail to adapt to a changing environment; and, of course, the question is: Why?

Let's consider some of the central sources for individual-level resistance to change in organizations. Organizational researchers have identified a number of central reasons that account for resistance to change. Some of the key reasons are cited in Exhibit 11.5.

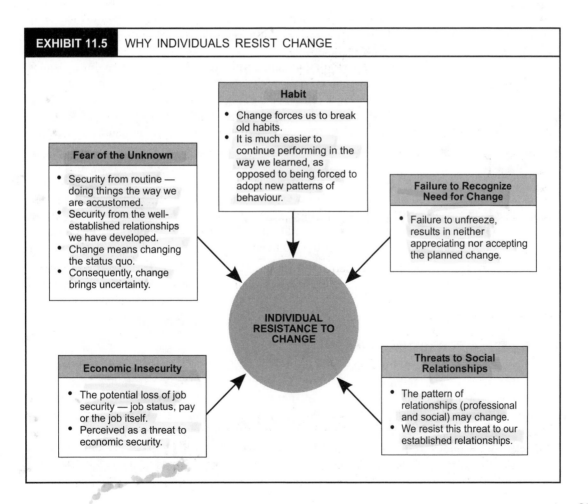

EXHIBIT 11.5 WHY INDIVIDUALS RESIST CHANGE

Habit
- Change forces us to break old habits.
- It is much easier to continue performing in the way we learned, as opposed to being forced to adopt new patterns of behaviour.

Fear of the Unknown
- Security from routine — doing things the way we are accustomed.
- Security from the well-established relationships we have developed.
- Change means changing the status quo.
- Consequently, change brings uncertainty.

Failure to Recognize Need for Change
- Failure to unfreeze, results in neither appreciating nor accepting the planned change.

INDIVIDUAL RESISTANCE TO CHANGE

Economic Insecurity
- The potential loss of job security — job status, pay or the job itself.
- Perceived as a threat to economic security.

Threats to Social Relationships
- The pattern of relationships (professional and social) may change.
- We resist this threat to our established relationships.

Why Do Organizations Resist Change?

Individuals are not the only sources of resistance to change. We can imagine certain structural features of the organization itself that can act as sources of resistance. Henry Mintzberg raises a number of interesting issues regarding the ability, or rather inability, of organizations to change. Certainly, Mintzberg underscores the desperate need for organizations to change their ways, so to speak. So, what, exactly, does Mintzberg say about organizational change?

Mintzberg reminds us that we are a society of organizations. That is, think about any aspect of our society — from our schools to our hospitals to our government — and you are really thinking about organizations. So, how organizations are designed says a lot about how our society is designed. Consequently, how adaptive organizations are to change says a lot about how readily adaptive our society is to change. And Mintzberg argues that how our organizations are designed is still being led by one dominant and traditional view — that is, when it comes to organizations, we still think in terms of **machine bureaucracy**.

Recall the nature of the machine bureaucracy and when it is most suitable. For tasks that can be made simple and repetitive, as in mass production processes, the machine bureaucracy is very suitable: through its formalization of rules, its standardization of tasks, its emphases on efficiency. However, given this, why are so many organizations whose work is not based on simple, repetitive tasks still structured like a machine bureaucracy? Moreover, given the changes occurring in our environment, why would organizations wish to maintain these rigid bureaucracies? Mintzberg suggests that the dominance of the machine bureaucratic mentality really stems from an irrational need for control. In Mintzberg's words, organizations are "irrationally" rational — there is a focus on maximizing efficiency through rules and regulations without a real critical evaluation of the process of managing.

Finally, Mintzberg suggests rather ominously that organizations "sow the seeds of their destruction". In other words, Mintzberg believes that any preoccupation with control to the degree that it emphasizes the machine bureaucracy over other forms tends to eventually become too rigid to adapt to change. In addition to Mintzberg's comments, management scholars have identified a number of central sources of resistance to change at the organizational level. (See Exhibit 11.6.)

Strategies for Facilitating Organizational Change

1. Communication and Negotiation

How can managers reduce resistance to change in order to facilitate a planned change? Given that fear of the unknown is a central source of resistance to change, the notion of communication seems to be a logical element of any change strategy: that is, keeping employees informed as to the nature of the change and progress made with regard to the change effort. A step further may involve appealing to the employees to "get on board" for the upcoming changes. This can involve a form of negotiation. That is, implementing change may require a negotiation of sorts between those implementing the change and those affected by the change. In other words, those who might face potential losses

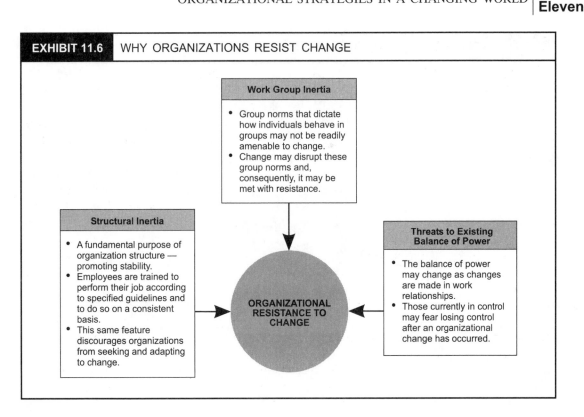

EXHIBIT 11.6 — WHY ORGANIZATIONS RESIST CHANGE

Work Group Inertia
- Group norms that dictate how individuals behave in groups may not be readily amenable to change.
- Change may disrupt these group norms and, consequently, it may be met with resistance.

Structural Inertia
- A fundamental purpose of organization structure — promoting stability.
- Employees are trained to perform their job according to specified guidelines and to do so on a consistent basis.
- This same feature discourages organizations from seeking and adapting to change.

ORGANIZATIONAL RESISTANCE TO CHANGE

Threats to Existing Balance of Power
- The balance of power may change as changes are made in work relationships.
- Those currently in control may fear losing control after an organizational change has occurred.

through the change may be given some sort of reward in exchange for the sacrifices made through the implementation of change.

2. Training

Of course, while communication and negotiation seem to be appealing aids to change, a critical component is to ensure that employees are prepared for the change. This may require re-training or upgrading present skills. Building self-confidence among employees with regard to their ability to manage in a changed workplace can also be facilitated by ensuring that employees, indeed, have the skills to cope with new roles or responsibilities. This may require the implementation of training programs to help employees learn their new job, so to speak, and by definition to break with the old routine or way of doing things.

3. Employee Involvement

Communication, negotiation and training are certainly useful considerations in the management of organizational change. However, what is more appealing from the employees' perspectives is to actually be involved in planning the change: that is, to participate in the

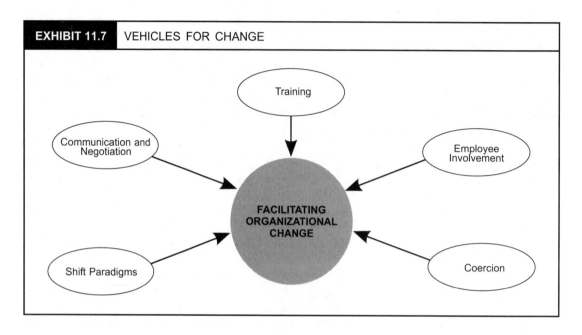

EXHIBIT 11.7 VEHICLES FOR CHANGE

content or the process of the change effort. In addition to reducing fear of the unknown, this also is simply better strategic planning. For example, observers of downsizings often note that poorly executed downsizings typically are those that failed to involve affected parties in the actual planning of the downsizing.

4. Coercion

One of the more direct, if not appealing, methods of reducing resistance to change is through coercion. The threat of punishment for those who resist change is one option. In other words, employees might simply be told that if they cannot accept the new way of doing things, they will be replaced. Of course, there are risks involved in using this alternative, including creating a negative morale, and hostility among employees, which might even result in greater resistance to the planned change. Organizations may be more likely to consider this alternative when other strategies have proven ineffective and where change is needed quickly.

5. Shift Paradigms

It would seem that radical organizational change can only come about when the members of an organization are encouraged to engage in double-loop learning — the concept we discussed above. It is akin to making a dramatic departure from the present way of doing things. This has also been referred to in the notion of "**shifting paradigms**". Joel Barker, a management consultant and author, in his book, *Paradigms*, talks about the failure of many organizations to adapt to change. Consider the case of the Swiss watchmakers. Way back in 1968, who dominated the watch industry? Yes — the Swiss, with about 65% of the unit sales in the world. And in fact, back then, if anyone was asked to predict who would remain the leader even 20 or 30 years later, they would probably say the Swiss. However, by 1980, who came to dominate the world watch market? You may have correctly guessed Seiko of Japan. By that year, the Swiss share had fallen to 10% of the market, while Japan (who held abut 1% of the market in 1968) was the dominant force, with Seiko owning about 33% of the world market. From 1979 to 1981 about 50,000 of the 62,000 Swiss watchmakers lost their jobs — a huge disaster for Switzerland. What happened? Well, Japan had focused on electronic technology — the electronic quartz was a natural outcome. Where did this technology come from that allowed Japan to demolish the Swiss's domination of the watch market? The technology came from the Swiss themselves — a research institute in Switzerland.

This story has a particularly ironic twist, because it suggests that the Swiss could have easily maintained their market leadership. However, when the Swiss researchers presented their new idea to Swiss manufacturers back in 1967 — the manufacturers rejected it! They considered it inferior — who would want to buy a watch that didn't have a mainspring, didn't need bearings, nor, almost, any gears, and it was electronic with battery power? So the manufacturers rejected it, but let their researchers display what they thought was useless technology at the world Watch Congress that year. Seiko, upon observing this invention, had a completely different view — and the result was a dramatic turnaround for Japan, and a dramatic failure for the Swiss. What happened here, according to Joel Barker, was a failure to make a **paradigm shift**.

In Barker's view, change is all about adopting new paradigms. What is this strange concept called a paradigm, and how did it cause the downfall of the Swiss watch industry at that time?

The term "paradigm" can be considered as referring to **our set of beliefs or mental framework for understanding how the world operates**. We see the world through our paradigms. You might also think of this as our theories, our assumptions, our beliefs or customs. As Joel Barker writes: "A paradigm in a sense tells you that there is a game, what the game is and how to play the game according to the rules." Barker argues that overcoming resistance to change is all about being able to do two things:

1. Recognize the current paradigms that govern our behaviour.
2. Shift to a new paradigm.

So, how does this apply to our example of the Swiss watch industry?

You might consider the Swiss manufacturers as being prisoners of their old paradigm — they could not conceive of the watch industry as ever changing, so it was the old, traditional Swiss watches that would always dominate the market. However, the industry did, in fact, experience a paradigm shift, brought about by Seiko, that did adapt their thinking to recognize new consumer tastes: the paradigm governing the rules of the watch industry game changed, but the Swiss still thought they could play the game by the old rules, based on the old paradigm. Consequently, they were victims of failing to adapt to changing conditions, failing to shift away from their old paradigm. The ability to critically examine our paradigms, how we see the world, is very much a part of our ability to accept change, both at the individual and at the organizational level.

ORGANIZATIONS AND TECHNOLOGICAL CHANGE

Technological change is a leading force in the changing face of business. Let us consider, then, some of the characteristics of technology: What is it? How does technology fare within the Canadian context? In what fundamental ways does technology change the nature of the workplace? We can address each of these questions below.

First, what is technology? **Technology** can be defined as the means by which we apply scientific discoveries and techniques to develop new and improved products and more efficient methods. For example, the term "information technology" has been used to describe the application of computer, audio, visual or telecommunications technology to the acquisition, analysis and display of information. And information technology includes the fields of computers, telecommunications and multi-media applications. Bio-technology refers to techniques in the biological sciences, and is the application of both science and technology to experiment with living cells or molecules. Research in biotechnology, including the area of genetic engineering, will lead to developments in diverse areas, such as food production, personal health and medical science.

Technology is a major driving force in most modern economies. In fact, in just about any industrialized nation, the role of technology is considered a key indicator of economic growth as well as a leading influence on the ratio of exports to imports. The Canadian economy is, indeed, shifting toward a greater emphasis on high-knowledge and high-technology industries. Many observers believe that this shift is critical, and it is one of Canada's central challenges to move from a resource-based economy to a knowledge-based economy. We can identify the contrast between the new knowledge-based era and previous eras. (See Exhibit 11.8.)

What's the Connection to Knowledge-Change?

Connected to Beck's observation of the three eras is a recognition that with each new era comes a new knowledge unique to that era and that distinguishes it from the era or economy that came before. Whether it stems from new technologies or new skills, in every new era exist opportunities for new products, new processes, new markets and, even, new industries. Just consider the new technologies of the three eras we considered. The tremendous prosperity experienced in the **commodity-processing era** was largely facilitated by the new technologies of the "batch system" of production. This system replaced the single craftsman or small group process of production, which generated only limited output (whether it was an article of clothing or a single machine). Batch production allowed the production of hundreds, even thousands, of the same product using machine reproduction of the original.

So, what we see is that a new knowledge base transformed the very nature of work, and transformed the so-called cottage industry into the factory system of production.

What we saw happening in the **mass-manufacturing era**, similarly, was the creation of new opportunities. The technology of that era essentially allowed manufacturers to integrate components into a single end-product. The result was the creation of a high-growth manufacturing economy. Finally, we have the **technology era**. What we saw was the displacement of the production worker as the centre of the industrial wheel with the

| EXHIBIT 11.8 | THE NEW ERA AND KNOWLEDGE WORK |

In her book entitled, *Shifting Gears*, Nuala Beck considers three fundamentally different eras from about 1850 to the present that have shaped our business enterprise system.

1. The Commodity-processing Era (1850–1918)

Beck suggests that in each era there has been at least one central ingredient, in abundant supply and at steadily falling cost, that helped facilitate the growth experienced during that era. The commodity-processing era had a vast supply of inexpensive steel. The central industries, those largely driving the economy at that time, included steel, railways, textiles and coal. So, around the mid-19th century, the economy was very much driven by commodities, transported by the newly constructed steamship lines and railways for processing in the mills. The new manufacturing processes played a central role in what became an era of great prosperity. Trade in products such as iron, steel and cotton accelerated.

2. The Mass-manufacturing Era (1918–1981)

In the era that followed, the mass-manufacturing era, it was energy and, specifically, the vast quantities of oil that facilitated the consumer-driven manufacturing boom that started around the turn of the century. The central industrial players during that era included: the auto industry, housing, machine tools and retailing. Businesses like that run by Henry Ford shaped consumer products out of the new technologies, and helped generate the era of mass production to satisfy mass demand. With inexpensive energy and innovative manufacturers, the ever increasing consumer demand for products could be met.

3. The Technology Era (1981–present)

The manufacturing era is steadily being superseded by the technology era. Today, we are in the technology era, which seems to have been largely facilitated by the development of the microchip and the semiconductor. And while the traditional leader in that industry has been Japan, North America is catching up, according to some observers. The rising players include the computer industry, as well as semiconductors and telecommunications. Canada is a strong supplier of many of the commodities needed by the technology-driven economy. For example, nickel and copper are important inputs into high-tech products, and Canada is a principal supplier of both. In fact, Beck argues that some of the economic turmoil that Canada has experienced is simply a temporary adjustment, as we shift from supplying commodities to the declining old economies to the new technology-driven economies.

Source: Based on Nuala Beck, *Shifting Gears: Thriving in the New Economy* (Toronto: Harper Collins, 1992).

implementation of automated assembly lines The key players in the new era are the professional, scientific and senior managerial employees. It is no longer production work that is the source of growth and opportunity: it is, rather, knowledge work!

What Is a Knowledge Worker?

In many of today's companies the most prized asset, unlike land, factories or equipment cannot even be measured on a company's balance sheet. That asset is knowledge. Beck describes knowledge workers as falling into one of three possible employment categories: professional, scientific/technical workers and management. (See Exhibit 11.9.)

EXHIBIT 11.9 KNOWLEDGE WORKERS

1. **Professionals.** This includes doctors, lawyers, engineers, accountants, and any other suppliers of information and specialized skills. The need for specialized skills has generated huge growth in professional services. Focus is on the development of ideas or of expert opinions.

2. **Scientific and technical workers.** Workers included in this broad category need not necessarily have high levels of education. For example, production workers can become knowledge workers through specialized training. So, members of this group might also be considered more specifically as data workers. Data occupations involve the manipulation of information. Data workers, such as those in clerical occupations, use, transmit or manipulate knowledge.

3. **Senior management.** The strategists and policy-makers are also knowledge workers who can critically affect organizational success through the decisions they make.

Beck underscores the opportunities for the knowledge worker in the technology era by pointing to employment differences between the knowledge worker and the manufacturing or production worker. According to Human Resource Development Canada, the fastest growing segment of workers in Canada in the last 25 years or so has been the knowledge worker. From 1971–1996, total employment was growing at an average rate of 2.1% annually. However, employment of knowledge workers grew at an average rate of 5.2% annually. This is roughly double the rate of growth for service workers, the second fastest growing segment of workers during that period. This is why many observers view the Canadian economy as becoming information intensive, in the sense that knowledge work is increasingly the source of employment.

Beck, however, points out that this doesn't mean all knowledge jobs are good and all manufacturing jobs are bad, so to speak. Clearly, many businesses that have entered the growing high-knowledge industry, like computers or pharmaceuticals, have failed. Similarly, some businesses in the manufacturing sector are prospering by generating new products and modernizing their facilities. That is, knowledge and knowledge work are available in both sectors, potentially. In fact, a recent study by Human Resources Development Canada also points out that growth in employment of knowledge workers has spread to all major industry groups — both high-tech and low-tech.

The Canadian Technology Scene

According to many observers, Canada traditionally has not been a strong competitor in the areas of technological research and development. Critics suggest that Canada does not engage in sufficient levels of research and development. (See Let's Talk Business 11.2.) Given the importance of operating in the global marketplace, the issue of Canada's competitiveness has become an increasingly key issue in recent years. At least one central factor in Canada's competitiveness is its ability to effectively employ advanced technology in the manufacturing of goods.

LET'S TALK BUSINESS 11.2 CANADA'S TECHNOLOGICAL STATUS

Why has Canada traditionally lagged in the area of research and innovation?

1. Canada's Traditional Dependence on Low Value-Added Exports

Canada has traditionally traded in largely undifferentiated products (coal, oil, gas, aluminum, copper, nickel, fisheries, agriculture, etc.) while not actively entering the high value-added sectors of raw materials, where technology is, in fact, an integral part of the production process. Canada fell into a role as supplier of unprocessed raw materials without efforts to apply technology to our products to create higher value-added export commodities. Unfortunately, Canada allowed its **imports** to become dominated by technology-intensive products.

2. Canada's Inadequate Technology Base

The development of secondary industry in Canada occurred in an artificial environment. Our industries were protected from foreign competition for many years through tariffs. Many observers believe that trade barriers can discourage domestic industry from innovating, given that there is less need to be competitive. Critics also suggest that, in contrast to the Canadian situation, many other countries developed a strong industrial sector by developing an infrastructure of technology-based industries. Foreign ownership has discouraged Canadian investment in research and development. The notion of the "branch plant" economy suggests that some of the central functions, such as strategic planning and research and development, are done in the multinational's home country, not in the host country of the subsidiary.

3. Canada's Limited Market and Company Size

Although Canada is large in land mass, it has a relatively small domestic market. Traditionally, then, there has been less incentive to innovate, given the small market. It is only more recently, with the reduction of trade barriers and the welcoming of global markets, that this issue is no longer a real impediment. In addition, the lack of size and stability in Canadian industrial laboratories is an obstacle to innovation. Many observers have noted that very few firms in Canada have sufficiently large research and development budgets. Among the minority is Northern Telecom, which, ironically, is being increasingly managed in the United States. Beyond the few, there are really no significant numbers of Canadian firms and no large sector of the Canadian economy to provide the driving force for research and development comparable to the large budgets of companies in the United States, Europe, and Japan.

4. Canada's Limited Spending on Research and Development

A central measure of a nation's innovation capacity is how much it spends in terms of research and development. In Canada, the amount of money spent on research and development has moved from 1.1% in the 1970s to 1.4% in the 1980s, to approximately 1.6% in the latter part of the 1990s. While that is an increase, how does it compare to what other nations are spending? The answer — it does **not** compare favourably! From 1995 to 1997, Japan spent almost 3% of their GDP on research and development, the United States spent about 2.5%, France and Germany both spent about 2.4%, Britain spent about 2.2%. So Canada has lagged in terms of research and development spending. A report issued by the Organization for Economic Co-operation and Development in 1998 indicated that the government financed only 7% of the cost of business research and development in Canada. This is in contrast with 17.3% in the United States, 12.7% in France, and 12% in Britain.

Source: McMillan & Jasson, 2001.

How Do Canadian Manufacturers Fare?

According to recent reports from Statistics Canada, approximately 70% of people who manage Canadian factories believe they are using production technologies that are at least as good as those employed by their foreign competitors. Of course, that may seem like a subjective measure; however, the researchers who conducted this survey confirmed this estimate with measures of actual technology use across five industries, and found supporting evidence for managers' claims.

High technology typically refers to the products that companies produce — electronic goods, computers, software, etc. As well, we can consider production or process technologies, which include the equipment used by the plant to produce its goods. The level of technology employed in the process of production might be high, even though the actual product produced is not a high-tech item per se. So, while you would typically find high-tech systems and equipment used in the production of computers or cars, you could also find such systems in the production of low-tech items, such as furniture or clothing.

Some observers suggest that free trade's push to become more competitive partly explains the increase in Canadian business's implementation of newer technology and modernizing of their plants. For example, in 1989, Canada's usage rate for industrial robots and computer-aided design and engineering (CAD/CAE) was about two-thirds that of employed in U.S. plants. By 1993, the two were the same. In addition, smaller advances also occurred in other technologies. Only approximately 58% of Canadian factories used at least one advanced technology in 1989, compared with 74% of U.S. factories. However, by 1993, 73% of Canadian factories employed at least one advanced technology, compared to 81% in the United States.

For technological progress to occur, research and development must take place.

Research = original investigation undertaken to acquire new knowledge

Development = application of research findings to create or improve products or processes.

Whether it is government, university or private sector research and development, the connection of research and development to the economy is pretty direct:

- Many observers have argued that, for almost any country, it is the export of technology-intensive commodities that is central to economic growth.
- In terms of the domestic welfare of a country, it has also been asserted that the ability of research and development to generate new products and services for a country will naturally improve the standard of living.
- Innovation through research and development may mean the creation of new employment opportunities.

CHAPTER SUMMARY ————————————————

Every organization must contend with a changing environment. These changes may stem from economic, competitive, legal/political, technological, or societal sources. This chapter emphasized the importance of understanding how organizations facilitate or resist change.

We considered the notion of double-loop and single-loop learning, and how organizations might effect these types of learning among their employees. Sources of resistance to change were specifically identified, as well as organizational responses to resistance. Finally, we drew attention to the importance of technology and innovation.

KEY TERMS

- organizational learning
- single-loop learning
- double-loop learning
- institutionalization
- cognitive scripts
- unfreezing
- change
- refreezing

- structural inertia
- paradigms
- The Commodity-processing Era
- The Mass-manufacturing Era
- The Technology Era
- knowledge worker
- research
- development

CASE APPLICATION   3M teaches change

[3M first] started with sandpaper: mineral and glue on a substrate. After years as an abrasives company, it morphed. A researcher left off the mineral, and adapted the glue and substrate to create a tape. After creating many varieties of sticky tape — electrical, medical — researchers created the first audio and videotapes. In their search to create better tape backings, other researchers happened on multilayer films that — surprise — have remarkable light management qualities. (In fact, these optical films have overturned a 200-year-old maxim of physics known as Brewster's Law.) This multilayer film technology is being used in brightness enhancement films, which are incorporated in the displays of virtually all laptops and palm computers.

In short, our 98-year history has been marked by twists and turns no one could have predicted. We did not foresee those changes, but we set up an infrastructure and tradition to allow them to occur. We planned for serendipity. We expect our company to change its shape — to adapt, to transform — at a steady and fairly rapid pace. In fact, one of our expectations is that we will derive 40 percent of our sales from products that have been introduced in the past four years. And each year, we also expect to derive 10 percent of sales from products introduced that year. These goals underscore our intention to live on what we have found most recently and not on the discoveries of the past.

This tradition differentiates 3M from many other companies — old and new. Older companies — those that have been around long enough to have a tradition — usually cling to what has worked in the past. Even though they may realize, in the abstract, that innovation is central to their survival, they shy away from change. They view innovation as a risky undertaking. They are partially correct, but they tend to ignore the fact that not innovating is even riskier. At 3M, we have a term for this misplaced loyalty to past models of success. We call it a competency trap. This is the same trap that opens up when someone says: We're pretty good at this — and we're making money, so why rock the boat? Newer companies haven't had the time to develop a tradition. If they are successful, they are undoubtedly standing at the leading edge. They've made several innovations; that's impressive, but not enough. Ahead they face the awesome challenge of keeping up with the pell-mell advance of the leading edge.

BUILDING A TRADITION OF INNOVATION

Because 3M has a tradition of innovation, we don't have to make conscious decisions at every step in the development of a process or technology. Things move quickly because the people know in their bones what's expected and how they should proceed. That knowledge isn't limited to a single industry or market. When 3M came up with a new super-weak adhesive that allows for repositionable Post-it® Notes, our tradition showed us how to bring a new-to-the-world product to a new market. When we created multilayer optical films, the tradition guided us and encouraged us. Our tradition also gives us courage when the climate changes and our current shape doesn't work as well as we'd like.

We know that we've been able to transform ourselves in the past — and that we have the resources to do it again. How is such a tradition created?

[1. **You require a sense of vision or direction that will lead organizational change or transformation.**

2. **You must understand the needs of those (e.g., customers) for whom the change is targeted.**

3. **You must set an appropriate pace for change, whether it is rapid or gradual.**]

. . . .

4. **You need to empower your people to make their own changes.** Transformation is a group process. The leader who tries to control evolution cell by cell is not going to succeed. One way in which we do this is by giving our employees the option to direct themselves for 15 percent of their time. During this time, they can work on projects of their own choosing, their own design, without management approval. We also acknowledge and reward the people who have succeeded through their own initiative. Our chairman and CEO, L. D. "Desi" DeSimone, frequently told the story of how he tried to kill — not once but three times the development of what became a popular 3M product. Each time, Desi gleefully pointed out, 3Mers found ways to circumvent his direction and bring the product to life. This celebration of dogged self-direction is held up as a model for our researchers. This didn't start with Desi, by the way. A half-century ago, long before empowerment became a corporate buzzword, 3M chairman William McKnight said that growth required people with initiative and that those people would make mistakes — but their mistakes would be less costly than the mistakes that came from dictatorial managers. McKnight's wisdom has been confirmed by our experience. Today, we can trace our most important products and technologies to self-initiated work by empowered employees.

5. **You need to create a climate of communication and sharing.** Discoveries need to be fully exploited, and this means sharing them with the others in the group. One person will use the discovery one way; one will use it another. At 3M, people know that products are developed by, and the profits are assigned to, the business unit. But technologies belong to everyone in the corporation. 3M researchers also know that career advancement comes faster to those who contribute to advances in several business units. We try to facilitate this communication by bringing together 3Mers from various cultures and various disciplines. We get them talking about problems and great results occur. This is how we discovered the optical opportunities in multilayer films and a thousand other advances.

6. **Finally, adapting organisms, if they have human consciousness, need psychic rewards.** They need to believe that their contributions matter and that they are appreciated by those around them. At 3M, we try to provide that recognition through peer-nominated award programs, a corporate technical "hall of fame" and other mechanisms.

RESIST THE URGE TO CONTROL

In addition to those six positive steps toward developing a tradition of innovation, companies should also try to avoid several behaviours. These "don'ts" are all designed to thwart the natural and counter-productive urge to control, structure and make clear those parts of business that inherently resist control and structure and clarity. First, don't fall in love with yourself. Companies, like individuals, need to know the difference between self-esteem and arrogance. You may have a good idea today, and you may have launched a popular new product, and you might be Wall Street's darling — but that doesn't mean you have a strong probability of long-term success. To survive and thrive, companies need to recreate themselves over and over. For that to happen, corporate leaders need to question their knowledge and the value of their business plan. And they need to be willing to chuck their current business model in favour of a strange and unproven strategy. They must adapt away from a known good into an unknown.

Second, in addition to questioning themselves, corporate leaders must question what their customers tell them. While they should be very attentive to what customers say, managers and product developers should never assume that customers fully understand their own needs and desires. If you take everything the customer says at face value, you will spend your career pursuing the same goals that your customer has described to every other supplier. And when you succeed, your customers will never be truly delighted because, after all, you simply did what they asked. On the other hand, if you give your customers something they didn't know they wanted, you will delight them. In other words, companies cannot clarify the murky business of product development by simply asking people what they want. No market research could have predicted Post-it® Notes, or multilayer optical film. Finally, don't try to control or make safe the fumbling, panicky, glorious adventure of discovery. Occasionally, one sees articles that describe how to rationalize this process, how to take the fuzzy front end and give it a nice haircut. This is self-defeating. We should allow the fuzzy front end to be as unkempt and as fuzzy as we can. Long-term growth depends on innovation, and innovation isn't neat. We stumble on many of our best discoveries. If you want to follow the rapidly moving leading edge, you must learn to live on your feet. And you must be willing to make necessary, healthy stumbles.

Source: By William E. Coyne from *Research Technology Management* (Mar./Apr. 2001) 44(2): 21–24. Reproduced with permission of Industrial Research Institute.

QUESTIONS

1. In what way do you think 3M represents a learning organization? How does it encourage double-loop learning?

2. With reference to your response to Question 1, do you think these qualities would also reduce resistance to change? In what ways?

3. Why might 3M's approach to change be difficult to apply in other types of organizations?

Canadian corporate change

READING I   THE NEWSPRINT LESSON

When we began our study of the Canadian economy in 1990, Canada was the third-richest country in the world (in GDP per capita) and had a dollar valued at 85 cents (U.S.). We released our report, *Canada at the Crossroads*, in 1991 and, a decade later, Canada is the fifth-richest country in the world and has [its] dollar valued at 65 cents (U.S.), a 23-percent international pay cut for all Canadians.

Why the substantial decline? Faced with two paths in 1991, the economy overall chose the less favourable path. This path hewed closely to the Canadian tradition of competing on the basis of lower-cost labour or raw materials and pursuing company strategies of replicating competitors elsewhere.

There is an alternative path — competing on the basis of uniqueness and innovation — which is the only path toward rising relative prosperity for Canada in the global economy. There is no question that Canadian firms can succeed at it. However, lulled by a steadily declining dollar, Canadian firms still face strong temptations toward more of the same.

Perhaps nothing could illustrate the contrast better than the trajectories of two industries that we studied in 1991, newsprint and telecommunications switches. In 1991, newsprint was one of Canada's leading export industries, with both impressive size ($5.5-billion in sales), and leading world export share (62 per cent). The Canadian industry featured seven large companies including the world's largest player, Abitibi-Price. The strength of the industry depended on three advantages: low wood fibre cost, low energy costs, and proximity to the world's largest market.

But these static advantages quickly came under pressure with the development of thermomechanical pulping, which facilitated the efficient use of low-cost fibre found in abundant supply in the southern U.S. and Latin America. Moreover, Canada lagged by a decade or more in implementing new processing technologies. Historically lax environmental regulation had also left firms unprepared for the heightening of environmental concerns about the forest products sector worldwide.

Since 1991, prices in the newsprint industry have drifted downward. In terms of world paper production, newsprint has dropped from 39 per cent to 30 per cent, as value-added grades of paper have grown. Meanwhile, Asia's growing appetite for newsprint has spurred investment in Asian production.

Winners in coping with these changes have been the Scandinavian firms, who invested heavily to upgrade themselves and their home industry through the 1990s. At home, they worked together through industry associations and universities to promote innovation. The average worker in the Scandinavian industry has a related university degree. Abroad, they invested heavily in North American assets.

Norway's Norske Skog purchased Canadian newsprint [player] Fletcher Challenge Canada and is in the process of acquiring Pacifica Papers, another Canadian newsprint

385

company. Swedish/Finnish firm Stora Enso and Finland's UPM-Kymmene also made major acquisitions abroad.

Unlike the Scandinavian industry, the Canadian pulp and paper sector, exemplified by newsprint, focused primarily on domestic consolidation rather than upgrading and globalizing. It also maintained its focus on the lowest-value-added, slowest-growing part of the marketplace: standard newsprint. And so, one of Canada's historical core industries has lost nine points of global share since 1991.

Today, the newsprint industry depends largely on the devalued Canadian dollar to stay profitable — shaky competitive ground indeed. At 65 cents (U.S.), the Canadian newsprint industry is right at the average of industry cost-competitiveness worldwide. At 85 cents (U.S.), Canada would be the least cost-competitive country in the world by far!

Contrast Canadian newsprint to the telecommunications switch industry. In 1991, the industry was Canada's most important high-technology sector. Nortel enjoyed the leading global market share in the important digital switch segment. Although things looked good for the industry back at the beginning of the 1990s, it was a target for worldwide competitors.

Yet the decade surprised us all. The market was transformed from digital switches for handling voice traffic for traditional phone companies such as Bell Canada, to optical transmission systems for handling data and Internet protocol traffic over alternative carrier networks, such as Qwest Corporation's all-fibre network.

Nortel and other members of the nascent Canadian cluster in 1991 could have continued a narrow definition of the industry and focused financial and managerial energy on consolidating it. Had it done so, the Canadian industry would have experienced a drift downward, as did newsprint.

However, the industry acted boldly and aggressively to innovate. Rather than attempt to maintain current positions — through replicating competitors and better management of the status quo — Canadian firms boldly chose innovative strategies with global aspirations, exploiting entirely new markets. They did well thanks to intense R & D, branding and managerial boldness. Despite the current capital markets challenges, Nortel, JDS Uniphase, Celestica and others are positioned to lead the next wave of innovation in the telecommunications equipment market.

At the turn of the millennium, Canada once again faces a fork in the road. If we are to compete and win on the world stage in the coming century, Canadian firms and governments must turn their backs on a culture of replication, and strive instead for uniqueness and innovation.

Innovation is the key today to global competitive advantage. Government at all levels must enhance Canada's commitment to creating a superior macroeconomic and microeconomic context for competitiveness. And our firms must develop more distinctive strategies based on relentless innovation.

If we all set our aspirations higher, Canada can not only prosper and succeed, but can become a leader in the global economy.

Source: Roger Martin and Michael Porter, "The road not taken" *The Globe and Mail* (April 26, 2001). Reproduced with permission of the authors.

READING II   THE BANK LESSON

The tepid pace of financial services consolidation may disappoint Bay Street's deal junkies and frustrate investors yearning for takeover premiums. So far as they are concerned, the lack of takeovers is more evidence that Canada is out of whack with the world trends.

In reality, the opposite is the case. Corporate Canada is growing up, getting out of the house and going global. For big companies, buying in Canada can be a quick and easy way to fill out the business portfolio. But it can also send the wrong message. Going local says that you're willing to play it safe by investing in a market with little to no growth. When you buy in Canada, you're buying a cost reduction opportunity, not necessarily a long-term expansion story.

The $7-billion takeover of Clarica last week by Sun Life Financial made news for a lot of reasons, not least of which was that it happened at all. Financial services consolidation looks like it has started and stopped with Clarica; the demutualized insurer attracted one bid only. Rival Canada Life has attracted none. Nor have Laurentian Bank or Quebec's National Bank. None of them is protected from takeover by Ottawa's recently overhauled financial services legislation. The Big Five banks, meanwhile, don't seem obsessed with merging with each other even though the financial services legislation theoretically allows them to do so. Bank mergers will probably happen, but the urgency is gone. Instead, the Big Five are looking beyond their borders.

In 1998, consolidation was the big story. Four of the Big Five banks announced merger plans for the simple reason, it appeared, that the Americans and Europeans were doing the same. When Finance Minister Paul Martin rejected the mergers, the banks cried like babies. In retrospect, though, Mr. Martin may have done them a favour. His decision forced them to step out of the Canadian sandbox. Toronto-Dominion Bank kept building its Waterhouse discount brokerage franchise in the United States. Bank of Montreal paid more attention to Harris Bank of Chicago, a franchise that the bank had owned for years but had paid scant attention to. Bank of Nova Scotia kept going in Latin America (although it wishes it had given Argentina a pass) and recently announced that it's looking for a retail bank south of the border.

Royal Bank of Canada went on a quiet though significant buying spree, picking up about $7-billion of insurance, banking and investment dealer companies across the United States. While none of RBC's acquisitions — among them Centura Banks of North Carolina — was a blockbuster, its plodding, middle-of-the-road acquisition strategy looks smart. The point is that medium-sized companies have a better chance of expanding than big companies. In less than a decade, RBC's U.S. presence will probably be larger than its Canadian one.

Buying outside of Canada comes with greater management and geopolitical risk, as Scotiabank faced in Argentina. But it also comes with potential rewards. Unlike the Canadian banks, HSBC, the former HongKong and Shanghai Bank, decided a couple of decades ago that it would go nowhere if it remained locked in the local market. Today, it is one of the few true global banking franchises. Manulife Financial, the Sun Life rival that was conspicuously absent from the Clarica bidding and is putting out signals that it will pass on Canada Life, seems to be a fan of the HSBC strategy. Its focus is Asia, notably Japan and China, where life insurance products are hot. While Sun Life showed a certain lack of imagination by buying Clarica, it does have a sizable American and overseas presence and has been pushing into India.

387

The banks' and Manulife's get-out-of-town strategy seems to have been confirmed by foreigners' lack of interest in Canada. If Canada is such a compelling place to invest, why didn't foreign companies bid for Clarica, Canada Life and National Bank? The answer, it appears, is the same reason why enlightened Canadian companies want to get out — lack of growth opportunities in the home market.

This leads to the next question: If all ownership restrictions are removed on financial services companies — no single shareholder, for instance, can own more than 20 per cent of a Big Five bank — will all the independent Canadian players vanish into foreign hands overnight? It seems doubtful. Buying in Canada doesn't exactly propel a company's globalization strategy to the next level. The good news is that the Canadian companies that can't attract bids will have to try harder to build value by stepping beyond their own little markets.

Source: Eric Reguly, "Smart firms should play in the global sandbox" *The Globe and Mail* (March 12, 2002): B10. Reproduced with permission from The Globe and Mail.

QUESTIONS

1. What does Reading I suggest with regard to the challenge faced by Canadian industry?

2. What do the banks (per Reading II) have in common with the newsprint industry (per Reading I)?

3. What do these readings imply about the challenges of organizational learning and change in Canada?

Notes

1. M.H. Bazerman, *Judgment in Managerial Decision Making*, 4th Ed. (New York: John Wiley, 1998).
2. A. Tversky and D. Kahneman, "Judgment under uncertainty: Heuristics and biases" *Science* 185: 1124–31.
3. D. Kahneman, P. Slovic and A. Tversky (eds.), *Judgment under Uncertainty: Heuristics and Biases* (New York: Cambridge University Press, 1982).
4. A. Newell and H. Simon, "Computer science as empirical inquiry: Symbols and search" in J. Haugeland (ed.), *Mind Design* (Cambridge, MA: MIT Press, 1981).
5. A. Tversky and D. Kahneman, "The belief in the 'law of small numbers'" *Psychological Bulletin* 76: 105–10; A. Tversky and D. Kahneman, "Subjective probability: A judgment of representativeness" *Cognitive Psychology* 3(3): 430–54.
6. Kahneman, Slovic & Tversky, ibid.
7. Tversky & Kahneman, "Judgment under uncertainty: Heuristics and biases," ibid.
8. A. Tversky and D. Kahneman, "Availability: A heuristic for judging frequency and probability" *Cognitive Psychology* 5: 207–32.
9. Tversky & Kahneman, "Judgment under uncertainty: Heuristics and biases," ibid.
10. Bazerman, ibid.
11. M. Alpert and H. Raiffa, "A progress report on the training of probability assessors" in Kahneman, Slovic & Tversky (eds.), ibid., pp. 294–305; B. Fischhoff, P. Slovic and S. Lichtenstein, "Knowing with certainty: The appropriateness of extreme confidence" *Journal of Experimental Psychology: Human Perception and Performance* 3: 552–64.
12. S. Lichtenstein, B. Fischhoff and L. Phillips, "Calibration of probabilities: The state of the art to 1980" in Kahneman, Slovic & Tversky (eds.), ibid., pp. 306–34.
13. M.H. Bazerman, *Judgment in Managerial Decision Making*, 2d Ed. (New York: John Wiley, 1990); Tversky & Kahneman, "Judgment under uncertainty: Heuristics and biases," ibid.
14. C.R. Schwenk, "The cognitive perspective on strategic decision making" *Journal of Management Studies* 25(1): 41–55.
15. R.H. Brockhaus, "Risk taking propensity of entrepreneurs" *Academy of Management Journal* 23: 509–20; M.B. Low and I.C. MacMillan, "Entrepreneurship: Past research and future challenges" *Journal of Management* 14(2): 139–61.
16. B.J. Bird, *Entrepreneurial Behaviour* (Glenview, IL: Scott, Foresman, 1989); E.J. Zajac and M.H. Bazerman, "Blind spots in industry and competitor analysis: Implications of interfirm (mis)perceptions for strategic decisions" *Academy of Management Review* 16(1): 37–56.
17. Brockhaus, "Risk taking propensity of entrepreneurs," ibid.
18. A.C. Cooper, W.C. Dunkelberg and C.Y. Woo, "Entrepreneurs' perceived chances for success" *Journal of Business Venturing* 3: 97–108.
19. E. Gatewood, K. Shaver and W. Gartner, "A longitudinal study of cognitive factors influencing start-up behaviors and success at venture creation" *Journal of Business Venturing* 10: 371–91; D.M. Ray, "The role of risk-taking in Singapore" *Journal of Business Venturing* 9(2): 157–77.
20. L.W. Busenitz, "Entrepreneurial risk and strategic decision making: It's a matter of perspective" *Journal of Applied Behavioral Science* 35(3): 325–40.
21. N. Krueger and P. Dickson, "How believing in ourselves increases risk taking: Perceived self-efficacy and opportunity recognition" *Decision Sciences* 25: 385–400.
22. D. Kahneman and D. Lovallo, "Timid choices and bold forecasts: A cognitive perspective on risk taking" *Management Science* 39(1): 17–31.
23. Bazerman, 1990, ibid.; Kahneman, Slovic & Tversky, ibid.

24. L.W. Busenitz and G.B. Murphy, "New evidence in the pursuit of locating new businesses" *Journal of Business Venturing* 2: 221–31; J.A. Katz, "A psychosocial cognitive model of employment status choice" *Entrepreneurship Theory and Practice* 17(1): 29–37.

25. Cooper, Dunkelberg & Woo, ibid.

26. C. Heath and A. Tversky, "Preferences and beliefs: Ambiguity and competence in choice under uncertainty" *Journal of Risk and Uncertainty* 4: 5–28.

27. Busenitz & Murphy, ibid.

28. Busenitz, ibid.: 328.

29. J.W. Fredrickson and A.L. Iaquinto, "Inertia and creeping rationality in strategic decision processes" *Academy of Management Journal* 32(3): 516–42; D. Miller and P.H. Friesen, *Organizations: A Quantum View* (Englewood Cliffs, NJ: Prentice Hall, 1984).

30. D. Kahneman and A. Tversky, "Prospect theory: An analysis of decision under risk" *Econometrica* 47: 263–91.

31. M.A. Neale and M.H. Bazerman, *Cognition and Rationality in Negotiation* (New York: Free Press, 1991).

32. Kahneman & Tversky, "Prospect theory: An analysis of decision under risk," ibid.; Glen Whyte, "Escalating commitment in individual and group decision making: A prospect theory approach" *Organizational Behaviour and Human Decision Process* 54(3): 430–55.

33. Kahneman & Tversky, "Prospect theory: An analysis of decision under risk," ibid.

34. R.M. Hogarth, *Judgement and Choice: The Psychology of Decisions* (New York: John Wiley, 1987).

35. Kahneman & Tversky, "Prospect theory: An analysis of decision under risk," ibid.

36. *The Eatons: The Rise and Fall of Canada's Royal Family*. © by Rod McQueen. Reproduced by permission of Stoddart Publishing Co. Limited.

37. B.M. Staw, "The escalation of commitment to a course of action" *Academy of Management Review* 6: 577–87.

38. Mark Keil and Ramiro Montealegre, "Cutting your losses: Extricating your organization when a big project goes awry" *Sloan Management Review* (Spring 2000) 41(3): 55–68.

39. Gareth Morgan, *Images of Organization* (Sage: Newbury Park, 1986).

40. J. Pfeffer and G.R. Salancik, *The External Control of Organizations* (New York: Harper & Row, 1978).

41. K. Weick, "Educational organizations as loosely coupled systems" *Administrative Science Quarterly* 21: 1–19.

42. E. Goffman, *Interaction Ritual* (Garden City, NY: Doubleday, 1967).

43. Pondy et al., *Organizational Symbolism* (Greenwich, CT: JAI Press, 1983).

44. J.D. Thompson, *Organizations in Action* (New York: McGraw-Hill, 1967); D. Katz and R.L. Kahn, *The Social Psychology of Organization*, 2d Ed. (New York: Wiley, 1978).

45. John A Challenger, "The transformed workplace: How can you survive" *The Futurist* (Nov./Dec. 2001) 35(6): 24–28. Originally published in the Nov./Dec. 2001 Issue of *The Futurist*. Used with permission from the World Future Society, 7910 Woodmont Avenue, Suite 450, Bethesda, Maryland 20814. Telephone: 301/656-8274; Fax: 301/951-0394; <http://www.wfs.org>.

46. A.D. Hall and R.E. Fagen, "Definition of system" *General Systems: The Yearbook of the Society for the Advancement of General Systems Theory* 1: 18–28.

47. Michael Hammer & James Champy, *Reengineering the Corporation* (New York, NY: HarperBusiness, 1993).

48. Varun Grover, William J Kettinger and James T.C. Teng, "Business process change in the 21st century" *Business and Economic Review* (Jan.–Mar. 2000) 46(2): 14–18. Reproduced with permission of the authors.

49. Ibid.

50. David Brown, "CIBC HR department halved as non-strategic roles outsourced" *Canadian HR Reporter* (June 4, 2001) 14(11): 1.

51. Heather Erickson, "Maybe organizational insider: Outsource payroll? Makes sense" *Canadian HR Reporter* (September 10, 2001) 14(15): G8.

52. Derek DeCloet, "CIBC to slash 400 jobs in brokerage" *Financial Post* (October 26, 2001).

53. "After the pink slip, Peter Kuitenbrouwer" *Financial Post* (September 27, 2001).

54. Kim Cameron, "Strategies for successful organizational downsizing" *Human Resource Management* 33 (Summer): 189–211 at 192.

55. Kim Cameron, "Strategies for successful organizational downsizing" *Human Resource Management* 33 (Summer): 189–211.

56. Dan Worrell, Wallace Davidson and Varinder Sharma, "Layoff announcements and shareholder wealth" *Academy of Management Journal* 34 (September): 662–78.

57. Peggy Lee, "A comparative analysis of layoff announcements and stock price reactions in the United States and Japan" *Strategic Management Journal* 18 (December): 879–94.

58. Wayne Cascio, "Downsizing? What do we know? What have we learned?" *Academy of Management Executive* 7 (February): 95–10

59. Terry H. Wagar, "Exploring the consequences of workforce reduction" *Canadian Journal of Administrative Sciences* (December 1998) 15(4): 300–309.

60. Mark Mone, "Relationships between self-concepts, aspirations, emotional responses, and intent to leave a downsizing organization" *Human Resource Management* 33 (Summer): 281–98; Lisa Ryan and Keith Macky, "Downsizing organizations: Uses, outcomes and strategies" *Asia Pacific Journal of Human Resources* 36 (Winter): 29–45.

61. Jeffery A. Tomasko, *Downsizing: Reshaping the Corporation of the Future* (New York: AMACON, 1990); Cascio, ibid.: 100; J. Brockner, "The effects of work layoff on survivors: Research, theory, and practice" *Research in Organizational Behaviour* 10(1): 213–56; Brockner et al., "Interactive effects of procedural justice and outcome negativity on victims and survivors of job loss" *Academy of Management Journal* 37 (June): 397–409; Sutton & D'Aunno, 1989; and K. McLellan and B. Marcolin, "Information technology outsourcing" *Business Quarterly* 59 (Autumn): 95–104.

62. Cascio, ibid.; Cameron, ibid.

63. Connie Wanberg, Larry Bunce and Mark Gavin, "Perceived fairness of layoffs among individuals who have been laid off: A longitudinal study" *Personnel Psychology* 52 (Spring): 59–84.

64. Marjorie Armstrong-Stassen, "Downsizing the federal government: A longitudinal study of managers' Reactions" *Canadian Journal of Administrative Sciences* 15 (December): 310–21.

65. Stephen Havlovic, France Bouthillette and Rena van der Wal. "Coping with downsizing and job loss: Lessons from the Shaughnessy Hospital closure" *Canadian Journal of Administrative Sciences* 15 (December): 322–32.

66. N. Doherty and J. Horsted, "Helping survivors to stay on board" *People Management* 1 (January): 26–31.

67. Wayne E. Baker, "Bloodletting and Downsizing Executive Excellence" *Provo* (May 1996) 13(5): 20.

68. P. DiMaggio and W. Powell, "The iron cage revisited: Institutional isomorphism and collective rationality in organizational fields" *American Sociological Review* 48(1): 147–60; J. Meyer and B. Rowan, "Institutional organizations: Formal structure as myth and ceremony" *American Journal of Sociology* 83: 440–63.

69. DiMaggio & Powell, ibid.

70. Meyer & Rowan, ibid.

71. K. Cameron, S. Freeman and A. Mishra, "Best practices in white-collar downsizing: Managing contradictions" *The Academy of Management Executive* 5(3): 58.

72. DiMaggio & Powell, ibid.; W. McKinley, C. Sanchez and A. Schick, "Organizational downsizing: Constraining, cloning, learning" *Academy of Management Executive* 9(3): 32–41.

73. McKinley, Sanchez & Schick, ibid.

74. Martin G. Evans, Hugh P. Gunz and R. Michael Jalland, "Implications of organizational downsizing for managerial careers" *Canadian Journal of Administrative Sciences* 14: 359–71.

75. McKinley, Sanchez & Schick, ibid.

76. K. Scott Shaver, "Person, process, choice: The psychology of new venture creation" *Entrepreneurship: Theory and Practice* 16(2): 23–45.

77. I.M. Kirzner, *Perception Opportunity and Profit: Studies in the Theory of Entrepreneurship* (Chicago: University of Chicago Press, 1979).

78. D. Hull, J. Bosley and G. Udell, "Renewing the hunt for the Heffalump: Identifying potential entrepreneurs by personality characteristics" *Journal of Small Business Management* 18(1): 11–18.

79. Jeffery A. Timmons, *New Venture Creation*, 4th Ed. (Homewood, IL: Irwin, 1994), p. 5.

80. J. Schumpeter, *The Theory of Economic Development* (Cambridge: Harvard University Press, 1936).

81. Ibid.

82. J.G. Kerr, *New Venture and Small Business Management* (Internet Course) (Toronto: Captus Press, 1997): Unit 2.

83. Taken from *Success* Magazine, February 1999: 12.

84. Bank of Canada, *Report on Small Business* (1994).

85. Canadian Federation of Business Information, *Small Business Primer* (July 1998).

86. Statistics Canada. 1998. *Small Business Quarterly, Labour Force Information* (Summer). Cat: #71-001.

87. Industry Canada, *Small Business in Canada* (1991): 3.

88. Industry Canada, *Small Business Quarterly Report* (2000).

89. Ibid.

90. Industry Canada and Statistics Canada, *Growing Small Business* (February 1994).

91. Industry Canada and Statistics Canada, *Small Business in Canada — A Statistical Overview* (January 1996).

92. Industry Canada and Statistics Canada, 1994, ibid.: 5.

93. Ibid.

94. Statistics Canada, *Canadian Economic Observer* (November 2000). Cat: #11-010-XPB.

95. S.J. Davis, J. Haltiwanger and S. Schuh, "Small business and job creation: Dissecting the myth and reassessing the facts" *Business Economics* 29(3): 13–21.

96. R. Levering, M. Moscowitz and M. Katz, *The 100 Best Companies to Work for in America* (Scarborough, New York: New American Library, 1985).

97. H.J. Pleitner, "Contributions of SME's to innovation" *Journal of Small Business and Entrepreneurship* 7(3): 14–22.

98. Michael Porter's "Five Forces Model" is described in *Competitive Strategy Techniques for Analyzing Industries and Competitors* (New York: Free Press, 1980) Chapter 11 and the "Diamond for National Advantage" was presented in a study prepared for the Business Council on National Issues and the government of Canada, October 1991 by Michael Porter and Monitor Company.

99. T.J. Peters and R.H. Waterman, *In Search of Excellence* (New York: Harper & Row, 1982).

100. Knight, R., *Entrepreneurship*, Ivy School of Business, December 1987.

101. D.C. McClelland, *The Achieving Society* (New York: Van Nostrand Reinhold, 1961).

102. D.C. McClelland, "Characteristics of Successful Entrepreneurs" *Journal of Creative Behaviour* 21: 219–33.

103. Ibid.

104. R.H. Brockhaus, "Risk taking propensity of entrepreneurs," ibid.

105. C.R. Anderson, "Locus of control, coping behaviors in a stress setting: A longitudinal study" *Journal of Applied Psychology* 62: 446–51.

106. Statistics Canada, *Canadian Economic Observer* (November 1997). Cat.: #11-010-XPB, January-December, V-10.

107. Knight, ibid.

108. M. Harvey and R. Evans, "Strategic windows in the entrepreneurial process" *Journal of Business Venturing* 10: 331–47.

109. Ibid.

110. R.W. Peacock, "A study of small enterprise intenders who do not proceed" *Journal of Small Business & Entrepreneurship* 8(4): 28–40.

111. G.R. Plaschka and H.P. Welsch, "Emerging structures in entrepreneurship education: Curricular designs and strategies" *Entrepreneurship Theory and Practice* 14(3): 55–71.

112. W.E. McMullan and W.A. Long, "Entrepreneurship education in the nineties" *Journal of Business Venturing* 52: 107–11.

113. J.N. Hood and J.E. Young, "Entrepreneurship's requisite areas of development: A survey of top executives in successful entrepreneurial firms" *Journal of Business Venturing* 8: 115–35.

114. D.W. Balderson, *Canadian Entrepreneurship and Small Business Management*, 4th Ed. (Toronto: McGraw-Hill Ryerson, 2000), p. 40.

115. Dun & Bradstreet, *Business Failure Record*. New York, 1999.

116. A. Cooper and K.W. Artz, "Determinants of satisfaction for entrepreneurs" *Journal of Business Venturing* 10: 439–57.

117. T. Bates, "Analysis of survival rates among franchise and independent small business startups" *Journal of Small Business Management* 33(2): 26–36.

118. B.A. Weisbrod, *The Voluntary Nonprofit Sector* (Lexington: D.C. Heath and Company, 1977).

119. Florence Heffron. *Organization Theory and Public Organizations: The Political Connection* (New Jersey: Prentice Hall, 1989).

120. To date, no universally accepted nomenclature for this sector exists. See Ronald Hirshhorn (ed.), *The Emerging Sector: In Search of A Framework* (Ottawa: Canadian Policy Research Networks Inc., 1997), p. 5.

121. This definition is based on the definition by N. Johnson, *Voluntary Social Services* (Oxford: Basil Blackwell, 1981); and L.M. Salamon and H.K. Anheier, *The Emerging Nonprofit Sector: An Overview* (Manchester: Manchester University Press, 1996).

122. Donald J. Bourgeois, *The Law of Charitable and Non-profit Organizations*, 2d Ed. (Toronto: Butterworths, 1995).

123. P.L. Browne, *Love in a Cold World? The Voluntary Sector in the Age of Cuts* (Ottawa: Canadian Centre for Policy Alternatives, 1996).

124. Ibid.

125. Figures are from Revenue Canada for 1998.

126. Walter Stewart, *The Charity Game: Waste and Fraud in Canada's $86-Billion-a-Year Compassion Industry* (Toronto: Douglas & McIntyre, 1996), p. 9; M. Hall and K.G. Banting, "The nonprofit sector in Canada: An introduction" in K.G. Banting (ed.), *The Nonprofit Sector in Canada* (Montreal and Kingston: School of Policy Studies, Queen's University, 2000).

127. D. Duchesne, *Giving Freely: Volunteers in Canada*. Statistics Canada, Labour Analytic Report. Cat: 71-535 No. 4. (Ottawa: Minister of Supply and Services Canada, 1989).

128. Kathleen M. Day and Rose Anne Devlin, "The Canadian nonprofit sector" in R. Hirshhorn (ed.), *The Emerging Sector: In Search of a Framework* (Ottawa: Canadian Policy Research Networks Inc., 1997), p. 63.

129. S. Martin, *An Essential Grace: Funding Canada's Health Care, Education, Welfare, Religion and Culture* (Toronto: McClelland and Stewart, 1985).

130. D.J. Tucker, J.V. Singh and A.G. Meinhard, "Organizational form, population dynamics and institutional change: A study of birth patterns of voluntary organizations" *Academy of Management Journal* 33: 151–78.

131. B.A. Weisbrod, *The Voluntary Nonprofit Sector* (Lexington: D.C. Heath and Company, 1977).

132. Ibid.

133. L.M. Salamon, *Partners in Public Service: Government-Nonprofit Relations in the Modern Welfare State* (Baltimore: The Johns Hopkins University Press, 1995).

134. Femida Handy, "Reputation as collateral: An economic analysis of the role of trust in nonprofit organizations" *Nonprofit and Voluntary Sector Quarterly* 24(4): 293–305.

135. J.J. Rice and M.J. Prince, *Changing Politics of Canadian Social Policy* (Toronto: University of Toronto Press, 2000).

136. Tucker, Singh & Meinhard, ibid.

137. S. McBride and J. Shields, *Dismantling a Nation: The Transition to Corporate Rule in Canada* (Halifax: Fernwood Publishing, 1997); B. Jeffrey, *Hard Right Turn: The New Face of Neo-Conservatism in Canada* (Toronto: HarperCollins Canada, 1999).

138. A.G. Meinhard and M.K. Foster, "Third sector strategic responses to Canada's changing social, political and economic climate: A comparative analysis." Paper presented at the Fourth International Conference of the International Society for Third Sector Research, Dublin, Ireland, 2000.

139. M.K. Foster and A.G. Meinhard, "Strategic responses of voluntary social service organizations to funding changes: The Ontario situation." Paper presented at the annual Academy of Management Conference, Toronto, Ontario, 2000; and Meinhard & Foster, ibid.

140. This section is based on the works of Neil Postman, *Technopoly: the Surrender of Culture to Technology* (New York: Random House, 1993); and H. Menzies, *Whose Brave New World? The Information Highway and the New Economy* (Toronto: Between the Lines, 1996).

141. This section is based on the following works: P.F. Drucker, "Lessons for successful nonprofit governance" *Nonprofit Management and Leadership* 1(1): 7–14; P.F. Drucker, "Introduction: Charitable and non-profit organizations" in Donald J. Bourgeois, *The Law of Charitable and Non-profit Organizations*, 2d Ed. (Toronto: Butterworths, 1995), pp. 1–30; Avner Ben-Ner and Theresa Van Hoomissen, "The governance of nonprofit organizations: Law and public policy" *Nonprofit Management and Leadership* 4(4): 393–414.

142. Based on John M. Bryson, *Strategic Planning for Public and Nonprofit Organizations*, Rev'd Ed. (San Francisco: Jossey-Bass, 1995).

143. A. Bedeian and R.F. Zammuto, *Organizations, Theory and Design* (Hinsdale, IL: Dryden Press, 1991).

144. Richard L. Daft, *Organizational Theory and Design*, 7th Ed. (Cincinnati, OH: South-Western College Publishing, 2001).

145. Bourgeois, ibid.; Michael O'Neil, 1992. "Ethical dimensions of nonprofit administration" *Nonprofit Management & Leadership*, 3(2): 199–213

146. This section based on works by: R. Herman and D. Heimovics, *Executive Leadership in Nonprofit Organizations: New Strategies for Shaping Executive-Board Dynamics* (San Francisco: Jossey-Bass, 1991); and J. Carver and M.M. Carver, *Reinventing Your Board* (San Francisco: Jossey-Bass, 1997).

147. B. O'Connell, *The Board Members Book* (New York: Foundation Center, 1985), p. 52.

148. Herman & Heimovics, ibid.; and Drucker, ibid.

149. Herman & Heimovics, ibid.: 58.

150. Herman & Heimovics, ibid: 59.

151. William A. Kleintop, "Information resources management for nonprofit organizations" in Tracy Connors (ed.), *The Nonprofit Handbook*, 2d Ed. (New York: John Wiley and Sons, 1997), pp. 535–54; and Carver & Carver, ibid.

152. G. Yukl, *Leadership in Organizations*, 3d Ed. (Engelwood Cliffs, NJ: Prentice Hall, 1994).

153. N. Tichy and M. Devana, *The Transformational Leader* (New York: John Wiley and Sons, 1986).

154. B. Bass, *Bass & Stogdill's Handbook of Leadership: Theory, Research and Managerial Applications* (New York: Free Press, 1990).

155. N. Tichy and D. Ulrich, "The leadership challenge — A call for the transformational leader" *Sloan Management Review* 26: 59–64.

156. J. Gregory Dees, "Enterprising nonprofits" *Harvard Business Review*, 55–67.

157. P. Kotler and A. Andreasen, *Strategic Marketing for Non-Profit Organizations* (Upper Saddle, NJ: Prentice Hall, 1996); B.L. McLeish, *Successful Strategies for Non-Profit Organizations* (New York: John Wiley and Sons, 1995); F. Rice, "What intelligent consumers want?" *Fortune* (Dec. 28, 1992), 57.

158. E. Johnson, "Marketing" in Connors, Tracy (ed.), *The Nonprofit Handbook*, 2d Ed. (New York: John Wiley and Sons, 1997), p. 378.

159. S. FitzRandolph and L. Miller, *Entrepreneurial Initiatives in the Nonprofit Sector*. CVSS Working paper series, 1998.

160. This discussion is based on the work of Brenda Zimmerman and Ray Dart, "Charities doing commercial ventures: Societal and organizational implications." Trillium Foundation and Canadian Policy Research Networks, Inc., Toronto, 1998.

161. M. Hall and L. Macpherson, "A provincial portrait of Canada's charities" *Canadian Centre for Philanthropy Research Bulletin*, Vol. 4 (1997).

162. M. Drumwright, P. Cunningham and I. Berger, "Social Alliances: Company/nonprofit collaboration" (2000, unpublished). Cambridge, MA: Marketing Science Institute Working Paper #00-101; P.N. Bloom and P.Y. Hussein, "Benefiting society and the bottom line" *Marketing Management* 4: 8–19; J.M. Handleman and S.J. Arnold, "The role of marketing actions with a social dimension: Appeals to the institutional environment" *Journal of Marketing* 63: 33–48; and S. Sagawa and E. Segal, *Common Interest, Common Good: Creating Value Through Business and Social Sector Partnerships* (Cambridge: Harvard Business School Press, 2000).

163. M. Sinclair and J. Galaskiewics. 1997. "Corporate-nonprofit partnerships: Varieties and covariates" *New York Law School Law Review* 41: 1059–90.

164. H. Schmid and A.G. Meinhard, "A comparative analysis of emerging partnerships between corporations and nonprofit social service organizations in Canada and Israel." Paper presented at the annual ARNOVA Conference, New Orleans, LA, 2000.

165. C. Cone, "Cause-Related Marketing Trends Report." (Boston: Cone Communications, Inc., 1997); and G. White, "The Not-for-profit and the private sectors in the 1990's . . . or how 'Birkenstock' and 'Pinstripe' need each other!" (Toronto: Market Vision Group, 1997).

166. M. Sinclair and J. Galaskiewics, "Corporate-nonprofit partnerships: Varieties and covariates" *New York Law School Law Review* 41: 1059–90.

167. S. Martin, *An Essential Grace: Funding Canada's Health Care, Education, Welfare, Religion and Culture* (Toronto: McClelland and Stewart, 1985).

168. Rice & Prince, ibid.

169. D. Hostland, *Structural Unemployment in Canada: Some Stylized Facts*. 1995. Web site: <http://www.hrdc-drhc.gc.ca/arb/publications/research/r-96-1e.pdf> (Last accessed: June 11, 2001).

170. Rice & Prince, ibid.

171. McBride & Shields, ibid.

172. Tucker, Singh, & Meinhard, ibid.

173. Rice & Prince, ibid.: 113.

174. Rice & Prince, ibid.; Meinhard & Foster, ibid.

175. R. Kramer, "A third sector in the third millennium?" *Voluntas* 11 (1): 1–23.

176. J.G. Stein, *The Cult of Efficiency* (Toronto: Anansi, 2001).

177. Meinhard & Foster, ibid.

178. John Gray, "Commentary" *Canadian Business* (April 16, 2001): 66.

179. Harry Sterling, "Is free trade a realistic option for East Asia?" *National Post* (March 13, 2001).

180. William Echikson, Jack Ewing and Inka Resrch, "Who'll get stomped in Europe's postal wars?" *BusinessWeek* (May 31, 1999).

181. Economic Council of Canada, *Responsible Regulation: An Interim Report* (Ottawa: Ministry of Supply and Services, 1979).

182. James Baxter, Southam News, "Majority against foreign-owned media: poll Decima research: But study finds foreign investment not opposed" (July 6, 2001).

183. Thomas L. Friedman, *The Lexus and the Olive Tree* (New York, NY: Farrar Strauss Giroux, 1999).

184. J. Luis Gausch and Robert W. Hahn, "The cost and benefits of regulation: implications for developing countries" *The World Bank Research Observer* 14(1): 137–58.

185. Garrett Wasney, "A new road for Canadian truckers" *World Trade* 10(2): 50.

186. Anonymous, "Deregulations' real winner: The consumer" *Railway Age* 202(1): 20.

187. Wasney, ibid.

188. Jordy Barnes, "Let banks fill low low-income insurance gap. Branch networks would make policies accessible, affordable" *National Post* (June 28, 2001).

189. Air Canada Article, *The Globe and Mail* (May 9, 2001).

190. Shaker A. Zahra and Carol Dianne Hansen, "Privatization, entrepreneurship, and global competitiveness in the 21st Century" *Competition Review* 10(1): 83–103.

191. William Megginson, "Privatization" *Foreign Policy* (Spring, 2000): 14.

192. D. Jones, 1997. "Doing the wrong thing: 48% of workers admit to unethical or illegal acts" *U.S.A. Today* (Apr. 4–6, 1997).

193. M. Mahar, "Unwelcome legacy: There's still a big unpaid tab for the S and L bailout" *Barron's* 72(48): 16.

194. Results of the PricewaterhouseCoopers Fifth Annual Global Survey were released in conjunction with the World Economic Forum held in New York, January 2002.

195. Poll results from Canadian Democracy and Corporate Accountability Commission report entitled, *The New Balance Sheet: Corporate Profits and Responsibility in the 21st Century*.

196. D.D. Runes, *Dictionary of Philosophy* (Littlefields: Adams and Co., 1964).

197. T.L. Beauchamp and N.E. Bowie, *Ethical Theory and Business* (Englewood Cliffs, NJ: Prentice Hall, 1983).

198. Richard T. De George, *Business Ethics*, 5th Ed. (Upper Saddle River, NJ: Prentice Hall, 1999).

199. P.V. Lewis, "'Defining business ethics': Like nailing jell-o to a wall" *Journal of Business Ethics* 4(5): 377–83.

200. J.R. Rest, *Moral Development: Advances in Research and Theory* (New York: Praeger, 1986).

201. T.M. Jones, "Ethical decision making by individuals in organizations: An issue-contingent model" *Academy of Management Review* 16(2): 367.

202. De George, ibid.

203. Mark Pastin, *The Hard Problems of Management: Gaining the Ethics Edge* (San Francisco: Jossey-Bass, 1986).

204. De George, ibid.

205. L.D. Molm, "Affect and social exchange: Satisfaction in power-dependence relations" *American Sociological Review* 56(4): 475–93.

206. M.R. Buckley, D.S. Wiese and M.G. Harvey, "An investigation into the dimensions of unethical behaviour" *Journal of Education for Business* 73(5): 284–90.

207. De George, ibid.

208. Jones, "Ethical decision making by individuals in organizations: An issue-contingent model," ibid.: 367.

209. B. Holstrom, "Moral hazard and observability" *Bell Journal of Economics* 10: 74–91.

210. G. Becker, *The Economic Approach to Human Behaviour* (Chicago: University of Chicago Press, 1976).

211. L.K. Trevino, "Ethical decision making in organizations: A person-situation interactionist model" *Academy of Management Review* 11(3): 601–17.

212. S.L. Grover, "Why professionals lie: The impact of professional role conflict on reporting accuracy" *Organizational Behaviour and Human Decision Processing* 55: 251–72.

213. W.H. Hegarty and H.P. Sims, "Some determinants of unethical decision behaviour: An experiment" *Journal of Applied Psychology* 63(4): 451–57.

214. M.L. Pava, "Religious business ethics and political liberalism: An integrative approach" *Journal of Business Ethics* 17(15): 1633–52.

215. J. Rawls, *Political Liberalism* (New York: Columbia University Press, 1993), p. 51.

216. L.K. Trevino and S.A. Youngblood, "Bad apples in bad barrels: A causal analysis of ethical decision making behaviour" *Journal of Applied Psychology* 75(4): 378–85.

217. S.L. Payne and R.A. Giacalone, "Social psychological approaches to the perception of ethical dilemmas" *Human Relations* 43: 649–65; Trevino, "Ethical decision making in organizations: A person-situation interactionist model," ibid.

218. A.M. Pettigrew, "On studying organizational cultures" *Administrative Science Quarterly* 24: 570–81.

219. Ibid.

220. Meyer & Rowan, ibid.

221. S.B. Knouse and R.A. Giacalone, "Ethical decision-making in business: Behavioral issues and concerns" *Journal of Business Ethics* 11: 369–77.

222. C.D. Stone, "The culture of the corporation" in W.M. Hoffman and J.M. Moore (eds.), *Business Ethics*, 2d Ed. (New York: McGraw-Hill, 1975).

223. R.D. Gatewood and A.B. Carroll, "Assessment of the ethical performance of organizational members: A conceptual framework" *Academy of Management Review* 16: 667–90.

224. G.B. Northcraft and M.A. Neale, *Organizational Behaviour* (Chicago: Dryden Press, 1994).

225. Gatewood & Carroll, ibid.

226. R.R. Sims, "The institutionalization of organizational ethics" *Journal of Business Ethics* 10: 493–511; L.J. Brooks, "Corporate codes of ethics" *Journal of Business Ethics* 8: 117–29.

227. K.E. Kram, P.C. Yeager and G.E. Reed, "Decisions and dilemmas: The ethical dimension in the corporate context" in J.E. Post (ed.), *Research in Corporate Social Performance and Policy*, Vol. 1 (Greenwich, CT: JAI Press, 1989), pp. 21–54.

228. J. Weber, "Manager's moral reasoning: Assessing their responses to the three moral dilemmas" *Human Relations* 43: 687–702.
229. Brooks, ibid.
230. R.S.J. Baumhart, "How ethical are businessmen?" *Harvard Business Review* 39: 6–31.
231. A. Higgins, C. Power and L. Kohlberg, "The relationship of moral atmosphere to judgments of responsibility" in W.M. Kurtines and J.L. Gewirtz (eds.), *Morality, Moral Behaviour and Moral Development* (New York: Wiley, 1984), pp. 74–106.
232. W.H. Hegarty and H.P. Sims, "Organizational philosophy, policies, and objectives related to unethical decision behaviour: A laboratory experiment" *Journal of Applied Psychology* 64(3): 331–38.
233. Weber, ibid.
234. L. Kohlberg, "Stage and sequence: The cognitive developmental approach to socialization" in D.A. Goslin (ed.), *Handbook of Socialization Theory and Research* (Chicago: Rand McNally, 1969), pp. 347–480; Knouse & Giacalone, ibid.; Trevino, ibid.
235. L.G. Zucker, "Institutionalization as a mechanism of cultural persistence" *American Sociological Review* 42(2): 726–42; Meyer & Rowan, ibid.
236. J.G. March, and H.A. Simon, *Organizations* (New York: Wiley, 1958).
237. C.J.G. Gersick and J.R. Hackman, "Habitual routines in task-performing groups" *Organizational Behaviour and Human Decision Processes* 47: 65–97.
238. Ibid.
239. R. Jackall, *Moral Mazes: The World of Corporate Managers* (New York: Oxford University Press, 1988).
240. Ibid.
241. H. Tajfel, *Human Groups and Social Categories: Studies in Social Psychology* (Cambridge, England: Cambridge University Press, 1981); H. Tajfel and J.C. Turner, "The social identity theory of intergroup behaviour" in S. Worchel and W.G. Austin (eds.), *Psychology of Intergroup Relations*, 2d Ed. (Chicago: Nelson Hall, 1985), pp. 7–24.
242. B.E. Ashforth and F. Mael, "Social identity theory and the organization" *Academy of Management Review* 14(1): 20–39.
243. J. Turner, "Towards a cognitive redefinition of the social group" in H. Tajfel (ed.), *Social Identity and Intergroup Relations* (Cambridge, England: Cambridge University Press, 1982), pp. 15–40.
244. Tajfel & Turner, ibid.
245. Ashforth & Mael, ibid.
246. R. Ricklee, "Ethics in America" *The Wall Street Journal* (October 31/November 3, 1985): 3; S. Milgram, *Obedience to Authority* (New York: Harper & Row, 1974).
247. E. Sutherland and D.R. Cressey, *Principles of Criminology* (Chicago: J.B. Lippincott, 1970).
248. Kahn et al., *Organizational Stress: Studies in Role Conflict and Ambiguity* (New York: John Wiley, 1964).
249. Merton, R.K. *Social Theory and Social Structure*, 2d Ed. (New York: Free Press, 1957).
250. Kahn et al., ibid.
251. Ashforth & Mael, ibid.
252. S. Stryker and R.T. Serpe, "Commitment, identity salience, and role behaviour: Theory research example" in W. Ickes and E.S. Knowles (ed.), *Personality, Roles and Social Behaviour* (New York: Springer-Verlag, 1982), pp. 199–218; Thoits, 1983.
253. Ashforth & Mael, ibid.
254. M. Friedman, *Capitalism and Freedom* (Chicago: University of Chicago Press, 1962); M. Friedman, "The social responsibility of business is to increase its profits" *New York Times Magazine* (September 13, 1970).
255. John Kenneth Galbraith, *The Affluent Society* (Boston: Houghton Mifflin Company, 1958).
256. Goodpaster, K.E., and J.B. Matthews, Jr., "Can a corporation have a conscience?" in T.L. Beauchamp and N.E. Bowie (eds.), *Ethical Theory and Business* (Englewood Cliffs, NJ: Prentice Hall, 1983).
257. Natasha Tarpley, "Levi's Mends the Social Fabric" *Fortune* (July 10, 2000). © 2001 Time Inc. All rights reserved.
258. A.Z. Carr, "Is business bluffing ethical?" *Harvard Business Review* 46: 127–34.
259. Carr, ibid.
260. *The Economist* (November 17, 2001): 70.
261. A.B. Carroll, "Linking business to behaviour in organizations" *SAM Advanced Management Journal* 43: 4–11.
262. Carr, ibid.
263. John Locke, *Second Treatise on Civil Government* (Cambridge: Cambridge University Press, 1690).
264. Immanuel Kant, *Grounding for the Metaphysics of Morals*. [First published in 1785.] Trans. James W. Ellington. (Indianapolis, IN: Hackett, 1993).

265. John A Challenger, "The transformed workplace: How can you survive." Originally published in Nov./Dec. 2001 Issue of *The Futurist*. Used with permission from the World Future Society, 7910 Woodmont Avenue, Suite 450, Bethesda, Maryland 20814. Telephone: 301/656-8274; Fax: 301/951-0394; <http://www.wfs.org>.

266. Challenger, ibid.

267. D.D. Warrick, "The illusion of doing well while the organization in regressing" *Organization Development Journal* 20(1): 56–61.

268. Challenger, ibid.

269. Challenger, ibid.

270. Timothy Taylor, "Thinking about a 'new economy'" *Public Interest* 143: 3–19.

271. Diane Rezendes Khirallah, "The tug of more Informationweek" *Manhasset* 883: 32–40.

272. Challenger, ibid.

273. Challenger, ibid.

274. J. Pedler, R. Burgoyne, and A. Boydell, *The Learning Company* (Maidenhead, Surrey: McGraw-Hill, 1997), p. 3.

275. W.L. French, C.H. Bell, Jr., and R.A. Zawacki (eds.), *Organization Development and Transformation: Managing Effective Change*, 4th ed. (Burr Ridge, IL: Irwin, 1994), p. 7.

276. C. Argyris and D.A. Schon, *Organizational Learning: A Theory of Action Perspective* (Reading, MA: Addison-Wesley Publishing Company, 1978).

277. Argyris & Schon, ibid.

278. Argyris & Schon, ibid: 4.

279. Argyris & Schon, ibid.

280. C. Argyris, *Reasoning, learning, and action* (San Francisco: Jossey-Bass, 1982), p. xii.

281. P. Senge, *The Fifth Discipline: The Art and Practice of the Learning Organization* (New York: Doubleday, 1990).

282. M. Dogson, "Organizational learning: A review of some literatures" *Organization Studies* 14: 375–94.

283. J.S. Glaser, "Connecting the workplace and adult development theory: Self directed work teams as a petri dish for adult development." Paper presented at the 7th Annual Meeting of the Society for Research in Adult Development, Toronto, Canada, June 1992.

284. D.H. Brundage and D. Mackeracher, *Adult Learning Principles and Their Application to Program Planning* (Toronto: Ministry of Education, 1980).

285. J. Mezirow, "Perspective transformation" *Adult Education* 28(2): 100–10.

286. R. Kegan, *The Evolving Self: Problem and Process in Human Development* (Cambridge: Harvard University Press, 1982).

287. M. Basseches, *Dialectical Thinking and Adult Development* (Norwood, NJ: Ablex, 1984).

288. E. Erikson, "Identity and the life cycle" *Psychological Issues Monograph* 1(1) (New York: International Universities Press, 1968).

289. Erickson, ibid.

290. E. Cell, *Learning to Learn from Experience* (Albany: State University of New York Press, 1945).

291. Argyris & Schon, ibid.

292. Meyer & Rowan, ibid.; Zucker, ibid.

293. Zucker, ibid.; Meyer & Rowan, ibid.

294. Meyer & Rowan, ibid.

295. J.P. Sims, Jr., D.A. Gioia, and Associates, *The Thinking Organization* (San Francisco: Jossey-Bass, 1986).

296. J. Piaget, *The Construction of Reality in the Child* (New York: Basic Books, 1954); Kohlberg, ibid.

297. John S. McCallum, "Managing in the new economy: Evolution or revolution?" *Ivey Business Journal* (Mar./Apr. 2001) 65(4): 28–30). © 2001 Ivey Management Services. One-time permission to reproduce granted by Ivey Management Services (December 18, 2001).

Glossary

adhocracy or innovative organization One of Mintzberg's five fundamental organizational configurations, the others being the simple or entrepreneurial structure, the machine bureaucracy, the professional bureaucracy and diversified/divisional. An "organic organization" unlike any of the others, where innovation and creativity flourish. *See* simple or entrepreneurial structure, machine bureaucracy, professional bureaucracy and diversified/divisional.

administrative inertia A structural obstacle to the acceptance or facilitation of changes in organizational strategy or in decision making. Organizational practices may be so embedded in the mindset of the organization as to prevent desirable change.

administrative management Henry Fayol's philosophy of management, one of the three major classical approaches (the others being the scientific and the bureaucratic), and focusing on the principles of division of work, unity of command, subordination of employees' individual interests to the common good, and *esprit de corps*. *See* bureaucratic management and scientific management.

availability heuristic The generation of probabilities by decision-makers, based on their familiarity with a certain task, idea or environment. Looking to the past for assistance, especially successful situations. Can lead to exclusion of consideration of the possibility of change, and thus false assumptions.

bailouts A type of government support of business, often in the form of a loan or loan guarantee. Common in the 1980s, but by the 1990s complete bailouts had become rare.

behavioural approaches to management Managerial perspectives that consider the social or human side of organizations and address the challenges of managing people. Assume that achieving maximum productivity requires understanding the human factor of organizations and creation of an environment that permits employees to fulfil social, not only economic, needs.

benchmarking The process of comparing one small business's performance to that of other, similar businesses.

borderless corporations A new term for multinational corporations that is not linked with one specific home country. Such an enterprise thus has no clear nationality.

bounded rationality The inability to absorb and process all information pertinent to a decision. Such is a criticism of the rational model of decision making, that our ability to gather and process all the information necessary for making a truly rational decision is limited by, for example, time constraints and relative lack of definition of the problem.

branch plants Subsidiaries (in one country, of companies in another country) that do not perform the complete range of functions necessary to offer a product in the marketplace. Typically, subsidiaries defer responsibility of higher-level strategic functions to the parent company.

bureaucratic management A classical approach to management (others including the scientific and the administrative) that focuses more broadly on the organization as a whole, and incorporates the ideas of rules and procedures, hierarchy of authority, division of labour, impersonality and selection and promotion. Associated with Max Weber. *See* scientific management and administrative management.

business enterprise system The system all developed countries possess that determines what goods and services are distributed to society, and how they are so produced and distributed. The decisions may be made by government or by business or by both.

business ethics Ethics is the study of morality or moral judgments, standards and rules of conduct. The notion of business ethics has been considered as comprising the rules, standards, principles, or codes giving guidelines for morally right behaviour in certain contexts.

capitalism An economic system based on the rights of the individual, on the rights of private property, on competition and on minimal government interference.

Categorical Imperative The assertion by the philosopher Immanuel Kant that moral actions are by definition actions that respect others.

centralization The degree to which decision-making authority in an organization is concentrated at the top level.

chain of command The line of authority that extends from the top of the organization to the lowest level. The administering function of the organization.

change The second phase of managing change. Action. Implementation of a program to move the organization and its members to a more adequate state. Preceded by unfreezing and followed by refreezing. *See* unfreezing and refreezing.

classical school of management The oldest of the formalized perspectives of management, which arose in the late 19th and early 20th centuries during a period of rapid industrialization of the U.S. and European business sector. Includes scientific, administrative and bureaucratic management. *See* scientific, administrative and bureaucratic management.

cloning forces Pressure on organizations to imitate the behaviour of industry leaders. "Jumping on the bandwagon", "keeping up with the corporate Joneses".

cognitive heuristics An aspect of non-rationality in decision making, where simple rules or guidelines are generated and employed in making decisions. They are "cognitive shortcuts" to reduce the amount of information that must be collected or processed.

cognitive scripts Mental pictures, usually unconscious, that serve to organize knowledge in some systematic fashion. Scripts or schema used by organizational members to help them function efficiently by reducing the amount of information they need to process as a means to guide their performance. Can generate obstacles to learning and change.

collaboration In behavioural approaches to management (particularly as formulated by Mary Parker Follett), the consequence of the discovery of the importance of managers and workers viewing themselves as collaborators or partners. Also emphasized by Chester Barnard, who felt that authority of managers over subordinates had to be earned.

common market Economic integration that goes beyond free trade areas and customs unions, and includes, for example, freer flow of labour and capital across members' borders and a common trade policy regarding non-members. *See* free trade area, customs union and economic union.

compartmentalizing In scientific management, the result of Frederick Taylor's pursuit of the one best method of performing a job, also called specializing, and involving breaking the job down into its most fundamental steps or components.

Competition Bureau The Competition Bureau operates under the Department of Industry/Industry Canada and is responsible for enforcing and administering the Competition Act. Its central aim is to help create and maintain equity in the marketplace among all the different and potentially competing interests, including: consumers and producers, wholesalers and retailers, dominant players and minor players, the public interest and the private interest.

competitive forces The competition an organization faces, both specific and general, and including, for example, globalization. They dictate changes in organization design and strategy.

constraining forces Practices that come to define what are perceived as legitimate management structures and activities and that, consequently, place pressure on organizations to conform to these institutional roles.

contingency approach The acknowledgement that there is no one best way to manage, and that different conditions and situations require the application of different approaches or techniques. Includes consideration of organization size, environmental uncertainty, etc.

corporate codes of conduct Codes that are necessary because external laws cannot cover all possible situations. They may be irrelevant if ethical behaviour is not rewarded and unethical behaviour tacitly encouraged.

corporate language The potential use of language to de-couple behaviour from its evaluation. To maintain external legitimacy organizations may adopt commonly accepted language for appearance but not relate them to how activities are really conducted.

corporate memory Individuals who are a central part of an organization's knowledge base. They can be eliminated by downsizing, but at significant cost, especially to the organization's ability to innovate.

corporate social responsibility Obligations or responsibilities of an organization to go beyond the production of goods or services at a profit, and beyond the requirements of competition, legal regulation or custom, thus acting in a way desirable in terms of the values and objectives of society.

Crown corporation Also called a public enterprise. An organization, federal or provincial, accountable, through a minister, to parliament for its operations. For example, Canada Post and the Liquor Control Board of Ontario.

customer departmentation Grouping work activities in an organization on the basis of the needs of different customers. *See* divisional, functional, geographic, hybrid and matrix departmentation.

customs union Economic integration with removal of trade barriers in international trade in goods and services among the member countries. A greater degree of integration than free trade areas, but with less member autonomy in how non-member countries are dealt with. *See* free trade area, common market and economic union.

decisional roles One of Mintzberg's three broad categories of roles that managers play, where information is processed and decisions made. Includes entrepreneur, disturbance handler, resource allocator and negotiator. *See* informational roles, interpersonal roles, entrepreneur, resource allocator and negotiator.

de-layering Flattening organizational hierarchies so that they have a wider span of control. *See* span of control. The elimination of hierarchical layers, often involving downsizing.

demographics Population trends, which have a significant effect on business planning and activities. Includes such phenomena as the baby boomers and the aging population.

departmentation The dividing or grouping of major functions or work activities into separate units on such bases as functional, divisional, hybrid and matrix. *See* functional, divisional, hybrid and matrix departmentation.

deregulation   Reduction in the number of laws or regulations affecting business activity. The potential benefit to consumers is increased competition, and the potential risk is exploitation in the form of reduction in quality of the product or service, or price increases.

discontinuance   When an entrepreneur or owner ceases operation. Not the same as failure. *See* small business failures. There are two paths to discontinuance: the business can be sold, or it can be folded. The probability of folding rather than selling increases as profitability declines.

disseminator   One of the three informational roles that managers play (the others being monitor and spokesperson), where the information obtained through monitoring is shared and distributed. *See* monitor and spokesperson.

disturbance handler   One of the four decisional roles that managers play (the others being entrepreneur, resource allocator and negotiator), where the manager deals with and attempts to resolve conflicts, such as with a difficult or unco-operative supplier. *See* informational and interpersonal roles, entrepreneur, resource allocator and negotiator.

diversified/divisional   One of Mintzberg's five fundamental organizational configurations, the others being the simple or entrepreneurial structure, the machine bureaucracy, the professional bureaucracy and the adhocracy or innovative organization. An organization where the middle line is the dominant component. Its strength is in its responsiveness to its environment. *See* simple or entrepreneurial structure, machine bureaucracy, professional bureaucracy and adhocracy or innovative organization.

divisional departmentation   Grouping employees according to the products or services produced. Especially useful in organizations that produce a wide variety of products or services. Variations are customer and geographic departmentation. *See* customer, divisional, geographic, hybrid and matrix departmentation.

double-loop learning   The assessment by individuals of whether an error or problem exists in an organization because the systems themselves need to be changed. Requires a deeper level of examination (than single-loop learning) and, typically, precedes significant organizational change. Uncovers root causes. *See* organizational learning and single-loop learning.

downsizing   The planned reduction in breadth of an organization's operations, typically involving terminating relatively large numbers of employees and/or decreasing the number of products or services the organization provides.

dynamic environment   One of the two (the other being "static") broad classifications of environments of organizations, containing relatively more uncertainty and change. *See* static environment.

economic union   A higher level of economic integration than a common market, with harmonization of fiscal, monetary and tax policies and, often, a common currency. There is comparably very little member autonomy. *See* free trade area, customs union and common market.

effectiveness   The pursuit and achievement of goals that are appropriate for an organization. Part of the manager's process of administering and coordinating resources in an effort to achieve the organization's goals and, as such, sometimes confused with efficiency. *See* efficiency.

efficiency   Using the fewest inputs to produce a given level of output. Part of the manager's process of administering and coordinating resources in an effort to achieve the organization's goals, and as such, sometimes confused with effectiveness. *See* effectiveness.

end-point ethics   *See* utilitarian ethics.

entrepreneur   (1) One of the four decisional roles that managers play (the others being disturbance handler, resource allocator and negotiator), where the manager, for example, develops and initiates new projects. *See* informational and interpersonal roles, disturbance handler, resource allocator and negotiator. (2) Usually applied to the founder of a new business but, alternatively, may also be seen as encompassing anyone who buys an existing business or manages the growth or turnaround of an existing business. Originally from a French word meaning "to undertake".

entrepreneurial skills Skills required to start or expand a business, including creativity, innovativeness, risk-taking and independence.

entrepreneurship No agreed-upon definition, but the features most often cited are opportunity recognition, organizational creation and risk-taking.

environmental uncertainty The rate at which market conditions and production technologies change, producing dynamic or static environments. *See* dynamic environment and static environment.

equity theory In modern behavioural approaches to management, the theory that motivation ensues from perception of fairness or unfairness. Employees compare their treatment to that of others in similar situations, and react to any inequity by pursuing the mode of inequity reduction that is personally least costly.

escalation of commitment to a failing course of action Departure from the last stage of the rational model of decision making, which is monitoring the decision to see if it is successful or not by gathering data or, simply, receiving feedback. A decision fiasco where loss or negative outcome is ignored, more resources are committed, and further losses experienced. The causes include social, structural and psychological determinants.

esprit de corps In administrative management, generating organizational cohesiveness and unity by encouraging team spirit and harmony among workers.

expansion The second stage in the small business life cycle, consisting of exponential growth and then slower growth. The other two stages are formation and stability. *See* formation and stability, small business life cycle, formation and stability.

expectancy theory Victor Vroom's theory of work motivation (and thus part of modern behavioural approaches) that people choose tasks and/or effort levels that they believe will most likely lead to valued outcomes. The model is composed of three central elements: the effort-performance expectancy, performance-reward instrumentality, and reward valence or value.

external context The environment of an organization, including the specific environment and the general environment. *See* internal context and specific environment and general environment.

figurehead One of the interpersonal roles that managers play (the others being leader and liaison). Typically ceremonial or symbolic, such as handing out "employee of the month" awards.

finance-related problems One of the three kinds of problems encountered by small businesses, the others being marketing-related and management-related. Usually, undercapitalization and locating financial resources. *See* management-related and marketing-related problems.

fluid organizations Organizations that tend to be organic rather than bureaucratic and by avoiding rigid adherence to rules realize the flexibility needed to be able to adapt quickly to changing environments. May use just-in-time inventory principles, for example.

foreign direct investment The purchase of physical assets or an amount of ownership in a company from another country in order to gain a measure of management control.

formalization Rules, regulations, procedures and so on governing how work is performed; the standardization of jobs in the organization. The greater the degree of formalization, the lower the reliance on individual discretion, and the greater the assurance of consistent and reliable performance.

formation The first stage in the small business life cycle, initiated with the idea for a new business and culminating when products or services based on that idea are sold to customers in the market-

403

place. The other stages are expansion and stability. *See* small business life cycle, expansion and stability.

franchising A method of distribution or marketing where a parent company (the franchisor) grants to another individual or company (the franchisee) the legal right to sell its products or services, with exclusive rights to a particular area or location.

free trade area The lowest degree of regional economic integration, where tariffs and non-tariff trade barriers on international trade in goods and services among the member countries are removed. *See* customs union, common market and economic union.

functional departmentation The grouping together of employees with the same or similar skills or expertise into one unit or department. The most traditional form of departmentation. *See* customer, divisional, geographical, hybrid and matrix departmentation.

functional specialization With social specialization, one of the two divisions of job specialization. The dividing-up of jobs into their smallest components, so that workers perform simple, specific and repetitive tasks. Job enrichment, on the other hand, requires a low degree of functional specialization. *See* horizontal differentiation and social specialization.

general environment The environment shared by all organizations in a society, such as the economic and political environments, and technological, societal and global forces. *See* specific environment, technological forces, societal forces and global forces.

geographical departmentation Grouping work activities in an organization to serve customers according to their geographical location. *See* customer, divisional, functional, hybrid and matrix departmentation.

global forces Forces that could be embedded in general economic, political, technological or societal forces, but are international in nature, such as international trade agreements. *See* technological forces and societal forces.

globalization No universally agreed-upon definition, but may be considered as a process involving the integration of national economies and the worldwide convergence of consumer preferences. The process of generating a single world economic system.

goal-setting theory In modern behavioural approaches to management, the result of the view that human behaviour is explainable in terms of reciprocality, in which the relative influences of behaviour, cognition, other personal factors and environmental events all vary in different settings. Managers need to manage with reference to performance expectations, set specific challenging goals and ensure that employees are committed to those goals.

government economic regulation The imposition of constraints, backed by the authority of the government, to significantly modify economic behaviour in the private sector. The motive may include protection of the consumer or of the environment, or protection of fair competition among businesses.

gross domestic product (GDP) The total value of a country's output of goods and services in a given year.

habitual routines Commonly accepted methods for performing a task, with, potentially, both functional and dysfunctional consequences. For example, once a routine has been established in a group, the behaviour involved will submit to normative control, without regard to actual effects. Unethical behaviour could be a consequence.

Hawthorne Effect The discovery that human nature is such that productivity can be enhanced by motivating employees by giving them special attention rather than by simply improving their physical working conditions. This is a key component of the human relations school of behavioural management, marking the transition to it from scientific management.

horizontal differentiation The degree of differentiation between horizontal units of the organization, based on, for example, the orientation of the members, the nature of their jobs and their education or training. Includes job specialization, which is divided into functional and social specialization. *See* vertical differentiation, functional specialization and social specialization.

human relations movement One of the schools of behavioural management, developed by Elton Mayo, who emphasized that social factors had a greater impact on productivity than actual working conditions. Focuses on organizations as social systems. *See* Hawthorne Effect.

hybrid departmentation Combining characteristics of functional, divisional, customer and/or geographical departmentation. *See* customer, divisional, functional, geographical, hybrid and matrix departmentation.

imperfect competition A fundamental shortcoming in the market system, necessitating government involvement. When fewer than the optimal number of competitors exist that are needed to ensure fair pricing and distribution of goods and services at the highest possible level of quality.

import quota Limitation on the amount of a product that can be imported to ensure that domestic producers retain an adequate share of consumer demand for their product.

informational roles One of Mintzberg's three broad categories of roles that managers play, where managers are communication sources for the organization, whether between parties in the organization or to parties outside it. Include monitor, disseminator and spokesperson roles. *See* decisional roles, interpersonal roles, monitor, disseminator and spokesperson.

innovation Entrepreneurial activities that involve creating something new, such as a new product, service or application of technology.

innovative organization *See* adhocracy.

institutionalization The processes by which shared beliefs take on a rule-like status. A social process through which individuals create a shared definition of what is appropriate or meaningful behaviour. May generate "accepted practices" that continue even when they are no longer functional.

institutional theory The theory that organizations are driven to incorporate practices and procedures defined by current concepts of work and those accepted or institutionalized by society. Taken-for-granted means of "getting things done" and, as such, not necessarily rational.

integrated organizations Organizations that focus on teams of workers rather than on individuals, unity of command or clear lines of authority; also, organizations with closer connections to their external environment, such as suppliers or other companies, to the extent of interdependence or alliance.

internal context Everything that happens inside an organization, including people (how they manage and are managed), structure (design and redesign of the organization) and strategy (pursuing goals and making decisions). *See* external context.

internal locus of control A quality entrepreneurs have been shown to possess whereby they perceive themselves as having an ability to influence events in their lives, and discount, for instance, luck or external forces.

interpersonal roles One of Mintzberg's three broad categories of roles that managers play. Those tasks that arise from the manager's formal authority base and involve relationships with either other organizational members or external parties. Include figurehead, leader and liaison roles. *See* decisional roles, informational roles, figurehead, leader and liaison.

joint venture An arrangement between two or more companies from different countries to produce a product or service together, or to collaborate in the research, development or marketing of that product or service. Also known as a strategic network or strategic alliance. *See* strategic alliance.

405

keiretsu The Japanese term for networking of major enterprises. Loosely affiliated collections of companies, common in Japanese industry and banking.

knowledge workers People employed in knowledge intensive industries such as the high-tech industries, where specialized and frequently changing knowledge is required. Knowledge work is thus harder to routinize than, for instance, service work.

leader One of the three interpersonal roles that managers play (the others being figurehead and liaison), wherein the manager may serve as a motivator, communicator and coordinator of subordinates' activities, such as by conducting performance appraisals. *See* informational roles, interpersonal roles, figurehead and liaison.

learning forces Lessons that result from institutionalized management practices and that are taught to future managers and business leaders in the course of their formal education.

liaison One of the three interpersonal roles that managers play (the others being figurehead and leader), including developing relationships with members of the organization outside the manager's area of authority, such as with other departments. *See* interpersonal roles, figurehead and leader.

licensing arrangements Arrangements whereby the owner of a product or process is paid a fee or royalty by another company in return for permission to produce or distribute the product or process. Can be a global business activity if the companies are in different countries.

machine bureaucracy One of Mintzberg's five fundamental organizational configurations, the others being simple or entrepreneurial structure, the professional bureaucracy, diversified/divisional, and the adhocracy or innovative organization. An organization with the technostructure dominant. Its strength is its efficiency. *See* simple or entrepreneurial structure, professional bureaucracy, diversified/divisional, adhocracy or innovative organization and technostructure.

management-related problems One of the three kinds of problems encountered by small businesses, the others being marketing-related and finance-related. Relate primarily to refinement of the business concept, but include organizational design and personnel management. *See* marketing-related and finance-related problems.

managerial skills Skills appropriate for maintaining the smooth running of an existing business, including skills in strategic and general management and in each of the functional areas, such as finance, marketing and human resource management.

marketing-related problems One of the three kinds of problems encountered by small businesses, the others being management and finance-related. Entail the difficulty of assessing the market and contacting the customer. *See* management-related and finance-related problems.

matrix departmentation Combining functional and divisional departmentation to exploit the strengths of both. Product managers and functional managers have equal authority, so that specialists from different divisions can be brought together for specific projects when needed. *See* customer, divisional, functional, geographical and hybrid departmentation.

mercantilism The trade theory that dominated economic thinking for the 15th, 16th and 17th centuries, where a country's wealth was believed to be a matter of its holdings of treasure, especially gold. The economic policy of accumulating this wealth through trade surpluses. *See* trade surpluses. In the modern era Japan has often been called a mercantilist country because of its high trade surpluses.

metaphors A creative form that produces its effect through a crossing of images; generating new meaning through the processes of comparison; generation of an image for studying a subject; a tool to help us understand the nature of organizations.

middle line One of Mintzberg's five organizational components, the others being the operating core, the strategic apex, the technostructure and the support staff. Managers occupying authority between the operating core and the strategic apex. *See* operating core, strategic apex, technostructure and support staff.

mixed boards One of three types of volunteer boards, the others being policy boards and working boards. Board members are responsible for strategic direction as well as daily operations. *See* policy boards and working boards.

modern behavioural science The discoveries of researchers with backgrounds in sociology, psychology and anthropology who studied the human element of organizations with particular attention to motivation, on the premise that motivating workers is preferable to controlling them. It has produced an enormous number of theories, including need-based and cognitive-based theories of motivation.

monitor One of the three informational roles that managers play (the others being disseminator and spokesperson), where the internal and external environments of the organization are constantly monitored for information useful in decision making. *See* disseminator, spokesperson, internal environment and external environment.

monopolistic competition When a large number of small firms have a product or service each of which is perceived as slightly different from the others, so that each firm has some influence on the price. Some retail operations are an example.

Multinational corporations Business enterprises that control assets, factories, etc., operated either as branch offices or affiliates in two or more foreign countries. It generates products or services through its affiliates in several countries, and maintains control over their operation, managing from a global perspective.

negotiator One of the four decisional roles that managers play (the others being entrepreneur, disturbance handler and resource allocator), involving negotiation in all its forms, whether with customers, employees or other departments. *See* informational and interpersonal roles, entrepreneur, disturbance handler and resource allocator.

networking Organizations engaging in co-operative relations with suppliers, distributors or competitors, with the aim of improving efficiency and flexibility in meeting consumer needs. Japanese version called keiretsu. *See* keiretsu.

non-programmed decisions Decisions for which there are no ready-made solutions and that may involve ill-defined problems, such as the merging of one organization with another. They are thus more common at higher managerial levels. *See* programmed decisions.

official goals The expression of the general aims of the organization, showing the organization's purpose. *See* operative goals.

open systems Organizations viewed as entities that are embedded in, and dependent on exchanges with, the environment within which they operate. The interdependence of elements means that the entity (the organization) is more than the sum of its parts; it interacts with its environment.

operating core One of Mintzberg's five organizational components, the others being the strategic apex, the middle line, the technostructure and the support staff. Employees who perform the basic work of producing the products or services. *See* strategic apex, middle line, support staff and technostructure.

operative goals More specific and measurable than the official goals, and pertaining to the primary tasks of an organization. *See* official goals.

organic and mechanistic Opposite extremes in organizational design, as exemplified by, respectively, the adhocracy (or innovative organization), and the machine bureaucracy. *See* adhocracy or innovative organization and machine bureaucracy.

organizational learning The detection and correction of error (Argyris and Schon). The collective experience of individuals within the organization, resulting in changes in organizational procedure. Consists of single-loop learning and double-loop learning. *See* single-loop learning and double-loop learning.

organizational role theory The theory that organizational roles have a psychological reality to individuals occupying them, whereby they fulfil role requirements based on internalized expectations concerning responsibilities of the role. Incompatible expectations produce role conflict, where the individual occupies more than one role.

outsourcing Hiring external organizations to conduct work in certain functions of the company, such as accounting. May be employed by corporations engaged in downsizing. *See* downsizing.

overconfidence heuristic The tendency of decision-makers to be too optimistic on the basis of initial assessments, especially when the decision-maker is unfamiliar with the problem or when there is significant uncertainty.

paradigms Our mental framework for understanding how the world operates. Our theories, our assumptions, our sets of beliefs, our customs. Overcoming resistance to change means recognizing the current paradigms that govern our behaviour, and shifting to a new paradigm.

paradox of entrepreneurs The paradox that entrepreneurs are willing to take on high risk, yet do not tend to exhibit higher-risk preferences than the rest of the population. Its explanation may be that entrepreneurs perceive risk differently from other people.

perfect competition A market situation where many firms all produce an indistinguishable product or service so that no single producer has the power to affect the price of that product or service.

piece-rate system In scientific management, motivating workers by tying compensation to performance, so that a standard level of performance produces a standard level of pay, and above-average performance produces above-average pay.

policy boards One of three types of volunteer boards, the others being working boards and mixed boards. They focus on strategic planning and decision making rather than on daily operations, and set limits for their executive directors and paid staff. *See* mixed boards and working boards.

prioritizing role demands A means of rationalizing behaviour when there is a role conflict. A potential method of ignoring ethical conflicts. Also called compartmentalizing, although not in the sense in which the term is used in scientific management.

private, non-governmental organizations A third category of organizations (after public and private sector) that serve the broader public interest, rely on private funding, government grants and volunteer labour, and are involved in a high degree of civic engagement. They range from research bodies to food banks.

privatization Divesting of government involvement in the operation, management or ownership of business activities, involving transfer of activities or functions from the government to the private sector. May involve selling a Crown corporation.

professional bureaucracy One of Mintzberg's five fundamental organizational configurations, the others being the simple or entrepreneurial structure, the machine bureaucracy, diversified/divisional, and the adhocracy or innovative organization. An organization in which the operating core is composed of professionals. Decisions are decentralized. Its strength rests in its professional skills. *See* operating core, simple or entrepreneurial structure, machine bureaucracy, diversified/divisional, and adhocracy or innovative organization.

programmed decisions Routine decisions that are made repeatedly using a pre-established set of alternatives. Typically, the outcomes of such decisions are relatively predictable. *See* non-programmed decisions.

prospect theory The theory that decisions can be framed as a choice between losses or gains. The choices we make very much depend on how the alternatives are framed. Risk aversion increases when options are framed as gains of different sizes, and decreases when they are framed as losses of different sizes.

pull factors Reasons a business would gain from entering the international context. Include the potential for sales growth and the opportunity of obtaining needed resources. *See* push factors.

push factors Forces that act on all businesses to create an environment where competing successfully means competing globally. Include the force of competition, the shift towards democracy, reduction in trade business, and improvements in technology. *See* pull factors.

rational model of decision making The model of decision making according to which we attempt to make decisions that will maximize the attainment of our goals, whether organizational or personal. There are six steps: identify problems and opportunities; choose the best decision style; develop alternative solutions; choose the best solution; implement the solution; monitor the results of the solution.

re-engineering The fundamental rethinking and radical redesign of business processes to achieve dramatic improvements in measures of performance. It often advocates the collection of individual tasks into a greater number of whole jobs.

refreezing The final phase of the planned change process, after unfreezing and change. When the newly developed behaviours, attitudes or structures become an enduring part of the organizational structure. *See* unfreezing and change.

representative heuristic The tendency of decision-makers to generate broad, and sometimes detailed, generalizations about a target individual, group, organization or situation based on only a few characteristics of that target. A form of stereotyping where small samples are perceived as representing actual probabilities.

resource allocator One of the four decisional roles that managers play (the others being entrepreneur, disturbance handler and negotiator), where it is decided how resources, such as money, equipment, personnel and time, will be allocated. *See* informational and interpersonal roles, entrepreneur, disturbance handler and negotiator.

restrictive or regulatory taxes One of two broad forms of taxes, the other being revenue taxes. Consist of two types, excise taxes and customs duties or tariffs. Excise taxes are applied to goods and services the purchase of which the government wants to restrict. *See* revenue taxes and tariffs.

revenue taxes One of two broad forms of taxes, the other being regulatory or restrictive taxes. Money collected to help fund government services and programs, including individual taxes, corporate income tax, property tax and sales tax. *See* restrictive or regulatory taxes.

rituals and myths Organizational rituals and myths contain messages that provide a shared experience and reinforcement of values for members. They are simply the established products, services, policies, etc., of the organization, and play a crucial role in establishing what is legitimate and what is unacceptable in the organizational culture. As such, they are important for that culture's ethics.

rule ethics Judging actions to be right or wrong according to absolute rules regardless of the consequences. Such rules may be based on religious beliefs, family values, education, experience, etc. *See* utilitarian or end-point ethics.

satisficing Choosing a solution to a problem that is the best readily available alternative but not necessarily the optimal solution. ("Satisfy" + "suffice" = "satisfice".) Once that alternative is chosen, the search for further alternatives is discontinued. It is thus in contrast to optimizing decisions.

scientific management Frederick Taylor's philosophy that the fundamental objective of management is "securing the maximum prosperity for the employer coupled with the maximum prosperity for each employee", by standardizing and compartmentalizing work practices. One of the three central classical approaches to management, the others being the administrative and the bureaucratic. *See* administrative and bureaucratic management.

self-management In behavioural approaches to management, the emphasis by Mary Parker Follett on the fact that the person doing a job is often the best one to decide how best to do it, rather than managers who are not familiar with it. One of three factors she highlights, the others being coordination and collaboration.

service sector Businesses that include an element of service, from hotels to restaurants to banking to social work, and in which an increasing proportion of the Canadian workforce is employed.

simple or entrepreneurial structure One of Mintzberg's five fundamental organizational configurations, the others being the machine bureaucracy, the professional bureaucracy, diversified/divisional, and the adhocracy, or innovative organization. The most basic form of organization, consisting of a strategic apex with a small operating core. Its strength is its simplicity. *See* adhocracy or innovative organization, diversified/divisional, machine bureaucracy, professional bureaucracy, operating core and strategic apex.

single-loop learning Simply, the correction of errors that employees find in organizational methods of performance in order to keep the system working. Assumes that the organization has the right systems established but simply needs to fine-tune them. Results in incremental improvements and improved efficiency. Addresses symptoms rather than root causes. *See* organizational learning and double-loop learning.

small business failures Not necessarily the same as bankruptcy. If failure is defined as involving a loss to creditors, only one percent of businesses fail annually.

small business life cycle The predictable pattern of sequential and progressive stages that any small business moves through as it faces internal and external challenges. One such model consists of formation, expansion and stability. *See* formation, expansion and stability.

social contract ethics This model of ethics posits that the rules by which people live are those that they would agree to live if given the opportunity to make a choice based on reason or knowledge. The idea of the social contract provided a basis for a new model of organizations that views them as networks of contracts.

social identity theory The theory that individuals classify themselves and others into social categories defined by typical characteristics of the members. Organizational identification is one form of social identification, with implications for ethical behaviour.

social specialization With functional specialization, one of the two divisions of job specialization. Specialization of individuals rather than specialization of jobs, accomplished through employment of professionals whose skills cannot be easily routinized. *See* functional specialization.

societal forces A wide range of influences, including, for example, changes in public opinion on ethical issues such as organizational justice (how employees are treated), that affect all organizations and to which business must respond.

span of control The number of employees reporting to a supervisor. It determines vertical differentiation. *See* horizontal and vertical differentiation.

specific or task environment The environment within which a particular organization operates, ultimately shaped by the general environment, and including stakeholders, customers, competitors, suppliers, etc. *See* general environment and stakeholders.

social context Acknowledgement of the fact that actions affect others and demand to be considered thus.

spokesperson One of the three informational roles that managers play (the others being monitor and disseminator), where information is transmitted to individuals outside the manager's area of authority. *See* decisional and interpersonal roles, monitor and disseminator.

stability The third and last stage in the small business life cycle, where daily operating practices become routine and institutionalized. Preceded by the stages of formation and expansion. *See* small business life cycle, formation and expansion.

stakeholders Individuals or groups who bear some kind of risk, whether financial, physical or other, as a result of a corporation's actions. Include such parties as suppliers, the government, and society in general. There are ethical as well as practical reasons to attend to all of their interests, even when they conflict. *See* general environment.

standardization In scientific management, the establishment of clear rules regarding how to perform the job, leaving little or no room for individual discretion, thus assuring consistent performance.

static environment One of the two (the other being dynamic) broad classifications of environments of organizations, exhibiting little, if any, change. *See* dynamic environment.

strategic alliance An alignment of different businesses meant to extend or enhance the core competencies of the businesses involved, obtain access to the expertise of another organization, and create new market opportunities for all parties involved. *See* joint venture.

strategic apex One of Mintzberg's five organizational components, the others being the operating core, the middle line, the technostructure and the support staff. The top-level managers, including the CEO, president, etc. *See* operating core, middle line, support staff and technostructure.

strategic planning The process by which an organization creates its own future. A function of the board, but not limited to board members and not necessarily including all of them. Often involves a SWOT analysis. (See SWOT analysis.)

subsidiaries Branch operations in foreign countries through which the enterprise can market goods and services. Either wholly owned or purchased as an existing firm in the host country, or built from scratch.

subsidies Government assistance to business possibly in the form of cash payments, low-interest loans or potentially reduced taxes. In the global context, they assist domestic industry in the competition against foreign business.

sunk costs Previous losses or costs. One of the psychological determinants of escalation of commitment to a failing course of action, when they enter into decision calculations. The desire to recoup them leads to self-justification for not evaluating performance objectively. *See* escalation of commitment to a failing course of action.

support staff One of Mintzberg's five organizational components, the others being the operating core, the strategic apex, the middle line and the technostructure. People who provide indirect support services, such as legal counsellors, payroll staff, etc. *See* operating core, middle line, strategic apex and technostructure.

SWOT analysis Analysis of strengths and weakness of the organization and of external opportunities and threats. In its light the strategic planning team needs to re-examine the mission statement.

tariff A tax on imported goods traditionally employed with the intent to ensure that they are not less expensive than domestically produced goods. *See* restrictive or regulatory taxes.

technological forces The technological environment that exerts influence across industries, playing a central role in how an organization functions, obtains resources, and competes, and changes in which permit and demand organizational change. *See* general environment.

technostructure One of Mintzberg's five organizational components, the others being the operating core, the strategic apex, the middle line and the support staff. Analysts who are concerned with planning and controlling the work of others, but whose job is more outside the hierarchy of authority. *See* operating core, middle line, strategic apex and support staff.

Theory X In Douglas McGregor's need-based theory of motivation (within modern behavioural approaches to management), the kind of managers who adopt an authoritarian attitude because they perceive their subordinates as essentially disinclined to work. They thus see their employees as needing to be threatened, coerced or directed by managers. *See* Theory Y.

Theory Y In Douglas McGregor's need-based theory of motivation (within modern behavioural approaches to management), the kind of managers who display a participatory style because they see their employees as inherently motivated by a desire to contribute, gaining satisfaction from doing their job well, and desiring responsibility and opportunities to exercise ingenuity and creativity. *See* Theory X.

time and motion studies In scientific management, the scientific analysis of work, often using a film taping and a stopwatch to closely scrutinize the elements of performing a task. *See* scientific management.

trade protectionism Protecting a country's domestic economy and businesses by restricting imports to prevent domestic producers from losing business to producers of low-priced foreign goods, and to prevent a trade deficit, where more money leaves the country than enters it because imports exceed exports.

trade surpluses When a country's exports exceed its imports, so that more money enters than leaves.

transactional leader A type of leadership role in a basically stable and knowable framework, with the aim of organizational maintenance. *See* transformational leader.

transformational leader A type of leadership role, particularly important in times of organizational change, that communicates a vision and inspires employees. *See* transactional leader.

unfreezing A recognition that the current state of affairs is inadequate. In practice, can occur as a result of any number of influences, from environmental pressures to the realization that performance is declining. Requires continuous monitoring of the environment by managers if it is to occur before it is too late to effect the correction. First phase of managing change, followed by change and refreezing. *See* change and refreezing.

unity of command In administrative management, avoiding confusion and conflicting instructions by having each employee report to only one boss, preferably at the upper levels of the organization. *See* administrative management.

utilitarian or end-point ethics Assessing the rightness or wrongness of an action by its outcomes. Its modern counterparts are cost-benefit and risk-benefit analysis. Can lead to taking the view that good ends justify bad means. *See* rule ethics.

vertical differentiation The number of managers and levels in the organizational hierarchy. *See* horizontal differentiation.

working boards One of three types of volunteer boards, the others being policy and mixed boards. Where board members do the organization's work or work closely with the staff. *See* policy boards and mixed boards.

work specialization One of the six defining elements of organizational structure, the others being chain of command, centralization, span of control, formalization and departmentation. Work is divided into horizontal differentiation, functional specialization and social specialization in order to achieve organizational goals. *See* horizontal differentiation, functional specialization, social specialization, chain of command, centralization, span of control, formalization and departmentation.

zero-sum gain The assumption of mercantilism that the world's wealth is a fixed amount, so that a nation can only increase its share by forcing other nations to reduce theirs. *See* mercantilism.

Bibliography

Adams, J.S. 1965. "Inequity in social exchanges" in L. Berkowitz (ed.), *Advances in Experimental Social Psychology*, pp. 267–300. New York: Academic Press.

Aldrich, H. 1979. *Organizations and Environments*. Englewood Cliffs, NJ: Prentice Hall.

Alpert, M., and H. Raiffa. 1982. "A progress report on the training of probability assessors" in D. Kahneman, P. Slovic, and A. Tversky (eds.), *Judgment under Uncertainty: Heuristics and Biases*, pp. 294–305. New York: Cambridge University Press.

Anderson, C.R. 1977. "Locus of control, coping behaviors in a stress setting: A longitudinal study." *Journal of Applied Psychology* 62: 446–51.

Andreason, A.R. 1996. "Find a corporate partner." *Harvard Business Review* 74: 47–56.

Anonymous. 1999. "The privatization of public services." *The Worklife Report* 11(4): 13–14.

Argyris, C. 1982. *Reasoning, learning, and action*. San Francisco: Jossey-Bass.

Argyris, C., and D.A. Schon. 1989. *Theory in Practice: Increasing Professional Effectiveness*. San Francisco: Jossey-Bass.

Argyris, C., and D.A. Schon. 1978. *Organizational Learning: A Theory of Action Perspective*. Reading, MA: Addison-Wesley Publishing Company.

Armstrong-Stassen, Marjorie. 1998. "Downsizing the federal government: A longitudinal study of managers' Reactions." *Canadian Journal of Administrative Sciences* 15 (December): 310–21.

Ashforth, B.E., and F. Mael. 1989. "Social identity theory and the organization." *Academy of Management Review* 14(1): 20–39.

Austin, J.E. 2000. "Strategic collaboration between nonprofits and businesses." *Nonprofit and Voluntary Sector Quarterly* 29(1) (Supplement 2000): 69–97.

Balderson, D.W. 2000. *Canadian Entrepreneurship and Small Business Management*, 4th Ed. Toronto: McGraw-Hill Ryerson.

Bandura, A. 1977. "Self-Efficacy: Toward a unifying theory of behavioral change." *Psychological Review* (May): 191–215.

Barker, J. 1993. *Paradigms: The Business of Discovering the Future*. New York: Harper Business.

Barnard, C. 1938. *The Functions of the Executive*. Cambridge, MA: Harvard University Press.

Barnard, C.I. 1976. "Foreword" in H.A. Simon, *Administrative Behaviour*, 3d Ed. New York: Free Press. (Original work published 1945.)

Bass, B. 1990. *Bass & Stogdill's Handbook of Leadership: Theory, Research and Managerial Applications*. New York: Free Press.

Basseches, M. 1986. "Cognitive-structural development on the conditions of employment." *Human Development* 29: 101–223.

Basseches, M. 1984. *Dialectical Thinking and Adult Development*. Norwood, NJ: Ablex.

Bates, T. 1995. "Analysis of survival rates among franchise and independent small business startups." *Journal of Small Business Management* 33(2): 26–36.

Bateson, G. 1972. *Steps to an Ecology of Mind*. New York: Ballantine Books.

Baumhart, R.S.J. 1961. "How ethical are businessmen?" *Harvard Business Review* 39: 6–31.

Bazerman, M.H. 1998. *Judgment in Managerial Decision Making*, 4th Ed. New York: John Wiley.

Bazerman, M.H. 1990. *Judgment in Managerial Decision Making*, 2d Ed. New York: John Wiley.

Bazerman, M.H., J.R. Curhan, D.A. Moore, and K.L. Valley. 2000. "Negotiation." *Annual Reviews Psychology* 51: 279–314.

Beauchamp, T.L., and N.E. Bowie. 1983. *Ethical Theory and Business*. Englewood Cliffs, NJ: Prentice Hall.

Becker, G. 1976. *The Economic Approach to Human Behaviour*. Chicago: University of Chicago Press.

Bedeian, A., and R.F. Zammuto. 1991. *Organizations, Theory and Design*. Hinsdale, IL: Dryden Press.

Ben-Ner, A., and T. Van Hoomissen. 1994. "The governance of nonprofit organizations: Law and public policy." *Nonprofit Management and Leadership* 4(4): 393–414.

Berger, I.E., and M.E. Drumwright. 2000. "The role of marketing in the development and distribution of social capital." Special Topic Session proposed for Marketing and Public Policy Conference 2001, Washington, DC.

Bird, B.J. 1989. *Entrepreneurial Behaviour.* Glenview, IL: Scott, Foresman.

Blau, P.M. 1970. "A formal theory of differentiation in organizations." *American Sociological Review* 35: 201–18.

Bloom, P.N., and P.Y. Hussein. 1995. "Benefiting society and the bottom line." *Marketing Management* 4: 8–19.

Bourgeois, D.J. 1995. *The Law of Charitable and Non-profit Organizations,* 2d Ed. Toronto: Butterworths.

Brockhaus, R.H. 1980. "Risk taking propensity of entrepreneurs." *Academy of Management Journal* 23: 509–20.

Brockner, J. 1992. "The escalation of commitment to a failing course of action: Toward theoretical progress." *Academy of Management Review* 17(1): 39–61.

Brockner, J. 1988. "The effects of work layoff on survivors: Research, theory, and practice." *Research in Organizational Behaviour* 10(1): 213–56.

Brockner, J., M. Konovsky, R. Schneider, R. Folger, M. Christopher, and R. Bies. 1994. "Interactive effects of procedural justice and outcome negativity on victims and survivors of job loss." *Academy of Management Journal* 37 (June): 397–409.

Brooks, L.J. 1989. "Corporate codes of ethics." *Journal of Business Ethics* 8: 117–29.

Brown, T.J., and P.A. Dacin. 1997. "The company and the product: Corporate association and consumer product responses." *Journal of Marketing* 61: 68–84.

Browne, P.L. 1996. *Love in a Cold World? The Voluntary Sector in the Age of Cuts.* Ottawa: Canadian Centre for Policy Alternatives.

Brundage, D.M. 1986. *The Maturation Process and Learning.* Proceedings of the Annual Conference of The Canadian Association for Studies on Adult Education, Winnipeg.

Brundage, D.H., and D. Mackeracher. 1980. *Adult Learning Principles and Their Application to Program Planning.* Toronto: Ministry of Education.

Bryson, J.M. 1995. *Strategic Planning for Public and Nonprofit Organizations,* Rev'd Ed. San Francisco: Jossey-Bass.

Buckley, M.R., D.S. Wiese, and M.G. Harvey. 1998. "An investigation into the dimensions of unethical behaviour." *Journal of Education for Business* 73(5): 284–90.

Bunner, P. 1999. "The next wave of privatization." *Report/Newsmagazine* (Alberta Edition) (December 6) 26(43): 10.

Burak, R. 1997. *Building the Ontario Public Service for the Future: A Framework for Action.* Toronto: O.P.S. Restructuring Secretariat, Government of Ontario.

Burgelman, R.A. 1983. "Corporate entrepreneurship and strategic management: Insights from a process study." *Management Science* 29(12): 1349–64.

Burgelman, R.A. 1985. "Managing the new venture division: Research findings and implications for strategic management." *Strategic Management Journal* 6(1): 39–54.

Burns, T., and G.M. Stalker. 1961. *The Management of Innovation.* London: Tavistock.

BusinessWeek, 1990. "The stateless corporation." (May 14), pp. 98–104.

Busenitz, L.W. 1999. "Entrepreneurial risk and strategic decision making: It's a matter of perspective." *Journal of Applied Behavioral Science* 35(3): 325–40.

Busenitz, L.W., and G.B. Murphy. 1996. "New evidence in the pursuit of locating new businesses." *Journal of Business Venturing* 2: 221–31.

Cameron, K. 1994. "Strategies for successful organizational downsizing." *Human Resource Management* 33 (Summer): 189–211.

Cameron, K., S. Freeman, and A. Mishra. 1991. "Best practices in white-collar downsizing: Managing contradictions." *The Academy of Management Executive* 5(3): 58.

Canada and the World Backgrounder. 2001. "Small is beautiful: Going further than deregulation, a major trend in government has been to sell off publicly owned assets in the hope of raising cash to help offset deficits." *Canada and the World Backgrounder* (March) 66(5): 12–15.

Carr, A.Z. 1968. "Is business bluffing ethical?" *Harvard Business Review* 46: 127–34.

Carroll, A.B. 1978. "Linking business to behaviour in organizations." *SAM Advanced Management Journal* 43: 4–11.

Carter, N. 1975. *Trends in Voluntary Support for Non-Governmental Social Service Agencies.* Ottawa: Canadian Council on Social Development.

Carter, N., W.B. Gartner, and P.D. Reynolds. 1996. "Exploring start-up events sequences." *Journal of Business Venturing* 2: 151–66.

Carver, J., and M.M. Carver. 1997. *Reinventing Your Board.* San Francisco: Jossey-Bass.

Cascio, W. 1993. "Downsizing? What do we know? What have we learned?" *Academy of Management Executive* 7 (February): 95–104.

416

Cell, E. 1945. *Learning to Learn from Experience*. Albany: State University of New York Press.

Chandler, A.D. Jr. 1962. *Strategy and Structure: Chapters in the History of the Industrial Enterprise*. Cambridge, MA: M.I.T. Press.

Clark, C. 1996. "Privatization and industrial policy as U.S. competitiveness strategies: Lessons from East Asia." *ACR* 4(1): 101–28.

Clark, P.B., and J.Q. Wilson. 1961. "Incentive systems: A theory of organizations." *Administrative Sciences Quarterly* 6: 129–66.

Clegg, S. 1990. *Modern Organizations*. Newbury Park, CA: Sage.

Cone, C. 1997. "Cause-Related Marketing Trends Report." Boston: Cone Communications, Inc.

Cooper, A., and K.W. Artz. 1995. "Determinants of satisfaction for entrepreneurs." *Journal of Business Venturing* 10: 439–57.

Cooper, A.C., W.C. Dunkelberg, and C.Y. Woo. 1988. "Entrepreneurs' perceived chances for success." *Journal of Business Venturing* 3: 97–108.

Craig, S.C., and J.M. McCann. 1979. "Assessing communications effects on energy conservation." *Journal of Consumer Research* 5: 82–88.

CUPE Report. 1999. "The privatization of public services." *Worklife* 11(4): 13–14.

Cyert, R.M., and J.G. March. 1963. *A Behavioral Theory of the Firm*. Englewood Cliffs, NJ: Prentice Hall.

Daft, R.L. 2001. *Organizational Theory and Design*, 7th Ed. Cincinnati, OH: South-Western College Publishing.

Daniels, J.D.J., and L.H. Radebaugh. 1998. *International Business: Environments and Operations*. Reading, MA: Addison-Wesley.

Davis, S.J., J. Haltiwanger, and S. Schuh. 1995. "Small business and job creation: Dissecting the myth and reassessing the facts." *Business Economics* 29(3): 13–21.

Day, K.M., and R.A. Devlin. 1997. "The Canadian nonprofit sector" in R. Hirshhorn (ed.), *The Emerging Sector: In Search of a Framework*. Ottawa: Canadian Policy Research Networks Inc.

Deal, T., and A. Kennedy. 1982. *Corporate Cultures: The Rites and Rituals of Corporate Life*. Reading, MA: Addison-Wesley.

De Castro, J.O., and K. Uhlenbruck. 1997. "Characteristics of privatization: Evidence from developed, less developed, and former communist countries." *Journal of International Business Studies* 28(1): 123–43.

Deci, E.L. 1975. *Intrinsic Motivation*. New York: Plenum.

Dees, J.G. 1998. "Enterprising nonprofits." *Harvard Business Review*, 55–67.

De George, R.T. 1999. *Business Ethics*, 5th Ed. Upper Saddle River, NJ: Prentice Hall.

DiMaggio, P., and W. Powell, 1983. "The iron cage revisited: Institutional isomorphism and collective rationality in organizational fields." *American Sociological Review* 48(1): 147–60.

DiMaggio, P.J., and H.K. Anheier. 1990. "The sociology of nonprofit organizations and sectors." *Annual Review of Sociology* 16: 137–59.

Dogson, M. 1993. "Organizational learning: A review of some literatures." *Organization Studies* 14: 375–94.

Doherty, N., and J. Horsted. 1995. "Helping survivors to stay on board." *People Management* 1 (January): 26–31.

Dollar, D. 1993. "What do we know about the long-term sources of comparative advantage?" *AEA Papers and Proceedings* (May): 431–35.

Douglas, J. 1987. "Political theories of nonprofit organization" in W.W. Powell (ed.), *The Nonprofit Sector: A Research Handbook*, pp. 43–54. New Haven: Yale University Press.

Drucker, P.F. 1995. "Introduction: Charitable and non-profit organizations" in Donald J. Bourgeois, *The Law of Charitable and Non-profit Organizations*, 2d Ed., pp. 1–30. Toronto: Butterworths.

Drucker, P.F. 1990. "Lessons for successful nonprofit governance." *Nonprofit Management and Leadership* 1(1): 7–14.

Drucker, P.F. 1973. *Management: Tasks, Responsibilities and Practices* (Chapter 7). New York: Harper & Row.

Drucker, P.F. 1967. *The Effective Executive*. New York: Harper & Row.

Drucker, P.F. 1954. *The Practice of Management*. New York: Harper & Row.

Duchesne, D. 1989. *Giving Freely: Volunteers in Canada*. Statistics Canada, Labour Analytic Report, Cat: 71-535 No. 4. Ottawa: Minister of Supply and Services, Canada.

The Economist. 1994. "The global economy" (October 1): 3–46.

Ellen, P., L. Mohr, and D. Web. 1997. "Can retailers benefit from cause marketing?" Working Paper, Georgia State University.

Erikson, E. 1968. "Identity and the life cycle." *Psychological Issues Monograph* 1(1). New York: International Universities Press.

Erikson, E.H. (ed.). 1976. *Adulthood*. New York: W.W. Norton.

Evans, B., and J. Shields, 1998. *Reinventing the State: Public Administration 'Reform' in Canada*. Halifax: Fernwood Publishing.

Evans, M.G., H.P. Gunz, and R.M. Jalland. 1997. "Implications of organizational downsizing for managerial careers." *Canadian Journal of Administrative Sciences* 14: 359–71.

Fayol, H. 1930. *Industrial and General Administration*. New York: Sir Isaac Pitman and Sons.

Ferrell, O.C., and L.G. Gresham. 1985. "A contingency framework for understanding ethical decision making in marketing." *Journal of Marketing* 49: 87–96.

Fiol, C., and M. Lyles. 1985. "Organizational learning." *Academy of Management Review* 10: 803–13.

Fischhoff, B., P. Slovic, and S. Lichtenstein. 1977. "Knowing with certainty: The appropriateness of extreme confidence." *Journal of Experimental Psychology: Human Perception and Performance* 3: 552–64.

FitzRandolph, S., and L. Miller. 1998. *Entrepreneurial Initiatives in the Nonprofit Sector*. CVSS Working paper series.

Flynn, J.P., and G.E. Web. 1975. "Women's incentives for community participation in policy issues." *Journal of Voluntary Action Research* 4: 137–45.

Follett, M.P. 1942. "Dynamic administration" in H. Metcalf and L.F. Urwick (eds.), *Dynamic Administration: The Collected Papers of Mary Parker Follett*. New York: Harper & Row.

Follett, M.P. 1934. *Creative Experience*. London: Longmans, Green.

Foster, M.K., and A.G. Meinhard. 2000. "Strategic responses of voluntary social service organizations to funding changes: The Ontario situation." Paper presented at the annual Academy of Management Conference, Toronto, Ontario.

Foster, M.K., and A.G. Meinhard. 1996. "Toward transforming social service organizations In Ontario." Presented at Babson Conference on Entrepreneurship, Seattle, WA.

Fredrickson, J.W., and A.L. Iaquinto. 1989. "Inertia and creeping rationality in strategic decision processes." *Academy of Management Journal* 32(3): 516–42.

French, W.L., C.H. Bell, Jr., and R.A. Zawacki. (eds.). 1994. *Organization development and transformation: Managing effective change*, 4th Ed. Burr Ridge, IL: Irwin.

Friedman, M. 1962. *Capitalism and Freedom*. Chicago: University of Chicago Press.

Friedman, T.L. 1999. *The Lexus and the Olive Tree*. New York, NY: Farrar Strauss Giroux.

Fulford, D. 2000. Personal communication, Director of Business Planning, Management Board Secretariat, Queen's Park, Toronto.

Gagnon, L. 1997. "In praise of state-owned liquor outlets." *The Globe and Mail* (December 27).

Galbraith, J.K. 1958. *The Affluent Society*. Boston: Houghton Mifflin Company.

Galbraith, J.R. 1977. *Organization Design*. Reading, MA: Addison-Wesley.

Galbraith, J.R. 1973. *Designing Complex Organizations*. Reading, MA: Addison-Wesley.

Garten, J.E. 1998. "Cultural imperialism is no joke." *BusinessWeek* (November 30).

Gatewood, E., K. Shaver, and W. Gartner. 1995. "A longitudinal study of cognitive factors influencing start-up behaviors and success at venture creation." *Journal of Business Venturing* 10: 371–91.

Gatewood, R.D., and A.B. Carroll. 1991. "Assessment of the ethical performance of organizational members: A conceptual framework." *Academy of Management Review* 16: 667–90.

Gausch, J.L., and R.W. Hahn. 1999. "The cost and benefits of regulation: implications for developing countries." *The World Bank Research Observer* 14(1): 137–58.

Gersick, C.J.G., and J.R. Hackman. 1990. "Habitual routines in task-performing groups." *Organizational Behaviour and Human Decision Processes* 47: 65–97.

Gidron, B., R.M. Kramer, and L.M. Salamon. 1992. *Government and the Third Sector: Emerging Relationships in Welfare States*. San Francisco: Jossey-Bass.

Gilbreth, F.B. 1911. *Principles of Scientific Management*. New York: Van Nostrand.

Gilmore, T.N., and R.K. Kazanjian. 1989. "Clarifying decision making in high-growth ventures: The use of responsibility charting." *Journal of Business Venturing* 4: 69–83.

Gioia, D.A. 1986. "Symbols, scripts, and sensemaking: Creating meaning in the organizational experience" in H.P. Sims, Jr., D.A. Gioia, and Associates, *The Thinking Organization: Dynamics of Organizational Social Cognition*, pp. 49–74. San Francisco: Jossey-Bass.

Glaser, J.S. 1992. "Connecting the workplace and adult development theory: Self directed work teams as a petri dish for adult development." Paper presented at the 7th Annual Meeting of the Society for Research in Adult Development, Toronto, Canada (June).

Gluck, R. 1975. "An exchange theory of incentive of urban political party organization." *Journal of Voluntary Action Research* 4: 104–15.

The Globe and Mail. 2001. "Who's minding the Crown corporations?" (March 5).

Goffman, E. 1967. *Interaction Ritual*. Garden City, NY: Doubleday.

Goodpaster, K.E., and J.B. Matthews, Jr. 1983. "Can a corporation have a conscience?" in T.L. Beauchamp and N.E. Bowie (eds.), *Ethical Theory and Business*. Englewood Cliffs, NJ: Prentice Hall.

Greider, W. 1997. *One World, Ready or Not: The Manic Logic of Global Capitalism*. New York: Simon & Schuster.

Griffin, R.W., and M.W. Pustay. 1998. *International Business: A Management Perspective*, 2d Ed. Reading, MA: Addison-Wesley.

Grover, S.L. 1993. "Why professionals lie: The impact of professional role conflict on reporting accuracy." *Organizational Behaviour and Human Decision Processing* 55: 251–72.

Hall, A.D., and R.E. Fagen. 1956. "Definition of system." *General Systems: The Yearbook of the Society for the Advancement of General Systems Theory* 1: 18–28.

Hall, M., and K.G. Banting. 2000. "The nonprofit sector in Canada: An introduction" in K.G. Banting (ed.), *The Nonprofit Sector in Canada*. Montreal and Kingston: School of Policy Studies, Queen's University.

Hall, M., and L. Macpherson. 1997. "A provincial portrait of Canada's charities." *Canadian Centre for Philanthropy Research Bulletin*, Vol. 4.

Hambrick, D.C., and L. Crozier. 1985. "Stumblers and stars in the management of rapid growth." *Journal of Business Venturing* 1(1): 31–45.

Hammer, M., and J. Champy. 1993. *Reengineering the Corporation*. New York, NY: HarperBusiness.

Handleman, J.M., and S.J. Arnold. 1999. "The role of marketing actions with a social dimension: Appeals to the institutional environment." *Journal of Marketing* 63: 33–48.

Handy, F. 1995. "Reputation as collateral: An economic analysis of the role of trust in nonprofit organizations." *Nonprofit and Voluntary Sector Quarterly* 24(4): 293–305.

Harvey, M., and R. Evans. 1995. "Strategic windows in the entrepreneurial process." *Journal of Business Venturing* 10: 331–47.

Havlovic, S., F. Bouthillette, and R. van der Wal. 1998. "Coping with downsizing and job loss: Lessons from the Shaughnessy Hospital closure." *Canadian Journal of Administrative Sciences* 15 (December): 322–32.

Heath, C., and A. Tversky. 1991. "Preferences and beliefs: Ambiguity and competence in choice under uncertainty." *Journal of Risk and Uncertainty* 4: 5–28.

Heffron, F. 1989. *Organization Theory and Public Organizations: The Political Connection*. New Jersey: Prentice Hall.

Hegarty, W.H., and H.P. Sims. 1979. "Organizational philosophy, policies, and objectives related to unethical decision behaviour: A laboratory experiment." *Journal of Applied Psychology* 64(3): 331–38.

Hegarty, W.H., and H.P. Sims. 1978. "Some determinants of unethical decision behaviour: An experiment." *Journal of Applied Psychology* 63(4): 451–57.

Heracleous, L. 1999. "Privatisation: Global trends and implications of the Singapore experience." *The International Journal of Public Sector Management* 12(5): 432–44.

Herman, R., and D. Heimovics. 1991. *Executive Leadership in Nonprofit Organizations: New Strategies for Shaping Executive-Board Dynamics*. San Francisco: Jossey-Bass.

Hertzberg, F., B. Mausner, and B. Snyderman. 1959. *The Motivation to Work*. New York: John Wiley.

Higgins, A., C. Power, and L. Kohlberg. 1984. "The relationship of moral atmosphere to judgments of responsibility" in W.M. Kurtines and J.L. Gewirtz (eds.), *Morality, Moral Behaviour and Moral Development*, pp. 74–106. New York: Wiley.

Hirschhorn, L., and T. Gilmore. 1992. "The new boundaries of the 'boundaryless' company." *Harvard Business Review* (May/June): 104–15.

Hirshhorn, R. (ed.) 1997. *The Emerging Sector: In Search of A Framework*. Ottawa: Canadian Policy Research Networks Inc.

Hogarth, R.M. 1987. *Judgement and Choice: The Psychology of Decisions*. New York: John Wiley.

Holstrom, B. 1979. "Moral hazard and observability." *Bell Journal of Economics* 10: 74–91.

Hood, J.N., and J.E. Young. 1993. "Entrepreneurship's requisite areas of development: A survey of top executives in successful entrepreneurial firms." *Journal of Business Venturing* 8: 115–35.

Huber, V.L., and M.A. Neale. 1987. "Effects of self and competitor's goals on performance in an interdependent bargaining task." *Journal of Applied Psychology* 72: 197–203.

Hull, D., J. Bosley, and G. Udell. 1980. "Renewing the hunt for the Heffalump: Identifying potential entrepreneurs by personality characteristics." *Journal of Small Business Management* 18(1): 11–18.

Hunt, S.D., and S. Vitell. 1986. "A general theory of marketing ethics." *Journal of Macromarketing* 6(1): 5–16.

Industry Canada and Statistics Canada. 1998. *Small Business Quarterly Report* (Summer).

Industry Canada. 1991. *Small Business in Canada*.

Jackall, R. 1988. *Moral Mazes: The World of Corporate Managers*. New York: Oxford University Press.

Janger, A.R. 1979. *Matrix Organizations of Complex Businesses*. New York: The Conference Board.

Janis, I.L., and L. Mann. 1977. *Decision Making: A Psychological Analysis of Conflict, Choice, and Commitment*. New York: Free Press.

Jeffrey, B. 1999. *Hard Right Turn: The New Face of Neo-Conservatism in Canada*. Toronto: HarperCollins Canada.

Johnson, E. 1997. "Marketing" in T. Connors (ed.), *The Nonprofit Handbook*, 2d Ed., pp. 376–413. New York: John Wiley and Sons.

419

Johnson, N. 1981. *Voluntary Social Services*. Oxford: Basil Blackwell.

Jones, T.M. 1991. "Ethical decision making by individuals in organizations: An issue-contingent model." *Academy of Management Review* 16(2): 366–95.

Kahn, R., D. Wolfe, R. Quinn, J. Snoek, and R. Rosenthal. 1964. *Organizational Stress: Studies in Role Conflict and Ambiguity*. New York: John Wiley.

Kahn, W.A. 1992. "To be fully there: Psychological presence." *Human Relations* 45(4).

Kahn, W.A. 1990a. "Toward an agenda for business ethics research." *Academy of Management Review* 15(2): 311–28.

Kahn, W.A. 1990b. "Psychological conditions of personal engagement and disengagement at work." *Academy Management Journal* 33(4): 692–724.

Kahneman, D. 1992. "Reference points, anchors, norms, and mixed feelings." *Organizational Behaviour Human Decision Process* 51: 269–312.

Kahneman, D., and D. Lovallo. 1993. "Timid choices and bold forecasts: A cognitive perspective on risk taking." *Management Science* 39(1): 17–31.

Kahneman, D., P. Slovic, and A. Tversky. (eds.) 1982. *Judgment under Uncertainty: Heuristics and Biases*. New York: Cambridge University Press.

Kahneman, D., and A. Tversky. 1979. "Prospect theory: An analysis of decision under risk." *Econometrica* 47: 263–91.

Kant, I. 1785. *Grounding for the Metaphysics of Morals*. Trans. James W. Ellington [1993]. Indianapolis, IN: Hackett.

Karakowsky, L. 1994. "The Influence of Organizational Context on Ethical Behaviour in the Workplace: Linking Institutionalization Theory to Individual-Level Behaviour." *Proceedings of the Administrative Sciences Association of Canada* 15(12): 21–30.

Karakowsky, L., and A.R. Elangovan. 2001. "Risky decision making in mixed-gender terms: Whose risk tolerance matters?" *Small Group Research* 32(1): 94–111.

Katz, J.A. 1992. "A psychosocial cognitive model of employment status choice." *Entrepreneurship Theory and Practice* 17(1): 29–37.

Katz, D., and R.L. Kahn. 1978. *The Social Psychology of Organization*, 2d Ed. New York: Wiley.

Kerr, J.G. 1997. *New Venture and Small Business Management* (Internet Course). Toronto: Captus Press.

Kegan, R. 1982. *The Evolving Self: Problem and Process in Human Development*. Cambridge: Harvard University Press.

Kegan, R. 1979. "The evolving self: A process conception for ego psychology." *The Counselling Psychologist* 8: 5–34.

Kikeri, S., J. Nellis, and M. Shirley. 1994. "Privatization: Lessons from market economies." *World Bank Research Observer*, 241–72.

Kirzner, I.M. 1979. *Perception Opportunity and Profit: Studies in the Theory of Entrepreneurship*. Chicago: University of Chicago Press.

Kleintop, W.A. 1997. "Information resources management for nonprofit organizations" in T. Connors (ed.), *The Nonprofit Handbook*, 2d Ed., pp. 535–54. New York: John Wiley and Sons.

Knight, R. 1987. *Entrepreneurship*. Ivy School of Business, December.

Kohlberg, L. 1969. "Stage and sequence: The cognitive developmental approach to socialization" in D.A. Goslin (ed.), *Handbook of Socialization Theory and Research*, pp. 347–480. Chicago: Rand McNally.

Kolb, D.A. 1984. *Experiential Learning: Experience as the Source of Learning and Development*. Englewood Cliffs, NJ: Prentice Hall.

Kotler, P., and A. Andreasen. 1996. *Strategic Marketing for Non-Profit Organizations*. Upper Saddle, NJ: Prentice Hall.

Kotler, P., and R.E. Turner. 1995. *Marketing Management*, Canadian 8th Ed. Toronto: Prentice Hall.

Knouse, S.B., and R.A. Giacalone. 1991. "Ethical decision-making in business: Behavioral issues and concerns." *Journal of Business Ethics* 11: 369–77.

Knox, A.B. 1977. *Adult Development and Learning*. San Francisco: Jossey-Bass.

Kohlberg, L. 1969. "Stage and sequence: The cognitive developmental approach to socialization" in D.A. Goslin (ed.), *Handbook of Socialization Theory and Research*, pp. 347–480. Chicago: Rand McNally.

Kram, K. 1985. *Mentoring at Work*. Glenview, IL: Scott Forseman.

Kram, K.E., P.C. Yeager, and G.E. Reed. 1989. "Decisions and dilemmas: The ethical dimension in the corporate context" in J.E. Post (ed.), *Research in Corporate Social Performance and Policy*, Vol. 1, pp. 21–54. Greenwich, CT: JAI Press.

Kramer, R. 2000. "A third sector in the third millennium?" *Voluntas* 11 (1): 1–23.

Kramer, R. 1981. *Voluntary Agencies in the Welfare State*. Berkeley: University of California Press.

Krueger, N., and P. Dickson. 1994. "How believing in ourselves increases risk taking: Perceived self-efficacy and opportunity recognition." *Decision Sciences* 25: 385–400.

Krugman, P.R., and M. Obstfeld. 1997. *International Economics: Theory and Policy*. Reading, MA: Addison-Wesley.

Kuhnle, S., and P. Selle. 1992. *Government and Voluntary Organizations: A Relational Perspective*. Aldershot: Avebury.

Lafond, A. Deputy Commissioner of Competition, Civil Matters Branch, Competition Bureau. 1999. "The roles and responsibilities of the industry regulator versus the Competition Bureau as regulated industries become competitive." Address to the Conference Board Regulatory Reform Program Meeting. February 19.

Lang, D. 1986. "Motivation in the voluntary sector." Unpublished Doctoral Dissertation. McMaster University.

Latham, G.P., and G.A. Yukl. 1975. "A review of research on the application of goal setting in organizations." *Academy of Management Journal* (December): 824–45.

Lawrence, P., and J. Lorsch. 1969. *Developing Organizations: Diagnosis and Action*. Reading, MA: Addison-Wesley.

Lawrence, P.R., and J.W. Lorsch. 1967a. *Organization and Environment*. Boston: Graduate School of Business Administration, Harvard University.

Lawrence, P.R., and J.W. Lorsch. 1967b. "Differentiation and integration in complex organizations." *Administrative Science Quarterly* (June): 1–47.

Lee, P. 1997. "A comparative analysis of layoff announcements and stock price reactions in the United States and Japan." *Strategic Management Journal* 18 (December): 879–94.

Leontief, W. 1954. "Domestic production and foreign trade; The American capital position re-examined." *Economia Internazionale* (February): 3–32.

Levac, M., and P. Wooldridge. Financial Markets Department. 1997. "The fiscal impact of privatization in Canada." *Bank of Canada Review* (Summer): 25–40.

Levering, R., M. Moscowitz, and M. Katz. 1985. *The 100 Best Companies to Work for in America*. Scarborough, New York: New American Library.

Levinson, D.J., C.N. Darrow, E.B. Klein, M.H. Levinson, and B. McKee. 1978. *The Seasons of a Man's Life*. New York: Ballatine Books.

Lewin, K. 1951. *Field Theory in Social Science*. New York: Harper & Row.

Lewis, P.V. 1985. "'Defining business ethics': Like nailing jell-o to a wall." *Journal of Business Ethics* 4(5): 377–83.

Lichtenstein, S., B. Fischhoff, and L. Phillips. 1982. "Calibration of probabilities: The state of the art to 1980" in D. Kahneman, P. Slovic, and A. Tversky (eds.), *Judgment under Uncertainty: Heuristics and Biases*, pp. 306–34. New York: Cambridge University Press.

Lipman, J. 1990. "When its commercial time, TV viewers prefer cartoons to celebrities any day." *The Wall Street Journal* (Feb. 16): B1, B4.

Locke, E.A. 1968. "Toward a theory of task motivation and incentives." *Organizational Behaviour and Human Performance* (May): 157–89.

Locke, E.A., L.M. Saari, and G.P. Latham. 1981. "Goal setting and task performance." *Psychological Bulletin* (January): 125–52.

Locke, John. 1690. *Second Treatise on Civil Government*. Cambridge: Cambridge University Press.

Low, M.B., and I.C. MacMillan. 1988. "Entrepreneurship: Past research and future challenges." *Journal of Management* 14(2): 139–61.

Luthans, F. 1973. "The contingency theory of management: A path out of the jungle." *Business Horizons* 16 (June): 62–72.

March, J.G., and H.A. Simon. 1958. *Organizations*. New York: Wiley.

Martin, S. 1985. *An Essential Grace: Funding Canada's Health Care, Education, Welfare, Religion and Culture*. Toronto: McClelland and Stewart.

Masi, D.A. 1981. *Organizing for Women: Issues, Strategies, and Services*. Lexington, MA: Lexington Books.

Maslow, A. 1954. *Motivation and Personality*. New York: Harper & Row.

McBride, S., and J. Shields. 1997. *Dismantling a Nation: The Transition to Corporate Rule in Canada*. Halifax: Fernwood Publishing.

McClelland, D.C. 1987. "Characteristics of Successful Entrepreneurs." *Journal of Creative Behaviour* 21: 219–33.

McClelland, D.C. 1961. *The Achieving Society*. New York: Van Nostrand Reinhold.

McGregor, D. 1960. *The Human Side of Enterprise* (pp. 33–58). New York: McGraw-Hill.

McKinley, W., C. Sanchez, and A. Schick. 1995. "Organizational downsizing: Constraining, cloning, learning." *Academy of Management Executive* 9(3): 32–41.

McLeish, B.L. 1995. *Successful Strategies for Non-Profit Organizations*. New York: John Wiley and Sons.

McLellan, K., and B. Marcolin. 1994. "Information technology outsourcing." *Business Quarterly* 59 (Autumn): 95–104.

McMillan, C.J., and E.M.V. Jasson. 2001. "Technology and the new economy: A Canadian strategy" in T. Wesson (ed.), *Canada and the New World Economic Order*, 2d Ed. Toronto: Captus Press.

McMullan, W.E., and W.A. Long. 1987. "Entrepreneurship education in the nineties." *Journal of Business Venturing* 52: 107–11.

McMurdy, Deirdre. 1995. "Rummage sales." *Maclean's* (July 24) 108(30): 32.

Meinhard, A.G., and M.K. Foster. 2000. "Third sector strategic responses to Canada's changing social, political and economic climate: A comparative analysis." Paper presented at the Fourth International Conference of the International Society for Third Sector Research, Dublin, Ireland.

Meinhard A.G., and M. Foster. 1997. "Responses of women's voluntary organizations to the changing social, political and economic environment." Paper presented at the Annual ARNOVA Conference, Indianapolis, IN.

Menzies, H. 1996. *Whose Brave New World? The Information Highway and the New Economy.* Toronto: Between the Lines.

Mertens, B. 1998. "The push for privatization." *Asian Business* 34(6): 42–45.

Merton, R.K. 1957. *Social Theory and Social Structure*, 2d Ed. New York: Free Press.

Meyer, J., and B. Rowan. 1977. "Institutional organizations: Formal structure as myth and ceremony." *American Journal of Sociology* 83: 440–63.

Mezirow, J. 1978. "Perspective transformation." *Adult Education* 28(2): 100–10.

Miles, R.E., and C.C. Snow. 1978. *Organizations: Strategy, Structure and Process.* New York: McGraw-Hill.

Milgram, S. 1974. *Obedience to Authority.* New York: Harper & Row.

Mill, J.S. 1861. *Utilitarianism.* Edited by Oskar Piest. [1948] New York: Liberal Arts Press.

Mill, J.S. 1859. *On Liberty.* Edited by Oskar Piest. [1975] New York: Norton.

Miller, D., and P.H. Friesen. 1984. *Organizations: A Quantum View.* Englewood Cliffs, NJ: Prentice Hall.

Mintzberg, H. 1979. *The Structuring of Organizational Structures.* Englewood Cliffs, NJ: Prentice Hall.

Mintzberg, H. 1974. "The manager's job: Folklore and fact." *Harvard Business Review* (July/August): 49–61.

Mintzberg, H. 1973. *The Nature of Managerial Work.* Englewood Cliffs, NJ: Prentice Hall.

Mitroff, I.I. 1983. *Stakeholders of the Organizational Mind: Toward a New View of Organizational Policy Making.* San Francisco: Jossey-Bass.

Molm, L.D. 1991. "Affect and social exchange: Satisfaction in power-dependence relations." *American Sociological Review* 56(4): 475–93.

Mone, M. 1994. "Relationships between self-concepts, aspirations, emotional responses, and intent to leave a downsizing organization." *Human Resource Management* 33 (Summer): 281–98.

Morgan, G. 1986. *Images of Organization.* Sage: Newbury Park.

Morrison, C. 2000. "Beyond booze." *Summit* 3(4): 21–22.

Murray, V. 1995. "Improving board performance." *The Philanthropist* 13(4).

Neale, M.A., and M.H. Bazerman. 1991. *Cognition and Rationality in Negotiation.* New York: Free Press.

Newell, A., and H. Simon. 1981. "Computer science as empirical inquiry: Symbols and search" in J. Haugeland (ed.), *Mind Design.* Cambridge, MA: MIT Press.

Nicolini, D., and M. Mezner. 1995. "The social construction of organizational learning: Conceptual and practical issues in the field." *Human Relations* 48(7): 727–47.

Northcraft, G., and M. Neale. 1994. *Organization Behaviour: A Management Challenge.* Chicago: Dryden Press.

Northcraft, G., and M. Neale. 1987. "Experts, amateurs, and real estate: An anchoring perspective on property pricing decisions." *Organizational Behaviour and Human Decision Processes* 39(1): 84–87.

Novelli, W.D. 1981. "Social Issues and direct marketing: What's the connection?" Paper presented at the Annual Conference of the Direct Mail/Marketing Association, Los Angeles, California, March 12.

O'Connell, B. 1985. *The Board Members Book.* New York: Foundation Center.

Ogilvy, D., and J. Raphaelson. 1982. "Research on advertising techniques that work and don't work." *Harvard Business Review* 60 (July–August): 14–18.

Ohlin, B. 1933. *Interregional and International Trade.* Cambridge, MA: Harvard University Press.

Olson, M. 1965. *The Logic of Collective Action; Public Goods and the Theory of Groups.* Cambridge: Harvard University Press.

O'Neil, M. 1992. "Ethical dimensions of nonprofit administration." *Nonprofit Management & Leadership* 3(2): 199–213.

Osborne, D., and T. Gaebler, 1993. *Reinventing Government: How the Entrepreneurial Spirit Is Transforming the Public Sector.* New York: Plume.

Ottesen, O. 1977. "The response function" in M. Berg (ed.), *Current Theories in Scandinavian Mass Communications Research.* Grena, Denmark: GMT.

Pal, L.A. 1997. "Civic re-alignment: NGOs and the contemporary welfare state" in Raymond B. Blake, Penny E. Bryden and J. Frank Strain (eds.), *The Welfare State in Canada: Past, Present and Future.* Concord, Ontario: Irwin Publishing.

Parson, H.M. 1974. "What happened at Hawthorne?" *Science* 183: 922–32.

Pastin, M. 1986. *The Hard Problems of Management: Gaining the Ethics Edge*. San Francisco: Jossey-Bass.

Pava, M.L. 1998. "Religious business ethics and political liberalism: An integrative approach." *Journal of Business Ethics* 17(15): 1633–52.

Payne, S.L., and R.A. Giacalone. 1990. "Social psychological approaches to the perception of ethical dilemmas." *Human Relations* 43: 649–65.

Peacock, R.W. 1991. "A study of small enterprise intenders who do not proceed." *Journal of Small Business & Entrepreneurship* 8(4): 28–40.

Pedler, J., R. Burgoyne, and A. Boydell. 1997. *The Learning Company*. Maidenhead, Surrey: McGraw-Hill.

Perrow, C. 1979. *Complex Organizations*, 2d Ed. Glenview, IL: Scott, Foresman.

Perry, W.G., Jr. 1970. *Forms of Intellectual and Ethical Development in the College Years*. New York: Holt, Rinehart, and Winston.

Peters, T.J., and R.H. Waterman. 1982. *In Search of Excellence*. New York: Harper & Row.

Pettigrew, A.M. 1979. "On studying organizational cultures." *Administrative Science Quarterly* 24: 570–81.

Pfeffer, J. 1982. *Organizations and Organizational Theory*. Boston: Pitman.

Pfeffer, J., and G.R. Salancik. 1978. *The External Control of Organizations*. New York: Harper & Row.

Piaget, J. 1954. *The Construction of Reality in the Child*. New York: Basic Books.

Plaschka, G.R., and H.P. Welsch. 1990. "Emerging structures in entrepreneurship education: Curricular designs and strategies." *Entrepreneurship Theory and Practice* 14(3): 55–71.

Pleitner, H.J. 1990. "Contributions of SME's to innovation." *Journal of Small Business and Entrepreneurship* 7(3): 14–22.

Pondy, L.R., P. Frost, G. Morgan, and T. Dandridge. (eds.) 1983. *Organizational Symbolism*. Greenwich, CT: JAI Press.

Porter, M.E. 1998. "Clusters and the new economics of competition." *Harvard Business Review* (November/December): 77–90.

Porter, M.E. 1990. *The Competitive Advantage of Nations*. New York: Free Press.

Porter, M.E. 1980. *Competitive Strategy: Techniques for Analyzing Industries and Competitors*. New York: Free Press.

Porter, M.E., and Monitor Company. 1991. A study prepared for the Business Council on National Issues and the government of Canada, October.

Postman, N. 1993. *Technopoly: the Surrender of Culture to Technology*. New York: Random House.

Pritchard, R.D., K.M. Campbell, and D.J. Campbell. 1977. "Effects of extrinsic financial rewards on intrinsic motivation." *Journal of Applied Psychology* (February): 9–15.

Rawls, J. 1993. *Political Liberalism*. New York: Columbia University Press.

Rawls, J. 1971. *A Theory of Justice*. Cambridge, MA: Harvard University Press.

Ray, D.M. 1994. "The role of risk-taking in Singapore." *Journal of Business Venturing* 9(2): 157–77.

Rein, I., P. Kotler, and M. Stoller. 1987. *High Visibility: How Executives, Politicians, Entertainers, Athletes and Other Professionals Create, Market and Achieve Successful Images*. New York: Dodd, Mead.

Rest, J.R. 1986. *Moral Development: Advances in Research and Theory*. New York: Praeger.

Reynolds, P., and B. Miller. 1992. "New firm gestation: Conception, birth, and implications for research." *Journal of Business Venturing* 7: 405–17.

Ricardo, D. 1996. *The Principles of Political Economy and Taxation*. [Originally published London, New York: J.M. Dent & Sons, 1911.] Amherst, NY: Prometheus Books.

Rice, J.J., and M.J. Prince. 2000. *Changing Politics of Canadian Social Policy*. Toronto: University of Toronto Press.

Rogers, C.R. 1961. *On Becoming a Person*. Boston: Houghton Mifflin.

Runes, D.D. 1964. *Dictionary of Philosophy*. Littlefields: Adams and Co.

Ryan, L., and K. Macky. 1998. "Downsizing organizations: Uses, outcomes and strategies." *Asia Pacific Journal of Human Resources* 36 (Winter): 29–45.

Ryan, W.P. 1999. "The new landscape for nonprofits." *Harvard Business Review* 77: 127–37.

Sagawa, S., and E. Segal. 2000. *Common Interest, Common Good: Creating Value Through Business and Social Sector Partnerships*. Cambridge: Harvard Business School Press.

Salamon, L.M. 1995. *Partners in Public Service: Government-Nonprofit Relations in the Modern Welfare State*. Baltimore: The Johns Hopkins University Press.

Salamon, L.M., 1987. "Partners in public service" in W.W. Powell (ed.), *The Nonprofit Sector: A Research Handbook*, pp. 107–17. New Haven: Yale University Press.

Salamon, L.M., and H.K. Anheier. 1996. *The Emerging Nonprofit Sector: An Overview*. Manchester: Manchester University Press.

Salamon, L., R. List, W. Sokolowski, S. Toepler, and H. Anheier. 1999. *Global Civil Society: Dimensions of the Nonprofit Sector*. Baltimore: John Hopkins University, Centre for Civil Society Studies.

Schein, E.M. 1985. *Organizational Culture and Leadership*. San Francisco: Jossey-Bass.

Schell, J. 1991. "In defence of the entrepreneur." *Inc.* 13(5): 28–30.

Schmid, H., and A.G. Meinhard. 2000. "A comparative analysis of emerging partnerships between corporations and nonprofit social service organizations in Canada and Israel." Presented at the annual ARNOVA Conference, New Orleans, LA.

Schumpeter, J. 1936. *The Theory of Economic Development*. Cambridge: Harvard University Press.

Schwenk, C.R. 1988. "The cognitive perspective on strategic decision making." *Journal of Management Studies* 25(1): 41–55.

Scott, J.T. 1997. "Defining the nonprofit sector" in R. Hirshhorn (ed.), *The Emerging Sector: In Search of a Framework*. Ottawa: Canadian Policy Research Networks Inc.

Scott, J.T. 1992. *Voluntary Sector In Crisis: Canada's Changing Public Philosophy of the State and Its Impact on Voluntary Charitable Organizations*. Ann Arbor: University Microfilms.

Scott, W.R. 1981. *Organizations: Rational, Natural, and Open Systems*. Englewood Cliffs, NJ: Prentice Hall.

Seidle, F.L. 1995. *Rethinking the Delivery of Public Services to Citizens*. Montreal: Institute for Research on Public Policy.

Selznick, P. 1943. "An approach to a theory of bureaucracy." *American Sociological Review* 8: 47–54.

Senge, P. 1990. *The Fifth Discipline: The Art and Practice of the Learning Organization*. New York: Doubleday.

Sethi, S.P. 1982. *Against the Corporate Wall*. Englewood Cliffs, NJ: Prentice Hall.

Shapira, Z. 1995. *Risk Taking: A Managerial Perspective*. New. York: Russell Sage Foundation.

Shaver, K. Scott. 1992. "Person, process, choice: The psychology of new venture creation." *Entrepreneurship: Theory and Practice* 16(2): 23–45.

Simon, H. 1957. *Models of Man*. New York, NY: Wiley.

Simon, H.A. 1945. *Administrative Behaviour*. New York: Free Press.

Sims, J.P. Jr., D.A. Gioia, and Associates. 1986. *The Thinking Organization*. San Francisco: Jossey-Bass.

Sims, R.R. 1991. "The institutionalization of organizational ethics." *Journal of Business Ethics* 10: 493–511.

Sinclair, M., and J. Galaskiewicz. 1997. "Corporate-nonprofit partnerships: Varieties and covariates." *New York Law School Law Review* 41: 1059–90.

Smalhout, James. 1999. "Keep the state out of business." *Euromoney* (March) 359: 36–41.

Smith, A. 1937. *The Wealth of Nations*. Edited by E. Cannan. [First Modern library edition 1937.] New York: Modern Library.

Smith, D.H. 1982. "Altruism, volunteers, and voluntarism" in J. Harmon (ed.), *Volunteerism in the Eighties: Fundamental Issues in Voluntary Action*. Washington DC: University Press of America.

Sonnenfeld, J.A. 1985. "Shedding light on the Hawthorne studies." *Journal of Occupational Behaviour* 6: 111–30.

Starbuck, W.H. 1976. "Organizations and their environments" in M.D. Dunnette (ed.), *Handbook of Industrial Psychology*, pp. 1069–123. Chicago: Rand McNally.

Staw, B.M. 1981. "The escalation of commitment to a course of action." *Academy of Management Review* 6: 577–87.

Staw, B.M., and J. Ross. 1987. "Behaviour in escalation situations: Antecedents, prototypes and solutions" in L.L. Cummings and B.M. Staw (eds.), *Research in Organization Behaviour* 9: 39–78. London: JAI Press.

Steers, R.M., and L.W. Porter. 1979. *Motivation and Work Behaviour*, 2d Ed. New York: McGraw-Hill.

Stein, J.G. 2001. *The Cult of Efficiency*. Toronto: Anansi.

Stene, E.O. 1940. "An approach to a science of administration." *American Political Science Review* 34: 1129ff.

Sternthal, B., R.R. Dholakia, and C. Levitt. 1978. "The persuasive effect of source credibility: Test of cognitive response." *Journal of Consumer Research* 4: 242–50.

Stewart, W. 1996. *The Charity Game: Waste and Fraud in Canada's $86-Billion-a-Year Compassion Industry*. Toronto: Douglas & McIntyre.

Stone, C.D. 1975. "The culture of the corporation" in W.M. Hoffman and J.M. Moore (eds.), *Business Ethics*, 2d Ed. New York: McGraw-Hill.

Stryker, S., and R.T. Serpe. 1982. "Commitment, identity salience, and role behaviour: Theory research example" in W. Ickes and E.S. Knowles (ed.), *Personality, Roles and Social Behaviour*, pp. 199–218. New York: Springer-Verlag.

Sutherland, E., and D.R. Cressey. 1970. *Principles of Criminology*. Chicago: J.B. Lippincott.

Sutton, R., and T. D'Aunno, 1989. "Decreasing organizational size: Untangling the effects of money and people." *Academy of Management Review* 14(2): 194–212.

Tajfel, H. 1981. *Human Groups and Social Categories: Studies in Social Psychology*. Cambridge, England: Cambridge University Press.

Tajfel, H., and J.C. Turner. 1985. "The social identity theory of intergroup behaviour" in S. Worchel and W.G. Austin (eds.), *Psychology of Intergroup Relations*, 2d Ed., pp. 7–24. Chicago: Nelson Hall.

Taylor, D.W., and A.A. Warrack. 1998. "Privatization of state enterprise: Policy drivers and lessons learned." *International Journal of Public Sector Management* 11(7): 524–35.

Taylor, D.W., A.A. Warrack, and M.C. Baetz. 1999. *Business and Government in Canada: Partners for the Future.* Scarborough, Toronto: Prentice Hall Canada, Inc.

Taylor, F. 1991. *Principles of Scientific Management.* New York: Harper & Row.

Taylor, F.W. 1947. *Scientific Management.* New York: Harper & Row.

Taylor, F.W. 1913. *Principles of Scientific Management.* New York: Harper & Brothers.

Taylor, M., J. Langan, and P. Hogget. 1995. *Encouraging Diversity: Voluntary and Private Organisations In Community Care.* Hampshire, England: Arena.

Theil, Rita. 1996. "Learning to apply the lessons of privatization." *International Financial Law Review* (April) 15(4): 51ff.

Thoits, P.A. 1983. "Multiple identities and psychological well-being: A reformulation and test of the social isolation hypothesis." *American Sociological Review* 48: 174–87.

Thompson, J.D. 1967. *Organizations in Action.* New York: McGraw-Hill.

Thompson, P. 1986/87. "Characteristics of the small business entrepreneur in Canada." *Journal of Small Business and Entrepreneurship* 4(3) (Winter).

Tichy, N., and M. Devana. 1986. *The Transformational Leader.* New York: John Wiley and Sons.

Tichy, N., and D. Ulrich. 1984. "The leadership challenge — A call for the transformational leader." *Sloan Management Review* 26: 59–64.

Timmons, Jeffery A. 1994. *New Venture Creation*, 4th Ed. Homewood, IL: Irwin.

Tolbert, P., and L.G. Zucker. 1983. "Institutional sources of change in the formal structure of organizations: The diffusion of civil service reform, 1880–1935." *Administrative Science Quarterly* 28(1): 22–39.

Tomasko, R. 1990. *Downsizing: Reshaping the Corporation of the Future.* New York: AMACON.

Trevino, L.K. 1986. "Ethical decision making in organizations: A person-situation interactionist model." *Academy of Management Review* 11(3): 601–17.

Trevino, L.K., and S.A. Youngblood. 1990. "Bad apples in bad barrels: A causal analysis of ethical decision making behaviour." *Journal of Applied Psychology* 75(4): 378–85.

Tsalikis, J., and D.J. Fritsche. 1989. "Business ethics: A literature review with a focus on marketing ethics." *Journal of Business Ethics* 8: 695–743.

Tucker, D., R. House, J. Singh, and A. Meinhard. 1984. *Voluntary Social Service Organizations: Their Births, Growth and Deaths.* Hamilton: McMaster University.

Tucker, D.J., J.V. Singh, and A.G. Meinhard. 1990. "Organizational form, population dynamics and institutional change: A study of birth patterns of voluntary organizations." *Academy of Management Journal* 33: 151–78.

Turner, J. 1982. "Towards a cognitive redefinition of the social group" in H. Tajfel (ed.), *Social Identity and Intergroup Relations*, pp. 15–40. Cambridge, England: Cambridge University Press.

Tversky, A., and D. Kahneman. 1974. "Judgment under uncertainty: Heuristics and biases." *Science* 185: 1124–31.

Tversky, A., and D. Kahneman. 1973. "Availability: A heuristic for judging frequency and probability." *Cognitive Psychology* 5: 207–32.

Tversky, A., and D. Kahneman. 1972. "Subjective probability: A judgment of representativeness." *Cognitive Psychology* 3(3): 430–54.

Tversky, A., and D. Kahneman. 1971. "The belief in the 'law of small numbers'." *Psychological Bulletin* 76: 105–10.

Useem, M. 1987. "Corporate philanthropy" in W.W. Powell (ed.), *The Nonprofit Sector: A Research Handbook.* New Haven: Yale University Press.

Van Til, J. 1988. *Mapping the Third Sector: Voluntarism in a Changing Social Economy.* New York: Foundation Center.

von Finckenstein, K. 1999. Q.C. Commissioner of Competition Bureau, Statement to the "Meet the Competition Bureau," Forum Insight Conference, Toronto, May 3.

Vroom, V.H. 1964. *Work and Motivation.* New York: John Wiley.

Wahba, M.A., and L.G. Bridwell. 1976. "Maslow reconsidered: A review of research on the need hierarchy theory." *Organizational Behaviour and Human Performance* (April): 212–40.

Wanberg, C., L. Bunce, and M. Gavin. 1999. "Perceived fairness of layoffs among individuals who have been laid off: A longitudinal study." *Personnel Psychology* 52 (Spring): 59–84.

Wasney, G. 1997. "A new road for Canadian truckers." *World Trade* 10(2): 48–50.

Weber, J. 1990. "Manager's moral reasoning: Assessing their responses to the three moral dilemmas." *Human Relations* 43: 687–702.

Weber, Joseph. 1998. "Does Canadian culture need this much protection?" *BusinessWeek* (June 18). Online: <http://www.bwarchive.businessweek.com>.

Weber, M. 1979. *Economy and Society*, eds. G. Roth and C. Wittich. Berkeley: University of California Press.

425

Weber, M. 1947. *The Theory of Social and Economic Organizations*. Edited and Translated by A.M. Henderson and T. Parsons. New York: Free Press.

Weber, M. 1946. *From Max Weber: Essays in Sociology*, eds. H.H. Gerth and C.W. Mills. New York: Oxford University Press.

Weber, M. 1927. *General Economic History*. Transl. F.H. Knight. London: Allen & Unwin.

Weick, K. 1979. *The Social Psychology of Organizing*. Reading, MA: Addison-Wesley.

Weick, K. 1976. "Educational organizations as loosely coupled systems." *Administrative Science Quarterly* 21: 1–19.

Weisbrod, B.A. 1995. "Do private firms, church-related nonprofits and other nonprofits behave differently?" Department of Economics, Northwestern University, Evanston, IL.

Weisbrod, B.A. 1977. *The Voluntary Nonprofit Sector*. Lexington: D.C. Heath and Company.

Weldon, P. 2000. Personal communication.

White, G. 1997. "The Not-for-profit and the private sectors in the 1990's . . . or how 'Birkenstock' and 'Pinstripe' need each other!" Toronto: Market Vision Group.

White, J.P., and R. Janzen. 2000. "The industrial relations implications of privatization: The case of Canada Post." *Industrial Relations* (Winter) 55(1): 36–55.

Whyte, G.. 1993. "Escalating commitment in individual and group decision making: A prospect theory approach." *Organizational Behaviour and Human Decision Process* 54(3): 430–55.

Wild, J.J., K.L. Wild, and J.C.Y. Han. 2000. *International Business: An Integrated Approach*. Upper Saddle River, NJ: Prentice Hall.

Winston, C. 1993. "Economic deregulation: Days of reckoning for economists." *Journal of Economic Literature* 31: 1263–89.

Woodward, J. 1965. *Industrial Organization: Theory and Practice*. London, NY: Oxford University Press.

World Bank. 1997. "Privatization revenue statistics by regions." Online: <http://worldbank.org/ecsp/finl/html/priv-regions.htm>.

Worrell, D., W. Davidson, and V. Sharma. 1991. "Layoff announcements and shareholder wealth." *Academy of Management Journal* 34 (September): 662–78.

Wren, D. 1979. *Evolution of Management Thought*, 2d Ed. New York: Wiley.

Young, D. 2000. "Alternative models of government-nonprofit sector relations: Theoretical and international perspectives." *Nonprofit and Voluntary Sector Quarterly* 29(1).

Yukl, G. 1994. *Leadership in Organizations*, 3d Ed. Engelwood Cliffs, NJ: Prentice Hall.

Zahra, S.A., and C.D. Hansen. 2000. "Privatization, entrepreneurship, and global competitiveness in the 21st Century." *Competition Review* 10(1): 83–103.

Zajac, E.J., and M.H. Bazerman. 1991. "Blind spots in industry and competitor analysis: Implications of interfirm (mis)perceptions for strategic decisions." *Academy of Management Review* 16(1): 37–56.

Zimmerman, B., and R. Dart. 1998. "Charities doing commercial ventures: Societal and organizational implications." Trillium Foundation and Canadian Policy Research Networks, Inc., Toronto.

Zucker, L.G. 1977. "Institutionalization as a mechanism of cultural persistence." *American Sociological Review* 42(2): 726–42.

Index